Program Authors

Dr. Diane August
Dr. Donald Bear
Dr. Janice A. Dole
Dr. Jana Echevarria
Dr. Douglas Fisher
Dr. David J. Francis
Dr. Vicki Gibson
Dr. Jan Hasbrouck
Margaret Kilgo
Dr. Scott G. Paris
Dr. Timothy Shanahan
Dr. Josefina V. Tinajero

Mc
Graw
Hill
Education

Also Available from McGraw-Hill Education

 TextEvaluator.

Cover and Title Pages: Nathan Love

www.mheonline.com/readingwonders

ISBN: 978-0-07-679834-6
MHID: 0-07-679834-8

Printed in the United States of America.

2 3 4 5 6 7 8 9 WEB 20 19 18 17 16   B

> "The students love their books. With this curriculum, we have fantastic informational text and a variety of genres."
>
> — Becky Boyle, Campbell Elementary, Lincoln, NE

> "I feel that my students are lucky to be exposed to Wonders. It makes a world of difference. The online piece has made my job easier and allowed me to become a better teacher."
>
> — Todd Kimmel, Horatio B. Hackett School, Philadelphia, PA

> "Students are able to do more than we thought they could. We have raised the rigor and they want more. The conversations that are happening between my students are more sophisticated."
>
> — Heather Griffith, Lakeside Farms Elementary, Lakeside, CA

PROGRAM AUTHORS

Dr. Diane August
American Institutes for Research, Washington, D.C.

Managing Researcher
Education Program

Dr. Donald R. Bear
Iowa State University

Professor, Iowa State University
Author of *Words Their Way, Words Their Way with English Learners, Vocabulary Their Way,* and *Words Their Way with Struggling Readers, 4-12*

Dr. Janice A. Dole
University of Utah

Professor, University of Utah
Director, Utah Center for Reading and Literacy
Content Facilitator, National Assessment of Educational Progress (NAEP)
CCSS Consultant to Literacy Coaches, Salt Lake City School District, Utah

Dr. Jana Echevarria
California State University, Long Beach

Professor Emerita, California State University
Author of *Making Content Comprehensible for English Learners: The SIOP Model*

Dr. Douglas Fisher
San Diego State University

Co-Director, Center for the Advancement of Reading, California State University
Author of *Language Arts Workshop: Purposeful Reading and Writing Instruction, Reading for Information in Elementary School;* coauthor of *Close Reading and Writing from Sources, Rigorous Reading: 5 Access Points for Comprehending Complex Text,* and *Text-Dependent Questions, Grades K-5* with N. Frey

Dr. David J. Francis
University of Houston

Director of the Center for Research on Educational Achievement and Teaching of English Language Learners (CREATE)

Consulting Authors

Kathy R. Bumgardner
National Literacy Consultant

Strategies Unlimited, Inc.
Gastonia, NC

Jay McTighe
Jay McTighe and Associates

Author of *Essential Questions: Opening Doors to Student Understanding, The Understanding by Design Guide to Creating High Quality Units* and *Schooling by Design: Mission, Action, Achievement* with G. Wiggins, and *Differentiated Instruction and Understanding By Design* with C. Tomlinson

Dr. Doris Walker-Dalhouse
Marquette University

Associate Professor, Department of Educational Policy & Leadership
Author of articles on multicultural literature, struggling readers, and reading instruction in urban schools

Dinah Zike
Educational Consultant

Dinah-Might Activities, Inc.
San Antonio, TX

Dr. Scott G. Paris
Educational Testing Service,
Vice President, Research Professor,
Nanyang Technological University,
Singapore, 2008–2011

Professor of Education and Psychology,
University of Michigan, 1978–2008

Dr. Timothy Shanahan
University of Illinois at Chicago

Distinguished Professor, Urban Education
Director, UIC Center for Literacy Chair,
Department of Curriculum & Instruction
Member, English Language Arts Work
Team and Writer of the Common Core
State Standards
President, International Reading
Association, 2006

Dr. Josefina V. Tinajero
University of Texas at El Paso

Professor of Bilingual Education &
Special Assistant to the Vice President
of Research

Dr. Vicki Gibson
Educational Consultant Gibson
Hasbrouck and Associates

Author of *Differentiated Instruction:
Grouping for Success, Differentiated
Instruction: Guidelines for Implementation,*
and *Managing Behaviors to Support
Differentiated Instruction*

Dr. Jan Hasbrouck
J.H. Consulting
Gibson Hasbrouck and Associates

Developed Oral Reading Fluency Norms for
Grades 1–8
Author of *The Reading Coach: A How-
to Manual for Success* and *Educators as
Physicians: Using RTI Assessments for
Effective Decision-Making*

Margaret Kilgo
Educational Consultant
Kilgo Consulting, Inc., Austin, TX

Developed Data-Driven Decisions
process for evaluating student
performance by standard
Member of Common Core State
Standards Anchor Standards
Committee for Reading and Writing

National Program Advisors

Mayda Bahamonde-Gunnell, Ed.D
Grand Rapids Public Schools
Rockford, MI

Maria Campanario
Boston Public Schools
Boston, MA

Sharon Giless Aguina
Waukegan Community Unit School District #60
Waukegan, IL

Carolyn Gore, Ph.D.
Caddo Parish School District
Shreveport, LA

Kellie Jones
Department of Bilingual/ESL Services
Brockton, MA

Michelle Martinez
Albuquerque Public Schools Curriculum and
Instruction
Albuquerque, NM

Jadi Miller
Lincoln Public Schools
Lincoln, NE

Matthew Walsh
Wissahickon School District
Ambler, PA

CONNECTED LITERACY TOOLS

Weekly Concept and Essential Question

The Keys to Unlock the Week

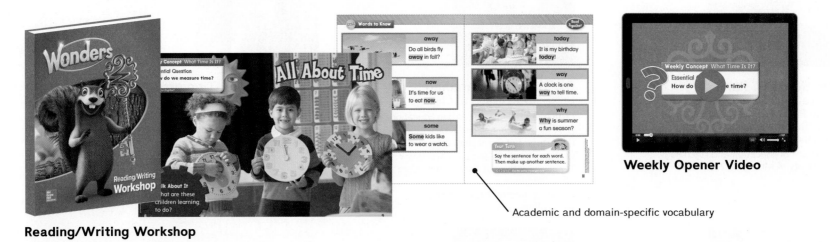

Reading/Writing Workshop

Weekly Opener Video

Academic and domain-specific vocabulary

Teach and Model

With Rich Opportunities for Collaborative Conversations

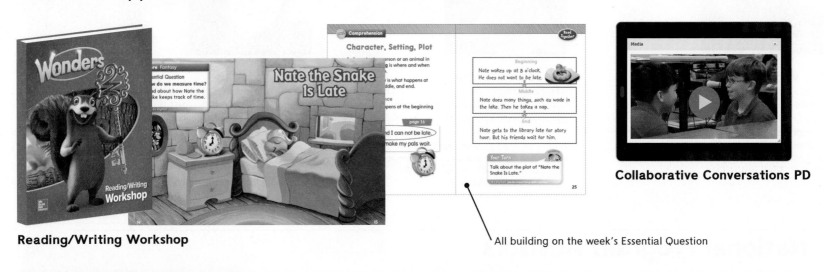

Reading/Writing Workshop

Collaborative Conversations PD

All building on the week's Essential Question

Practice and Apply

Close Reading, Writing to Sources, Grammar, Spelling, and Phonics

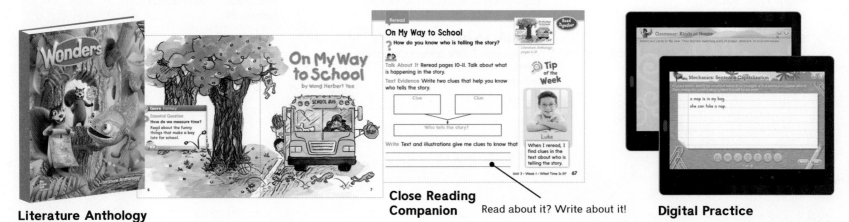

Literature Anthology

Close Reading Companion

Read about it? Write about it!

Digital Practice

Build Knowledge and Skills at Every Level

Differentiate to Accelerate

Move students ahead as soon as they're ready

Over 6500 more leveled readers online!

Nonfiction Leveled Readers

Fiction Leveled Readers

Also available:
- WonderWorks
- Wonders for English Learners
- Wonders Adaptive Learning

Adaptive Learning

Foundational Skills

Build phonemic awareness, phonics, word recognition and fluency

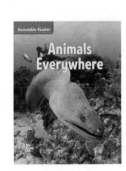

Decodable Readers

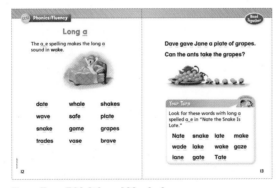

Reading/Writing Workshop

Visual Vocabulary Cards

Retelling Cards

Assess

Specific skills and standards for every student, assignment, and class

Specific recommendations for every skill and standard.

Weekly, Unit, Benchmark Assessments

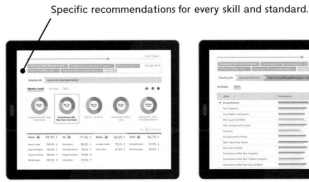

Data Dashboard

Proficiency Report

PROGRAM COMPONENTS
Print and Digital

Reading/Writing Workshop

Literature Big Books

Literature Anthology

Close Reading Companion

Interactive Read-Aloud Cards

Teacher Editions

Teaching Poster

Decodable Readers

Leveled Readers

Leveled Reader Lesson Cards

Classroom Library Trade Books

Your Turn Practice Book

Leveled Workstation Activity Cards

Retelling Cards

Visual Vocabulary Cards

Sound-Spelling Cards

Photo Cards

High-Frequency Word Cards

Weekly Assessment

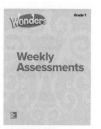
Unit Assessment

Benchmark Assessment

Additional Digital Resources

For You

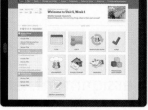

 Plan Customizable Lesson Plans

 Assess Online Assessments Reports and Scoring

 Professional Development Model Lessons and PD Videos

 Teach Classroom Presentation Tools Instructional Lessons

 Collaborate Online Class Conversations Interactive Group Projects

Additional Online Resources
- Leveled Practice
- Grammar Practice
- Phonics/Spelling
- ELL Activities
- Genre Study
- Reader's Theater
- Tier 2 Intervention
- Instructional Routine Handbook

 Manage and Assign Student Grouping and Assignments

 School to Home Activities and Messages

For Your Students

 My To Do List Assignments Assessment

Words to Know Build Vocabulary

 Read e Books Interactive Texts

Play Interactive Games

Write Interactive Writing

School to Home Support
- Activities for Home
- Messages from the Teacher

www.connected.mcgraw-hill.com

Together We Can

Unit Planning

Weekly Lessons

Model Lesson Extended Complex Text

Program Information

(t to b) Jim West/Alamy; LWA/The Image Bank/Getty Images; Derek Croucher/Alamy; Monalyn Gracia/Corbis; Ron Sherman/Stone/Getty Images

UNIT OVERVIEW

Week 1	Week 2	Week 3
TAKING ACTION	**MY TEAM**	**WEATHER TOGETHER**

READING

Week 1 — TAKING ACTION

ESSENTIAL QUESTION
How can we work together to make our lives better?

Build Background

CCSS Oral Vocabulary
L.I.5c *argument, conflict, fair, risk, shift*

CCSS Word Work
RF.I.2 Phonemic Awareness: Phoneme Identity/Segmentation/Substitution, Rhyme, Syllable Deletion
RF.I.3 Phonics/Spelling: Variant Vowel /ü/
RF.I.3 Structural Analysis: Suffixes *-ful, -less*
RF.I.3g High-Frequency Words: *answer, brought, busy, door, enough, eyes* Vocabulary Words: *demand, emergency*
L.I.5 Synonyms

CCSS Comprehension
RL.I.I Strategy: Reread
RL.I.2 Skill: Theme
Genre: Fantasy

CCSS Fluency
RF.I.4b Dialogue

Week 2 — MY TEAM

ESSENTIAL QUESTION
Who helps you?

Build Background

CCSS Oral Vocabulary
L.I.5c *decision, distance, inspire, respect, swiftly*

CCSS Word Work
RF.I.2 Phonemic Awareness: Phoneme Categorization/Reversal/Blending/Segmentation/Substitution
RF.I.3 Phonics/Spelling: Variant Vowel /ô/
RF.I.3 Structural Analysis: Vowel Team Syllables
RF.I.3g High-Frequency Words: *brother, father, friend, love, mother, picture* Vocabulary Words: *accept, often*
L.I.5 Antonyms

CCSS Comprehension
RL.I.I Strategy: Reread
RI.2.6 Skill: Author's Purpose
Genre: Informational Nonfiction

CCSS Fluency
RF.I.4b Intonation

Week 3 — WEATHER TOGETHER

ESSENTIAL QUESTION
How can weather affect us?

Build Background

CCSS Oral Vocabulary
L.I.5c *creative, cycle, frigid, predict, scorching*

CCSS Word Work
RF.I.2 Phonemic Awareness: Phoneme Categorization/Segmentation/Substitution
RF.I.3 Phonics/Spelling: Silent Letters
RF.I.3 Structural Analysis: Compound Words
RF.I.3g High-Frequency Words: *been, children, month, question, their, year* Vocabulary Words: *country, gathers*
L.I.4 Similes

CCSS Comprehension
RL.I.7 Strategy: Visualize
RL.I.3 Skill: Plot: Cause and Effect
Genre: Realistic Fiction

CCSS Fluency
RF.I.4b Phrasing

LANGUAGE ARTS

Week 1

CCSS Writing
W.I.5 Write to Sources
Trait: Sentence Fluency

CCSS Grammar
RF.I.I Pronouns
L.I.2 Mechanics: Capitalize *I*

Week 2

CCSS Writing
W.I.5 Write to Sources
Trait: Voice

CCSS Grammar
RF.I.I Possessive Pronouns
L.I.2 Mechanics: Days, Months, Holidays

Week 3

CCSS Writing
W.I.5 Write to Sources
Trait: Voice

CCSS Grammar
RF.I.I Special Pronouns
L.I.2 Mechanics: Commas in Dates and Letters

Together We Can

Review and Assess

Week 4	Week 5	Week 6
SHARING TRADITIONS	**CELEBRATE AMERICA!**	

Week 4 — SHARING TRADITIONS

ESSENTIAL QUESTION
What traditions do you know about?

Build Background

CCSS Oral Vocabulary
L.I.5c ancient, drama, effort, movement, tradition

CCSS Word Work
RF.I.2 Phonemic Awareness: Syllable Addition, Phoneme Segmentation/Blending/Substitution
RF.I.3 Phonics/Spelling: Three-Letter Blends
RF.I.3 Structural Analysis: Inflectional Endings -ed, -ing
RF.I.3g High-Frequency Words: *before, front, heard, push, tomorrow, your*
Vocabulary Words: *difficult, nobody*
L.I.4b Compound Words

CCSS Comprehension
RL.I.4 Strategy: Visualize
RL.I.2 Skill: Theme
Genre: Realistic Fiction

CCSS Fluency
RF.I.4b Phrasing

Week 5 — CELEBRATE AMERICA!

ESSENTIAL QUESTION
Why do we celebrate holidays?

Build Background

CCSS Oral Vocabulary
L.I.5c design, display, pride, purpose, represent

CCSS Word Work
RF.I.2 Phonemic Awareness: Phoneme Reversal/Blending/Deletion/Addition, Syllable Deletion/Addition
Phonics/Spelling: Words with /âr/
RF.I.3 Structural Analysis: r-Controlled Vowel Syllables
RF.I.3g High-Frequency Words: *favorite, few, gone, surprise, wonder, young*
Vocabulary Words: *nation, unite*
L.I.5 Metaphors

CCSS Comprehension
RI.I.I Strategy: Reread
RI.2.6 Skill: Author's Purpose
Genre: Informational Nonfiction

CCSS Fluency
RF.I.4b Phrasing

Week 6

CCSS Reader's Theater
RF.I.4 Assign Roles
Fluency: Phrasing, Rate, and Expression

CCSS Reading Digitally
RI.I.5 Take Notes
W.I.6 Access Interactive Elements Navigate Links

CCSS Research and Inquiry
W.I.7 Retell Information
Unit Projects
Presentation of Ideas

> **Unit 6 Assessment**
>
> **Unit Assessment Book**
> pages 125–150
>
> **Fluency Assessment**
> pages 50–61

Week 4 — Writing

CCSS Writing
W.I.5 Write to Sources
Trait: Sentence Fluency

CCSS Grammar
RF.I.I Using *I* and *me*
L.I.2 Mechanics: Commas in Dates and Letters

Week 5 — Writing

CCSS Writing
W.I.5 Write to Sources
Trait: Ideas

CCSS Grammar
RF.I.I Adverbs That Tell *How*
L.I.2 Mechanics: Abbreviation

Week 6 — Writing

CCSS Writing
W.I.5 Write to Sources
Publishing Celebrations
Portfolio Choice

UNIT OPENER

Unit 6
Together We Can!

214

Together

Together is better,
Whatever we do,

You get so much more done,
When someone helps you.

If someone is lonely,
And not having fun,
Just ask them to play;

Two is better than one.

And books sound much better,
When shared with a friend,

Together is better,
Beginning to end.

—by Constance A. Kareme

The Big Idea

How does teamwork help us?

215

READING/WRITING WORKSHOP, pp. 214–215

Reading/Writing Workshop

The Big Idea *How does teamwork help us?*

Talk About It

Have children read the Big Idea aloud. Ask them about a time they worked with others to reach a goal. Have them describe the experience and their role. Children may mention group projects in school, team sports, or family trips.

Ask: *How do you work with others?* Have children discuss with partners or in groups, then share their ideas with the class. Let children know that they will discuss the Big Idea throughout the unit. Each week they will talk, read, and write about an Essential Question related to the Big Idea.

Read the Poem: "Together"

Read aloud "Together." Ask children questions to explore the theme.

- Why does the writer think together is better?
- What things are better with more than one person?
- Why is reading better with a friend?

Structure Read the poem aloud again. Show students the beginning and ending. Ask them to identify the examples the writer uses to support the idea "together is better." (*getting things done, loneliness, reading*) Have them think of more times when being together with others is better.

RESEARCH AND INQUIRY WRITING

Weekly Projects Each week children will produce a project related to the Essential Question. They will then develop one of these projects more fully for the Unit Research Project. Through their research, children will focus their attention on:

- brainstorming topic ideas.
- conducting interviews.
- finding information in print and online sources.
- working with a partner or group.

Shared Research Board You may wish to develop a Shared Research Board. Children can post ideas and information about the unit theme. Children can post materials, notes, or facts they gather as they do their research. They can also post notes with questions they have as they conduct their research.

WEEKLY PROJECTS

Children work in pairs or small groups.

Week 1 Illustrated Plan Proposal, T44
Week 2 Informative Newspaper, T122
Week 3 Illustrated Mini Tornado, T200
Week 4 Informative Poster, T278
Week 5 Illustrated Flag, T356

WEEK 6

Children work in small groups to complete and present one of the following projects.

- Skit
- Thank-You Letters
- Safety Poster
- Persuasive Letter
- Holiday Song

Write About the Text Throughout the unit children will respond to writing prompts on a variety of texts. As students practice close reading by reading and rereading a text, they take notes and cite text evidence. After reading, children write briefly about what they recall about the text in order to build writing fluency. Through the scaffolded instruction in writing about text in Shared Writing, the teacher then guides the class to respond to a writing prompt, using sentence frames as needed. In Interactive Writing the children analyze a student model response that includes the weekly writing trait before they respond to a new prompt together. In Independent Writing, children write independently, applying their close reading skills and the trait to their own writing.

WEEKLY WRITING TRAITS

Week 1 Sentence Fluency: Vary Sentence Length, T28
Week 2 Voice: Use Your Own Voice, T106
Week 3 Ideas: Main Idea, T184
Week 4 Sentence Fluency: Varying Sentence Types, T262
Week 5 Voice: Author's Voice, T340

COLLABORATE
Post children's questions and monitor student online discussions. Create a Shared Research Board.

www.connected.mcgraw-hill.com

WRITER'S WORKSPACE
Ask children to work through their writing using the online tools for support.

www.connected.mcgraw-hill.com

WEEKLY OVERVIEW

Build Knowledge
Taking Action

? Essential Question:
How can we work together to make our lives better?

Teach and Model
Close Reading and Writing

Big Book and Little Book

Reading Writing Workshop

Super Tools, 222–231
Genre Fantasy Lexile 430

Interactive Read Aloud

"The Cat's Bell"
Genre Fable

Practice and Apply
Close Reading and Writing

Literature Anthology *Click, Clack, Moo,* 270–293
Genre Fantasy Lexile 380

Paired Read

"March On!," 296–301
Genre Nonfiction Lexile 510

Differentiated Texts

APPROACHING
Lexile 290

ON LEVEL
Lexile 500

BEYOND
Lexile 480

ELL
Lexile 350

Leveled Readers

Extended Complex Texts

Frog and Toad Together
Genre Fiction
Lexile 330

Ling & Ting—Not Exactly the Same!
Genre Fiction
Lexile 510

Classroom Library

UNIT 6 WEEK 1

Student Outcomes

Close Reading of Complex Text

- Cite relevant evidence from text
- Demonstrate understanding of theme or central message
- Retell the text

RL.1.2

Writing

Write to Sources

- Draw evidence from fiction text
- Write narrative text
- Conduct short research on taking action

W1.3, W.1.7

Speaking and Listening

- Engage in collaborative conversation about taking action
- Retell and discuss *Super Tools*
- Present information on how we can work together to make our lives better

SL.1.1c, SL.1.2, SL.1.3

Content Knowledge

- Explore how people can change their world.

Language Development

Conventions

- Use pronouns: *I, you, he, she, it, we, they*

Vocabulary Acquisition

- Develop oral vocabulary

fair	conflict	shift
risk	argument	

- Acquire and use academic vocabulary

demand	emergency

- Use context clues to understand synonyms

L.1.1d, L.1.4, L.1.6, L.4.5c

Foundational Skills

Phonics/Word Study/Spelling

- Variant vowel spellings with digraphs: *oo, u, u_e, ew, ue, ui, ou*
- Suffixes *-ful and -less*
- moon, tune, flew, blue, fruit, soup, toy, coin, enough, door

High-Frequency Words

answer   brought   busy   door   enough   eyes

Fluency

- Expression

Decodable Text

- Apply foundational skills in connected text

RF.1.3c, L.1.4b, RF.1.3g, RF.1.4a, RF.1.4b, RF.1.4c

Professional Development

- See lessons in action in real classrooms.
- Get expert advice on instructional practices.
- Collaborate with other teachers.
- Access PLC Resources

Go Digital! www.connected.mcgraw-hill.com.

INSTRUCTIONAL PATH

1 Talk About Working Together

Guide children in collaborative conversations.

Discuss the essential question: *How can we work together to make our lives better?*

Develop academic language.

Listen to "The Cat's Bell" to summarize the story.

2 Read *Super Tools*

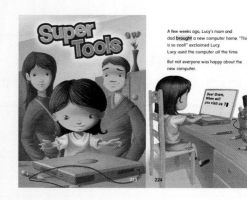

Apply foundational skills in connected text. Model close reading.

Read

Super Tools to learn about Lucy's writing tools working together, citing text evidence to answer text-dependent questions.

Reread

Super Tools to analyze text, craft, and structure, citing text evidence.

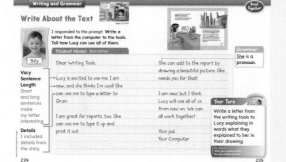

3 Write About *Super Tools*

Model writing to a source.

Analyze a short response student model.

Use text evidence from close reading to write to a source.

4 Read and Write About Working Together

Practice and apply close reading of the anchor text.

> **Read**

Click, Clack, Moo: Cows That Type to learn about cows that type.

> **Reread**

Click, Clack, Moo: Cows That Type and use text evidence to understand how the author uses text, craft, and structure to develop a deeper understanding of the story.

> **Integrate**

Information about how protestors made their lives better.

Write to a Source, citing text evidence to write a letter from ducks to the farmer.

5 Independent Partner Work

Gradual release of support to independent work

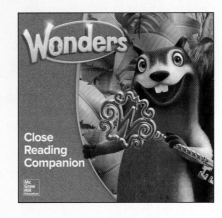

- Text-Dependent Questions
- Scaffolded Partner Work
- Talk with a Partner
- Cite Text Evidence
- Complete a sentence frame.
- Guided Text Annotation

6 Integrate Knowledge and Ideas

Connect Texts

Text to Text Discuss how each of the texts answers the question: How can we work together to make our lives better?

Text to Photography Compare information about taking action in the texts read with the photograph.

Conduct a Short Research Project

Create a plan proposal for working together.

DEVELOPING READERS AND WRITERS

Write to Sources: Narrative

Day 1 and Day 2

Shared Writing

- Write about the characters in the story, p. T18

Interactive Writing

- Analyze a student model, p. T28

- Write a new letter from the characters in the story, p. T29

- Find Text Evidence

- Apply Writing Trait: Sentence Fluency: Varying Sentence Length, p. T29

- Apply Grammar Skill: Pronouns *I, you, he, she, it, we, they,* p. T29

Day 3, Day 4 and Day 5

Independent Writing

- Write a new letter modeled on what the cows wrote in *Click, Clack, Moo: Cows That Type,* p. T36

- Provide scaffolded instruction to meet student needs, p. T36

- Find Text Evidence, p. T36

- Apply Writing Trait: Sentence Fluency: Varying Sentence Length, p. T36

- Prewrite and Draft, p. T36

- Revise and Edit, p. T42

- Final Draft, p. T43

- Present, Evaluate, and Publish, p. T48

Grammar

Pronouns

- Use pronouns to tell about what is happening, pp, T19, T29, T37, T43, T49
- Apply grammar to writing, pp. T19, T37, T42, T49

Mechanics: Capitalize *I*

- Use capitaliziation on *I*, pp. T37, T43, T49

Online PDFs

Grammar Practice, pp. 126–130

Online Grammar Games

Spelling

Words with Variant Vowel /ü/

- Spell words with Variant Vowel /ü/

Online PDFs

Phonics/Spelling blms
pp. 126–130

Online Spelling Games

SUGGESTED LESSON PLAN

	READING		DAY 1	DAY 2
Whole Group	**Teach, Model and Apply** Wonders Reading/Writing Workshop Workshop	**Core**	**Build Background** Taking Action, T8–T9 **Oral Vocabulary** *fair, conflict,* T8 **Word Works** T12–T15 • Fluency: Sound-Spellings • Phonemic Awareness: Phoneme Identity • Phonics/Spelling: Introduce Variant Vowel /ü/ • High-Frequency Words: *answer, brought, busy, door, enough, eyes* • Vocabulary: *demand, emergency* **Shared Read** *Super Tools,* T16–T17	**Oral Language** Taking Action, T20 **Oral Vocabulary** *shift, risk, argument, fair, conflict,* T20 **Word Work** T22–T25 • Phonemic Awareness: Phoneme Segmentation • Structural Analysis: Suffixes *-ful* and *-less* • Vocabulary: *demand, emergency* **Shared Read** *Super Tools,* T26–T27 • Genre: Fantasy, T26 • Skill: Theme, T27
		Options	**Listening Comprehension** "The Cat's Bell," T10–T11	**Listening Comprehension** "The Cat's Bell," T21 **Word Work** T22–T25 • Phonics/Spelling: Review Variant Vowel /ü/ • High-Frequency Words
	LANGUAGE ARTS			
	Writing **Grammar**	**Core**	**Shared Writing** T18 **Grammar** Pronouns, T19	**Interactive Writing** T28 **Grammar** Pronouns, T29
		Options		

DIFFERENTIATED INSTRUCTION

Use your data dashboard to determine each student's needs. Then select instructional supports options throughout the week.

APPROACHING LEVEL

Leveled Reader
Two Hungry Elephants, T52–T53
"Dogs Helping People," T53
Literature Circles, T53

Phonemic Awareness
Identify and Generate Rhyme, T54 (TIER 2)
Phoneme Identity, T54
Phoneme Segmentation, T55
Syllable Deletion, T55

Phonics
Connect *oo, u, u_e, ew, ue, ui, ou, to* /ü/, T56 (TIER 2)
Blend Words with Variant Vowel /ü/, T56 (TIER 2)
Blend Words with Variant Vowel /ü/, T57
Build Fluency with Phonics, T57

Structural Analysis
Review Suffixes *-ful* and *-less*, T58

Words to Know
Review, T59

Comprehension
Read for Fluency, T60 (TIER 2)
Identify Plot, T60 (TIER 2)
Review Theme, T61
Self-Selected Reading, T61

ON LEVEL

Leveled Reader
What a Feast!, T62–T63
"Helpers Bring Food," T63
Literature Circles, T63

Phonics
Build Words with Variant Vowel /ü/, T64

DAY 3	DAY 4	DAY 5
Fluency Expression, T31 **Word Work** T32–T35 • Phonemic Awareness: Identify and Generate Rhyme • Phonics/Spelling: Blend Words with Variant Vowel /ü/ • Vocabulary Strategy: Synonyms **Close Reading** *Click, Clack, Moo: Cows That Type*, T35A–T35N	**Extend the Concept** T38–T39 • Text Feature: Captions, T38 • Close Reading: "March On!," T39–T39B **Word Work** T40–T41 • Phonemic Awareness: Syllable Deletion • Structural Analysis: Suffixes *-ful* and *-less* **Integrate Ideas** • Research and Inquiry, T44–T45	**Word Work** T46–T47 • Phonemic Awareness: Phoneme Segmentation/ Substitution • Phonics/Spelling: Blend and Build Words with Variant Vowel /ü/ • Structural Analysis: Suffixes *-ful* and *-less* • High-Frequency Words • Vocabulary: *demand, emergency* **Integrate Ideas** • Text Connections, T50–T51
Oral Language Taking Action, T30 **Word Work** T32–T35 • Structural Analysis: Suffixes *-ful* and *-less* • High-Frequency Words	**Word Work** T40–T41 • Fluency: Sound-Spellings • Phonics/Spelling: Build Words with Variant Vowel /ü/ • High-Frequency Words • Vocabulary: *demand, emergency* **Close Read** *Click, Clack, Moo: Cows That Type*, T35A–T35N	**Word Work** T46-T47 • Fluency: Expression **Integrate Ideas** • Research and Inquiry, T50 • Speaking and Listening, T51
Independent Writing T36 **Grammar** Mechanics: Capitalize *I*, T37	**Independent Writing** T42 **Grammar** Mechanics: Capitalize *I*, T43	**Independent Writing** T48 **Grammar** Pronouns, T49
Grammar Pronouns, T37	**Grammar** Pronouns, T43	**Grammar** Mechanics: Capitalize *I*, T49

Words to Know
Review Words, T64

Comprehension
Review Theme, T65
Self-Selected Reading, T65

BEYOND LEVEL

Leveled Reader
Beware of the Lion!, T66–T67
"Pete Seeger," T67
Literature Circles, T67

Vocabulary
Antonyms, T68

Comprehension
Review Theme, T69
Self-Selected Reading, T69

Gifted and Talented

ENGLISH LANGUAGE LEARNERS

Shared Read
Super Tools, T70–T71

Leveled Reader
What A Feast!, T72–T73
"Helpers Bring Food," T73
Literature Circles, T73

Vocabulary
Preteach Oral Vocabulary, T74
Preteach ELL Vocabulary, T74

Words to Know
Review Words, T75
Reteach High-Frequency Words, T75

Writing/Spelling
Writing Trait: Sentence Fluency, T76
Words with Variant Vowel /ü/, T76

Grammar
Pronouns, T77

DIFFERENTIATE TO ACCELERATE

  A C T   Scaffold to   **A**ccess **C**omplex **T**ext

IF ▶ the text complexity of a particular selection is too difficult for children

THEN ▶ see the references noted in the chart below for scaffolded instruction to help children Access Complex Text.

Qualitative — Quantitative
Reader and Task
TEXT COMPLEXITY

	Reading/Writing Workshop	Literature Anthology	Leveled Readers	Classroom Library

			Approach · On Level · Beyond · ELL	
Quantitative	*Super Tools* **Lexile** 430	*Click, Clack, Moo: Cows That Type* **Lexile** 380 "*March On!*" **Lexile** 510	**Approaching Level** **Lexile** 290 **Beyond Level** **Lexile** 480 — **On Level** **Lexile** 500 **ELL** **Lexile** 350	*Frog and Toad Together* **Lexile** 330 *Ling & Ting: Not Exactly the Same!* **Lexile** 390
Qualitative	**What Makes the Text Complex?** **Foundational Skills** • Decoding with variant vowel spellings with digraphs: *oo, u, u_e, ew, ue, ui, ou,* T12–T13 • Reading words with suffixes *-ful* and *-less,* T23 • Identifying high-frequency words, T14–T15 *See Scaffolded Instruction in Teacher's Edition, T12–T13, T14–T15, and T23.*	**What Makes the Text Complex?** • **Text Organization,** T35B, T35C • **Connection of Ideas,** T35B, T35J • **Specific Vocabulary,** T35H **A C T** *See Scaffolded Instruction in Teacher's Edition, T35B, T35C, T35J, and T35H.*	**What Makes the Text Complex?** **Foundational Skills** • Decoding with variant vowel spellings with digraphs: *oo, u, u_e, ew, ue, ui, ou* • Reading words with suffixes *-ful* and *-less* • Identifying high-frequency words *answer brought busy door enough eyes* *See Level Up lessons online for Leveled Readers.*	**What Makes the Text Complex?** • **Purpose** • **Specific Vocabulary** • **Prior Knowledge** • **Sentence Structure** • **Organization** • **Connection of Ideas** • **Genre** **A C T** *See Scaffolded Instruction in Teacher's Edition, T413–T415.*
Reader and Task	**The** Introduce the Concept lesson on pages T8–T9 will help determine the reader's knowledge and engagement in the weekly concept. See pages T16–T17, T26–T27, T44–T45 and T50-T51 for questions and tasks for this text.	**The** Introduce the Concept lesson on pages T8–T9 will help determine the reader's knowledge and engagement in the weekly concept. See pages T35A–T35N, T39–T39B, T44–T45 and T50-T51 for questions and tasks for this text.	**The** Introduce the Concept lesson on pages T8–T9 will help determine the reader's knowledge and engagement in the weekly concept. See pages T52–T53, T62–T63, T66–T67, T72–T73, T44–T45 and T50-T51 for questions and tasks for this text.	**The** Introduce the Concept lesson on pages T8–T9 will help determine the reader's knowledge and engagement in the weekly concept. See pages T413–T415 for questions and tasks for this text.

Monitor and *Differentiate*

✔ Quick Check

To differentiate instruction, use the Quick Checks to assess students' needs and select the appropriate small group instruction focus.

Comprehension Strategy Reread, T11

Comprehension Skill Theme, T27

Phonics Words with Variant Vowel /ü/, T15, T25, T35, T41, T47

High-Frequency Words and Vocabulary T15, T25, T35, T41, T47

If No →

| Approaching Level | Reteach T52–T61 |
| ELL | Develop T70–T77 |

If Yes →

| On Level | Review T62–T65 |
| Beyond Level | Extend T66–T69 |

Using Weekly Data

Check your data Dashboard to verify assessment results and guide grouping decisions.

Level Up with Leveled Readers

IF children can read their leveled text fluently and answer comprehension questions

THEN work with the next level up to accelerate children's reading with more complex text.

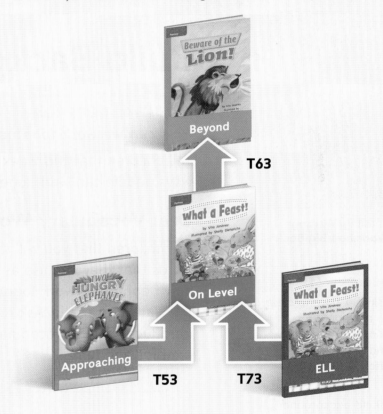

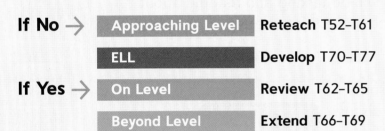

ELL ENGLISH LANGUAGE LEARNERS

Small Group Instruction

Use the ELL small group lessons in the *Wonders* Teacher's Edition to provide focused instruction.

Language Development
Vocabulary preteaching, oral vocabulary preteaching, high-frequency word review and reteach, pp. T74–T75

Close Reading
Interactive Question-Response routines for scaffolded text-dependent questioning for reading and rereading the Shared Read and Leveled Reader, pp. T70–T73

Writing
Focus on the writing trait, grammar, and spelling, pp. T76–T77

Additional ELL Support

Use Wonders for English Learners for ELD instruction that connects to the core.

Language Development
My Language Book for ample opportunities for discussions and scaffolded language support

Close Reading
Guided support for the Shared Read, Big Books, and Interactive Read Alouds. Differentiated texts about the weekly concept

Writing
Guided support in Interactive and Independent Writing and writing to sources

Wonders for ELs Teacher Edition and My Language Book

Materials

Reading/Writing Workshop
VOLUME 4

Reading/Writing Workshop Big Book
UNIT 6

Visual Vocabulary Cards

argument
conflict
fair
risk
shift

High-Frequency Word Cards
answer   door
brought   enough
busy   eyes

Vocabulary Cards
demand   emergency

a **b** **c**

Word-Building Cards

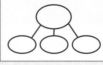

Teaching Poster

Interactive Read-Aloud Cards

When I read ___ I had to reread...

Think Aloud Clouds

oo u_e u
ew ue
ou u_u
spoon

Sound-Spelling Cards

→ Introduce the Concept

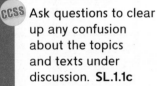

Reading/Writing Workshop Big Book

OBJECTIVES

CCSS Ask questions to clear up any confusion about the topics and texts under discussion. **SL.1.1c**

• Build background knowledge
• Discuss the Essential Question

ACADEMIC LANGUAGE

• *action, disagreement, reasonable*
• Cognates: *acción, razonable*

MINILESSON

5 Mins

Build Background

ESSENTIAL QUESTION

How can we work together to make our lives better?

Tell children that this week they will be talking and reading about ways people can work together to make things better.

Oral Vocabulary Words

Tell children that you will share some words that they can use as they discuss how people can work together. Use the Define/Example/Ask routine to introduce the oral vocabulary words **conflict** and **fair**.

Visual Vocabulary Cards

Oral Vocabulary Routine

<u>Define:</u> A **conflict** is a disagreement or problem between two or more people.

<u>Example:</u> Both children wanted to play with the ball, but they settled their conflict by taking turns.

<u>Ask:</u> Have you ever had a conflict with a friend?

<u>Define:</u> If something is **fair**, it is reasonable and follows the rules.

<u>Example:</u> Jon did not think it was fair that his sister got a bigger cup of hot chocolate than he did.

<u>Ask:</u> Which is fair: each child in the class gets one cracker, or one child gets all the crackers?

Discuss the theme of "Taking Action." Have children tell about a time when they worked with others to make something better. *What did you do? Was it easy to work together?*

Go Digital

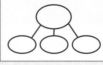

Taking Action

Video

school

Visual Glossary

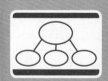

Graphic Organizer

Reading/Writing Workshop, pp. 216–217

Talk About It: Taking Action

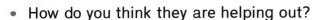

Guide children to discuss how the boys are working together.

- What are the boys doing? How are they working together?
- How do you think they are helping out?

Use Teaching Poster 40 and prompt children to complete the Word Web by sharing words that describe how the people in the photograph are working together. Discuss how they are making their community a better place.

Have children look at page 217 of their Reading/Writing Workshop and do the Talk About It activity with a partner.

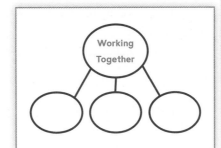

Teaching Poster

Collaborative Conversations

Ask and Answer Questions As children engage in partner, small-group, and whole-group discussions, encourage them to:

- ask questions about ideas they do not understand.
- give others a chance to think after asking a question.
- write down questions they want to ask the teacher or the whole class.

ELL

ENGLISH LANGUAGE LEARNERS SCAFFOLD

Beginning

Use Visuals Point to the children in the photograph. *The children are helping to paint the wall. Are they working together, or alone? Are other people in the photograph working together? Show me.* Repeat children's responses in complete sentences.

Intermediate

Describe Ask children to describe what the boys are doing. *How are the boys working together?* Correct the meaning of children's responses as needed.

Advanced/High

Discuss Have children elaborate on working together. *What are the boys doing? How are they making things better?* Repeat children's responses slowly and clearly to the class.

→ # Listening Comprehension

MINILESSON
10
Mins

Read the Interactive Read Aloud

Connect to Concept: Taking Action

Tell children that they will now read about some mice who have to do something dangerous. Ask: *What dangers do mice face?*

"The Cat's Bell"

Focus on Oral Vocabulary

Review the oral vocabulary words *fair* and *conflict*. Use the Define/Example/Ask routine to introduce the oral vocabulary words *argument, risk, shift*. Prompt children to use the words as they discuss how people can work together.

Oral Vocabulary Routine

Define: An **argument** is a fight that uses words.

Example: The two friends had an argument about who won the game.

Ask: Have you and your friends ever had an argument? What was it about?

Define: A **risk** is a danger or the possibility that something bad may happen.

Example: If you walk through deep mud, there is a risk your shoe will get stuck.

Ask: What risks do you take when you walk in the rain?

Define: If I **shift** something, I move it a little bit from one place to another.

Example: I will shift this chair to make room for another one.

Ask: What does it look like to shift your feet?

Visual Vocabulary Cards

Go Digital

"The Cat's Bell"

When I read ____, I had to reread...

Reread

school

Visual Glossary

Retell

Set a Purpose for Reading

- Display the Interactive Read-Aloud Cards.
- Read aloud the title.
- Tell children that you will be reading a story about some mice with a big problem. Tell children to read to find out how the mice work together.

Strategy: Reread

1 Explain Tell children that if they do not understand something as they read or listen to a story, they can go back and read the text again. This is called rereading. They can also reread to help them remember important information. This can help them understand the text better.

Think Aloud Rereading parts of a story can help me to better understand it. Today, as we read "The Cat's Bell," I will pay attention to which parts I do not understand or want to make sure I remember. Then I will go back and reread those parts.

2 Model Read the selection. As you read, use the Think Aloud Cloud to model the strategy.

Think Aloud Remember that you can reread parts of the text to make sure you understood correctly. I found the beginning confusing. I am not sure that I understood why the mice can't go and eat the food on the table. When I reread the text, I understand that they are afraid of the cat.

3 Guided Practice As you continue to read, pause to ask children which parts of the story they find confusing. *What parts did you have trouble understanding? What can you do to better understand them?* Guide children in rereading parts of the text they did not understand.

Respond to Reading

After reading, prompt children to retell "The Cat's Bell." Discuss what parts they needed to reread and how it helped them understand the story events. Prompt children to discuss how the mice worked together to make their lives better.

ENGLISH LANGUAGE LEARNERS SCAFFOLD

Beginning

Engage Display Card 2 of "The Cat's Bell." *I didn't understand this part. Let's reread it.* Reread the card. *Do the mice have a problem? Are the mice having an argument?*

Intermediate

Describe Display Card 2 of "The Cat's Bell." *I do not understand why the mice do not get a dog. Let's reread the page.* Reread the card. *Why don't the mice get a dog?*

Advanced/High

Describe Display Card 3 of "The Cat's Bell." *I do not understand why the mice are arguing again. Let's reread this part.* Reread the card. *Explain what the mice are arguing about.*

Monitor and *Differentiate*

✓ **Quick Check**

Can children apply the reread strategy?

⬇

Small Group Instruction

If No →	Approaching	Reteach pp. T52–53
	ELL	Develop pp. T70–73
If Yes →	On Level	Review pp. T62–63
	Beyond Level	Extend pp. T66–67

 → # Word Work

Quick Review

Build Fluency: Sound-Spellings
Display the **Word-Building Cards** *oo, u, u_e, ew, ue, ui, ou, oy, oi, ar, ore, oar, er, ir, ur, ey, igh, oa, oe, ee, ea, ai, ay, e_e, u_e, o_e, dge, i_e, a_e, _ce.* Have children say the sounds aloud.

 5 Mins

Phonemic Awareness

OBJECTIVES

CCSS Isolate and pronounce initial, medial vowel, and final sounds (phonemes) in spoken single-syllable words. **RF.1.2c**

CCSS Decode regularly spelled one-syllable words. **RF.1.3b**

Phoneme Identity

1 Model Show children how to identify the same sound in a group of words. *Listen as I say three words:* fruit, noon, chew. *These words have one sound that is the same. I hear /ü/ in* fruit, noon, *and* chew.

2 Guided Practice/Practice Have children practice identifying the same sound or sounds in word sets. Do the first one together.

moose, hoop, juice   house, cow, town   glued, zoom, mood

flew, too, shoo   stork, corn, board   boot, goose, drew

10 Mins

Phonics

Introduce Variant Vowel /ü/

Sound-Spelling Card

1 Model Display the *Spoon* **Sound-Spelling Card.**
Teach /ü/ spelled *oo, u, u_e, ew, ue, ui,* and *ou* using *spoon, truth, rule, chew, glue, fruit,* and *you. This is the* Spoon *Sound-Spelling Card. The sound is /ü/. This is the sound in the middle of the word* spoon. Listen: */spüüün/. The /ü/ sound can be spelled:* oo, u, u_e, ew, ue, ui, *and* ou. *Say it with me: /ü/. I'll say /ü/ as I write the different spellings.*

2 Guided Practice/Practice Have children practice connecting *oo, u, u_e, ew, ue, ui,* and *ou* to the sound /ü/. *Now do it with me. Say /ü/ as I write:* oo, u, u_e, ew, ue, ui, *and* ou. *This time, write the different spellings five times as you say /ü/.*

SKILLS TRACE

VARIANT VOWEL /ü/

Introduce Unit 6 Week 1 Day 1

Review Unit 6 Week 1 Days 2, 3, 4, 5

Assess Unit 6 Week 1

Go Digital

Phonemic Awareness

Spoon

Phonics

Handwriting

Blend with Variant Vowel /ü/

1 **Model** Display the **Word-Building Cards** *s, o, o, n.* Model how to blend the sounds. *This is the letter* s. *It stands for /s/. These are the letters* oo. *Together they stand for /ü/. This is the letter* n. *It stands for /n/. Listen as I blend these sounds together: /sssüüünnn/. Say it with me.*

Continue by modeling the words *truth, flute, new, true, suit, you.*

2 **Guided Practice/Practice** Display the Day 1 Phonics Practice Activity. Read each word in the first row, blending the sounds; for example: */sssüüüp/. The word is* soup. Have children blend each word with you. Prompt children to read the connected text, sounding out the decodable words.

soup	room	soon	tools	super	cool
rude	drew	new	blue	juice	you
look	loop	rode	rude	stay	stew
coin	mouse	town	corn	hurt	boys

Duke wore a blue suit and brown boots.

Lucy jumped into her new pool.

A moose from the zoo was on the loose!

Also online

Day 1 Phonics Practice Activity

Corrective Feedback

Sound Error Model the sound that children missed, then have them repeat the sound. Say: *My turn.* Tap under the letters and say: *Sound? /ü/. What's the sound?* Return to the beginning of the word. Say: *Let's start over.* Blend the word with children again.

 Daily Handwriting

Throughout the week teach uppercase and lowercase letters *Qq* using the Handwriting models.

ENGLISH LANGUAGE LEARNERS

Phonemic Awareness: Minimal Contrasts Focus on articulation. Say /ü/ and note your mouth position. Have children repeat. Use the Sound-Spelling Cards. Repeat for the variant vowel /ů/ sound. Have children say the sounds and notice the difference. Continue with the words *hoop/hook, tooth/took, boot/book.*

Phonics: Variations in Language There is only an approximate transfer for the /ü/ sound in Cantonese and Vietnamese. Emphasize /ü/, and show correct mouth position. Practice with Approaching Level phonics lessons.

ON-LEVEL PRACTICE BOOK p. 271

The letters **oo** can stand for the sound you hear in the middle of **moon**.

The underlined letters in the words below show some other ways to spell the same sound.

| truth | blue | new | tube | fruit | you |

Read the first word. Then circle another word in the row with the same ending sounds.

1. spoon   sock   (noon)   both

2. grew   peg   goat   (flew)

3. clue   (glue)   call   nice

4. Ruth   scarf   pail   (truth)

5. group   game   (soup)   walk

APPROACHING	BEYOND	ELL
p. 271	p. 271	p. 271

Word Work

Quick Review

High-Frequency Words: Read, Spell, and Write to review last week's high-frequency words: *above, build, fall, knew, money, toward.*

MINILESSON 5 Mins · Spelling

OBJECTIVES

CCSS Recognize and read grade-appropriate irregularly spelled words. **RF.1.3g**

CCSS Use conventional spelling for words with common spelling patterns and for frequently occurring irregular words. **L.1.2d**

Words with /ü/ Spellings

Dictation Use the Spelling Dictation routine for each word to help children transfer their knowledge of sound-spellings to writing.

Pretest After dictation, pronounce each spelling word. Say a sentence for each word and pronounce the word again. Ask children to say each word softly, stretching the sounds, before writing it. After the pretest, display the spelling words and write each word as you say the letter names. Have children check their words.

moon	tune	flew	blue	fruit
soup	toy	coin	enough	door

For Approaching Level and Beyond Level children, refer to the Differentiated Spelling Lists for modified word lists.

Go Digital

Spelling Word Routine

High-Frequency Word Routine

Visual Glossary

MINILESSON 5 Mins · High-Frequency Words

answer, brought, busy, door, enough, eyes

1 Model Display **High-Frequency Word Cards** *answer, brought, busy, door, enough, eyes.* Use the Read/Spell/Write routine to teach each word.

ELL

ENGLISH LANGUAGE LEARNERS

Pantomime Review the meaning of these words by using pictures, pantomime, or gestures when possible. Have children repeat or act out the word.

- **Read** Point to and say the word *answer. This is the word* answer. *Say it with me:* answer. *Did you answer the question?*

- **Spell** *The word* answer *is spelled* a-n-s-w-e-r. *Spell it with me.*

- **Write** *Let's write the word in the air as we say each letter:* a-n-s-w-e-r.

- Follow the steps to introduce *brought, busy, door, enough, eyes.*

- As children spell each word with you, point out the irregularities in sound-spellings, such as the silent *w* in the word *answer.*

 · Have partners create sentences using each word.

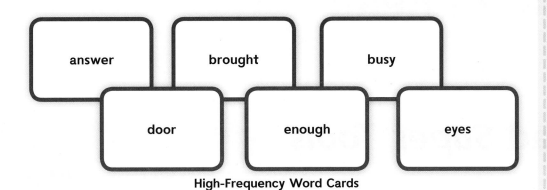

High-Frequency Word Cards

2 **Guided Practice** Have children read the sentences. Prompt them to identify the high-frequency words in connected text and to blend the decodable words.

1. I will **answer** the phone.
2. Sam **brought** his flute home from school.
3. We had a **busy** day at school today.
4. Who opened the **door**?
5. Do we have **enough** time to play this game?
6. My **eyes** are brown.

MINILESSON 5 Mins

Introduce Vocabulary

demand, emergency

1 **Model** Introduce the new words using the routine.

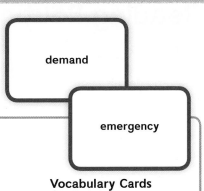

Vocabulary Cards

Vocabulary Routine

<u>Define:</u> If you **demand** someone do something, you ask forcefully or strongly.

<u>Example:</u> *My parents demand that I do my homework.*

<u>Ask:</u> What do people demand that you do? EXAMPLES

<u>Define:</u> An **emergency** is something that you do not expect and need to take care of right away.

<u>Example:</u> *The police helped us during the emergency.*

<u>Ask:</u> How do you feel during an emergency? PRIOR KNOWLEDGE

2 **Review** Use the routine to review last week's vocabulary words.

Monitor and *Differentiate*

 Quick Check

Can children read and decode words with variant vowel /ü/?

Can children recognize and read high-frequency and vocabulary words?

Small Group Instruction

If No →	Approaching	Reteach pp.T56–59
	ELL	Develop pp. T70–77
If Yes→	On Level	Review pp. T64–65
	Beyond Level	Extend pp. T68–69

→ **Shared Read**

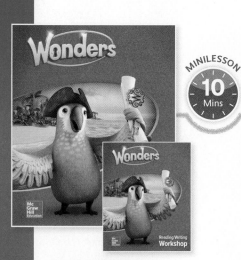

Reading/Writing Workshop Big Book and Reading/Writing Workshop

OBJECTIVES

CCSS Decode regularly spelled one-syllable words. **RF.1.3b**

CCSS Recognize and read grade-appropriate irregularly spelled words. **RF.1.3g**

Understand nonfiction genre

ACADEMIC LANGUAGE

• *nonfiction, wild, survive*
• Cognate: *no ficción*

See pages T70–T71 for Interactive Question-Response routine for the Shared Read.

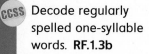

Read *Super Tools*

Focus on Foundational Skills

Review with children the words and letter-sounds in *Super Tools*.

• Have children use pages 218–219 to review high-frequency words *brought, door, busy, enough, eyes, answer,* and vocabulary words *demand* and *emergency*.

• Have children use pages 220–221 to review that the letters *ui, u, ew, oo, u_e, ou,* and *ue* can stand for the /ü/ sound. Guide them to blend the sounds to read the words.

• Display the story words *writing, watched, picture, draw, drawing,* and *drawn.* Spell each word and model reading it. Tell children they will be reading the words in the selection.

Read Guide children in reading *Super Tools.* Point out the high-frequency words, vocabulary words, and words in which *oo, u, u_e, ew, ue, ui,* and *ou* stand for the /ü/ sound.

Close Reading Routine

Read DOK 1–2

• Identify key ideas and details about how the writing tools work together.
• Take notes and retell.
• Use ACT prompts as needed.

Reread DOK 2–3

• Analyze the text, craft, and structure.
• Use the Reread minilessons.

Integrate DOK 4

• Integrate knowledge and ideas.
• Make text-to-text connections.
• Use the Integrate Lesson.

Genre: Fantasy Tell children that *Super Tools* is a fantasy. A fantasy is a made-up story that could not happen in real life; often has characters who are not people, but talk and act like real people; and has a beginning, a middle, and an end.

Go Digital

Super Tools

Super Tools

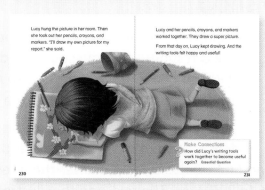

READING/WRITING WORKSHOP, pp. 222–231 **Lexile** 430

Connect to Concept: Taking Action

ESSENTIAL QUESTION Explain to children that as they read *Super Tools,* they will look for key ideas and details that will help them answer the Essential Question: *How can we work together to make our lives better?*

- Pages 224–225: What new thing does Lucy get?
- Pages 226–227: How do her writing tools help with her report?
- Pages 228–229: What does seeing the picture make Lucy wish?
- Pages 230–231: What does Lucy decide to do for her report?

Focus on Fluency

With partners, have children read *Super Tools* to develop fluency. Remind them that they can ask themselves questions to understand what they are reading. Have them use both text and illustrations to answer their questions.

Retell Have partners use key ideas and details to retell *Super Tools.* Invite them to tell how Lucy's computer and writing tools are super tools.

Make Connections

Read together Make Connections on page 231. Use this sentence starter to help partners talk about how Lucy's writing tools worked together:

> *First, the pencils . . .*

Guide children to connect what they have read to the Essential Question.

OBJECTIVES

CCSS Write informative/ explanatory texts in which they name a topic, supply some facts about the topic, and provide some sense of closure. **W.1.2**

CCSS Use personal, possessive, and indefinite pronouns (e.g., *I, me, my; they, them, their, anyone, everything*). **L.1.1d**

CCSS Use personal (subject, object), possessive, and indefinite pronouns (e.g., *I, me, my; they, them, their; anyone, everything*). **CA L.1.1d**

ACADEMIC LANGUAGE

• *persuade, pronoun, sentence, text*

• Cognates: *persuadir, texto*

Write About the Reading/Writing Workshop

Analyze the Prompt Tell children that today the class will work together to write a response to a question. Read the prompt aloud. *How did the writing tools persuade Lucy to use them again?* Say: *To respond to this question, we need to look at the text and illustrations in* Super Tools.

Find Text Evidence Explain that you will reread the text to find evidence and take notes to help answer the question. Read aloud pages 226 to 227. Say: *The text and the illustrations tell me that the writing tools work together to persuade Lucy to use them again. On page 226, the tools are watching while Lucy finishes her report about birds on the computer. I see in the illustration that they don't look happy. Then on page 227, the writing tools work together to draw a picture to go with Lucy's report. They want to show Lucy that she can use her computer and her writing tools. These are details that will help us answer the prompt. Let's write them in our notes.*

Write to a Prompt Reread the prompt to children. *How did the writing tools persuade Lucy to use them again?* Say: *Let's use some of the words from the prompt for our first sentence: The writing tools worked together to persuade Lucy to use them again.* Write the sentence. *As we read our notes, think about which notes tell us how the writing tools worked together to persuade Lucy to use them again.* Track the print as you reread the notes.

Guide children to dictate complete sentences for you to record. Read the final response as you track the print.

Go Digital

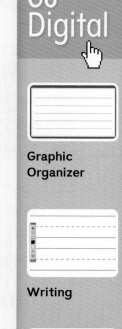

Graphic Organizer

Writing

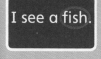

I see a fish.

Grammar

Grammar

Pronouns

1 Explain Review that a noun is a person, place, thing, or idea. Explain that pronouns are words that take the place of nouns. Display the following sentences:

My name is ____. I am your teacher. Your name is ____. You are one student in this class. John is a boy. He is in our class. Myra is a girl. She is in our class.

You and I are in this room. We are in this room. The kids are sitting in the corner. They are sitting in the corner.

Circle the pronouns and explain that a pronoun can stand for a certain person or group of people.

2 Guided Practice/Practice Display the paragraph below and read it aloud. Have children identify the pronouns.

We got fruit at the farm stand. (we) They will make a fruit pie. (they) You can help, too. (you) She cuts up a plum. (she) He makes the crust. (he) I know it will taste good! (I, it)

Talk About It Have partners use their own names in oral sentences, and then replace them with the pronoun *I*. Then have them make sentences using *you, he, she, it, we,* and *they.*

Link to Writing Say: *Let's look back at our writing and see if we used any pronouns to tell how the writing tools persuaded Lucy.* Review the Shared Writing for the correct use of pronouns. If pronouns are not in the Shared Writing, work with children to add them and reread the response together.

ENGLISH LANGUAGE LEARNERS SCAFFOLD

Beginning

Demonstrate Comprehension Reread the sentences in the Practice section. As you circle each pronoun, point to children to demonstrate its meaning. Instruct children to point to themselves and say "I." Then have them point to you and say "you."

Intermediate

Explain Write the pronouns on individual cards. Have the child pick a card and tell what the pronoun stands for. Repeat correct answers slowly and clearly.

Advanced/High

Expand Have groups of children practice using pronouns by standing in different arrangements. For example, have one child point to another child and say "you." Then have the two children stand together and say "we."

Daily Wrap Up

- Encourage children to discuss the Essential Question using the oral vocabulary words. Ask: *How do we work together in our classroom?*

- Prompt children to share the skills they learned. Ask: *What reading skills did you use today?*

Materials

Reading/Writing Workshop
VOLUME 4

Reading/Writing Workshop Big Book
UNIT 6

Visual Vocabulary Cards

argument   risk
conflict   shift
fair

High-Frequency Word Cards

answer   door
brought   enough
busy   eyes

Teaching Poster

Spelling Word Cards

| a | b | c |

Word-Building Cards

demand

Vocabulary Cards
demand   emergency

Interactive Read-Aloud Cards

Sound-Spelling Cards

→ Build the Concept

Go Digital

MINILESSON
5 Mins

Oral Language

COLLABORATE

ESSENTIAL QUESTION

Remind children that this week you've been talking and reading about how people can make things better by working together. Remind them of how the mice tried to solve their problem and how the writing tools worked together. Guide children to discuss the Essential Question using information from what they read and discussed on Day 1.

Oral Vocabulary Words

Review the oral vocabulary words. Use the Define/Example/Ask routine to review the oral vocabulary words *argument, conflict, fair, risk,* and *shift.*

- When you have an argument with a friend, how do you solve the problem?
- What conflict do the writing tools have in *Super Tools*?
- How does it feel when someone does not treat you in a fair way?
- If you had to shift something big, would it be easier to do together with another person? Why?
- Can you name some story characters who take risks?

OBJECTIVES

CCSS

Ask and answer questions about key details in a text read aloud or information presented orally or through other media. **SL.1.2**

- Discuss the Essential Question
- Build concept understanding

ACADEMIC LANGUAGE

- *reread, problem, solution*
- Cognates: *problema, solución*

school

Visual Glossary

"The Cat's Bell"

Listening Comprehension

MINILESSON 5 Mins

Reread the Interactive Read Aloud

Strategy: Reread

Remind children that as they listen, they can reread parts of the text that they did not understand the first time.

Tell children that you will reread "The Cat's Bell." Display the Interactive Read-Aloud Cards. Pause as you read to model the strategy.

"The Cat's Bell"

Think Aloud When I read, I can go back and read parts of the text again to make sure I understood everything. The first time I read "The Cat's Bell," I wasn't sure I understood what the mice wanted to do to the cat, so I reread that part of the story. After I reread, I understood that they wanted to put a bell on the cat so they would hear it and know when the cat was close by.

Make Connections

Discuss partners' responses to "The Cat's Bell."

- *Do you think the mice came up with a good solution to their problem?*

- *Do you think the mice could have done a better job of working together? How?*

- *Help children to recall story details to support their responses.*

Write About It Have children come up with another possible solution to the mice's problem and describe it in their Writer's Notebooks. Guide children by asking questions such as, *Is there a way the mice could work together to scare the cat away? Is there another way the mice could make a warning system?* Have children write continuously for six minutes.

 **Word Work**

Quick Review

Build Fluency: Sound-Spellings
Display the **Word-Building Cards:** *oo, u, u_e, ew, ue, ui, ou, oy, oi, ar, ore, oar, er, ir, ur, ey, igh, oa, oe, ee, ea, ai, ay, e_e, u_e, o_e, dge, i_e, a_e, _ce.* Have children say the sounds.

Phonemic Awareness

Go Digital

Phoneme Segmentation

OBJECTIVES

CCSS Segment spoken single-syllable words into their complete sequence of individual sounds (phonemes). **RF.1.2d**

CCSS Decode regularly spelled one-syllable words. **RF.1.3b**

1 **Model** Show children how to segment words into phonemes. *Listen as I say a word:* moose. *How many sounds do you hear in* moose? *Listen: /m/ /ü/ /s/. I hear three sounds in* moose.

2 **Guided Practice/Practice** Have children segment the words and say the number of sounds. Do the first one together.

school	flew	broom	group
tooth	prune	grew	bruise

Phonemic Awareness

Phonics

Review Variant Vowel /ü/

1 **Model** Display the *Spoon* **Sound-Spelling Card**. Review the sound /ü/ spelled *oo, u, u_e, ew, ue, ui,* and *ou* using the words *spoon, truth, tube, grew, true, juice,* and *group.*

2 **Guided Practice/Practice** Have children practice connecting the letters and sound. Point to the letters *oo, u, u_e, ew, ue, ui,* and *ou* on the Sound-Spelling Card. *What are these letters? What sound do they stand for?*

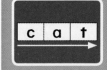

Phonics

Structural Analysis

Handwriting

Blend with Variant Vowel /ü/

1 Model Display **Word-Building Cards** *b, l, u, e* to form the word *blue*. Model how to generate and blend the sounds to say the word. *This is the letter* b. *It stands for /b/. This is the letter* l. *It stands for /l/. These are the letters* ue. *Together they stand for /ü/. Listen as I blend these sounds together: /blllüüü/. Say it with me:* blue. Continue by modeling the words *root, fruit,* and *news*.

2 Guided Practice/Practice Repeat the routine with children with *soup, flew, roof, tune, hoop, drew, scoop, noon, suit, true.*

Build with Variant Vowel /ü/

1 Model Display the Word-Building Cards *m, o, o, n.* Blend: /m/ /ü/ /n/, /mmmüüünnn/, *moon.*

Replace *n* with *d* and repeat with *mood.*

Change *m* to *f* and repeat with *food.*

2 Guided Practice/Practice Continue with *fool, tool, too, zoo, zoom, room, root, fruit, suit, sue, due, dew, drew, grew, group.*

ENGLISH LANGUAGE LEARNERS

Build Vocabulary Review the meanings of example words that can be explained or demonstrated in a concrete way. For example, ask children to point to something *blue,* a piece of *fruit,* or the *roof* of a building. Model the actions for *flew* and *drew* as you say, *"A bird flew away. I drew a picture of it."* Have children repeat. Provide sentence starters, such as, *"At noon I ____ "* for children to complete. Correct grammar and pronunciation as needed.

MINILESSON 5 Mins

Structural Analysis

Suffixes *-ful* and *-less*

1 Model Write and read *help, helpful,* and *helpless.* Explain that some word parts added to the end of words are called suffixes. Underline *-ful.* Tell children that the suffix *-ful* means "full" or "full of." Explain that when you add *-ful* to the end of *help,* the new word *helpful* means "full of help." Use *helpful* in a sentence.

Read *helpless.* Underline *-less.* Tell children that the suffix *-less* means "without." Explain that when you add *-less* to the end of *help,* the new word *helpless* means "without help." Use *helpless* in a sentence.

2 Guided Practice/Practice Write the following words: *fearful, joyful, toothless, useless.* For each word, help children identify the root word and suffix, blend the word, tell what it means, and use it in a sentence.

Word Work

MINILESSON 5 Mins

Spelling

Word Sort with /ü/ Spellings

1 Model Display the **Spelling Word Cards** from the Teacher's Resource Book, one at a time. Have children read each word, listening for the /ü/ sound.

Make cards for *food, rule, grew, glue, suit,* and *group* to create a six-column chart. Say each word, and have children spell them.

2 Guided Practice/Practice Have children place each Spelling Word Card in the column with the same spelling for /ü/. Have children read the words. Then call out a word. Have a child find the word card and point to it as the class spells the word.

ANALYZE ERRORS/ARTICULATION SUPPORT

Use children's pretest errors to analyze spelling problems and provide corrective feedback. For example, some children might have difficulty using different spellings for the same sound. They might spell *moon,* for example, with an alternate /ü/ spelling.

Have children make word cards for each spelling word. Ask them to trace the letters that stand for /ü/ in a color. Suggest they use a different color for each spelling. As children say and spell each word, have them use their fingers to trace the /ü/ spelling.

Go Digital

Spelling Word Sort

High-Frequency Word Routine

school
Visual Glossary

MINILESSON 5 Mins

High-Frequency Words

answer, brought, busy, door, enough, eyes

1 Guided Practice Say each word and have children Read/Spell/Write it. Ask children to picture the word in their minds and write it the way they see it. Display the words for children to self-correct.

- Point out irregularities in sound-spellings, such as the /i/ sound spelled *u* in *busy* or the /f/ sound spelled *gh* in *enough.*

2 Practice Add the high-frequency words *answer, brought, busy, door, enough,* and *eyes* to the cumulative word bank.

- Have partners create sentences using the words.

- Have children look at the words and compare their sounds and spellings to words from previous weeks.

- Suggest that children write about how they can work together to make their lives easier.

Cumulative Review Review last week's words using the Read/Spell/Write routine.

- Repeat the above routine, mixing the words and having children say each one.

MINILESSON
5 Mins

Reinforce Vocabulary

demand, emergency

1 Guided Practice Use the **Vocabulary Cards** to review this week's and last week's vocabulary words. Work together with children to generate a new context sentence for each word.

2 Practice Have children work with a partner to orally complete each sentence stem on the Day 2 Vocabulary Practice Activity using this week's and last week's vocabulary words.

> emergency   demand   balance   section

1. One ____ of the road is closed today.
2. Can you ____ yourself on one leg?
3. Did you ____ that she give back your book?
4. Call 9-1-1 when you have an ____.   Also online

Day 2 Vocabulary Practice Activity

ON-LEVEL PRACTICE BOOK p. 272

Complete each sentence. Use one of the words in the box.

> answer   brought   busy   door   enough   eyes

1. Dad said, "Please ____answer____ me now."

2. We use our ____eyes____ to see.

3. Gram ____brought____ me a gift today.

4. Mom is too ____busy____ to go to the park today.

5. Do we have ____enough____ eggs to make the cupcakes?

6. Please close the ____door____ when you come in.

APPROACHING p. 272	BEYOND p. 272	ELL p. 272

Monitor and *Differentiate*

✓ **Quick Check**

Can children read and decode words with variant vowel /ü/?

Can children recognize and read high-frequency and vocabulary words?

⬇

Small Group Instruction

If No → Approaching Reteach pp.T56–59
         ELL   Develop pp. T70–77
If Yes→ On Level   Review pp. T64–65
        Beyond Level Extend pp. T68–69

Comprehension

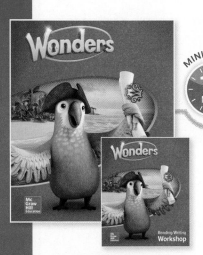

Reading/Writing Workshop Big Book and Reading/Writing Workshop

---

OBJECTIVES

CCSS Retell stories, including key details, and demonstrate understanding of their central message or lesson. **RL.1.2**

Understand fantasy genre

ACADEMIC LANGUAGE
- *fantasy, theme*
- Cognates: *fantasía, tema*

MINILESSON
10
Mins

Reread *Super Tools*

Genre: Fantasy

1 Model Tell children they will now reread the fantasy selection *Super Tools*. Explain that as they read, they will look for information in the text to help them understand the selection.

Review the characteristics of a fantasy. It:

- is a made-up story that could not happen in real life.

- often has characters that are animals or objects that look and act like people.

- has a beginning, a middle, and an end.

Tell children that the characters in a fantasy story often act like real people. *A fantasy is a made-up story with a setting and characters. Sometimes the characters in a fantasy are animals or objects that talk and act like real people.*

Display pages 224–225: *At the beginning of this story, Lucy has a new computer. The illustration shows that Lucy's pencils, crayons, and markers are having a meeting. The text tells what they are saying. These writing tools are acting like people. That tells us that this is a fantasy.*

2 Guided Practice/Practice Display pages 226 and 227 of *Super Tools*. Read page 227 aloud. Say: *This is the middle of the story. These writing tools are doing things that pencils, crayons, and markers could not really do. Could the events in this story really happen? What does that tell us about the story?*

Go Digital

Super Tools

Genre

Theme

SKILLS TRACE

THEME

Introduce	Unit 6 Week 1
Review	Unit 6 Weeks 3, 4
Assess	Unit 6 Weeks 1, 4

Skill: Theme

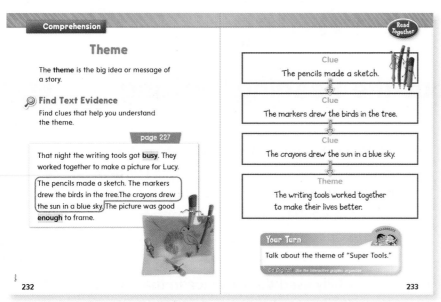

Reading/Writing Workshop, pp. 232–233

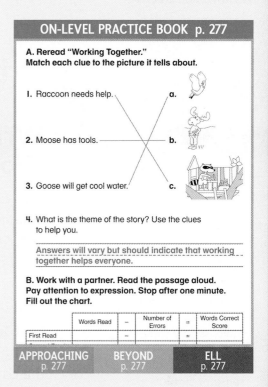

A. Reread "Working Together."
Match each clue to the picture it tells about.

1. Raccoon needs help.   a.

2. Moose has tools.   b.

3. Goose will get cool water.   c.

4. What is the theme of the story? Use the clues to help you.

Answers will vary but should indicate that working together helps everyone.

B. Work with a partner. Read the passage aloud. Pay attention to expression. Stop after one minute. Fill out the chart.

	Words Read	–	Number of Errors	=	Words Correct Score
First Read		–		=	

APPROACHING p. 277	BEYOND p. 277	ELL p. 277

1 Model Tell children that when they read a fantasy, they can think about the message that the author wants to share. Have children look at pages 232–233 in their Reading/Writing Workshop. Read together the definition of theme. *The theme is the big idea or message of a story.*

2 Guided Practice/Practice Read together the Find Text Evidence section and model using clues to find the theme of *Super Tools.*
Point out the information added to the graphic organizer. *The illustration and the text on page 227 tells us that the pencils made a sketch. That clue is added to the Theme chart. The information gives us a clue about the message of the story. What other clues can we find in the story to help us understand the theme?*

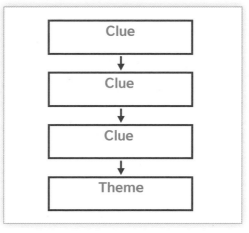

Teaching Poster

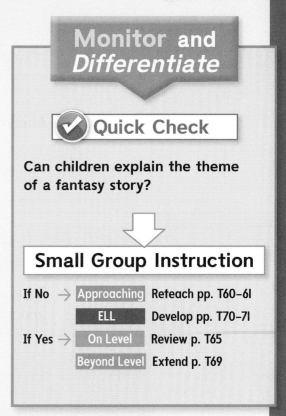

Monitor and *Differentiate*

✓ Quick Check

Can children explain the theme of a fantasy story?

Small Group Instruction

If No → **Approaching** Reteach pp. T60–6I

ELL Develop pp. T70–7I

If Yes → **On Level** Review p. T65

Beyond Level Extend p. T69

Write About the Reading/Writing Workshop

Reading/Writing Workshop

OBJECTIVES

CCSS Write informative/ explanatory texts in which they name a topic, supply some facts about the topic, and provide some sense of closure. **W.1.2**

CCSS Use personal, possessive, and indefinite pronouns (e.g., *I, me, my; they, them, their, anyone, everything*). **L.1.1d**

ACADEMIC LANGUAGE

• *letter, details, text, sentence length*
• Cognates: *detalles, texto*

Analyze the Model Prompt Have children turn to page 234 in the **Reading/Writing Workshop.** Billy responded to the prompt: *Write a letter from the computer to the writing tools. Tell how Lucy can use all of them.* Say: *The prompt is asking Billy to write a letter from the computer to the writing tools. To answer this prompt, Billy looked for text evidence in* Super Tools.

Find Text Evidence Explain that Billy used the evidence in the text and illustrations to take notes. Then, he used his note to write a letter from the computer explaining how Lucy could use both the computer and the writing tools.

Graphic Organizer

Writing

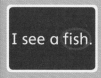

Grammar

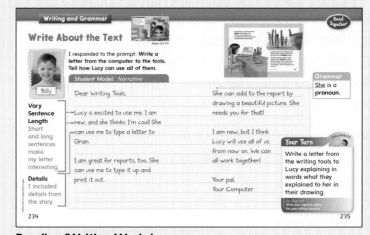

Reading/Writing Workshop

Analyze the Student Model Read the model. Discuss the callouts.

• **Vary Sentence Length** Billy used both short sentences and long sentences to add variety to his letter. **Trait: Sentence Fluency**

• **Details** Billy included details from the story to explain how Lucy could use both the computer and writing tools. **Trait: Ideas**

• **Pronouns** Billy correctly used pronouns to take the place of nouns. **Grammar**

Point out that Billy began his letter with a greeting to the writing tools and ended it with a closing by the computer.

Your Turn: Write a Letter Say: *Now we will write to a new prompt.* Have children turn to page 235 of the **Reading/Writing Workshop**. Read the Your Turn prompt together: *Write a letter from the writing tools to Lucy explaining in words what they explained to her in their drawing.*

Find Text Evidence Say: *To respond to this prompt, we need to look back at the story and the illustrations and take notes. We're looking for details that help us imagine what the writing tools would say to Lucy. On page 225, the writing tools meet and decide to remind Lucy how great they are. On 227, they work together to draw a bird to show her they can help with her report, too. These are details we can use in our letter.*

Write to a Prompt Say: *First, we need to write a greeting to Lucy. Let's write a greeting followed by a comma: Dear Lucy.* Write the greeting. Say: *Now let's use our notes to write our first two sentences: We just want to remind you that writing tools are great! We can help with your report, too.* Write the sentences. Tell children you will reread the notes to help them add sentences to the letter. Track the print as you reread the notes. Say: *Let's look back and see if we used both short and long sentences. Did we include details from the story and end with a closing by the writing tools?* Read the final response as you track the print.

For additional practice with the writing traits, have children turn to page 282 of the **Your Turn Practice Book**.

Grammar

5 Mins

Pronouns

① **Review** Remind children that the pronouns *I, he, she,* and *it* stand for one noun; *we* and *they* stand for more than one; and *you* can stand for one or more.

② **Guided Practice/Practice** Display the sentences below and read them aloud. Have children choose which pronoun could replace the underlined subject of each sentence.

> <u>Bruce and Ruth</u> were born on the same day. (They, She) (They) <u>Bruce</u> wants to have a party. (I, He) (He) <u>Ruth</u> wants to go skating. (They, She) (She) <u>Luke and I</u> think they should have a skating party. (It, We) (We)

Talk About It Have partners work together to come up with oral sentences about Bruce and Ruth's party that use the pronouns *I, you,* and *it.*

Daily Wrap Up

- Discuss the Essential Question and encourage children to use the oral vocabulary words. Ask: *How could we work together to make our classroom better?*

- Prompt children to discuss what they learned today by asking: *How did the skills you learned today help you?*

Materials

Reading/Writing Workshop
VOLUME 4

Literature Anthology
VOLUME 4

Visual Vocabulary Cards

argument	answer
conflict	brought
fair	busy
risk	door
shift	enough
demand	eyes
emergency	

Teaching Poster

Response Board

Word-Building Cards

Sound-Spelling Cards

Interactive Read-Aloud Cards

Spelling Word Cards

→ Build the Concept

Oral Language
5 Mins

OBJECTIVES
Read grade-level text orally with accuracy, appropriate rate, and expression. **RF.1.4b**

Review point of view

ACADEMIC LANGUAGE
- *point of view, illustration, character*
- Cognate: *ilustración*

ESSENTIAL QUESTION

Remind children that this week you have been talking and reading about working together to make things better. Remind them of the mice working together to find a way to avoid the cat and how Lucy's tools worked together. Guide children to discuss the question using information from what they have read and talked about throughout the week.

Review Oral Vocabulary

Review the oral vocabulary words *argument, conflict, fair, risk,* and *shift* using the Define/Example/Ask routine. Prompt children to use the words as they discuss how we can work together to make our lives better.

Visual Vocabulary Cards

Comprehension/ Fluency

Point of View

1 Explain Tell children they have been learning about identifying theme to help them understand the stories they read. Remind them they have also learned how to determine the point of view of the characters in a story. *As we read, we can use text and illustrations to understand how a character thinks and feels. Understanding a character's point of view can help us better understand why the character does things.*

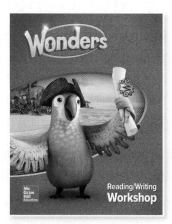

Reading/Writing Workshop

2 Model Display pages 224 and 225 of *Super Tools. I read in the text that Lucy's tools are not happy about her new computer. They feel sad and useless. In the illustration on page 224, I can see that they look sad. This helps us understand their point of view: they miss being used by Lucy.*

3 Guided Practice/Practice Reread *Super Tools*. Use text evidence to identify the point of view of the tools and of Lucy.

Expression: Dialogue

1 Explain Tell children as you read the passage, you will read the dialogue with lots of expression to show how the characters are feeling. You will also change your voice slightly to show that different characters are speaking.

2 Model Read a section of the *Super Tools* with dialogue. *I read the words between the quotation marks with different voices and expression to show how the characters feel.* Point out how the expression you use is different for each character.

3 Guided Practice/Practice Have children reread the passage chorally. Remind them to read the dialogue with feeling and with different voices for each character.

Fluency Practice Children can practice using Practice Book passages.

ENGLISH LANGUAGE LEARNERS

Retell Guide children to retell by using a question prompt on each page. *What are the tools doing? Why?* Provide sentence starters for children to complete orally. *The tools feel ____. They want to ____.*

→ # Word Work

Quick Review

Build Fluency: Sound-Spellings

Display the Word-Building Cards: *oo, u, u_e, ew, ue, ui, ou, oy, oi, ar, ore, oar, er, ir, ur, ey, igh, oa, oe, ee, ea, ai, ay, e_e, u_e, o_e, dge, i_e, a_e, _ce.* Have children say the sounds.

Phonological Awareness

OBJECTIVES

CCSS Decode regularly spelled one-syllable words. **RF.1.3b**

CCSS Use frequently occurring affixes as a clue to the meaning of a word. **L.1.4b**

Identify and generate rhyming words

Identify and Generate Rhyme

1 Model Review with children how to identify and then generate rhyming words. *Listen carefully as I say three words:* pool, stool, bill. *Pool and* stool *rhyme because they both end with the same sounds: /ül/. What is another word that rhymes with* pool *and* stool? *Rule ends with /ül/ too, so* rule *rhymes with* pool *and* stool.

2 Guided Practice/Practice Have children practice identifying and generating rhyming words. Do the first one with them.

soon, could, noon   loose, tube, goose

boy, too, you   school, coop, group

Phonics

Blend with Variant Vowel /ü/

1 Model Display **Word-Building Cards** *s, u, i, t.* Model how to blend the sounds. *This is the letter* s. *It stands for /s/. These are the letters* ui. *Together they stand for /ü/. This is the letter* t. *It stands for /t/. Let's blend all three sounds: /süüüt/. The word is* suit. Continue by modeling the words *flute, spool, stew,* and *truth.*

2 Guided Practice/Practice Review the words and sentences on the Day 3 Phonics Practice Activity with children. Read each word in the first row, blending the sounds; for example: */f/ /ü/ /d/; /füüüd/. The word is* food.

• Have children blend each word with you. Prompt children to read the connected text, sounding out the decodable words.

Go Digital

Phonological Awareness

Phonics

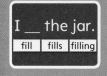

Structural Analysis

Handwriting

food	too	new	moo	snoop
room	rule	grew	group	youth
juice	zoom	blue	tool	truth
painful	endless	hopeful	useful	clueless
helpless	harmful	useless	spoonful	cloudless

Luke and June found glue at school.

Ruby used a spoon to stir the stew.

Also online

Day 3 Phonics Practice Activity

Decodable Reader Have children read "Rooster and Goose" (pages 1–4), "The Flute Youth" (9–12), "Lewis and His New Suit" (17–20), and "Sue and Lucy" (25–28) to practice decoding words in connected text.

MINILESSON 5 Mins

Structural Analysis

Suffixes *-ful* and *-less*

1 Model Write and read *spoon* and *spoonful*. Review with children that the suffix *-ful* means "full" or "full of" so *spoonful* means "a spoon that is full." Use *spoonful* in a sentence. Repeat with *cloud* and *cloudless*. Remind children that *-less* means "without."

2 Practice/Apply Write these words: *pain, hope, use,* and *harm*. Read the words with children. As you point to each word, ask children to add *-ful,* blend the new word, tell what it means, and use it in a sentence. Repeat with *-less*.

Corrective Feedback

Corrective Feedback Say: *My turn.* Then lead children in blending the sounds. Say: *Do it with me.* You will respond with children to offer support. Then say: *Your turn. Blend.* Have children chorally blend. Return to the beginning of the word. Say: *Let's start over.*

→ # Word Work

MINILESSON
5 Mins

Spelling

OBJECTIVES

CCSS Recognize and read grade-appropriate irregularly spelled words. **RF.1.3g**

CCSS Use conventional spelling for words with common spelling patterns and for frequently occurring regular words. **L.1.2d**

Word Sort with /ü/ Spellings

❶ **Model** Make index cards for *oo, u_e, ew, ue, ui,* and *ou* and form six columns in a pocket chart. Say the sound with children.

Hold up the *moon* **Spelling Word Card**. Say and spell *moon.* Pronounce each sound clearly: /m/ /ü/ /n/. Blend the sounds, stretching the vowel sound: /müüün/. Place the word below the *oo* card.

❷ **Guided Practice/Practice** Have children spell the word. Repeat the process with the *u_e, ew, ue, ui,* and *ou* words.

Display the words *toy, coin, enough,* and *door* in a separate column. Read and spell the words together with children. Point out that these spelling words do not contain the /ü/ sound.

Conclude by asking children to orally generate additional words that rhyme with each word. Write down the additional words.

Go Digital

Spelling Word Sort

school

Visual Glossary

MINILESSON
5 Mins

High-Frequency Words

answer, brought, busy, door, enough, eyes

PHONICS/SPELLING PRACTICE BOOK p. 128

❶ **Guided Practice** Say each word and have children Read/Spell/Write it. Point out irregularities in sound-spellings, such as the spelling of *eyes.*

• Display **Visual Vocabulary Cards** to review this week's words.

| moon | tune | flew | blue |
| fruit | soup | enough | door |

Find the spelling words in the puzzle. Draw a circle around each word.

f	r	u	i	t	p	s	x	u
n	w	m	g	t	b	v	m	j
f	t	k	i	u	s	o	u	p
l	r	t	m	n	n	w	u	z
e	m	l	b	e	h	t	d	m
w	k	b	l	u	e	m	o	l
m	v	t	g	r	m	f	o	l
e	n	o	u	g	h	r	r	e
p	r	f	c	o	m	o	o	n
q	r	m	f	j	z	a	d	h

Visual Vocabulary Cards

❷ **Practice** Repeat the activity with last week's words.

Build Fluency: Word Automaticity

Have children read the following sentences aloud together at the same pace. Repeat several times.

The bell rings. I open my eyes. "Who is there?" I ask.

"We are," Gram and Gramps answer.

I open the door.

"Are you and Dad busy?" they ask. "We brought lunch. We have enough food for all of us."

Vocabulary

demand, emergency

Review Use the **Visual Vocabulary Cards** to review this week's words using the Define/Example/Ask routine. Have partners generate context sentences for each vocabulary word.

Visual Vocabulary Cards

Strategy: Synonyms

❶ **Model** Tell children that some words have almost the same meaning as other words. Point out that you can find synonyms in a dictionary or a thesaurus. Use *Super Tools* to discuss synonyms.

Think Aloud In *Super Tools*, we read the word *exclaimed* in the sentence: "This is so cool!,' exclaimed Lucy." The word *exclaimed* is another way to say *said*, but with great excitement. The two words have similar meanings. What other words can you write for *said*?

❷ **Guided Practice** Work with children to create a list of synonyms for such words from the story as *said, happy, sad,* and *cool.* Help children use a dictionary or thesaurus, as needed or appropriate.

❸ **Practice** Have partners find the word *demand* in the story and discuss what it means. Then have them brainstorm synonyms for *demand.* Help them use a dictionary or a thesaurus to find synonyms, such as *ask* and *request.* Remind children that entries in a dictionary are in alphabetical order and that children should look at the first letter to help them locate a word. Repeat for *emergency.*

Monitor and *Differentiate*

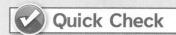

✓ **Quick Check**

Can children read and decode words with variant vowel /ü/?

Can children recognize and read high-frequency and vocabulary words?

⬇

Small Group Instruction

If No → Approaching   Reteach pp. T56–59

         ELL   Develop pp. T70–77

If Yes → On Level   Review pp. T64–65

         Beyond Level   Extend pp. T68–69

WORD WORK   **T35**

Genre Fantasy

Essential Question

How can we work together to make our lives better?

Read about how some smart cows and hens get what they want.

Go Digital!

Click, Clack, Moo Cows That Type

by Doreen Cronin

illustrated by Betsy Lewin

270

271

LITERATURE ANTHOLOGY, pp. 270–271

Wonders

Literature Anthology

Click, Clack, Moo: Cows That Type

Lexile 380

Close Reading Routine

Read   DOK 1–2

- Identify key ideas and details about how the animals take action.
- Take notes and retell.
- Use **ACT** prompts as needed.

Reread   DOK 2–3

- Analyze the text, craft, and structure.
- Use *Close Reading Companion*, pp. 166–168.

Integrate   DOK 4

- Integrate knowledge and ideas.
- Make text-to-text connections.
- Use the Integrate Lesson.

Read

ESSENTIAL QUESTION

Read aloud the Essential Question: *How can we work together to make our lives better?* Read aloud the title. Ask: *What do you predict this story is about?* Tell children that as they read, they should think about how the animals work together.

Story Words Read, spell, and define the words *impossible, sincerely, typewriter, impatient, strike, neutral,* and *ultimatum.* Explain that they will read these words in the selection.

Note Taking: Graphic Organizer As children read the selection, guide them to fill in **Your Turn Practice Book** page 274.

Farmer Brown has a problem.
His cows like to type.
All day long he hears
Click, clack, **moo.**
Click, clack, **moo.**
Clickety, clack, **moo.** **1** **2**

272

At first, he couldn't believe his ears.
Cows that type.
Impossible!
Click, clack, **moo.**
Click, clack, **moo.**
Clickety, clack, **moo.**

273

LITERATURE ANTHOLOGY, pp. 272–273

1 **Strategy: Reread**

Teacher Think Aloud I read that Farmer Brown hears "Click, clack, moo" sounds. What is happening on this page? I know that cows "moo" and typewriters make "click, clack" sounds. I'll reread to see if I missed something. I read that the farmer's cows like to type. Now I understand that the cows are making the sounds as they type.

2 **Skill: Theme**

Remember, the theme of a story is the message the author wants to share. What characters say and do can help us figure out the theme. As we read this story, we'll fill in a Theme chart.

A C T **Access Complex Text**

▶ **What makes this text complex?**

Text Organization An understanding of what a letter is and how to distinguish letters within a story is needed for children to understand the story.

Connection of Ideas As children read the story, they will need to understand that the animals are trying to bargain with the farmer.

What have you learned so far about what the cows in the story like to do? (The cows like to type.)

Build Vocabulary page 272
problem: trouble to fix

Then, he couldn't believe his **eyes**. ③

Dear Farmer Brown,
The barn is very cold at night.
We'd like some electric blankets.

Sincerely,
The Cows

274   275

LITERATURE ANTHOLOGY, pp. 274–275

Read

③ Ask and Answer Questions

Remember, when you ask yourself a question about something you read in the text, you can usually find the answer if you keep reading. On page 274, you read that the farmer couldn't believe his eyes. What question could you ask? (What did the farmer see that he could not believe?) On page 275, the picture shows a letter tacked to the barn door. The cows wrote the letter asking for blankets. What does this tell you? (The letter is what the farmer saw.)

A C T Access Complex Text

▶ **Text Organization**

Children might need help recognizing the part of the story that is a letter.

- Help children understand that part of the story's action is told through a letter. Call attention to the greeting (who it is written to), body (what it says), closing, and signature (who wrote it).

- Guide children to understand that the cows wanted to communicate to the farmer that they are unhappy with their working conditions and what he can do to make their lives better.

It was bad **enough** the cows had found the old typewriter in the barn, now they wanted electric blankets! "No way," said Farmer Brown. "No electric blankets."

So the cows went on strike. They left a note on the barn **door**.

Sorry.
We're closed.
No milk today. **4**

276

277

LITERATURE ANTHOLOGY, pp. 276–277

4 Skill: Theme

Let's look for clues about the theme. What do the characters say and do? What happens in the story? Let's add these clues to our chart.

> Reread   *Close Reading Companion,* 166

Author's Craft: Word Choice

Reread pages 276–277. Why does the author begin the cow's new letter with the word *Sorry*? (The cows wrote *Sorry* because they are saying they will not give milk to Farmer Brown.)

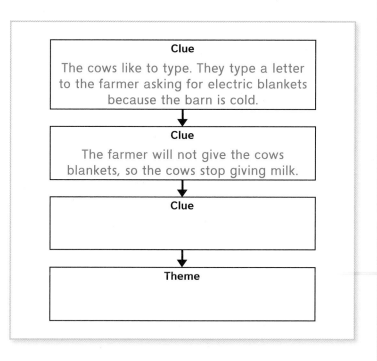

Clue
The cows like to type. They type a letter to the farmer asking for electric blankets because the barn is cold.

↓

Clue
The farmer will not give the cows blankets, so the cows stop giving milk.

↓

Clue

↓

Theme

LITERATURE ANTHOLOGY, pp. 278–279

Read

⑤ Repetition

Sometimes words or sounds are repeated in different places throughout the story. This can help us know an action is being repeated. What words do you see on page 278 that you have read earlier in the story? (*Click, clack, moo. Click, clack, moo. Clickety, clack, moo.*) What is happening each time these words are repeated? (*The cows are typing.*)

Build Vocabulary page 278
background: the space behind

⑥ Retell

The plot is what happens at the beginning, middle, and end of a story. What happened in the beginning of this story? (The cows typed a letter to the farmer saying they wanted electric blankets and the farmer said no. So, the cows went on strike.)

⑦ Strategy: Reread

Teacher Think Aloud On page 280, I read that the cows were growing impatient with the farmer. I don't understand why, so I will reread. On page 279, I read that the cows wrote another letter to the farmer. I did not read a letter from the farmer, so I think the cows were growing impatient waiting for the farmer to respond.

The cows were growing impatient with the farmer. They left a new note on the barn door.

Closed.
No milk.
No eggs.

"No eggs!" cried Farmer Brown. **7** In the background he heard them.

Click, clack, **moo.**
Click, clack, **moo.**
Clickety, clack, **moo.** **8**

280

281

LITERATURE ANTHOLOGY, pp. 280–281

8 Skill: Theme

What did the hens do when they didn't get the blankets they wanted? Let's add this clue to our Theme chart.

> Reread *Close Reading Companion,* 167

Illustrator's Craft

Reread pages 278–279. How do the illustrations help you understand that the cows and hens are working together? (On page 278, I see the cows typing a letter. On page 279, I see Farmer Brown reading the letter and a cow and some hens watching him. This tells me that both groups of animals are waiting to hear what Farmer Brown will say.)

Clue
The cows like to type. They type a letter to the farmer asking for electric blankets because the barn is cold.

↓

Clue
The farmer will not give the cows blankets, so the cows stop giving milk.

↓

Clue
The hens don't get the blankets they want, so they stop giving eggs.

↓

Theme

"Cows that type. Hens on strike! Whoever heard of such a thing? How can I run a farm with no milk and no eggs!" Farmer Brown was furious. **9** **10**

282

283

LITERATURE ANTHOLOGY, pp. 282–283

Read

9 Maintain Skill: Point of View

Remember, the point of view is the way a character thinks or feels. What characters say helps us understand their point of view. What does the farmer say on page 283? (that he has never heard of cows that type or hens that go on strike) What does this tell you about the farmer's point of view about the cows and the hens? (It tells us he thinks they are not behaving the way cows and hens should.)

Build Vocabulary page 283
run: work
furious: very angry

10 Cause and Effect

COLLABORATE

We read that Farmer Brown was furious. He was furious as an effect of something that happened. What happened that caused Farmer Brown to be furious? Turn to a partner and discuss what caused Farmer Brown to be furious.

Farmer Brown got out his own typewriter.

Dear Cows and Hens:
There will be no electric blankets.
You are cows and hens.
I **demand** milk and eggs.

Sincerely,
Farmer Brown

284

Duck was a neutral party, so he brought the ultimatum to the cows. **11**

285

LITERATURE ANTHOLOGY, pp. 284–285

⑪ Use a Dictionary

Teacher Think Aloud If I don't know the meaning of a word, I can look up the word in a dictionary. I am not sure what *neutral* means. Entries in a dictionary are in alphabetical order, so I look at the first letter to help me locate the word. The dictionary tells me that *neutral* means "not on either side in an argument." I know that the cows and hens are arguing with the farmer. The definition helps me understand that the duck is neutral because he isn't involved in the argument— he's not on the side of the farmer or on the side of the cows and hens.

A C T Access Complex Text

▶ **Specific Vocabulary**

Children may not be familiar with the word *ultimatum.*

- Point out the word *ultimatum* and explain that it is a kind of demand, usually made after a series of requests.

- Tell children to imagine that a parent has asked a child over and over to pick up his toys, but the child doesn't do it. Finally, the parent says, "Pick up your toys or you can't go out to play." Explain that this is an ultimatum.

The cows held an emergency meeting. All the animals gathered around the barn to snoop, but none of them could understand Moo.
All night long, Farmer Brown waited for an answer. 12 13
286
287

LITERATURE ANTHOLOGY, pp. 286–287

Read

12 Skill: Theme

We read Farmer Brown typed his own letter to the cows and hens and had the Duck deliver it. What did Farmer Brown's letter say? What do the cows do when they get the letter? Let's add these clues to our chart.

13 Make and Confirm Predictions

What do you predict will happen at the cows' meeting? Let's read on to see whether your predictions are correct.

Build Vocabulary page 287
snoop: to sneak in to find information

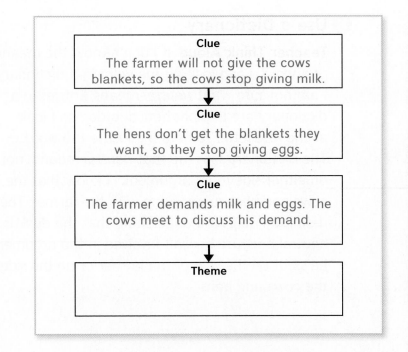

Clue
The farmer will not give the cows blankets, so the cows stop giving milk.

↓

Clue
The hens don't get the blankets they want, so they stop giving eggs.

↓

Clue
The farmer demands milk and eggs. The cows meet to discuss his demand.

↓

Theme

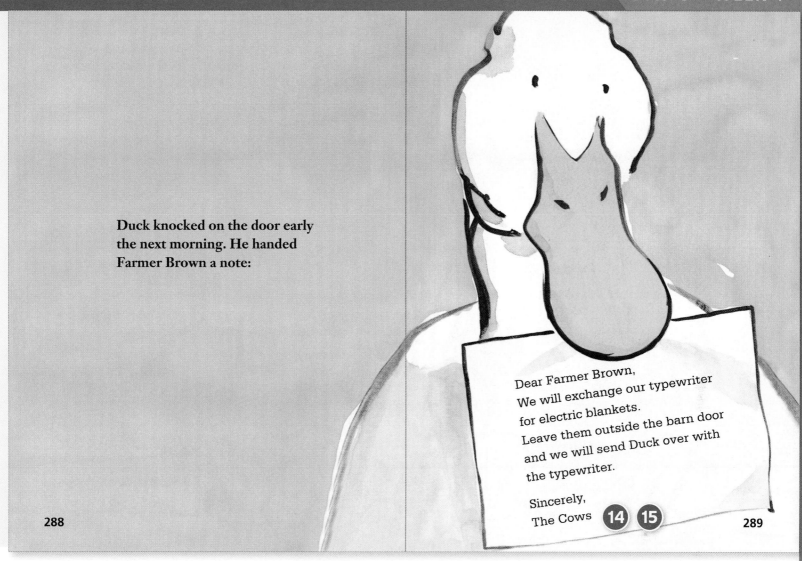

Duck knocked on the door early
the next morning. He handed
Farmer Brown a note:

Dear Farmer Brown,
We will exchange our typewriter
for electric blankets.
Leave them outside the barn door
and we will send Duck over with
the typewriter.

Sincerely,
The Cows

288

289

LITERATURE ANTHOLOGY, pp. 288–289

⑭ Make and Confirm Predictions

What did you predict would happen at the cows'
meeting? Was your prediction correct?

⑮ Genre: Fantasy

This is a fantasy story. What couldn't really
happen? (Animals can't type and make demands.
They don't talk and act like people.) What could
really happen? (Cows give milk. Hens give eggs.)

Reread

Illustrator's Craft

Why is the illustration on pages 286–287 in black
and white? (because it is night time)

A C T Access Complex Text

▶ Connections of Ideas

Prompt children to understand that the animals are
trying to bargain with the farmer.

- Remind children of what the cows and hens want
  and what the farmer wants. Discuss the idea that
  when people want different things, sometimes
  they have to compromise. That means they each
  give up something to get what they want.

- Guide children to understand that although the
  cows are having fun using the typewriter, they
  are willing to give it up to get the blankets they
  want.

Farmer Brown decided this was a good deal.

He left the blankets next to the barn door and waited for Duck to come with the typewriter. **16**

290   291

LITERATURE ANTHOLOGY, pp. 290–291

Read

16 **Skill: Theme**

What did Farmer Brown think of the cows' deal? What did he do? Let's add these clues to our Theme chart.

Reread   *Close Reading Companion,* 168

Author's Craft: Events

Reread pages 291–293. How does the author let you know that Duck learned something important? (Duck didn't return the typewriter. Instead, he typed Farmer Brown a letter saying the ducks wanted a diving board. The illustration on page 293 shows me that Duck's idea worked.)

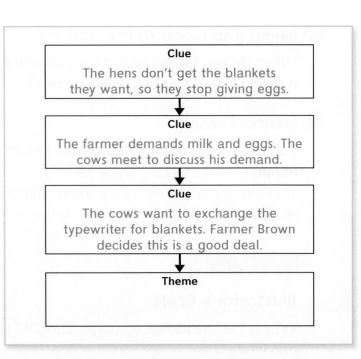

Clue

The hens don't get the blankets they want, so they stop giving eggs.

↓

Clue

The farmer demands milk and eggs. The cows meet to discuss his demand.

↓

Clue

The cows want to exchange the typewriter for blankets. Farmer Brown decides this is a good deal.

↓

Theme

The next morning he got a note:

Dear Farmer Brown,
The pond is quite boring.
We'd like a diving board.

Sincerely,
The Ducks

Click, clack, **quack.**
Click, clack, **quack.**
Clickety, clack, **quack.**

292

293

LITERATURE ANTHOLOGY, pp. 292–293

Skill: Theme

Review and discuss with children the clues they added to the Theme chart. *Think about what the characters said and did in the story. Think about what happened in the story. What message does the author want to give? Let's add the theme to our Theme chart.*

Return to Purposes

Review children's predictions. Ask children if their predictions were correct. Guide them to use evidence in the text to confirm whether their predictions were accurate.

Clue
The hens don't get the blankets they want, so they stop giving eggs.

↓

Clue
The farmer demands milk and eggs. The cows meet to discuss his demand.

↓

Clue
The cows want to exchange the typewriter for blankets. Farmer Brown decides this is a good deal.

↓

Theme
The animals worked together to make their lives better.

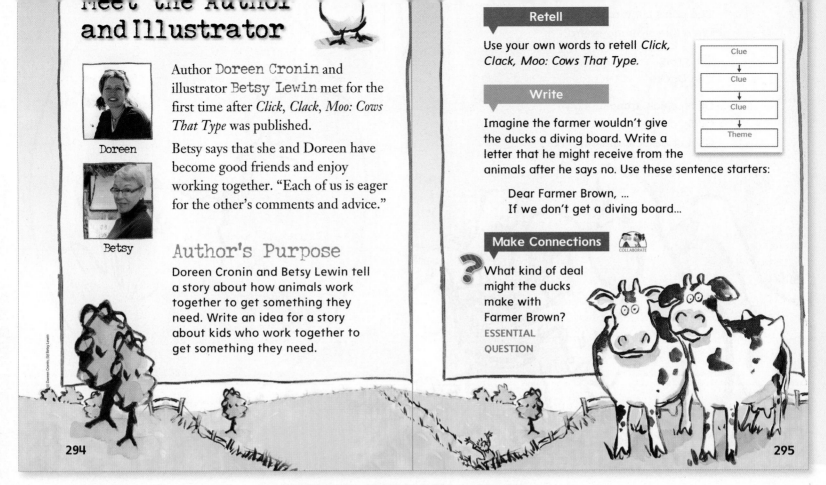

LITERATURE ANTHOLOGY, pp. 294–295

Meet the Author and Illustrator

Doreen Cronin and Betsy Lewin

Read aloud page 294 with children. Ask them why they think Doreen Cronin and Betsey Lewin wrote and illustrated a story about cows that type. Do you think they came up with a creative way to tell a story about working together to get something you want?

Author's Purpose

Have children write a sentence or two in their Response Journals expressing a story idea. *Some kids need ____. To get it, they work together by ____. My story will have____.*

AUTHOR'S CRAFT

Focus on Text Structure

Discuss the different text formats and structures Doreen Cronin used to tell her story.

- On pages 275–277, point out the author formatted the text as letters.

- On pages 278–279, point out the author has used dialogue, sentences that describe events, words that describe sounds, and a letter.

- Guide children to think about how they can use these different text formats in their own writing.

Respond to the Text

Retell

Guide children in retelling the story. Remind them that as they read the story, they looked for clues about the theme. Have children use the information they recorded on their chart to help them retell the story.

Reread

Analyze the Text

After children read and retell the selection, have them reread *Click, Clack, Moo: Cows That Type* to develop a deeper understanding of the text by answering the questions on pages 166–168 of the *Close Reading Companion*. For students who need support finding text evidence to support their responses, use the scaffolded instruction from the Reread prompts on pages T35D–T35K.

Write About the Text

Review the writing prompt with students. Remind them to use their responses from the *Close Reading Companion* and cite text evidence to support their answers.

For a full lesson on writing a response supported by text evidence, see pages T36–T37.

Answer: The ducks should tell the farmer they want a diving board because the pond is boring. They should also tell the farmer that they will keep their eggs from him and convince other farm animals to go on strike too until they get what they want. Evidence: On pages 276–277, the cows will not give the farmer their milk until they get blankets. On pages 278–281, the cows convince the hens to go on strike. On pages 292–293, the ducks tell why they want the diving board for the pond.

Integrate

Make Connections
COLLABORATE

Essential Question Answer: The cows and hens went on strike together to get the electric blankets they wanted. Evidence: On page 276, first the cows go on strike and refuse to give Farmer Brown milk. On page 279, the cows asked for blankets for the hens, too. The hens refuse to give Farmer Brown eggs. By the end, Farmer Brown gives them blankets.

ENGLISH LANGUAGE LEARNERS

Retell Help children by looking at each page of the selection and asking a prompt, such as: *Who is in the story on these pages? What is happening?* Provide sentence starters with characters' names to help children retell the story, such as: *Farmer Brown is ____. The cows ____.*

CONNECT TO CONTENT
MAKING A BETTER COMMUNITY

Remind children that they have been reading about ways people can work together to make their community a better place. Prompt children to discuss how the cows cooperate to make their lives better. Talk together about ways children might work together to make their school and community a better place, too.

Literature Anthology

OBJECTIVES

CCSS Write narratives in which they recount two or more appropriately sequenced events, include some details regarding what happened, use temporal words to signal event order, and provide some sense of closure. **W.1.3**

CCSS Use personal, possessive, and indefinite pronouns (e.g., *I, me, my; they, them, their, anyone, everything*). **L.1.1d**

ACADEMIC LANGUAGE

- *details, explain, variety, pronoun*
- Cognates: *detalles, explicar, variedad*

MINILESSON 5 Mins

Independent Writing

Write About the Literature Anthology

Analyze the Prompt Have children turn to page 295 in the **Literature Anthology.** Read the prompt: *Imagine the farmer wouldn't give the ducks a diving board. Write a letter the farmer might receive from the animals after he says no.* Say: *The prompt is asking you to imagine what the animals might write to the farmer if he refuses to give the ducks a diving board. The next step in answering the prompt is to find text evidence and make inferences about how the animals can help the ducks get what they want.*

Find Text Evidence Say: *To answer the prompt, we need to find evidence in the text and the illustrations. What can we use from the story to help us figure out what the animals would say to the farmer? Look at pages 279–281. When the hens wanted electric blankets, the cows helped. How did the cows and hens work together to get what they wanted?* (The cows wrote a new letter telling that the hens were cold and wanted blankets, too. Then both groups went on strike while they waited for the farmer's reply.)

Write to the Prompt Guide children as they begin their writing.

- **Prewrite** Have children review their notes and plan their writing. Guide them to brainstorm ways the animals can convince the farmer to get the ducks a diving board. Then guide children to organize their ideas and choose details to support their writing.

- **Draft** Have children write a response to the prompt. Remind them to begin their letter with a greeting to the farmer. As children write their drafts, have them focus on the week's skills.

  - **Vary Sentence Length** Use both short sentences and long sentences. **Trait: Sentence Fluency**

  - **Details** Use details from the story. **Trait: Ideas**

  - **Pronouns** Use pronouns to take the place of nouns correctly. **Grammar**

Tell children they will continue to work on their responses on Day 4.

Go Digital

Present the Lesson

Graphic Organizer

Writing

I see a fish.

Grammar

Grammar

Pronouns

1 Review Have children look at page 235 in the **Reading/Writing Workshop.** Remind them that pronouns take the place of nouns. Have children identify the pronouns in the model sentence.

Ask: *Which pronoun is in this sentence?* She can add to the report by drawing a beautiful picture. Say: She *is a pronoun. It takes the place of the noun* Lucy.

2 Guided Practice/Practice Guide children to identify other pronouns in Billy's writing. Have children work with partners to identify the pronouns and write new sentences with *I, me, us,* and *you.*

Talk About It Have partners work together to explain why Billy used each pronoun.

Mechanics: Capitalize *I*

1 Explain Explain that the pronoun *I* is always written with a capital letter. It stands for our own name.

2 Guided Practice Prompt children to correct each sentence.

My mom and i are going to the zoo. (My mom and I are going to the zoo.)

i had soup for lunch. (I had soup for lunch.)

Daily Wrap Up

- Review the Essential Question and encourage children to discuss using the oral vocabulary words. Ask: *What did we read about animals working together?*

- Prompt children to review and discuss the skills they used today.

Materials

Literature Anthology
VOLUME 4

Visual Vocabulary Cards

argument   answer
conflict   brought
fair   busy
risk   door
shift   enough
demand   eyes
emergency

Teaching Poster

moon

**Spelling Word
Cards**

a b c
**Word-Building
Cards**

Our Plan

FOLDABLES
Dinah Zike's

Dinah Zike's Foldables®

(→) # Extend the Concept   CLOSE READING

MINILESSON
5 Mins

March On!

ESSENTIAL QUESTION

Remind children that this week they have been learning about how we can work together to make life better. Guide children to discuss the question using information from what they have read and discussed. Use the Define/Example/Ask routine to review the oral vocabulary words *argument, conflict, fair, risk,* and *shift*. Then review last week's oral vocabulary words *structure, project, contented, intend,* and *marvelous.*

Text Feature: Captions

1 Explain Tell children they can use informational text selections to find facts and details. Explain that informational text often has photographs. These photographs often have captions—short descriptions giving information about the photograph.

2 Model Display Teaching Poster 18. Read the top right caption: "*The park is a place to rest or play.*" This caption tells us where the people are and what they are doing.

3 Guided Practice/Practice Read together the caption: "*City buildings shine brightly at night.*" Guide children to discuss the information in the caption. *What does the caption tell us? What information is in the caption, but not in the photograph? If we wanted to write a new caption for this photograph, what could it say?* Tell children to look for captions as they read informational text selections.

OBJECTIVES

CCSS Use the illustrations and details in a text to describe its key ideas. **RI.1.7**

Review vocabulary

ACADEMIC LANGUAGE

• *caption, photograph, information, description*

• Cognates: *fotografía, información, descripción*

Go Digital

school

Visual Glossary

Teaching Poster

"March On!"

Genre Nonfiction

Compare Texts

Read about how people made their lives better.

100 years ago only men could vote. **1**

March On!

How can people make their lives better? One way is to work together.

One hundred years ago, women in America were not allowed to vote. That meant they could not pick their leaders or help decide on laws and rules.

296

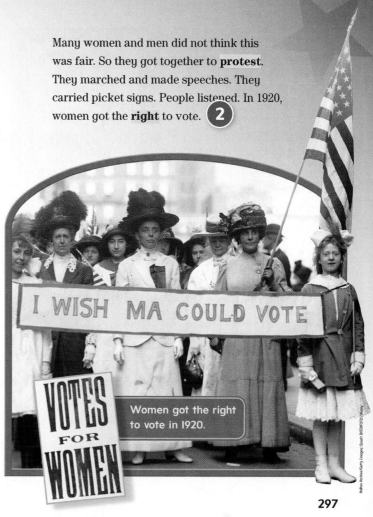

Many women and men did not think this was fair. So they got together to **protest**. They marched and made speeches. They carried picket signs. People listened. In 1920, women got the **right** to vote. **2**

I WISH MA COULD VOTE

VOTES FOR WOMEN

Women got the right to vote in 1920.

297

LITERATURE ANTHOLOGY, pp. 296–297

Lexile 510

Compare Texts

As you read and reread "March On!," encourage children to think about the Essential Question: *How can we work together to make our lives better?* Review with children that when they read *Click, Clack, Moo: Cows That Type,* they read a fantasy story about animals working together. Now they will read a story about ways real people worked together to make lives better. Point out the words *protest, rights,* and *improve.*

Read

1 Text Features: Captions

Teacher Think Aloud In this picture, I see men in old-fashioned clothes. From the caption, I learn that 100 years ago, only men could vote. The caption helps me understand the information in the picture.

2 Skill: Key Details

What key details have you read on pages 296–297? (One hundred years ago, women could not vote. Many people thought this was unfair so they protested, marched, and made speeches. Women got the right to vote in 1920.)

Many people did not think this was fair. So they got together and marched. Leaders like Martin Luther King, Jr. made speeches. He said all people should have the same rights.

People listened. Laws were passed that said all people must be treated equally. **4**

In some places black and white people could not eat lunch together. **3**

People from all over came to support equal rights.

For many years, black people in our country did not have the same rights as other people. Some businesses would not hire black people. Some stores would not let black people shop, and some schools would not let black children in.

298

299

LITERATURE ANTHOLOGY, pp. 298–299

Read

❸ Text Features: Captions

What information does the caption tell you that the rest of the text does not tell? (It tells another example of a way African-American people did not have the same rights as other people.)

❹ Strategy: Reread

Teacher Think Aloud What does the author mean about laws stating all people must be treated equally? I will reread these pages to make sure I didn't miss an important point. Now I understand. For many years, African-American people in our country were not treated the same way as other people. Laws were passed that said all people must have the same rights and be treated the same way.

❺ Text Features: Captions

Teacher Think Aloud When I look at the photograph, I see men working. I am not sure what kind of work they are doing. The caption gives me this information. From the caption I learn that the men are picking crops.

Retell

Guide children to use key details to retell the selection.

In the 1960s people all over the country got together to help farm workers. Many of these workers came to this country to pick crops. But they did not get much money. They did not have good places to live or schools for their children.

Farm workers picked crops for very little money.

5

300

People worked together to change this. Leaders like César Chávez organized the workers. People all over the country marched with them. The farmers listened. They gave the workers more pay and better homes. It is possible to **improve** our lives if we work together!

Make Connections
How are the animals in *Click, Clack, Moo: Cows That Type* like the people in "March On!"?
Essential Question

César Chávez organized farm workers to fight for better lives.

301

LITERATURE ANTHOLOGY, pp. 300–301

Reread

After children retell, have them reread to develop a deeper understanding of the text by annotating and answering the questions on pages 169–171 of the *Close Reading Companion*. For children who need support citing text evidence, use these Reread questions:

- How does the author organize the information in this selection?

- How does the title "March On!" help you understand the main idea of the selection?

- How is "March On!" like *Click, Clack, Moo: Cows That Type?* How is it different?

Integrate

Make Connections
COLLABORATE

Essential Question Encourage children to use text evidence from both selections.

SOCIAL STUDIES CONNECT TO CONTENT
CITIZENS WORKING TOGETHER

Remind children that this week they have been learning about how people can work together to make things better. How did people working together help the fight for equal rights? (Laws were passed that said all people had to be treated equally.) How did people working together help farm workers? (Farmers agreed to give better pay and better living conditions.)

→ # Word Work

OBJECTIVES

CCSS Decode regularly spelled one-syllable words. **RF.1.3b**

CCSS Read words with inflectional endings. **RF.1.3f**

CCSS Recognize and read grade-appropriate irregularly spelled words. **RF.1.3g**

Delete syllables in words to form new words

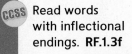

5 Mins MINILESSON

Phonological Awareness

Syllable Deletion

1 Model Show children how to delete syllables in words to form new words. *Listen carefully as I say a word:* harmless. *I will delete the last syllable, or part, of the word:* less. *What word do I have if I take* less *away from* harmless? Harmless *without* less *is harm.*

2 Guided Practice/Practice Have children practice syllable deletion. Do the first one together.

cheerful without *ful*   *helpless* without *less*   *cowboy* without *cow*

roomy without *y*   *undo* without *un*   *sandwich* without *wich*

10 Mins MINILESSON

Phonics/Structural Analysis

Build Words with Variant Vowel /ü/

Review *The sound /ü/ can be represented by the letters* oo, u, u_e, ew, ue, ui, *and* ou. *We'll use* **Word-Building Cards** *to build words with the /ü/ sound.*

Place the letters r, o, o, f. *Let's blend the sounds together and read the word: /rrrüüüfff/. Now let's change the* f *to* t. *Blend the sounds and read the word:* root. *Continue with* boot, hoot, shoot, shoo, moo, boo, blew, blue, glue, grew, drew, dew, dune, tune.

Decodable Reader   Have children read "Choose a Room" (pages 5–8), "Group Rules" (13–16), "A Cruise Crew" (21–24), and "A True Team" (29–32) to practice decoding words in connected text.

Suffixes *-ful, -less*

Review Remind children that *-ful* means "full" or "full of" and *-less* means "without." Write: *hopeless, graceful, playful, harmless, thankful, clueless.* Have partners sort the words by suffix. Have them identify the root word and suffix, blend the word, tell its meaning, and use it in a sentence.

Go Digital

Phonological Awareness

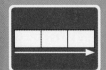

Phonics

Structural Analysis

Spelling Word Sort

Visual Glossary

Spelling

Word Sort with /ü/ Spellings

Review Provide pairs with copies of the **Spelling Word Cards**. While one partner reads the words one at a time, the other partner should orally segment the word and then write the word.

Have children correct their own papers. Then have them sort the words by sound-spelling.

High-Frequency Words

answer, brought, busy, door, enough, eyes

Review Display **Visual Vocabulary Cards** for the words. Have children Read/Spell/Write each word.

- Point to a word and call on a child to use it in a sentence.
- Review last week's words using the same procedure.

Expand Vocabulary

demand, emergency

Use the Visual Vocabulary Cards to review *demand* and *emergency*.

1 Explain Remind children that words have different forms. Explain that nouns have forms that mean "one" and "more than one" and verbs have forms that tell if something is happening now or happened in the past. Write these endings: *-ed, -ing, -s, -es.* Review the meanings of each ending.

2 Model Using a two-column chart, model how to add an ending to *emergency.* Write *emergency.* Then write *emergencies* in the next column. Read the words. Point out you changed *y* to *i* before adding *-es.* Then discuss how the ending changed the meaning of *emergency.* Have children use both words in sentences.

3 Guided Practice Have partners fill in a four-column chart for *demand.* Remind them they can add the endings *-s, -ing,* and *-ed.* Then have them share sentences using different forms of the word.

Monitor and *Differentiate*

 Quick Check

Can children read and decode words with variant vowel /ü/?

Can children recognize and read high-frequency and vocabulary words?

Small Group Instruction

If No →	Approaching	Reteach pp. T56–59
	ELL	Develop pp. T70–77
If Yes →	On Level	Review pp. T64–65
	Beyond Level	Extend pp. T68–69

Language Arts

Independent Writing

Literature Anthology

OBJECTIVES

CCSS With guidance and support from adults, focus on a topic, respond to questions and suggestions from peers, and add details to strengthen writing as needed. **W.1.5**

CCSS Use personal, possessive, and indefinite pronouns (e.g., *I, me, my; they, them, their, anyone, everything*). **L.1.1d**

CCSS Build on others' talk in conversations by responding to the comments of others through multiple exchanges. **SL.1.1b**

ACADEMIC LANGUAGE

• *details, length, edit, revise*
• Cognates: *detalles, editar, revisar*

Write About the Literature Anthology

Revise

Reread the prompt about the story *Click, Clack, Moo: Cows That Type: Imagine the farmer wouldn't give the ducks a diving board. Write a letter that the farmer might receive from the animals after he says no.* Have children read their drafts to see if they responded to the prompt. Then have them check for:

• **Vary Sentence Length** Did children use both short and long sentences to make their letters interesting? **Trait: Sentence Fluency**

• **Details** Did children include details from the story in their letter? **Trait: Ideas**

• **Pronouns** Did children correctly use pronouns to take the place of nouns? **Grammar**

Peer Review Have children work in pairs to do a peer review and read their partner's draft. Ask partners to check that the response includes pronouns, details from the story, and sentences of different lengths. They should take notes about what they liked most about the writing, questions they have for the author, and additional ideas they think the author could include. Have partners discuss these topics by responding to each other's comments. Provide time for them to make revisions.

Proofread/Edit

Have children check for the following:

• Pronouns are used correctly.

• All sentences are complete.

• Frequently occurring prepositions are used.

Peer Edit Next, have partners exchange their drafts and take turns reviewing them against the checklist. Encourage partners to discuss and fix errors together.

Go Digital

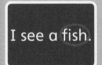

Writing

> ▬ Make a capital letter.
> ⋀ Add.
> ⏚ Take out.

Proofreader's Marks

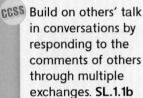

I see a fish.

Grammar

Final Draft

After children edit their writing and finish their peer edits, have them write their final draft. Tell children to write neatly so others can read their writing. Or, work with children to explore a variety of digital tools to produce and publish their writing, including collaborating with peers. Have them include details that help make their writing clear and interesting and to add a drawing if needed to make their ideas clear.

Teacher Conference As children work, conference with them to provide guidance. Check to make sure they are including details from the story and varied sentence lengths in their letter.

MINILESSON
5 Mins

Grammar

Pronouns

❶ Review Remind children the pronouns *I, he, she,* and *it* stand for one noun; *we* and *they* stand for more than one; and *you* can stand for one or more.

❷ Practice Display the following sentences. Have children choose which pronoun could replace the underlined part of each sentence.

> <u>The tuba</u> is fun to play in the marching band. (It, He) (It)
>
> <u>Mom</u> answered the door. (They, She) (She)
>
> <u>The kids</u> are shooting hoops at the park. (He, They) (They)
>
> <u>Bruce</u> is making soup. (He, It) (He)
>
> <u>Miss Dowd and I</u> live next door to each other. (She, We) (We)

Talk About It Have partners work together to orally generate sentences with *you* and *I*.

COLLABORATE

Mechanics: Capitalize *I*

❶ Review Remind children that the pronoun *I* is always capitalized.

❷ Practice Display sentences with errors. Read each aloud. Have children work together to fix the sentences.

> sue and i are going to the pool? (Sue and I are going to the pool.)
>
> i like To swim. (I like to swim.)

Daily Wrap Up

- Have children discuss the Essential Question using the oral vocabulary words. Ask: *What are ways you can work together with others to help out?*

- Prompt children to discuss the skills they practiced and learned today by asking, *What skills did you use today in your reading and writing?*

→ Integrate Ideas

OBJECTIVES

 CCSS Participate in shared research and writing projects (e.g., explore a number of "how-to" books on a given topic and use them to write a sequence of instructions). **W.1.7**

- Build background knowledge
- Research information using technology

ACADEMIC LANGUAGE

- *plan, proposal, change, action*
- Cognates: *plan, propuesta, acción*

SOCIAL STUDIES

RESEARCH AND INQUIRY

Make a Plan Proposal

Tell children that today partners will do a research project on how they can make their lives better at school. Review the steps in the research process below.

STEP 1 ## Choose a Topic

Have partners choose one way to make their lives better at school. They should think of an idea, reasons why it would make things better, and a plan for making it happen.

STEP 2 ## Find Resources

Discuss how to use the selections, reference materials, and online sources to find ideas for plans and how to put them into action. Have them use the Research Process Checklist online.

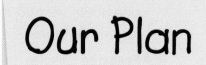

Our Plan

STEP 3 ## Keep Track of Ideas

Have children record their ideas in a Matchbook Foldable®. Model recording details.

Dinah Zike's
FOLDABLES

Go Digital

Resources:
Research and
Inquiry

Collaborative Conversations

Ask and Answer Questions Review with children that as they engage in partner, small-group, and whole-group discussions, they should:

- ask questions about ideas they do not understand.
- give others a chance to think after asking a question.
- write down questions they want to ask the teacher or the whole class.

STEP 4 **Create the Project: Plan Proposal**

Explain the characteristics of a proposal.

- **Idea** A proposal should state the idea. In this proposal, the idea will be what change you want to make and how you could make it happen.

- **Reason** A proposal should explain why you think the idea will make things in school better.

- **Plan** The proposal should explain what steps need to be done to make the idea happen.

Have children write their plan proposal.

- Guide them to write sentences explaining their proposal to make their lives better at school and how they could make this happen. They should explain the idea, the reasons why it would make things better, and a plan for making it happen.

- Have children share their plan proposals with the class and discuss each other's plans.

Art Supplies

Idea: New art supplies;

Reason: Art supplies will make our lives better in school;

Plan: We will have a bake sale to make money.

ILLUSTRATED PLAN PROPOSAL

ENGLISH LANGUAGE LEARNERS

ELL SCAFFOLD

Beginning	Intermediate	Advanced/High
Use Sentence Frames Use sentence frames to help children discuss their plan. For example: ____ will make our lives better.	**Discuss** Guide children to focus on the most important details about their plan. Ask: *Who will make this happen? Will it cost money? How can you raise money for this plan?*	**Describe** Prompt children to elaborate on their plan. Ask them to explain how their plan will improve their lives at school.

Materials

Reading/Writing Workshop
VOLUME 4

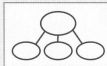

Literature Anthology
VOLUME 4

Visual Vocabulary Cards

answer
brought
busy
door
enough
eyes
demand
emergency

Teaching Poster

moon

Spelling Word Cards

a b c

Word-Building Cards

→ Word Work/Fluency

 Phonemic Awareness
MINILESSON 5 Mins

OBJECTIVES

CCSS Segment spoken single-syllable words into their complete sequence of individual sounds (phonemes). **RF.1.2d**

CCSS Decode regularly spelled one-syllable words. **RF.1.3b**

CCSS Recognize and read grade-appropriate irregularly spelled words. **RF.1.3g**

Phoneme Segmentation

Review Guide children to segment sounds in words. *I am going to say a word. I want you to say each sound in the word.*

| zoo | soup | chew | fruit | moon | blue | spoon |

Phoneme Substitution

Review Guide children to substitute sounds in words. *Now I am going to say a word. Then I'll tell you a sound to change to make a new word. Let's do one together:* suit/boot.

Continue with: fool/pool; room/root; tooth/tool.

Phonemic Awareness

Phonics/Structural Analysis
MINILESSON 10 Mins

Blend and Build with Variant Vowel /ü/

Review Have children read and say the words *soon, news, rule, truth, blue, you,* and *fruit.* Then have children follow the word building routine with **Word-Building Cards** to build *clue, glue, blue, sue, suit, soup, soon, moon, mood, food, fool, cool, pool, spool, spoon.*

Word Automaticity Display decodable words and point to each word as children chorally read it. Test how many words children can read in one minute. Model blending words children miss.

Phonics

Suffixes *-ful, -less*

Review Have children explain what *-ful* and *-less* mean. Then have them read words such as *useful, helpful, painless,* and *clueless.*

Structural Analysis

Visual Glossary

Fluency: Word Automaticity

Spelling

Word Sort with /ü/ Spellings

Review Have children use the **Spelling Word Cards** to sort the weekly words by spellings for /ü/. Remind children that four of the words do not have the /ü/ sound.

Assess Assess children on their abilities to spell /ü/ words. Say each word and provide a sentence. Allow them time to write the words. To challenge them, provide an additional word for each sound-spelling.

High-Frequency Words

answer, brought, busy, door, enough, eyes

Review Display **Visual Vocabulary Cards** for the words. Have children Read/Spell/Write each word and write a sentence with each.

Review Vocabulary

demand, emergency

Review Write each word and point to it. Ask children to use the word in a sentence. Write the sentences and reinforce word meanings as necessary. Repeat with last week's words or other previously taught words children need to review.

Fluency

Expression

Review Review that quotation marks indicate a character is speaking. Children should change their voice for each character.

Read aloud from the Shared Read. Have children echo each sentence. Point out how you read dialogue with different expression for different characters. Then have partners reread the selection, working on how they read dialogue.

Quick Review

Build Fluency: Sound-Spellings
Display the **Word-Building Cards:** *oo, u, u_e, ew, ue, ui, ou, oy, oi, ar, ore, oar, er, ir, ur, ey, igh, oa, oe, ee, ea, ai, ay, e_e, u_e, o_e, dge, i_e, a_e, _ce.* Have children say the sounds.

Monitor and *Differentiate*

 Quick Check

Can children read and decode words with variant vowel /ü/?

Can children recognize and read high-frequency and vocabulary words?

Small Group Instruction

If No → | Approaching | Reteach pp. T56–59
| ELL | Develop pp. T70–77
If Yes → | On Level | Review pp. T64–65
| Beyond Level | Extend pp. T68–69

Literature Anthology

OBJECTIVES

CCSS With guidance and support from adults, use a variety of digital tools to produce and publish writing, including in collaboration with peers. **W.1.6**

CCSS Ask and answer questions about key details in a text read aloud or in information presented orally or through other media. **SL.1.2**

CCSS Describe people, places, things, and events with relevant details, expressing ideas and feelings clearly. **SL.1.4**

ACADEMIC LANGUAGE

• *present, evaluate, magazine*
• Cognates: *presentar, evaluar*

Write About the Literature Anthology

Prepare

Tell children they will plan what they will say about their finished writing and drawing to the class. Remind children to:

• Think about why they chose certain details to include in their letter.

• Think about how they used both short and long sentences to add variety to their letter.

Present

Have children take turns giving presentations of their responses to the prompt about the story *Click, Clack, Moo: Cows That Type: Imagine the farmer wouldn't give the ducks a diving board. Write a letter that the farmer might receive from the animals after he says no.* If possible, record their presentations so children can self-evaluate. Tell children to:

• Express their ideas clearly using relevant details.

• Ask and answer questions about key details in their letters.

• Listen carefully and quietly to the presenter.

Evaluate

Have children discuss their own presentations and evaluate their performance using the presentation rubric.

Use the teacher's rubric to evaluate children's writing. Have children add their writing to their Writer's Portfolio. Encourage children to look back at previous writing. Then have them discuss what they would like to improve about their writing. Have them share their observations with a partner.

Publish

After children finish presenting their letters, discuss how the class will publish the letters in an online class magazine. Guide children to use digital tools to publish their writing. Present children's magazines so children can see how they look. Suggest that they add illustrations if they have not done so already. Allow children to help with ordering the letters in the magazine.

Go Digital

Writing

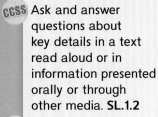

Checklists

Grammar

Grammar

Pronouns

1 **Review** Have children describe when the pronouns *I, you, he, she, it, we,* and *they* are used. Write the following sentences and have children identify the pronouns:

> Jan and I are going to the zoo. It is a fun place. We like the snake house. Would you like to go too? (I, it, We, you)

2 **Practice** Ask: What pronoun takes the place of *Jan and I*? What takes the place of *zoo*? How many nouns does *I* stand for?

Have children work in pairs to write sentences using *he, she, it,* and *they*.

Mechanics: Capitalize *I*

1 **Review** Remind children that the pronoun *I* is capitalized.

2 **Practice** Write the following sentences. Read each aloud. Have children fix the sentences.

> MoM, dad, and i, like to play board games? (Mom, Dad, and I like to play board games.)

> When i get home, from School, i'll eat a snack. (When I get home from school, I'll eat a snack.)

Daily Wrap Up

- Review the Essential Question and encourage children to discuss using the oral vocabulary words.

- Review with children that the theme is the big idea of a story. Remind them they can reread parts of a story to understand it better or remember important information.

- Review words with variant vowel spellings of /ü/.

- Use the Visual Vocabulary Cards to review the Words to Know.

- Remind children that a story has a theme or message.

Integrate Ideas

Close Reading Routine

- Identify key ideas and details about working together for change.
- Take notes and retell.
- Use A C T prompts as needed.

Reread   DOK 2–3

- Analyze text, craft, and structure.

Integrate   DOK 4

- Integrate knowledge and ideas and make text-to-text connections.
- Use the Integrate Lesson.
- Use *Close Reading Companion*, p. 172.

TEXT CONNECTIONS

Connect to the Essential Question

Write the essential question on the board: *How can we work together to make our lives better?* Read the essential question aloud. Tell children that they will think about all of the information that they have learned about how people work together. Say: *We have read many selections on this topic. We will compare the information from this week's* **Leveled Readers** *and* Super Tools, **Reading/Writing Workshop** *pages 222–231.*

Evaluate Text Evidence Guide children to review the selections and their completed graphic organizers. Have children work with partners to compare information from all the week's reads. Children can record notes using a Foldable®. Guide them to record information from the selections that helps them to answer the Essential Question.

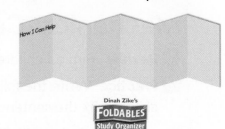

Dinah Zike's
FOLDABLES
Study Organizer

Taking Action

OBJECTIVES

CCSS Participate in shared research and writing projects. **W.1.7**

Go Digital

Collaborate

RESEARCH AND INQUIRY

Have children create a checklist and review their plan proposals:

- Does their proposal tell what change they want to make? Does it tell how to make the change happen?
- Do they wish to make any last minute changes to the text or the images?
- Have they correctly explained the steps to make the idea happen?
- Have they taken notes about what they would like to talk about when presenting their proposals to the class?

Guide partners to practice sharing their plan proposals with each other. Children should practice speaking and presenting their information clearly.

Guide children to share their work. Prompt children to ask questions to clarify when something is unclear: *What plan did you research? What steps do you want the proposal to show? How does your plan help to make lives better at school?* Have children use the Presentation Checklist online.

OBJECTIVES

CCSS Identify basic similarities and differences between two texts on the same topic (e.g., in illustrations, descriptions, or procedures). **RI.1.9**

Text to Photography

Read aloud with children the Integrate activity on page 172 of the *Close Reading Companion*. Have partners share reactions to the photograph. Then guide them to discuss how it is similar to the selections they read earlier in the week. Have partners collaborate to complete the Integrate page by following the prompts.

Present Ideas and Synthesize Information

When children finish their discussions, ask for a volunteer from each pair to share the information from their Foldable® and their Integrate pages. After each pair has presented their ideas, ask: *How does learning about these ways to work together help you answer the Essential Question, How can we work together to make our lives better?* Lead a class discussion asking students to use the information from their charts to answer the Essential Question.

SPEAKING AND LISTENING

OBJECTIVES

CCSS Participate in collaborative conversations with diverse partners about grade 1 topics and texts with peers and adults in small and larger groups. **SL.1.1**

CCSS Give, restate, and follow simple two-step directions. **SL.1.2a**

CCSS Ask and answer questions about what a speaker says in order to gather additional information or clarify something that is not understood. **SL.1.3**

As children work with partners in their *Close Reading Companion* or on their proposals, make sure that they actively participate in the conversation and, when necessary, remind them to use these speaking and listening strategies:

Speaking Strategies

- Have conversations about their work with both peers and adults.
- Work together with diverse partners in small and large groups.
- Give directions about what steps need to be done to make the idea happen.

Listening Strategies

- Restate directions about what steps need to be done to make the idea happen, to make sure the directions are understood.
- Ask questions to get additional information or to clarify something that they might not have understood the first time.
- Pay attention when having a conversation with someone and look at the person who is speaking.

→ Approaching Level

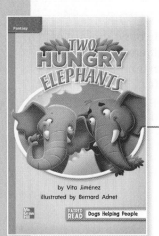

Lexile 290

OBJECTIVES

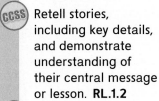 Retell stories, including key details, and demonstrate understanding of their central message or lesson. **RL.1.2**

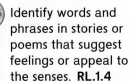 Identify words and phrases in stories or poems that suggest feelings or appeal to the senses. **RL.1.4**

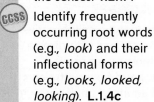 Identify frequently occurring root words (e.g., *look*) and their inflectional forms (e.g., *looks, looked, looking*). **L.1.4c**

Leveled Reader:
Two Hungry Elephants

Go Digital

Two Hungry Elephants

Graphic Organizer

Retell

Before Reading

Preview and Predict

Have children turn to the title page. Read the title and the author's name and have children repeat. Preview the selection's illustrations. Prompt children to predict what the selection might be about.

Review Genre: Fantasy

Have children recall that a fantasy has invented characters, settings, or other elements that could not exist in real life.

ESSENTIAL QUESTION

Remind children of the Essential Question: *How can we work together to make our lives better?* Set a purpose for reading: *Let's read to find out how the elephants worked together to make their lives better.*

Remind children that as they read a selection, they can ask questions about what they do not understand or what they want to know more about.

During Reading

Guided Comprehension

As children whisper read *Two Hungry Elephants,* monitor and provide guidance, correcting blending and modeling the key strategies and skills. Guide children to identify frequently occurring root words and their inflectional forms; for example, *eat/eating* and *starve/starving.*

Strategy: Reread

Remind children that they can reread to be sure they understand what is happening in a selection. Model the strategy on page 2. Say: *I don't know why Lucy is dizzy.* Reread the page. *Now I see. She hadn't eaten.*

Skill: Theme

Remind children that the theme is the message the author wants to share with the reader. As you read, say: *Let's look for clues that will help us figure out the theme.* Display a Theme chart for children to copy.

Model recording children's answers in the boxes. Have children record the answers in their own charts.

Think Aloud On pages 10 and 11, I read that Tom held the branch down while Lucy picked the leaves. Then they weren't hungry anymore. I'll write these events as clues. Then I can find the theme.

Guide children to use the text and illustrations to complete the chart.

After Reading

Respond to Reading

Have children complete the Respond to Reading on page 12.

Retell

Have children take turns retelling the selection, using the **Retelling Cards** as a guide. Help children make a personal connection by saying: *Think about when you work with a partner in class. How does working together help you both?*

Model Fluency

Read the sentences, one at a time. Have children chorally repeat. Point out to children how you use proper expression to read dialogue.

Apply Have partners practice reading. Provide feedback as needed.

PAIRED READ ...

Leveled Reader

"Dogs Helping People"

Make Connections: Write About It *Analytical Writing*

Before reading, ask children to note that the genre of this text is informational text. Then discuss the Compare Texts direction. Ask children to make connections between information in "Dogs Helping People" and *Two Hungry Elephants*. Provide a sentence frame such as: *We read about animals helping ____ and animals helping ____.*

Analytical Writing

COMPARE TEXTS
• Have children use text evidence to compare fantasy to informational text.

Literature Circles

Lead children in conducting a literature circle using the Thinkmark questions to guide the discussion. You may wish to discuss what children have learned about how animals help to make lives better from both selections in the Leveled Reader.

Level Up

Level-up lessons available online.

IF children can read *Two Hungry Elephants,* Approaching Level with fluency and correctly answer the Respond to Reading questions,

THEN tell children that they will read another story about animals working together.

• Use pages 7–11 of *What a Feast!* On Level to model using Teaching Poster 37 to list clues to the theme.

• Have children read the selection, checking their comprehension by using the graphic organizer.

Phonological Awareness

IDENTIFY AND GENERATE RHYME

TIER 2

OBJECTIVES

CCSS Isolate and pronounce initial, medial vowel, and final sounds (phonemes) in spoken single-syllable words. **RF.1.2c**

Identify and generate rhyming words

 I Do Explain to children that they will be identifying rhyming words. *Listen as I say two words:* moon, tune. Moon *and* tune *rhyme because they end with the same sounds. Listen: /m/ /ün/; /t/ /ün/. Now listen to this word:* soon. Soon *ends with /ün/.* Soon *rhymes with* moon *and* tune.

 We Do *Repeat:* boot, root. *Listen for the ending sounds: /b/ /üt/, /r/ /üt/. Do* boot *and* root *have the same ending sounds? Yes! That means they rhyme. What is another word that rhymes with* boot *and* root? Hoot *ends in /üt/.* Hoot *rhymes with* boot *and* root.

 You Do *It's your turn. Tell which two words in each group rhyme. Then say another word that rhymes with them.*

too, blue, soon   goose, fool, cool   soup, stool, hoop

Repeat the rhyming routine with additional /ü/ rhyming words.

PHONEME IDENTITY

TIER 2

OBJECTIVES

CCSS Isolate and pronounce initial, medial vowel, and final sounds (phonemes) in spoken single-syllable words. **RF.1.2c**

 I Do Explain to children that they will be identifying the same sound in words. *Listen as I say three words:* boot, grew, soon. *I hear one sound that is the same in* boot, grew, *and* soon. *Listen: /büüüt/, /grüüü/, /süüün/. The sound that is the same in* boot, grew, *and* soon *is /ü/.*

 We Do *Repeat these words:* rude, flute, new. *What sound is the same in /rüüüd/, /flüüüt/, and /nüüü/? The sound is /ü/.*

 You Do *It's your turn. I will say three words. What sound is the same in all three words?*

room, hoop, suit   bird, chirp, nurse   pool, tune, moose

Repeat the identity routine with additional /ü/ words.

PHONEME SEGMENTATION

OBJECTIVES

 CCSS Segment spoken single-syllable words into their complete sequence of individual sounds (phonemes). **RF.1.2d**

 I Do Explain to children that they will be saying the sounds in words. *Listen as I say a word:* suit. *I hear three sounds: /s/, /ü/, and /t/. There are three sounds in* suit: */s/, /ü/, and /t/.*

 We Do *Let's do some together. I am going to say a word:* new. *How many sounds do you hear? What are the sounds? There are two sounds in* new. *The sounds are /nnn/ and /üüü/.*

Repeat this routine with the following words:

food   tool   juice   blue   broom   truth   chew

 You Do *I'll say a word. Tell me how many sounds you hear. Then tell me the sounds.*

cool   moon   fruit   dew   stew   prune   glue

SYLLABLE DELETION

OBJECTIVES

Delete syllables in words.

 I Do Explain to children that they will be deleting, or taking away, parts of words to make new words. *Listen as I say a word:* duty. *I will take away the last syllable, or part, of the word* duty. *I will take away /tē/ from* duty. Duty *without /tē/ is* dew.

 We Do *Let's do some together. I am going to say a word:* reuse. *I will take away one part: /rē/. What is the new word?* Reuse *without /rē/ is* use.

 You Do *I'll say a word. Then I will tell you to take away one part. Tell me the new word.*

movie without /vē/   *cookie* without /ē/

cabin without /cab/   *robot* without /bot/

 ENGLISH LANGUAGE LEARNERS

For the **children** who need **phonemic awareness, phonics,** and **fluency** practice, use scaffolding methods as necessary to ensure children understand the meaning of the words. Refer to the Language Transfer Handbook for phonics elements that may not transfer in children's native languages.

Approaching Level

Phonics

CONNECT *oo, u, u_e, ew, ue, ui, ou* TO /ü/

 OBJECTIVES
Know and apply grade-level phonics and word analysis skills in decoding words. **RF.1.3**

 I Do Display the **Word-Building Card** *oo*. These letters are both lowercase o. *Together they can stand for the /ü/ sound. I am going to trace the letters* oo *while I say /ü/.* Trace the letters *oo* while saying /ü/ five times. Repeat with Word-Building Cards for *u, u_e, ew, ue, ui, ou.*

 We Do *Now do it with me.* Have children take turns saying /ü/ while using their fingers to trace lowercase *oo*. Then have them say /ü/ as they use their fingers to trace the letters *oo* five more times. Repeat for *u, u_e, ew, ue, ui, ou.*

 You Do Have children connect the letters *oo* to the sound /ü/ by saying /ü/ as they trace lowercase *oo* on paper five to ten times. Then ask them to write the letters *oo* while saying /ü/ five to ten times. Repeat for *u, u_e, ew, ue, ui, ou.*

Repeat, connecting the letters to the sound /ü/ throughout the week.

BLEND WORDS WITH VARIANT VOWEL /ü/

 OBJECTIVES
Decode regularly spelled one-syllable words. **RF.1.3b**

 I Do Display Word-Building Cards *s, oo, n*. *This is the letter s. It stands for /s/. These are the letters o, o. Together they stand for /ü/. This is the letter n. It stands for /n/. I'll blend the sounds together: /süüün/,* soon.

 We Do Guide children to blend the sounds and read: *fool, tune, blue, suit, group, chew, truth.*

 You Do Have children blend and decode: *zoo, fruit, grew, clue, rule, soup, stool, news, you, juice, rude.*

Repeat, blending additional /ü/ words.

BUILD WORDS WITH VARIANT VOWEL /ü/

OBJECTIVES

CCSS Decode regularly spelled one-syllable words. **RF.1.3b**

 Display Word-Building Cards *f, l, ew.* *These are the letters* f, l, *and* e, w. *They stand for* /f/, /l/, *and* /ü/: /flüüü/, flew. *The word is* flew.

 Now let's do one together. Change the letter *f* in *flew* to *b. Let's blend the new word:* /b/ /l/, /ü/, blew.

 Have children build the words *glue, goo, food, fool, tool, tune, tube, too, true.*

Repeat, building additional words with /ü/.

BLEND WORDS WITH VARIANT VOWEL /ü/

OBJECTIVES

CCSS Decode regularly spelled one-syllable words. **RF.1.3b**

 Display Word-Building Cards *n, ew.* *This is the letter* n. *It stands for* /n/. *These are the letters* e *and* w. *Together they stand for* /ü/. *Listen as I blend the sounds:* /nü/, new. *The word is* new.

 Let's do some together. Blend and read *moon, rule, group, suit.*

 Display the words to the right. Have children blend and read the words.

Decodable Reader Have children read "Rooster and Goose" (1–4), "The Flute Youth" (9–12), "Lewis and His New Suit" (17–20), and "Sue and Lucy" (25–28).

soup	flew	true	fruit	dew	youth
hoop	July	tube	loose	clue	zoom
look	loop	rude	rode	stew	stay
night	key	coin	nudge	mouse	froze

A moose and a goose were on the news.
Duke wore a blue suit and brown boots.
June jumped into the new pool at noon.

BUILD FLUENCY WITH PHONICS

Sound-Spellings Fluency

Display the following Word-Building Cards: *oo, u, u_e, ew, ue, ui, ou, oy, oi, ar, ore, oar, er, ir, ur, ey, igh, oa, oe, ee, ea, ai, ay, e_e, u_e, o_e, dge, i_e, a_e, _ce.* Have children chorally say the sounds. Repeat and vary the pace.

Fluency in Connected Text

Decodable Reader Have children read "Choose a Room" (pages 5–8), "Group Rules" (13–16), "A Cruise Crew" (21–24), and "A True Team" (29–32).

Have partners reread the stories for fluency.

Structural Analysis

REVIEW SUFFIXES *-ful, -less*

OBJECTIVES

Use frequently occurring affixes as a clue to the meaning of a word. **L.1.4b**

I Do

Write and read *"helpful." I look at the word* helpful *and see a word I know,* help. Underline *-ful. The suffix* -ful *means "full" or "full of" so the word* helpful *means "full of help."* Repeat with *helpless.* Remind children that *-less* means "without." Use *helpful* and *helpless* in sentences.

We Do

Write and read *"hopeful." Do you see a word you know? Yes,* hope. Underline *-ful. We know that* -ful *is a suffix that means "full" or "full of." Let's blend* hope *and* -ful: hopeful. *Use* hopeful *in a sentence.* Repeat with *hopeless.*

You Do

Write these words on the board: *useful, spoonful, useless, endless.* Have partners identify each base word and suffix. Ask them to blend the words, tell what they mean, and use the words in sentences.

Repeat Have partners read more words with *-ful* and *-less*, identify the suffix, and use the word in a sentence.

RETEACH SUFFIXES *-ful, -less*

OBJECTIVES

Use frequently occurring affixes as a clue to the meaning of a word. **L.1.4b**

I Do

Remind children that they can add suffixes to the ends of some words. Write *-ful. This is the suffix* -ful. *It means "full" or "full of."* Write *playful. I see the word* play *and the suffix* -ful *in this word. I can blend* play *and* -ful *to read* playful. *My puppy is playful. She likes to play.* Repeat with *-less.* Use the word *spotless.*

We Do

Write *use. Let's read this word:* use. *Now let's add* -ful *to* use. Write *useful. Let's blend* use *and* ful *to read this word:* useful. *What does* useful *mean? Yes, it means "full of use." Now let's use* useful *in a sentence.* Have children add *-less* to *use* and repeat.

You Do

Have partners add *-ful* to *help, hope,* and *spoon.* Ask them to blend the new words, tell what they mean, and use them in sentences.

Repeat for *-less* with *help* and *hope.*

Words to Know

REVIEW HIGH-FREQUENCY WORDS

OBJECTIVES

 Recognize and read grade-appropriate irregularly spelled words. **RF.1.3g**

 I Do Use the **High-Frequency Word Cards** to **Read/Spell/Write** each. Use each word orally in a sentence.

 We Do Guide children to Read/Spell/Write each word on their **Response Boards.** Help them generate oral sentences for the words.

 You Do Have partners work together to Read/Spell/Write the words *answer, brought, busy, door, enough,* and *eyes.* Ask them to say sentences for the words.

CUMULATIVE REVIEW

OBJECTIVES

 Recognize and read grade-appropriate irregularly spelled words. **RF.1.3g**

Review previously taught high-frequency words

 I Do Display the **High-Frequency Word Cards** from the previous weeks. Use the Read/Spell/Write routine to review each word.

 We Do Guide children as they Read/Spell/Write the words on their Response Boards. Have children complete sentence frames for the words. *I thought you knew ____. Let's guess whether ____.*

Have partners take turns displaying and reading the words. Ask them to use the words in sentences.

 You Do **Fluency** Display the High-Frequency Word Cards. Point to words in random order. Have children chorally read each word. Repeat at a faster pace.

REVIEW VOCABULARY WORDS

OBJECTIVES

 Identify real-life connections between words and their use (e.g., note places at home that are *cozy*). **L.1.5c**

 I Do Display **Visual Vocabulary Cards** for *demand* and *emergency.* Review each word using the Define/Example/Ask routine.

 We Do Invite children to act out or tell what they do when they demand something and when they are in an emergency. Then work with them to complete these sentence starters: *(1) Does your mom demand that ____? (2) We had an emergency when ____.*

 You Do Have partners write two sentences on their own, using each of the words.

Comprehension

READ FOR FLUENCY

OBJECTIVES

CCSS Read on-level text orally with accuracy, appropriate rate, and expression on successive readings. **RF.1.4b**

 I Do Read the first page of the Practice Book story aloud. Model using appropriate expression when you read what the characters say.

 We Do Read the second page aloud and have children repeat each sentence after you. Point out how you use appropriate expression when you read what Racoon and Moose say.

 You Do Have children read the rest of the story aloud. Remind them to slightly change their voice when they read what different characters say.

IDENTIFY PLOT

OBJECTIVES

CCSS Describe characters, settings, and major events in a story, using key details. **RL.1.3**

 I Do Remind children that they have been reading a fantasy story. *When I read a story, I think about the plot. The plot is what happens at the beginning, middle, and end of the story.*

 We Do Read the first page of the Practice Book story aloud. Pause to discuss the plot. *We read the beginning of the story. In the beginning, Raccoon is busy. What is he doing? What does he need?*

 You Do Guide children as they read the rest of the Practice Book story. Prompt them to tell what happens in the middle and end of the story.

REVIEW THEME

OBJECTIVES

 Retell stories, including key details, and demonstrate understanding of their central message or lesson. **RL.1.2**

 I Do Remind children that the theme of a story is the important message that the author wants to share. *The theme is the big idea or message of a story. When I read a fantasy story, I look for clues to help me figure out the theme. I think about what the characters say and do. I think about what happens in the story, too.*

 We Do Read the first two pages of the Practice Book story together. Pause to discuss what the characters say and do. *We read that Raccoon is building a tree house and needs help. What does Moose do? These events are clues that will help me figure out the theme.*

 You Do *What are some clues that we read so far that will help us figure out the theme?* Record the events on a Theme chart. Continue by guiding children as they continue to read. Have them discuss more clues and the theme.

SELF-SELECTED READING

OBJECTIVES

With prompting and support, read prose and poetry of appropriate complexity for grade 1. **RL.1.10**

Apply the strategy and skill to read a text

Read Independently

Have children pick a fantasy story for sustained silent reading. Remind them that:

- they should think about what the characters say and do to identify the theme of the story.
- they should reread to help them understand the events in the story.

Read Purposefully

Have children record clues about the theme in a Theme chart. After reading, guide children to participate in a group discussion about the story they read. Guide children to:

- share the information they recorded on their Theme charts.
- tell whether they like the theme.
- discuss what parts they reread to help them find and understand clues about the theme.

On Level

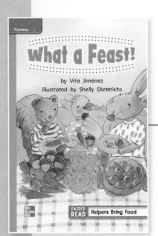

Lexile 500

OBJECTIVES

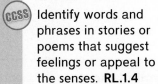 Retell stories, including key details, and demonstrate understanding of their central message or lesson. **RL.1.2**

Identify words and phrases in stories or poems that suggest feelings or appeal to the senses. **RL.1.4**

Identify frequently occurring root words (e.g., *look*) and their inflectional forms (e.g., *looks, looked, looking*). **L.1.4c**

Leveled Reader:
What a Feast!

Before Reading

Preview and Predict

Have children turn to the title page. Read the title and the author's name and have children repeat. Preview the selection's illustrations. Prompt children to predict what the selection might be about.

Review Genre: Fantasy

Have children recall that a fantasy has invented characters, settings, or other elements that could not exist in real life.

ESSENTIAL QUESTION

Remind children of the Essential Question: *How can we work together to make our lives better?* Set a purpose for reading: *Let's read to find out how the animals help each other to make a feast.* Remind children to ask questions while they are reading.

During Reading

Guided Comprehension

As children whisper read *What a Feast!,* monitor and provide guidance, correcting blending and modeling the key strategies and skills. Guide children to identify frequently occurring root words and their inflectional forms, for example *eat/eating* and *stop/stopped.*

Strategy: Reread

Remind children to reread to make sure they understand the text correctly. Model the strategy on page 3: *I'm confused. Is Squirrel tired because the nut was too heavy? I'll reread this page.* Reread the page. *What was squirrel tired of?*

Skill: Theme

Remind children that the theme is the message of a story. As you read, ask: *What are some clues that tell us about the theme of this story?* Display a Theme chart for children to copy.

Go Digital

What a Feast!

Graphic Organizer

Retell

Model recording answers for children. Have children copy the answers into their own charts.

Think Aloud As I read, I will look for clues that tell what the characters do to help each other. I can see what happens as a result of their actions. Then I can use the clues to figure out the theme.

As children read, prompt them to complete the chart.

After Reading

Respond to Reading

Have children complete the Respond to Reading on page 12.

Retell

Have children take turns retelling the selection using the **Retelling Cards** as a guide. Help children make a connection by asking: *Tell about a time you shared something with someone. What did you share? How did sharing help both of you?*

Model Fluency

Read the sentences one at a time. Have children chorally repeat. Point out to children how you read dialogue to make the characters' words sound like someone talking.

Apply Have partners practice reading. Provide feedback as needed.

PAIRED READ ...

Leveled Reader

"Helpers Bring Food"

Make Connections:
Write About It ✏ *Analytical Writing*

Before reading, ask children to note that the genre of this text is informational. Then discuss the Compare Texts direction. After reading, ask children to make connections between the information they learned from "Helpers Bring Food" and *What a Feast!*

✏ *Analytical Writing*

COMPARE TEXTS

- Have children use text evidence to compare fantasy to informational text.

Literature Circles

Lead children in conducting a literature circle using the Thinkmark questions to guide the discussion. You may wish to discuss what children have learned about helping from both selections in the Leveled Reader.

Level Up

Level-up lessons available online.

IF children can read *What a Feast!* On Level with fluency and correctly answer the Respond to Reading questions,

THEN tell children that they will read another story about animals helping each other.

- Use pages 8–11 of *Beware of the Lion!* Beyond Level to model using Teaching Poster 37 to list clues to identifying the theme.

- Have children read the selection, checking their comprehension by using the graphic organizer.

On Level

Phonics

BUILD WORDS WITH VARIANT VOWEL /ü/

OBJECTIVES

 Decode regularly spelled one-syllable words. **RF.1.3b**

 I Do Display **Word-Building Cards** f, oo, d. *These are the letters* f, o, o, *and* d. *The two o's together stand for one sound,* /ü/, *so the letters stand for* /f/ /ü/ *and* /d/. *I will blend* /f/ /ü/ /d/ *together:* /fffüüüd/, food. *The word is* food.

 We Do *Now let's do one together.* Change the letter f to m. *Let's blend and read the new word:* /m/ /ü/ /d/, /müüüd/, mood. *The new word is* mood.

 You Do Have children build and blend these words: *rude, root, boot, boo, blue, blew, grew, glue, sue, suit, fruit, flute*

Repeat with additional /ü/ words. **Decodable Reader** Have children read "Rooster and Goose," "Choose a Room," "The Flute Youth," "Group Rules," "Lewis and His New Suit," "A Cruise Crew," "Sue and Lucy," and "A True Team" (pages 1–32).

Words to Know

REVIEW WORDS

OBJECTIVES

 Recognize and read grade-appropriate irregularly spelled words. **RF.1.3g**

Review high-frequency words *answer, brought, busy, door, enough, eyes* and vocabulary words *demand* and *emergency*

 I Do Use the **Read/Spell/Write** routine to teach each high-frequency and vocabulary word. Use each word orally in a sentence.

 We Do Guide children to Read/Spell/Write each word using their **Response Boards**. Then work with them to generate oral sentences for the words.

 You Do Have partners use the Read/Spell/Write routine on their own using the high-frequency words *answer, brought, busy, door, enough,* and *eyes* and the vocabulary words *demand* and *emergency.* Have partners write sentences about ways people can work together to help out. Tell them that each sentence should contain at least one high-frequency or vocabulary word.

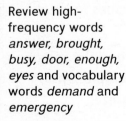

Comprehension

REVIEW THEME

OBJECTIVES

 Retell stories, including key details, and demonstrate understanding of their central message or lesson. **RL.1.2**

 I Do Remind children that the theme of a fantasy story is an important message that the author wants to share. *When I read a story, I look for clues about the theme. I ask: What do characters do and say? What happens in the story? What message does the author want to give?*

 We Do Read the first two pages of the Practice Book story aloud. Pause to discuss what the characters say and do. *We read that Raccoon is making a tree house and wants some help. What does Moose say and do? What do you think the theme might be?*

 You Do Guide children to read the rest of the Practice Book story. Have them fill in a Theme chart as they read. Remind them to think about what characters say and do. Then invite children to discuss the theme.

SELF-SELECTED READING

OBJECTIVES

With prompting and support, read prose and poetry of appropriate complexity for grade 1. **RL.1.10**

Apply the strategy and skill to read a text

Read Independently

Have children pick a fantasy story for sustained silent reading. Remind them to:

- pay attention what the characters say and do and to events in the story.
- reread to help them find clues about the theme.

Read Purposefully

Have children record details on a Theme chart. After reading, guide partners to:

- share the information they recorded on their Theme chart.
- tell what clues helped them identify the theme.
- reread parts to check their understanding of the story and the theme.

→ Beyond Level

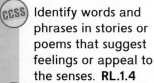

Lexile 480

OBJECTIVES

CCSS Retell stories, including key details, and demonstrate understanding of their central message or lesson. **RL.1.2**

CCSS Identify words and phrases in stories or poems that suggest feelings or appeal to the senses. **RL.1.4**

CCSS Identify frequently occurring root words (e.g., *look*) and their inflectional forms (e.g., *look, looked, looking*). **L.1.4**

Leveled Reader:
Beware of the Lion!

Before Reading

Preview and Predict

Read the title and the author's name. Have children preview the title page and the illustrations. Ask: *What do you think this book will be about?*

Review Genre: Fantasy

Have children recall that a fantasy has invented characters, settings, or other elements that could not exist in real life. Prompt children to name key characteristics of a fantasy. Tell them to look for these as they read the Leveled Reader.

ESSENTIAL QUESTION

Remind children of the Essential Question: *How can we work together to make our lives better?* Set a purpose for reading: *Let's find out how the animals make their lives better.*

During Reading

Guided Comprehension

Have children whisper read *Beware of the Lion!* Have them place self-stick notes next to difficult words. Remind children that when they come to an unfamiliar word, they can look for familiar spellings. They will need to break longer words into smaller chunks and sound out each part.

Monitor children's reading. Stop periodically and ask open-ended questions to facilitate rich discussion, such as *How do the animals feel? Why?* Build on children's responses to develop deeper understanding of the text. Guide children to identify frequently occurring root words and their inflectional forms, for example *eat/eating* and *ask/asked.*

Strategy: Reread

Remind children that sometimes they may misread a word or miss an important point. Say: *If you get confused or do not understand what is happening, you should go back and reread the page or a section.*

Go Digital

Beware of the Lion!

Graphic Organizer

Skill: Theme

Remind children the theme is the big idea or message in a story. As you read, ask: *What clues help you figure out the theme?* Display a Theme chart for children to copy.

Model how to record the information. Have children fill in their charts as they read.

Think Aloud As I read, I look for clues that tell what happens as a result of the characters' words and actions. All of the animals in the story are afraid of Lion, but they know something needs to be done. This may be a clue to the theme of the story.

After Reading

Respond to Reading

Complete the Respond to Reading on page 12 after reading.

Retell

Have children take turns retelling the selection. Help children make a personal connection by writing about a time they worked in a group or on a team. *How did working together help everyone?*

PAIRED READ ...

"Pete Seeger"

Make Connections:
Write About It  *Analytical Writing*

Leveled Reader

Before reading "Pete Seeger," have children preview the title page and prompt them to identify the genre. Discuss the Compare Texts direction. After reading, have partners discuss the information in "Pete Seeger" and *Beware of the Lion!* Ask children to make connections by comparing and contrasting how the characters helped others in each selection. Prompt children to discuss how helping each other can improve people's lives.

Analytical Writing

COMPARE TEXTS

- Have children use text evidence to compare fantasy to informational text.

Literature Circles

Lead children in conducting a literature circle using the Thinkmark questions to guide the discussion. You may wish to discuss what children have learned about helping one another from both selections in the Leveled Reader.

Gifted and Talented

SYNTHESIZE Challenge children to write about someone they know, or someone famous, who has helped others solve a problem.

EXTEND Have them use facts they learned from the week or do additional research to find out more about the person or the problem that was solved.

Vocabulary

OBJECTIVES

CCSS Produce complete sentences when appropriate to task and situation. **SL.1.6**

 I Do Review the meaning of the oral vocabulary word *fair*.

Remind children that an antonym means the opposite of another word. *If you are fair, you are just and honest. You treat everyone equally. We can add a word part to the word* fair *to make its antonym:* unfair.

 We Do Have children take turns using the words *fair* and *unfair* in sentences.

 You Do Have partners share their sentences with the group.

 Gifted and Talented **Extend** Have children do a skit about a situation, rule, or experience that they think is unfair and what could be done to make it fair.

VOCABULARY WORDS: ANTONYMS

OBJECTIVES

CCSS Produce complete sentences when appropriate to task and situation. **SL.1.6**

 I Do Review with children the meaning of the vocabulary word *demand*. Write the sentence *I demand that you clean your room.* Read the sentence aloud, and have children repeat. Discuss what *demand* means in the sentence.

Remind children that an antonym means the opposite of another word. *When you demand people do things, you command them. What is the opposite of* demand? *Antonyms for* demand *might be* yield *or* surrender.

 We Do Have children complete sentence frames using the two words: *I demand that you ____. I had to surrender when ____.*

 You Do Have partners use the words *yield* and *demand* in sentences that show their relationship.

Comprehension

REVIEW THEME

OBJECTIVES

 Retell stories, including key details, and demonstrate understanding of their central message or lesson. **RL.1.2**

I Do Discuss with children how they can determine the theme of a fantasy story. Prompt them to explain that they can look for clues that help them figure out the story's message.

We Do Guide children in reading the first two pages of the Practice Book story aloud. Pause to prompt children to discuss clues to the theme of the story. *What is Raccoon doing? What does Moose offer to do?*

You Do Have children read the rest of the Practice Book story independently and fill out a Theme chart. Remind them to look for clues that will help them figure out the theme. Then invite children to discuss the theme.

SELF-SELECTED READING

OBJECTIVES

 With prompting and support, read prose and poetry of appropriate complexity for grade 1. **RL.1.10**

Apply the strategy and skill to read a text

Read Independently

Have children pick a fantasy story for sustained silent reading. Tell them that they should use a Theme chart to record clues about the theme. Remind them to reread to help them figure out things they do not understand.

Read Purposefully

Have children record details on a Theme chart. After reading, guide children to:

- share the information they recorded on their Theme charts with partners.
- record their thoughts about the theme of the story in a reading response journal.

Independent Study Have children draw a scene from the book that illustrates the author's message or theme. Have them state the theme in their own words as a caption.

→ English Language Learners

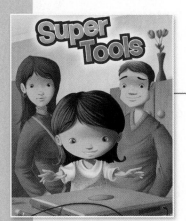

Reading/Writing Workshop

OBJECTIVES

 Retell stories, including key details, and demonstrate understanding of their central message or lesson. **RL.1.2**

Shared Read:
Super Tools

Go Digital

Super Tools

Graphic Organizer

Before Reading

Build Background

Read the Essential Question: *How can we work together to make our lives better?*

- Explain the meaning of the Essential Question: *When people work together, they can share ideas. They can work together to get a job done. It's fun to work together!*

- **Model an answer:** *We work together to clean up our classroom. The job gets done quickly. Everyone does their share of the work. Our school day is easier when our classroom is neat and clean.*

- Ask children a question that ties the Essential Question to their own background knowledge. *How do you work together with family and friends?* Ask partners to share their answers.

During Reading

Interactive Question-Response

- Ask questions that help children understand the meaning of the text after each paragraph.

- Reinforce the meanings of key vocabulary by providing meanings embedded in the questions.

- Ask children questions that require them to use key vocabulary.

- Reinforce the comprehension strategies and skills of the week by modeling.

Super Tools

Pages 222–223

Point to the title. *Listen as I read the title of this fantasy story.* Point to each word as you read it, and then point to the word *Tools. Tools are things that help us do a job. Read the title with me.*

Point to the illustration. *This is Lucy. Say her name with me:* Lucy. *What do Mom and Dad have?* (computer and printer) *A computer is a tool that Lucy can use to write and draw. What other tools are on Lucy's desk?* (pencils, crayons, markers) *Lucy can also use these tools to write and draw.*

Pages 224–225

Point to the illustration on page 224. *What is Lucy doing?* (using the computer) *She looks very busy.* Point to the pencils, crayons, and markers in the illustration on page 225. *These writing tools have faces, and they can talk! Now we know that this story couldn't really happen. Listen as I read what they say:* "Lucy hasn't used us in weeks!" cried the markers. "Can we demand to be used?" asked the crayons. "No, that would be rude. But we can remind her how great we are," said the pencils. *How do the writing tools feel?*

 Why are the writing tools upset? (Lucy isn't using them anymore.)

Explain and Model the Skill *I don't know yet what the theme is, but it seems important that the drawing tools are unhappy. I think it is a clue.*

Pages 226–227

Lucy is using her computer to write a report. But the writing tools have a plan. Listen as I read the beginning of page 227. What was their plan? (draw a picture for Lucy)

Now look at the picture. What are the pencils doing? (drawing) *What are the markers and crayons doing?* (coloring)

Explain and Model Phonics Write the words: *Lucy, drew, blue.* Say each word and have children repeat it. *What sound is the same in all of these words?* (/ü/) Circle *u, ew,* and *ue. These letters stand for the /ü/ sound in these words.*

 What did the tools draw? (tree; birds in a nest)

Pages 228–229

Let's look at the picture on page 228. How do you think Lucy feels? (surprised) *Point to the last sentence. Let's read this sentence together:* "Who drew this great picture?" she asked.

Mom and Dad thought that Lucy drew the picture. Point to the last sentence. *Let's read this sentence together:* "It is fun to draw," she said. *Lucy was reminded how much fun it was to use the markers, crayons, and pencils.*

Explain and Model High-Frequency Words Point to the word *eyes* and have children say it with you. *Point to your eyes. What do your eyes help you to do?* (see things)

 What tools do you like to draw with?

Pages 230–231

Look at the picture. What does Lucy decide to do? (draw) *What tools does she use?* (markers, pencils, crayons) *Let's read the last sentence together:* "And the writing tools felt happy and useful!"

Explain and Model the Strategy *If something in the story doesn't make sense, you can reread and figure it out. You can also look at the pictures to help. If you don't understand how Lucy and the tools worked together, you can reread page 231. You can also look at what the tools are doing in the picture.*

After Reading

Make Connections

- Review the Essential Question.

English Language Learners

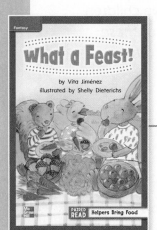

Lexile 350

OBJECTIVES

(ccss) Retell stories, including key details, and demonstrate understanding of their central message or lesson. **RL.1.2**

(ccss) Identify words and phrases in stories or poems that suggest feelings or appeal to the senses. **RL.1.4**

(ccss) Identify frequently occurring root words (e.g., *look*) and their inflectional forms (e.g., *look, looked, looking*). **L.1.4c**

Leveled Reader
What a Feast!

What a Feast!

Before Reading

Preview

Read the title. Ask: *What is the title? Say it again.* Repeat with the author's name. Preview the illustrations. Have children describe the pictures. Use simple language to tell about each page. Follow with questions, such as: *What food does this animal like?*

ESSENTIAL QUESTION

Remind children of the Essential Question: *How can we work together to make our lives better?* Say: *Let's read to find out how the animals in this story work together to help each other.* Encourage children to ask for help when they do not understand a word or phrase.

Graphic Organizer

During Reading

Interactive Question-Response

Pages 2–3 *Why did Squirrel gather so many nuts? Listen as I reread this sentence: "He wanted to save enough nuts for an emergency." An emergency is an unexpected event that causes a problem. What emergency might Squirrel have?* (It might snow and he won't be able to find more food.) *Point to wanted. What root word do you see?* (want)

Pages 4–5 *How are Squirrel and Bird alike?* (gather food) *What food does Squirrel gather?* (nuts) *What does Bird gather?* (seeds and berries) *Tell your partner why Squirrel and Bird want something different to eat.*

Pages 6–7 *Bunny eats different food. Look at the picture on page 6 for Bunny's food. What is it?* (carrots and lettuce) *Bunny asks Bird and Squirrel what's wrong. Let's find what Bird says.* ("We're sad.")

Pages 8–9 *Bird and Squirrel's bellies want different food. Look at the picture. Let's read the label: bellies. Which character can solve this problem? Bunny says.* ("I have the answer!")

Page 10 *What is Bunny's idea?* (They all will put their food together so they have something different to eat.) *Talk to your partner about what Squirrel and Bird think of Bunny's idea.*

Page 11 *The friends had a great feast. Why was the feast so great?* (They shared their food.) *Could this be a clue to the theme of the story?*

Retell

After Reading

Respond to Reading

Revisit the Essential Question. Ask children to work with partners to fill in the graphic organizer and answer the questions on page 12. Pair children with peers of varying language abilities.

Retell

Model retelling using the **Retelling Card** prompts. Say: *Look at the illustrations. Use details to help you retell the story.* Help children make personal connections by asking: *When did you share something? How did it help you? How did it help the person with whom you shared?*

Expression Fluency: Read Dialogue

Read the pages in the book, one at a time. Help children echo-read the pages expressively and with appropriate phrasing. Remind them to use proper expression when reading dialogue.

Apply Have children practice reading with partners. Pair children with peers of varying language abilities. Provide feedback as needed.

PAIRED READ ...

"Helpers Bring Food"

Make Connections: Write About It

Leveled Reader

Before reading, tell children to note that this selection is informational text. Then discuss the Compare Texts direction.

After reading, ask children to make connections between the information they learned from "Helpers Bring Food" and *What a Feast!* Prompt children by providing a sentence frame: *Sharing food is helpful because ____.*

Analytical Writing

COMPARE TEXTS
- Have children use text evidence to compare fantasy to informational text.

Literature Circles

Lead children in conducting a literature circle using the Thinkmark questions to guide the discussion. You may wish to discuss what children have learned about how sharing helps to make lives better from both selections in the Leveled Reader.

Level Up

Level-up lessons available online.

IF children can read *What a Feast!* **ELL Level** with fluency and correctly answer the Respond to Reading questions,

THEN tell children that they will read a more detailed version of the story.

- Use pages 9–11 of *What a Feast!* **On Level** to model using Teaching Poster 37 to identify clues to the theme.

- Have children read the selection, checking their comprehension by using the graphic organizer.

Vocabulary

PRETEACH ORAL VOCABULARY

OBJECTIVES

 Produce complete sentences when appropriate to task and situation. **SL.1.6**

LANGUAGE OBJECTIVE

Use oral vocabulary words

 I Do Display images from the **Visual Vocabulary Cards** one at a time and follow the routine to review the Oral Vocabulary words *fair* and *conflict*.

 We Do Display each image again and explain how it illustrates or demonstrates the word. Model using sentences to describe the image.

You Do Display the word again and have partners discuss how this picture demonstrates the word.

Beginning	Intermediate	Advanced/High
Use the words in sentences about a picture from *Super Tools* and have children repeat.	Provide sentence frames for children to complete about pictures from *Super Tools*.	Challenge partners to use the words to describe pictures from *Super Tools* or stories they have read.

PRETEACH VOCABULARY

OBJECTIVES

 Identify real-life connections between words and their use (e.g., note places at home that are *cozy*). **L.1.5c**

LANGUAGE OBJECTIVE

Use vocabulary words

 I Do Display images from the **ELL Visual Vocabulary Cards** one at a time and follow the routine to review the vocabulary words *collecting* and *answer*. Say each word and have children repeat it. Define the word in English.

 We Do Display the image again and explain how it illustrates or demonstrates the word. Model using sentences to describe the image.

  You Do Display each word again and have children say the word and then spell it. Provide opportunities for children to use the words in speaking and writing. Provide sentence starters.

Beginning	Intermediate	Advanced/High
Say a sentence about an image. Have children repeat the sentence and match it to its picture.	Say sentences about the images, leaving out the words. Have children repeat, inserting the correct words.	Ask children to use the words to say sentences about the images.

Words to Know

REVIEW WORDS

OBJECTIVES

Recognize and read grade-appropriate irregularly spelled words. **RF.1.3g**

LANGUAGE OBJECTIVE

Use high-frequency and vocabulary words

 I Do Display the **High-Frequency Word** and **Vocabulary Cards** for *answer, brought, busy, door, enough, eyes* and *demand* and *emergency*. Read each word. Use the **Read/Spell/Write** routine to teach each word. Have children write the words on their **Response Boards**.

 We Do Write sentence frames on separate lines. Track the print as children read and complete the sentences: *(1) I will answer the _____. (2) When Dad came home, he brought _____. (3) Are you busy _____? (4) If you go through this door, _____. (5) We need to buy enough _____. (6) Open your eyes and see _____. (7) I demand that _____. (8) An emergency is _____.*

 You Do Display the High-Frequency Word Cards from the previous weeks. Display one card at a time as children chorally read the word. Mix and repeat. Note words children need to review. Repeat with vocabulary words.

Beginning	Intermediate	Advanced/High
Say each word and have children repeat. Use gestures or pantomime to demonstrate the word.	Have children use the words in sentences about the word cards.	Challenge partners to use the words in sentences to tell about stories they have read.

RETEACH HIGH-FREQUENCY WORDS

OBJECTIVES

Recognize and read grade-appropriate irregularly spelled words. **RF.1.3g**

LANGUAGE OBJECTIVE

Use high-frequency words

 I Do Display the Visual Vocabulary Card and say the word aloud. Define the word in English and, if appropriate, in Spanish. Identify any cognates.

 We Do Point to the image again and explain how it illustrates or demonstrates the word. Ask children to repeat the word. Engage children in structured partner-talk about the image as prompted on the back of the card. Ask children to chorally say the word three times.

 You Do Display each visual in random order, hiding the word. Have children identify the word and define it in their own words.

Beginning	Intermediate	Advanced/High
Say a word. Have children find its picture. Use the word in a sentence, and have children repeat.	Have children complete sentence frames for the words.	Have children say a sentence but leave out the word. Have others say what word completes it.

Writing/Spelling

WRITING TRAIT: SENTENCE FLUENCY

OBJECTIVES

 Produce and expand complete simple and compound declarative, interrogative, imperative, and exclamatory sentences in response to prompts. **L.1.1j**

LANGUAGE OBJECTIVE

Write sentences of varying lengths

 Explain that authors vary the length of their sentences to make writing more interesting. Write and read: *Lucy got something new. It was a computer. Lucy really liked it.* Then show children these sentences: *Lucy looked at what Mom and Dad had brought. It was a new computer! Lucy was surprised!* Point out the different lengths and how they make the writing more interesting.

 Read page 226 in *Super Tools.* Discuss the variety of sentence types and how they make the writing more interesting. Repeat with page 231.

 Have children write sentences about a drawing they made. Remind them to use both short and long sentences.

Beginning	Intermediate	Advanced/High
Use sentences of different lengths to tell about *Super Tools.* Have children repeat the sentences.	Have children tell about *Super Tools.* Provide sentence frames of different lengths as necessary.	Have children write sentences of different lengths about *Super Tools* or another story they know.

WORDS WITH VARIANT VOWEL /ü/

OBJECTIVES

 Use conventional spelling for words with common spelling patterns and for frequently occurring irregular words. **L.1.2d**

LANGUAGE OBJECTIVE

Spell words with variant vowel /ü/

 Read aloud the first Spelling Word on page T14, *moon.* Segment the word into sounds and attach a spelling to each sound. Point out the /ü/ sound and spelling. Read aloud, segment, and spell the remaining words and have children repeat.

 Say a sentence for *moon.* Then say *moon* slowly and ask children to repeat. Have them write the word. Repeat the process for the remaining words.

 Display the words. Have children work with partners to check their spelling lists. Have children correct misspelled words on their lists.

Beginning	Intermediate	Advanced/High
Help children say the words and copy them with the correct spelling.	After children have corrected their words, have pairs quiz each other.	Challenge children to think of other words that have the /ü/ sound.

Grammar

PRONOUNS

OBJECTIVES

 CCSS Use personal **(subject, object)**, possessive, and indefinite pronouns (e.g., *I, me, my; they, them, their; anyone, everything*). **L.1.1d**

LANGUAGE OBJECTIVE

Recognize and use the personal pronouns *I, you, he, she, it, we, they*

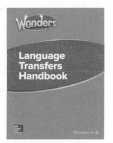

Language Transfers Handbook

TRANSFER SKILLS

Speakers of Cantonese, Haitian Creole, Hmong, Korean, Spanish, and Khmer may use pronouns of the inappropriate gender. *(He is my mom.)* Provide extra support. Have them point to a girl and say *she*, a boy and say *he*, and an object and say *it*.

 I Do Remind children that pronouns take the place of nouns, or words that name people, places, things, or ideas. Then review the pronouns *I, you, he, she, it,* we, and *they*. Say sentences as you demonstrate each pronoun. For example, point to yourself and say *I am (your name)* or point to a boy and say: *He is a boy.*

 We Do Write the sentence pairs on the board. Have children read the sentences and tell what pronouns stand for the underlined words.

Judy is on the swing. She is happy.

"I am hungry," said Roy.

Sue and Luke are in a race. They run fast.

The cat is black. It has a white nose.

Jane is late. Where is she?

 You Do Write the following sentence frames on the board:

I like to dance. _____ is fun. (It, We) (It)

Jake ran home. _____ is tired. (They, He) (He)

Mom and Dad went to the market. _____ got fruit. (He, They) (They)

My brother is too tall. _____ hit his head on the door! (It, He,) (He)

Sue and I walk to school. _____ live close by. (She, We) (We)

Have partners complete each sentence frame with the correct pronoun. Circulate, listen in, and take note of each child's language use and proficiency.

Beginning	Intermediate	Advanced/High
Help children describe a story picture. Point to a character or object. Use a pronoun in a sentence to tell about it. Have children repeat the sentence as they point to the person or object in the picture the pronoun stands for.	Help children describe a story picture. Say a sentence with a noun. Have children repeat the sentence but substitute a pronoun for the noun.	Ask partners to write or say sentences about story pictures. Have them use a noun in one sentence and the pronoun that stands for it in a second sentence.

PROGRESS MONITORING

Unit 6 Week 1 Formal Assessment	Standards Covered	Component for Assessment
Comprehension • Theme • Point of View	• RL.1.2 • RL.2.6	• *Selection Test* • *Weekly Assessment*
Vocabulary Strategy Synonyms	L.4.5c	• *Selection Test* • *Weekly Assessment*
Phonics Variant Vowel Spellings with Digraphs: *oo, u, u_e, ew, ue, ui, ou*	RF.1.3c	*Weekly Assessment*
Structural Analysis Suffixes -*ful* and -*less*	RF.1.3	*Weekly Assessment*
High-Frequency Words *answer, brought, busy, door, enough, eyes*	RF.1.3g	*Weekly Assessment*
Writing Writing About Text	RL.1.2	*Weekly Assessment*
Unit 6 Week 1 Informal Assessment		
Research/Listening/Collaborating	SL.1.1c, SL.1.2, SL.1.3	• *RWW* • *Teacher's Edition*
Oral Reading Fluency (ORF) **Fluency Goal:** 13-33 words correct per minute (WCPM) **Accuracy Rate Goal:** 95% or higher	RF.1.4a. RF.1.4b, RF.1.4c	*Fluency Assessment*

Using Assessment Results

Weekly Assessment Skills	If . . .	Then . . .
COMPREHENSION	Children answer 0–3 multiple-choice items correctly . . .	. . . assign Lessons 31–33 on Theme from the *Tier 2 Comprehension Intervention online PDFs*.
VOCABULARY	Children answer 0–2 multiple-choice items correctly . . .	. . . assign Lesson 115 on Synonyms from the *Tier 2 Vocabulary Intervention online PDFs*.
PHONICS/ STRUCTURAL ANALYSIS/HFW	Children answer 0–6 multiple-choice items correctly . . .	. . . assign Lesson 95 on Variant Vowels Spelled *oo*, Lesson 96 on Variant Vowel /ü/ (*ue ou, ew*), Lesson 97 on Variant Vowel /ü/ (*u, ui, u_e*), and Lesson 101 on Suffixes (*-ful, -less*) from the *Tier 2 Phonics/ Word Study Intervention online PDFs*.
WRITING	Children score less than "2" on the constructed response . . .	. . . reteach necessary skills using Section 13 on Write About Reading from the *Tier 2 Comprehension Intervention online PDFs*.
FLUENCY	Children have a WCPM score of 13 . . .	. . . assign a lesson from Section 1, 9, or 10 of the *Tier 2 Fluency Intervention online PDFs*.
	Children have a WCPM score of 0–12 . . .	. . . assign a lesson from Sections 2–8 of the *Tier 2 Fluency Intervention online PDFs*.

Using Weekly Data

Check your data Dashboard to verify assessment results and guide grouping decisions.

Response to Intervention

Use the children's assessment results to assist you in identifying children who will benefit from focused intervention.

Data-Driven Recommendations

Use the appropriate sections of the *Placement and Diagnostic Assessment* to designate children requiring:

TIER 2 Intervention Online PDFs

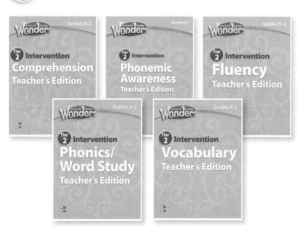

TIER 3 WonderWorks Intervention Program

My Team

Teach and Model
Close Reading and Writing

Big Book and Little Book

Reading Writing Workshop

All Kinds of Helpers, 242–251
Genre Nonfiction Lexile 530

Interactive Read Aloud

"Anansi's Sons"
Genre: Folktale

Practice and Apply
Close Reading and Writing

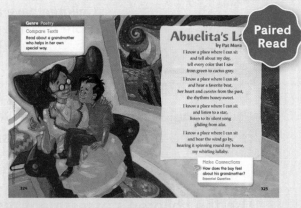

Literature Anthology

Meet Rosina, 302–321
Genre Nonfiction Lexile 420

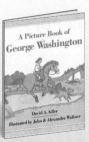

Paired Read

"Abuelita's Lap," 324–325
Genre Poetry Lexile NP

Differentiated Texts

APPROACHING
Lexile 310

ON LEVEL
Lexile 400

BEYOND
Lexile 540

ELL
Lexile 290

Leveled Readers

Extended Complex Texts

A Picture Book of George Washington
Genre Nonfiction
Lexile 750

How People Learned to Fly
Genre Nonfiction
Lexile 630

Classroom Library

Student Outcomes

Close Reading of Complex Text
- Cite relevant evidence from text
- Identify author's purpose
- Retell the text

RI.2.6, RI.1.2

Writing

Write to Sources
- Draw evidence from nonfiction text
- Write informative text
- Conduct short research on teams

W.1.2, W.1.7

Speaking and Listening
- Engage in collaborative conversation about who helps you
- Retell and discuss *All Kinds of Helpers*
- Present information on how your team helps you

SL.1.1c, SL.1.2, SL.1.3

Content Knowledge
- Explore different elements of fair play and good sportsmanship

Language Development

Conventions
- Use possessive pronouns

Vocabulary Acquisition
- Develop oral vocabulary

inspire	respect	distance
swiftly	decision	

- Acquire and use academic vocabulary

accept	often

- Use context clues to understand antonyms

L.1.1d, L.1.4, L.1.6, L.4.5c

Foundational Skills

Phonics/Word Study/Spelling
- Variant vowel spellings with digraphs: *a, aw, au, augh, al*
- Vowel team syllables
- haul, cause, saw, claw, paw, dawn, moon, soup, love, friend

High-Frequency Words
brother   father   friend   love   mother   picture

Fluency
- Intonation

Decodable Text
- Apply foundational skills in connected text

RF.1.3, RF.1.3d, RF.1.3e, RF.1.3g, RF.1.4a, RF.1.4b, RF.1.4c

Professional Development
- See lessons in action in real classrooms.
- Get expert advice on instructional practices.
- Collaborate with other teachers.
- Access PLC Resources

Go Digital! www.connected.mcgraw-hill.com.

INSTRUCTIONAL PATH

1 Talk About Who Helps You

Guide children in collaborative conversations.

Discuss the essential question: *Who helps you?*

Develop academic language.

Listen to "Anansi's Sons" and reread to understand the story.

2 Read *All Kinds of Helpers*

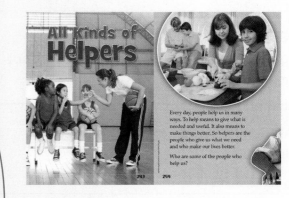

Apply foundational skills in connected text. Model close reading.

Read

All Kinds of Helpers to learn about the different ways people help, citing text evidence to answer text-dependent questions.

Reread

All Kinds of Helpers to analyze text, craft, and structure, citing text evidence.

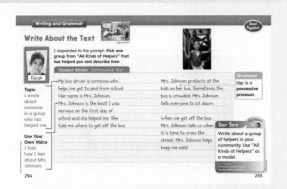

3 Write About *All Kinds of Helpers*

Model writing to a source.

Analyze a short response student model.

Use text evidence from close reading to write to a source.

4 ## Read and Write About *Meet Rosina*

Practice and apply close reading of the anchor text.

Read

Meet Rosina to learn about people who help her.

Reread

Meet Rosina and use text evidence to understand how the author uses text, craft, and structure to develop a deeper understanding of Rosina and her life.

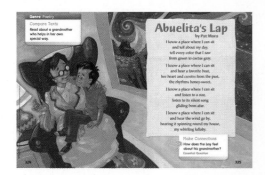

Integrate

Information about the people who help us.

Write to a Source, citing text evidence to write about people in your community who help you.

5 ## Independent Partner Work

Gradual release of support to independent work

- Text-Dependent Questions
- Scaffolded Partner Work
- Talk with a Partner
- Cite Text Evidence
- Complete a sentence frame.
- Guided Text Annotation

6 ## Integrate Knowledge and Ideas

Connect Texts

Text to Text Discuss how each of the texts answers the question: Who helps you?

Text to Poetry Compare information about who helps us in the texts read with the poem "What Does the Little Birdie Say?"

Conduct a Short Research Project

Create a newspaper article.

DEVELOPING READERS AND WRITERS

Write to Sources: Informative

Day 1 and Day 2

Shared Writing

- Write about *All Kinds of Helpers,* p. T96

Interactive Writing

- Analyze a student model, p. T106
- Write about *All Kinds of Helpers,* p. T107
- Find Text Evidence
- Apply Writing Trait: Voice: Use Your Own Voice, p. T107
- Apply Grammar Skill: Possessive Pronouns, p. T107

Day 3, Day 4 and Day 5

Independent Writing

- Write about *Meet Rosina,* p. T114
- Provide scaffolded instruction to meet student needs, p. T114
- Find Text Evidence, p. T114
- Apply Writing Trait: Voice p. T114
- Prewrite and Draft, p. T114
- Revise and Edit, p. T120
- Final Draft, p. T120
- Present, Evaluate, and Publish, p. T126

Grammar

Possessive Pronouns

- Use possessive pronouns to tell about what is happening, pp. T97, T107, T115, T121, T127

- Apply grammar to writing, pp. T97, T114, T120, T127

Mechanics: Capitalize Days, Months, and Holidays

- Use capitalization in days, months, and holidays, pp. T115, T121, T127

Online PDFs

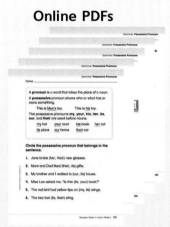

Grammar Practice, pp. 131–135

Online Grammar Games

Spelling

Words with Variant Vowel /ô/

- Spell words with variant vowel /ô/

Online PDFs

Phonics/Spelling blms
pp. 131–135

Online Spelling Games

SUGGESTED LESSON PLAN

READING		DAY 1	DAY 2
Teach, Model and Apply Reading/Writing Workshop	Core	**Build Background** My Team, T86–T87 **Oral Vocabulary** *inspire, respect,* T86 **Word Work** T90–T93 • Fluency: Sound-Spellings • Phonemic Awareness: Phoneme Categorization • Phonics/Spelling: Introduce Variant Vowel /ô/ • High-Frequency Words: *brother, father, friend, love, mother, picture* • Vocabulary: *accept, often* **Shared Read** *All Kinds of Helpers,* T94–T95	**Oral Language** My Team, T98 **Oral Vocabulary** *decision, distance, inspire, respect, swiftly,* T98 **Word Work** T100–T103 • Phonemic Awareness: Phoneme Reversal • Structural Analysis: Vowel Team Syllables • Vocabulary: *accept, often* **Shared Read** *All Kinds of Helpers,* T104–T105 • Genre: Informational Text/Nonfiction, T104 • Skill: Author's Purpose, T105
	Options	**Listening Comprehension** "Anansi's Sons," T88–T89	**Listening Comprehension** "Anansi's Sons," T99 **Word Work** T100–T103 • Phonics/Spelling: Review Variant Vowel /ô/ • High-Frequency Words

LANGUAGE ARTS			
Writing **Grammar**	Core	**Shared Writing** T96 **Grammar** Possessive Pronouns, T97	**Interactive Writing** T106 **Grammar** Possessive Pronouns, T107
	Options		

DIFFERENTIATED INSTRUCTION
Use your data dashboard to determine each student's needs. Then select instructional supports options throughout the week.

APPROACHING LEVEL

Leveled Reader
Helping Me, Helping You!, T130–T131
"Fire!," T131
Literature Circles, T131

Phonemic Awareness
Phoneme Blending, T132 TIER 2
Phoneme Categorization, T132 TIER 2
Phoneme Reversal, T133
Phoneme Substitution, T133

Phonics
Connect *a, aw, au, augh, al* to /ô/ T134 TIER 2
Blend Words with Variant Vowel /ô/, T134 TIER 2
Build Words with Variant Vowel /ô/, T135
Build Fluency with Phonics, T135

Structural Analysis
Review Vowel Team Syllables, T136

Words to Know
Review, T137

Comprehension
Read for Fluency, T138 TIER 2
Identify Main Idea, T138 TIER 2
Review Author's Purpose, T139
Self-Selected Reading, T139

ON LEVEL

Leveled Reader
Helping Me, Helping You!, T140–T141
"Fire!," T141
Literature Circles, T141

Phonics
Build Words with /ô/, T142

DAY 3

Fluency Intonation, T109
Word Work T110–T113
• Phonemic Awareness: Phoneme Blending
• Phonics/Spelling: Blend Words with Variant Vowel /ô/
• Vocabulary Strategy: Antonyms
Close Reading *Meet Rosina,* T113A–T113L

Oral Language My Team, T108
Word Work T110–T113
• Structural Analysis: Vowel Team Syllables
• High-Frequency Words

Independent Writing T114
Grammar Mechanics: Capitalize Days, Months, Holidays, T115

Grammar Possessive Pronouns, T115

DAY 4

Extend the Concept T116–T117
• Literary Element: Sensory Words, T116
• Close Reading: "Abuelita's Lap," T117
Word Work T118–T119
• Phonemic Awareness: Phoneme Categorization
• Structural Analysis: Vowel Team Syllables
Integrate Ideas
• Research and Inquiry, T122–T123

Word Work T118–T119
• Fluency: Sound-Spellings
• Phonics/Spelling: Word Sort with /ô/
• High-Frequency Words
• Vocabulary: *accept, often*
Close Reading *Meet Rosina,* T113A–T113L

Independent Writing T120
Grammar Mechanics: Capitalize Days, Months, Holidays, T121

Grammar Possessive Pronouns, T121

DAY 5

Word Work T124–T125
• Phonemic Awareness: Phoneme Segmentation/ Substitution
• Phonics/Spelling: Blend and Build Words with Variant Vowel /ô/
• Structural Analysis: Vowel Team Syllables
• High-Frequency Words
• Vocabulary: *accept, often*
Integrate Ideas
• Text Connections, T128–T129

Word Work T124–T125
• Fluency: Intonation
Integrate Ideas
• Research and Inquiry, T128
• Speaking and Listening, T129

Independent Writing T126
Grammar Possessive Pronouns, T127

Grammar Mechanics: Capitalize Days, Months, Holidays, T127

Words to Know
Review Words, T142

Comprehension
Review Author's Purpose, T143
Self-Selected Reading, T143

BEYOND LEVEL

Leveled Reader
Helping Me, Helping You!, T144–T145
"Fire!," T145
Literature Circles, T145

Vocabulary
Context Clues, T146

Comprehension
Review Author's Purpose, T147
Self-Selected Reading, T147 *Gifted and Talented*

ENGLISH LANGUAGE LEARNERS

Shared Read
All Kinds of Helpers, T148–T149

Leveled Reader
Helping Me, Helping You! T150–T151
"Fire!," T151
Literature Circles, T151

Vocabulary
Preteach Oral Vocabulary, T152
Preteach ELL Vocabulary, T152

Words to Know
Review Words, T153
Reteach High-Frequency Words, T153

Writing/Spelling
Writing Trait: Voice, T154
Words with Variant Vowel /ô/, T154

Grammar
Possessive Pronouns, T155

DIFFERENTIATE TO ACCELERATE

  Scaffold to **A**ccess **C**omplex **T**ext

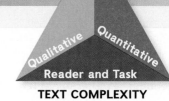

IF	the text complexity of a particular selection is too difficult for children
THEN	see the references noted in the chart below for scaffolded instruction to help children Access Complex Text.

Qualitative Quantitative
Reader and Task
TEXT COMPLEXITY

	Reading/Writing Workshop	**Literature Anthology**	**Leveled Readers**	**Classroom Library**

Quantitative	*All Kinds of Helpers* **Lexile** 530	*Meet Rosina* **Lexile** 420 "Abuelita's Lap" **Lexile** NP	**Approaching Level** **Lexile** 310 **Beyond Level** **Lexile** 540 **On Level** **Lexile** 400 **ELL** **Lexile** 290	*A Picture Book of George Washington* **Lexile** 750 *How People Learned to Fly* **Lexile** 630
Qualitative	**What Makes the Text Complex?** **Foundational Skills** • Decoding with variant vowel spellings with digraphs: *a, aw, au, augh, al,* T90–T91 • Reading words with vowel team syllables, T101 • Identifying high-frequency words, T92–T93 *See Scaffolded Instruction in Teacher's Edition, T90 –T91, T92–T93, and T101.*	**What Makes the Text Complex?** • **Purpose of Text,** T113B, T113E • **Organization,** T113B, T113F **A C T** *See Scaffolded Instruction in Teacher's Edition , T113B, T113E, and T113F.*	**What Makes the Text Complex?** **Foundational Skills** • Decoding with variant vowel spellings with digraphs: *a, aw, au, augh, al* • Reading words with vowel team syllables • Identifying high-frequency words *brother father friend love mother picture* *See Level Up lessons online for Leveled Readers.*	**What Makes the Text Complex?** • **Purpose** • **Specific Vocabulary** • **Prior Knowledge** • **Sentence Structure** • **Organization** • **Connection of Ideas** • **Genre** **A C T** *See Scaffolded Instruction in Teacher's Edition, T413–T415.*
Reader and Task	**The** Introduce the Concept lesson on pages T86–T87 will help determine the reader's knowledge and engagement in the weekly concept. See pages T94–T95, T104–T105, T122–T123 and T128-T129 for questions and tasks for this text.	**The** Introduce the Concept lesson on pages T86–T87 will help determine the reader's knowledge and engagement in the weekly concept. See pages T113A–T113L, T117, T122–T123 and T128-T129 for questions and tasks for this text.	**The** Introduce the Concept lesson on pages T86–T87 will help determine the reader's knowledge and engagement in the weekly concept. See pages T130–T131, T140–T141, T144–T145, T150–T151, T122–T123 and T128-T129 for questions and tasks for this text.	**The** Introduce the Concept lesson on pages T86–T87 will help determine the reader's knowledge and engagement in the weekly concept. See pages T413–T415 for questions and tasks for this text.

Monitor and *Differentiate*

✓ Quick Check

To differentiate instruction, use the Quick Checks to assess students' needs and select the appropriate small group instruction focus.

Comprehension Strategy Reread, T89

Comprehension Skill Author's Purpose, T105

Phonics Words with ô, T93, T103, T113, T119, T125

High-Frequency Words and Vocabulary T93, T103, T113, T119, T125

If No →

| Approaching Level | Reteach T130–T139 |
| ELL | Develop T148–T155 |

If Yes →

| On Level | Review T140–T143 |
| Beyond Level | Extend T144–T147 |

Using Weekly Data

Check your data Dashboard to verify assessment results and guide grouping decisions.

Level Up with Leveled Readers

IF children can read their leveled text fluently and answer comprehension questions

THEN work with the next level up to accelerate children's reading with more complex text.

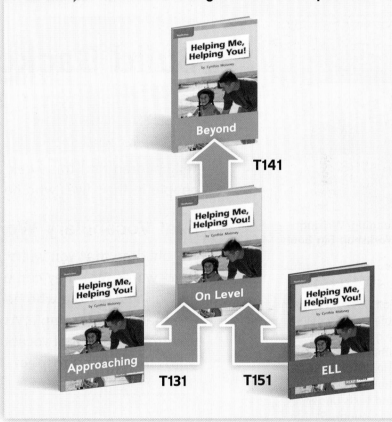

Beyond — T141

On Level

Approaching — T131

ELL — T151

ELL ENGLISH LANGUAGE LEARNERS

Small Group Instruction

Use the ELL small group lessons in the *Wonders* Teacher's Edition to provide focused instruction.

Language Development
Vocabulary preteaching, oral vocabulary preteaching, high-frequency word review and reteach, pp. T152–T153

Close Reading
Interactive Question-Response routines for scaffolded text-dependent questioning for reading and rereading the Shared Read and Leveled Reader, pp. T148–T151

Writing
Focus on the writing trait, grammar, and spelling, pp. T154–T155

Additional ELL Support

Use Wonders for English Learners for ELD instruction that connects to the core.

Language Development
My Language Book for ample opportunities for discussions and scaffolded language support

Close Reading
Guided support for the Shared Read, Big Books, and Interactive Read Alouds. Differentiated texts about the weekly concept

Writing
Guided support in Interactive and Independent Writing and writing to sources

Wonders for ELs Teacher Edition and My Language Book

WHOLE GROUP

DAY 1

Materials

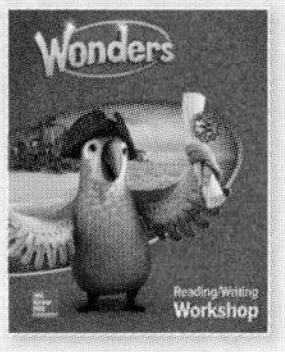

Reading/Writing Workshop
VOLUME 4

Reading/Writing Workshop Big Book
UNIT 6

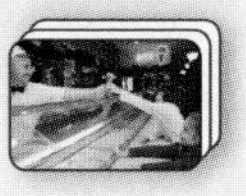

Visual Vocabulary Cards
decision
distance
inspire
respect
swiftly

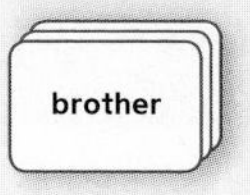

High-Frequency Word Cards
brother love
father mother
friend picture

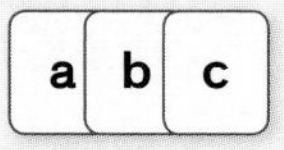

Word-Building Cards

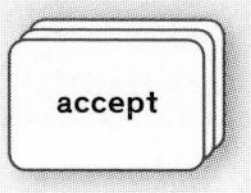

Vocabulary Cards
accept
often

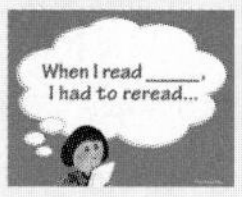

Think Aloud Clouds

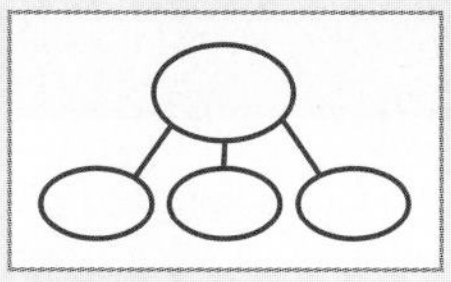

Teaching Poster

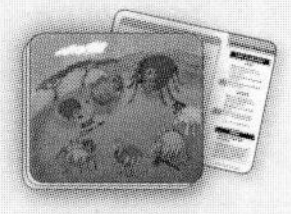

Interactive Read-Aloud Cards

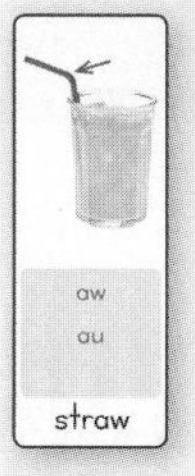

Sound-Spelling Cards

Introduce the Concept

Reading/Writing Workshop Big Book

OBJECTIVES

CCSS Follow agreed-upon rules for discussions (e.g., listening to others with care, speaking one at a time about the topics and texts under discussion). **SL.1.1a**

- Build background knowledge
- Discuss the Essential Question

ACADEMIC LANGUAGE

- *team, vocabulary, admire*
- Cognates: *vocabulario, admirar*

MINILESSON 5 Mins

Build Background

ESSENTIAL QUESTION

Who helps you?

Tell children that this week they will be talking and reading about the people in their lives who help them.

Oral Vocabulary Words

Tell children that you will share some words that they can use as they discuss people who help them. Use the Define/Example/Ask routine to introduce the oral vocabulary words **inspire** and **respect**.

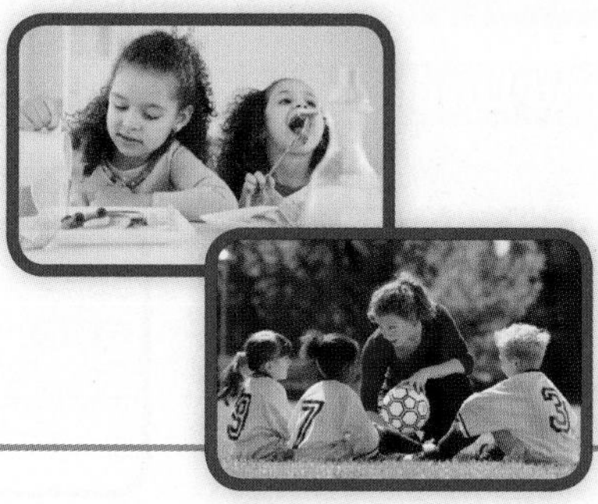

Visual Vocabulary Cards

Oral Vocabulary Routine

Define: To **inspire** is to make someone want to do something.

Example: The smell of breakfast inspires the sleepy children to get out of bed.

Ask: Who has inspired you to do something special?

Define: When you **respect** someone, you admire and look up to him or her.

Example: The players respect Coach Dotson because she is a great soccer player and treats everyone fairly.

Ask: Whom do you respect?

Discuss the theme of "My Team." Have children tell about a time someone helped them. *Why did you need help? What did this person do to help you?*

Go Digital

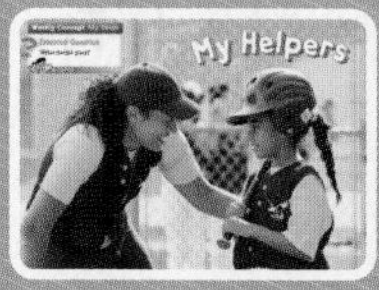

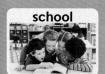

My Team

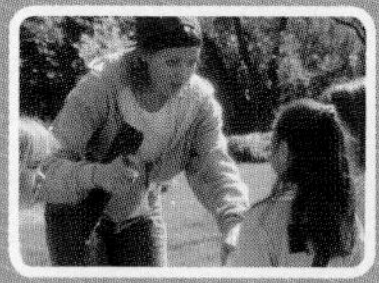

Video

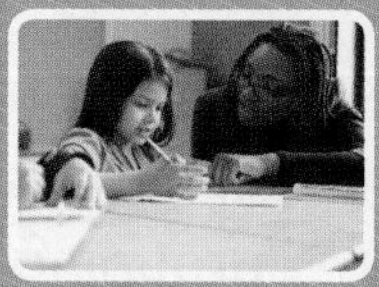

Photos

school

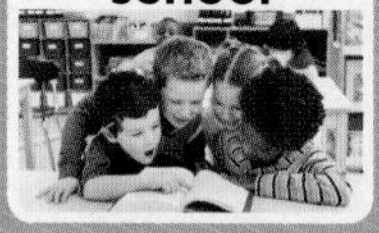

Visual Glossary

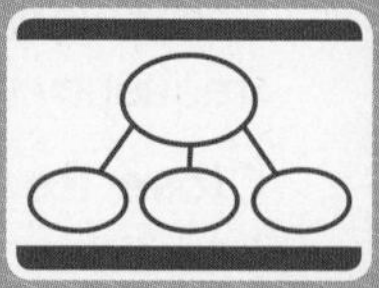

Graphic Organizer

Reading/Writing Workshop, pp. 236–237

Talk About It: My Team

Guide children to discuss the photograph of the player and the coach.

- What sport is this child playing?
- How might the coach help her?

Use Teaching Poster 40 and prompt children to complete the Word Web by telling how coaches can help athletes.

Children can look at page 237 of their Reading/Writing Workshop and do the Talk About It activity with a partner.

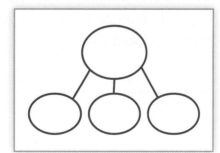

Teaching Poster

Collaborative Conversations

Listen Carefully As children engage in partner, small-group, and whole-group discussions, encourage them to:

- always look at the speaker.
- respect others by not interrupting them.
- repeat others' ideas to check understanding.

ENGLISH LANGUAGE LEARNERS SCAFFOLD

Beginning

Use Visuals Tell children: *This girl is playing baseball. This is her coach. Does the coach help the girl?* Help children come up with other words to describe what coaches do, such as *teach* and *lead.*

Intermediate

Describe Ask children to describe what the coach is doing. *Is the coach helping the girl? How?* Elicit more details to support children's answers.

Advanced/High

Discuss Have children elaborate on how the coach helps the girl. *What kinds of rules do you think the coach would explain and enforce? How do coaches help?* Model correct pronunciation as needed.

→ Listening Comprehension

MINILESSON
10 Mins

Read the Interactive Read Aloud

"Anansi's Sons"

OBJECTIVES

CCSS Participate in a collaborative conversation with diverse partners about *grade 1 topics and texts* with peers and adults in small and larger groups. **SL.1.1**

• Develop concept understanding

• Develop reading strategy: Reread

ACADEMIC LANGUAGE

• *reread, event, detail*

• Cognate: *detalle*

Connect to Concept: My Team

Tell children that they will now read a folktale about six sons who work together to help their father when he is in danger.
Ask: *How do you think children can help their parents?*

Focus on Oral Vocabulary

Review the oral vocabulary words *inspire* and *respect*. Use the Define/Example/Ask routine to introduce the oral vocabulary words *decision, distance,* and *swiftly*. Prompt children to use the words as they discuss the people who help them.

Visual Vocabulary Cards

Oral Vocabulary Routine

<u>Define:</u> When you make a **decision**, you make a choice.

<u>Example:</u> After looking at all the flavors, Amy made a decision: she would have vanilla.

<u>Ask:</u> What decisions have you made today?

<u>Define:</u> **Distance** is how far one thing is from another or the space between two things.

<u>Example:</u> It was a long distance from the house to the pond.

<u>Ask:</u> How can you measure the distance between your chair and the door?

<u>Define:</u> When something moves **swiftly**, it moves fast.

<u>Example:</u> When the rabbit saw the fox, it ran swiftly to its den.

<u>Ask:</u> When do you move swiftly?

Go Digital

"Anansi's Sons"

Reread

school

Visual Glossary

Retell

Set a Purpose for Reading

- Display the Interactive Read-Aloud Cards.
- Read aloud the title.
- Tell children that you will be reading a folktale about a spider whose six sons each have a special ability. Say: *Anansi, the father, is a character in many folktales. He is always a spider.* Tell children to read to find out what special abilities his sons have.

Strategy: Reread

1 Explain Remind children that if they do not understand something as they read or listen to a story, they can go back and read the text again. They can also read parts again to remember important information. This is called rereading. This can help them understand the text better.

Think Aloud Rereading tricky parts of a story can help me to better understand it. Today, as we read "Anansi's Sons," I will make a note of the parts I do not understand. Then I will go back and reread those parts.

2 Model Read the selection. As you read, use the Think Aloud Cloud to model applying the strategy.

Think Aloud Remember that you can reread parts of the text to make sure you understood correctly or remember them right. There are a lot of details in this text. I am not sure that I understood why the sons have such strange names. When I reread the pages, I understand that each son is named for his special ability.

3 Guided Practice As you continue to read, pause to ask children which parts of the story they find confusing. *What parts did you have trouble understanding? What can you do to better understand them?* Guide children in rereading parts of the text they did not understand.

Respond to Reading

After reading, prompt children to retell "Anansi's Sons." Guide them to talk about how each son helped Anansi. Discuss how rereading helped children understand the story events.

ENGLISH LANGUAGE LEARNERS SCAFFOLD

Beginning

Engage Display Card 1 of "Anansi's Sons." *I didn't understand this part. Let's reread it.* Reread the card. *Is Anansi a spider? Does he have six sons? Show me Anansi's sons.*

Intermediate

Describe Display Card 2 of "Anansi's Sons." *I do not understand why Road Builder builds a road to the river. Let's reread the card.* Reread the card. *Why does Road Builder build a road to the river?*

Advanced/High

Describe Display Card 2 of "Anansi's Sons." *I do not understand why See Trouble climbs the tree. Let's reread this part.* Reread the card. *Can you explain why See Trouble climbs the tree? What does he see?*

Monitor and *Differentiate*

 Quick Check

Can children apply the reread strategy?

↓

Small Group Instruction

If No →	Approaching	Reteach pp. T130–131
	ELL	Develop pp. T148–151
If Yes →	On Level	Review pp. T140–141
	Beyond Level	Extend pp. T144–145

→ Word Work

 MINILESSON **5** Mins

Phonemic Awareness

OBJECTIVES

 CCSS Isolate and pronounce initial, medial vowel, and final sounds (phonemes) in spoken single-syllable words. **RF.1.2c**

CCSS Decode regularly spelled one-syllable words. **RF.1.3b**

Phoneme Categorization

1 Model Show children how to categorize phonemes. *Listen as I say three words:* jaw, draw, glue. Jaw *and* draw *have the /ô/ sound.* Glue *does not have the /ô/ sound.* Glue *does not belong.* Repeat with *lawn, match, cause.*

2 Guided Practice/Practice Have children practice categorizing phonemes. Do the first one together. *I will say three words. Tell me which word does not belong and why.*

dawn, hole, pause   wait, saw, game   mouth, yawn, couch

talk, yawn, moon   sauce, cause, join   row, law, claw

 MINILESSON **10** Mins

Phonics

Introduce Variant Vowel /ô/

aw
au
straw

Sound-Spelling Card

1 Model Display the *Straw* **Sound-Spelling Card.** Teach /ô/ spelled *a, aw, au, augh,* and *al* using *ball, saw, haul, caught,* and *walk. This is the* Straw *Sound-Spelling Card. The sound is /ô/. This is the sound at the end of the word* straw. *Listen: /ssstrrrôôô/. The /ô/ sound can be spelled with the letters* a, aw, au, augh, *and* al. *Say the sound with me: /ô/. I'll say /ô/ as I write the letters* a, aw, au, augh, *and* al *several times.*

2 Guided Practice/Practice Have children practice connecting the letters *a, aw, au, augh,* and *al* to the sound /ô/ by writing them. *Now do it with me. Say /ô/ as I write the letters* a, aw, au, augh, *and* al. *This time, write each spelling five times as you say the /ô/ sound.*

Go Digital

Phonemic Awareness

Straw

Phonics

Handwriting

SKILLS TRACE

VARIANT VOWEL /ô/

Introduce Unit 6 Week 2 Day 1

Review Unit 6 Week 2 Days 2, 3, 4, 5

Assess Unit 6 Week 2

Blend with Variant Vowel /ô/

1 **Model** Display the **Word-Building Cards** *s, a, w.* Model how to blend the sounds. *This is the letter* s. *It stands for /s/. These are the letters* a *and* w. *Together they stand for /ô/. Listen as I blend these sounds together: /sssôôô/. Say it with me:* saw. Continue by modeling the words *small, haul, taught,* and *walk.*

2 **Guided Practice/Practice** Display the Day 1 Phonics Practice Activity. Read each word in the first row, blending the sounds; for example: */fffôôôlll/. The word is* fall. Have children blend each word with you. Prompt children to read the connected text, sounding out the decodable words.

fall	paw	fault	talk	claw	caught
mall	lawn	cause	crawl	bald	sauce
call	cool	yarn	yawn	false	face
shout	point	toys	grew	spoon	awful

Paul saw a hawk in the big tree.

He taught his daughter to draw.

My dog almost caught the ball in her paws.

> Also online

Day 1 Phonics Practice Activity

Corrective Feedback

Sound Error Model the sound that children missed, then have them repeat the sound. Say: *My turn.* Tap under the letters and say: *Sound? /ô/. What's the sound?* Return to the beginning of the word. Say: *Let's start over.* Blend the word with children again.

Daily Handwriting

Throughout the week teach uppercase and lowercase letters *Bb* using the Handwriting models.

ON-LEVEL PRACTICE BOOK p. 283

Say **paw**. The same vowel sound can be spelled with **a** as in **mall**, **au** as in **fault**, **augh** as in **taught**, and **al** as in **talk**.

Write the words from the box that have the same sound-spelling as the name of the picture.

stalk	taught	fall	haul	claw
small	chalk	cause	paw	naughty

1. crawl — paw — claw

2. call — small — fall

3. sauce — cause — haul

4. caught — naughty — taught

5. walk — stalk — chalk

APPROACHING p. 283	BEYOND p. 283	ELL p. 283

Word Work

Quick Review

High-Frequency Words: Read, Spell, and Write to review last week's high-frequency words: *answer, brought, busy, door, enough, eyes.*

MINILESSON
5 Mins

Spelling

OJBECTIVES

CCSS Recognize and read grade-appropriate irregularly spelled words. **RF.1.3g**

CCSS Use conventional spelling for words with common spelling patterns and for frequently occurring irregular words. **L.1.2d**

Words with Variant Vowel /ô/

Dictation Use the Spelling Dictation routine for each word to help children transfer their growing knowledge of sound-spellings to writing.

Pretest After dictation, pronounce each spelling word. Say a sentence for each word and pronounce the word again. Ask children to say each word softly, stretching the sounds, before writing it. After the pretest, display the spelling words and write each word as you say the letter names. Have children check their words.

haul	cause	saw	claw	paw
dawn	moon	soup	love	friend

For Approaching Level and Beyond Level children, refer to the Differentiated Spelling Lists for modified word lists.

Go Digital

Spelling Word Routine

High-Frequency Word Routine

school

Visual Glossary

MINILESSON
10 Mins

High-Frequency Words

brother, father, friend, love, mother, picture

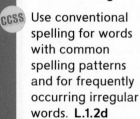

ENGLISH LANGUAGE LEARNERS

Pantomime Review the meaning of these words by using pictures, pantomime, or gestures when possible. Have children repeat or act out the word.

1 Model Display the **High-Frequency Word Cards** *brother, father, friend, love, mother,* and *picture*. Use the Read/Spell/Write routine to teach each word.

- **Read** Point to and say the word *brother. This is the word* brother. *Say it with me:* brother. *Sam is my brother.*

- **Spell** *The word* brother *is spelled* b-r-o-t-h-e-r. *Spell it with me.*

- **Write** *Let's write the word in the air as we say each letter:* b-r-o-t-h-e-r.

- Follow the routine to introduce *father, friend, love, mother, picture.*

- As children spell each word with you, point out the irregularities in sound-spellings, such as the /u/ sound spelled *o* in the word *brother*.

- Have partners create sentences using each word.

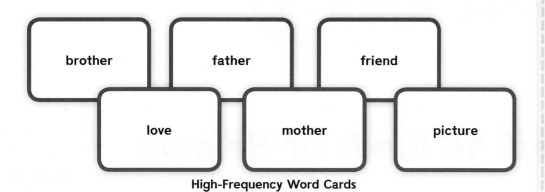

High-Frequency Word Cards

2 Guided Practice Have children read the sentences. Prompt them to identify the high-frequency words in connected text and to blend the decodable words.

1. This is a **picture** of Tom's **brother** Tim.

2. Jake's **father** and **mother** coach his baseball team.

3. My **friend** and I **love** to play baseball.

Introduce Vocabulary

accept, often

1 Model Introduce the new words using the routine.

Vocabulary Routine

<u>Define:</u> If you **accept** something, you take it or agree to it.

<u>Example:</u> *Will Mom accept my apology?*

<u>Ask:</u> What are some things you accept? EXAMPLES

<u>Define:</u> If you do something **often**, you do it a lot.

<u>Example:</u> *How often do you walk to school?*

<u>Ask:</u> What are some things you do often? What are some things you do not do often? COMPARE AND CONTRAST

Vocabulary Cards

2 Review Use the routine to review last week's vocabulary words.

Monitor and *Differentiate*

✓ **Quick Check**

Can children read and decode words with variant vowel /ô/?

Can children recognize and read high-frequency and vocabulary words?

Small Group Instruction

If No → Approaching Reteach pp. T134–137

ELL Develop pp. T148–155

If Yes → On Level Review pp. T142–143

Beyond Level Extend pp. T146–147

→ **Shared Read**

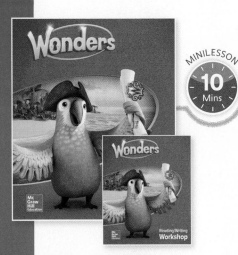

Reading/Writing Workshop Big Book and Reading/Writing Workshop

OBJECTIVES

CCSS Decode regularly spelled one-syllable words. **RF.1.3b**

CCSS Recognize and read grade-appropriate irregularly spelled words. **RF.1.3g**

Understand nonfiction genre

ACADEMIC LANGUAGE
• *nonfiction, helpers*
• Cognate: *no ficción*

See pages T148–T149 for Interactive Question-Response routine for the Shared Read.

Read *All Kinds of Helpers*

Focus on Foundational Skills

Review with children the words and letter-sounds they will see in *All Kinds of Helpers.*

• Have children use pages 238–239 to review high-frequency words *love, mother, father, brother, picture,* and *friend,* and vocabulary words *accept* and *often.*

• Have children use pages 240–241 to review that the letters *a, aw, au, augh,* and *al* can stand for the /ô/ sound. Guide them to blend the sounds to read the words.

• Display the words *either, social, idea, police,* and *special.* Spell each word and model reading it. Tell children they will be reading the words in the selection.

Read Guide children in reading *All Kinds of Helpers.* Point out the high-frequency words, vocabulary words, and words in which *a, aw, au, augh,* and *al* stand for the /ô/ sound.

Close Reading Routine

Read   DOK 1–2

• Identify key ideas and details about people who help.
• Take notes and retell.
• Use **ACT** prompts as needed.

Reread   DOK 2–3

• Analyze the text, craft, and structure.
• Use the Reread minilessons.

Integrate   DOK 4

• Integrate knowledge and ideas.
• Make text-to-text connections.
• Use the Integrate lesson.

Genre: Informational Text/Nonfiction Tell children that *All Kinds of Helpers* is a nonfiction selection. Remind children that nonfiction tells about real people, places, things, or events; presents facts and information; and often uses photos, illustrations, and text to give information.

Go Digital

All Kinds of Helpers

All Kinds of Helpers

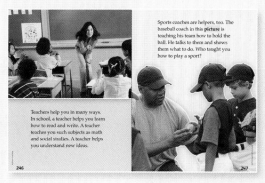
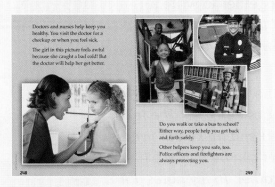

READING/WRITING WORKSHOP, pp. 242–251 **Lexile** 530

Connect to Concept: My Team

Essential Question Explain to children that as they read *All Kinds of Helpers,* they will look for key ideas and details that will help them answer the Essential Question: *Who helps you?*

- Pages 244–245: What do helpers do? How does the boy's family help?
- Pages 246–247: How does a teacher help?
- Pages 248–249: What helpers protect you?
- Pages 250–251: How can grownups help boys and girls?

Focus on Fluency

Have children read *All Kinds of Helpers* to develop fluency. With a partner, remind them that they can ask questions to make sure they understand what they are reading. Have them use both text and photographs to answer their questions.

Retell Have partners use key ideas and details to retell *All Kinds of Helpers.* Invite children to act out the different ways helpers help people.

Make Connections

Read together Make Connections on page 251. Have partners talk about how people in the community help them.

SHARED READ **T95**

→ Language Arts

Reading/Writing Workshop

OBJECTIVES

 Write informative/ explanatory texts in which they name a topic, supply some facts about the topic, and provide some sense of closure. **W.1.2**

 Use personal, possessive, and indefinite pronouns (e.g., *I, me, my; they, them, their, anyone, everything*). **L.1.1d**

ACADEMIC LANGUAGE

• *different, topic, pronoun, possessive*

• Cognates: *diferente, posesivo*

MINILESSON
5 Mins

Shared Writing

Write About the Reading/Writing Workshop

Analyze the Prompt Tell children you will work together to write a response to a prompt. Read aloud the prompt: *What are some different kinds of helpers?* Say: *To respond to this prompt, we need to look at the text and photographs in* All Kinds of Helpers.

Find Text Evidence Explain that you will reread the text and take notes to help answer the question. Read aloud pages 244–245. *The text says helpers are people who give us what we need and make our lives better. On page 245, the text tells me that families can be helpers. I see a photograph of a boy helping his younger brother. In my notes, I'll write that families are one kind of helper.*

Write to a Prompt Reread the prompt to children. *What are some different kinds of helpers?* Say: *Our first sentence should tell our topic, or what we are writing about. Let's write our first sentence together: There are different kinds of helpers.* Write the sentence. *Now let's look at our notes to find the different kinds of helpers we read about in the selection. Our next sentences will tell about them.* Track the print as you reread the notes.

Guide children to dictate complete sentences for you to record. Read the final response as you track the print.

Go Digital

Graphic Organizer

Writing

I see a fish.

Grammar

Grammar

5 Mins

Possessive Pronouns

1 Explain/Model Review that pronouns are words that take the place of nouns. Explain that a possessive pronoun shows who or what has or owns something. Some possessive pronouns are used before nouns. Display the following sentences:

<u>My</u> house is white.   <u>Your</u> mother just called.

<u>His</u> coat is too small.   Julie lost <u>her</u> tooth.

The dog sleeps in <u>its</u> bed.   Gran stayed at <u>our</u> house.

They put <u>their</u> spelling tests in the basket.

Explain that *my, your, his, her, its, our,* and *their* are possessive pronouns.

2 Guided Practice/Practice Display the sentences below and read them aloud. Have partners identify the possessive pronouns.

The school has its own pool. (its)

Miss Dawson helped me with my math. (my)

Susie likes her new skirt. (her)

Jack left his flute on the lawn. (his)

COLLABORATE

Talk About It Have partners make sentences using *his, our,* and *their.*

Link to Writing Say: *Let's look at our writing and see if we used possessive pronouns correctly.* Review the Shared Writing for possessive pronouns. If there are no possessive pronouns, work with children to add them and reread the response together.

ELL

ENGLISH LANGUAGE LEARNERS SCAFFOLD

Beginning

Demonstrate Comprehension Read aloud the Model sentences. For each, ask a question: *Does* my *show whose house it is? Does* just *show whose mother it is?* Continue asking *yes* and *no* questions for each.

Intermediate

Explain Distribute a marker to each child. Then ask each child, "Whose marker is this?" Prompt children to respond in a complete sentence using *my.* Then have children ask one another, responding using *your, his,* and *her.*

Advanced/High

Expand Have a child use one of the possessive pronouns in a sentence. For example, *I like to play with my dog.* Then have another child asks a *Whose* question in response, such as "Whose dog?" Continue until children have practiced the possessive pronouns.

Daily Wrap Up

- Encourage children to discuss the Essential Question using the oral vocabulary words. Ask: *How did someone help you today?*

- Prompt children to share the skills they learned today.

LANGUAGE ARTS **T97**

Materials

  Wonders **Reading/Writing Workshop** VOLUME 4

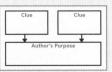  Wonders **Reading/Writing Workshop Big Book** UNIT 6

 brother
High-Frequency Word Cards
brother   love
father   mother
friend   picture

 a b c
Word-Building Cards

Clue   Clue
Author's Purpose
Teaching Poster

 accept
Vocabulary Cards
accept   often

haul
Spelling Word Cards

Interactive Read-Aloud Cards

 aw
au
straw
Sound-Spelling Cards

→ # Build the Concept

 MINILESSON 5 Mins

Oral Language

Go Digital

 **school**
Visual Glossary

"Anansi's Sons"

OBJECTIVES

 CCSS Ask and answer questions about key details in a text read aloud or information presented orally or through other media. **SL.1.2**

- Discuss the Essential Question
- Build concept understanding

ACADEMIC LANGUAGE
reread

ESSENTIAL QUESTION

Remind children that this week you've been talking and reading about the people who help them. Remind them of Anansi and his sons and how the people in different jobs help the children. Guide children to discuss the Essential Question using information from what they read and discussed on Day 1.

Oral Vocabulary Words

Review the oral vocabulary words. Use the Define/Example/Ask routine to review the oral vocabulary words *decision, distance, inspire, respect,* and *swiftly.*

- What is a big decision you have made?
- Which distance is greater, the distance from our classroom to the playground or the distance from our classroom to the lunchroom?
- What kind of music inspires you to dance?
- How can you show respect to someone you admire?
- What animals move swiftly?

Listening Comprehension

MINILESSON 5 Mins

Reread the Interactive Read Aloud

Strategy: Reread

Remind children that as they listen, they can reread parts of the text that they did not understand the first time or want to remember better.

Tell children that you will reread "Anansi's Sons." Display the Interactive Read-Aloud Cards. Pause as you read to model applying the strategy.

"Anansi's Sons"

Think Aloud When I read, I can go back and read parts of the text again to make sure I understood everything. The first time I read "Anansi's Sons," I wasn't sure I understood why Road Builder built a road to the river, so I reread that part of the story. After rereading, I understood that he built a road to the river because See Trouble had seen that their father was in the river and needed help.

Make Connections

Discuss partners' responses to "Anansi's Sons."

- Which son do you think helped Anansi the most?
- Do you think Anansi made a good decision by putting the shining sphere up in the sky?
- Help children to recall story details to support their responses.

Write About It Have children draw a picture of their favorite part of the folktale and write a sentence about it in their Writer's Notebooks. Guide children by asking questions such as, *Which son's special ability would you want to have? Which event would be the most exciting to see?* Have children write continuously for six minutes.

 **Word Work**

Quick Review

Build Fluency: Sound-Spellings
Display the **Word-Building Cards:** *aw, au, augh, al, ew, ue, ui, ow, oy, oi, ar, ore, oar, er, ir, ur, ey, igh, oa, oe, ee, ea, ai, ay, e_e, u_e, o_e, dge, i_e, a_e.*
Have children say the sounds. Repeat, and vary the pace.

MINILESSON 5 Mins
Phonemic Awareness

OBJECTIVES

CCSS Decode regularly spelled one-syllable words. **RF.1.3b**

CCSS Decode two-syllable words following basic patterns by breaking the words into syllables. **RF.1.3e**

Reverse sounds to form new words

Phoneme Reversal

1 Model Show children how to reverse phonemes to form new words. *Listen as I blend these sounds: /n/ /e/ /t/, /nnneeet/, net. Now I will say the sounds backward and blend them to make a new word. Listen: /t/ /e/ /n/, /teeennn/, ten.* Repeat with *tell/let.*

2 Guided Practice/Practice Have children reverse the sounds in the following words. Do the first one together. *Now I am going to say more sounds. Blend the sounds to say a word. Then say the sounds backward and blend them to make another word.*

/p/ /o/ /t/   /b/ /a/ /k/   /ch/ /i/ /p/   /z/ /ü/   /t/ /ô/ /t/

MINILESSON 5 Mins
Phonics

Review Variant Vowel /ô/

1 Model Display the *Straw* **Sound-Spelling Card.** Review the sound /ô/ spelled *a, aw, au, augh,* and *al* using the words *wall, paw, cause, caught,* and *talk.*

2 Guided Practice/Practice Have children practice connecting the spellings for /ô/ to the sound. Point to the letters on the Sound-Spelling Card. *What are these letters? What sound do they stand for?*

Go Digital

Phonemic Awareness

Phonics

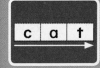

Structural Analysis

Handwriting

Blend with Variant Vowel /ô/

1 **Model** Display **Word-Building Cards** *d, r, a, w* to form the word *draw*. Model how to generate and blend the sounds to say the word. *This is the letter* d. *It stands for* /d/. *This is the letter* r. *It stands for* /r/. *These are the letters* a *and* w. *Together they stand for* /ô/. *Listen as I blend these sounds together:* /drrrôôô/. *Say it with me:* draw. Continue by modeling the words *walk, wash, jaw, caught,* and *haul.*

2 **Guided Practice/Practice** Repeat the routine with children with *chalk, crawl, hawk, sauce, wall, taught, small, talk, salt, yawn.*

Build with Variant Vowel /ô/

1 **Model** Display the Word-Building Cards *s, a, w.* Blend: /s/ /ô/, /sssôôô/, *saw.*

Replace *s* with *l* and repeat with *law.*

Add *n* after *law* and repeat with *lawn.*

2 **Guided Practice/Practice** Continue with *dawn, drawn, draw, raw, jaw, paw, pause, cause, clause, claw, call, wall, walk, talk.*

Structural Analysis

Vowel Team Syllables

1 **Model** Write and read *down*. Underline *ow*. Remind children that the letters *ow* stand for the vowel sound /ou/. Point out that when children see the letters for a vowel spelling in a word, the letters act as a team and must therefore stay together in the same syllable. Write *downtown*. Divide the word into syllables, then blend the syllables to read the word.

Write and read *rain, draw,* and *boat*. Underline the vowel team in each word. Tell children that the vowel team stays together in the same syllable. Then write *rainbow, drawing,* and *boathouse.* Work with children to divide the word into syllables, then blend the syllables to read the words. Remind children that sometimes it will be necessary to approximate sounds to read multisyllabic words.

2 **Guided Practice/Practice** Write the following words: *joyful, repeat, hauling, railroad.* For each word, work with children to identify the vowel teams. Have children identify each syllable, then blend the syllables to read the words.

ENGLISH LANGUAGE LEARNERS

Build Vocabulary Review the meanings of example words that can be explained or demonstrated in a concrete way. For example, ask children to point to *chalk,* their *jaw,* or a *wall.* Model the actions for *walk, crawl,* and *yawn* as you say, *"I yawn as I walk. I can crawl on the floor."* Have children repeat. Provide sentence starters such as "You taught me ____." for children to complete. Correct grammar and pronunciation as needed.

→ # Word Work

MINILESSON 5 Mins

Spelling

OBJECTIVES

 Recognize and read grade-appropriate irregularly spelled words. **RF.1.3g**

 Use conventional spelling for words with common spelling patterns and for frequently occurring irregular words. **L.1.2d**

Word Sort with /ô/

1 Model Display the **Spelling Word Cards** from the Teacher's Resource Book one at a time. Have children read each word, listening for the /ô/ sound.

Make cards for *sauce* and *jaw* to create a two-column chart. Say each word and pronounce the sounds. Ask children to spell each word.

2 Guided Practice/Practice Have children place each Spelling Word Card in the column with the word containing the same /ô/ spelling.

When completed, have children read the words in each column. Then call out a word. Have a child point to the word card as the class spells the word.

ANALYZE ERRORS/ARTICULATION SUPPORT

Use children's pretest errors to analyze spelling problems and provide corrective feedback. For example, some children might have difficulty using different spellings for the same sound. They might spell *dawn*, for example, with an alternate /ô/ spelling.

Have children make word cards for the spelling words. Ask them to trace the letters that stand for /ô/. Suggest they use a different color for each spelling. Then write additional /ô/ words. Have children sort the words and analyze the spelling patterns.

Go Digital

Spelling Word Sort

High-Frequency Word Routine

school

Visual Glossary

ENGLISH LANGUAGE LEARNERS

Provide Clues Practice spelling by helping children generate more words with the /ô/ sound. Provide clues: *Think of a word that begins with l and rhymes with* dawn. Write the word and have children practice reading it. Correct their pronunciation if needed.

MINILESSON 5 Mins

High-Frequency Words

brother, father, friend, love, mother, picture

1 Guided Practice Say each word and have children Read/Spell/Write it. Ask children to picture the word in their minds and write it the way they see it. Display the words for children to self-correct.

- Point out irregularities in sound-spellings, such as /u/ spelled *o_e* in *love*. Remind children that they saw this spelling in *come*.

2 Practice Add the high-frequency words *brother, father, friend, love, mother,* and *picture* to the cumulative word bank.

- Have partners create sentences using the words.
- Have children look at the words and compare their sounds and spellings to words from previous weeks.
- Suggest children write about how people can help one another.

Cumulative Review Review last week's words using the Read/Spell/Write routine.

- Repeat, mixing the words and having children chorally say each one.

Reinforce Vocabulary

MINILESSON
5 Mins

accept, often

1 Guided Practice Use the **Vocabulary Cards** to review this week's and last week's vocabulary words. Work together with children to generate a new context sentence for each word.

2 Practice Have children work with a partner to orally complete each sentence stem on the Day 2 Vocabulary Practice Activity using this week's and last week's vocabulary words.

demand	emergency	accept	often

1. We had an ____ fire drill at school.
2. We go to the park ____.
3. The teacher had to ____ that we stop talking.
4. We had to ____ the new rules.   Also online

Day 2 Vocabulary Practice Activity

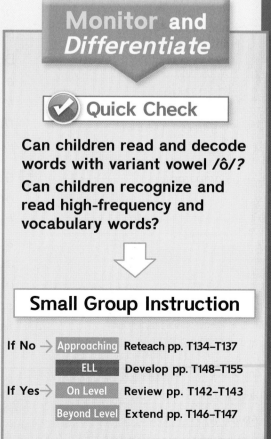

ON-LEVEL PRACTICE BOOK p. 284

A. Complete each sentence. Use one of the words in the box.

brother	father	friend	love	mother	picture

1. My ____friend____ Liz goes to my school.

2. I ____love____ to run around the park.

3. I smiled for my class ____picture____.

4. My ____mother____ and ____father____ tell me to go to bed. Word order may vary.

5. Paul's ____brother____ is the same age as I am.

B. Write your own sentence using a word from the box.

6. Responses will vary.

APPROACHING p. 284	BEYOND p. 284	ELL p. 284

Monitor and *Differentiate*

✓ **Quick Check**

Can children read and decode words with variant vowel /ô/?

Can children recognize and read high-frequency and vocabulary words?

⬇

Small Group Instruction

If No →	Approaching	Reteach pp. T134–T137
	ELL	Develop pp. T148–T155
If Yes →	On Level	Review pp. T142–T143
	Beyond Level	Extend pp. T146–T147

Comprehension

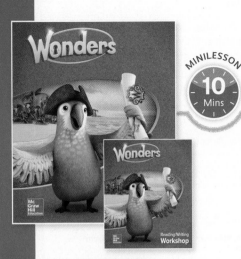

Reading/Writing Workshop Big Book and Reading/Writing Workshop

---

OBJECTIVES

CCSS Identify the main purpose of a text, including what the author wants to answer, explain, or describe. **RI.2.6**

Understand nonfiction genre

ACADEMIC LANGUAGE
• *organized, compare*
• Cognates: *organizado/a, comparar*

SKILLS TRACE

AUTHOR'S PURPOSE

Introduce Unit 6 Week 2

Review Unit 6 Week 5

Assess Unit 6 Week 2

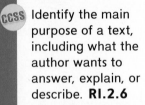

MINILESSON
10 Mins

Reread *All Kinds of Helpers*

Genre: Informational Text/Nonfiction

1 Model Tell children they will now reread the nonfiction selection *All Kinds of Helpers*. Explain that as they read, they will look for information in the text to help them understand the selection.

Review the characteristics of nonfiction text. It:

• tells about real people, places, or things.

• gives information and facts.

• can have illustrations and photographs related to the information.

• can be organized to compare information.

Explain that informational nonfiction tells about real people, places, things, or events. *Nonfiction selections often give information about real people. The text and the photographs provide interesting facts and details. Sometimes authors organize the text to compare information.*

Display pages 246 and 247: *The text on page 247 explains what a coach does. The photograph gives additional information. These facts help me understand what coaches do. The information shows that the selection is nonfiction. All of the information is about how coaches are helpers.*

2 Guided Practice/Practice Display pages 248 and 249 of *All Kinds of Helpers*. Read page 249. *The text explains about people who help us stay safe. The photograph gives more details about how a crossing guard helps us.* Prompt children to discuss how the author has organized the information to compare different kinds of helpers. *What is the information on this page about? How is a crossing guard like a firefighter? How is he or she like a coach? How has the author organized the information?*

Go Digital

All Kinds of Helpers

Genre

Author's Purpose

Skill: Author's Purpose

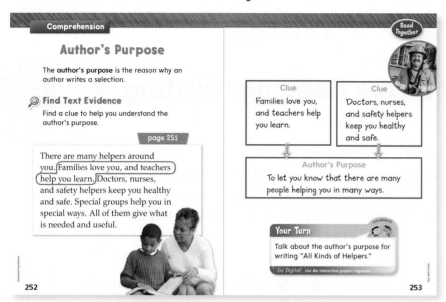

Reading/Writing Workshop, pp. 252-253

ON-LEVEL PRACTICE BOOK p. 289

A. Read the story and follow the directions.

1. Why did the author write "Coaches"? Choose the best answer.

● to tell what coaches do

ⓑ to tell about sports

ⓒ to tell about how to play soccer

2. Write words from the story that tell you what coaches show players.

Possible responses:

| throw | rules | run fast |

3. What makes a good team? Choose the best answer.

ⓐ They do not work hard.

ⓑ They like to lose.

● They work together.

B. Work with a partner. Read the passage aloud. Pay attention to intonation. Stop after one minute. Fill out the chart.

	Words Read	−	Number of Errors	=	Words Correct Score
First Read		−		=	
Second Read		−		=	

| APPROACHING p. 289 | BEYOND p. 289 | ELL p. 289 |

❶ Model Tell children that often authors write nonfiction selections because they want to share information. Have children look at pages 252–253 in their Reading/Writing Workshop. Read together the definition of Author's Purpose. *The author's purpose is the reason why an author writes a selection.*

❷ Guided Practice/Practice Read together the Find Text Evidence section and model finding the author's purpose in *All Kinds of Helpers*. Point out the information added to the graphic organizer. *On page 251, we read about how families and teachers help. This information gives a clue about the author's purpose. It has been added to the Author's Purpose chart. What other clues can we find in the text to help us understand the author's purpose?*

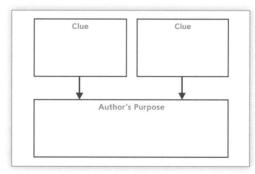

Teaching Poster

Monitor and *Differentiate*

✓ **Quick Check**

Can children identify the author's purpose in a nonfiction selection?

⬇

Small Group Instruction

If No → Approaching   Reteach pp. T138–139

ELL   Develop pp. T148–155

If Yes → On Level   Review p. T143

Beyond Level   Extend p. T147

Write About the Reading/Writing Workshop

Go Digital

Reading/Writing Workshop

OBJECTIVES

CCSS Write informative/ explanatory texts in which they name a topic, supply some facts about the topic, and provide some sense of closure. **W.1.2**

CCSS Use personal, possessive, and indefinite pronouns (e.g., *I, me, my; they, them, their, anyone, everything*). **L.1.1d**

ACADEMIC LANGUAGE

· *describe, topic, voice, model, possessive*
· Cognates: *describir, voz, modelo, posesivo*

Analyze the Model Prompt Have children turn to page 254 in the **Reading/Writing Workshop**. Farah responded to the prompt: *Pick one group from* All Kinds of Helpers *that has helped you and describe how.* Explain to children that the prompt has two parts. Say: *To respond to this prompt, first Farah used the text to find an example of a kind of helper who has helped her, and then she told how that person helped her.*

Find Text Evidence Explain that Farah took notes on the different kinds of helpers in the text. Then, to respond to the prompt, she used her notes to pick a kind of helper who helped her.

Graphic Organizer

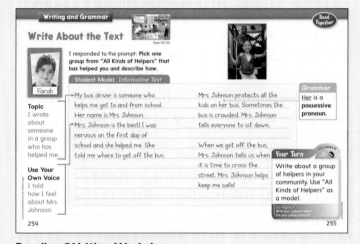

Reading/Writing Workshop

Writing

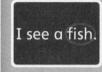

I see a fish.

Grammar

Analyze the Student Model Read the model. Discuss the callouts.

- **Topic** Farah's first sentence told the topic of her response. It named the kind of helper she picked. **Trait: Organization**

- **Use Your Own Voice** Farah's writing showed what she thinks and how she feels about her bus driver, Mrs. Johnson. **Trait: Voice**

- **Possessive Pronouns** Farah used the possessive pronoun *her* before the word *bus* to show that it is Mrs. Johnson's bus. **Grammar**

Point out that Farah also included facts about her topic.

Your Turn: Write About the Text Say: *Now we will write to a new prompt*. Have children turn to page 255 of the **Reading/Writing Workshop**. Read the Your Turn prompt together. *Write about a group of helpers in your community. Use* All Kinds of Helpers *as a model.*

Find Text Evidence Say: *To respond to this prompt, we will take notes about the information we learn about in the text and how it is organized. We'll use our notes to make inferences about helpers in our community and how we can use* All Kinds of Helpers *as our model for writing.*

Write to a Prompt Invite children to use the notes to brainstorm a group of helpers in your community they would like to write about. Track the print as you reread the notes. Say: *We saw that many paragraphs in the selection begin with a topic sentence. Let's start our writing with a topic sentence that tells what group of helpers we are writing about*. Write a topic sentence using children's ideas, such as: Firefighters are important helpers in our community. Guide children to expand on the topic sentence in complete sentences as you share the pen with them. Say: *Let's reread our response. Does our first sentence tell the topic? Did we include details about how the helpers help our community?* Read the final response as you track the print.

For additional practice with the writing traits, have children turn to page 294 of the **Your Turn Practice Book**.

ENGLISH LANGUAGE LEARNERS

Explain Read aloud the Model sentences and ask questions: *Does* mine *tell whose book it is? Does* his *tell whose it is? Whose bat is it? Whose baseballs are they?*

Contrast Have a child contrast his hair type or color with another boy's hair using *his* and *mine*. For example, *His hair is redder than mine*. Then have the child contrast his hair with a girl using *hers* and with a group using *theirs*. Clarify children's responses as needed by providing vocabulary.

Grammar

Possessive Pronouns

❶ **Explain** Remind children that some possessive pronouns are used before nouns. Then explain that some possessive pronouns can stand alone. Display the following sentences:

> Is this book <u>yours</u>? It is not <u>mine</u>. It is <u>his</u>.
>
> The bat is <u>theirs</u>. Only the baseballs are <u>ours</u>.
>
> This shirt is just like <u>hers</u>.

Explain that *mine, yours, his, hers, ours,* and *theirs* are possessive pronouns.

❷ **Guided Practice/Practice** Display the sentences below and read them aloud. Have partners identify the possessive pronouns that stand alone.

> That soup tastes better than mine. (mine)
>
> This school is smaller than theirs. (theirs)

Talk About It Have partners make sentences using *yours* and *ours.*

Daily Wrap Up

- Discuss the Essential Question and encourage children to use the oral vocabulary words. Ask: *Who helps you at home?*

- Prompt children to discuss what they learned today by asking: *How did the skills you learned today help you read and write?*

Materials

Reading/Writing Workshop
VOLUME 4

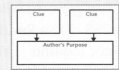
Literature Anthology
VOLUME 4

Visual Vocabulary Cards

accept   love
brother   mother
decision   often
distance   picture
father   respect
friend   swiftly
inspire

Teaching poster

Clue	Clue
Author's Purpose	

Interactive Read-Aloud Cards

Response Board

haul

Spelling Word Cards

a b c
Word-Building Cards

 → # Build the Concept

Go Digital

school
Visual Glossary

All Kinds of Helpers

MINILESSON
5 Mins

Oral Language

ESSENTIAL QUESTION

Remind children this week you have been talking and reading about the people in their lives who help them. Remind them of how Anansi's sons helped save him and all the different kinds of helpers you have read about. Guide children to discuss the question using information from what they have read and discussed throughout the week.

Review Oral Vocabulary

Review the oral vocabulary words *decision, distance, inspire, respect,* and *swiftly* using the Define/Example/Ask routine. Prompt children to use the words as they discuss those who help them.

Visual Vocabulary Cards

OBJECTIVES

CCSS Describe the connection between two individuals, events, ideas, or pieces of information in a text. **RI.1.3**

CCSS Read grade-level text orally with accuracy, appropriate rate, and expression. **RF.1.4b**

Review problem and solution

ACADEMIC LANGUAGE

• *problem, solution, intonation, question*

• Cognates: *problema, solución, entonación*

Comprehension/ Fluency

MINILESSON
10 Mins

Connections Within Text: Problem and Solution

1 **Explain** Tell children they have been learning about using author's purpose to help them understand the selections they read. Remind them they have also learned how to look for problems and solutions. *As we read, we can think about the problems presented in the text. We can also look for the solutions offered for the problems.*

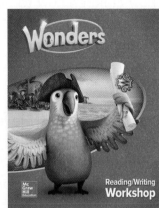

Reading/Writing Workshop

2 **Model** Display page 248 of *All Kinds of Helpers. I see this child is sick. This is a problem. What are the people doing to solve the problem? The child is visiting the doctor. The doctor will solve the problem by giving the child medicine.*

3 **Guided Practice/Practice** Reread *All Kinds of Helpers* with children. Use text evidence to identify problems and solutions.

MINILESSON
5 Mins

Intonation: Questions

1 **Explain** Tell children as you read the passage, you will look for sentences that end in question marks. You will make your voice rise when you read the questions. This signals to listeners that you are asking a question.

2 **Model** Model reading the question on page 244 of the Shared Read. *This sentence has a question mark. I read the words in front of the question mark as though I am asking something.* Point out how your voice rises. Reread the whole page and point out how you pause for punctuation.

3 **Guided Practice/Practice** Have children reread the passage. Remind them to raise their voice when they read questions.

Fluency Practice Children can practice using Practice Book passages.

 → **Word Work**

MINILESSON 5 Mins

Phonemic Awareness

OBJECTIVES

 Orally produce
single-syllable
words by blending
sounds (phonemes),
including consonant
blends. **RF.1.2b**

CCSS Decode two-syllable
words following basic
patterns by breaking
the words into
syllables. **RF.1.3e**

Phoneme Blending

1 Model Show children how to blend sounds using the **Response
Board.** *I will say three sounds. I will put one marker in each box as
I say each sound.* Put a marker in a box as you say each sound: /d/
/ô/ /n/. *Now I will blend the sounds to form a word:* /d/ /ô/ /n/,
/dôôônnn/, dawn.

2 Guided Practice/Practice Have children practice blending
phonemes. Guide practice with the first three. *Let's do some together.
I will say one sound at a time. Place a marker for each sound you
hear. Then we will blend the sounds to say a word.*

/j/ /ô/ /b/ /ô/ /l/ /w/ /ô/ /k/ /h/ /ô/ /l/

/k/ /l/ /ô/ /k/ /ô/ /z/ /k/ /r/ /ô/ /l/ /f/ /ô/ /l/ /t/

MINILESSON 5 Mins

Phonics

Blend with Variant Vowel /ô/

1 Model Display **Word-Building Cards** *h, a, w, k.* Model blending.
This is the letter h. *It stands for* /h/. *These are the letters* a *and* w.
Together they stand for /ô/. *This is the letter* k. *It stands for* /k/. *Let's
blend:* /hôôôk/, hawk. Continue with: *salt, launch,* and *chalk.*

2 Guided Practice/Practice Review the words and sentences on the
Day 3 Phonics Practice Activity with children. Read each word in the
first row, blending the sounds; for example: /k/ /ô/ /l/; /kôôôlll/. *The
word is* call. Have children blend each word with you. Prompt children
to read the connected text, sounding out the decodable words.

Go Digital

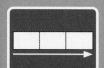

Phonemic Awareness

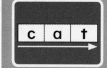

Phonics

Structural Analysis

Handwriting

call	sauce	talk	yawn	haul
ball	bald	caught	also	haunt
drawing	awful	because	oatmeal	daughter
August	auto	always	hallway	sleepless
join	June	shoot	shout	untrue

Did you draw a hawk, a fawn, or a walrus?

Mrs. Paul's daughter crawled on the lawn.

Also online

Day 3 Phonics Practice Activity

Decodable Reader Have children read "Paul's Paw" (pages 33–36), "Not Too Small" (41–44), and "A Walk With Mayor Moose" (49–52) to practice decoding words in connected text.

MINILESSON
5 Mins

Structural Analysis

Vowel Team Syllables

1 Model Write and read *laundry*. Circle the *au*. Review with children that when the letters *au* come together in a word, they act as a vowel team and must stay in the same syllable. Blend the first syllable with children: /lllôôônnn/. Then blend the second syllable: /drrrēēē/. Finally blend the two syllables to read *laundry*. Repeat with *explain, awful,* and *soaking*. Remind children that when reading multisyllabic words, it is often necessary to approximate sounds.

2 Practice/Apply Write and read: *launching, faucet, jigsaw, lawyer, raccoon, oatmeal*. Point to each word and help children blend each syllable. Blend the syllables to read the words. Have children identify the letters for the vowel spelling in each vowel team syllable.

Corrective Feedback

Corrective Feedback Say: *My turn*. Model blending. Then lead children in blending. Say: *Do it with me*. Respond with children to offer support. Then say: *Your turn. Blend*. Have children chorally blend. Return to the beginning of the word. Say: *Let's start over*.

→ # Word Work

Quick Review

High-Frequency Words: Read, Spell, and Write to review this week's high-frequency words: *brother, father, friend, love, mother, picture.*

MINILESSON

5 Mins

Spelling

OBJECTIVES

CCSS Recognize and read grade-appropriate irregularly spelled words. **RF.1.3g**

CCSS Use conventional spelling for words with common spelling patterns and for frequently occurring irregular words. **L.1.2d**

Word Sort with /ô/

❶ **Model** Make index cards for *aw* and *au* and form two columns in a pocket chart. Say the sound with children.

Hold up the *haul* **Spelling Word Card**. Say and spell *haul*. Pronounce each sound clearly: /h/ /ô/ /l/. Blend the sounds: /hôôôl/. Place the word below the *au* card. Repeat with *cause*.

❷ **Guided Practice/Practice** Have children spell each word. Repeat the process with the *aw* words.

Display *moon, soup, love, friend* in a separate column. Read and spell the words with children. Point out that these words do not contain /ô/.

Conclude by asking children to orally generate additional words that rhyme with each word. Write down the additional words.

MINILESSON

5 Mins

High-Frequency Words

PHONICS/SPELLING PRACTICE BOOK p. 133

brother, father, friend, love, mother, picture

❶ **Guided Practice** Say each word and have children Read/Spell/Write it. Point out irregularities in sound-spellings, such as /e/ spelled *ie* in *friend*.

- Display **Visual Vocabulary Cards** to review this week's words.

haul	cause	saw	claw
paw	dawn	love	friend

A. Read the spelling words in the box. Fill in the blanks below with spelling words that match each spelling pattern.

aw		au	
I. ___saw___		5. ___haul___	
2. ___claw___		6. ___cause___	
3. ___paw___			
4. ___dawn___			

In I–4 and 5–6, order of words may vary.
B. Write the spelling word that begins with I.

7. ___love___

Write the spelling word that ends with **nd.**

8. ___friend___

Go Digital

er | ir | or | ur
her
girl curb — word

Spelling Word Sort

school

Visual Glossary

Visual Vocabulary Cards

❷ **Practice** Repeat the activity with last week's words.

Build Fluency: Word Automaticity

Have children read the following sentences aloud together at the same pace. Repeat several times.

My **brother** is my best **friend**.

My brother and I **love** our **mother** and **father**.

We have a **picture** of all four of us together.

Word Bank

Review the current and previous words in the word bank. Encourage children to suggest which words should be removed or added back.

Vocabulary

5 Mins

accept, often

Review Use the **Visual Vocabulary Cards** to review this week's words using the Define/Example/Ask routine. Have partners generate context sentences for each vocabulary word.

Visual Vocabulary Cards

Strategy: Antonyms

1 Model Tell children that some words have opposite meanings. Words with opposite meanings are called antonyms. Point out that you can often find antonyms in a dictionary or a thesaurus. Use *All Kinds of Helpers* to discuss antonyms for words.

Think Aloud I read the sentence: "The girl in this picture feels awful because she caught a bad cold." The word *awful* means "very bad" or "terrible." The opposite of *awful* is *wonderful*. Thinking about the opposite helps me understand the meaning of *awful*.

2 Guided Practice Help children generate antonyms for other words in the story: *useful, better, healthy, safe,* and *always*. Discuss how these words would change the meaning of the sentences.

3 Practice Have partners find the word *accept* in the story, discuss what it means, and brainstorm antonyms. Help them use a dictionary or a thesaurus to find antonyms such as *reject* and *refuse*. Repeat for *often;* antonyms might include *rarely* and *never*.

Monitor and *Differentiate*

✓ **Quick Check**

Can children read and decode words with variant vowel /ô/?

Can children recognize and read high-frequency and vocabulary words?

Small Group Instruction

If No → **Approaching** Reteach pp. T134–137

ELL Develop pp. T148–155

If Yes → **On Level** Review pp. T142–143

Beyond Level Extend pp. T146–147

Genre Nonfiction

Essential Question
Who helps you?
Read about a girl who is a lot like you!

Go Digital!

Meet
Rosina

by George Ancona

302   303

LITERATURE ANTHOLOGY, pp. 302–303

Literature Anthology

Meet Rosina   CLOSE READING

Lexile 420

Close Reading Routine

Read   DOK 1–2

- Identify key ideas and details about people who help.
- Take notes and retell.
- Use **A C T** prompts as needed.

Reread   DOK 2–3

- Analyze the text, craft, and structure.
- Use *Close Reading Companion*, pp. 173–175.

Integrate   DOK 4

- Integrate knowledge and ideas.
- Make text-to-text connections.
- Use the Integrate lesson.

Read

ESSENTIAL QUESTION

Read aloud the Essential Question: *Who helps you?* Tell children to think about how teachers, families, and community workers help them as they read. Read aloud the title. Ask: *What do you think this selection will be about?*

Story Words Read, spell, and define the words *American, special, language, library, guacamole,* and *deaf.* Explain that they will read these words in the selection.

Note Taking: Graphic Organizer As children read the selection, guide them to fill in **Your Turn Practice Book** page 286.

I am deaf, so I talk with my hands. ① ②

304   305

LITERATURE ANTHOLOGY, pp. 304–305

---

① Strategy: Reread

Teacher Think Aloud On page 305, I read that Rosina talks with her hands. I don't understand what that means, so I will reread. On page 304, I see Rosina making gestures and the text tells what she is saying. Now I understand: Rosina talks with her hands by making hand signs to communicate.

② Skill: Author's Purpose

The author's purpose is the reason why an author writes a selection. We can look for details to help us understand the author's purpose. What detail did you read on these pages? (Rosina is deaf.)

A C T   Access Complex Text

▶ **What makes this text complex?**

Purpose of Text The purpose of the selection is to describe the activities of a deaf girl's day, some of which relate to her being deaf, some of which do not. Knowing that someone who is deaf cannot hear is key to understanding.

Organization The selection describes parts of Rosina's life, at school and at home, in no particular order. Children might need help to understand that the events described occur in a typical day, but not necessarily all in one day.

I go to a special school for deaf children. All of our teachers teach with American Sign Language. We call this signing.

We study math, writing, reading, and art. It's the same as in other schools.

My **brother** Emilio also goes to my school. We play basketball during recess. **3**

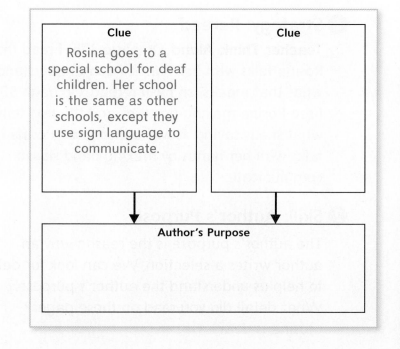

307

LITERATURE ANTHOLOGY, pp. 306–307

Read

3 Skill: Author's Purpose

Teacher Think Aloud When I read nonfiction, I look for what the author wants readers to know. I read that Rosina goes to a special school for deaf children. Her teachers use signing to teach, but she studies the same subjects and plays the same games at recess as children in other schools. I ask myself why the author wrote these facts. These are clues that will help us understand the author's purpose. Let's add them to our Author's Purpose chart.

Build Vocabulary page 307
recess: break time

Clue	Clue
Rosina goes to a special school for deaf children. Her school is the same as other schools, except they use sign language to communicate.	

Author's Purpose

My **mother** and aunt are deaf, too. They both work at my school. Mom is a teacher's helper.

308

My Aunt Carla shows us **pictures** of students who used to go to the school. My mom was one of them. My aunt **often** tells stories about when my parents were young. **4**

309

LITERATURE ANTHOLOGY, pp. 308–309

---

4 Strategy: Reread

Teacher Think Aloud I realize I am not sure who the adults are in the photographs. I'll reread the pages. Now I understand Rosina's mother and aunt both work at her school. They are the women in the photographs. What can you reread to check your understanding?

Student Think Aloud First, I read about Rosina at school. Now I'm reading about her mother and aunt. Is Rosina still at school? If so, why are her mother and aunt there? I'm going to reread these pages to be sure I understand. When I reread, I notice some information I missed at first, like that Rosina's mother and aunt both work at her school. Now I understand that Rosina is still at school.

Read

Genre: Nonfiction

How do we know this is a nonfiction selection? (It is about real people and places. It uses photographs instead of illustrations.)

Reread

Author's Purpose: Photographs

Reread pages 306–309. How do the photographs help you understand more about the author's purpose? (The photos show Rosina doing activities like writing and playing, just like other children do.)

Hedy is good at telling stories. She makes us feel as if we're in the story. The story can make us feel sad, scared, worried, or happy. **6**

Sometimes we go to the school library. Our librarian, Hedy, signs stories from the books in the library. **5**

310

311

LITERATURE ANTHOLOGY, pp. 310–311

Read

5 Maintain Skill: Problem and Solution

We know that people who are deaf cannot hear someone read aloud a story. How does the librarian at Rosina's school solve this problem? (She signs the story.)

6 Key Details

Turn to a partner and talk about the information on pages 310–311. What details can you find about what happens in Rosina's school library?

Build Vocabulary page 310

librarian: a person who works in a library

A C T **A**ccess **C**omplex **T**ext

▶ **Purpose of the Text**

The selection describes some activities that relate to Rosina being deaf, and some that do not.

- Look at pages 310–311. Discuss what the children in the picture are doing. *Do we go to the library at our school?*

- Point out that the librarian is reading the story to the children by signing it. Explain that this selection tells ways that Rosina's school is both similar to and different from other schools.

I **love** going to art class. I like to paint. Here I am painting a picture of myself! **7**

312

Our class made up a story. It is about a deaf **father** who woke up one day with four arms. We wrote it and did all the drawings. Then we made it into a book called *Too Many Hands*.

313

LITERATURE ANTHOLOGY, pp. 312–313

7 Cause and Effect

Why does Rosina love going to art class? (because she likes to paint)

> **Reread**   *Close Reading Com.panion,* 173

Photographs

Reread pages 310–311. How do the photos help explain the way Hedy helps? (The photos show how Hedy uses sign language to read a story.)

Point of View

Why does the author write using the words *I, we,* and *our*? (The author writes from Rosina's point of view, as if she were writing the selection.)

A C T Access Complex Text

▶ **Organization**

The selection does not describe a sequence of events in Rosina's day.

- Ask children to recall the things they have read that Rosina does at school.

- Help children understand that the selection tells about different things Rosina does, but she doesn't do all these things in one day.

I like sports. We are playing rugby. The way we play is to tag the person carrying the ball. Then he or she throws it to another player on the team. By running fast we can get away and cross the goal line.

8

314

Our team played other schools. We beat all of the other teams and **accepted** a big trophy.

We were so happy! We splashed our coach in water. Some of us got wet, too. We are all **friends** so no one got mad.

9

315

LITERATURE ANTHOLOGY, pp. 314–315

Read

8 **Context Clues**

If we don't know what *rugby* means, we can look for context clues. The photograph shows children in uniforms. They look like they are playing a team sport. What do the first two sentences tell you? (Rugby is a team sport.)

9 **Skill: Author's Purpose**

What facts did you learn about Rosina on these pages? (Rosina likes to play sports. She plays on a rugby team. Her team won a trophy and then celebrated.) Let's add these clues to our chart.

Build Vocabulary pages 314–315
trophy: a special statue; a prize
coach: a person who helps a team

Clue	Clue
Rosina goes to a special school for deaf children. Her school is the same as other schools, except they use sign language to communicate.	Rosina likes to play sports. The players on her team are all friends.

Author's Purpose

At home we all help Mom cook meals. I chop lettuce. Emilio cuts up cheese. Dad makes guacamole. 10 11

After school I shower and change clothes for dinner. Mom likes to fix my hair. She puts it up in a bun like her mother did.

316

317

LITERATURE ANTHOLOGY, pp. 316–317

10 Ask and Answer Questions

As you read, you can ask questions about the text. Turn to a partner and discuss what you want to learn about Rosina's family. Then you can continue reading to find the answers.

11 Word Categories

To help us understand the words in a selection, we can sort them into categories. What category can the words *cook, chop,* and *cuts* be put into? (cooking words) What category might you put the word *guacamole* into? (food words)

Build Vocabulary page 317
chop: to cut

Reread   *Close Reading Companion,* 174

Author's Craft: Details

Reread page 315. How does the author help you know that Rosina's coach is a good helper? (I read that her team beat all the other teams. Also, the team was so happy that they splashed their coach with water. They must like having him for a coach.)

Author's Craft

Reread pages 316–317. What clues help you know Rosina's family helps one another? (The text tells me that Rosina's mother helps her fix her hair and that everyone helps cook meals. I see the family working together this way in the photographs.)

After dinner, Dad and I play a game of chess. Emilio roots for me. **12**

Mom, Dad, Emilio, and me. That's my family—but there are many more, too. **13**

318

319

LITERATURE ANTHOLOGY, pp. 318–319

Read

12 Make and Confirm Predictions

Remember, we can make predictions about what might happen next. Here we see that Rosina is playing chess with her father. Her brother, Emilio, roots for her. Can you predict what will happen next? Let's read on to find out.

13 Skill: Author's Purpose

What does the author want readers to know on these pages? Let's add that clue to our Author's Purpose chart.

Build Vocabulary page 318
roots: cheers

Clue	Clue
Rosina goes to a special school for deaf children. Her school is the same as other schools, except they use sign language to communicate.	Rosina likes to play sports. The players on her team are all friends. Rosina spends time with her family. They play games.

Author's Purpose

We are a big family. I have lots of aunts, cousins, grandpas, and grandmas. Most of my mom's family is deaf. My whole family uses sign language to talk to each other.

320

This is how we sign "goodbye."

321

LITERATURE ANTHOLOGY, pp. 320–321

Skill: Author's Purpose

Prompt children to review and discuss the clues they recorded on the Author's Purpose chart. What information did you read about Rosina? Why did the author write these facts? What does the author want readers to learn about? Let's use the clues to figure out the author's purpose.

Return to Purposes

Review children's predictions. Ask children if their predictions were correct. Guide them to use information in the text to confirm if their predictions were accurate. Discuss what children learned about Rosina by reading the selection.

Clue	Clue
Rosina goes to a special school for deaf children. Her school is the same as other schools, except they use sign language to communicate.	Rosina likes to play sports. The players on her team are all friends. Rosina spends time with her family. They play games.

Author's Purpose

to give information about a girl who is deaf, goes to a special school, and talks with her hands, but whose activities and interests are the same as other children her age

Meet George Ancona

George Ancona wrote the words and took the photographs for this piece. He learned how to take photographs from his father when he was growing up. His father developed pictures in their bathroom!

Today, George likes to photograph people in their everyday lives. Before George wrote this book, he already knew some sign language. In this picture, he is signing, "I love you!"

Author's Purpose
George Ancona shows how Rosina spends a day. Write a journal entry about what you did yesterday.

Respond to the Text

Retell
Use your own words to retell *Meet Rosina*.

Write
Rosina has a special community that works together. How do the people in your community work together to help you? Use these sentence starters:

I get help from...
They help me by...

Make Connections
How does Rosina's family help her? Who else helps her? ESSENTIAL QUESTION

322   323

LITERATURE ANTHOLOGY, pp. 322–323

Meet the Author/Photographer

George Ancona

Read aloud page 322 with children. Ask them how George Ancona learned to take photographs. *In his picture, what is George Ancona signing?*

Author's Purpose

Have children write an entry in their Response Journals about what they did yesterday.

The first thing I did yesterday was ____. Then I ____.

PHOTOGRAPHER'S CRAFT

Focus on Details

Explain that in *Meet Rosina* the photographs help tell information. The photographs show readers things that might be difficult to understand with just words.

- For example, on page 304, the photographs show how Rosina signs each letter of her name. These pictures help readers see what sign language looks like.

Respond to the Text

Retell

Guide children in retelling the selection. Remind them that as they read *Meet Rosina*, they paid attention to the facts in the selection to determine what the author wanted the readers to learn. Have children use the information they recorded on their Author's Purpose chart to help them retell the selection.

Reread

Analyze the Text

After children read and retell the selection, have them reread *Meet Rosina* to develop a deeper understanding of the text by answering the questions on pages 173–175 of the *Close Reading Companion*. For children who need support finding text evidence to support their responses, use the scaffolded instruction from the Reread prompts on pages T113D–T113H.

Write About the Text

Review the writing prompt with children. Remind them to use their responses from the *Close Reading Companion* and to cite text evidence to support their answers.

For a full lesson on writing a response supported by text evidence, see pages T114–T115.

<u>Answer:</u> Children's responses will vary, but children should tell about how people in their own community work together to help them.
<u>Evidence:</u> On pages 306–311, the text tells about school helpers, including teachers, teacher aides, and a librarian. Pages 314–315 show children playing as a team. Pages 316–317 show Rosina's family and describe how they work together to prepare a meal.

Integrate

Make Connections

Essential Question <u>Answer:</u> Rosina's mom and aunt both help by working at her school. Another person who helps Rosina is the librarian. <u>Evidence:</u> On page 308, I read that both her mom and aunt work at her school. On pages 310–311, I read that the librarian is good at telling stories with sign language.

ENGLISH LANGUAGE LEARNERS

Retell Help children by looking at each page of the selection and asking a prompt, such as: *What is Rosina doing? Why is she doing that?* Point to and identify the characters. *How does the teacher help the children?* Provide sentence starters to help children retell the selection, such as: *At school, Rosina ____.*

CONNECT TO CONTENT
COMMUNITY RULES AND RESPONSIBILITIES

Guide children to talk about the different people who help Rosina in her school and community. Prompt them to name some of the rules they might find in Rosina's school and how those rules could help all the students. Talk together about how rules and laws in school and the community help everyone get the help they need.

→ # Language Arts

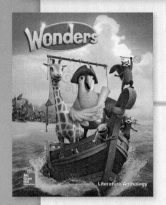

Literature Anthology

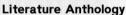

OBJECTIVES

CCSS Write informative/ explanatory texts in which they name a topic, supply some facts about the topic, and provide some sense of closure. **W.1.2**

CCSS Use personal, possessive, and indefinite pronouns (e.g., *I, me, my; they, them, their, anyone, everything*). **L.1.1d**

ACADEMIC LANGUAGE

• topic, inference, voice, pronoun, proper noun
• Cognates: *voz, inferencia*

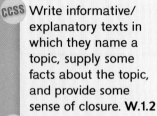

Independent Writing

Write About the Literature Anthology

Analylyze the Prompt Have children turn to page 323 in the **Literature Anthology**. Read the prompt: *Rosina has a special community that works together. How do the people in your community work together to help you?* Say: *In* Meet Rosina, *we read about how people in Rosina's community work together to help. The prompt asks how people work together in your community to help you. To respond to the prompt, we need to find text evidence and make inferences.*

Find Text Evidence Say: *We can look for evidence in the text and photographs about how people in Rosina's community help her.* Say: *Look at page 306. What do we learn about the teachers at Rosina's school?* (All the teachers teach with American Sign Language.) *Why is this a way for them to help?* (because all the children at her school are deaf and use sign language) Remind children that they can use text evidence to make inferences about ways people in their community do things to help them. Have children take notes as they look for evidence to respond to the prompt.

Write to the Prompt: Guide children as they begin their writing.

• **Prewrite** Have children review their notes and plan their writing. Guide them to decide which people in the community they want to write about and which details they will include in their response.

• **Draft** Remind children they can use some words from the prompt as they write their topic sentence. As children write their drafts, have them focus on the week's skills.

  • **Topic** Have children check that their first sentence states the topic and their sentences stay focused on the topic. **Trait: Organization**

  • **Use Your Own Voice** Remind children that their writing should show what they think and how they feel about the topic. **Trait: Voice**

  • **Possessive Pronouns** Remind children that they can use possessive pronouns to show who or what has something. **Grammar**

Tell children they will continue to work on their responses on Day 4.

Go Digital

Present the Lesson

Graphic Organizer

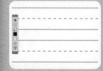

Writing

I see a fish.

Grammar

Grammar

Possessive Pronouns

1 Review Have children look at page 253 in the **Reading/Writing Workshop**. Remind them that possessive pronouns show who or what has or owns something.

Ask: *Which possessive pronoun is in the following sentence?* Mrs. Johnson protects all the kids on her bus. Her *is a possessive pronoun. It tells whose bus it is.*

2 Guided Practice/Practice Guide children to identify more possessive pronouns in Farah's response. Have children work with partners to identify the possessive pronouns and write new sentences with them.

Talk About It Have partners work together to explain why Farah used each possessive pronoun.

Mechanics: Days, Months, and Holidays

1 Explain Review the days of the week and months of the year with children. Review that the days of the week and months of the year are proper nouns and begin with capital letters.

2 Guided Practice Prompt children to correct the sentences.

Will you be home on saturday or sunday? (Saturday, Sunday)

The game is on the third friday of october. (Friday, October)

Their birthdays are in july and august. (July, August)

ENGLISH LANGUAGE LEARNERS SCAFFOLD

Beginning

Demonstrate Comprehension Provide sentence frames for partners as they write their responses: *People in my community help by ____. They also ____.* Correct the meaning of children's responses as needed.

Intermediate

Explain Encourage children to talk about words they used to express their feelings. Provide sentence frames, then have children complete and read them.

Advanced/High

Expand After children complete their responses, ask: *What did you do to show how you feel? What details or words can you add to your response to show your voice?* Repeat correct answers slowly and clearly to the class.

Daily Wrap Up

- Review the Essential Question and encourage children to discuss using the oral vocabulary words. Ask: *What do you do to help others?*

- Prompt children to review and discuss the skills they used today.

Materials

Literature Anthology
VOLUME 4

Visual Vocabulary Cards

accept
brother
decision
distance
father
friend
inspire

love
mother
often
picture
respect
swiftly

Teaching Poster

haul

Spelling Word Cards

a b c

Word-Building Cards

Dinah Zike's
FOLDABLES

Dinah Zike's Foldables®

→ Extend the Concept

CLOSE READING

MINILESSON

5 Mins

Abuelita's Lap

OBJECTIVES

CCSS Identify words and phrases in stories or poems that suggest feelings or appeal to the senses. **RL.1.4**

Review vocabulary

ACADEMIC LANGUAGE

• *sensory, poetry, poem, experience, sense*

• Cognates: *sensorial, poesía, poema, experiencia*

ESSENTIAL QUESTION

Remind children that this week they have been learning about the people in their lives who help them. Guide children to discuss the question using information from what they have read and discussed. Use the Define/Example/Ask routine to review the oral vocabulary words *decision, distance, inspire, respect,* and *swiftly.* Then review last week's oral vocabulary words *fair, conflict, shift, risk,* and *argument.*

Literary Element: Sensory Words

1 Explain Tell children they can read poetry selections for information and enjoyment. Explain that poems often include sensory words—words that describe what we experience with our senses of touch, hearing, sight, smell, and taste.

2 Model Display Teaching Poster 24. Read the first two lines. *The words* clicks *and* squeaks *tell us what the bat sounds like when it flies. These words describe what we experience with our sense of hearing.*

3 Guided Practice/Practice Read together lines 3 and 4 of the poem. *What words tell us what the moon looks like? Do these words describe what we experience with our sense of hearing, sight, or smell?* Tell children to look for sensory words as they read poems.

Close Reading

Compare Texts

Tell children they should think about how the boy in the poem is like Rosina in *Meet Rosina.*

After reading, work with children to memorize the poem. Guide them to recite it with expression, emphasizing the sensory words.

Go Digital

Visual Glossary

Teaching Poster

"Abuelita's Lap"

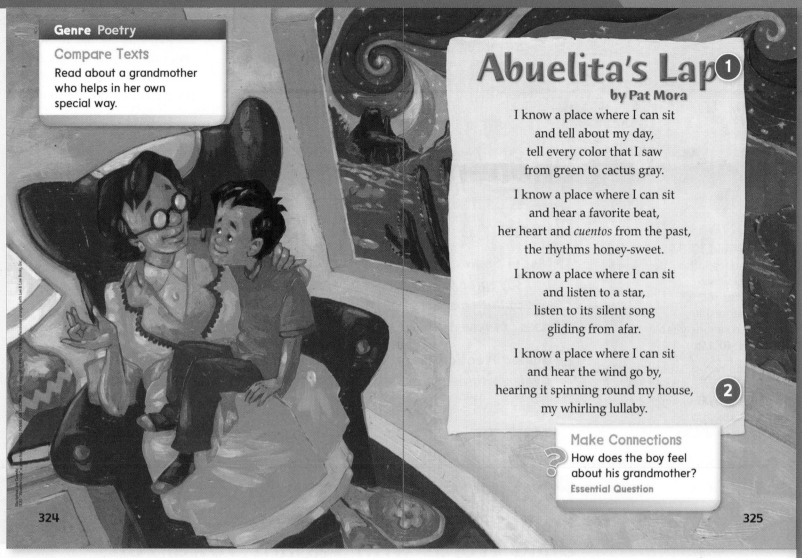

Genre Poetry

Compare Texts

Read about a grandmother who helps in her own special way.

Abuelita's Lap ①
by Pat Mora

I know a place where I can sit
and tell about my day,
tell every color that I saw
from green to cactus gray.

I know a place where I can sit
and hear a favorite beat,
her heart and *cuentos* from the past,
the rhythms honey-sweet.

I know a place where I can sit
and listen to a star,
listen to its silent song
gliding from afar.

I know a place where I can sit
and hear the wind go by,
hearing it spinning round my house,
my whirling lullaby.

②

Make Connections

? How does the boy feel about his grandmother?
Essential Question

324   325

LITERATURE ANTHOLOGY, pp. 324–325

Read

❶ Skill: Key Details

Reread the title and look at the illustration. Where is the boy sitting? (in his grandmother's lap) What things does the boy do while sitting in his grandmother's lap? (tells about his day; hears songs and stories; listens to sounds)

❷ Literary Element: Sensory Words

What words in the poem describe things the boy hears? *(rhythms honey-sweet, silent song gliding, wind spinning, whirling lullaby)*

Retell

Guide children to retell the poem.

Reread

After children retell, have them reread to develop a deeper understanding of the poem by answering questions on *Close Reading Companion* pages 176–178.

For children who need support citing text evidence, use these Reread questions:

- How does the title "Abuelita's Lap" help you understand the poem?

- Where do you think Abuelita lives?

Integrate

Make Connections

COLLABORATE **Essential Question** Have children use text evidence to tell how the boy feels about Abuelita.

EXTEND THE CONCEPT/LITERATURE ANTHOLOGY **T117**

 **Word Work**

Quick Review
Build Fluency: Sound-Spellings
Display the **Word-Building Cards:** *aw, au, augh, al, ew, ue, ui, ow, oy, oi, ar, ore, oar, er, ir, ur, ey, igh, oa, oe, ee, ea, ai, ay, e_e, u_e, o_e, dge, i_e, a_e.* Have children say the sounds.

5 Mins MINILESSON

Phonemic Awareness

OBJECTIVES

CCSS Isolate and pronounce initial, medial vowel, and final sounds (phonemes) in spoken single-syllable words. **RF.1.2c**

CCSS Decode two-syllable words following basic patterns by breaking the words into syllables. **RF.1.3e**

Phoneme Categorization

1 Model Show children how to categorize words by vowel sound. *Listen as I say three words:* pause, yawn, tool. *Two of the words have the /ô/ sound. One does not.* Pause *and* yawn *have the /ô/ sound.* Tool *does not have the /ô/ sound.* Tool *does not belong.*

2 Guided Practice/Practice Have children practice. Do one together. *I will say three words. Tell me which word does not belong and why.*

clown, jaws, sauce   draw, lawn, boy   hope, coat, dawn

flute, call, soon   mall, chalk, rope   day, raw, pain

10 Mins MINILESSON

Phonics/Structural Analysis

Build Words with Variant Vowel /ô/

Review *The sound /ô/ can be represented by the letters* a, aw, au, augh, *and* al. *We'll use* **Word-Building Cards** *to build words with /ô/.*

Place the letters l, a, w, n. *Let's blend the sounds together and read the word: /lllôôônnn/. Now take away the* n. *Blend. Continue with* laws, paws, pause, cause, calls, call, mall, small, stall, tall, fall, fawn, dawn.

> **Decodable Reader** Have children read "Thank You Authors!" (pages 37–40), "My Baseball Coach" (45–48), and "Teacher Talk" (53–56) to practice decoding words in connected text.

Vowel Team Syllables

Review Remind children that when they see letters for a vowel spelling in a word, those letters act as a team and must stay together in the same syllable. Write *crawling.* Have children identify the letters *a, w* as standing for the vowel sound; have them blend and read the word.

Write these words: *because, daughter, railroad, tallest, zooming, hallway.* Have partners blend and read the words. Then have them use the words in sentences.

Go Digital

Phonemic Awareness

Phonics

Structural Analysis

Spelling Word Sort

school
Visual Glossary

Spelling

Word Sort with /ô/

Review Provide pairs of children with copies of the **Spelling Word Cards**. While one partner reads the words one at a time, the other partner should orally segment the word and then write the word. After reading all the words, partners should switch roles.

Have children correct their own papers. Then have them sort the words by spelling pattern.

High-Frequency Words

brother, father, friend, love, mother, picture

Review Display **Visual Vocabulary Cards** for high-frequency words *brother, father, friend, love, mother, picture*. Have children Read/Spell/Write each word.

- Point to a word and call on a child to use it in a sentence.
- Review last week's words using the same procedure.

Expand Vocabulary

accept, often

Use the Visual Vocabulary Cards to review *accept* and *often*.

1 **Explain** Remind children that words have different forms. Explain that verbs have forms that tell if something is happening now or happened in the past. Write these endings: *-ed, -ing, -s*. Review the meanings of each ending.

2 **Model** Draw a four-column chart. Model how to add *-s* to *accept*. Write *accept* in the first column. Then write *accepts* in the next column. Read the words. Discuss when you would use each word. Guide children in using both words in sentences.

3 **Guided Practice** Have partners fill in the chart for *-ed* and *-ing*. Then have them use the new words in sentences.

Monitor and *Differentiate*

 Quick Check

Can children read and decode words with variant vowel /ô/?

Can children recognize and read high-frequency and vocabulary words?

⬇

Small Group Instruction

If No →	Approaching	Reteach pp. T134–T137
	ELL	Develop pp. T148–T155
If Yes →	On Level	Review pp. T142–T143
	Beyond Level	Extend pp. T146–T147

Write About the Literature Anthology

Revise

Reread the prompt about the selection *Meet Rosina: Rosina has a special community that works together. How do the people in your community work together to help you?* Have children read their drafts to see if they responded to the prompt. Then have them check for:

Literature Anthology

OBJECTIVES

CCSS With guidance and support from adults, focus on a topic, respond to questions and suggestions from peers, and add details to strengthen writing as needed. **W.1.5**

CCSS Capitalize dates and names of people. **L.1.2a**

CCSS Ask questions to clear up any confusion about the topics and texts under discussion. **SL.1.1b**

ACADEMIC LANGUAGE

- *edit, revise, pronoun, proper noun*
- Cognates: *editar, revisar*

- **Topic** Does their first sentence tell their topic? Do their other sentences focus on the topic? **Trait: Organization**

- **Use Your Own Voice** Did they show what they think and how they feel in their writing? **Trait: Voice**

- **Possessive Pronouns** Did they use possessive pronouns correctly? **Grammar**

Peer Review Have children work in pairs to do a peer review and read their partner's draft. Ask partners to check that the response focuses on the topic, shows the writer's voice, and uses possessive pronouns correctly. They should take notes about what they liked most about the writing, questions they have for the author about anything that confused them, and additional ideas they think the author could include. Have partners discuss these topics. Provide time for them to make revisions.

Writing

— Make a capital letter.

∧ Add.

𝒴 Take out.

Proofreader's Marks

Proofread/Edit

Have children check for the following:

- Possessive pronouns are used correctly.

- Frequently occurring conjunctions are used correctly.

- Proper nouns are capitalized.

Peer Edit Next, have partners exchange their drafts and take turns reviewing them against the checklist. Encourage partners to discuss and fix errors together.

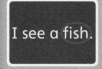

I see a fish.

Grammar

Final Draft

After children edit their writing and finish their peer edits, have them write their final draft. Tell children to write neatly so others can read their writing. Or, work with children to explore a variety of digital tools to produce and publish their writing, including collaborating with peers. Have them include details that help make their writing clear and interesting and add a drawing if needed to make their ideas clear.

Teacher Conference As children work, conference with them to provide guidance. Make sure children write a topic sentence and stay focused on their topic, and that their writing expresses how they feel.

Grammar

Possessive Pronouns

1 Review Remind children that possessive pronouns show who or what has or owns something.

2 Practice Display the following possessive pronouns: *my, your, his, her, its, our, their, mine, yours, his, hers, ours, theirs.* Have pairs of children use each word in a sentence.

Talk About It Have partners discuss their responses to the writing prompt using the possessive pronouns they learned.

Mechanics: Days, Months, and Holidays

1 Explain Explain to children that the names of holidays are proper nouns. Remind them that proper nouns begin with capital letters.

2 Practice Display the sentences below. Read each aloud. Then have children fix each sentence.

> i helped my mom on mother's day? (I helped my mom on Mother's Day.)

> The third sunday in june is father's Day. (The third Sunday in June is Father's Day.)

Daily Wrap Up

- Have children discuss the Essential Question using the oral vocabulary words. Ask: *Who do you respect in your community?*

- Prompt children to discuss the skills they practiced and learned today by asking, *What skills did you use today?*

→ Integrate Ideas

My Team

RESEARCH AND INQUIRY

Make a Newspaper

Review the steps in the research process. Tell children they will do a research project to write a newspaper article about someone who helps others. Children will work with a group to put the articles together to make a newspaper.

STEP 1 ### Choose a Topic

Guide children to think of the people who help them in their lives and choose one to write about.

STEP 2 ### Find Resources

With children, review print and online newspapers. Encourage children to interview family and community members to get information. Have them use the Research Process Checklist online.

STEP 3 ### Keep Track of Ideas

Have children record their ideas in a Four-Tab Foldable®. Model recording details they can include in their article.

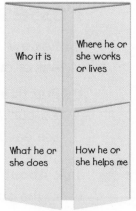

Who it is | Where he or she works or lives

What he or she does | How he or she helps me

Dinah Zike's
FOLDABLES

Go Digital

Resources Research and Inquiry

Collaborative Conversations

Listen Carefully Review with children that as they engage in partner, small-group, and whole-group discussions, they should:

- always look at the speaker.
- respect others by not interrupting them.
- repeat others' ideas to check understanding.

STEP 4 **Create the Project: Newspaper**

Explain the characteristics of a newspaper.

- **Articles** A newspaper has articles about interesting topics. In this project, the articles will give information about people who help you.

- **Images** A newspaper can have images that illustrate the articles. Your newspaper can have images of the people you write about in the articles.

Have children write articles and create a newspaper.

- Prompt children to use the information from their interviews to write an article about a person who helps them.

- Guide them to include a drawing of the person they write about.

- Have groups put their articles together to form a newspaper. Encourage groups to read each other's newspapers.

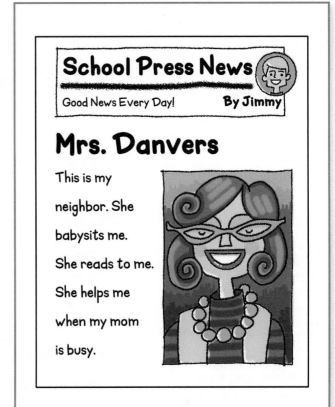

INFORMATIVE NEWSPAPER

ELL **ENGLISH LANGUAGE LEARNERS**
SCAFFOLD

Beginning	Intermediate	Advanced/High
Use Sentence Frames Use sentence frames to help children discuss the person they write about. For example: ____ helps me. She helps me ____.	**Discuss** Guide children to focus on the most important details in their articles. Ask: *How do you know this person? Does this person help you often? What does he or she do?*	**Describe** Prompt children to elaborate on how the person helps them. Ask them how they feel about this person and what they have learned from him or her.

Materials

Reading/Writing Workshop
VOLUME 4

Literature Anthology
VOLUME 4

 Visual Vocabulary Cards
accept
brother
father
friend
love
mother
often
picture

 **Teaching Poster**

haul **Spelling Word Cards**

| a | b | c |
Word-Building Cards

→ # Word Work/Fluency

Go Digital

MINILESSON 5 Mins
Phonemic Awareness

Phonemic Awareness

Phoneme Segmentation

Review Guide children to segment sounds in words. *I am going to say a word. I want you to say each sound in the word.*

paw   fault   small   clause   taught

Phoneme Substitution

Review Have children substitute sounds in words. *I am going to say a word. Then I'll tell you to change a sound to make a new word.* Do *talk/chalk* together. Continue with: *fawn/yawn; raw/jaw; ball/mall.*

| m | a |
| n | t | p |

Phonics

MINILESSON 10 Mins
Phonics/Structural Analysis

Blend and Build with /ô/

Review Have children blend and read the words *hawk, walk, launch, small,* and *daughter*. Then follow the word-building routine with **Word-Building Cards** to build *yawn, dawn, drawn, draw, raw, saw, sauce, salt, halt, hall, wall, mall.*

Word Automaticity Display decodable words and point to each word as children chorally read it. Test how many words children can read in one minute. Model blending words children miss.

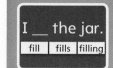
I __ the jar.
| fill | fills | filling |

Structural Analysis

Vowel Team Syllables

Review Have children explain why a vowel team stays in the same syllable in a longer, multisyllabic word. Then have children practice writing and reading two-syllable words with vowel team syllables, such as *awful, laundry, because, drawing,* and *August.*

school
Visual Glossary

Fluency: Word Automaticity

Spelling

Word Sort with /ô/ Spellings

Review Have children use the **Spelling Word Cards** to sort the weekly words by spellings for /ô/. Remind children that four of the words do not have the /ô/ sound.

Assess Assess children on their ability to spell words with /ô/ spellings. Say each word and provide a sentence. Then allow them time to write down the words. To challenge children, provide an additional word for each sound-spelling.

High-Frequency Words

brother, father, friend, love, mother, picture

Review Display **Visual Vocabulary Cards** for the words. Have children Read/Spell/Write each word and write a sentence with each.

Review Vocabulary

accept, often

Review Write *accept* and *often*. Point to each word and ask children to use the word in a sentence. Write the sentences and reinforce word meanings as necessary. Repeat with last week's words or other previously taught words that children need to review.

Fluency

Intonation

Review Review that a question mark indicates a question is being asked. Remind them their voices should go up at the end of a question.

Read aloud from the Shared Read. Have children echo each sentence. Point out how your voice goes up slightly at the end of questions. Then have partners reread, working on how they read questions. Provide feedback as needed.

Quick Review

Build Fluency: Sound-Spellings
Display the **Word-Building Cards:** *aw, au, augh, al, ew, ue, ui, ow, oy, oi, ar, ore, oar, er, ir, ur, ey, igh, oa, oe, ee, ea, ai, ay, e_e, u_e, o_e, dge, i_e, a_e.* Have children say the sounds. Repeat, and vary the pace.

Monitor and *Differentiate*

 Quick Check

Can children read and decode words with variant vowel /ô/?

Can children recognize and read high-frequency and vocabulary words?

Small Group Instruction

If No →	Approaching	Reteach pp. T134–T137
	ELL	Develop pp. T148–T155
If Yes →	On Level	Review pp. T142–T143
	Beyond Level	Extend pp. T146–T147

Literature Anthology

OBJECTIVES

CCSS With guidance and support from adults, use a variety of digital tools to produce and publish writing, including in collaboration with peers. **W.1.6**

CCSS Follow agreed-upon rules for discussions (e.g., listening to others with care, speaking one at a time about the topics and texts under discussion). **SL.1.1a**

CCSS Describe people, places, things, and events with relevant details, expressing ideas and feelings clearly. **SL.1.4**

ACADEMIC LANGUAGE

- *topic, evaluate, blog, capitalize*
- Cognate: *evaluar*

MINILESSON 5 Mins Independent Writing

Write About the Literature Anthology

Prepare

Tell children they will plan what they will say about their finished writing and drawing to the class. Remind children to:

- Think about how they focused every sentence on their topic.
- Think about how they expressed their feelings in their writing.

Present

Have children take turns giving presentations of their responses to the prompt about *Meet Rosina: How do the people in your community work together to help you?* If possible, record their presentations so children can self-evaluate. Tell children to:

- Listen carefully and quietly while others speak.
- Take turns speaking one at a time.
- Express their ideas and feelings clearly.

Evaluate

Have children discuss their own presentations and evaluate their performance using the presentation rubric.

Use the teacher's rubric to evaluate children's writing. Have children add their writing to their Writer's Portfolio. Encourage children to look back at their previous writing. Guide children to discuss what they liked best about their writing. Have children share their observations with a partner.

Publish

After children finish presenting their work, discuss how the class will publish a blog of their responses. If possible, scan children's writing and encourage them to view and discuss the responses. Guide children to use digital tools to publish writing.

Go Digital

Writing

Checklists

I see a fish.

Grammar

Grammar

Possessive Pronouns

1 Review Have children describe when possessive pronouns are used. Write the following sentences and have children identify the possessive pronouns:

I went fishing with my mom and dad. Mom put her fish in a bucket. I caught a fish that is bigger than hers. Dad caught a fish that is bigger than mine. His is bigger than both of ours! (my, her, hers, mine, his, ours)

2 Practice Ask: *What do pronouns take the place of?* (nouns) *What do possessive pronouns show?* (They show who or what has or owns something.)

Have children work in pairs to write sentences using *your, its, our, their,* and *mine.*

Mechanics: Days, Months, and Holidays

1 Review Remind children that all days, months, and holidays are capitalized.

2 Practice Write the following sentences. Read each aloud. Have children fix the sentences.

We planted a Tree on arbor day. (We planted a tree on Arbor Day.)

let's make a play date for tuesday, july 22. (Let's make a play date for Tuesday, July 22.)

Daily Wrap Up

- Review the Essential Question and encourage children to discuss using the oral vocabulary words.

- Review with children that authors write to entertain readers, to try to convince them of something, or to give information. Children can identify the author's purpose as they read and reread selections.

- Review words with variant vowel /ô/.

- Use the Visual Vocabulary Word Cards to review the Words to Know.

- Remind children that an author's voice is the feeling the author shows.

→ # Integrate Ideas

Close Reading Routine

Read   DOK 1–2

- Identify key ideas and details about people who help them.
- Take notes and retell.
- Use **A C T** prompts as needed.

Reread   DOK 2–3

- Analyze text, craft, and structure.

Integrate   DOK 4

- Integrate knowledge and ideas and make text-to-text connections.
- Use the Integrate Lesson.
- Use *Close Reading Companion*, p. 179.

 CLOSE READING

TEXT CONNECTIONS

 COLLABORATE
Connect to the Essential Question

Write the essential question on the board: *Who helps you?* Read the essential question aloud. Tell children that they will think about all of the information that they have learned about people that help. Say: *We have read many selections on this topic. We will compare the information from this week's* **Leveled Readers** *and* All Kinds of Helpers, **Reading/Writing Workshop** *pages 242–251.*

Evaluate Text Evidence Guide children to review the selections and their completed graphic organizers. Have children work with partners to compare information from all the week's reads. Children can record notes using a Foldable®. Guide them to record information from the selections that helps them to answer the Essential Question.

Dinah Zike's
FOLDABLES
Study Organizer

My Team

OBJECTIVES

CCSS Participate in shared research and writing projects. **W.1.7**

Go Digital

Collaborate

RESEARCH AND INQUIRY

COLLABORATE
Have children create a checklist and review their newspaper articles:

- Is their newspaper article about someone that helps them?
- Do they wish to make any last minute changes to the newspaper article or the images?
- Have they correctly given information about someone that helps them?
- Have they taken notes about what they would like to talk about when presenting their newspaper articles to the class?

Guide partners to practice sharing their articles with each other. Children should practice speaking and presenting their information clearly.

Guide children to share their work. Prompt children to ask questions to clarify when something is unclear: *Who did you interview? What do you want this article to tell about? How does this person help you?* Have children use the Presentation Checklist online.

OBJECTIVES

CCSS Identify basic similarities and differences between two texts on the same topic (e.g., in illustrations, descriptions, or procedures). **RI.1.9**

Text to Poetry

Read aloud with children the Integrate activity on page 179 of the *Close Reading Companion*. Have partners share reactions to the poem. Then guide them to discuss how it is similar to the selections they read earlier in the week. Have partners collaborate to complete the Integrate page by following the prompts.

Present Ideas and Synthesize Information

When children finish their discussions, ask for a volunteer from each pair to share the information from their Foldable® and their Integrate pages. After each pair has presented their ideas, ask: *How does learning about these people help you answer the Essential Question, Who helps you?* Lead a class discussion asking students to use the information from their charts to answer the Essential Question.

SPEAKING AND LISTENING

As children work with partners in their *Close Reading Companion* or on their articles, make sure that students actively participate in the conversation and, when necessary, remind them to use these speaking and listening strategies:

Speaking Strategies

- Describe the places and things that they are discussing with relevant details.
- Use words that express their ideas and feelings clearly.
- Add drawings to their presentations to clarify their ideas, thoughts, and feelings.

Listening Strategies

- Ask questions to clear up any confusion about what they have heard.
- Listen carefully for specific information in a text read aloud or information presented orally.
- Listen quietly as a presenter speaks and wait until the speaker has finished before asking questions.

OBJECTIVES

CCSS Ask questions to clear up any confusion about the topics and texts under discussion. **SL.1.1c**

CCSS Describe people, places, things, and events with relevant details, expressing ideas and feelings clearly. **SL.1.4**

CCSS Add drawings or other visual displays to descriptions when appropriate to clarify ideas, thoughts, and feelings. **SL.1.5**

Approaching Level

Lexile 310

OBJECTIVES

Identify the main purpose of a text, including what the author wants to answer, explain, or describe. **RI.2.6**

Leveled Reader:
Helping Me, Helping You!

Before Reading

Preview and Predict

Have children turn to the title page. Read the title and the author's name and have children repeat. Preview the selection's photographs. Prompt children to predict what the selection might be about.

Review Genre: Informational Text/Nonfiction

Have children recall that informational text gives facts and information about real people, places, things, or events.

ESSENTIAL QUESTION

Remind children of the Essential Question: *Who helps you?* Set a purpose for reading: *Let's read to find out how family and people in our neighborhood help us.*

Remind children that as they read a selection, they can ask questions about what they do not understand or want to know more about.

During Reading

Guided Comprehension

As children whisper read *Helping Me, Helping You!,* monitor and provide guidance, correcting blending and modeling the key strategies and skills.

Strategy: Reread

Remind children that sometimes they may misread a word or miss an important point. They can reread a passage to make sure they understand. Model the strategy on page 3: *I read too quickly. I don't know who reads together with the girl.* Reread the page. *Now I see. It's her mother.*

Skill: Author's Purpose

Remind children the author's purpose is the reason why an author writes a text, such as to entertain, to inform, or to persuade. As you read, say: *What clues tell us why the author wrote this selection? What did she want readers to know?* Display an Author's Purpose chart for children to copy.

Go Digital

Helping Me, Helping You!

Graphic Organizer

Retell

Model recording children's answers in the boxes. Have children record the answers in their own charts.

Think Aloud As I read I'll look for clues to show why the author wrote this text. On pages 4 and 5, I read about how family members help each other. I think these details give clues about why the author wrote this.

Guide children to use the text and illustrations to complete the chart.

After Reading

Respond to Reading

Have children complete the Respond to Reading on page 12.

Retell

Have children take turns retelling the selection, using the **Retelling Cards** as a guide. Help children make a personal connection by saying: *How does someone in your family or neighborhood help you?*

Model Fluency

Read the sentences, one at a time. Have children chorally repeat. Point out to children how your voice goes up at the end of a question.

Apply Have children practice repeated readings with partners. Provide feedback as needed.

Literature Circles

Lead children in conducting a literature circle using the Thinkmark questions to guide the discussion. You may wish to discuss what children have learned about people who help them from both selections in the Leveled Reader.

Level Up

Level-up lessons available online.

IF children can read *Helping Me, Helping You!* Approaching Level with fluency and correctly answer the Respond to Reading questions,

THEN tell children that they will read a more detailed version of this selection.

- Use pages 4–5 of *Helping Me, Helping You!* On Level to model using Teaching Poster 38 to record clues to the author's purpose.

- Have children read the selection, checking their comprehension by using the graphic organizer.

PAIRED READ …

Leveled Reader

"Fire!"

Make Connections: Write About It • Analytical Writing

Before reading, ask children to note that the genre of this text is poetry. Then read the Compare Texts direction together. After reading the poem, ask children to make connections between the information they learned from "Fire!" and *Helping Me, Helping You!* Provide a sentence frame such as: _____ and _____ are people in my neighborhood who help me.

FOCUS ON SOCIAL STUDIES

Children can extend their knowledge of people who help them by completing the social studies activity on page 16.

Phonemic Awareness

PHONEME BLENDING

TIER 2

OBJECTIVES

 Orally produce single-syllable words by blending sounds (phonemes), including consonant blends. **RF.1.2b**

I Do Explain to children that today they will blend sounds to form words. *Listen as I say the sounds in a word: /h/ /ô/ /l/. Now I will blend the sounds together and say the word: /hhhôôôlll/,* haul. *Let's say the word together:* haul.

We Do *Let's do some together. Listen as I say some sounds: /k/ /ô/ /t/. Let's blend and say the word: /kôôôt/,* caught.

Repeat this routine with the following words:

/t/ /ô/ /k/   /k/ /ô/ /l/   /l/ /ô/ /n/   /p/ /ô/

You Do *It's your turn. I'll say some sounds. Blend and say the word.*

/r/ /ô/   /k/ /r/ /ô/ /l/   /s/ /ô/ /s/   /k/ /ô/ /z/

Repeat the blending routine with additional /ô/ words.

PHONEME CATEGORIZATION

TIER 2

OBJECTIVES

 Isolate and pronounce initial, medial vowel, and final sounds (phonemes) in spoken single-syllable words. **RF.1.2c**

I Do *Listen as I say three words:* ball, chalk, pain. *The words* ball *and* chalk *have the /ô/ sound. The word* pain *does not. It doesn't belong.*

We Do *Let's do some together. I will say three words:* law, star, paw. *Say them with me:* law, star, paw. *Star does not have /ô/. It does not belong.* Repeat this routine with the following words:

taught, ride, stalk   rail, haunt, dawn   park, ball, lawn

You Do *It's your turn. I will say three words. Tell me which does not belong and why.*

pause, turn, fault   boy, raw, claw   yawn, steak, fake

Repeat the categorization routine with additional words.

PHONEME REVERSAL

OBJECTIVES

 Orally produce single-syllable words by blending sounds (phonemes), including consonant blends. **RF.1.2b**

 I Do Explain that today children will listen to sounds, blend them, and then reverse them. *Listen as I blend these sounds: /t/ /a/ /k/,* tack. *Now I will say the sounds backward: /k/ /a/ /t/, /kat/,* cat. *The word is* cat.

 We Do *Let's do some together. Listen: /k/ /ô/ /t/ Let's blend the sounds: /kôt/,* caught. *Now let's blend the sounds backward to make another word: /t/ /ô/ /k/, /tôk/,* talk.

Repeat this routine with the following sounds.

| /k/ /a/ /b/ | /d/ /o/ /k/ | /t/ /ô/ /t/ | /p/ /o/ /t/ /s/ |

 You Do *It's your turn. I will say some sounds. Blend the sounds to make a word. Then say the sounds backward and blend them to make another word.*

| /l/ /ô/ /w/ | /s/ /ô/ /s/ | /ü/ /z/ | /p/ /a/ /n/ |

PHONEME SUBSTITUTION

OBJECTIVES

 Isolate and pronounce initial, medial vowel, and final sounds (phonemes) in spoken single-syllable words. **RF.1.2c**

 I Do *Listen as I say a word:* hot. *I hear /o/ in the middle of* hot. *I'm going to change /o/ to /a/. Here is the new word: /h/ /a/ /t/,* hat. *I made a new word,* hat.

 We Do *Do it with me. Listen to this word: /wāāāk/,* wake. *Say the word with me:* wake. *Now change /ā/ to /i/: /wiiik/,* wick. *The new word is* wick.

Repeat with these words:

| cat, caught | loan, lawn | squeak, squawk |

 You Do *Now you do it. Change a sound to create a new word.*

| close, claws | chip, chop | fun, fawn | song, sing |

ELL ENGLISH LANGUAGE LEARNERS

For the **children** who need **phonemic awareness, phonics,** and **fluency** practice, use scaffolding methods as necessary to ensure children understand the meaning of the words. Refer to the Language Transfers Handbook for phonics elements that may not transfer in children's native languages.

Phonics

CONNECT a, aw, au, augh, al TO /ô/

OBJECTIVES

CCSS Decode regularly spelled one-syllable words. **RF.1.3b**

 I Do Display the **Word-Building Card** *aw*. *These are the lowercase letters* a *and* w. *I am going to trace* a *and* w *while I say /ô/.* Trace the letters *a, w* while saying /ô/ five times. Repeat for *a, au, augh,* and *al.*

 We Do *Now do it with me.* Have children trace the lowercase *a and w* on the Word-Building Cards with their finger while saying /ô/. Trace the letters *aw* five times and say /ô/ with children. Repeat for *a, au, augh,* and *al.*

 You Do Have children connect *aw* to the sound /ô/ by tracing lowercase *aw* with their finger, while saying /ô/. Once children have traced on paper five to ten times, they should then write the letters *aw* while saying /ô/ five to ten times. Repeat for *a, au, augh,* and *al.*

Repeat, connecting the letters *a, aw, au, augh,* and *al* to the sound /ô/ throughout the week.

BLEND WORDS WITH VARIANT VOWEL /ô/

OBJECTIVES

CCSS Decode regularly spelled one-syllable words. **RF.1.3b**

 I Do Display Word-Building Cards *w, al, k. This is the letter* w. *It stands for /w/. These are the letters* a, l. *They stand for /ô/. This is the letter* k. *It stands for /k/. Let's blend: /wôôôk/,* walk.

 We Do Guide children to blend and read: *paw, call, taught, haunt.*

 You Do Have children blend and read: *saw, all, claw, cause, law, fault, caught, brawl, pause, halt, stalk, mall.*

Repeat, blending additional words with variant vowel /ô/.

You may wish to review Phonics with ELL using this section.

BUILD WORDS WITH VARIANT VOWEL /ô/

OBJECTIVES
Decode regularly spelled one-syllable words. **RF.1.3b**

 I Do Display Word-Building Cards *al, l. These are the letters* a, l, l. *They stand for /ô/ and /l/. I will blend /ô/ and /l/: /ôl/,* all. *The word is* all.

 We Do Add *t* to *all. Let's build a new word. I am going to add* t *to the word* all. *Let's blend and read: /tôôôl/,* tall.

 You Do Have children continue building: *small, call, mall, malt, salt, halt, haul, haunt, haunts, flaunts, flaunt.*

Repeat, building additional words with /ô/.

BLEND WORDS WITH VARIANT VOWEL /ô/

OBJECTIVES
Decode regularly spelled one-syllable words. **RF.1.3b**

 I Do Display Word-Building Cards l, aw. *This is* l. *It stands for /l/. These are the letters* a, w. *They stand for /ô/. Listen: /lôôô/,* law. *The word is* law.

 We Do *Let's blend some words.* Blend and read *haul, taught, salt, walk.*

 You Do Display the words to the right. Have children blend and read the words.

Decodable Reader Have children read "Thank You Authors!" (pages 37–40), "My Baseball Coach" (45–48), and "Teacher Talk" (53–56).

saw	fall	walk	paw	cause	hawk
mall	salt	caught	ball	fault	claw
pawn	call	lawn	pause	malt	brawl
flute	crowd	chalk	crew	tools	taught

The tall girl talks as she makes the sauce.

The walk will dry after the thaw.

Paul will haul the dirt from the lawn.

BUILD FLUENCY WITH PHONICS

Sound-Spellings Fluency

Display the following Word-Building Cards: *aw, au, augh, al, ew, ue, ui, ow, oy, oi, ar, ore, oar, er, ir, ur, ey, igh, oa, oe, ee, ea, ai, ay, e_e, u_e, o_e, dge, i_e, a_e.* Have children chorally say the sounds. Repeat and vary the pace.

Fluency in Connected Text

Have children review the **Decodable Reader** selections. Identify words with the /ô/ sound and blend words as needed.

Have partners reread the selections for fluency.

Structural Analysis

REVIEW VOWEL TEAM SYLLABLES

OBJECTIVES

Decode two-syllable words following basic patterns by breaking the words into syllables. **RF.1.3e**

I Do Remind children that a syllable is a word part that has a vowel sound. Write *explain*. *I see the vowel team* ai. *It stands for one vowel sound. When I divide the word into syllables, the* a *and* i *stay together. I'll divide the word between the middle consonants. The first syllable is closed: ex. I'll blend the syllables together: /ex/ /plān/, explain.*

We Do Write *teamwork*. *I see the vowel team* ea, *which stands for the sound /ā/. I know a vowel team stays together in one syllable. I blend the first syllable: /t/ /ā/ /m/; team. Then I blend the last syllable: /w/ /ur/ /k/; work. Blend the syllables: /tām/ /wurk/; teamwork.*

You Do Give partners two-syllable words with vowel teams, such as *painless, sleepy,* and *sealing*. Have them break each into syllables and read each word.

Repeat Have children read additional words with vowel team syllables.

RETEACH VOWEL TEAM SYLLABLES

OBJECTIVES

Decode two-syllable words following basic patterns by breaking the words into syllables. **RF.1.3e**

I Do Explain to children that when a syllable in a word has a vowel team, the vowels stand for one sound. Write *be<u>cause</u>*. *The letters* b *and* e *stand for /b/and /ā/: be. Au stands for /ô/. So the second syllable is /k/ /ô/ /z/; cause. I can blend the two syllables together: /bā/ /côz/; because.*

Repeat with *August* and *teacher*.

We Do Repeat the routine by reading each syllable and blending the syllables with children with these words:

raincoat   feeling   author   soaking

You Do *Now it's your turn. Read each syllable and blend the syllables to read the word.*

saucer   lawyer   repeat   daydream   pigtail

Words to Know

REVIEW HIGH-FREQUENCY WORDS

OBJECTIVES

 CCSS Recognize and read grade-appropriate irregularly spelled words. **RF.1.3g**

 I Do   Use the **High-Frequency Word Cards** to **Read/Spell/Write** each high-frequency word. Use each word orally in a sentence.

 We Do   Guide children to Read/Spell/Write each word on their **Response Boards**. Work together to generate oral sentences using the words.

 You Do   Have children work with a partner to do the Read/Spell/Write routine on their own using the words *brother, father, friend, love, mother, picture.*

CUMULATIVE REVIEW

OBJECTIVES

 CCSS Recognize and read grade-appropriate irregularly spelled words. **RF.1.3g**

Review previously taught high-frequency words

 I Do   Display High-Frequency Word Cards from the previous weeks, such as *began, better, guess, learn, right, sure.* Review each word using the Read/Spell/Write routine.

 We Do   Have children write the words on their Response Boards. Complete sentences for each word, such as: *This game is better than____* or *In school we learn ____.*

 You Do   Show each card and have children chorally read. Mix and repeat.

Fluency Display the High-Frequency Word Cards. Point to the words in random order. Have children chorally read. Repeat at a faster pace.

REVIEW VOCABULARY WORDS

OBJECTIVES

 CCSS Identify real-life connections between words and their use (e.g., note places at home that are *cozy*). **L.1.5c**

 I Do   Display the **Visual Vocabulary Cards** for *accept* and *often*. Review each word using the Define/Example/Ask routine.

 We Do   Invite children to act out each word. Then work with them to complete these sentence starters: *(1) Did you accept ____? (2) We often go to ____.*

 You Do   Have partners write two sentences on their own, using each of the words. Provide assistance as needed.

Comprehension

READ FOR FLUENCY

TIER 2

OBJECTIVES

 Read grade-level text orally with accuracy, appropriate rate, and expression. **RF.1.4b**

 I Do Read the first page of the Practice Book selection. Model using appropriate intonation.

 We Do Read the rest of the Practice Book selection and have children repeat each sentence after you. Point out how your voice changes slightly as you read each sentence.

 You Do Have children work with a partner and take turns rereading the passage aloud. Remind them to use proper intonation as they read.

IDENTIFY MAIN IDEA

TIER 2

OBJECTIVES

 Identify the main topic and retell key details of a text. **RI.1.2**

 I Do Remind children that they have been reading informational text. Tell them that readers can use key details and illustrations to help them figure out the main idea of a selection. *Key details in an informational text tell all about the main idea, or what the selection is mainly about.*

 We Do Read the first page of the Practice Book selection aloud. Model identifying details to help figure out the main idea. *What do coaches help people do? Yes, they help people learn a sport. What else do they do? That's right, they teach people the rules of the sport. These details tell about what coaches do.*

 You Do Guide children to read the rest of the Practice Book selection. Prompt them to identify important details that can help them figure out the main idea. Help children explain the main idea.

REVIEW AUTHOR'S PURPOSE

OBJECTIVES

Identify the main purpose of a text, including what the author wants to answer, explain, or describe. **RI.2.6**

 I Do Remind children that the author's purpose is the reason why the author wrote the selection. Most informational texts are written to give information about a person, place, thing, or idea. *It is important to understand the author's purpose because it helps the reader understand the subject.*

 We Do Read the Practice Book selection together. Pause to identify the information the selection gives. *What does the author want us to know about coaches? Yes, she wants us to know what coaches do. What are some things coaches do?*

 You Do Have partners reread the selection together. Have them work together as you guide them to complete an Author's Purpose chart.

SELF-SELECTED READING

OBJECTIVES

 With prompting and support, read informational texts appropriately complex for grade 1. **RI.1.10**

Apply the strategy and skill to read a text

Read Independently

Have children pick an informational text for sustained silent reading. Remind them to:

- reread any parts they do not understand the first time they read or want to make sure they remember.
- identify the author's purpose for writing the text.

Read Purposefully

Have children record the clues and author's purpose on an Author's Purpose chart. After reading, guide children to participate in a group discussion about the selection they read. Guide children to:

- share their charts.
- tell how they could tell that the selection was informational text.
- share facts they learned from their selection.

On Level

Nonfiction
Helping Me, Helping You!
by Cynthia Moloney

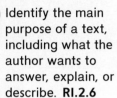
PAIRED READ Poetry

Lexile 400

OBJECTIVES

 Identify the main purpose of a text, including what the author wants to answer, explain, or describe. **RI.2.6**

Leveled Reader:
Helping Me, Helping You!

Go Digital

Helping Me, Helping You!

Graphic Organizer

Before Reading

Preview and Predict

Have children turn to the title page. Read the title and the author's name and have children repeat. Preview the selection's photographs. Prompt children to predict what the selection might be about.

Review Genre: Informational Text/Nonfiction

Have children recall that informational text gives facts and information about real people, places, things, or events.

ESSENTIAL QUESTION

Remind children of the Essential Question: *Who helps you?* Set a purpose for reading: *Let's read to find out about family and neighborhood helpers.*

Remind children that as they read a selection, they can ask questions about what they do not understand or want to know more about.

Retell

During Reading

Guided Comprehension

As children whisper read *Helping Me, Helping You!,* monitor and provide guidance, correcting blending and modeling the key strategies and skills.

Strategy: Reread

Remind children that sometimes they may misread a word or miss an important point. They can reread the passage or an earlier part to be sure they understand. Model using the strategy on page 2. Say: *I read this page but I still don't understand who the people on a team are.* Reread the page. *What did the author mean by "the people on your team"?*

Skill: Author's Purpose

Remind children that the author's purpose is the reason why an author writes a text, such as to entertain, to inform, or to persuade. As you read, ask: *What clues tell us about the author's purpose?* Display an Author's Purpose chart for children to copy.

Model recording answers for children. Have children copy the answers into their own charts.

Think Aloud As I read, I will look for clues to help me understand the author's purpose. On page 3, I see that the author gives information about what the mother does. I'll write this clue in my chart. I'll look to see if other details also give information.

Prompt children to fill in their charts as they read.

After Reading

Respond to Reading

Have children complete the Respond to Reading on page 12.

Retell

Have children take turns retelling the selection, using the **Retelling Cards** as a guide. Help children make a connection: *Who helps you in your life? What does this helper do for you?*

Model Fluency

Read the sentences one at a time. Have children chorally repeat. Point out to children how your voice goes up when reading questions.

Apply Have partners practice reading. Provide feedback as needed.

PAIRED READ ...

"Fire!"

Make Connections: Write About It 🖊 *Analytical Writing*

Before reading, ask children to note that the genre of this text is poetry. Then discuss the Compare Texts direction. After reading, ask children to make connections between the information they learned from "Fire!" and *Helping Me, Helping You!*

Leveled Reader

Literature Circles

Lead children in conducting a literature circle using the Thinkmark questions to guide the discussion. You may wish to discuss what children have learned about people who help them from both selections in the Leveled Reader.

Level Up

Level-up lessons available online.

IF children can read *Helping Me, Helping You!* `On Level` with fluency and correctly answer the Respond to Reading questions,

THEN tell children that they will read a more detailed version of this selection.

• Use pages 2–4 of *Helping Me, Helping You!* `Beyond Level` to model using Teaching Poster 38 to list clues to the author's purpose.

• Have children read the selection, checking their comprehension by using the graphic organizer.

🌐 **FOCUS ON SOCIAL STUDIES**

Children can extend their knowledge of the people who help them by completing the social studies activity on page 16.

Phonics

OBJECTIVES

Decode regularly spelled one-syllable words. **RF.1.3b**

I Do

Display **Word-Building Cards** *m, al, l. These are letters* m, a, l, l. *They stand for* /m/ /ô/ *and* /l/. *I will blend* /m/ /ô/ *and* /l/ *together:* /môôl/, mall. *The word is* mall.

We Do

Now let's do one together. Make the word *mall* using Word-Building Cards. Place the letter *s* at the end of *mall. Let's blend:* /m/ /ô/ /l/ /z /, /môôlz/; malls. *Now there is a new word,* malls.

I am going to change the letter m *to* c. *Let's blend and read the new word:* /k/ /ô/ /l/ /z/, /kôôlz/; calls. *The new word is* calls.

You Do

Have children build and blend the words: *call, fall, tall, talk, walk, chalk, bawl, brawl, shawl.*

Repeat with additional words with /ô/ spelled *a, aw, au, aug, al.*

Decodable Reader Have children read "Paul's Paw," "Thank You Authors!," "Not Too Small," "My Baseball Coach," "A Walk With Mayor Moose," and "Teacher Talk" (pages 33–56).

Words to Know

OBJECTIVES

Recognize and read grade-appropriate irregularly spelled words. **RF.1.3g**

Review high-frequency words *brother, father, friend, love, mother, picture* and vocabulary words *accept* and *often*

I Do

Use the **Read/Spell/Write** routine to teach each high-frequency and vocabulary word. Use each word orally in a sentence.

We Do

Guide children to Read/Spell/Write each word using their **Response Boards**. Then work together to generate oral sentences using the words.

You Do

Have partners work together using the Read/Spell/Write routine with the high-frequency words *brother, father, friend, love, mother,* and *picture,* and the vocabulary words *accept* and *often.* Have partners write sentences about this week's stories. Each sentence must contain at least one high-frequency word or vocabulary word.

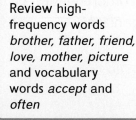

Comprehension

REVIEW AUTHOR'S PURPOSE

OBJECTIVES

Identify the main purpose of a text, including what the author wants to answer, explain, or describe. **RI.2.6**

 I Do Remind children that the author's purpose is the reason why the author wrote the text: to inform, entertain, or persuade. *When we read an informational text, we look for what the author wants readers to know. We pay attention to the facts in the selection and read to find out how the author feels about the subject.*

 We Do Read the first two pages of the Practice Book selection aloud. Pause to point out the different things coaches do. *We read that coaches help people learn to play a sport and they teach the rules. Why did the author write these facts? What does the author want readers to learn about?*

 You Do Guide children to read the rest of the Practice Book selection. Remind them to identify other facts the author gives. Then have partners decide whether the author wanted to entertain the reader, inform the reader about a topic, or persuade the reader to do something.

SELF-SELECTED READING

OBJECTIVES

With prompting and support, read informational texts appropriately complex for grade 1. **RI.1.10**

Apply the strategy and skill to read a text

Read Independently

Have children pick an informational selection for sustained silent reading. Remind them to:

- reread any parts that they do not understand the first time or want to remember.
- identify the author's purpose for writing the selection.

Read Purposefully

Have children record clues that tell them the author's purpose on an Author's Purpose chart. After completing the chart, guide partners to:

- share and compare their charts.
- tell what parts they reread and why.
- identify the parts of the selection that showed them that it was informational.

Beyond Level

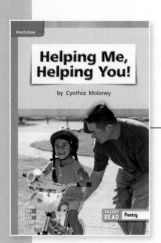

Lexile 540

OBJECTIVES

Identify the main purpose of a text, including what the author wants to answer, explain, or describe. **RI.2.6**

Leveled Reader:
Helping Me, Helping You!

Before Reading

Preview and Predict

Read the title and the author's name. Have children preview the title page and the photographs. Ask: *What do you think this selection will be about?*

Review Genre: Informational Text/Nonfiction

Have children recall that informational text gives facts and information about real people, places, things, or events. Prompt children to name key characteristics of informational text. Tell them to look for these characteristics as they read the Leveled Reader.

ESSENTIAL QUESTION

Remind children of the Essential Question: *Who helps you?* Set a purpose for reading: *Let's find out how family and neighborhood people help.*

During Reading

Guided Comprehension

Have children whisper read *Helping Me, Helping You!* Have them place self-stick notes next to difficult words. Remind children that when they come to an unfamiliar word, they can look for familiar spellings. They will need to break longer words into smaller chunks and sound out each part.

Monitor children's reading. Stop periodically and ask open-ended questions to facilitate rich discussion, such as, *What does the author want you to know about helpers in this part of the text?* Build on children's responses to develop deeper understanding of the text.

Strategy: Reread

Remind children that sometimes they may misread a word or miss an important point. *Remember, if you do not understand what is happening, you should go back and reread the page or a passage.*

Go Digital

Helping Me, Helping You!

Graphic Organizer

Skill: Author's Purpose

Remind children the author's purpose is the reason why an author wrote a text, such as to entertain, to inform, or to persuade. As you read, ask: *What are some clues that helped you identify the author's purpose?* Display an Author's Purpose chart for children to copy. Model how to record the information.

Think Aloud As I read, I look for the details the author gives. Then I think about what those details tell me about the reason the author wrote the text. I will add the clues to my chart.

Have children fill in their charts as they read.

After Reading

Respond to Reading

Have children complete the Respond to Reading on page 12.

Retell

Have children take turns retelling the selection. Help them make a personal connection by writing about a person who has helped them. *Tell who the person is and how he or she helped you.*

PAIRED READ ...

Leveled Reader

"Fire!"

Make Connections:
Write About It  *Analytical Writing*

Before reading "Fire!" have children preview the title page and prompt them to identify the genre. Discuss the Compare Texts direction. After reading, have children work with a partner to discuss the information they learned in "Fire!" and *Helping Me, Helping You!* Ask children to make connections by comparing and contrasting the helpers in each selection. Prompt children to discuss what helpers they learned about from both selections.

FOCUS ON SOCIAL STUDIES

Children can extend their knowledge about people who help them by completing the social studies activity on page 16.

Literature Circles

Lead children in conducting a literature circle using the Thinkmark questions to guide the discussion. You may wish to discuss what children have learned about different helpers from both selections in the Leveled Reader.

Gifted and Talented

SYNTHESIZE Challenge children to choose a kind of helper they are curious about or whose work they think might be interesting to do as a job. Encourage them to use ideas from the selection.

EXTEND Have them use facts they learned from the week or do additional research to find out more about this particular helper.

Vocabulary

ORAL VOCABULARY: CONTEXT CLUES

OBJECTIVES

Use sentence-level context as a clue to the meaning of a word or phrase. **L.1.4a**

 I Do Tell children that if they are not sure of what a word means, they should look at the other words in the sentence. Say: *A good story can inspire you to read more.* Discuss how the information in the sentence can help them figure out the meaning of *inspire.* Say: *If a story is good, it makes me want to read more, so* inspire *must mean "to make someone want to do something."*

 We Do *Let's look for context clues together.* Say: *I respect, or admire, people who help others who are in need.* Ask: *Which words in the sentence help you understand what the word* respect *means?*

 You Do Have partners make up oral sentences with the words *inspire* and *respect* that include strong context.

 Gifted and Talented **Extend** Have partners tell each other about a person they respect and explain why they do. Encourage them to use the words *respect* and *inspire.* Challenge partners to then share with the group what their partner said.

VOCABULARY WORDS: CONTEXT CLUES

OBJECTIVES

Use sentence-level context as a clue to the meaning of a word or phrase. **L.1.4a**

 I Do Remind children that they can use context clues, or other words in a sentence, to help them figure out the meaning of words they do not understand. Write and read aloud the sentence: *"The best artist will accept the prize for first place."* Explain how context clues help make the meaning of *accept* clear. *A person usually agrees to take a prize, so* accept *probably means "to agree to take."*

 We Do *Let's use context clues together.* Write: *I love peaches, so I eat them often.* Ask: *If you do something you like often, do you do it a lot or a little? How do the words in the sentence help you understand what* often *means?*

 You Do Have children work with a partner to come up with and write down two sentences, one using *accept* and one that uses *often.* Tell them to try to include context clues for the words.

Comprehension

REVIEW AUTHOR'S PURPOSE

OBJECTIVES

Identify the main purpose of a text, including what the author wants to answer, explain, or describe. **RI.2.6**

 I Do

Discuss with children how they can understand the author's purpose for writing a selection. *To understand the author's purpose, I look for clues that tell me what the author wants readers to know. I look at the key details to find out how the author feels about the subject.*

We Do

Guide children in reading the first two pages of the Practice Book selection aloud. Prompt them to discuss the information the author gives. *What is this selection about? How do you know? Does the author want to entertain, inform, or persuade readers about being a coach?*

You Do

Have children read the rest of the Practice Book selection independently. Remind them to use the clues to determine the author's purpose for writing the selection.

SELF-SELECTED READING

OBJECTIVES

With prompting and support, read informational texts appropriately complex for grade 1. **RI.1.10**

Apply the strategy and skill to read a text

Read Independently

Have children pick an informational selection for sustained silent reading. Remind them to reread any parts of the selection that they do not understand the first time or want to make sure they remember. Encourage children to focus on the author's purpose for writing the selection.

Read Purposefully

Have children record clues to the author's purpose in an Author's Purpose chart. After reading, guide children to:

- share their charts with a partner and why they think the author wrote the selection.
- record information about the selection and what they learned in a reading response journal.

 Gifted and Talented **Independent Study** Ask children to write a letter to the author of the book they read, telling him or her what they liked best about the book. Encourage children to include something they learned from their reading that they think is important.

English Language Learners

Reading/Writing Workshop

Shared Read:
All Kinds of Helpers

Go
Digital

All Kind of Helpers

Before Reading

Build Background

Read the Essential Question: *Who helps you?*

- Explain the meaning of the Essential Question: *When you help someone, you might make a job easier. You might do something that needs to be done. Or, you might make something better.*

- **Model an answer:** *Many people help me at school. The school secretary answers questions. The librarian helps me find books for our classroom. Our principal helps me order materials. I am grateful for everyone's help.*

- Ask children a question that ties the Essential Question to their own background knowledge. *Who helps you at home? Who helps you at school?* Ask partners to share their answers.

Graphic Organizer

During Reading

Interactive Question-Response

- Ask questions that help children understand the meaning of the text after each paragraph.

- Reinforce the meanings of key vocabulary by providing meanings embedded in the questions.

- Ask children questions that require them to use key vocabulary.

- Reinforce the comprehension strategies and skills of the week by modeling.

OBJECTIVES

(CCSS) Identify the main purpose of a text, including what the author wants to answer, explain, or describe. **RI.2.6**

All Kinds of Helpers

Pages 242–243

Point to the title. *Listen as I read the title of this nonfiction selection.* Point to each word as you read it, and then point to the word *Helpers. Helpers take care of others. They can do a job. They can make a job easier. Read the title with me:* All Kinds of Helpers.

Point to the photo. *Who are the helpers in this photo?* (coaches) *How does a coach help?* (teaches us how to play a sport; encourages us; keeps us safe when we are playing a sport)

Pages 244–245

Point to the photos on pages 244 and 245. *Who are the people in these photos?* (Mom, Dad, brothers) *Yes, they are a family. How are the people in the photos helping each other?* (making dinner; helping with homework) Point to the last sentence on page 245. *Listen as I read this sentence:* "His mother and father help him learn about the world." *Now reread that sentence with me. Moms and dads can help us know what to do. They can help us learn new things.*

 What are other ways families help each other?

Pages 246–247

Who do you see in this photo? (teacher) *What is she doing?* (teaching the children) *Let's read the last sentence on this page together:* A teacher helps you understand new ideas.

Now let's look at the photo on page 247. This man is a baseball coach. Say those words with me: baseball coach. *He is showing the team how to hold a baseball. Now listen as I read the last question:* "Who taught you how to play a sport?" *Can you answer the question?*

Explain and Model Phonics *Write these words:* talks, taught. *Say each word and have children repeat it. Circle* al *and* au. *Say: These letters stand for the /ô/ sound in these words.*

Pages 248–249

Look at the photo on page 248. This girl has a bad cold! Who will help her? (doctor and nurse)

Let's look at page 249. There are three different community helpers in the photos. Who are they? (bus driver; police officer; firefighter) *Listen to this sentence:* "Police officers and firefighters are always protecting you." *How do police officers help?* (They can help if you have a problem or if you are in danger.) *How do firefighters help?* (They put out fires.)

Explain and Model the Skill *This selection has lots of good information. The author's purpose is to give information about people who help us. What did the author tell us on this page?*

Explain and Model the Strategy *If something doesn't make sense, reread to help you understand. I'm not sure what the author means with* "Either way, people help you get back and forth safely." *Back and forth where? If I read the sentence before and look at the picture, I see the author is talking about getting to school.*

 Who helps you get to school?

Pages 250–251

Let's look at the photo on page 250. What are the people doing? (playing soccer) *Let's read the pages together to see who else helps out in a community.* (grown-ups; doctors; families; teachers) *People can help us in many different ways.*

Explain and Model High-Frequency Words
Point to the word *friend* and have children say it. *Let's say the letters in this word:* f, r, i, e, n, d. *Who are some of your friends?*

 What people have helped you today?

After Reading

Make Connections

- Review the Essential Question.

English Language Learners

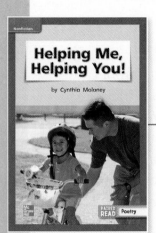

Lexile 290

OBJECTIVES

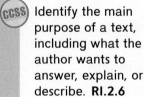
Identify the main purpose of a text, including what the author wants to answer, explain, or describe. **RI.2.6**

Leveled Reader:
Helping Me, Helping You!

Before Reading

Preview

Read the title. Ask: *What is the title? Say it again*. Repeat with the author's name. Preview the photographs. Have children describe the photos. Use simple language to tell about each page. Follow with questions, such as: *What does this helper do?*

ESSENTIAL QUESTION

Remind children of the Essential Question: *Who helps you?* Say: *Let's read to find out how people in our family and in the neighborhood help us.* Encourage children to ask for help when they do not understand a word or phrase.

During Reading

Interactive Question-Response

Pages 2–3 *Look at the photos on page 2. These people help us. Who do you see? We'll find out more about them as we read. Now look at the photo on page 3. Tell your partner how the girl's mother helps her.*

Pages 4–5 *What family members did we read about? Find the words* brother *and* father *and let's read them together:* brother, father. *What's another word that means "father"?* (dad, papa)

Pages 6–7 *Let's read these pages together. Who are the helpers in the photos?* (grandmother; dentist) *Talk with your partner about how they help.*

Pages 8–9 *What two helpers did we read about on these pages?* (librarian and sitter) *What do you think the author wanted you to learn in this part of the selection?* (Sample answer: the different ways a librarian and a sitter can help us)

Pages 10–11 *Let's reread the labels together as I point to what they show in the photos:* fire truck, hard hat. *How do these things help us?* (Sample answer: Fire trucks have ladders to rescue people in danger and hoses to put out a fire. Hard hats protect workers from falling debris.)

Now let's read the question together: Who helps you? *Tell your partner about the people who help you.*

Helping Me, Helping You!

Graphic Organizer

Retell

Go Digital

After Reading

Respond to Reading

Revisit the Essential Question. Ask children to work with partners to fill in the graphic organizer and answer the questions on page 12. Pair children with peers of varying language abilities.

Retell

Model retelling using the **Retelling Card** prompts. Say: *Look at the photographs. Use details to help you retell the selection.* Help children make personal connections by asking, *Who are people in your family who help you? Who are people in your neighborhood who help you?*

Intonation Fluency: Questions

Read the pages in the book, one at a time. Help children echo read the pages expressively and with appropriate phrasing. Remind them to make their voice go up at the end of a question.

Apply Have children practice reading with partners. Pair children with peers of varying language abilities. Provide feedback as needed.

PAIRED READ ...

Leveled Reader

"Fire!"

Make Connections: Write About It *Analytical Writing*

Before reading, tell children to note that this text is poetry. Then discuss the Compare Texts direction.

After reading, ask children to make connections between the information they learned from "Fire!" and *Helping Me, Helping You!* Prompt children by providing sentence frames: ____ *and* ____ *help me. They* ____.

FOCUS ON SOCIAL STUDIES

Children can extend their knowledge of people who help them by completing the social studies activity on page 16.

Literature Circles

Lead children in conducting a literature circle using the Thinkmark questions to guide the discussion. You may wish to discuss what children have learned about different ways people help us from both selections in the Leveled Reader.

Level Up

Level-up lessons available online.

IF children can read *Helping Me, Helping You!* ELL Level with fluency and correctly answer the Respond to Reading questions,

THEN tell children that they will read a more detailed version of this selection.

• Use pages 2–3 of *Helping Me, Helping You!* On Level to model using Teaching Poster 38 to list clues to the author's purpose.

• Have children read the selection, checking their comprehension by using the graphic organizer.

Vocabulary

PRETEACH ORAL VOCABULARY

CCSS

OBJECTIVES

Produce complete sentences when appropriate to task and situation. **SL.1.6**

LANGUAGE OBJECTIVE

Use oral vocabulary words

 I Do Display images from the **Visual Vocabulary Cards** one at a time to review the Oral Vocabulary words *inspire* and *respect.*

 We Do Display the image again and explain how it illustrates or demonstrates the word. Model using sentences to describe the image.

 You Do Display the word again. Have partners talk about how the picture shows the word.

Beginning	Intermediate	Advanced/High
Say the word and have children point to the image. Give sentence starters for them to repeat and complete: *I respect ____. I admire ____.*	Have children use the words *inspire* and *respect* in complete sentences to tell about each image.	Have partners use the words in questions to ask and answer.

PRETEACH VOCABULARY

CCSS

OBJECTIVES

Identify real-life connections between words and their use (e.g., note places at home that are *cozy*). **L.1.5c**

LANGUAGE OBJECTIVE

Use vocabulary words

 I Do Display images from the **ELL Visual Vocabulary Cards** one at a time to review the vocabulary words *knit* and *helpers* and follow the routine. Say the word and have children repeat it. Define the word in English.

 We Do Display the image again and explain how it illustrates or demonstrates the word. Model using sentences to describe the image.

 You Do Display the word again and have children say the word, then spell it. Provide opportunities for children to use the words in speaking and writing. Provide sentence starters.

Beginning	Intermediate	Advanced/High
Help children find examples of or act out each word.	Spell each word and have children identify the word you spelled, then spell it for you.	Have children use their own words to tell what each word means.

Words to Know

REVIEW WORDS

OBJECTIVES

 Recognize and read grade-appropriate irregularly spelled words. **RF.1.3g**

LANGUAGE OBJECTIVE

Use high-frequency words *brother, father, friend, love, mother, picture,* and vocabulary words *accept, often*

 I Do Display the **High-Frequency Word** and **Vocabulary Cards** for *brother, father, friend, love, mother, picture,* and *accept* and *often*. Read each word. Use the **Read/Spell/Write routine** to teach each word. Have children write the words on their **Response Boards**.

 We Do Write sentence frames on separate lines. Track the print as you guide children to read and complete the sentences: *(1) My brother wants to ____. (2) Our father is ____. (3) Does your friend ____? (4) I love to ____! (5) My mother makes ____. (6) The picture is ____. (7) I accept your ____. (8) We often go to ____.*

 You Do Display the High-Frequency Word Cards from the previous weeks. Display one card at a time as children chorally read the word. Mix and repeat. Note words children need to review. Repeat with Vocabulary words.

Beginning	Intermediate	Advanced/High
Have children echo read each word. Ask yes/no questions for children to answer in complete sentences: *Is a father a man? Yes, a father is a man.*	Have children complete sentences with correct word choices, then repeat the sentence: *My ____ (friend, picture) and I play together.*	Have children write sentences using each other words. Encourage them to share their sentences with the group.

RETEACH HIGH-FREQUENCY WORDS

OBJECTIVES

 Recognize and read grade-appropriate irregularly spelled words. **RF.1.3g**

LANGUAGE OBJECTIVE

Use high-frequency words

 I Do Display each Visual Vocabulary Card and say the word aloud. Define the word in English, then in Spanish if appropriate, identifying any cognates.

 We Do Point to the image and explain how it illustrates the word. Have children repeat the word. Engage children in structured partner-talk about the image as prompted on the back of the card. Ask children to chorally say the word three times.

 You Do Display each visual card in random order, hiding the word. Have children identify and define the word in their own words.

Beginning	Intermediate	Advanced/High
Have children echo read each word while pointing to its Visual Vocabulary card.	Have children say an original oral sentence for each high-frequency word.	Challenge children to write a sentence for each high-frequency word.

Writing/Spelling

WRITING TRAIT: VOICE

OBJECTIVES

CCSS With guidance and support from adults, focus on a topic, respond to questions and suggestions from peers, and add details to strengthen writing as needed. **W.1.5**

LANGUAGE OBJECTIVE

Use your own voice to write a sentence

 I Do Explain that writers use their own voice to show their feelings in their writing. Write and read: *Our team won the game. Our team is good. Hooray for our team! We are the champs!* Point out how the writer's voice comes through in the second pair of sentences.

 We Do Read page 245 of *All Kinds of Helpers. How do you think the author feels about helpers? How do you know?* Explain that a writer often chooses to include certain information and uses words to show how he or she feels about a topic. Help children identify what information and words tell how the author feels.

 You Do Have children write a sentence about helping someone. Remind them to use their own voice: *Use words that show how you feel.*

Beginning	Intermediate	Advanced/High
Have children add voice to simple oral sentences: *I like/don't like dogs.*	Have children use voice to complete simple written sentences: *Dogs are ____.*	Encourage children to emphasize their voice to tell about classroom items.

WORDS WITH VARIANT VOWEL /ô/

OBJECTIVES

CCSS Use conventional spelling for words with common spelling pattern and for frequently occurring irregular words. **L.1.2d**

LANGUAGE OBJECTIVE

Spell words with /ô/

 I Do Read the first Spelling Word, *haul*, on page T92. Segment the word into sounds and attach a spelling to each sound. Point out /ô/ spelled *au*. Read aloud, segment, and spell the remaining words and have children repeat.

 We Do Say a sentence for *haul*. Then, read *haul* slowly and have children repeat. Have them write the word. Repeat the process for the remaining words.

 You Do Display the words. Have children work with a partner to check their spelling lists. Have children correct misspelled words on their list.

Beginning	Intermediate	Advanced/High
Help children copy the words with correct spelling and say the word.	After children have corrected their words, have pairs quiz each other.	Challenge children to think of other words that have /ô/ spelled *aw* or *au*.

Grammar

POSSESSIVE PRONOUNS

OBJECTIVES

Use personal, possessive, and indefinite pronouns. **L.1.1d**

Language Transfers Handbook

TRANSFER SKILLS

Cantonese and Hmong speakers may omit the final *n* sound. This may cause confusion between *my* and *mine*. For example: *This desk is my*. Provide additional practice by having children hold up objects that belong to them and complete each sentence by naming the object: *This is my ____. This ____ is mine.*

 Review that a possessive pronoun shows who or what has or owns something. Some possessive pronouns take the place of a noun, while others can stand alone.

 Write the following sentences on the board. *This is mother's hat.* Underline mother's. Say: *We can use a possessive pronoun to take the place of* mother's *or we can use a possessive pronoun that will stand alone.* Write and read: *This is <u>her</u> hat. This hat is <u>hers</u>.*

Write the words and sentences below on the board. Have children echo read the sentence and guide them to choose the correct possessive pronoun to replace the underlined noun in each. Have them reread the sentence with the correct possessive pronoun.

theirs   **his**   **her**

<u>Mike's</u> friend needs help.

<u>Ann's</u> bike is stuck in the mud.

The other bikes are <u>their bikes.</u>

 Write the following sentences on the board.

Paul's dad taught him to ride a bike. ____ dad is helpful.

My friends lent me some books. The books are ____.

Pair children and have them complete each sentence by providing possessive pronouns. Circulate, listen in, and take note of each child's language use and proficiency.

Beginning	Intermediate	Advanced/High
Ask yes/no questions using possessive pronouns. Have children answer in complete sentences.	Ask questions using possessive pronouns. Have children answer in complete sentences.	Have children create sentences using possessive pronouns to describe characters in selection illustrations.

PROGRESS MONITORING

Unit 6 Week 2 Formal Assessment	Standards Covered	Component for Assessment
Comprehension Author's Purpose	RI.2.6	• *Selection Test* • *Weekly Assessment*
Vocabulary Strategy Antonyms	L.4.5c	• *Selection Test* • *Weekly Assessment*
Phonics Variant Vowel /ô/ (aw, au, a, augh, al, ough)	RF.1.3	*Weekly Assessment*
Structural Analysis Vowel-Team Syllables	RF.1.3d, RF.1.3e	*Weekly Assessment*
High-Frequency Words *brother, father, friend, love, mother, picture*	RF.1.3g	*Weekly Assessment*
Writing Writing About Text	RI.2.6	*Weekly Assessment*
Unit 6 Week 2 Informal Assessment		
Research/Listening/Collaborating	SL.1.1c, SL.1.2, SL.1.3	• *RWW* • *Teacher's Edition*
Oral Reading Fluency (ORF) **Fluency Goal:** 13-33 words correct per minute (WCPM) **Accuracy Rate Goal:** 95% or higher	RF.1.4a. RF.1.4b, RF.1.4c	*Fluency Assessment*

Using Assessment Results

Weekly Assessment Skills	If . . .	Then . . .
COMPREHENSION	Children answer 0–3 multiple-choice items correctly . . .	. . . assign Lessons 82–84 on Author's Purpose from the *Tier 2 Comprehension Intervention online PDFs*.
VOCABULARY	Children answer 0–2 multiple-choice items correctly . . .	. . . assign Lesson 116 on Antonyms from the *Tier 2 Vocabulary Intervention online PDFs*.
PHONICS/ STRUCTURAL ANALYSIS/HFW	Children answer 0–6 multiple-choice items correctly . . .	. . . assign Lesson 98 on Variant Vowel /ô/ spelled *aw, au, a, augh, al, ough* and Lesson 110 on Vowel Team Syllables from the *Tier 2 Phonics/Word Study Intervention online PDFs*.
WRITING	Children score less than "2" on the constructed response . . .	. . . reteach necessary skills using Section 13 on Write About Reading from the *Tier 2 Comprehension Intervention online PDFs*.
FLUENCY	Children have a WCPM score of 13 . . .	. . . assign a lesson from Section 1, 9, or 10 of the *Tier 2 Fluency Intervention online PDFs*.
	Children have a WCPM score of 0–12 . . .	. . . assign a lesson from Sections 2–8 of the *Tier 2 Fluency Intervention online PDFs.*

Using Weekly Data

Check your data Dashboard to verify assessment results and guide grouping decisions.

Response to Intervention

Use the children's assessment results to assist you in identifying children who will benefit from focused intervention.

Data-Driven Recommendations

Use the appropriate sections of the *Placement and Diagnostic Assessment* to designate children requiring:

TIER 2 Intervention Online PDFs   **TIER 3** WonderWorks Intervention Program

WEEKLY OVERVIEW

Build Knowledge
Weather Together

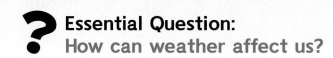

? Essential Question:
How can weather affect us?

Teach and Model
Close Reading and Writing

Big Book and Little Book

Reading Writing Workshop

Wrapped in Ice, 262–271
Genre Realistic Fiction **Lexile** 320

Interactive Read Aloud

"Paul Bunyan and the Popcorn Blizzard"
Genre Folktale

Practice and Apply
Close Reading and Writing

Literature Anthology

Rain School, 326–355
Genre Realistic Fiction **Lexile** 440

Paired Read

"Rainy Weather," 358–361
Genre Nonfiction **Lexile** 470

Differentiated Texts

APPROACHING
Lexile 390

ON LEVEL
Lexile 460

BEYOND
Lexile 420

ELL
Lexile 370

Leveled Readers

Extended Complex Texts

Frog and Toad Together
Genre Fiction
Lexile 330

Ling & Ting—Nat Exactly the Same!
Genre Fiction
Lexile 390

Classroom Library

FROG AND TOAD TOGETHER. Used by permission of HarperCollins Publishers.

Student Outcomes

Close Reading of Complex Text

- Cite relevant evidence from text
- Describe plot events: cause and effect
- Retell the text

RL.1.3, RL.1.2

Writing

Write to Sources

- Draw evidence from fiction text
- Write informative text
- Conduct short research on the weather

W.1.2, W.1.7

Speaking and Listening

- Engage in collaborative conversation about weather
- Retell and discuss *Rain School*
- Present information on how the weather can affect us

SL.1.1c, SL.1.2, SL.1.3

Content Knowledge

- Explore how weather affects the ways people live

Language Development

Conventions

- Use special pronouns

Vocabulary Acquisition

- Develop oral vocabulary

predict	cycle	creative
frigid	scorching	

- Acquire and use academic vocabulary

country	gathers

- Use context clues to understand similes

L.1.1d, L.1.4, L.4.5a, L.1.6

Foundational Skills

Phonics/Word Study/Spelling

- Silent letters *wr, kn, gn*
- Compound words
- gnat, gnu, know, knife, been, write, wrong, cause, dawn, their

High-Frequency Words

been	children	month	question
their	year		

Fluency

- Intonation

Decodable Text

- Apply foundational skills in connected text

RF.1.3, RF.1.3e, RF.1.3g, RF.1.4a, RF.1.4b, RF.1.4c

Professional Development

- See lessons in action in real classrooms.
- Get expert advice on instructional practices.
- Collaborate with other teachers.
- Access PLC Resources

Go Digital! www.connected.mcgraw-hill.com.

INSTRUCTIONAL PATH

1 ## Talk About Weather

Guide children in collaborative conversations.

Discuss the essential question: *How can weather affect us?*

Develop academic language.

Listen to "Paul Bunyan and the Popcorn Blizzard" to visualize the story.

2 ## Read *Wrapped in Ice*

Apply foundational skills in connected text. Model close reading.

Read

Wrapped in Ice to learn how the snow affects Kim's neighborhood, citing text evidence to answer text-dependent questions.

Reread

Wrapped in Ice to analyze text, craft, and structure, citing text evidence.

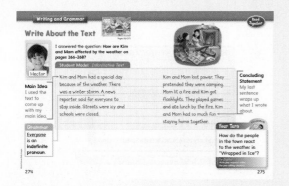

3 ## Write About *Wrapped in Ice*

Model writing to a source.

Analyze a short response student model.

Use text evidence from close reading to write to a source.

4 Read and Write About *Rain School*

Practice and apply close reading of the anchor text.

Read

Rain School to learn about how weather affects a school in Chad, Africa.

Reread

Rain School and use text evidence to understand how the author uses text, craft, and structure to develop a deeper understanding of the story.

Integrate

Information about how rain can be both helpful and harmful.

Write to a Source, citing text evidence to explain what children in *Rain School* learn from their first lesson.

5 Independent Partner Work

Gradual release of support to independent work

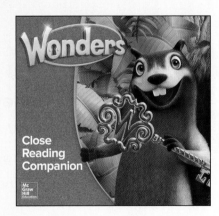

- Text-Dependent Questions
- Scaffolded Partner Work
- Talk with a Partner
- Cite Text Evidence
- Complete a sentence frame.
- Guided Text Annotation

6 Integrate Knowledge and Ideas

Connect Texts

Text to Text Discuss how each of the texts answers the question: How can weather affect us?

Text to Fine Art Compare information about weather in the texts read with the piece of fine art.

Conduct a Short Research Project

Create an illustrated mini tornado.

DEVELOPING READERS AND WRITERS

Write to Sources: Informative

Day 1 and Day 2

Shared Writing

• Write about *Wrapped in Ice*, p. T174

Interactive Writing

• Analyze a student model, p. T184

• Write about *Wrapped in Ice*, p. T185

• Find Text Evidence

• Apply Writing Trait: Voice, p. T185

• Apply Grammar Skill: Special Pronouns, p. T185

Day 3, Day 4 and Day 5

Independent Writing

• Write about *Rain School*, p. T192

• Provide scaffolded instruction to meet student needs, p. T192

• Find Text Evidence, p. T192

• Apply Writing Trait: Voice, T192

• Prewrite and Draft, p. T192

• Revise and Edit, p. T198

• Final Draft, p. T198

• Present, Evaluate, and Publish, p. T204

Grammar

Indefinite Pronouns

- Use indefinite pronouns to tell about what is happening, pp, T175, T185, T193, T199, T205

- Apply grammar to writing, pp. T175, T192, T198, T205

Mechanics: Commas in Dates and Letters

- Use commas in dates and letters, pp. T194, T199, T205

Online PDFs

Grammar Practice, pp. 136–140

Online Grammar Games

Spelling

Words with Silent Letters *wr, kn, gn*

- Spell words with silent letters *wr, kn, gn*

Online PDFs

Phonics/Spelling blms
pp. 136–140

Online Spelling Games

SUGGESTED LESSON PLAN

READING		DAY 1	DAY 2
Teach, Model and Apply	**Core**	**Build Background** Weather Together, T164–T165 **Oral Vocabulary** *predict, cycle,* T164 **Word Work** T168–T171 • Fluency: Sound-Spellings • Phonemic Awareness: Phoneme Categorization • Phonics/Spelling: Introduce Silent Letters *wr, kn, gn* • High-Frequency Words: *been, children, month, question, their, year* • Vocabulary: *country, gathers* **Shared Read** *Wrapped in Ice,* T172–T173	**Oral Language** Weather Together, T176 **Oral Vocabulary** *creative, frigid, scorching, cycle, predict,* T176 **Word Work** T178–T181 • Phonemic Awareness: Phoneme Segmentation • Structural Analysis: Compound Words • Vocabulary: *country, gathers* **Shared Read** *Wrapped In Ice,* T182–T183 • Genre: Realistic Fiction, T182 • Skill: Plot/Cause and Effect, T183
	Options	**Listening Comprehension** "Paul Bunyan and the Popcorn Blizzard," T166–T167	**Listening Comprehension** "Paul Bunyan and the Popcorn Blizzard," T177 **Word Work** T178–T181 • Phonics/Spelling: Review Silent Letters *wr, kn, gn* • High-Frequency Words

LANGUAGE ARTS			
Writing **Grammar**	**Core**	**Shared Writing** T174 **Grammar** Special Pronouns, T175	**Interactive Writing** T184 **Grammar** Special Pronouns, T185
	Options		

DIFFERENTIATED INSTRUCTION
Use your data dashboard to determine each student's needs. Then select instructional supports options throughout the week.

APPROACHING LEVEL

Leveled Reader
Snow Day, T208–T209
"A Mountain of Snow," T209
Literature Circles, T209

Phonemic Awareness:
Phoneme Categorization, T210 **TIER 2**
Phoneme Segmentation, T210 **TIER 2**
Phoneme Substitution, T211

Phonics
Connect to Silent Letters, T212 **TIER 2**
Blend Words with Silent Letters, T212 **TIER 2**
Build Words with Silent Letters, *wr, kn, gn,* T213
Build Fluency with Phonics, T213

Structural Analysis
Review Compound Words, T214

Words to Know
Review, T215
Review Vocabulary Words, T215 **TIER 2**

Comprehension
Read for Fluency, T216
Identify Plot, T216 **TIER 2**
Review Plot: Cause and Effect, T217
Self-Selected Reading, T217

ON LEVEL

Leveled Reader
Heat Wave, T218–T219
"Stay Safe When It's Hot," T219
Literature Circles, T219

Phonics
Build Words with Silent Letters *wr, kn, gn,* T220

CUSTOMIZE YOUR OWN LESSON PLANS

www.connected.mcgraw-hill.com

WEEK 3

DAY 3	DAY 4	DAY 5
Fluency Intonation, T187 **Word Work** T188–T191 • Phonemic Awareness: Phoneme Substitution • Phonics/Spelling: Blend Words with Silent Letters *wr, kn, gn* • Vocabulary Strategy: Similes **Close Reading** *Rain School,* T191A–T191R	**Extend the Concept** T194–T195 • Text Feature: Headings, T195 • Close Reading: "Rainy Weather," T195A–T195B **Word Work** T196–T197 • Phonemic Awareness: Phoneme Categorization • Structural Analysis: Compound Words **Integrate Ideas** • Research and Inquiry, T200–T201	**Word Work** T202–T203 • Phonemic Awareness: Phoneme Segmentation/ Substitution • Phonics/Spelling: Blend and Build Words with Silent Letters *wr, kn, gn* • Structural Analysis: Compound Words • High-Frequency Words • Vocabulary: *country, gathers* **Integrate Ideas** • Text Connections, T206–T207
Oral Language Weather Together, T186 **Word Work** T188–T191 • Structural Analysis: Compound Words • High-Frequency Words	**Word Work** T196–T197 • Fluency: Sound-Spellings • Phonics/Spelling: Build Words with Silent Letters *wr, kn, gn* • High-Frequency Words • Vocabulary: *country, gathers* **Close Reading** *Rain School,* T191A–T191R	**Word Work** T202–T203 • Fluency: Intonation **Integrate Ideas** • Research and Inquiry, T206 • Speaking and Listening, T207
Independent Writing T192 **Grammar** Mechanics: Commas in Dates and Letters, T193	**Independent Writing** T198 **Grammar** Special Pronouns, T199	**Independent Writing** T204 **Grammar** Special Pronouns, T205
Grammar Special Pronouns, T193	**Grammar** Mechanics: Commas in Dates and Letters, T199	**Grammar** Mechanics: Commas in Dates and Letters, T205

BEYOND LEVEL

Words to Know
Review Words, T220

Comprehension
Review Plot/Cause and Effect, T221
Self-Selected Reading, T221

Leveled Reader
Rainy Fun Day, T222–T223
"Let's Stay Dry!," T223
Literature Circles, T223

Vocabulary
Multiple-Meaning Words, T224

Comprehension
Review Plot: Cause and Effect, T225
Self-Selected Reading, T225

 Gifted and Talented

ENGLISH LANGUAGE LEARNERS

Shared Read
Wrapped In Ice, T226–T227

Leveled Reader
Heat Wave, T228–T229
"Stay Safe When It's Hot," T229
Literature Circles, T229

Vocabulary
Preteach Oral Vocabulary, T230
Preteach ELL Vocabulary, T230

Words to Know
Review Words, T231
Reteach High-Frequency Words, T231

Writing/Spelling
Writing Trait: Idea, T232
Silent Letters *wr, kn, gn,* T232

Grammar
Special Pronouns, T233

DIFFERENTIATE TO ACCELERATE

 Scaffold to **A**ccess **C**omplex **T**ext

IF ➤ the text complexity of a particular selection is too difficult for children

THEN ➤ see the references noted in the chart below for scaffolded instruction to help children Access Complex Text.

Reader and Task

TEXT COMPLEXITY

Reading/Writing Workshop	Literature Anthology	Leveled Readers	Classroom Library

Quantitative

Wrapped in Ice **Lexile** 320	*Rain School* **Lexile** 440 "Rainy Weather" **Lexile** 470	**Approaching Level** **Lexile** 390 **Beyond Level** **Lexile** 420	**On Level** **Lexile** 460 **ELL** **Lexile** 370	*Library Lion* **Lexile** 470 *Ling & Ting: Not Exactly the Same!* **Lexile** 390

Qualitative

What Makes the Text Complex?	What Makes the Text Complex?	What Makes the Text Complex?	What Makes the Text Complex?
Foundational Skills • Decoding with silent letters *wr, kn, gn,* T168–T169 • Reading compound words, T179 • Identifying high-frequency words, T170–T171 *See Scaffolded Instruction in Teacher's Edition, T168–T169, T170–T171, and T179.*	• Prior Knowledge, T191B, T191F, T191L **ACT** *See Scaffolded Instruction in Teacher's Edition, T191B, T191F, and T191L.*	**Foundational Skills** • Decoding with silent letters *wr, kn, gn* • Reading compound words • Identifying high-frequency words *been children month question their year* *See Level Up lessons online for Leveled Readers.*	• Purpose • Specific Vocabulary • Prior Knowledge • Sentence Structure • Organization • Connection of Ideas • Genre **ACT** *See Scaffolded Instruction in Teacher's Edition, T413–T415.*

Reader and Task

The Introduce the Concept lesson on pages T164–T165 will help determine the reader's knowledge and engagement in the weekly concept. See pages T172–T173, T182–T183, T200-T201 and T206-T207 for questions and tasks for this text.	**The** Introduce the Concept lesson on pages T164–T165 will help determine the reader's knowledge and engagement in the weekly concept. See pages T191A–T191R, T195A–T195B, T200-T201 and T206-T207 for questions and tasks for this text.	**The** Introduce the Concept lesson on pages T164–T165 will help determine the reader's knowledge and engagement in the weekly concept. See pages T208-T209, T218-T219, T222-T223, T228-T229, T200-T201 and T206-T207 for questions and tasks for this text.	**The** Introduce the Concept lesson on pages T164–T165 will help determine the reader's knowledge and engagement in the weekly concept. See pages T413–T415 for questions and tasks for this text.

Monitor and *Differentiate*

✓ Quick Check

To differentiate instruction, use the Quick Checks to assess students' needs and select the appropriate small group instruction focus.

Comprehension Strategy Visualize, T167

Comprehension Skill Plot: Cause and Effect, T183

Phonics Silent Letters: *wr, kn, gn,* T171, T181, T191, T197, T203

High-Frequency Words and Vocabulary T171, T181, T191, T197, T203

If No →

| Approaching Level | Reteach T208–T217 |
| ELL | Develop T226–T233 |

If Yes →

| On Level | Review T218–T221 |
| Beyond Level | Extend T222–T225 |

Using Weekly Data

Check your data Dashboard to verify assessment results and guide grouping decisions.

Level Up with Leveled Readers

 IF children can read their leveled text fluently and answer comprehension questions

THEN work with the next level up to accelerate children's reading with more complex text.

T219

Beyond

On Level

Approaching T209   T229   ELL

ENGLISH LANGUAGE LEARNERS

Small Group Instruction

Use the ELL small group lessons in the *Wonders* Teacher's Edition to provide focused instruction.

Language Development
Vocabulary preteaching, oral vocabulary preteaching, high-frequency word review and reteach, pp. T230–T231

Close Reading
Interactive Question-Response routines for scaffolded text-dependent questioning for reading and rereading the Shared Read and Leveled Reader, pp. T226–T229

Writing
Focus on the writing trait, grammar, and spelling, pp. T232–T233

Additional ELL Support

Use Wonders for English Learners for ELD instruction that connects to the core.

Language Development
My Language Book for ample opportunities for discussions and scaffolded language support

Close Reading
Guided support for the Shared Read, Big Books, and Interactive Read Alouds. Differentiated texts about the weekly concept

Writing
Guided support in Interactive and Independent Writing and writing to sources

Wonders for ELs Teacher Edition and My Language Book

Materials

Reading/Writing Workshop
VOLUME 4

Reading/Writing Workshop Big Book
UNIT 6

Visual Vocabulary Cards
creative
cycle
frigid
predict
scorching

High-Frequency Word Cards
been   question
children their
month   year

Vocabulary Cards
country
gathers

Teaching Poster

Rr

rose

Sound-Spelling Cards

a b c
Word-Building Cards

Think Aloud Clouds

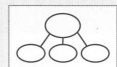
Interactive Read-Aloud Cards

(→) # Introduce the Concept

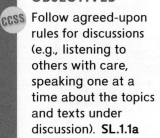
Reading/Writing Workshop Big Book

OBJECTIVES

(CCSS) Follow agreed-upon rules for discussions (e.g., listening to others with care, speaking one at a time about the topics and texts under discussion). **SL.1.1a**

- Build background knowledge
- Discuss the Essential Question

ACADEMIC LANGUAGE
weather, affect

MINILESSON
5 Mins

Build Background

ESSENTIAL QUESTION

How can weather affect us?

Tell children that this week they will be talking and reading about different kinds of weather and how it affects our lives.

Oral Vocabulary Words

Tell children that you will share some words that they can use as they discuss the weather and its effects. Use the Define/Example/Ask routine to introduce the oral vocabulary words **cycle** and **predict**.

Visual Vocabulary Cards

Oral Vocabulary Routine

<u>Define:</u> A **cycle** is a series of events that repeats in the same order.

<u>Example:</u> A butterfly begins its life cycle as a caterpillar.

<u>Ask:</u> What is the cycle of weather over a year?

<u>Define:</u> When you **predict**, you use clues to guess what will happen in the future.

<u>Example:</u> When Ken reads a story, he predicts what will happen next.

<u>Ask:</u> What do you predict will happen when you go home today?

Discuss the theme of "Weather Together." Have children tell how weather affects them. *What do you like to do when the weather is sunny and warm? What do you like to do when the weather is rainy? What can't you do when the weather is rainy?*

Go Digital

Weather Together

Video

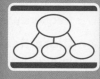
school
Visual Glossary

Graphic Organizer

READING/WRITING WORKSHOP, pp. 256–257

Talk About It: Weather Together

Guide children to discuss the weather in the photo.

- How does the weather affect the people in this photograph?

- How does the weather affect the cars? What other effects could it have?

Use Teaching Poster 40 and prompt children to complete the Word Web by sharing words to describe how the weather affects everyone in the photograph.

Have children look at page 257 of their Reading/Writing Workshop and do the Talk About It activity with a partner.

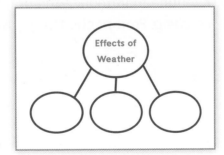

Teaching Poster

Collaborative Conversations

Take Turns Talking As children engage in partner, small-group, and whole-group discussions, encourage them to:

- take turns talking and not speak over others.

- raise their hand if they want to speak.

- ask others to share their ideas and opinions.

INTRODUCE THE CONCEPT **T165**

→ Listening Comprehension

Read the Interactive Read Aloud

OBJECTIVES

CCSS Participate in collaborative conversations with diverse partners about grade 1 topics and texts with peers and adults in small and larger groups. **SL.1.1**

• Develop concept understanding

• Develop reading strategy visualize

ACADEMIC LANGUAGE

• *tall tale, visualize, events, characters*

• Cognate: *visualizar*

Connect to Concept: Weather Together

Tell children that they will now read about an unusual snowstorm. Ask: *What do you do in a snowstorm?*

Focus on Oral Vocabulary

Review the oral vocabulary words *cycle* and *predict*. Use the Define/Example/Ask routine to introduce the oral vocabulary words *creative, frigid,* and *scorching*. Prompt children to use the words as they discuss weather.

"Paul Bunyan and the Popcorn Blizzard"

Oral Vocabulary Routine

<u>Define:</u> When you are **creative**, you use your imagination to make something new and different.

<u>Example:</u> Greg is very creative; he paints and writes stories.

<u>Ask:</u> What are some ways you like to be creative?

<u>Define:</u> **Frigid** means "very, very cold."

<u>Example:</u> We don't swim in the river in the winter because the water is frigid.

<u>Ask:</u> What do we wear when the weather is frigid?

<u>Define:</u> **Scorching** means "very, very hot."

<u>Example:</u> The puddle dried up under the scorching sun.

<u>Ask:</u> What do we wear when the weather is scorching?

Visual Vocabulary Cards

Go Digital

"Paul Bunyan and the Popcorn Blizzard"

I was able to picture in my mind...

Visualize

school

Visual Glossary

Retell

Set a Purpose for Reading

- Display the Interactive Read-Aloud Cards.
- Read aloud the title.
- Tell children that you will be reading a tall tale about Paul Bunyan. Say: *Paul Bunyan is a character who was much, much bigger than a real person. There are many tall tales about him. A tall tale is a made-up story with characters and events so exaggerated they could not have happened.* Tell children to listen to find out how unusual weather created an unusual storm.

Strategy: Visualize

1 Explain to children that as they read or listen to a story, they can use the words and illustrations to visualize, or create pictures in their minds, of the story events. This can help them understand the story.

Think Aloud Visualizing the characters and events in the stories you read can help you better understand what's happening in a story. As we read, pay attention to the author's words and study the illustrations. Then close your eyes and use the words and illustrations to create a picture in your mind. As we continue reading, change the picture in your mind so that the story makes sense.

2 **Model** Read the selection. As you read, use the Think Aloud Cloud to model applying the strategy.

Think Aloud Remember, visualizing the information in your mind as you read can help you understand the text. I look at the picture and read the words, "... forty bowls of porridge he ate for breakfast." When I think about these words, I am able to picture in my mind a kitchen piled with 40 empty porridge bowls. That image helps me understand how much porridge that would be. As I read, I will continue visualizing to help myself understand the information.

3 **Guided Practice** As you continue to read, pause to encourage children to visualize. *What do you see in your mind? What do the words and illustrations make you see?* Guide children in using the details in the text and illustrations to visualize what is happening in the story.

Respond to Reading

After reading, prompt children to retell "Paul Bunyan and the Popcorn Blizzard." Discuss what they pictured in their minds as they read.

ENGLISH LANGUAGE LEARNERS SCAFFOLD

Beginning

Engage Display Card 1. *In your mind, can you see a big baby eating many bowls of porridge? Show me how big Paul was when he was a baby.*

Intermediate

Describe Display Card 1. Ask children to describe the illustration. Then have them close their eyes. *What do you see in your mind? Describe it.*

Advanced/High

Describe Have children look at the illustrations in the story. Then have children close their eyes and retell the story events by describing what they visualize. Elicit details to support their answers.

Monitor and *Differentiate*

 Quick Check

Can children apply the strategy visualize?

Small Group Instruction

If No →	Approaching	Reteach pp. T208–209
	ELL	Develop pp. T226–229
If Yes →	On Level	Review pp. T218–219
	Beyond Level	Extend pp. T222–223

Word Work

MINILESSON 5 Mins

Phonemic Awareness

OBJECTIVES

CCSS Isolate and pronounce initial, medial vowel, and final sounds (phonemes) in spoken single-syllable words. **RF.1.2c**

CCSS Decode regularly spelled one-syllable words. **RF.1.3b**

Phoneme Categorization

1 Model Show children how to categorize words by phoneme. *Listen carefully as I say three words:* wrap, rough, sing. *Which word does not belong? That's right,* sing *does not begin with the /r/ sound like the words* wrap *and* rough *do.* Sing *does not belong.*

2 Guided Practice/Practice Have children practice phoneme categorization. Guide practice with the first set. *Listen to the following words. Tell me which word does not belong and why.*

sick, wall, knit	strap, draw, flip	cause, bought, slide
grape, broil, grill	now, ripe, sign	thing, flush, these

MINILESSON 10 Mins

Phonics

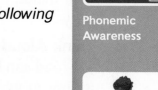
Sound-Spelling Card

Introduce Silent Letters
wr, kn, gn

1 Model Display the *Rose* and *Nest* **Sound-Spelling Cards.** Teach that when the consonants *wr, kn,* or *gn* appear together at the beginning of a word or syllable, the first letter is silent. *This is the* Rose *Sound-Spelling Card. The sound is /r/. This is the sound at the beginning of the word* rose. *The sound /r/ is sometimes spelled with the letters* wr *as in* write. *Write the word* write, *and underline* w. *The letter* w *is silent.* Repeat for *kn* and *gn.*

2 Guided Practice/Practice Have children practice connecting the letters *wr* to the sound /r/ and the letters *kn* and *gn* to the sound /n/ by writing the spellings. *Now do it with me. Say /r/ as I write the letters* wr. *This time, write the letters* wr *five times as you say the /r/ sound.* Repeat for *kn* and *gn.*

Go Digital

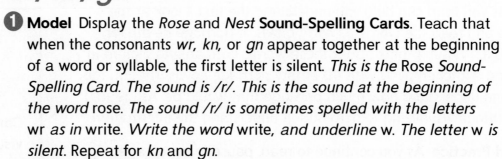
Phonemic Awareness

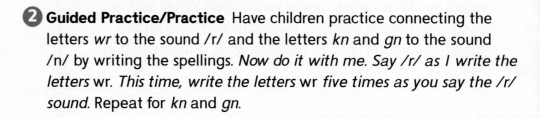
Rose
Phonics

Handwriting

Blend Words with Silent Letters *wr, kn, gn*

❶ Model Display **Word-Building Cards** *k, n, e, e*. Model how to blend the sounds. *These are the letters* kn. *Together they stand for /n/. These are the letters* ee. *Together they stand for /ē/. Listen as I blend these sounds together: /nnnēēē/. Say it with me*. Continue by modeling the words *knob, wreck*, and *gnome*.

❷ Guided Practice/Practice Display the Day 1 Phonics Practice Activity. Read each word in the first row, blending the sounds, for example, /rrriiit/. The word is *write*. Have children blend each word with you. Prompt children to read the connected text, sounding out the decodable words.

write	kneel	wrote	knife	knit	wrong
gnaw	wrap	gnat	wrist	knot	wren
ring	wring	no	gnome	new	knew
taught	smaller	grew	fearful	blue	suit

He cut the knot with a knife.

I knew a mouse gnawed on the cheese.

Wrap the cloth on your wrist.

Also online

Day 1 Phonics Practice Activity

Corrective Feedback

Sound Error Model the sound that children missed, then have them repeat the sound. Say: *My turn*. Tap under the letter and say: *Sound? What's the sound?* Return to the beginning of the word. Say: *Let's start over*. Blend the word with children again.

 Daily Handwriting

Throughout the week teach uppercase and lowercase letters *Zz* using the Handwriting models.

ENGLISH LANGUAGE LEARNERS

Phonemic Awareness: Minimal Contrasts Focus on articulation. Say the /n/ sound and note your mouth position. Have children repeat. Use Sound-Spelling Cards. Repeat for /r/. Have children say both sounds, noticing the differences. Continue with *knight/write, wrote/note, gnat/rat*.

Phonics: Variations in Language In some languages, including Cantonese, Vietnamese, Hmong, and Korean, there is no direct sound transfer for /r/. Emphasize /r/ and show correct mouth position. Practice with Approaching Level phonics lessons.

ON-LEVEL PRACTICE BOOK p. 295

When you see **wr, kn, gn** at the beginning of a word or syllable, the first letter is silent.

wrap   knit   gnaw

A. Circle the word that names each picture.

1. right (write) 2. (knot) not

3. rats (gnats) 4. need (knead)

B. Use words from the box to complete each sentence. Write the word on the line.

| knew | wrap | knock | wring |

5. I will ___knock___ on the door.

6. Can you ___wring___ out the wet shirt?

| APPROACHING p. 295 | BEYOND p. 295 | ELL p. 295 |

WORD WORK T169

Quick Review
High-Frequency Words: Read, Spell, and Write to review last week's high-frequency words: *brother, father, friend, love, mother, picture.*

→ # Word Work

MINILESSON 5 Mins
Spelling

Go Digital

OBJECTIVES

CCSS Recognize and read grade-appropriate irregularly spelled words. **RF.1.3g**

CCSS Use conventional spelling for words with common spelling patterns and for frequently occurring irregular words. **L.1.2d**

Words with *wr, kn, gn*

Dictation Use the Dictation Routine for each word to help children transfer their growing knowledge of sound-spellings to writing.

Pretest After dictation, pronounce each spelling word. Say a sentence for each word and pronounce the word again. After the pretest, display the spelling words and write each word as you say the letter names. Have children check their words.

gnat	gnu	know	knife	been
write	wrong	cause	dawn	their

For Approaching Level and Beyond Level children, refer to the Differentiated Spelling Lists for modified word lists.

Spelling Word Routine

they	together
how	eat

High-Frequency Routine

school

Visual Glossary

MINILESSON 5 Mins
High-Frequency Words

been, children, month, question, their, year

1 Model Display the **High-Frequency Word Cards**. Use the Read/Spell/Write routine to teach each word.

- **Read** Point to and say the word *been. This is the word* been. *Say it with me:* been. *She has been sick all week.*

- **Spell** *The word* been *is spelled* b-e-e-n. *Spell it with me.*

- **Write** *Let's write the word* been *in the air as we say each letter* b-e-e-n.

- Follow the same steps for *children, month, question, their, year.*

- As children spell each word with you, point out irregularities in sound-spellings, such as the /i/ sound spelled *ee* in *been.*

- Have partners create sentences using each word.

ENGLISH LANGUAGE LEARNERS

Pantomime Review the meaning of these words by using pictures, pantomime, or gestures when possible. Have children repeat or act out the word.

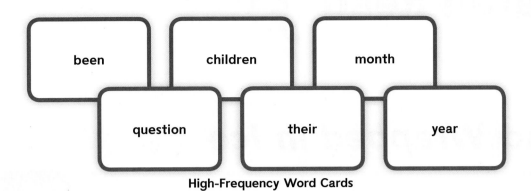

High-Frequency Word Cards

2 **Guided Practice/Practice** Have children read the sentences. Prompt them to identify the high-frequency words and to blend the decodable words.

1. The **children** have **been** here all day.

2. This is the first **month** in the **year**.

3. **Their** group has a **question** it would like to ask.

MINILESSON 5 Mins Introduce Vocabulary

country, gathers

1 **Model** Introduce the new words using the routine.

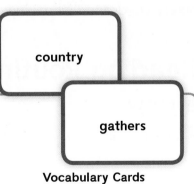

Vocabulary Cards

Vocabulary Routine

<u>Define:</u> A **country** is a land where a group of people live.

<u>Example:</u> *Canada is the country north of the U.S.*

<u>Ask:</u> What country do you live in? EXAMPLE

<u>Define:</u> **Gathers** means "brings or comes together in one place."

<u>Example:</u> *She gathers shells at the beach.*

<u>Ask:</u> Name a word that means something similar to gathers. SYNONYM

2 **Review** Use the routine to review last week's vocabulary words.

Monitor and *Differentiate*

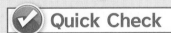 **Quick Check**

Can children read and decode words with silent letters *wr, kn, gn*?

Can children recognize and read high-frequency and vocabulary words?

Small Group Instruction

If No → Approaching Reteach pp. T212–215

ELL Develop pp. T226–233

If Yes → On Level Review pp. T220–221

Beyond Level Extend pp. T224–225

DAY 1

→ **Shared Read**

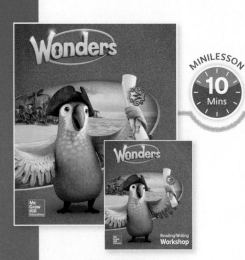

Reading/Writing Workshop Big Book and Reading/Writing Workshop

---

OBJECTIVES

CCSS Decode regularly spelled one-syllable words. **RF.I.3b**

CCSS Recognize and read grade-appropriate irregularly spelled words. **RF.I.3g**

Understand realistic fiction genre

ACADEMIC LANGUAGE

• *realistic fiction, ice, weather*

• Cognates: *ficción, realista*

See pages T226–T227 for Interactive Question-Response routine for the Shared Read.

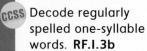

Read *Wrapped in Ice*

Focus on Foundational Skills

Review the words and letter-sounds in *Wrapped in Ice*.

• Have children use pages 258–259 to review the high-frequency words *been, children, month, question, their, year,* and the vocabulary words *country* and *gathers.*

• Have children use pages 260–261 to review that the letter combinations *wr, gn,* and *kn* have silent letters *w, g, k.* Guide them to blend the sounds to read the words.

• Display the story words *everyone, neighbors, science, something, surfaces,* and *worried.* Spell each word and model reading it. Tell children they will be reading the words in the selection.

Read Guide children in reading *Wrapped in Ice.* Point out high-frequency words, vocabulary words, and words in which *w, g,* and *k* are silent.

Close Reading Routine

Read DOK 1-2

• Identify key ideas and details about how weather affects Kim and her mom.
• Take notes and retell.
• Use A C T prompts as needed.

Reread DOK 2–3

• Analyze the text, craft, and structure.
• Use the Reread minilessons.

Integrate DOK 4

• Integrate knowledge and ideas.
• Make text-to-text connections.
• Use the Integrate Lesson.

Genre: Realistic Fiction Tell children that *Wrapped in Ice* is realistic fiction. Realistic fiction is a made-up story about characters and events; has events that could happen in real life; and has characters who behave like real people.

Go Digital

Wrapped in Ice

Wrapped in Ice

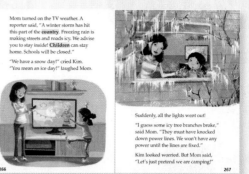

READING/WRITING WORKSHOP, pp. 262–271 Lexile 320

Connect to Concept: Weather Together

ESSENTIAL QUESTION Explain to children that as they read *Wrapped in Ice*, they will look for key ideas and details that will help them answer the Essential Question: *How can weather affect us?*

- Pages 264–265: What does Kim see outside the window?
- Pages 266–267: What happens to the lights because of the ice storm?
- Pages 268–269: What do Kim and her mom do together?
- Pages 270–271: What happens after the ice storm?

Focus on Fluency

With partners, have children read *Wrapped in Ice.* Remind them that they can ask themselves questions to understand what they are reading. Have them use both text and illustrations to answer their questions.

Retell Have partners use key ideas and details to retell *Wrapped in Ice.* Invite them to tell how the weather made the day special.

Make Connections

Read together Make Connections on page 271. Use this sentence starter to help partners talk about how the icy weather changed Kim and her neighborhood:

> *After the ice storm, everyone. . .*

Guide children to connect what they have read to the Essential Question.

Reading/Writing Workshop

McGraw Hill Education

Reading/Writing Workshop

OBJECTIVES

CCSS Write informative/ explanatory texts in which they name a topic, supply some facts about the topic, and provide some sense of closure. **W.1.2**

CCSS Use personal, possessive, and indefinite pronouns (e.g., *I, me, my; they, them, their, anyone, everything*). **L.1.1d**

ACADEMIC LANGUAGE

- *text, illustrations, events, order, pronoun*
- Cognates: *texto, ilustraciónes, orden*

Write About the Reading/Writing Workshop

Analyze the Prompt Tell children that today the class will work together to write a response to a prompt. Read the prompt aloud. *What happened in* Wrapped In Ice? Say: *To respond to this prompt, we need to look at the text and illustrations in* Wrapped In Ice.

Find Text Evidence Explain that you will reread the text and take notes to help respond to the prompt. Read aloud pages 264–265. Say: *The text and the illustrations tell me what happened in the story. For example, Kim heard a strange sound. She looked outside and saw everything coated in ice. In the illustration, I see that the tree branches and roads are covered in ice. Kim asked her mom about the ice storm. These are details that will help us answer the question. Let's write them down in our notes.*

Write to a Prompt Reread the prompt to children. *What happened in* Wrapped In Ice? Say: *We need to tell what happened in the story in order of sequence of events. Let's start by writing a sentence about the first event: At the beginning of the story, Kim heard a strange sound and looked out the window.* Write the sentence. *Now, we will read our notes and use them to tell what else happened in the story in order.* Track the print as you reread the notes.

Guide children to dictate complete sentences for you to record based on their notes. Read the final response as you track the print.

Go Digital

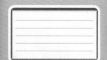

Graphic Organizer

Writing

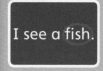

I see a fish.

Grammar

Grammar

5 Mins MINILESSON

Special Pronouns

① Explain/Model Explain that some pronouns do not refer to a specific person, place, thing, or number. Explain that *anyone* means "any person" and *everyone* means "all people." Display the following sentences:

> Does anyone know what time it is?
>
> Everyone thought the joke was funny.

Explain that *anything* means "no special thing," *everything* means "all things," and *nothing* means "no thing."

> You can have anything you want for lunch.
>
> There is nothing in the mailbox.

② Guided Practice/Practice Display the paragraph below and read it aloud. Have children identify the pronouns.

> Does anyone know what is in the box? Everyone thinks the box is filled with peanuts. "I do not think there is anything to eat in that box," said Nate. The children looked in. Nothing was in the box! (anyone, everyone, I, anything, nothing)

Talk About It Have partners orally generate sentences using *anyone, everyone, anything, everything,* and *nothing.*

Link to Writing Say: *Let's look back at our writing and see if we used any special pronouns. Did we use them correctly?* If special pronouns are not in the Shared Writing, work with children to add them and reread the response together.

ENGLISH LANGUAGE LEARNERS SCAFFOLD

Beginning

Demonstrate Comprehension Read aloud the Model sentences. Ask children questions to check their understanding of the words. *What does* anyone *mean? Does* nothing *mean "no thing" or "all things"?*

Intermediate

Explain Write the pronouns *anyone, everyone, anything, everything,* and *nothing* on individual cards. Have children pick a card and tell what the pronoun means.

Advanced/High

Expand Have partners come up with sentences for *anyone, everyone, anything, everything,* and *nothing.* Then have them substitute the words' meanings in the sentences to check that they used the correct words.

Daily Wrap Up

- Encourage children to discuss the Essential Question using the oral vocabulary words. Ask: *How did the weather affect us today?*

- Prompt children to share the skills they learned and used today.

Materials

Reading/Writing Workshop
VOLUME 4

Reading/Writing Workshop Big Book
UNIT 6

 been
High-Frequency Word Cards
been question
children their
month year

 a b c
Word-Building Cards

 country
Vocabulary Cards
country
gathers

 gnat
Spelling Word Cards

Cause → Effect
Teaching Poster

Interactive Read-Aloud Cards

 Rr
r
wr_
rose
Sound-Spelling Cards

→ Build the Concept

Go
Digital

MINILESSON 5 Mins Oral Language

Visual Glossary

"Paul Bunyan and the Popcorn Blizzard"

OBJECTIVES

CCSS Ask and answer questions about key details in a text read aloud or information presented orally or through other media. **SL.1.2**

• Discuss the Essential Question
• Build concept understanding

ACADEMIC LANGUAGE

• *visualize*
• Cognate: *visualizar*

ESSENTIAL QUESTION

Remind children that this week you've been talking and reading about weather and how it affects people. Remind them of Paul Bunyan and the popcorn snow and what happened during the ice storm. Guide children to discuss the Essential Question using information from what they read and discussed on Day 1.

Oral Vocabulary Words

Review the oral vocabulary words. Use the Define/Example/Ask routine to review the oral vocabulary words *creative, cycle, frigid, predict,* and *scorching.*

• What creative activities do you enjoy?
• What is something that happens in a cycle?
• Which gets frigid: something in the freezer or something in the oven?
• When you predict, do you tell what already happened or what is going to happen?
• Name something that can feel scorching hot.

Listening Comprehension

Reread the Interactive Read Aloud

MINILESSON
5 Mins

Strategy: Visualize

Remind children that as they listen, they can pay attention to the words and illustrations and then close their eyes and visualize the story events. When they visualize, they create a picture in their mind.

"Paul Bunyan and the Popcorn Blizzard"

Tell children that you will reread "Paul Bunyan and the Popcorn Blizzard." Display the Interactive Read-Aloud Cards. Pause as you read to model applying the strategy.

Think Aloud When I read or listen to a story, I can read the text and look at the illustrations. Then I can use the information to picture the story events in my mind. When I first read the story, I noticed that the illustration shows Paul pulling a blue ox out of a mountain of snow. I read the words, "Paul searched in a snowdrift that was as tall as a mountain. Then he pulled out the biggest, bluest baby ox he had ever seen." When I thought about these words, I saw a picture in my mind of a huge pile of snow. I saw Paul reaching into it and pulling out the blue ox.

Make Connections

Discuss partners' responses to "Paul Bunyan and the Popcorn Blizzard."

COLLABORATE

- *What kinds of weather did Paul experience?*
- *What problems did the weather cause?*
- *How did the lumberjacks feel about the weather? How did Paul feel?*

Write About It Have children write an opinion as to whether they think the events in the story could really happen. Guide children to use details from the text to support their argument that the story could or could not really happen. Have children write continuously for six minutes.

 Word Work

Quick Review

Build Fluency: Sound-Spellings
Display the **Word-Building Cards:** *wr, kn, gn, au, aw, augh, ew, ue, ui, ow, oy, oi, ar, ore, oar, er, ir, ur, ey, igh, oa, oe, ee, ea, ai, ay, e_e, u_e, o_e, _ge.* Have children say the sounds.

Phonemic Awareness

OBJECTIVES

 Segment spoken single-syllable words into their complete sequence of individual sounds (phonemes). **RF.1.2d**

 Decode two-syllable words following basic patterns by breaking the words into syllables. **RF.1.3e**

Phoneme Segmentation

1 Model Use the **Response Board** to show children how to segment words. *I am going to say the sounds in the word* knob. *Listen: /n/ /o/ /b/. The first sound is /n/. The second sound is /o/. The last sound is /b/. I'll place a marker in a box for each sound I hear. This word has three sounds: /n/ /o/ /b/. Say the word with me:* knob.

2 Guided Practice/Practice Have children segment words. Do the first two together. *I am going to say some more words. Place a marker in a box to stand for each sound. Then tell me the sounds.*

wrote	flaw	knock	booth	choice
house	wreck	snore	know	threw

Phonics

Review Silent Letters *wr, kn, gn*

1 Model Display the *Nest* and *Rose* **Sound-Spelling Cards**. Review what children learned about silent letters. Review the sound /n/ spelled *kn* using the words *knot* and *gnat*, and the sound /r/ spelled *wr* using the word *write*.

2 Guided Practice/Practice Have children practice connecting the letters and sounds. Point to the Sound-Spelling Cards. *What are these letters? What sound do they stand for?*

Go Digital

Phonemic Awareness

Phonics

Structural Analysis

Handwriting

Blend with Silent Letters *wr, kn, gn*

1 Model Display **Word-Building Cards** *g, n, a, t* to form the word *gnat*. Model how to generate and blend the sounds to say the word. *These are the letters* g and n. *Together they stand for /n/. This is the letter* a. *It stands for /a/. This is the letter* t. *It stands for /t/. Let's blend: /nnnaaat/. The word is* gnat. Continue with *knee* and *write*.

2 Guided Practice/Practice Repeat the routine with children with *know, wrong, gnome, knob, wrist, knock, wrap, wreck, knight, wrench.*

Build with Silent Letters *wr, kn, gn*

1 Model Display the Word-Building Cards *k, n, a, c, k*. Blend: /n/ /a/ /k/, /nnnaaak/, *knack*.

- Replace *a* with *o* and repeat with *knock*.
- Replace *ck* with *b* and repeat with *knob*.

2 Guided Practice/Practice Continue with *know, known, knot, knit, knife, knee, kneel.*

ENGLISH LANGUAGE LEARNERS

Build Vocabulary Review the meanings of example words that can be explained or demonstrated in a concrete way. For example, ask children to point to their *knee* and to their *wrist*. Model the meaning of *knock* and *knob*, saying, "*I can knock on the door and then turn the knob to open the door.*" Have children repeat. Provide sentence starters, such as, "*I know how to ___*" for children to complete. Correct grammar and pronunciation as needed.

MINILESSON
5 Mins

Structural Analysis

Compound Words

1 Model Write and read aloud *bird, house,* and *birdhouse*. Explain to children that *birdhouse* is a compound word. A compound word is a longer word made up of two smaller words they may know. The word *birdhouse* is made up of the words *bird* and *house*. Tell children that looking for smaller words in longer words can sometimes help them pronounce and figure out the meaning of the longer word. A *birdhouse* is a house for a bird to live in.

2 Guided Practice/Practice Write the following compound words: *bookbag, daydream, wristwatch, homework, baseball.* Have children name the two smaller words in each compound word and then use each compound word in a sentence.

→ # Word Work

Quick Review

High-Frequency Words: Read, Spell, and Write to review this week's high-frequency words: *been, children, month, question, their, year.*

MINILESSON 5 Mins — Spelling

Go Digital

Spelling Word Sort

they	together
how	eat

High-Frequency Word Routine

school

Visual Glossary

OBJECTIVES

CCSS Recognize and read grade-appropriate irregularly spelled words. **RF.1.3g**

CCSS Use conventional spelling for words with common spelling patterns and for frequently occurring irregular words. **L.1.2d**

Word Sort with *wr, kn, gn*

1 Model Display the **Spelling Word Cards** from the Teacher's Resource Book. Have children read each word, listening for the beginning sound.

Use cards for *wr, kn,* and *gn* to create a three-column chart. Say the silent letter pairs and pronounce the sound for each spelling. Have children repeat the spelling and pronunciation of each letter pair.

2 Guided Practice/Practice Have children place each Spelling Word Card in the column with the same silent letters. When completed, have children read the words in each column. Then call out a word. Have a child find the word card and point to it as the class spells the word.

> ### ANALYZE ERRORS/ARTICULATION SUPPORT
>
> Use children's pretest errors to analyze spelling problems and provide corrective feedback. For example, some children will leave out the silent letter *w, k,* or *g.* Or, they might write the homophone for the word (e.g., *right/write*).
>
> Give a clue to one of the spelling words, including the definition. Example: *The word has five letters. It starts with the /n/ sound. It is something you cut with.* Have children write and read the word.

ENGLISH LANGUAGE LEARNERS

Provide Clues Practice spelling by helping children generate more words with silent letter *wr, kn,* and *gn* spelling patterns. Provide clues: *Think of a word that begins with* kn *and rhymes with* rock. Write the word and have children practice reading it. Correct their pronunciation, if needed.

MINILESSON 5 Mins — High-Frequency Words

been, children, month, question, their, year

1 Guided Practice Say each word and have children Read/Spell/Write it. Ask children to close their eyes, picture the word in their minds, and write it the way they see it. Display the high-frequency words for children to self-correct.

- Point out irregularities in sound-spellings such as the /u/ sound spelled *o* in *month.*

2 Practice Add the high-frequency words *been, children, month, question, their,* and *year* to the cumulative word bank.

- Have children work with a partner to create sentences using the words.

- Have children look at the words and compare their sounds and spellings to words from previous weeks.

- Suggest that they write about weather.

Cumulative Review Review last week's words using the Read/Spell/Write routine.

- Repeat the above routine, mixing the words and having children chorally say each one.

MINILESSON 5 Mins
Reinforce Vocabulary

country, gathers

1 Guided Practice Use the **Vocabulary Cards** to review this week's and last week's vocabulary words. Work together with children to generate a new context sentence for each word.

2 Practice Have children work with a partner to orally complete each sentence stem on the Day 2 Vocabulary Practice Activity using this week's and last week's vocabulary words.

| accept | often | country | gathers |

1. She ____ wood for the campfire.
2. Will you ____ this gift from me?
3. The U.S.A. is a large ____.
4. I ____ go shopping with my mother.

Also online

Day 2 Vocabulary Practice Activity

ON-LEVEL PRACTICE BOOK p. 296

Complete each sentence. Use the words from the word box.

| been | children | month | question | their | year |

1. Raise your hand if you want to ask a __question__.

2. The __children__ are making a fort.

3. We have __been__ playing all day.

4. June is the name of a __month__.

5. All the kids have __their__ books.

6. Last __year__, we were in kindergarten.

| APPROACHING p. 296 | BEYOND p. 296 | ELL p. 296 |

Monitor and *Differentiate*

✓ Quick Check

Can children read and decode words with silent letters *wr, kn, gn?*

Can children recognize and read high-frequency and vocabulary words?

Small Group Instruction

If No → Approaching Reteach pp. T212–215

ELL Develop pp. T226–233

If Yes → On Level Review pp. T220–221

Beyond Level Extend pp. T224–225

Comprehension

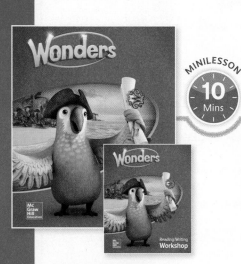

Reading/Writing Workshop Big Book and Reading/Writing Workshop

---

OBJECTIVES

CCSS Describe characters, settings, and major events in a story, using key details. **RL.1.3**

Understand realistic fiction genre

ACADEMIC LANGUAGE

• realistic fiction, cause and effect

• Cognates: *ficción, realista, causa y efecto*

SKILLS TRACE

PLOT

Introduce Unit 3 Week 1

REVIEW Unit 3 Weeks 2, 3; Unit 4 Weeks 1, 4; Unit 5 Weeks 1, 2, 4; Unit 6 Weeks 3, 4

ASSESS Unit 3 Weeks 1, 2, 3; Unit 4 Week 1; Unit 5 Weeks 2, 4; Unit 6 Week 3

MINILESSON
10 Mins

Reread *Wrapped in Ice*

Genre: Realistic Fiction

1 **Model** Tell children they will now reread the realistic fiction selection *Wrapped in Ice*. Explain that as they read, they will look for information in the text to help them understand the selection.

Review the characteristics of realistic fiction. It:

• is a made-up story about characters and events.

• has events that could happen in real life.

• has characters who are like real people.

• has a beginning, a middle, and an end.

Point out that realistic fiction selections have a setting, characters, and a plot. *Realistic fiction selections are made-up stories that could happen in real life. The characters talk and act like real people and the events could really happen. Realistic fiction usually has a beginning, a middle, and an end. Often the characters have a problem that they want to solve, or a situation that they want to change.*

Display pages 264–265. *This is the beginning of the story. The illustration shows where the story is taking place, which is the setting of the story. Kim is in her house. Everything outside is covered in ice. A storm like this could really happen. These details help me understand why the story is realistic fiction.*

2 **Guided Practice/Practice** Display pages 266 and 267 of *Wrapped in Ice*. Read page 267 aloud. *What part of the story is this? Yes, it is the middle of the story. The illustration shows that Kim's house is without electricity. The text explains that icy tree branches knocked down power lines. Could these events really happen? Yes, they could. What does that tell us about the genre of the story?*

Go Digital

Wrapped in Ice

Genre

Cause and Effect

Skill: Plot/Cause and Effect

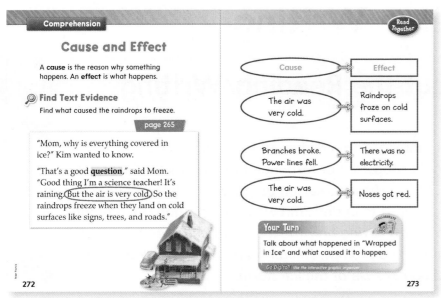

Reading/Writing Workshop, pp. 272–273

1 Model Tell children that in stories, one event causes another event to happen. Have children look at pages 272–273 in their Reading/Writing Workshop. Read together the definition of cause and effect. *A cause is the reason why something happens. An effect is what happens.*

2 Guided Practice/Practice Read together the Find Text Evidence section and model finding a cause and an effect in *Wrapped in Ice.* Point out the information that was added to the graphic organizer. *On page 265, we read that the air was very cold. This information is the cause—it explains why other things will happen. Raindrops froze when they landed on cold surfaces. This is an effect— something that happens. The information is added to the Cause and Effect chart. What other cause and effect relationships can we find in the story?*

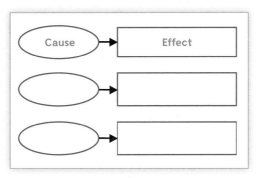

Teaching Poster

Monitor and *Differentiate*

✓ Quick Check

Can children identify causes and effects in a realistic fiction story?

⬇

Small Group Instruction

If No →	Approaching	Reteach pp. T216–217
	ELL	Develop pp. T226–233
If Yes →	On Level	Review p. T221
	Beyond Level	Extend p. T225

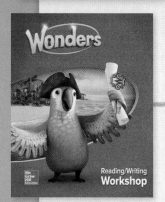

Interactive Writing

OBJECTIVES

CCSS Write informative/ explanatory texts in which they name a topic, supply some facts about the topic, and provide some sense of closure. **W.1.2**

CCSS Use personal, possessive, and indefinite pronouns (e.g., *I, me, my; they, them, their, anyone, everything*). **L.1.1d**

ACADEMIC LANGUAGE

- *idea, concluding statement, evidence, pronoun*
- Cognates: *idea, evidencia*

Write About the Reading/Writing Workshop

Analyze the Model Prompt Have children turn to page 274 in the **Reading/Writing Workshop.** Hector responded to the prompt: *How are Kim and Mom affected by the weather on pages 266–268?* Explain to children that the first step is to understand what information the prompt is asking for. *The prompt is asking how the ice storm changes what Kim and Mom do. To answer this prompt, Hector found text evidence about what Kim and Mom do because of the ice storm.*

Find Text Evidence Explain that Hector used evidence in the text and illustrations to take notes. Then, he used his notes to make an inference that Kim and her mom had a special day because of the weather.

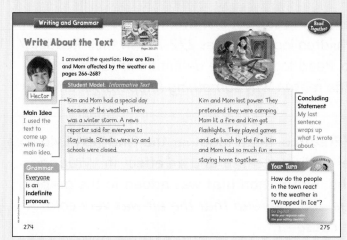

Reading/Writing Workshop

Go Digital

Graphic Organizer

Writing

I see a fish.

Grammar

Analyze the Student Model Read the model. Discuss the callouts.

- **Special Pronouns** Hector correctly used the special pronoun *everyone.* **Grammar**

- **Main Idea** Hector used text evidence to write his main idea in his first sentence. **Trait: Ideas**

- **Concluding Statement** Hector finished his writing with a sentence that wrapped up his ideas. **Trait: Organization**

Point out that Hector included details from the story to explain his main idea that Kim and Mom had a special day because of the storm.

Your Turn: Write About the Text Say: *Now we will write to a new prompt.* Have children turn to page 275 of the **Reading/Writing Workshop**. Read the Your Turn prompt together. *How do the people in the town react to the weather in* Wrapped in Ice?

Find Text Evidence Say: *To answer this question, we need to look back at the story and the illustrations and take notes. This time we will look for information about how people in the town react to the ice storm. Let's look at page 269. What does everyone do when the storm is over?* (They work together to put sand on the sidewalks and break up the ice. Then Mom invites the neighbors over.)

Write to a Prompt: Say: *Let's use our notes to write our first sentence: Everyone went outside after the storm to help clean up.* Write the sentence. Tell children you will reread the notes to help them tell how the people in the town reacted. Track the print as you reread the notes. Then guide children in forming complete sentences as you share the pen in writing them. Say: *Let's look back to see if we told our main idea in our first sentence and ended with a concluding statement that wraps up our writing.* Read the final response as you track the print.

For additional practice with the Writing Trait, have children turn to page 306 of the **Your Turn Practice Book**.

Grammar

MINILESSON 5 Mins

Special Pronouns

❶ Review Explain that there are pronouns that do not refer to a specific person, place, thing, or number. Explain that *nobody* means "no person," *somebody* means "no special person," and *anybody* means "any person." *Anybody* means the same as *anyone.* Display the following sentences:

> I knocked on the door, but nobody came.

> Somebody got my backpack by mistake.

> I didn't know anybody at my new school.

❷ Guided Practice/Practice Display the paragraph below and read it aloud. Have children identify the special pronouns and explain what they mean in the sentences.

> Paul said, "Nobody wants to play ball. I wish I could find somebody who wants to play. Luke, do you know anybody who wants to play?" (nobody, somebody, anybody)

Talk About It Have partners orally generate sentences using *nobody, somebody,* and *anybody.*

Daily Wrap Up

- Discuss the Essential Question and encourage children to use the oral vocabulary words. *What can you do in sunny weather? in rainy weather?*

- Prompt children to discuss the skills they learned today. How do those skills help them?

Materials

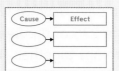

Reading/Writing Workshop
VOLUME 6

Literature Anthology
VOLUME 6

Visual Vocabulary Cards

creative   been
cycle   children
frigid   month
predict   question
scorching   their
country   year
gathers

Teaching Poster

Cause	→	Effect

| a | b | c |

Word-Building Cards

gnat

Spelling Word Cards

→ # Build the Concept

MINILESSON
5 Mins

Oral Language

 OBJECTIVES

CCSS Read grade-level text orally with accuracy, appropriate rate, and expression. **RF.1.4b**

Review theme

ACADEMIC LANGUAGE
• *theme, message, comma, pause*
• Cognates: *tema, mensaje, coma*

ESSENTIAL QUESTION

Remind children that this week you have been talking and reading about how weather affects us. Remind them of how the hot and cold weather affected Paul Bunyan and the effects of the ice storm. Guide children to discuss the question using information from what they have read and discussed throughout the week.

Review Oral Vocabulary

Review the oral vocabulary words *creative, cycle, frigid, predict,* and *scorching* using the Define/Example/Ask routine. Prompt children to use the words as they discuss weather.

Visual Vocabulary Cards

Comprehension/ Fluency

ENGLISH LANGUAGE LEARNERS

Retell Guide children to retell by using a question prompt on each page. *What does Kim see? What does she do?* Provide sentence starters for children to complete orally. *Kim sees lots of ____.*

MINILESSON
10 Mins

Theme

1 **Explain** Tell children they have been learning about using cause and effect to help them understand the plot of stories. Remind them they have also learned how to look for the theme of a story. *As we read, we can think about the big idea or message the author wants to share. Understanding the theme can help us to better understand the story.*

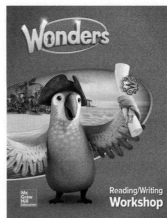

Reading/Writing Workshop

2 **Model** Display pages 268 and 269 of *Wrapped in Ice. I see the ice has caused problems for everyone. The electricity is off, and the roads are slippery. I also see all the neighbors are working together to solve the problems. These are clues to the theme of the story.*

3 **Guided Practice/Practice** Reread *Wrapped in Ice*. Use text evidence to identify clues and use them to determine the theme.

MINILESSON
5 Mins

Intonation

1 **Explain** Tell children as you read, you will change your voice to express the feelings in the words you read. Explain exclamation marks are used to show strong emotion and question marks are used to show the sentence asks something.

2 **Model** Model reading a section of the Shared Read that has exclamation marks. *This sentence has an exclamation mark. I'll read it with more feeling than the other sentences.* Model reading a section that has question marks. *This sentence has a question. I'll read it as though I am asking something.* Also point out how you pause for commas and other punctuation.

3 **Guided Practice/Practice** Have children reread the passage chorally. Remind them to show feeling and expression.

Fluency Practice Children can practice using Practice Book passages.

 → # Word Work

Quick Review

Build Fluency: Sound-Spellings

Display the **Word-Building Cards**: wr, kn, gn, au, aw, augh, ew, ue, ui, ow, oy, oi, ar, ore, oar, er, ir, ur, ey, igh, oa, oe, ee, ea, ai, ay, e_e, u_e, o_e, _ge. Have children say the sounds.

Phonemic Awareness

OBJECTIVES

(CCSS) Decode regularly spelled one-syllable words. **RF.1.3b**

- Recognize and read compound words
- Substitute sounds in words

Phoneme Substitution

1 Model Show children how to substitute phonemes. *I'm going to say a word and its sounds: gnat, /n/ /a/ /t/. Change the /a/ to /i/. The new word is /n/ /i/ /t/,* knit.

2 Guided Practice/Practice Have children practice substituting phonemes with these examples. *For each word, change the sound and say the new word.*

write/wrote	wreck/rack	gnaw/knew
wring/rung	knight/note	quite/quote

Phonics

Blend with Silent Letters *wr, kn, gn*

1 Model Display **Word-Building Cards** w, r, a, p. Model how to blend the sounds. *These are the letters* wr. *Together they stand for /r/. This is the letter* a. *It stands for /a/. This is the letter* p. *It stands for /p/. Let's blend the sounds: /rrraaap/. Say it with me:* wrap.

Continue with *gnu* and *known*.

2 Guided Practice/Practice Review the words and sentences on the Day 3 Phonics Practice Activity with children. Read each word in the first row, blending the sounds, for example: /r/ /ī/ /t/ /s/; /rrrīīītsss/. The word is *writes*.

Have children blend each word with you. Prompt children to read the connected text, sounding out the decodable words.

Go Digital

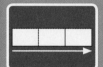

Phonemic Awareness

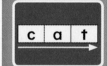

Phonics

Structural Analysis

Handwriting

writes	knee	knock	wrong	wrote	gnat
knight	wrist	wrap	gnaw	wreck	gnu

kneepad	snowball	wristwatch	moonlight
baseball	daydream	homework	doghouse
caught	strawberry	suitcase	toothbrush

I wrote the wrong date on my test.

Do you know how to knit a scarf?

Also online

Day 3 Phonics Practice Activity

Decodable Reader Have children read "Miss Wright's Job" (pages 57–60) and "Know About Snowstorms" (65–68) to practice decoding words in connected text.

MINILESSON
5 Mins

Structural Analysis

Compound Words

1 Model Write the word *lunchtime* and read it with children. Remind children that compound words are made up of two smaller words. *Lunchtime* is a compound word made up of the words *lunch* and *time*. The two smaller words often help us figure out the meaning of the compound word.

2 Practice/Apply Write the following compound words: *classroom, snowstorm, kneepad, sunlight, rainfall*. Have children name the two smaller words in each compound. Help children blend the words. Point out that compound words have more than one syllable.

Corrective Feedback

Corrective Feedback Say: *My turn*. Model blending. Then lead children in blending the sounds. Say: *Do it with me*. Respond with children to offer support. Then say: *Your turn. Blend*. Have children chorally blend. Return to the beginning of the word. Say: *Let's start over*.

Word Work

MINILESSON 5 Mins Spelling

OBJECTIVES

CCSS Recognize and read grade-appropriate irregularly spelled words. **RF.1.3g**

CCSS Use conventional spelling for words with common spelling patterns and for frequently occurring irregular words. **L.1.2d**

CCSS Explain the meanings of simple similes and metaphors (e.g., as pretty as a picture) in context. **L.4.5**

Word Sort with *wr, kn, gn*

1 Model Make index cards for *wr, kn,* and *gn* to form three columns in a pocket chart. Say or blend the sounds with children.

Hold up the *gnat* **Spelling Word Card**. Say and spell it. Pronounce the sounds clearly. Blend sounds, emphasizing the initial consonant sound. Repeat with *gnu*. Place the words below the *gn* card.

2 Guided Practice/Practice Have children spell each word. Repeat the process with the other silent letter spellings.

Display the words *cause, dawn, been,* and *their* in a separate column. Read and spell the words together with children. Point out that these spelling words do not contain silent letters.

Conclude by asking children to orally generate additional words that rhyme with each word or start with the same silent letters. Write the additional words.

Go Digital

er	ir	or	ur
her			
girl curb			word

Spelling Word Sort

school

Visual Glossary

MINILESSON 5 Mins High-Frequency Words

PHONICS/SPELLING PRACTICE BOOK p. 138

been, children, month, question, their, year

1 Guided Practice Say each word and have children Read/Spell/Write it.

- Display **Visual Vocabulary Cards** to review this week's high-frequency words.

A. Read the words in the box. Say each word. Then complete each word to make a spelling word.

gnat	gnu	know	knife
write	wrong	been	their

1. g n at
2. k n ow
3. w r ong
4. k n ife
5. b e e n
6. t h eir
7. w r ite
8. g n u

B. Write your own sentence. Use one or two words from the box. Check that your capital and lowercase letters are clear.

9. Check letter formation.

Possible response: I know how to write my name.

Visual Vocabulary Cards

2 Practice Repeat the activity with last week's words.

Build Fluency: Word Automaticity

Have children read the following sentences aloud together at the wsame pace. Repeat several times.

The children have **been** running outside.

Their **question** is about what to write.

What is the first month of the **year**?

Word Bank

Review the current and previous words in the word bank. Discuss with children which words should be removed or added back.

Vocabulary

MINILESSON 5 Mins

country, gathers

Review Use the **Visual Vocabulary Cards** to review this week's words using the Define/Example/Ask routine. Have partners generate context sentences for each vocabulary word.

Visual Vocabulary Cards

Strategy: Similes

1 Model Explain that a simile is a figure of speech that compares one thing to another. A simile uses the word *like* or *as* to help readers picture what something looks, sounds, or feels like. Use *Wrapped in Ice* to model how to identify a simile and its meaning.

Think Aloud In *Wrapped in Ice*, a simile is used in this sentence: "The driveway was like a skating rink." I know that a skating rink is made of ice. That must mean that the driveway was either covered in ice or was very slippery. The word "like" tells me that this is a simile comparing the driveway to an ice rink.

2 Guided Practice Help children use the strategy to identify the simile and meaning of these sentences: *It was like an oven outside. He was as brave as a lion.*

3 Practice Have children create a simile with the word *country* or look for similes in other stories they have read.

Monitor and *Differentiate*

✓ **Quick Check**

Can children read and decode words with silent letters *wr, kn, gn?*

Can children recognize and read high-frequency and vocabulary words?

Small Group Instruction

If No → Approaching Reteach pp. T212–215

ELL Develop pp. T226–233

If Yes → On Level Review pp. T220–221

Beyond Level Extend pp. T224–225

WORD WORK **T191**

Genre Realistic Fiction

Essential Question
How can weather affect us?
Read about why a school has to be rebuilt every year.

Go Digital!

Rain School
by James Rumford

326

327

LITERATURE ANTHOLOGY, pp. 326–327

Literature Anthology

Rain School

CLOSE READING

Lexile 440

Close Reading Routine

Read   **DOK 1–2**

- Identify key ideas and details about how weather affects the school.
- Take notes and retell.
- Use Ⓐ Ⓒ Ⓣ prompts as needed.

Reread   **DOK 2–3**

- Analyze the text, craft, and structure.
- Use *Close Reading Companion*, pp. 180–182.

Integrate   **DOK 4**

- Integrate knowledge and ideas
- Make text-to-text connections.
- Use the Integrate Lesson.

Read

ESSENTIAL QUESTION

Read aloud the Essential Question: *How can weather affect us?* Tell children that as they read they should think about why the story is named *Rain School.* Ask: *What do you predict will happen in this story?*

Story Words Read, spell, and define the words *Chad, sapling, arrives, knowledge,* and *disappears.* Tell children they will read these words in the selection.

Note Taking: Graphic Organizer As children read the selection, guide them to fill in the graphic organizer on **Your Turn Practice Book** page 298.

In the **country** of Chad, it is the first day of school. The dry dirt road is filling up with **children**. ① ②

Big brothers and big sisters are leading the way.

328

329

LITERATURE ANTHOLOGY, pp. 328–329

① Strategy: Visualize

Teacher Think Aloud The text tells us the road is "dry dirt." If I close my eyes, I can visualize the dirt road. It is very dry. I can imagine that it is dusty and that the dry dust kicks up as children walk on it.

② Skill: Cause and Effect

Teacher Think Aloud I remember a cause is the reason why something happens and an effect is what happens. I think about why children are walking on the road. I read it is the first day of school. That is the cause for the children to be walking on the road. They are walking to school.

Build Vocabulary page 329
leading the way: showing where to go

A C T **A**ccess **C**omplex **T**ext

▶ **What makes this text complex?**

Prior Knowledge This story takes place in the African country of Chad. Children may be unfamiliar with the way of life in Chad.

Reread

Author's Purpose

Reread pages 328–329. How does the author's text help you understand the illustration? (The text says that big brothers and sisters lead the way. The illustration shows children walking in a line. Most of the bigger children are in front. They must be brothers and sisters to the younger children.)

LITERATURE ANTHOLOGY **T191B**

"Will they give us a notebook?" Thomas asks.

"Will they give us a pencil?"

"Will I learn to read like you?"

"Stop asking so many **questions** and keep up," say the big brothers and big sisters. **3**

330

331

LITERATURE ANTHOLOGY, pp. 330–331

Read

❸ Ask and Answer Questions

Teacher Think Aloud Sometimes when I don't understand what I am reading, it can be helpful to ask a question, look for details, and try to find the answer. I ask myself, "Why is Thomas asking all these questions?"

To answer my question, I will use the details in the text and pictures. Thomas's questions show that he does not know what goes on at school. And, the picture shows that he is smaller than the other children. I think this is Thomas's first day at school and that is why he is asking so many questions.

❹ Compound Words

If we don't know the meaning of a longer word, we can see if it is made up of smaller words. Name the two smaller words in *schoolyard*. (*school* and *yard*) These words help us know the meaning of the word. A schoolyard is the yard around a school. What are the two words in *classroom*? (*class* and *room*) What do you think *classroom* means? (a room for having a class)

Build Vocabulary page 330
notebook: a blank book for writing

Thomas arrives at the schoolyard, **4** but there are no classrooms.

There are no desks.

It doesn't matter.

There is a teacher.

"We will build our school," she says. "This is the first lesson." **5**

332

333

LITERATURE ANTHOLOGY, pp. 332–333

5 Skill: Cause and Effect

Teacher Think Aloud I read that the first lesson is to build the school. This seems like an effect. What was the reason or cause that led the teacher to make this the first lesson. They don't have a school is the cause. Let's put this on our chart.

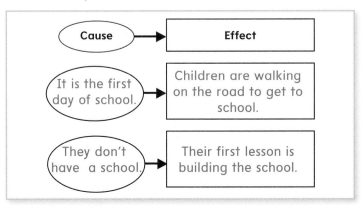

Cause → **Effect**

It is the first day of school. → Children are walking on the road to get to school.

They don't have a school. → Their first lesson is building the school.

Reread

Dialogue

Reread page 330. How does the dialogue help you know how Thomas feels? (He asks a lot of questions. He must be excited about going to school.)

Author's Purpose

Reread pages 332–333. How does the author help you know what is most important to the children about school? (The text says it doesn't matter that there are no classrooms or desks because there is a teacher. That lets me know that the teacher is the most important part of school.)

Build Vocabulary page 333
lesson: something to be learned

Thomas learns to make mud bricks and dry them in the sun. **6** **7**

334   335

LITERATURE ANTHOLOGY, pp. 334–335

Read

6 Key Details

Remember, we can get key details from the text and from the illustrations. What do you learn from the words and picture on pages 334–335? (bricks can be made from mud; everyone is working together to build the school.)

7 Genre: Realistic Fiction

Teacher Think Aloud This story is about children in a country I do not know much about. But the characters act like real people. The events in the beginning of the story could really happen. These are clues that the story is realistic fiction.

Build Vocabulary page 334
brick: a block of hard clay or mud for building

8 Skill: Cause and Effect

Turn to a partner and discuss what happens as a result of Thomas working with the others to build the school. (He learns to make bricks and to build walls and desks from mud.)

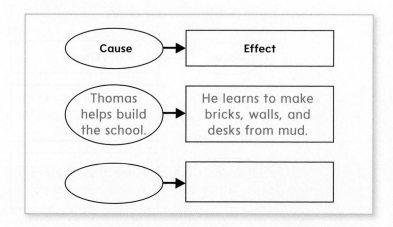

Cause	→	Effect
Thomas helps build the school.	→	He learns to make bricks, walls, and desks from mud.
	→	

He learns to build mud walls and mud desks. **8**

336 337

LITERATURE ANTHOLOGY, pp. 336–337

Reread *Close Reading Companion,* 180

Author's Purpose

How do the text and illustrations help you understand what the first lesson is about? (The text tells me that Thomas learns to make bricks and build walls and desks. The illustrations show all the children and some grownups working to build the school. This helps me know that the lesson is about how to make things, but also about how to work together.)

Author's Craft: Repetition

Reread pages 334–337. Why does the author repeat the word *mud* on these pages? (to help us know that everything the children are building is made from the earth)

A C T Access Complex Text

▶ **Prior Knowledge**

Guide children to understand that the story takes place in a part of the country of Chad where they do not have construction workers with tools and big machines to build buildings.

- Review the details in the text and illustrations that tell you about how the people are building the school.

- Point out that the people are making a wooden frame and are using bricks made of mud. These are natural materials they can get where they live.

He **gathers** grass and saplings with the other children, and they make a roof. **9**

338

339

LITERATURE ANTHOLOGY, pp. 338–339

Read

9 Strategy: Visualize

Teacher Think Aloud As I read, I use the words and pictures to visualize, or picture in my mind, what is happening in this part of the story. What do you visualize when you read pages 338–339?

Student Think Aloud I read that Thomas gathers grass and saplings to help make a roof for the school. I close my eyes and picture Thomas being up on the grass roof. I can imagine him working to put the grass and saplings together to make a roof.

10 Author's Craft: Word Choice

Teacher Think Aloud The author uses interesting words and phrases to describe the school. He says that the inside of the school smells of earth and of fields ready for planting. Those words help me imagine what it is like inside a building made of mud, grass, and saplings. Mud is earth and comes from the fields. Grass and saplings grow in the fields.

Inside it is cool. It smells of the earth. It smells of the fields ready for planting. **10**

Thomas helps bring in little wooden stools.

Everyone sits down.

This is the moment they have **been** waiting for. **11**

LITERATURE ANTHOLOGY, pp. 340–341

11 Make and Confirm Predictions

Now that we are about halfway through the story, let's see if our predictions were correct. Since the story is called *Rain School*, I had predicted it would be about children learning about weather. My prediction was not correct. I will revise my prediction. We have learned about children building their own school. We read on page 340 that this is the moment the children have been waiting for. Now let's predict what that moment is, and make a new prediction about why the story is called *Rain School*. What do you predict will happen next?

Build Vocabulary page 340
stool: a seat on legs without arms or a back

Reread   *Close Reading Companion,* 181

Illustrator's Craft: Point of View

Reread pages 338–339. How does the illustration show that the children are enjoying their work? (I see Thomas up on the roof waving to the children down below. The other children on the roof are smiling. I think they are having fun doing their job!)

Author's Craft: Word Choice

Reread pages 340–341. How do the author's words help you know how the children feel about their school? (The author says that the school smells of the earth and the fields ready for planting. This helps me know the children are comfortable and at home in their school.)

LITERATURE ANTHOLOGY **T191H**

The teacher brings in a blackboard.
On it she writes a letter.
"A!" says the teacher.
"A!" says Thomas with the other children.

The teacher writes the letter with big strokes in the air.
The students do the same, over and over.
"Wonderful," says the teacher. **12**

342

343

LITERATURE ANTHOLOGY, pp. 342–343

Read

12 Skill: Cause and Effect

What are the children doing? (They are writing letters in the air.) Let's add this to our chart as a cause. What effect do you think will happen from them writing letters in the air? (They will learn the letters of the alphabet.) Let's add the effect to our Cause and Effect chart.

Build Vocabulary page 343
blackboard: a large board for writing on
stroke: a smooth swinging motion

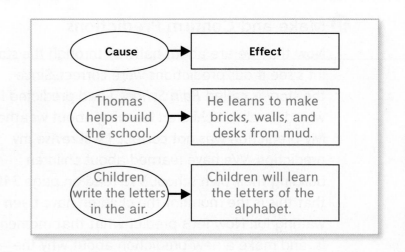

Cause	→	Effect
Thomas helps build the school.	→	He learns to make bricks, walls, and desks from mud.
Children write the letters in the air.	→	Children will learn the letters of the alphabet.

She hands out notebooks and pencils.

"Page one," says the teacher. Thomas opens his notebook to the first page and holds his pencil ready and waiting.

"Now write the letter A. Beautiful!" says the teacher as she looks at the students' work. **13** **14**

344

345

LITERATURE ANTHOLOGY, pp. 344–345

13 Strategy: Visualize

Remember, when you visualize, you use the words and pictures to make a picture in your mind. As you read pages 344–345, what do you visualize in this part of the story? What do you think the teacher saw that made her say "Beautiful!"?

14 Root Words and Suffixes

When we see a word we are not familiar with, we can check to see if the word has a root we know. I see the word *beautiful*. I can tell that the root of the word is *beauty*. The suffix is *-ful*. We can use the root and the suffix to figure out what the word means. What do you think *beautiful* means? (full of beauty)

15 Every day Thomas learns something new. Every day the teacher cheers him and the other children on. "Excellent job," she says. "Perfect, my learning friends!" 16

346

347

LITERATURE ANTHOLOGY, pp. 346–347

Read

15 Repetition

What phrase does the author repeat? (Every day) What does this phrase tell you? (It tells us that time is passing in the story.) Why do you think the author repeats this phrase? (to reinforce what Thomas does in school every day)

Build Vocabulary page 346
excellent: very good

16 Shades of Meaning

The word *excellent* is an adjective. The teacher used it to describe the students' work. This adjective is very positive. We can think of other adjectives the teacher might have used to be a little less positive, such as *good* or *nice*. What is an adjective that is even more positive than *excellent*? (Possible answer: fabulous, stupendous)

The nine **months** of the school **year** fly by.

The last day has come. The students' minds are fat with knowledge. **Their** notebooks are rumpled from learning.

Thomas and the other children call out, "Thank you, Teacher."

She smiles and says, "Well done, my hard-working friends! See you next year."

Thomas and the other children race home. **17**

348

349

LITERATURE ANTHOLOGY, pp. 348–349

---

17 **Maintain Skill: Theme**

Remember that the theme is the big idea or message of a story. As we read, we look for clues that help us understand the theme. What clues have we learned so far that tell us what the theme of the story is? Turn to a partner and name some clues.

Reread

Author's Craft: Sensory Words

Reread page 349. Why did the author say the students minds are "fat with knowledge" and their notebooks are "rumpled with learning?" (This is an interesting way to help me understand that the children learned a lot and worked very hard during the school year.)

A C T **A**ccess **C**omplex **T**ext

▶ Prior Knowledge

Help children understand schooling in Chad.

• *What are ways being a student in Chad is different from being a student in the United States?* (Possible responses: Children build a school, desks and walls are made of mud, the roof is made of grass and saplings.)

• *How is it the same?* (Possible responses: There is a teacher, the school has a blackboard, children learn letters, reading, social studies.)

Build Vocabulary page 349
rumpled: wrinkled

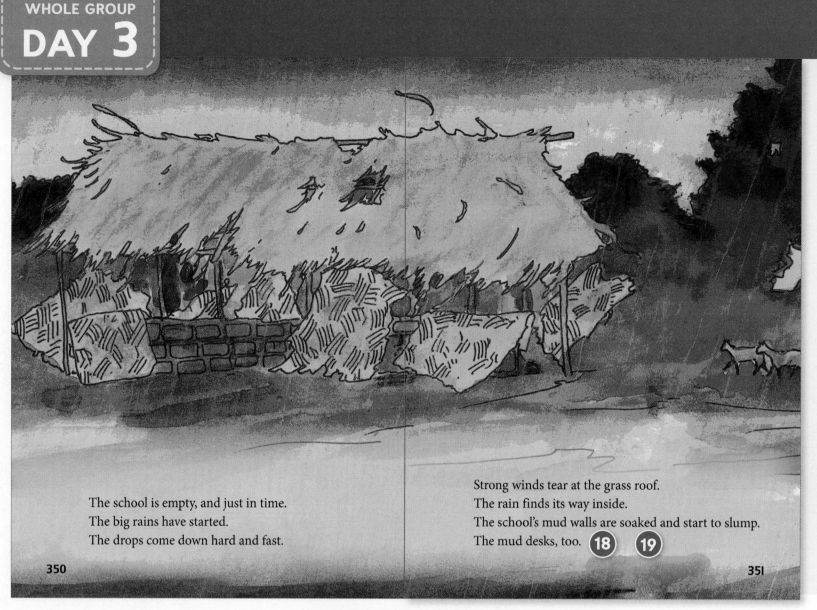

The school is empty, and just in time.
The big rains have started.
The drops come down hard and fast.

350

Strong winds tear at the grass roof.
The rain finds its way inside.
The school's mud walls are soaked and start to slump.
The mud desks, too. **18** **19**

351

LITERATURE ANTHOLOGY, pp. 350–351

Read

18 Skill: Cause and Effect

Turn to a partner and discuss what happened on pages 350–351. What causes the mud walls to get soaked? (heavy rain) What effect does this have on the school building? (It causes the building to start falling down.) We can add this to our chart.

Build Vocabulary page 351
slump: to fall

19 Word Categories

We can think about the words in a story by sorting them into categories. The word *rain* names something in nature. What other words on this page name something in nature? (wind, mud) What words fit into the category of man-made objects? (school, walls, desks) We can also think about the attributes of the words we sort. Rain is something in nature that falls from the sky.

Slowly, the school disappears until there is almost nothing left. **20**

It doesn't matter. The letters have been learned and the knowledge taken away by the children.

352   353

LITERATURE ANTHOLOGY, pp. 352–353

20 Skill: Cause and Effect

Teacher Think Aloud To find the cause and effect, I begin by asking myself *What happened?* and *Why did it happen?* Let's answer the questions and add our answers to the chart.

Student Think Aloud I read the first sentence and look at the picture. What happens is that the school disappears. I ask myself, *What causes this to happen?* It happens because rain and wind tear it down.

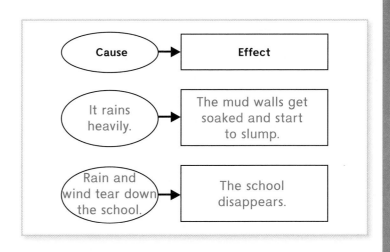

Come September, school will start over. Thomas will be a big brother then, leading the children on their first day to school. They will all stand in front of their smiling teachers, ready to build their school again.

354

355

LITERATURE ANTHOLOGY, pp. 354–355

Read

Skill: Cause and Effect

Display the chart. *What is the last cause and effect we read on page 354? Let's add it to the chart.* Read the completed chart with children. Remind them the plot of the story is the events that take place. Point out cause-and-effect relationships make up the events that make up the plot of the story.

Return to Purposes

Review children's predictions. Guide them to use text evidence to confirm whether their predictions were accurate. Discuss what children learned about how weather affects the children in Chad by reading the selection.

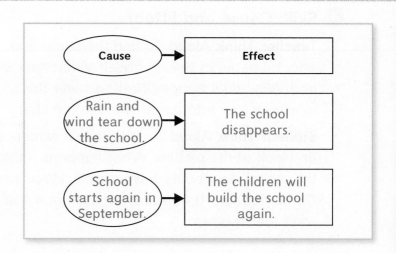

Cause	→	Effect
Rain and wind tear down the school.	→	The school disappears.
School starts again in September.	→	The children will build the school again.

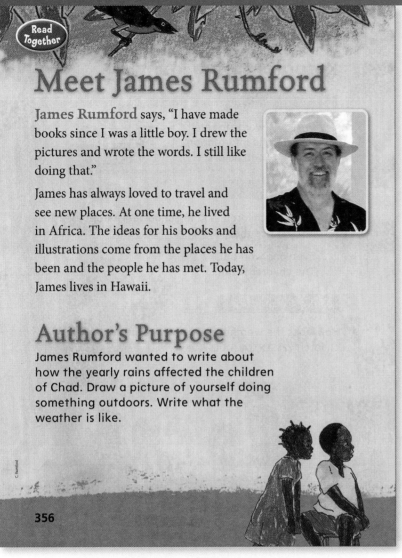

Meet James Rumford

James Rumford says, "I have made books since I was a little boy. I drew the pictures and wrote the words. I still like doing that."

James has always loved to travel and see new places. At one time, he lived in Africa. The ideas for his books and illustrations come from the places he has been and the people he has met. Today, James lives in Hawaii.

Author's Purpose

James Rumford wanted to write about how the yearly rains affected the children of Chad. Draw a picture of yourself doing something outdoors. Write what the weather is like.

356

LITERATURE ANTHOLOGY, p. 356

Meet the Author/Illustrator

James Rumford

Read aloud page 356 with children. Ask them why they think James Rumford wrote a story set in Africa. *Where does he get his ideas for the stories he writes? How do you think he knows about the rainy season in Chad?*

Author's Purpose

Have children draw a picture of themselves doing something outdoors. Have them write in their Response Journals a description of what the weather was like when they were outdoors. *I ____ outdoors. The weather was ____ that day.*

ILLUSTRATOR'S CRAFT

Focus on Color in Graphics

Tell children James Rumford used different colors to portray different kinds of weather. The colors make readers look at the illustrations and help them understand what is going on in the story.

- *What colors does Rumford use to show dry weather on pages 328–333?* (yellow/orange)
- *What color does he use to show rainy weather on 350–351?* (blue)
- *What do the colors on pages 354–355 show the reader?* (It is the dry season again.)

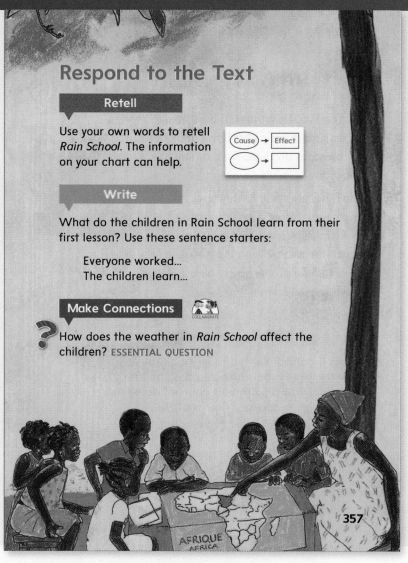

Respond to the Text

Retell

Use your own words to retell *Rain School*. The information on your chart can help.

Cause → Effect

Write

What do the children in Rain School learn from their first lesson? Use these sentence starters:

Everyone worked...
The children learn...

Make Connections

? How does the weather in *Rain School* affect the children? ESSENTIAL QUESTION

LITERATURE ANTHOLOGY, p. 357

Respond to the Text

Read

Retell

Guide children in retelling the selection. Remind them that as they read *Rain School*, they identified causes and effects and visualized what was happening in the story. Have children use the information they recorded on the Cause and Effect chart to help them retell the selection.

Reread

Analyze the Text

After children read and retell the selection, have them reread *Rain School* to develop a deeper understanding of the text by answering the questions on pages 180–182 of the *Close Reading Companion*. For students who need support finding text evidence to support their responses, use the scaffolded instruction from the Reread prompts on pages T191D–T191H.

Write About the Text

Review the writing prompt with students. Remind them to use their responses from the *Close Reading Companion* and cite text evidence to support their answers.

For a full lesson on writing a response supported by text evidence, see pages T192-T193.

<u>Answer:</u> The children learn what it means to build something important together as a community.

<u>Evidence:</u> On pages 332–333, we see that there is no school and learn that the children will be building one from scratch. On pages 334–337, we see Thomas and the other children working together to build the school. On pages 338–339, we see that the children are enjoying the work. On pages 340–341, the author includes details that help us know the children appreciate their new school and feel at home in it.

Integrate

Make Connections
COLLABORATE

Essential Question Answers will vary, but remind children to use text evidence from *Rain School* to help them tell how weather affects the children in the story.

<u>Answer:</u> The big rains and strong winds destroy the school the children worked together to build with their teacher.

<u>Evidence:</u> On pages 350-351, we see the rain and wind tearing apart the school. On pages 352-353, we see that the school has disappeared after the rain.

ENGLISH LANGUAGE LEARNERS

Retell Help children by looking at each page of the selection and asking a prompt, such as: *What is the weather like? What are the children doing?* Provide sentence starters to help children retell the selection, such as: *The children go to_____. The children worked together to _____. The weather _____.*

SOCIAL STUDIES

CONNECT TO CONTENT
WEATHER SEASONS AND CYCLES

Remind children that they have been learning about how weather affects people. Talk about the weather in the story and explain that the events described happen every year. Guide children to understand that the weather cycle in Chad has a rainy season each year. The story explains how the rainy season affects some people in Chad.

Write About the Literature Anthology

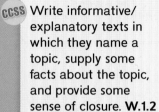

Literature Anthology

OBJECTIVES

CCSS Write informative/ explanatory texts in which they name a topic, supply some facts about the topic, and provide some sense of closure. **W.1.2**

CCSS Use personal, possessive, and indefinite pronouns (e.g., *I, me, my; they, them, their, anyone, everything*). **L.1.1d**

ACADEMIC LANGUAGE

• *idea, illustrations, concluding statement, pronoun*

• Cognates: *idea, ilustraciónes*

Analyze the Prompt Have children turn to page 357 in the **Literature Anthology**. Read the prompt: *What do the children in* Rain School *learn from their first lesson?* Explain that the first step in answering the prompt is to understand what the prompt is asking for. *The prompt is asking what the children learn from their first lesson at school. The next step in answering the prompt is to find text evidence and make inferences.*

Find Text Evidence Say: *To answer the prompt, we need to find evidence in the text and the illustrations about the children's first lesson at school. Look at pages 332–333. The text tells us that when the students arrive, there are no classrooms or desks. What does the teacher tell them their first lesson will be?* (She tells them their first lesson will be building their school.) **Have children take notes as they look for evidence to respond to the prompt. Remind them they will have to make inferences to tell what the children learn from their first lesson.**

Write to the Prompt Guide children as they begin their writing.

• **Prewrite** Have children review their notes and plan their writing. Guide them to think of their main idea and then choose details to support their main idea.

• **Draft** Have children write a response to the prompt. Remind them that they can use some of the words from the prompt in their first sentence. As children write their drafts, have them focus on the week's skills.

  • **Special Pronouns** Use special pronouns such as *everyone, anyone,* and *everything* correctly. **Grammar**

  • **Main Idea** Begin their writing with a sentence that tells their main idea. **Trait: Ideas**

  • **Concluding Statement** Add a concluding sentence that wraps up their writing and retells the main idea. **Trait: Organization**

Tell children they will continue to work on their responses on Day 4.

Go Digital

Present the Lesson

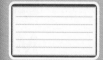

Graphic Organizer

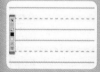

Writing

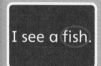

I see a fish.

Grammar

Grammar

Special Pronouns

1 Review Have children look at page 274 in the **Reading/Writing Workshop**. Remind them that the pronouns *anyone, everyone, anything, everything,* and *nothing* name a person, place, thing, or number that is not particular, or specific. Have children identify the special pronoun in the student model.

Say: *Name the pronoun in this sentence:* A news reporter said for everyone to stay inside. *The word* everyone *is the pronoun.*

2 Guided Practice/Practice Guide children to write a new sentence about how the weather affected Mom and Kim using a special pronoun and explain what the word means in the sentence.

Talk About It Have partners orally generate sentences using *nobody, somebody,* and *anybody.*

Mechanics: Commas in Dates and Letters

1 Explain Remind children that commas separate the date and year when writing a date. Explain that commas are also used after the greeting and closing in a letter.

2 Guided Practice Prompt children to identify the commas in the following letter:

May 1, 20__

Dear Anna,

I can knit! My mom showed me how. I am making a red and green scarf. I will wrap it when I am done. I will send it to you. It will keep the cold off your neck.

Your friend,

Paula

ELL

ENGLISH LANGUAGE LEARNERS SCAFFOLD

Beginning

Demonstrate Comprehension Provide sentence frames for partners as they write their responses: *The children learn _____ from their first lesson. They also learn ____.* Correct the meaning of children's responses as needed.

Intermediate

Explain Encourage children to begin their responses by stating their main idea. *What are you writing about?* Provide sentence frames, then have children complete and read them.

Advanced/High

Expand After children complete their responses, ask: *Did you state your main idea? Did you use special pronouns?* Elicit more details to support children's main ideas.

Daily Wrap Up

- Review the Essential Question and encourage children to discuss using the oral vocabulary words. Ask: *What types of weather did we read about?*

- Prompt children to review and discuss the skills they used today. Say: *Give examples of how you used each skill today.*

Materials

Literature Anthology
VOLUME 4

Visual Vocabulary Cards

creative	been
cycle	children
frigid	month
predict	question
scorching	their
country	year
gathers	

Teaching Poster

gnat

Spelling Word Cards

 a b c

Word-Building Cards

Tornado Facts

Dinah Zike's
FOLDABLES

Dinah Zike's Foldables®

→ Extend the Concept

CLOSE READING

MINILESSON
5 Mins
Rainy Weather

OBJECTIVES

CCSS Know and use various text features (e.g., headings, tables of contents, glossaries, electronic menus, icons) to locate key facts or information in a text. RI.1.5

Review vocabulary

ACADEMIC LANGUAGE

• *head, informational, information, section*
• Cognates: *informativo, información, sección*

ESSENTIAL QUESTION

Remind children that this week they have been learning about weather and how it affects us. Guide children to discuss the question using information from what they have read and discussed. Use the Visual Vocabulary Cards and the Define/Example/Ask routine to review the oral vocabulary words *creative, cycle, frigid, predict*, and *scorching*.

Guide children to use each word as they talk about what they have read and learned about weather. Prompt children by asking questions.

• When are you being more creative: when you draw a picture or when you watch television?

• What cycles do you know about?

• What do you do when the weather is frigid?

• Can you predict what would happen if you put a cup of water in the freezer?

• How do you feel when the sun is scorching?

Review last week's oral vocabulary words *inspire, respect, distance, swiftly*, and *decision*.

Go Digital

Visual Glossary

Teaching Poster

"Rainy Weather"

Text Feature: Headings

1 **Explain** Tell children they can use informational selections to find facts and details. Explain that informational text often has headings—words or phrases at the beginning of a section of text. The headings tell what information is in the section. Explain that headings are usually larger than the rest of the text.

2 **Model** Display Teaching Poster 21. Read together the first heading and the text that follows it. Guide children to discuss the information in the heading and in the section. *The heading gives information about the text in this section. It tells me the section will be about spring and summer. As I read the section, I see that all the sentences are about what happens in spring and summer.*

3 **Guided Practice/Practice** Read the second heading and the text that follows it. *What does the heading tell us? What details do we learn in the section? Can you think of a sentence we could add to this section?* Tell children to look for headings as they read informational text selections.

ENGLISH LANGUAGE LEARNERS SCAFFOLD

Beginning

Use Sentence Frames Use sentence frames to help children discuss the information. *The heading is "____ and ____." This section tells us about ____.*

Intermediate

Discuss Ask children to explain how headings can help them locate information in a text. Ask them what other illustrations could go with each section.

Advanced/High

Describe For each section, have children tell what all the sentences have in common. Ask: *Is this a good heading for this section? Why or why not?*

Genre Nonfiction

Compare Texts
Read about how rain affects some people and places.

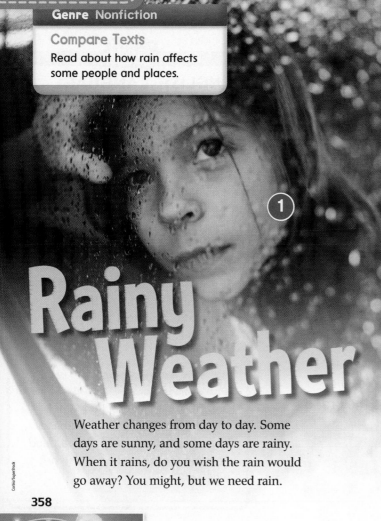

Rainy Weather

1

Weather changes from day to day. Some days are sunny, and some days are rainy. When it rains, do you wish the rain would go away? You might, but we need rain.

358

How Rain Helps   2

All living things need water. Rain helps plants grow, so that people and animals have food. Rain falls on ponds, lakes, and rivers. Then animals can drink water all year long. People need water to drink, too. We also use it for cooking and cleaning.

359

LITERATURE ANTHOLOGY, pp. 358–359

Literature Anthology

Rainy Weather   CLOSE READING   Lexile 470

Compare Texts

As you read and reread "Rainy Weather," encourage children to think about the Essential Question. Tell children to think about the good and bad things caused by rain. Point out the words *storms, damage,* and *predict.*

Read

❶ Strategy: Visualize

Teacher Think Aloud On page 358, I see a girl who looks unhappy that it is raining. I use the picture and the words to visualize what the girl is seeing and hearing.

❷ Text Feature: Headings

Teacher Think Aloud I know this selection is about rainy weather. The selection is divided into sections. The headings let me know what each section is about.

❸ Text Features: Headings

What will the section of text on page 360 be about? (stormy weather) How do you know? (The heading is "Stormy Weather.")

Retell

Guilde children to use key details to retell the selection.

Stormy Weather

We need rain, but rain can mean **storms,** and storms can mean problems. In a thunderstorm, thunder crashes! Lightning flashes! Lightning can strike trees or buildings.

A hurricane is a bigger storm. Heavy rains can cause a lot of **damage**. Winds can blow so hard that trees bend and break. There may be a flood. When it's over, people help each other clean it up.

360

Ready and Safe

Weather people can **predict** if a storm is on the way. Then we can stay safe.

In a thunderstorm or hurricane, the best place to be is inside. People may buy extra food, drinking water, and flashlights. Then they do not have to go outside. Soon the sun will be out. And then there will come another rainy day.

The red and yellow on this map show a storm.

Make Connections
How did the rain affect people in *Rain School*?
Essential Question

361

LITERATURE ANTHOLOGY, pp. 360–361

Reread

After children retell, have them reread to develop a deeper understanding of the text by annotating and answering the questions on pages 183–185 of the *Close Reading Companion*. For children who need support citing text evidence, use these Reread questions:

- Why did the author write "Rainy Weather"?
- How is the information in this selection organized?
- How do the photographs help you understand the selection?

Integrate

Make Connections

Essential Question Have children use text evidence to make connections between "Rainy Weather" and how rain affected people in *Rain School.*

CONNECT TO CONTENT
THE EFFECTS OF WEATHER

Remind children that this week they have been learning about ways weather affects us. *Have we had any of the weather described in "Rainy Weather" this week? If so, how did it affect you? If not, what can you do to prepare for it?*

STEM

 → # Word Work

Quick Review

Build Fluency: Sound-Spellings
Display the **Word-Building Cards:**
wr, kn, gn, au, aw, augh, ew, ue, ui,
ow, oy, oi, ar, ore, oar, er, ir, ur, ey,
igh, oa, oe, ee, ea, ai, ay, e_e, u_e,
o_e, _ge. Have children say the sounds.

Phonemic Awareness

OBJECTIVES

CCSS Isolate and pronounce initial, medial vowel, and final sounds (phonemes) in spoken single-syllable words. **RF.1.2c**

CCSS Decode regularly spelled one-syllable words. **RF.1.3b**

CCSS Recognize and read grade-appropriate irregularly spelled words. **RF.1.3g**

Phoneme Categorization

1 **Model** Show children how to categorize phonemes. *Listen:* knee, knot, rope. *Which word does not belong?* Knee *and* knot *both start with the /n/ sound.* Rope *does not start with the /n/ sound. It does not belong.*

2 **Guided Practice/Practice** Have children practice categorizing phonemes. Do the first set together. *Now I'll say a group of words. Listen carefully, then tell me which word does not belong and why.*

germ, hurt, toil   know, cup, nice   farm, card, join

Phonics/Structural Analysis

Build with Silent Letters *wr, kn, gn*

Review *The spellings* wr, kn, *and* gn *all contain silent letters. The spelling* wr *stands for the sound /r/; the spellings* kn *and* gn *stand for /n/. We'll use* **Word-Building Cards** *to build words with* wr, kn, *and* gn.

Place the letters *w, r, e, c, k. Let's blend the sounds together and read the word: /rrreeek/. Now let's change the* ck *to* n. Blend the sounds and read the word. Continue with *wrench, wrong, wring, wrist, write, wrote, note, knot, knit, knight, knew, gnome.*

> **Decodable Reader** Have children read "A Lighthouse Stops Wrecks" (pages 61–64) and "The Rusty Knight" (69–72) to practice decoding words in connected text.

Compound Words

Review Write the compound word *snowflake* and read it with children. Remind children that a compound word is a longer word made up of two smaller words. The word *snowflake* is made up of the words *snow* and *flake.* Remind children that you can often use the two smaller words to figure out the meaning of the compound word.

Write the following compound words: *meatball, birthday, popcorn, sundown, playground.* Have partners identify the two smaller words in each compound, then write sentences with each compound word.

Go Digital

Phonemic Awareness

Phonics

Structural Analysis

Spelling Word Sort

Visual Glossary

Spelling

5 Mins

Word Sort with *wr, kn, gn*

Review Provide partners with copies of the **Spelling Word Cards**. While one partner reads the words one at a time, the other partner should orally segment the word and then write the word.

Have children correct their own papers. Then have them sort the words by silent letter spelling pattern.

High-Frequency Words

5 Mins

been, children, month, question, their, year

Review Display **Visual Vocabulary Cards** for high-frequency words *been, children, month, question, their, year*. Have children Read/ Spell/Write them.

- Point to a word and call on a child to use it in a sentence.
- Review last week's words using the same procedure.

Expand Vocabulary

5 Mins

country, gathers

Use the Visual Vocabulary Cards to review *country* and *gathers*.

❶ Explain Explain to children that words have different forms. Help children generate different forms of this week's words by adding, changing, or removing inflectional endings *-ed, -ing,* and *-s* or *-es*. Review the meaning of each ending.

❷ Model Draw a four-column chart. Model how to remove and add endings to the word *gather*. Write *gathers* in the first column. Then write *gather, gathered,* and *gathering* in the next three columns. Read the words with children. Point out how the different endings change the meaning of *gathers*.

❸ Guided Practice Have partners fill in a two-column chart for *country*. Have them share sentences with the different word forms.

 Monitor and *Differentiate*

 Quick Check

Can children read and decode words with silent letters *wr, kn, gn*?

Can children recognize and read high-frequency and vocabulary words?

Small Group Instruction

If No → | Approaching | Reteach pp. T212–215
| ELL | Develop pp. T226–233

If Yes → | On Level | Review pp. T220–221
| Beyond Level | Extend pp. T224–225

WORD WORK **T197**

OBJECTIVES

 CCSS Participate in shared research and writing projects (e.g., explore a number of "how-to" books on a given topic and use them to write a sequence of instructions). **W.1.7**

- Build background knowledge
- Research information using technology

ACADEMIC LANGUAGE

- *tornado, form, mini, food coloring*
- Cognates: *tornado, mini*

 SCIENCE

RESEARCH AND INQUIRY

 COLLABORATE

Make a Mini Tornado

Review the steps in the research process. Tell children that today they will do a research project with a partner to learn more about tornadoes.

STEP 1 Choose a Topic

Discuss with children what they know about tornadoes. Ask what children find interesting about them. Then guide partners to begin researching tornadoes and how they form.

STEP 2 Find Resources

Discuss how to use reference materials and online resources to find facts about tornadoes. Have them use the Research Process Checklist online.

STEP 3 Keep Track of Ideas

Have children record what they learn about tornadoes in a Matchbook Foldable®. Model recording details.

Tornado Facts

Dinah Zike's
FOLDABLES

Go Digital

Resources: Research and Inquiry

Collaborative Conversations

Take Turns Talking Review with children that as they engage in partner, small-group, and whole-group discussions, they should:

- take turns talking and not speak over others.
- raise their hand if they want to speak.
- ask others to share their ideas and opinions.

STEP 4 **Create the Project: Mini Tornado**

Explain the characteristics of a mini tornado.

- Bottles A mini tornado is made of two clear plastic bottles taped together securely.
- Water One of the bottles is filled 3/4 full with water.
- Food Coloring Add a few drops of food coloring to the water so you can see the tornado clearly.

Have children create their own mini tornados.

- Guide children to fill one bottle 3/4 full with water. Help them add a few drops of food coloring to the water.
- Help them tape the bottles spout to spout.
- Have children turn the bottles over and swirl them.
- Have partners write about the results of their tornado.
- Have partners write three facts they learned about tornadoes.

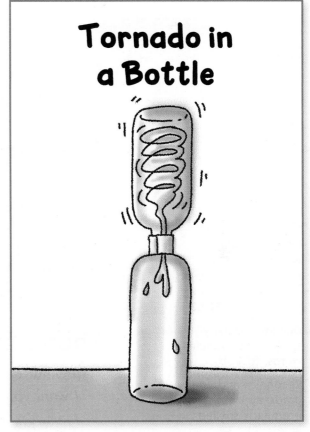

ILLUSTRATED MINI TORNADO

 ENGLISH LANGUAGE LEARNERS SCAFFOLD

Beginning	Intermediate	Advanced/High
Use Sentence Frames Use sentence frames to help children discuss tornadoes. For example: *I put ____ inside the bottles of my mini tornado. A real tornado is made up of ____.*	**Discuss** Guide children to focus on the most important details about tornadoes. Ask: *What kind of weather brings tornadoes? Is there a lot of wind when there is a tornado? What are the effects?*	**Describe** Prompt children to elaborate on tornadoes. Ask them to describe tornadoes they have seen in a movie or on television and to tell what happens when a tornado touches the ground.

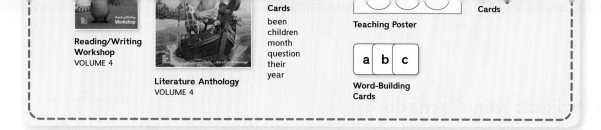

Reading/Writing
Workshop
VOLUME 4

Literature Anthology
VOLUME 4

Cards
been
children
month
question
their
year

Teaching Poster

a b c

Word-Building
Cards

Word Work/Fluency

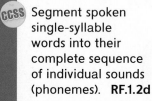

Phonemic Awareness

OBJECTIVES

CCSS Segment spoken single-syllable words into their complete sequence of individual sounds (phonemes). **RF.1.2d**

CCSS Decode regularly spelled one-syllable words. **RF.1.3b**

CCSS Recognize and read grade-appropriate irregularly spelled words. **RF.1.3g**

- Read compound words
- Recognize and read high-frequency and vocabulary words

Phoneme Segmentation

Review Guide children to segment words into phonemes. *I am going to say a word. I want you to say each sound in the word.*

wrist   mouse   flight   cheese   know   graze

Phoneme Substitution

Review Guide children to substitute phonemes. *I will say a word. I want you change the sound and say the new word.*

gnaw/knew   write/wrote   night/note   blue/blow

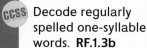

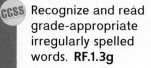

Phonics/Structural Analysis

Blend and Build with *wr, kn, gn*

Review Have children read and say the words *knee, write,* and *gnaw.* Then have children follow the word building routine with **Word-Building Cards** to build *wrong, wrote, wrist, wring, wren, wrench.*

Word Automaticity Help children practice word automaticity. Display decodable words and point to each word as children chorally read it. Test how many words children can read in one minute. Model blending words children miss.

Compound Words

Review Have children explain what a compound word is and how to form one. Then have them practice writing and reading compound words: *kneepad, haircut, toenail, doghouse,* and *football.*

Go
Digital

Phonemic Awareness

m a
n t p

Phonics

I ___ the jar.
fill | fills | filling

Structural Analysis

school

Visual Glossary

Fluency: Word Automaticity

Spelling

Word Sort with *wr, kn, gn*

Review Have children use the **Spelling Word Cards** to sort the weekly words by silent letter patterns.

Assess Assess children on their abilities to spell words with silent letters *wr, kn,* and *gn.* Say each word and provide a sentence. Then allow them time to write down the words. To challenge children, provide an additional word in each family.

High-Frequency Words

been, children, month, question, their, year

Review Display **Visual Vocabulary Cards** for the words. Have children Read/Spell/Write each word and write a sentence with each.

Review Vocabulary

country, gathers

Review Write the words and ask children to use each in a sentence. Write the sentences and reinforce word meanings as needed. Repeat the activity with last week's words or other previously taught words that children need to review.

Fluency

Intonation

Review what it means to read with expression when you read aloud and that when you come to a comma, you should pause briefly.

Read aloud the first few pages of the Shared Read. Have children echo read each sentence. Point out how you pause for each comma. Then have partners reread the selection, pausing for commas. Provide feedback as needed.

Monitor and *Differentiate*

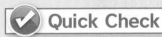

✓ Quick Check

Can children read and decode words with silent letters *wr, kn, gn*?

Can children recognize and read high-frequency and vocabulary words?

Small Group Instruction

If No →	Approaching	Reteach pp. T212–215
	ELL	Develop pp. T226–233
If Yes →	On Level	Review pp. T220–221
	Beyond Level	Extend pp. T224–225

Literature Anthology

OBJECTIVES

CCSS With guidance and support from adults, use a variety of digital tools to produce and publish writing, including in collaboration with peers. **W.1.6**

CCSS Follow agreed-upon rules for discussions (e.g., listening to others with care, speaking one at a time about the topics and texts under discussion). **SL.1.1a**

CCSS Describe people, places, things, and events with relevant details, expressing ideas and feelings clearly. **SL.1.4**

ACADEMIC LANGUAGE

• *present, evaluate, publish*
• Cognates: *presentar, evaluar*

MINILESSON 5 Mins

Independent Writing

Write About the Literature Anthology

Prepare

Tell children they will plan what they will say about their finished writing and drawing to the class. Remind children to:

- Think about how they stated their main idea in their first sentence, and included sentences to support their main idea.
- Think about how their concluding sentence retells their main idea.

Present

Have children take turns giving presentations of their responses to the prompt about the story *Rain School: What do the children in* Rain School *learn from their first lesson?* If possible, record their presentations so children can self-evaluate. Tell children to:

- Describe what the children in *Rain School* learned using relevant details.
- Listen carefully and quietly while others speak.
- Ask and answer questions to gather additional information.

Evaluate

Have children discuss their own presentations and evaluate their performance using the presentation rubric.

Use the teacher's rubric to evaluate children's writing. Have children add their writing to their Writer's Portfolio. Encourage children to look back at previous writing. Guide children to discuss what they would like to improve about their writing. Have children share their observations with a partner.

Publish

After children finish presenting their response, discuss how the class will post them in a bulletin board display. Add a map of Africa with the country of Chad highlighted to the display. Suggest that children add illustrations to their responses if they have not already done so. Guide children to use digital tools to create the bulletin board.

Go Digital

Writing

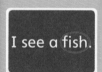

Checklists

I see a fish.

Grammar

Grammar

Special Pronouns

1 Review Have children describe how this week's special pronouns are alike. Write the following sentences and have children identify the special pronouns:

I like everything about playing outside. I will play anything that has running and jumping. Nobody likes it when it rains. But if somebody thinks of a good indoors game, everyone can still have fun! (everything, anything, nobody, somebody, everyone)

2 Practice Have children work in pairs to write sentences using *anyone, nothing,* and *anybody.*

Mechanics: Commas in Dates and Letters

1 Review Remind children that commas are used in dates, and after the greeting and closing in a letter.

2 Practice Display the letter below. Read it aloud. Have children work in pairs to fix the letter.

June 4 20__ (June 4, 20__)

Dear Miss Wall (Dear Miss Wall,)

Thank you for helping me with my reading. I can read better now. I read faster than I used to. Can you come to lunch at my house on Saturday June 7 20__? My mom and dad would like to thank you too.
(Saturday, June 7, 20__)

Sincerely (Sincerely,)

Drew

Daily Wrap Up

- Review the Essential Question and encourage children to discuss using the oral vocabulary words.

- Review with children that looking for causes and effects and visualizing story events can help them better understand what they read.

- Review words with silent letters.

- Use the Visual Vocabulary Cards to review the Words to Know.

- Remind children that realistic fiction is a made-up story that could happen in real life.

→ Integrate Ideas

Close Reading Routine

Read DOK 1–2

- Identify key ideas and details about how weather affects people.
- Take notes and retell.
- Use **A C T** prompts as needed.

Reread DOK 2–3

- Analyze text, craft, and structure.

Integrate DOK 4

- Integrate knowledge and ideas and make text-to-text connections.
- Use the Integrate Lesson.
- Use *Close Reading Companion*, p. 186.

TEXT CONNECTIONS

Connect to the Essential Question

COLLABORATE

Write the essential question on the board: *How can weather affect us?* Read the essential question aloud. Tell children that they will think about all of the information that they have learned about how weather affects us Say: *We have read many selections on this topic. We will compare the information from this week's **Leveled Readers** and* Wrapped in Ice, **Reading/Writing Workshop** *pages 262–271.*

Evaluate Text Evidence Guide children to review the selections and their completed graphic organizers. Have children work with partners to compare information from all the week's reads. Children can record notes using a Foldable®. Guide them to record information from the selections that helps them to answer the Essential Question.

Dinah Zike's
FOLDABLES
Study Organizer

Weather Together

OBJECTIVES

CCSS Participate in shared research and writing projects. **W.1.7**

RESEARCH AND INQUIRY

COLLABORATE

Have children create a checklist and review their projects:

- Does their mini tornado show how a real tornado looks?
- Do they wish to make any last minute changes to their mini tornado or the sentences about the results?
- Have they correctly written three facts they learned about tornadoes?
- Have they taken notes about what they would like to talk about when presenting their projects to the class?

Guide partners to practice sharing their projects with each other. Children should practice speaking and presenting their information clearly.

Guide students to share their work. Prompt children to ask questions to clarify when something is unclear: *What did you learn about tornadoes from the project? What were the results of the project? How is your tornado like real tornadoes?* Have children use the Presentation Checklist online.

Go Digital

Collaborate

Text to Fine Art

Read aloud with children the Integrate activity on page 186 of the *Close Reading Companion*. Have partners share reactions to the painting. Then guide them to discuss how it is similar to the selections they read earlier in the week. Have partners collaborate to complete the Integrate page by following the prompts.

Present Ideas and Synthesize Information

When children finish their discussions, ask for a volunteer from each pair to share the information from their Foldable® and their Integrate pages. After each pair has presented their ideas, ask: *How does learning about weather help you answer the Essential Question, How can weather affect us?* Lead a class discussion asking students to use the information from their charts to answer the Essential Question.

OBJECTIVES

CCSS Identify basic similarities and differences between two texts on the same topic (e.g., in illustrations, descriptions, or procedures). **RI.1.9**

SPEAKING AND LISTENING

As children work with partners in their *Close Reading Companion* or on their projects, make sure that students actively participate in the conversation and, when necessary, remind them to use these speaking and listening strategies:

Speaking Strategies

- Use agreed-upon rules for discussions, such as listening to others with care, speaking one at a time, and sticking to the subject that is being discussed.

- Try to speak in complete sentences when that is appropriate to the task.

- Include important details when answering questions asked by others.

Listening Strategies

- Listen carefully to text read aloud or information presented orally in order to ask questions about the information.

- Listen carefully to text read aloud or information presented orally in order to answer questions about the information.

- Listen quietly as the presenter speaks and wait until the speaker has finished before asking questions.

OBJECTIVES

CCSS Follow agreed-upon rules for discussions. **SL.1.1a**

CCSS Ask and answer questions about key details in a text read aloud or information presented orally or through other media. **SL.1.2**

CCSS Produce complete sentences when appropriate to task and situation. **SL.1.6**

→ Approaching Level

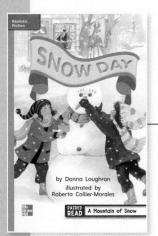

by Donna Loughran
illustrated by
Roberta Collier-Morales

PAIRED READ A Mountain of Snow

Lexile 390

OBJECTIVES

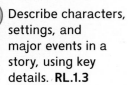 Describe characters, settings, and major events in a story, using key details. **RL.1.3**

• Visualize story events

• Recognize causes and effects

Leveled Reader:
Snow Day

Before Reading

Preview and Predict

Have children turn to the title page. Read the title and the author's name and have children repeat. Preview the selection's illustrations. Prompt children to predict what the selection might be about.

Review Genre: Realistic Fiction

Have children recall that realistic fiction is a made-up story that could happen in real life.

ESSENTIAL QUESTION

Remind children of the Essential Question: *How can weather affect us?* Set a purpose for reading: *Let's read to find out what happens on a snow day.*

Remind children that as they read a selection, they can ask questions about what they do not understand or want to know more about.

During Reading

Guided Comprehension

As children whisper read *Snow Day*, monitor and provide guidance, correcting blending and modeling the key strategies and skills.

Strategy: Visualize

Remind children that they can use the words and pictures in the story to help them picture in their minds what is happening. Model using the strategy on page 2. Say: *If I close my eyes, I see the swirling snow and one of the girls with her nose pressed to the window. It looks cold outside, but inside the house is still warm.*

Skill: Plot/Cause and Effect

Remind children that a cause is the reason why something happens. An effect is what happens. As you read, ask: *What caused Rosie and Tess to put on warm clothes?* Display a Cause and Effect chart for children to copy.

Go Digital

Snow Day

Graphic Organizer

Retell

Model recording children's answers in the boxes. Have children record the answers in their own charts.

Think Aloud On page 5 I read that the girls put on their warmest clothes. What causes them to do this? They are going out in the snow. I will write that cause and effect in my chart.

Guide children to use the text and illustrations to fill in the rest of the chart.

After Reading

Respond to Reading

Have children complete the Respond to Reading on page 12.

Retell

Have children take turns retelling the selection, using the **Retelling Cards** as a guide. Help children make a personal connection by saying: *What is your favorite kind of weather? What do you like to do in it?*

Model Fluency

Read the sentences, one at a time. Have children chorally repeat. Point out to children how you pause when you come to a comma.

Apply Have partners practice reading. Provide feedback as needed.

PAIRED READ ...

"A Mountain of Snow"

Make Connections:
Write About It *Analytical Writing*

Leveled Reader

Before reading, ask children to note that the genre of this text is informational text. Then read the Compare Texts direction together. After reading the selection, ask children to make connections between the information they learned from "A Mountain of Snow" and *Snow Day*. Provide a sentence frame such as: *I learned that when it snows people can ____.*

FOCUS ON SCIENCE

Children can extend their knowledge of weather by completing the science activity on page 16. **STEM**

Literature Circles

Lead children in conducting a literature circle using the Thinkmark questions to guide the discussion. You may wish to discuss what children have learned about snow from both selections in the Leveled Reader.

Level Up

Level-up lessons available online.

IF children can read *Snow Day*, Approaching Level with fluency and correctly answer the Respond to Reading questions,

THEN tell children that they will read a story about a different type of weather.

• Use page 4 of *Heat Wave* On Level to model using Teaching Poster 32 to list causes and effects.

• Have children read the selection, checking their comprehension by using the graphic organizer.

Approaching Level

Phonemic Awareness

PHONEME CATEGORIZATION

 TIER 2

 OBJECTIVES

Isolate and pronounce initial, medial vowel, and final sounds (phonemes) in spoken single-syllable words. **RF.1.2c**

 I Do
Explain to children that today they will be categorizing phonemes. *Listen as I say three words:* wrap, write, gate. Wrap *and* write *begin with the /r/ sound.* Gate *begins with the /g/ sound.* Gate *does not belong.*

 We Do
Let's do it together. Listen: knee, cat, knit. Knee *and* knit *begin with /n/.* Cat *does not. It does not belong.*

Repeat this routine with the following words:

write, red, night   kneel, soup, nose   new, gnat, bud

 You Do
I'll say three words. Which word does not belong?

coat, knife, not   knit, knot, sound   wool, write, wrap

PHONEME SEGMENTATION

TIER 2

 OBJECTIVES

Segment spoken single-syllable words into their complete sequence of individual sounds (phonemes). **RF.1.2d**

 I Do
Explain to children that they will be segmenting words into phonemes. *Listen as I say a word:* write. *I hear three sounds in* write: /r/ /ī/ /t/.

 We Do
Let's do it together. Listen as I say a word: know. *How many sounds do you hear in that word? Hold up a finger for each sound. Yes, there are two sounds:* /n/ /ō/.

Repeat this routine with the following words:

rage, gnat, zoo, wrote, proud

 You Do
It's your turn. Hold up a finger to show how many sounds you hear. Then say the sounds.

rent, knock, scout, gnash, cute, gnaw

PHONEME CATEGORIZATION

OBJECTIVES

CCSS Isolate and pronounce initial, medial vowel, and final sounds (phonemes) in spoken single-syllable words. **RF.1.2c**

 I Do Explain that children will be categorizing phonemes. *Listen carefully as I say three words:* bet, tend, robe. Bet *and* tend *have the /e/ sound.* Robe *does not.*

 We Do *Let's do it together. Listen to these words:* cod, wrap, gnat. Wrap *and* gnat *have the /a/ sound in the middle of the word.* Cod *does not.*

Repeat this routine with the following words:

wife, cake, knight   hill, chart, dark   most, road, sock

 You Do *I'll say three words. You say the word with a different middle sound. That word does not belong in the group.*

home, cot, wrote   rest, web, height   bird, turn, fork

PHONEME SUBSTITUTION

OBJECTIVES

CCSS Isolate and pronounce initial, medial vowel, and final sounds (phonemes) in spoken single-syllable words. **RF.1.2c**

 I Do Explain that children will substitute phonemes. *Listen carefully as I say a word:* knit. *I'll change /i/ to /o/ to make a new word: /n/ /o/ /t/. The new word is* knot.

 We Do *Let's do some together. Listen as I say the word. The word is* wrench*: /r/ /e/ /n/ /ch/. Say the word with me:* wrench. *Now let's change /e/ to /a/. The new word is* ranch. Repeat this routine with the following words:

write, wrote   fan, ran   form, farm

It's your turn. Make the changes and say the new word.

 You Do dirt/dart   gnaw/know   gnome/name   flow/fly

ELL ENGLISH LANGUAGE LEARNERS

For the **children** who need **phonemic awareness, decoding,** and **fluency** practice, use scaffolding methods as necessary to ensure children understand the meaning of the words. Refer to the Language Transfer Handbook for phonics elements that may not transfer in children's native languages.

Phonics

CONNECT TO SILENT LETTERS

OBJECTIVES

 Know the spelling-soundcorrespondences for common consonant digraphs (two letters that represent one sound). **RF.1.3a**

 I Do Display the **Word-Building Card** *wr. These are the lowercase letters* w, r. *I am going to trace the letters* wr *while I say /r/.* Trace the letters *wr* while saying /r/ five times. Remind children that you will not say a sound for the *w* because in this letter pattern the *w* is silent. Repeat with *kn* and *gn*.

 We Do *Now do it with me.* Have children trace the lowercase *wr* with their finger while saying /r/. Trace the letters *wr* five times and say /r/ with children. Continue with *kn* and *gn*.

 You Do Have children connect the letters *wr* to the sound /r/ by writing lowercase *wr*, while saying /r/. After children have written *wr* on paper five to ten times, continue with *kn* and *gn*.

Repeat connecting the letters *wr, kn, gn* to the sounds /r/ and /n/ throughout the week.

BLEND WORDS WITH SILENT LETTERS

TIER 2

OBJECTIVES

 Decode regularly spelled one-syllable words. **RF.1.3b**

 I Do Display Word-Building Cards *wr, a, p. These are the letters* w, r. *Together they stand for the /r/ sound. This is the letter* a. *It stands for the /a/ sound. This is the letter* p. *It stands for /p/. I'll blend the sounds together: /rrraaap/,* wrap.

 We Do *Do it with me.* Display the Word-Building Cards *kn, i, t. These are the letters* kn. *Together they stand for the /n/ sound. The letters* i *and* t *stand for /i/ and /t/. Let's blend the sounds together: /nnniiit/,* knit. *The word is* knit.

 You Do Have children blend the sounds and read: *wreck, write, knee, know, gnat.* Provide help as needed.

Have children blend and decode: *kneel, knock, wren, wrote, gnome, gnash.*

You may wish to review Phonics with **ELL** using this section.

BUILD WORDS WITH SILENT LETTERS

CCSS

OBJECTIVES

Decode regularly spelled one-syllable words. **RF.1.3b**

 I Do Display **Word-Building Cards** *kn, o, t. The* k *and* n *together stand for /n/. The* o *and* t *stand for /o/ and /t/. I'll blend these sounds:* /nnnooot/, knot.

 We Do *Let's build a different word.* Point to the cards forming *knot* and repeat the word. *Now I am going to change the letter* t *in* knot *to the letter* w. *Let's blend and read the new word:* /n//ō/, /nnnōōō/, know.

 You Do Have children continue building and blending words: *knock, knot, gnat, gnome, wrong, wring, wrist.*

Repeat building additional words with silent letters *wr, kn, gn.*

BLEND WORDS WITH SILENT LETTERS: *wr, kn, gn*

CCSS

OBJECTIVES

Decode regularly spelled one-syllable words. **RF.1.3b**

 I Do Display Word-Building Cards *gn, o, m, e. The letters* gn *together stand for the /n/ sound. Listen:* /nnnōōōmmm/, gnome. *The word is* gnome.

 We Do *Let's do some words together.* Blend and read the words *wrong, wrote, knife, known, gnash, gnaw.*

 You Do Display the words to the right. Have children blend and read the words.

Decodable Reader Have children read "A Lighthouse Stops Wrecks" (pages 61–64) and "The Rusty Knight" (69–72).

wrench	wring	write	wrap	wreck
knack	knee	knight	knob	known
gnaw	gnash	gnat	kneel	knock
caught	steam	few	oat	toil

There is a gnat on my knee.

Knock and twist the knob.

The knight was known to have a gold knife.

BUILD FLUENCY WITH PHONICS

Sound-Spellings Fluency

Display Word-Building Cards: *wr, kn, gn, au, aw, augh, ew, ue, ui, ow, oy, oi, ar, ore, oar, er, ir, ur, ey, igh, oa, oe, ee, ea, ai, ay, e_e, u_e, o_e, _ge.* Have children chorally say the sounds. Repeat and vary the pace.

Fluency in Connected Text

Have children review the **Decodable Reader** selections. Identify words with silent letters and blend words as needed.

Have partners reread the selections for fluency.

Structural Analysis

REVIEW COMPOUND WORDS

OBJECTIVES

Know and apply grade-level phonics and word analysis skills in decoding words. **RF.1.3**

Recognize smaller words in compound words

 I Do
Write the word *kneecap* on the board. *Some words are made up of two smaller words. These are called compound words. The word* kneecap *is made up of two smaller words:* knee *and* cap. Draw a line between the two words. Then point to your kneecap and say, *This is my kneecap.*

 We Do
Write *homework. I see the word* home. Underline *home. What other word do you see? Yes,* work. *Let's say this compound word together:* homework.

Repeat with *birdhouse, knapsack, wristband, knockout.*

 You Do
Find the two smaller words in each compound word. Have children work with partners. Give them several compound words and have them find words in each.

Repeat Have children find compound words as they read during the week. Keep a list of words that they find.

RETEACH COMPOUND WORDS

OBJECTIVES

Know and apply grade-level phonics and word analysis skills in decoding words. **RF.1.3**

Read and write compound words

 I Do
Explain that a compound word is a word made up of two smaller words. *When you identify the two words, you can often figure out the meaning of the larger word.*

Write the word *pancake. When I look at this word, I see the words* pan *and* cake. *A pancake might be a cake that is cooked in a pan.*

 We Do
Write *lunchtime. What two small words do you see in this word? Yes,* lunch *and* time. *Think about what these words mean. What does* lunchtime *mean?*

 You Do
Continue with *tugboat, backpack, daydream, bathrobe.* Have partners write one or two compound words and draw a picture showing what they mean. Provide support as needed.

Repeat Have partners create a list of other compound words.

Words to Know

REVIEW HIGH-FREQUENCY WORDS

OBJECTIVES

 Recognize and read grade-appropriate irregularly spelled words. **RF.1.3g**

Review high frequency words *been, children, month, question, their, year*

 I Do Use the **High-Frequency Word Cards** to **Read/Spell/Write** each high-frequency word. Use each word orally in a sentence.

 We Do Guide children to Read/Spell/Write each word on their **Response Boards**. Work together to generate oral sentences using the words.

 You Do Have children work with a partner to do the Read/Spell/Write routine on their own using the words *been, children, month, question, their, year*.

CUMULATIVE REVIEW

OBJECTIVES

 Recognize and read grade-appropriate irregularly spelled words. **RF.1.3g**

Review previously taught high-frequency words

 I Do Display the **High-Frequency Word Cards** from the previous weeks. Review each word using the Read/Spell/Write routine.

 We Do Have children write the words on their Response Boards. Complete sentences for each word, such as *Let's use blocks to build _____.* Show each card and have children chorally read. Mix and repeat.

 You Do **Fluency** Display the High-Frequency Cards. Point to the words in random order. Have children chorally read. Repeat at a faster pace.

REVIEW VOCABULARY WORDS

OBJECTIVES

 Identify real-life connections between words and their use (e.g., note places at home that are *cozy*). **L.1.5c**

 I Do Display the **Visual Vocabulary Cards** for *country* and *gathers*. Review each word using the Define/Example/Ask routine.

 We Do Invite children to act out each word. Then work with them to complete these sentence starters: *(1) We walked in the country and saw _____. (2) A squirrel gathers _____.*

 You Do Have partners write two sentences of their own, using each of the words. Provide assistance as needed.

Comprehension

READ FOR FLUENCY

OBJECTIVES

Read with sufficient accuracy and fluency to support comprehension. **RF.1.4**

Read grade-level text orally with accuracy, appropriate rate, and expression. **RF.1.4b**

I Do Read the first two pages of the Practice Book selection. Model using appropriate intonation. *When I see exclamation marks or question marks, my voice changes to show excitement or ask a question.*

We Do Read the rest of the Practice Book selection and have children echo-read each sentence after you. Point out how your voice changes when you see an exclamation mark or a question mark.

You Do Have children work with a partner and take turns rereading the passage aloud. Remind them to use intonation as they read, showing excitement when they see an exclamation mark or changing their voice to ask a question.

IDENTIFY PLOT

OBJECTIVES

Describe characters, settings, and major events in a story, using key details. **RL.1.3**

Identify important events in a story

I Do Remind children that they have been reading a realistic fiction selection. Point out that the plot is the events that take place in a story. *The plot tells what the characters do. It describes where they go and what happens to them during the story.*

We Do Read the first page of the Practice Book selection aloud. Model identifying and describing the major events. *We learn something important on the first page of the story. What does Mom tell Dad and Paul?*

You Do Guide children to read the rest of the Practice Book selection. Prompt them to describe what happens and why it happens.

REVIEW PLOT: CAUSE AND EFFECT

OBJECTIVES

 Describe characters, settings, and major events in a story, using key details. **RL.1.3**

 I Do Remind children that stories have characters, a setting, and a plot. The plot includes what the characters do, where they go, and what happens during the story. Point out that often one thing that happens in the story, an event, can cause something else to happen.

 We Do Read the Practice Book passage together. Pause to point out the characters, what they do, where they are, and what happens. *At the beginning we learn a storm is coming. What does this cause the family to do?*

 You Do Have partners reread the selection together. Have them work together as you guide them to complete a Cause and Effect chart.

SELF-SELECTED READING

OBJECTIVES

Describe characters, settings, and major events in a story, using key details. **RL.1.3**

Apply the strategy and skill to read a text

Read Independently

Have children pick a realistic fiction selection for sustained silent reading. Remind them to:

- recall or predict what the reading will be about.
- identify the characters and setting.
- identify the events that happen during the story.

Read Purposefully

Have children record the important events on a Cause and Effect chart. After reading, guide children to participate in a group discussion about the selection they read. Guide children to:

- share their charts.
- explain how they know the story is realistic fiction.
- discuss why certain events happen as a result of other events.

→ On Level

by Donna Loughran
illustrated by Laura Ferraro Close

PAIRED READ Stay Safe When It's Hot

Lexile 460

OBJECTIVES

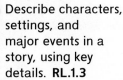 Describe characters, settings, and major events in a story, using key details. **RL.1.3**

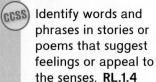 Identify words and phrases in stories or poems that suggest feelings or appeal to the senses. **RL.1.4**

With guidance and support from adults, demonstrate understanding of figurative language, word relationships, and nuances in word meanings. **L.1.5**

• Visualize story events

• Recognize causes and effects

Leveled Reader:
Heat Wave

Before Reading

Preview and Predict

Have children turn to the title page. Read the title and the author's name and have children repeat. Preview the selection's illustrations. Prompt children to predict what the selection might be about.

Review Genre: Realistic Fiction

Have children recall that realistic fiction is a made-up story that could happen in real life. Discuss the features of realistic fiction.

ESSENTIAL QUESTION

Remind children of the Essential Question: *How can weather affect us?* Set a purpose for reading: *Let's read to find out what the children do to stay cool in a heat wave.* Remind children to ask questions as they read.

During Reading

Guided Comprehension

As children whisper read *Heat Wave,* monitor and provide guidance, correcting blending and modeling the key strategies and skills. Guide children in identifying figurative language in the story, such as "I'm as hot as a hot dog on a grill," on page 2.

Strategy: Visualize

Remind children they can use the words and pictures in the story to help them picture in their minds what is happening. Model the strategy on page 3. Say: *I see a sunny day and lots of people in the pool. They are playing. Outside it is hot! What do you visualize?*

Skill: Plot/Cause and Effect

Remind children that a cause is an event that makes something happen. An effect is what happens. As you read, ask: *What are some effects the heat wave has on the children?* Display a Cause and Effect chart for children to copy.

Go Digital

Heat Wave

Graphic Organizer

Retell

Literature Circles

Lead children in conducting a literature circle using the Thinkmark questions to guide the discussion. You may wish to discuss what children have learned about hot weather from both selections in the Leveled Reader.

Model recording answers for children. Have children copy the answers into their own charts.

Think Aloud As I read, I will look for events that cause other things to happen. I read on page 4 Jamal's yard is yellow because it hasn't rained. I'll write this cause and effect in my chart.

Once the selection is finished, prompt children to complete the chart.

After Reading

Respond to Reading

Have children complete the Respond to Reading on page 12.

Retell

Have children take turns retelling the selection, using the **Retelling Cards** as a guide. Help children make a connection by asking: *What are some things you do to stay cool when it is very hot out?*

Model Fluency

Read the sentences one at a time. Have children chorally repeat. Point out to children how you pause when you come to a comma.

Apply Have partners practice reading. Provide feedback as needed.

Level Up

Level-up lessons available online.

IF children can read *Heat Wave* On Level with fluency and correctly answer the Respond to Reading questions,

THEN tell children that they will read a story about another type of weather.

• Use page 6 of *Rainy Day Fun* Beyond Level to model using Teaching Poster 32 to list causes and effects.

• Have children read the selection, checking their comprehension by using the graphic organizer.

PAIRED READ ...

Leveled Reader

"Stay Safe When It's Hot"

Make Connections: Write About It ✏ *Analytical Writing*

Before reading, ask children to note that the genre of this text is nonfiction. Then read the Compare Texts direction together. After reading the selection, ask children to make connections between the information they learned from "Stay Safe When It's Hot" and *Heat Wave*.

🧪 **FOCUS ON SCIENCE**

Children can extend their knowledge of weather by completing the science activity on page 16. **STEM**

On Level
Phonics

BUILD WORDS WITH SILENT LETTERS: *wr, kn, gn*

OBJECTIVES

Know the spelling-soundcorrespondences for common consonant digraphs (two letters that represent one sound). **RF.1.3a**

I Do

Display **Word-Building Cards** *kn, o, b. These are letters* k, n, o, b. *They stand for* /n/ /o/ *and* /b/. *Remember the* k *is silent when* k *and* n *are together. I will blend* /n/, /o /, *and* /b/ *together:* /nnnooob/, knob. *The word is* knob.

We Do

Now let's do one together. Make the word *write* using Word-Building Cards. *Let's blend the sounds to say the word. Remember that the* w *is silent when* w *and* r *are together:* /rrrīīīt/, write.

Change the letter *i* to *o. I am going to change the letter* i *to* o. *Let's blend and read the new word:* /rrrōōōt/, wrote. *The new word is* wrote.

You Do

Have children build and blend the words: *wring, wrist, wreck, wrack, knack, knit, knot, gnat, gnome.*

Repeat with additional words with silent letters *wr, kn, gn.* **Decodable Reader** Have children read "Miss Wright's Job," "A Lighthouse Stops Wrecks," "Know About Snowstorms," and "The Rusty Knight" (pages 57–72).

Words to Know

REVIEW WORDS

OBJECTIVES

Recognize and read grade-appropriate irregularly spelled words. **RF.1.3g**

Review high-frequency words *been, children, month, question, their, year* and vocabulary words *country* and *gathers*

I Do

Use the Read/Spell/Write routine to teach each high-frequency word and vocabulary word. Use each word orally in a sentence.

We Do

Guide children to Read/Spell/Write each word using their **Response Boards**. Work together to generate oral sentences using the words.

You Do

Have partners work together using the Read/Spell/Write routine with the words *been, children, month, question, their,* and *year* and the vocabulary words *country* and *gathers.* Have partners then write sentences about a place they have been. Each sentence must contain at least one high-frequency or vocabulary word.

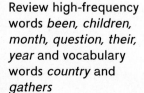

Comprehension

REVIEW PLOT: CAUSE AND EFFECT

OBJECTIVES

Describe characters, settings, and major events in a story, using key details. **RL.1.3**

I Do

Remind children that a story has characters, a setting, and a plot. *When we read a story, we look for the important events. We think about what happens and why it happens. Some events cause other events to happen.*

We Do

Read the first two pages of the Practice Book selection aloud. Pause to point out who the characters are and what they are doing. *What did Paul's family just learn? Yes, the coming storm is an important event. What do they decide to do?*

You Do

Guide children to read the rest of the Practice Book selection. Remind them to identify what happens during the story and why these events happen. Then have partners talk about the characters, setting, and plot.

SELF-SELECTED READING

OBJECTIVES

With prompting and support, read prose and poetry of appropriate complexity for grade 1. **RL.1.10**

Apply the strategy and skill to read a text

Read Independently

Have children pick a realistic fiction selection for sustained silent reading. Remind them to:

- visualize the story events as they read.
- identify the characters and setting.
- identify the important events and notice what happens during the story and why.

Read Purposefully

Have children record the important events of the plot on a Cause and Event chart. After completing the chart, guide partners to:

- share and compare their charts.
- discuss the important events in the story.

→ Beyond Level

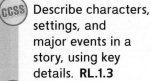

Lexile 420

Leveled Reader:
Rainy Day Fun

Rainy Day Fun

Before Reading

Preview and Predict

Read the title and author name. Have children preview the title page and the photographs. Ask: *What do you think you will learn about?*

Review Genre: Realistic Fiction

Have children recall that realistic fiction is a made-up story that could happen in real life. Prompt children to name key characteristics of realistic fiction. Tell them to look for these features as they read.

ESSENTIAL QUESTION

Remind children of the Essential Question: *How can weather affect us?* Set a purpose for reading: *Let's find out what happens to the characters on a very rainy day.*

During Reading

Guided Comprehension

Have children whisper read *Rainy Day Fun.* Have them place self-stick notes next to difficult words. Remind children that when they come to an unfamiliar word, they can look for familiar spellings. They will need to break longer words into smaller chunks and sound out each part.

Monitor children's reading. Stop periodically and ask open-ended questions to facilitate rich discussion, such as *How does the weather affect the plot?* Build on children's responses to develop deeper understanding of the text. Guide children in identifying figurative language in the story, such as "Thunder roared like a lion," on page 6.

Strategy: Visualize

Remind children that they can use the words and pictures in the story to help them picture in their minds what is happening. Model the strategy on pages 2–3: *I see everyone in the back room standing around Grandpa. Through the windows, I see gray sky and streaks of rain. There are plants all over the room. What do you see?*

Go Digital

Graphic Organizer

OBJECTIVES

(CCSS) Describe characters, settings, and major events in a story, using key details. **RL.1.3**

(CCSS) Identify words and phrases in stories or poems that suggest feelings or appeal to the senses. **RL.1.4**

(CCSS) With guidance and support from adults, demonstrate understanding of figurative language, word relationships, and nuances in word meanings. **L.1.5**

• Visualize story events
• Recognize causes and effects

Skill: Plot/Cause and Effect

Remind children that a cause is an event that makes something happen. An effect is what happens. As you read, ask: *What caused Dina to be shy?* Display a Cause and Effect chart for children to copy.

Model how to record the information. Have children fill in their chart.

Think Aloud On page 3, I read Dina was too shy to smile back. I'll write that she was shy in the Effect box. I'll continue reading to see what caused her to be so shy.

After Reading

Respond to Reading

Have children complete the Respond to Reading on page 12.

Retell

Have children take turns retelling the selection. Help children make a personal connection by writing about a time they were stuck inside during a rainstorm. *What did you do while it was raining?*

Leveled Reader

PAIRED READ ...

"Let's Stay Dry!"

Make Connections: Write About It *Analytical Writing*

Before reading "Let's Stay Dry!" have children preview the title page and prompt them to identify the genre. Discuss the Compare Texts direction. After reading, have children work with a partner to discuss the information they learned in *Rainy Day Fun* and "Let's Stay Dry!" Ask children to make connections by comparing and contrasting each selection. Prompt children to discuss what they learned about rainy weather from both selections.

Literature Circles

Lead children in conducting a literature circle using the Thinkmark questions to guide the discussion. You may wish to discuss what children have learned about rain from both selections in the Leveled Reader.

Gifted and Talented

SYNTHESIZE Challenge children to write about advantages and disadvantages of rain. Encourage them to include personal experiences.

EXTEND Have them use facts they learned from the week or do additional research to find out more about rain.

FOCUS ON SCIENCE

Children can extend their knowledge of weather by completing the science activity on page 16. STEM

ORAL VOCABULARY: MULTIPLE-MEANING WORDS

OBJECTIVES

CCSS Produce complete sentences when appropriate to task and situation. **SL.1.6**

Understand multiple-meaning words

 I Do
Remind children that sometimes a word has more than one meaning. *Sometimes a familiar word can have a new meaning. I know that the word* cycle *can mean "to ride a bike." The word* cycle *can also mean "a series of events that happen over and over." What cycles can you think of?*

 We Do
We know that scorching *can mean "very, very hot." Scorched can also mean "destroyed or devastated." The building was scorched by the fire.*

 You Do
Have partners work together to create two oral sentences, each using a different meaning of the words *cycle* and *scorch*. Ask them to share their sentences with the group.

 Gifted and Talented
Extend Have partners make up a collaborative story about a cycle, either a seasonal cycle or a cycle that one rides. Challenge them to use *cycle* with its other meaning in the story as well.

VOCABULARY WORDS: MULTIPLE-MEANING WORDS

OBJECTIVES

CCSS Produce complete sentences when appropriate to task and situation. **SL.1.6**

Understand multiple-meaning words

 I Do
Review the meaning of the vocabulary word *gathers* with children. Then remind children that some words have more than one meaning.

 We Do
The word gather *can mean "to bring or come together." The class gathers every weekday morning.* Gather *can also mean "to form an opinion." If the sky has dark clouds, what might you gather?* (It will rain.)

 You Do
Have partners work together to write sentences for both meanings of the word *gather*. Ask them to share their sentences with the group.

Comprehension

REVIEW PLOT: CAUSE AND EFFECT

OBJECTIVES
Describe characters, settings, and major events in a story, using key details. **RL.1.3**

 I Do Remind children that identifying the characters and setting and understanding the plot helps readers understand and enjoy a story. *The plot is the events that happen in the beginning, middle, and end of the story. Usually one event causes something else to happen.*

 We Do Guide children in reading the first two pages of the Practice Book selection aloud. Prompt them to discuss the characters and events in the beginning of the story. *Who are the characters? What is the first event in the story? What is the family going to do about this problem?*

 You Do Have children read the rest of the Practice Book selection independently. Remind them to ask themselves: *What happened? Why did it happen?*

SELF-SELECTED READING

OBJECTIVES
With prompting and support, read prose and poetry of appropriate complexity for grade 1. **RL.1.10**

Apply the strategy and skill to read a text

Read Independently

Have children pick a realistic fiction selection for sustained silent reading. Remind them to think about the characters, setting, and events in the story.

Read Purposefully

Have children record events in the Cause and Effect chart. After reading, guide children to:

- share their charts with a partner and discuss how one event caused something else to happen.
- record information about the story and what they liked most about it in a reading response journal.

 Independent Study Have children explain how weather played a role in the story they read. If it didn't, challenge them to rewrite their favorite part and incorporate a storm or other weather phenomenon that does affect the plot.

→ English Language Learners

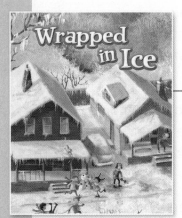

Reading/Writing Workshop

 OBJECTIVES

Describe characters, settings, and major events in a story, using key details. **RL.1.3**

Shared Read:
Wrapped in Ice

Go Digital

Wrapped in Ice

Graphic Organizer

Before Reading

Build Background

Read the Essential Question: *How can weather affect us?*

- Explain the meaning of the Essential Question: *The weather explains what it is like outside. It can be hot or cold. It can be sunny or cloudy, or wet or dry. Sometimes the weather plays a part in what people plan or do.*

- **Model an answer:** *When the weather is warm and sunny, people in my community like to be outside. They play and garden. They walk their dogs and go to the park. When the weather is windy and stormy, most people stay indoors. Sometimes neighbors help each other during a storm.*

- Ask children a question that ties the Essential Question to their own background knowledge. *What do people in your neighborhood do when it is warm and sunny? What do they do if it is windy and stormy?* Ask partners to share their answers.

During Reading

Interactive Question-Response

- Ask questions that help children understand the meaning of the text after each paragraph.

- Reinforce the meanings of key vocabulary by providing meanings embedded in the questions.

- Ask children questions that require them to use key vocabulary.

- Reinforce the comprehension strategies and skills of the week by modeling.

Wrapped in Ice

Pages 262–263

Point to each word in the title as you read it aloud. Then have children say the title with you. *This story is about an ice storm. When water freezes, it becomes ice. What does ice feel like?* (cold and smooth)

Point to the illustration. *The setting of this story is a neighborhood. What is the weather like?* (cold and icy) *The title,* Wrapped in Ice, *means that the neighborhood is covered in ice.*

Pages 264–265

Point to the illustration on page 264. *This is Kim. What does she see outside?* (Ice covers the yard, the car, and the trees.) Point to the italicized words. *These words tell how the ice sounds on Kim's window: "Ping! Ping, ping!" Say those words with me.*

Kim wants to know why everything is covered in ice. Mom says: "The air is very cold. So the raindrops freeze when they land on cold surfaces like signs, trees, and roads." Raindrops freeze when it is cold.

Explain and Model Phonics Write these words: *wrapped, design, signs.* Say each word; have children repeat it. Circle *wr* and *gn. These letter pairs have silent letters. The* w *and* g *are silent.*

Have you ever seen an ice storm? What was it like? Compare the ice storm you saw to what Kim sees out her window.

Pages 266–267

Look at the illustration. *Who do you see?* (reporter and weather map) *The reporter tells people to stay inside. Even school is closed! Let's read what Kim says: "We have a snow day!"*

Let's read page 267 together. What happened? (The lights went out.) *How do you think Kim feels about her dark house?* (worried, nervous) *Show me how your face looks when you are worried.*

Explain and Model the Skill *The lights suddenly went out at Kim's house. But what caused this to happen? Mom explains icy branches knocked down power lines. A power line is like a thick rope. It carries electricity to people's homes. The icy branches hitting the power lines are a cause. What is the effect?* (The lights went out.)

What would you do if the lights went out at home? Tell your partner what the effect would be.

Pages 268–269

Let's look at the picture on page 268. What do Mom and Kim use for light? (flashlights, fire) *What are they doing?* (eating lunch and playing games) *How do you think Kim feels now?* (happy, relieved)

Now let's look at page 269. What are the neighbors doing? (breaking ice, putting sand on the sidewalk) *Why are people's noses red? Their noses are red because it is really cold outside!*

Explain and Model the Strategy *You can make a picture in your mind to help you understand the story. Use the words and pictures to imagine the neighbors working together outside.*

Tell your partner what you visualize the neighbors doing outside.

Pages 270–271

Let's look at the picture. It looks like everyone is having fun! What are the neighbors doing? (having snacks, talking) *They had an ice party!*

Explain and Model High-Frequency Words Point to *month* and *year* and have children say them. Display a classroom calendar and point to the current month and year. *What month is it? What is the year?*

After Reading

Make Connections

• Review the Essential Question.

→ English Language Learners

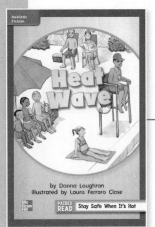

Lexile 370

OBJECTIVES

 Describe characters, settings, and major events in a story, using key details. **RL.1.3**

 Identify words and phrases in stories or poems that suggest feelings or appeal to the senses. **RL.1.4**

 With guidance and support from adults, demonstrate understanding of figurative language, word relationships, and nuances in word meanings. **L.1.5**

- Visualize story events
- Recognize causes and effects

Leveled Reader:
Heat Wave

Before Reading

Preview

Read the title. Ask: *What is the title? Say it again.* Repeat with the author's name. Preview the photographs. Have children describe the photos. Use simple language to tell about each page. Follow with questions, such as, *How are the boys trying to stay cool?*

ESSENTIAL QUESTION

Remind children of the Essential Question: *How can weather affect us?* Say: *Let's read to find out what friends do in a heat wave.* Encourage children to ask for help when they do not understand a word or phrase.

During Reading

Interactive Question-Response

Pages 2–3 *Let's visualize, or picture in your mind, the children who are hot in the story. First look at the pictures. Then listen as I read these pages. Who is the hottest?* (Martin) *Yes, Martin says, "I'm the hottest. I'm as hot as a hot dog!" Notice how Martin compares himself to a hot food. This is the author using figurative language. Martin must be really hot!*

Pages 4–5 *How do the boys feel on this day?* (very hot) *Martin asks to swim. But what does he need to put on first? Let's read the label on page 5 together: sunscreen. Sunscreen helps protect our skin from the sun. Why did the children put on sunscreen?* (It is hot and sunny. They don't want to get sunburned.)

Pages 6–7 *Look at the pictures. What do the boys think about in order to stay cool?* (ice cubes and ice cream) *Now talk with your partner about what you visualize when you think of the boys' ideas.*

Pages 8–9 *What are the boys talking about?* (places that are cold) *Have you ever heard of Iceland or the North Pole? What do you know about either place?* Show children where these places are on a map.

Pages 10–11 *The boys think of more ways to stay cool. Ty's mom has a way. Let's find the words she says.* ("You need to drink water in this heat.") *What do the boys do?* (go to the water fountain)

Go Digital

Heat Wave

Graphic Organizer

Retell

After Reading

Respond to Reading

Revisit the Essential Question. Ask children to work with partners to fill in the graphic organizer and answer the questions on page 12. Pair children with peers of varying language abilities.

Retell

Model retelling using the **Retelling Card** prompts. Say: *Look at the illustrations. Use details to help you retell the selection.* Help children make personal connections by asking, *Do you like hot weather? Why or why not? What are some ways you keep cool when you are hot?*

Intonation Fluency: Punctuation

Read the pages in the book, one at a time. Help children echo-read the pages with appropriate intonation. Remind them to read with excitement when they see an exclamation point.

Apply Have children practice reading with partners. Pair children with peers of varying language abilities. Provide feedback as needed.

PAIRED READ ...

"Stay Safe When It's Hot"

Make Connections: Write About It *Analytical Writing*

Before reading, tell children to note that this selection is informational text. Then discuss the Compare Texts direction.

Leveled Reader

After reading, ask children to make connections between the information they learned from "Stay Safe When It's Hot" and *Heat Wave.* Prompt children by providing a sentence frame: *When it's hot we should ____.*

Literature Circles

Lead children in conducting a literature circle using the Thinkmark questions to guide the discussion. You may wish to discuss what children have learned about hot weather from both selections in the Leveled Reader.

Level Up

Level-up lessons available online.

IF children can read *Heat Wave* ELL Level with fluency and correctly answer the Respond to Reading questions,

THEN tell children that they will read a more detailed version of the story.

- Use page 5 of *Heat Wave* On Level to model using Teaching Poster 32 to list causes and effects.

- Have children read the selection, checking their comprehension by using the graphic organizer.

FOCUS ON SCIENCE

Children can extend their knowledge of weather by completing the science activity on page 16. STEM

Vocabulary

OBJECTIVES

 CCSS Produce complete sentences when appropriate to task and situation. **SL.1.6**

LANGUAGE OBJECTIVE

Use oral vocabulary words

 I Do Display images from the **Visual Vocabulary Cards** one at a time to review the oral vocabulary words *predict* and *cycle*.

 We Do Display each image again and explain how it illustrates or demonstrates the word. Model using sentences to describe the image.

 You Do Display the word again. Have partners talk about how the picture shows the word.

Beginning	Intermediate	Advanced/High
Display the Visual Vocabulary Cards and say the words together. Use each word in a sentence for children to repeat.	Help children dictate a sentence using each word. Write their sentences. Read the sentences together.	Have partners each write a sentence for one of the words. Help partners read each other's sentences.

OBJECTIVES

 CCSS Identify real-life connections between words and their use (e.g., note places at home that are *cozy*). **L.1.5c**

LANGUAGE OBJECTIVE

Use vocabulary words

 I Do Display images from the **ELL Visual Vocabulary Cards** one at a time to review the vocabulary words *cool* and *sunscreen* and follow the routine. Say the word and have children repeat it. Define the word in English.

 We Do Display each image again and explain how it illustrates or demonstrates the word. Model using sentences to describe the image.

 You Do Display the word again and have children say the word, then spell it. Provide opportunities for children to use the words in speaking and writing. Provide sentence starters.

Beginning	Intermediate	Advanced/High
Help children find pictures in classroom books that relate to each word. Then have them use the word in a sentence.	Display the Visual Vocabulary Cards. Ask children to spell and repeat each word.	Have children explain the meaning of each word.

Words to Know

REVIEW WORDS

OBJECTIVES

Recognize and read grade-appropriate irregularly spelled words. **RF.1.3g**

LANGUAGE OBJECTIVE

Use high-frequency words *been children, month, question, their, year,* and vocabulary words *country* and *gathers*

 I Do

Display the **High-Frequency Word Cards:** *been, children, month, question, their, year, country,* and *gathers*. Use the Read/Spell/Write routine. Have children write words on their **Response Boards**.

 We Do

Write sentence frames on separate lines. Track as children read and complete sentences: **(1)** *We have been to _____.* **(2)** *The children ran _____.* **(3)** *This month is _____.* **(4)** *Do you have a question about _____?* **(5)** *Their pet is _____.* **(6)** *This year we will _____.* **(7)** *This country is called _____.* **(8)** *The class gathers to _____.*

 You Do

Display High-Frequency Word Cards from the previous weeks. Display one card at a time as children chorally read the word. Mix and repeat. Note words children need to review. Repeat with vocabulary words.

Beginning	Intermediate	Advanced/High
Display a calendar with pictures. Use the words in sentences about the pictures. Repeat.	Ask questions with each word. Have children use the word in answers: *What are you reading? I am reading about pets.*	Challenge partners to make up sentences using two or more words: *The children asked a question.*

RETEACH HIGH-FREQUENCY WORDS

OBJECTIVES

Recognize and read grade-appropriate irregularly spelled words. **RF.1.3g**

LANGUAGE OBJECTIVE

Use high-frequency words

 I Do

Display each **Visual Vocabulary Card** and say the word aloud. Define the word in English, then in Spanish if appropriate, identifying any cognates.

 We Do

Point to the image and explain how it illustrates the word. Have children repeat the word. Engage children in structured partner-talk with prompts on the back of the card. Ask children to chorally say the word three times.

 You Do

Display each card in random order, hiding the word. Have children identify and define words in their own words.

Beginning	Intermediate	Advanced/High
Write two sets of words on index cards. Mix the cards and place in a grid. Children match cards and read the words.	Have children draw a picture that illustrates some of the words and label pictures with the words.	List the words and read them together. Have partners look for the words in classroom books.

Writing/Spelling

WRITING TRAIT: IDEA

OBJECTIVES

 Write informative/ explanatory texts in which they name a topic, supply some facts about the topic, and provide some sense of closure. **W.1.2**

LANGUAGE OBJECTIVE

Write details to support a main idea

 I Do Explain that writers focus on a main idea and use details to support that idea. Write and read: *I blow out candles and eat cake. I open gifts. Then I play games. I have fun at my party.* Have children reread and tell the main idea.

 We Do Read aloud pages 264–266 of *Wrapped in Ice.* What details did you read? (Kim woke up to see trees and cars covered in ice. Kim has no school.) What is the main idea? (Kim and her mother get to stay home and have a special day together.) Repeat with pages 266–271.

 You Do Have children write three details and a main idea to tell about a day when they had a rainy or snowy day.

Beginning	Intermediate	Advanced/High
Have children act out how they spent a snowy or rainy day. Say a sentence about what they do, and have them repeat.	Have children act out how they spent a snowy or rainy day. Have them tell what they do. Provide sentence frames as necessary.	Have partners take turns acting and guessing how they spent a snowy or rainy day. Make sure they use complete sentences.

SILENT LETTERS: *gn, kn, wr*

OBJECTIVES

 Use conventional spelling for words with common spelling patterns and for frequently occurring irregular words. **L.1.2d**

LANGUAGE OBJECTIVE

Spell words with silent letters: *gn, kn, wr*

 I Do Read aloud the Spelling Words on page T170. Segment the first word into sounds and attach a spelling to each sound. Point out /n/ spelled *gn*. Read aloud, segment, and spell remaining words and have children repeat.

 We Do Say a sentence for *gnat*. Then say *gnat* slowly and ask children to repeat. Have them write the word. Repeat the process for the remaining words.

 You Do Display the words. Have children work with a partner to check their spelling lists. Have children correct misspelled words on their lists.

Beginning	Intermediate	Advanced/High
Guide children to trace or copy the words. Then have them repeat each word.	List the words. Then make another list of the words with missing letters. Help children to write the missing letters and read each word.	Challenge children to find and list other words with silent letters *gn, kn, wr.*

Grammar

SPECIAL PRONOUNS

OBJECTIVES

Use personal, possessive, and indefinite pronouns (*e.g., I, me, my; they, them, their; anyone, everything*). **L.1.1d**

LANGUAGE OBJECTIVE

Use indefinite pronouns correctly

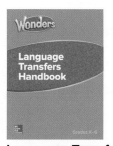

Language Transfers Handbook

TRANSFER SKILLS

Korean and Spanish children may omit subject pronouns. Write sentence frames to reinforce the subject pronoun: Everyone went to lunch. Then ask: *Who went to lunch?* Have children repeat the answer, emphasizing the subject pronoun.

 Remind children that pronouns take the place of nouns. Explain that some pronouns do not refer to a specific person or thing. Write: *Anyone can play the game.* Read the sentence together and underline the pronoun. *This pronoun does not refer to a particular person.*

Change the word *anyone* to *everyone.* Read the sentence and underline the pronoun. *Does this pronoun refer to a particular group of people? No, it does not.*

 Write the following sentences and help children read them. Underline the pronoun. Reinforce their understanding by saying: *This pronoun does not refer to a specific person or thing.*

Anyone can ride the bus.

Everything is in my knapsack.

Nothing is in the bag.

We have looked everywhere.

 List these indefinite pronouns and read them together: *anyone, everyone, anything, everything, nothing, nobody, somebody, anybody.*

Write the following sentence frames.

____ *came to the dance.*

____ *is on the rug.*

Pair children and have them complete each sentence frame by providing an indefinite pronoun from the list. Circulate, listen in, and take note of each child's language use and proficiency.

Beginning	Intermediate	Advanced/High
Help children use indefinite pronouns to complete sentences about pictures in a selection read this week.	Display selection pictures and have children describe what they see. Guide them to use indefinite pronouns.	Display each picture in a recently read selection and have children retell the story. Encourage them to use indefinite pronouns.

PROGRESS MONITORING

Unit 6 Week 3 Formal Assessment	Standards Covered	Component for Assessment
Comprehension Plot: Cause and Effect	RL.1.3	• *Selection Test* • *Weekly Assessment*
Vocabulary Strategy Similes	L.4.5a	• *Selection Test* • *Weekly Assessment*
Phonics Silent Letters *wr, kn, gn*	RF.1.3	*Weekly Assessment*
Structural Analysis Compound Words	RF.1.3e	*Weekly Assessment*
High-Frequency Words *been, children, month, question, their, year*	RF.1.3g	*Weekly Assessment*
Writing Writing About Text	RL.1.3	*Weekly Assessment*
Unit 6 Week 3 Informal Assessment		
Research/Listening/Collaborating	SL.1.1c, SL.1.2, SL.1.3	• *RWW* • *Teacher's Edition*
Oral Reading Fluency (ORF) **Fluency Goal:** 13-33 words correct per minute (WCPM) **Accuracy Rate Goal:** 95% or higher	RF.1.4a. RF.1.4b, RF.1.4c	*Fluency Assessment*

Using Assessment Results

Weekly Assessment Skills	If . . .	Then . . .
COMPREHENSION	Children answer 0–3 multiple-choice items correctly . . .	. . . assign Lessons 28-30 on Identify Plot Events and Lessons 37-39 on Sequence (fiction) from the *Tier 2 Comprehension Intervention online PDFs*.
VOCABULARY	Children answer 0–2 multiple-choice items correctly . . .	. . . assign Lesson 112 on Similes from the *Tier 2 Vocabulary Intervention online PDFs*.
PHONICS/ STRUCTURAL ANALYSIS/HFW	Children answer 0–6 multiple-choice items correctly . . .	. . . assign Lesson 56 on Silent Letters and Lesson 84 on Compound Words from the *Tier 2 Phonics/ Word Study Intervention online PDFs*.
WRITING	Children score less than "2" on the constructed response . . .	. . . reteach necessary skills using Section 13 on Write About Reading from the *Tier 2 Comprehension Intervention online PDFs*.
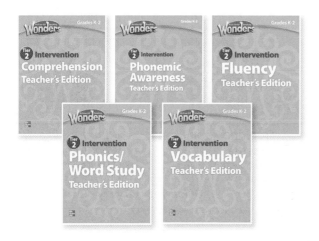 FLUENCY	Children have a WCPM score of 13 . . .	. . . assign a lesson from Section 1, 9, or 10 of the *Tier 2 Fluency Intervention online PDFs*.
	Children have a WCPM score of 0–12 . . .	. . . assign a lesson from Sections 2–8 of the *Tier 2 Fluency Intervention online PDFs*.

Using Weekly Data

Check your data Dashboard to verify assessment results and guide grouping decisions.

Data-Driven Recommendations

Response to Intervention

Use the children's assessment results to assist you in identifying children who will benefit from focused intervention.

Use the appropriate sections of the *Placement and Diagnostic Assessment* to designate children requiring:

 Intervention Online PDFs

 WonderWorks Intervention Program

Sharing Traditions

What traditions do you know about?

Teach and Model
Close Reading and Writing

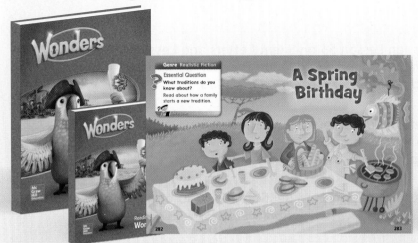

Big Book and Little Book

Reading Writing Workshop

A Spring Birthday, 282–291
Genre Realistic Fiction **Lexile** 380

Interactive Read Aloud

"Let's Dance"
Genre: Nonfiction

Practice and Apply
Close Reading and Writing

Literature Anthology   *Lissy's Friends*, 362–391
Genre Fiction **Lexile** 460

Paired Read

"Making Paper Shapes," 394–397
Genre Nonfiction **Lexile** 510

Differentiated Texts

APPROACHING
Lexile 380

ON LEVEL
Lexile 410

BEYOND
Lexile 440

ELL
Lexile 290

Leveled Readers

Extended Complex Texts

Frog and Toad Together
Genre Fiction
Lexile 330

Ling & Ting—Not Exactly the Same!
Genre Fiction
Lexile 390

Classroom Library

Ken Karp/McGraw-Hill Education

Student Outcomes

Close Reading of Complex Text
- Cite relevant evidence from text
- Demonstrate understanding of theme or central message
- Retell the text

RL.1.2

Writing
Write to Sources
- Draw evidence from fiction text
- Write narrative text
- Conduct short research on traditions

W.1.3, W.1.7

Speaking and Listening
- Engage in collaborative conversation about traditions
- Retell and discuss *A Spring Birthday*
- Present information on what traditions you know about

SL.1.1c, SL.1.2, SL.1.3

Content Knowledge
- Explore how people of different backgrounds are all part of the same world

Language Development
Conventions
- Use *I* and *me*

Vocabulary Acquisition
- Develop oral vocabulary

  tradition   effort   ancient

  movement   drama

- Acquire and use academic vocabulary

  difficult   nobody

- Use context clues to understand compound words

L.1.1, L.1.4, L.1.6, L.2.4d

Foundational Skills
Phonics/Word Study/Spelling
- Three-letter blends *scr, spl, spr, str, thr, shr*
- Inflectional endings *-ed, -ing*
- strike, spray, splash, split, scrape, three, know, write, your, heard

High-Frequency Words
before   front   heard   push

tomorrow   your

Fluency
- Appropriate phrasing

Decodable Text
- Apply foundational skills in connected text

RF.1.3, RF.1.3f, RF.1.3g, RF.1.4a, RF.1.4b, RF.1.4c

Professional Development
- See lessons in action in real classrooms.
- Get expert advice on instructional practices.
- Collaborate with other teachers.
- Access PLC Resources

Go Digital! www.connected.mcgraw-hill.com.

INSTRUCTIONAL PATH

1 Talk About Sharing Traditions

Guide children in collaborative conversations.

Discuss the essential question: *What traditions do you know about?*

Develop academic language.

Listen to "Let's Dance" to visualize how traditional dances are passed from parents to children.

2

Read *A Spring Birthday*

Apply foundational skills in connected text. Model close reading.

> **Read**

A Spring Birthday to learn about a family starts a new tradition, citing text evidence to answer text-dependent questions.

> **Reread**

A Spring Birthday to analyze text, craft, and structure, citing text evidence.

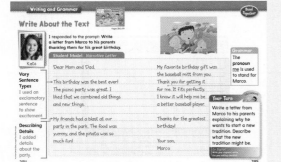

Write About *A Spring Birthday*

3

Model writing to a source.

Analyze a short response student model.

Use text evidence from close reading to write to a source.

4 Read and Write About Traditions

Practice and apply close reading of the anchor text.

> **Read**

Lissy's Friends to learn about a family tradition that helps someone make friends.

> **Reread**

Lissy's Friends and use text evidence to understand how the author presents information about a young girls family tradition.

> **Integrate**

Information about traditions.

Write to a Source, citing text evidence to write a letter from Lissy to her friends.

5 Independent Partner Work

Gradual release of support to independent work

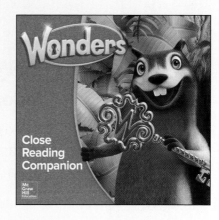

- Text-Dependent Questions
- Scaffolded Partner Work
- Talk with a Partner
- Cite Text Evidence
- Complete a sentence frame.
- Guided Text Annotation

6 Integrate Knowledge and Ideas

Connect Texts

Text to Text Discuss how each of the texts answers the question: What traditions do you know about?

Text to Photography Compare information about traditions in the texts read with the photograph.

Conduct a Short Research Project

Create a poster about a tradition.

DEVELOPING READERS AND WRITERS

Write to Sources: Narrative

Day 1 and Day 2

Shared Writing

- Write a letter from a character in the story inviting a friend, p. T252

Interactive Writing

- Analyze a student model, p. T262
- Write a letter from the same character thanking his parents, p. T263
- Find Text Evidence
- Apply Writing Trait: Sentence Fluency: Varying Sentence Types, p. T263
- Apply Grammar Skill: *I* and *Me*, p. T263

Day 3, Day 4 and Day 5

Independent Writing

- Write a letter telling what happens next from a character in *Lissy's Friends,* p. T270
- Provide scaffolded instruction to meet student needs, p. T270
- Find Text Evidence, p. T270
- Apply Writing Trait: Sentence Fluency: Varying Sentence Types, p. T270
- Prewrite and Draft, p. T270
- Revise and Edit, p. T276
- Final Draft, p. T277
- Present, Evaluate, and Publish, p. T282

Grammar

Using *I* and *Me*

- Use *I* and *me* to tell what is happening, pp, T253, T263, T271, T276, T283
- Apply grammar to writing, pp. T253, T262, T270, T283

Mechanics: Commas in Dates and Letters

- Use commas in dates and letters, pp. T271, T277, T283

Online PDFs

Grammar Practice, pp. 141–145

Online Grammar Games

Spelling

Words with Three-Letter Blends

- Spell words with three-letter blends

Online PDFs

Phonics/Spelling blms
pp. 141–145

Online Spelling Games

SUGGESTED LESSON PLAN

READING		DAY 1	DAY 2
Teach, Model and Apply *Reading/Writing Workshop*	Core	**Build Background** Sharing Traditions, T242–T243 **Oral Vocabulary** *tradition, effort,* T242 **Word Work** T246–T249 • Fluency: Sound-Spellings • Phonemic Awareness: Syllable Addition • Phonics/Spelling: Introduce Three-Letter Blends • High-Frequency Words: *before, front, heard, push, tomorrow, your* • Vocabulary: *difficult, nobody* **Shared Read** *A Spring Birthday,* T250–T251	**Oral Language** Sharing Tradition, T254 **Oral Vocabulary** *ancient, movement, effort, tradition, drama,* T254 **Word Work** T256–T259 • Phonemic Awareness: Phoneme Segmentation • Structural Analysis: Inflectional Endings *-ed, -ing* • Vocabulary: *difficult, nobody* **Shared Read** *A Spring Birthday,* T260–T261 • Genre: Realistic Fiction, T260 • Skill: Theme, T261
	Options	**Listening Comprehension** "Let's Dance!," T244–T245	**Listening Comprehension** "Let's Dance!," T255 **Word Work** T256–T259 • Phonics/Spelling: Review Three-Letter Blends • High-Frequency Words
LANGUAGE ARTS			
Writing **Grammar**	Core	**Shared Writing** T252 **Grammar** *I* and *Me,* T253	**Interactive Writing** T262 **Grammar** *I* and *Me,* T263
	Options		

DIFFERENTIATED INSTRUCTION

Use your data dashboard to determine each student's needs. Then select instructional supports options throughout the week.

APPROACHING LEVEL

Leveled Reader
The Quilt, T286–T287
"Making a Quilt Square," T287
Literature Circles, T287

Phonemic Awareness
Phoneme Blending, T288 
Phoneme Segmentation, T288
Syllable Addition, T289
Phoneme Substitution, T289

Phonics
Connect Three-Letter Blends and Letters, T290
Blend Words with Three-Letter Blends, T290
Build Words with Three-Letter Blends, T291
Build Fluency with Phonics, T291

Structural Analysis
Review Inflectional Endings *-ing -ed,* T292

Words to Know
Review, T293

Comprehension
Read for Fluency, T294
Identify Plot, 294
Review Theme, T295
Self-Selected Reading, T295

ON LEVEL

Leveled Reader
Latkes for Sam, T296–T297
"What is a Taco?," T297
Literature Circles, T297

Phonics
Build Words with Three-Letter Blends, T298

DAY 3	**DAY 4**	**DAY 5**
Fluency Phrasing, T265	**Extend the Concept** T272–T273	**Word Work** T280–T281
Word Work T266–T269	• Text Feature: Directions, T273	• Phonemic Awareness: Phoneme Blending/
• Phonemic Awareness: Phoneme Blending	• Close Reading: "Making Paper Shapes,"	Substitution
• Phonics/Spelling: Blend Words with Three-Letter	T273A–T273B	• Phonics/Spelling: Blend and Build Words with
Blends	**Word Work** T274–T275	Three-Letter Blends
• Vocabulary Strategy: Compounds Words	• Phonemic Awareness: Phoneme Segmentation	• Structural Analysis: Inflectional Endings -ed, -ing
Close Reading Lissy's Friends, T269A–T269R	• Structural Analysis: Inflectional Endings -ed, -ing	• High-Frequency Words
	Integrate Ideas	• Vocabulary: difficult, nobody
	• Research and Inquiry, T278–T279	**Integrate Ideas**
		• Text Connections, T284–T285
Oral Language Sharing Traditions, T264	**Word Work** T274–T275	**Word Work** T280–T281
Word Work T266–T269	• Fluency: Sound-Spellings	• Fluency: Phrasing
• Structural Analysis: Inflectional Endings -ed, -ing	• Phonics/Spelling: Build Words with Three-Letter	**Integrate Ideas**
• High-Frequency Words	Blends	• Research and Inquiry, T284
	• High-Frequency Words	• Speaking and Listening, T285
	• Vocabulary: difficult, nobody	
	Close Reading Lissy's Friends, T269A–T269R	
Independent Writing T270	**Independent Writing** T276	**Independent Writing** T282
Grammar Mechanics: Commas in Dates and	**Grammar** Mechanics: Commas in Dates and	**Grammar** I and Me, T283
Letters, T271	Letters, T277	
Grammar I and Me, T271	**Grammar** I and Me, T277	**Grammar** Mechanics: Commas in Dates and Letters, T283

BEYOND LEVEL		ENGLISH LANGUAGE LEARNERS	
Words to Know Review Words, T298	**Leveled Reader** Patty Jumps!, T300–T301 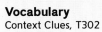 "How to Play Four Square," T301 Literature Circles, T301	**Shared Read** A Spring Birthday, T304–T305 **Leveled Reader** Latkes for Sam, T306–T307 "What is a Taco?," T307 Literature Circles, T307	**Words to Know** Review Words, T309 Reteach High-Frequency Words, T309
Comprehension Review Theme, T299 Self-Selected Reading, T299	**Vocabulary** Context Clues, T302 **Comprehension** Review Theme, T303 Self-Selected Reading, T303 Gifted and Talented	**Vocabulary** Preteach Oral Vocabulary, T308 Preteach ELL Vocabulary, T308	**Writing/Spelling** Writing Trait: Sentence Fluency, T310 Three-Letter Blends, T310 **Grammar** I and Me, T311

DIFFERENTIATE TO ACCELERATE

  Scaffold to **A**ccess **C**omplex **T**ext

IF the text complexity of a particular selection is too difficult for children

THEN see the references noted in the chart below for scaffolded instruction to help children Access Complex Text.

Qualitative   Quantitative
Reader and Task
TEXT COMPLEXITY

	Reading/Writing Workshop	Literature Anthology	Leveled Readers	Classroom Library
			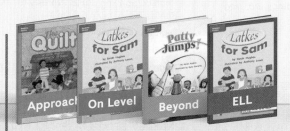	
Quantitative	*A Spring Birthday* **Lexile** 380	*Lissy's Friends* **Lexile** 460 "Making Paper Shapes" **Lexile** 510	**Approaching Level** **Lexile** 380 **Beyond Level** **Lexile** 440	**On Level** **Lexile** 410 **ELL** **Lexile** 290	*Library Lion* **Lexile** 470 *Ling & Ting: Not Exactly the Same!* **Lexile** 390
Qualitative	**What Makes the Text Complex?** **Foundational Skills** • Decoding with three-letter blends *scr, spl, spr, str, thr, shr,* T246–T247 • Reading words with inflectional endings *-ed, -ing,* T257 • Identifying high-frequency words, T248–T249 *See Scaffolded Instruction in Teacher's Edition, T246–T247, T248–T249, and T257.*	**What Makes the Text Complex?** • Connection of Ideas, T269B, T269G • Genre, T269B, T269C **ACT** *See Scaffolded Instruction in Teacher's Edition, T269B, T269C, and T269G.*	**What Makes the Text Complex?** **Foundational Skills** • Decoding with three-letter blends *scr, spl, spr, str, thr, shr* • Reading words with inflectional endings *-ed, -ing* • Identifying high-frequency words *before front heard push tomorrow your* *See Level Up lessons online for Leveled Readers.*		**What Makes the Text Complex?** • Purpose • Specific Vocabulary • Prior Knowledge • Sentence Structure • Organization • Connection of Ideas • Genre **ACT** *See Scaffolded Instruction in Teacher's Edition, T413–T415.*
Reader and Task	**The** Introduce the Concept lesson on pages T242–T243 will help determine the reader's knowledge and engagement in the weekly concept. See pages T250–T251, T260–T261, T278–T279 and T284–T285 for questions and tasks for this text.	**The** Introduce the Concept lesson on pages T242–T243 will help determine the reader's knowledge and engagement in the weekly concept. See pages T269A–T269R, T273A–T 273B, T278–T279 and T284–T285 for questions and tasks for this text.	**The** Introduce the Concept lesson on pages T242–T243 will help determine the reader's knowledge and engagement in the weekly concept. See pages T286–T287, T296–T297, T300–T301, T306–T307, T278–T279 and T284–T285 for questions and tasks for this text.		**The** Introduce the Concept lesson on pages T242–T243 will help determine the reader's knowledge and engagement in the weekly concept. See pages T413–T415 for questions and tasks for this text.

Monitor and *Differentiate*

Quick Check

To differentiate instruction use the Quick Checks to assess students' needs and select the appropriate small group instruction focus.

Comprehension Strategy Visualize, T245

Comprehension Skill Theme, T261

Phonics Three-Letter Blends, T249, T259, T269, T275, T281

High-Frequency Words and Vocabulary T249, T259, T269, T275, T281

If No → | **Approaching Level** | Reteach T286–T295
| **ELL** | Develop T304–T311

If Yes → | **On Level** | Review T296–T299
| **Beyond Level** | Extend T300–T303

Using Weekly Data

Check your data Dashboard to verify assessment results and guide grouping decisions.

Level Up with Leveled Readers

IF children can read their leveled text fluently and answer comprehension questions

THEN work with the next level up to accelerate children's reading with more complex text.

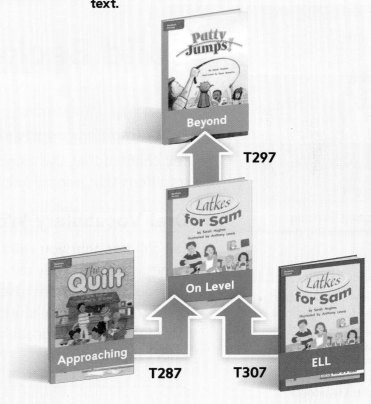

Beyond — T297

On Level

Approaching — T287

ELL — T307

ENGLISH LANGUAGE LEARNERS

Small Group Instruction

Use the ELL small group lessons in the *Wonders* Teacher's Edition to provide focused instruction.

Language Development
Vocabulary preteaching, oral vocabulary preteaching, high-frequency word review and reteach, pp. T308–T309

Close Reading
Interactive Question-Response routines for scaffolded text-dependent questioning for reading and rereading the Shared Read and Leveled Reader, pp. T304–T307

Writing
Focus on the writing trait, grammar, and spelling, pp. T310–T311

Additional ELL Support

Use Wonders for English Learners for ELD instruction that connects to the core.

Language Development
My Language Book for ample opportunities for discussions and scaffolded language support

Close Reading
Guided support for the Shared Read, Big Books, and Interactive Read Alouds. Differentiated texts about the weekly concept

Writing
Guided support in Interactive and Independent Writing and writing to sources

Wonders for ELs Teacher Edition and My Language Book

Materials

Reading/Writing Workshop
VOLUME 4

Reading/Writing Workshop Big Book
UNIT 6

Visual Vocabulary Cards
ancient
drama
effort
movement
tradition

 before

High-Frequency Word Cards
before   push
front   tomorrow
heard   your

 difficult

Vocabulary Cards
difficult
nobody

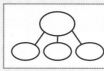
Teaching Poster

 a b c
Word-Building Cards

Think Aloud Clouds

Interactive Read-Aloud Cards

Photo Cards

Reading/Writing Workshop Big Book

OBJECTIVES

CCSS Follow agreed-upon rules for discussions (e.g., listening to others with care, speaking one at a time about the topics and texts under discussion). **SL.1.1a**

• Build background knowledge
• Discuss the Essential Question

ACADEMIC LANGUAGE

• *traditions, celebrate*
• Cognates: *tradiciones, celebrar*

 → # Introduce the Concept

Build Background

MINILESSON 5 Mins

ESSENTIAL QUESTION

What traditions do you know about?

Tell children that this week they will be talking and reading about traditions that people follow and pass down.

Oral Vocabulary Words

Tell children that you will share some words that they can use as they discuss traditions. Use the Define/Example/Ask routine to introduce the oral vocabulary words **effort** and **tradition**.

Visual Vocabulary Cards

Oral Vocabulary Routine

<u>Define:</u> When you make an **effort**, you try very hard to do something.

<u>Example:</u> Liz made an effort to finish her chores quickly so she could go outside to play.

<u>Ask:</u> Which takes more effort: climbing a tree or sitting under a tree?

<u>Define:</u> A **tradition** is a custom or holiday that is passed down from the past to the present.

<u>Example:</u> It's a tradition in Jorge's family to have a big party on the first day of summer.

<u>Ask:</u> Can you think of some traditions that your family follows?

Discuss the theme of "Sharing Traditions." Have children tell about traditions their families enjoy. *Are there special holidays your family celebrates? How do you celebrate?*

Go Digital

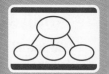
Sharing TraditiAons

Video

school
Visual Glossary

Graphic Organizer

Reading/Writing Workshop, pp. 276–277

Talk About It: Sharing Traditions

Guide children to discuss what the grandmother and her grandson are doing in this photo.

- What is the grandmother teaching her grandson?

- Why do you think she is passing along this tradition?

Use Teaching Poster 40 and prompt children to complete the Word Web by sharing words to describe the tradition being shared in the photograph.

Have children look at page 276 of their Reading/Writing Workshop and do the Talk About It activity with a partner.

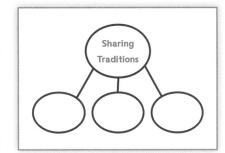

Teaching Poster

Collaborative Conversations

Add New Ideas As children engage in partner, small-group, and whole-group discussions, encourage them to:

- stay on topic.

- connect their own ideas to the comments of others.

- look for ways to connect their experiences to the conversation.

ELL

ENGLISH LANGUAGE LEARNERS SCAFFOLD

Beginning

Use Visuals Help children to describe the photo of the grandmother and grandson. *They are knitting. What colors are they knitting? Who is teaching? Who is learning?* Repeat responses as complete sentences.

Intermediate

Describe Ask children to describe the activity that the grandmother and grandson are sharing. *Can you tell what they are making? Who is helping whom? How can you tell?* Clarify children's responses as needed by providing vocabulary.

Advanced/High

Discuss Have children elaborate on what is happening in the photo. Describe something you have learned from a family member. Elicit more details to support children's answers.

→ # Listening Comprehension

CLOSE READING

Read the Interactive Read Aloud

MINILESSON
10 Mins

OBJECTIVES

CCSS Participate in collaborative conversations with diverse partners about *grade 1 topics and texts* with peers and adults in small and larger groups. **SL.1.1**

• Develop concept understanding

• Develop reading strategy: Visualize

ACADEMIC LANGUAGE

• *visualize, tradition, dance*

• Cognates: *visualizar, tradición*

Connect to Concept: Sharing Traditions

Tell children that they will now read about some special traditional dances. Ask: *Do you know any special dances? What are they like?*

"Let's Dance!"

Focus on Oral Vocabulary

Review the oral vocabulary words *effort* and *tradition*. Use the Define/Example/Ask routine to introduce the oral vocabulary words *ancient, drama,* and *movement.* Prompt children to use the words as they discuss traditions.

Go Digital

"Let's Dance!"

I was able to picture in my mind...
Visualize

school
Visual Glossary

Retell

Oral Vocabulary Routine

<u>Define:</u> **Ancient** means "very, very old."

<u>Example:</u> The ancient tree was planted by my great-grandfather.

<u>Ask:</u> What can you think of that might be ancient?

<u>Define:</u> If something has **drama**, it gives you a feeling of surprise and excitement.

<u>Example:</u> The movie about the superhero saving the world had a lot of drama.

Visual Vocabulary Cards

<u>Ask:</u> Which movie scene has more drama: a scene of a man working at a computer or a scene of a man being chased by a lion?

<u>Define:</u> A **movement** is a way that someone or something moves.

<u>Example:</u> The bird was startled by the movement of the flag blowing in the wind.

<u>Ask:</u> Show me a movement you can make with your hands.

Set a Purpose for Reading

- Display the Interactive Read-Aloud Cards.
- Read aloud the title.
- Tell children that you will be reading an informational selection about traditional dances. Say: *Traditional dances are passed on from parents to children.* Tell children to read to find out who does traditional dances.

Strategy: Visualize

1 Explain to children that as they read or listen to a text, they can use the words and illustrations to visualize, or create pictures in their minds, of the important details. This can help them understand the text.

Think Aloud Visualizing the details and facts in the text you read can help you better understand the text. As we read, think about the author's words and look at the illustrations. Then close your eyes and create a picture in your mind. As we read, change the picture in your mind using the words in the selection.

2 **Model** Read the selection. As you read, use the Think Aloud Cloud to model applying the strategy.

Think Aloud I look at the photograph and read the words, "In the Jingle Dance, women decorate their skirts with small metal cones. The cones jingle as the women dance." When I think about the details in these words and the photograph, I am able to picture in my mind a woman wearing an outfit that has metal cones on it. I see the cones hitting each to make a jingling sound as the woman dances.

3 **Guided Practice** As you continue to read, pause to encourage children to visualize. *What do you see in your mind? What do the words and illustrations make you see?* Guide children in using the details in the text and illustrations to visualize what is happening in the text.

Respond to Reading

After reading, prompt children to retell "Let's Dance!" Guide them to discuss the traditions that they learned about. Discuss what they pictured in their minds as they listened.

ENGLISH LANGUAGE LEARNERS SCAFFOLD

Beginning

Engage Display Card 1. *In your mind, can you see clothes with animal bones, hides, and feathers? Are the people dancing? Does the dance look fun? Repeat responses in complete sentences.*

Intermediate

Describe Display Card 1. Have children look at the illustration and then close their eyes. *What do you see in your mind? Describe it.*

Advanced/High

Describe Have children look at the illustrations in the selection. Then have children close their eyes and retell the selection as they visual each part of the text. Encourage them to describe the details they see in their minds.

Monitor and *Differentiate*

 Quick Check

Can children apply the strategy visualize?

Small Group Instruction

If No →	Approaching	Reteach pp. T286–287
	ELL	Develop pp. T304–307
If Yes →	On Level	Review pp. T296–297
	Beyond Level	Extend pp. T300–301

→ # Word Work

MINILESSON 5 Mins

Phonological Awareness

OBJECTIVES

CCSS Decode regularly spelled one-syllable words. **RF.1.3b**

Add syllables to words

Syllable Addition

1 Model Model adding syllables to words to form new words. *Listen as I say a word:* pup. *Now I will add the syllable* pet *to the end of* pup *and blend the sounds to make a new* word: pup-pet. *The new word is* puppet. Puppet *has two syllables, or word parts,* pup *and* pet.

2 Guided Practice/Practice Have children practice adding syllables to words to form new words. *I will say a word and a syllable to add to the word. You blend the word chunks and tell me the new word. Let's do the first one together.*

Add /ten/ to the end of kit.   *Add /ed/ to the end of* taste.

Add /ing/ to the end of bake.   *Add /not/ to the end of* can.

MINILESSON 10 Mins

Phonics

Photo Cards

Introduce Three-Letter Blends

1 Model Display **Word-Building Cards** *s, p, l, i, t.* Teach that when three consonants appear together in a word, we often blend the three sounds together. *These are the letters* s, p, *and* l. *I'll blend the sounds to get /spl/. Say it with me: /spl/. These are the sounds at the beginning of the word* split. *Listen: /s/ /p/ /l/ /i/ /t/.* Repeat with *scr, spr, str, thr,* and *shr.* Point out the digraph /th/ *th* in *thr* and the digraph /sh/ *sh* in *shr.*

2 Guided Practice/Practice Have children practice connecting the letters *s, p,* and *l* to the /spl/ sounds by writing the spelling. *Now do it with me. Say /spl/ as I write the letters* s, p, *and* l. *This time, write the letters* s, p, *and* l *five times as you say the /spl/ sounds.* Repeat for *scr, spr, str, thr,* and *shr.* Remind children that the three-letter blends *thr* and *shr* are made up of a digraph and *r.*

Go Digital

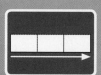

Phonological Awareness

Phonics

Handwriting

Blend with Three-Letter Blends

1 Model Display **Word-Building Cards** *s, t, r, e, e, t*. Model how to blend the sounds. *These are the letters* s, t, *and* r. *Together they stand for /str/. These are the letters* ee. *Together they stand for /ē/. This is the letter* t. *It stands for /t/. Listen as I blend these sounds together: /ssstrrrēēēt/. Say it with me.* Continue by modeling the words *scrap, splash, sprout, three,* and *shrug.*

2 Guided Practice/Practice Display the Day 1 Phonics Practice Activity. Read each word in the first row, blending the sounds, for example, /ssstrrrooong/. The word is *strong.* Have children blend each word with you. Prompt children to read the connected text, sounding out the decodable words.

strong	street	scrub	spray	threw
split	throne	straw	shrink	screen
spread	strike	scrap	throat	strange
writers	glued	taught	kneepad	bedspread

Is thread as strong as string?

We will stroll down the street.

Three fish splashed in the stream. | Also online

Day 1 Phonics Practice Activity

Corrective Feedback

Sound Error Model the sounds that children missed, then have them repeat the sounds. Say: *My turn.* Tap under the letters and say: *Sounds? What are the sounds?* Return to the beginning of the word. Say: *Let's start over.* Blend the word with children again.

 Daily Handwriting

Throughout the week teach uppercase and lowercase letters *Jj* using the Handwriting models.

ENGLISH LANGUAGE LEARNERS

Phonological Awareness: Minimal Contrasts Focus on articulation. Say each blend, clearly pronouncing the individual sounds. Have children repeat. Then say two similar words with three-letter blends and have children pronounce each one: *scrap/strap, sprawl/scrawl, thread/spread, shrill/thrill.*

Phonics: Variations in Language In many Asian languages, including Cantonese, Vietnamese, Hmong, and Korean, there is no direct sound transfer for /r/. Emphasize /r/ and show correct mouth position when pronouncing each blend containing *r*. Practice with Approaching Level phonics lessons.

ON-LEVEL PRACTICE BOOK p. 307

Sometimes three consonants form a **blend**.

scrap splash spray street three shrub

Read the first word. Then circle another word in the line with the same three-letter blend.

1. street   (straw)   tree   sharp

2. shrub   (shred)   should   both

3. scrap   cry   (scratch)   school

4. three   thing   (threw)   tree

5. spray   spot   soap   (spring)

6. splash   seat   play   (split)

APPROACHING p. 307	BEYOND p. 307	ELL p. 307

→ # Word Work

Quick Review

High-Frequency Words: Read, Spell, and Write to review last week's high-frequency words: *been, children, month, question, their, year.*

MINILESSON 5 Mins

Spelling

OBJECTIVES

CCSS Recognize and read grade-appropriate irregularly spelled words. **RF.1.3g**

CCSS Use conventional spelling for words with common spelling patterns and for frequently occurring irregular words. **L.1.2d**

Words with Three-Letter Blends

Dictation Use the Spelling Dictation routine for each word to help children transfer their knowledge of sound-spellings to writing.

Pretest Pronounce each spelling word. Say a sentence for each word and pronounce the word again. Ask children to say each word, stretching the sounds, before writing it. After the pretest, display the spelling words and write each word as you say the letter names. Have children check their words.

strike	spray	splash	split	scrape
three	know	write	your	heard

For Approaching Level and Beyond Level children, refer to the Differentiated Spelling Lists for modified word lists.

Go Digital

Spelling Word Routine

High-Frequency Word Routine

MINILESSON 5 Mins

High-Frequency Words

before, front, heard, push, tomorrow, your

1 Model Display the **High-Frequency Word Cards** *before, front, heard, push, tomorrow,* and *your*. Use the Read/Spell/Write routine.

ENGLISH LANGUAGE LEARNERS

Pantomime Review the meaning of these words by using pictures, pantomime, or gestures when possible. Have children repeat or act out the word.

- **Read** Point to and say the word *before*. *This is the word* before. *Say it with me:* before. *I got to school before you.*

- **Spell** *The word* before *is spelled* b-e-f-o-r-e. *Spell it with me.*

- **Write** *Write the word in the air as we say the letters:* b-e-f-o-r-e.

- Follow the same steps to introduce *front, heard, push, tomorrow,* and *your.*

- As children spell each word with you, point out irregularities in sound-spellings, such as the /ûr/ sound spelled *ear* in *heard*.

COLLABORATE
- Have partners create sentences using each word.

school

Visual Glossary

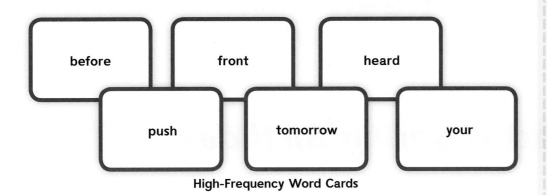

| before | front | heard |
| push | tomorrow | your |

High-Frequency Word Cards

2 Guided Practice Have children read the following sentences. Prompt them to identify the high-frequency words in connected text and to blend the decodable words.

1. My name comes **before your** name in ABC order.

2. **Push** the cart in **front** of you.

3. Had you **heard** that the plane will fly **tomorrow**?

MINILESSON
5 Mins

Introduce Vocabulary

difficult, nobody

1 Model Introduce the new words using the routine.

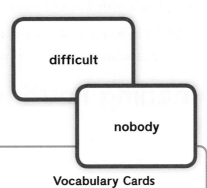

difficult

nobody

Vocabulary Cards

Vocabulary Routine

<u>Define:</u> Something that is **difficult** is not easy.

<u>Example:</u> *It is difficult to learn to speak a new language.*

<u>Ask:</u> Name a word that means something similar to difficult. SYNONYM

<u>Define:</u> **Nobody** means "no person."

<u>Example:</u> *We came to visit, but nobody was home.*

<u>Ask:</u> Why might nobody be home? EXPLANATION

2 Review Use the routine to review last week's vocabulary words.

Monitor and *Differentiate*

✓ **Quick Check**

Can children read and decode words with three-letter blends?

Can children recognize and read high-frequency and vocabulary words?

Small Group Instruction

If No → Approaching Reteach pp. T290–293

ELL Develop pp. T304–311

If Yes → On Level Review pp. T298–299

Beyond Level Extend pp. T302–303

WORD WORK **T249**

→ # Shared Read

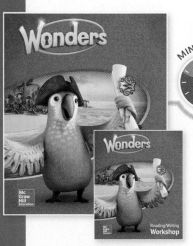

Reading/Writing Workshop Big Book and Reading/Writing Workshop

---

OBJECTIVES

CCSS Decode regularly spelled one-syllable words. **RF.1.3b**

CCSS Recognize and read grade-appropriate irregularly spelled words. **RF.1.3g**

Understand realistic fiction genre

ACADEMIC LANGUAGE

• *realistic fiction, tradition*
• Cognates: *ficción realista, tradición*

See pages T304–T305 for Interactive Question-Response routine for the Shared Read.

MINILESSON
10 Mins

Read *A Spring Birthday*

Focus on Foundational Skills

Review with children the words and letter-sounds they will see in *A Spring Birthday*.

• Have children use pages 278–279 to review high-frequency words *before, front, heard, push, tomorrow, your,* and vocabulary words *difficult* and *nobody*.

• Have children use page 280–281 to review the three-letter blends *scr, spl, spr, str, thr,* and *shr*. Guide them to blend the sounds to read the words.

• Display the story words *bought, celebrate, everyone, family, Mexican, and tradition*. Spell each word and model reading it. Then display and read the words *empanadas, feliz cumpleaños, piñata,* and *las mañanitas,* and explain that these are Spanish words. Tell children they will be reading the words in the selection.

Read Guide children in reading *A Spring Birthday*. Point out the high-frequency words, vocabulary words, and words with three-letter blends.

Close Reading Routine

Read   DOK 1–2

• Identify key ideas and details about birthday traditions.
• Take notes and retell.
• Use (A C T) prompts as needed.

Reread   DOK 2–3

• Analyze the text, craft, and structure.
• Use the Reread minilessons.

Integrate   DOK 4

• Integrate knowledge and ideas.
• Make text-to-text connections.
• Use the Integrate Lesson.

Genre: Realistic Fiction Tell children that *A Spring Birthday* is realistic fiction. Realistic fiction is a made-up story about characters and events; could happen in real life; and has a beginning, a middle, and an end.

Go Digital

A Spring Birthday

A Spring Birthday

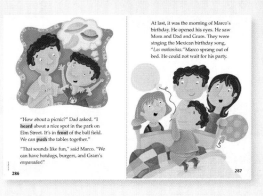

READING/WRITING WORKSHOP, pp. 282–291   Lexile 380

Connect to Concept: Up In the Sky

ESSENTIAL QUESTION Explain to children that as they read *A Spring Birthday*, they will look for key ideas and details that will help them answer the Essential Question: *What traditions do you know about?*

- Pages 284–285: What is Marco's family's birthday tradition?
- Pages 286–287: What new type of birthday party does Marco's Dad suggest?
- Pages 288–289: What do Marco and his friends take turns doing?
- Pages 290–291: What is Marco's birthday present?

Focus on Fluency

With partners, have children read *A Spring Birthday* to develop fluency. Remind them that they can ask themselves questions to make sure they understand what they are reading. Have them use both text and illustrations to answer their questions.

Retell Have partners use key ideas and details to retell *A Spring Birthday*. Invite them to act out their favorite part of the story.

Make Connections

Read together Make Connections on page 291. Have children turn to a partner and talk about what traditions they know from other places in the world. Use this sentence starter to guide discussion:

> A tradition I know about is . . .

Guide children to connect what they have read to the Essential Question.

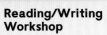

→ # Language Arts

 MINILESSON 5 Mins

Shared Writing

Write About the Reading/Writing Workshop

Analyze the Prompt Tell children that today the class will work together to write a response to a prompt. Read the prompt aloud. *Write a letter from Marco inviting his friend Jacob to his birthday party.* Say: *To respond to this prompt, we need to look at the text and illustrations in* A Spring Birthday.

Find Text Evidence Explain that you will reread the text and take notes to help respond to the prompt. Read aloud pages 286–287. Say: *Earlier I read that Marco wants to invite his friends to his birthday party. The text and the illustrations tell me some of the plans for his party. His dad suggests that they have a picnic at a park. Marco wants to have hotdogs, burgers, and his Gram's special empanadas. I can see these foods in the illustration as Marco imagines them. These are details we can use to write Marco's invitation letter to Jacob. Let's write them in our notes.*

Write to a Prompt Reread the prompt to children. *Write a letter from Marco inviting his friend Jacob to his birthday party.* Say: *First, we will begin the letter with a greeting: Dear Jacob.* Write the greeting. *We will add a comma after the greeting.* Add a comma. *Next, we will imagine being Marco, and tell Jacob the reason we are writing: I would like to invite you to my birthday party.* Write the sentence. *As I read our notes, think about which notes tell us details about the party that we can add to the invitation letter.* Track the print as you reread the notes.

Guide children to dictate complete sentences for you to record. Read the final response as you track the print.

OBJECTIVES

CCSS Write narratives in which they recount two or more appropriately sequenced events, include some details regarding what happened, use temporal words to signal event order, and provide some sense of closure. **W.1.3**

CCSS Use personal, possessive, and indefinite pronouns (e.g., *I, me, my; they, them, their, anyone, everything*). **L.1.1d**

ACADEMIC LANGUAGE

• notes, details, greeting, comma

• Cognates: *notas, detalles, coma*

Go Digital

Graphic Organizer

Writing

I see a fish.

Grammar

Grammar

I and *Me*

① Explain/Model Remind children that the subject of a sentence is what a sentence is about. Explain that we use the pronoun *I* as the subject of a sentence. Explain that we use the pronoun *me* after a verb or a word such as *for, at, of, with, to,* or *between.* Display the following sentences:

> I like to play ball.
>
> Will likes to play ball with me.

② Guided Practice/Practice Display the sentences below and read them aloud. Have children identify the pronouns *I* and *me.*

> I can throw the ball. (I)
>
> My dad and I play catch. (I)
>
> My dad showed me how to catch the ball. (me)
>
> He helps me get ready for the game. (me)

Talk About It Have partners orally generate sentences that use the pronouns *I* or *me.*

Link to Writing Say: *Let's look back at our writing and see if we used any pronouns in our note. Did we use them correctly?* Review the Shared Writing for the correct use of the pronouns *I* and *me.*

ENGLISH LANGUAGE LEARNERS SCAFFOLD

Beginning

Demonstrate Comprehension Read aloud the first Model sentence. Ask: *Is* I *the subject of the sentence?* Read aloud the second sentence. Ask: *What is the pronoun? Is it the subject of the sentence?* Me *comes after* with, *so it is not the subject. Will is the subject.*

Intermediate

Explain Have children tell why *I* is used in the first Model sentence and why *me* is used in the second Model sentence. Model correct pronunciation as needed.

Advanced/High

Expand Have one child change *I* to *me* in the Model sentence and have the partner explain why it is wrong. Have them repeat with the second Model sentence, changing *me* to *I.*

Daily Wrap Up

- Encourage children to discuss the Essential Question using the oral vocabulary words. Ask: *What are some school traditions we have?*

- Prompt children to share the skills they learned today.

Materials

Reading/ Writing Workshop VOLUME 4

Reading/Writing Workshop Big Book UNIT 6

Visual Vocabulary Cards
ancient
drama
effort
movement
tradition

High-Frequency Word Cards
before
front
heard
push
tomorrow
your

Vocabulary Cards
difficult
nobody

Teaching Poster

Spelling Word Cards

a b c
Word-Building Cards

Interactive Read-Aloud Cards

3
Photo Cards

→ Build the Concept

MINILESSON 5 Mins
Oral Language

OBJECTIVES
CCSS Ask and answer questions about key details in a text read aloud or information presented orally or through other reading. **SL.1.2**

• Discuss the Essential Question
• Build concept understanding

ACADEMIC LANGUAGE
• *visualize*
• Cognate: *visualizar*

ESSENTIAL QUESTION
Remind children that this week you've been talking and reading about traditions. Remind them of the traditional dances and the family birthday traditions. Guide children to discuss the Essential Question using information from what they read and discussed on Day 1.

Oral Vocabulary Words

Review the oral vocabulary words. Use the Define/Example/Ask routine to review the oral vocabulary words *ancient, drama, effort, movement,* and *tradition*.

• Can you name something that is ancient?
• If a dance has a lot of drama, is it boring or exciting?
• Would it take a lot of effort to chop down a big tree? Why?
• How are a rabbit's movements different from an elephant's?
• Is a tradition something people do often or just once?

Listening Comprehension

Reread the Interactive Read Aloud

Strategy: Visualize

Remind children that as they listen, they can use details in the text and illustrations to visualize the story events. When they visualize, they create a picture in their mind.

Tell children that you will reread "Let's Dance!" Display the Interactive Read-Aloud Cards.

"Let's Dance!"

Think Aloud When I read, I pay attention to the text and the illustrations. Then I use what I read and see to visualize what is happening in the story. When I first read the words, "The hora is a very cheerful dance. Dancers hold hands and dance sideways in a circle," I pictured in my mind a group of people holding hands and dancing in a circle. I saw them laughing and smiling as they danced.

Make Connections

Discuss partners' responses to "Let's Dance!"

- *Have you done any of the dances before? Which dance would you most like to do?*

- *Which traditional clothing did you enjoy seeing?*

- *Which dance looks the most difficult? Which dance looks the most fun?*

Write About It Have children write a few sentences about their favorite of the four dances in their Writer's Notebooks. Guide children by asking questions, such as *Which photograph do you like best? Which clothes would you like to wear?* Have children write continuously for six minutes.

 **Word Work**

 MINILESSON 5 Mins

Phonemic Awareness

OBJECTIVES

CCSS Segment spoken single-syllable words into their complete sequence of individual sounds (phonemes). **RF.1.2d**

CCSS Read words with inflectional endings. **RF.1.3f**

Phoneme Segmentation

❶ **Model** Use the **Response Boards** to model how to segment words into phonemes. Say: *Listen as I say a word:* strap. *I want to know how many sounds are in the word* strap. *I will place a marker in a box for each sound I hear: /s/ /t/ /r/ /a/ /p/. I will place five markers because I hear five sounds in* strap.

❷ **Guided Practice/Practice** Have children practice segmenting phonemes in the following words. Do the first two together. Say: *Listen as I say some words. Place one marker in a box for each sound you hear. Then tell me how many sounds are in each word.*

scream (5)	spray (4)	sprang (5)	throne (4)	splash (5)
scrap (5)	street (5)	throb (4)	thrill (4)	stripe (5)

 MINILESSON 5 Mins

Phonics

Review Three-Letter Blends

❶ **Model** Display **Word-Building Cards** *s, c, r, u, b.* Review the sounds /skr/ spelled *scr* using the word *scrub.* Repeat with these three-letter blends: *spl, spr, str, thr,* and *shr.*

❷ **Guided Practice/Practice** Have children practice connecting the letters and sounds. Point to the Word-Building Cards for the three-letter blends. Say: *What are these letters? What sounds do they stand for?*

Go Digital

Phonemic Awareness

Phonics

I __ the jar.
fill | fills | filling
Structural Analysis

Handwriting

Blend with Three-Letter Blends

1 **Model** Display **Word-Building Cards** *s, p, r, a, y to* form the word *spray*. Model how to generate and blend the sounds to say the word. Say: *These are the letters* spr. *Together they stand for /spr/. These are the letters* ay. *Together they stand for /ā/. Let's blend these sounds together: /ssssprrrāāā/. Say it with me:* spray. Continue by modeling the words *scream, split, stroke, three,* and *shrink*.

2 **Guided Practice/Practice** Repeat the routine with children with *scratch, straw, throat, stretch, splash, throw, strand, stream, spring*.

Build with Three-Letter Blends

1 **Model** Display the Word-Building Cards *s, c, r, a, t, c, h*. Blend the sounds: /s/ /k/ /r/ /a/ /ch/, /ssskrrrach/, scratch.

- Replace *tch* with *wl* and repeat with *scrawl*.

- Replace *wl* with *p* and repeat with *scrap*.

2 **Guided Practice/Practice** Continue with *strap, strand, streak, stream, street, string, spring, sprint, splint, split*.

Structural Analysis

Inflectional Endings *-ed, -ing*

1 **Model** Write and read aloud *stretch, stretched,* and *stretching*. Underline the *-ed* and *-ing*. Remind children that when *-ed* is added to a verb, or action word, it tells about something that has already happened. When *-ing* is added to a verb, it tells about something that is happening now.

Repeat with *scrape, scraped, scraping* and *scrub, scrubbed, scrubbing*. Remind children of the rules they learned for dropping final *e* and doubling final consonants.

2 **Guided Practice/Practice** Write the following words on the board: *thrill, splash, strip, scrape*. Have children add *-ed* and *-ing* to each word and then use each word in a sentence.

ENGLISH LANGUAGE LEARNERS

Build Vocabulary Review the meanings of example words that can be explained or demonstrated in a concrete way. For example, ask children to point to their *throat* and to a *strand* of hair. Model the meaning of *scratch* saying, "*I use my fingers to scratch my arm.*" and have children repeat. Provide sentence starters, such as, *I see three* ____. for children to complete. Correct grammar and pronunciation as needed.

 → # Word Work

Quick Review

High-Frequency Words: Read, Spell, and Write to review this week's high-frequency words: *before, front, heard, push, tomorrow, your.*

MINILESSON
5 Mins

Spelling

OBJECTIVES

CCSS Recognize and read grade-appropriate irregularly spelled words. **RF.1.3g**

CCSS Use conventional spelling for words with common spelling patterns and for frequently occurring irregular words. **L.1.2d**

Word Sort with Three-Letter Blends

❶ **Model** Display the **Spelling Word Cards** from the Teacher's Resource Book. Have children read each word, listening for the beginning blend.

Use cards for *str, spr, spl, scr,* and *thr* to create a five-column chart. Say the letters and blend the sounds for each three-letter blend. Ask children to spell each blend.

❷ **Guided Practice/Practice** Have children place each Spelling Word Card in the column with the same three-letter blend. When completed, have children read the words. Then call out a word. Have a child find the word card and point to it as the class spells the word.

ANALYZE ERRORS/ARTICULATION SUPPORT

Use children's pretest errors to analyze spelling problems and provide corrective feedback. For example, some may leave out one of the letters in a three-letter blend. Work with children to recognize the difference in sounds and spellings in minimal contrast pairs, such as *spit/split, slash/splash, shed/shred,* and *read/thread.*

Say each word. Have children repeat. Isolate the three-letter blend and have children orally segment the sounds.

ENGLISH LANGUAGE LEARNERS

Provide Clues Practice spelling by helping children generate more words with three-letter blends. Provide clues: *Think of a word that begins with* spr *and rhymes with* day. Write the word and have children practice reading it. Correct their pronunciation, if needed.

MINILESSON
5 Mins

High-Frequency Words

before, front, heard, push, tomorrow, your

❶ **Guided Practice** Say each word and have children Read/Spell/Write it. Ask children to picture the word in their minds, and write it the way they see it. Display the words for children to self-correct.

• Point out irregularities in sound-spellings such as the /u/ sound spelled *o* in *front.*

Go Digital

Spelling Word Sort

High-Frequency Word Routine

school

Visual Glossary

2 Practice Add the high-frequency words *before, front, heard, push, tomorrow,* and *your* to the cumulative word bank.

COLLABORATE

- Have partners create sentences using the words.

- Have children look at the words and compare their sounds and spellings to words from previous weeks.

- Suggest that they write about traditions they know.

Cumulative Review Review last week's words using the Read/Spell/Write routine.

- Repeat the above routine, mixing the words and having children say each one.

MINILESSON
5 Mins

Reinforce Vocabulary

difficult, nobody

1 Guided Practice Use the **Vocabulary Cards** to review this week's and last week's vocabulary words. Work together with children to generate a new context sentence for each word.

2 Practice Have children work with a partner to orally complete each sentence stem on the Day 2 Vocabulary Practice Activity using this week's and last week's vocabulary words.

---

country	gathers	difficult	nobody

1. Making origami is an art form from the ____ of Japan.
2. Most of the time, ____ wants to be last in line.
3. It is ____ for the baby to sit quietly.
4. A crowd of people ____ to watch the parade.

Also online

Day 2 Vocabulary Practice Activity

ON-LEVEL PRACTICE BOOK p. 308

Complete each sentence. Use one of the words in the box.

before	front	heard	push	tomorrow	your

1. Let's wash up _____ before _____ we eat lunch.

2. Is this _____ your _____ book or mine?

3. I helped Mom paint the _____ front _____ door.

4. We _____ heard _____ the thunder.

5. Will you _____ push _____ me on the swing?

6. I have art class today and soccer _____ tomorrow _____

APPROACHING p. 308	BEYOND p. 308	ELL p. 308

Monitor and *Differentiate*

✓ **Quick Check**

Can children read and decode words with three-letter blends?

Can children recognize and read high-frequency and vocabulary words?

⬇

Small Group Instruction

If No → Approaching Reteach pp. T290–293

ELL Develop pp. T304–311

If Yes → On Level Review pp. T298–299

Beyond Level Extend pp. T302–303

Comprehension

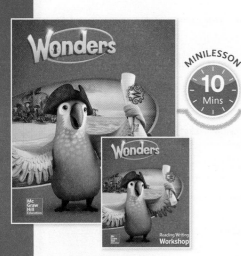

Reading/Writing Workshop Big Book and Reading/Writing Workshop

---

OBJECTIVES

CCSS Retell stories, including key details, and demonstrate understanding of their central message or lesson. **RI.1.2**

Understand realistic fiction genre

ACADEMIC LANGUAGE

• *realistic fiction, theme*

• Cognates: *ficción realista, tema*

MINILESSON 10 Mins Reread *A Spring Birthday*

Genre: Realistic Fiction

❶ **Model** Tell children they will now reread the realistic fiction selection *A Spring Birthday*. Explain that as they read, they will look for information in the text to help them understand the selection.

Review the characteristics of realistic fiction. It:

• is a made-up story about characters and events.

• has events that could happen in real life.

• has a beginning, a middle, and an end.

Tell children that realistic fictional stories have a setting, characters, and a plot. *In realistic fiction, the characters talk and act like real people. Realistic fiction often has a beginning, a middle, and an end. The beginning of the story usually sets up the situation that is described in the middle and end.*

Display pages 284 and 285 and read the pages aloud. *This is the beginning of the story. The characters in the story are talking and acting just like real people. Marco wants to do something new on his birthday. This could happen in real life, so I know the story is realistic fiction.*

❷ **Guided Practice/Practice** Display pages 286 and 287 of *A Spring Birthday*. Read page 286 aloud. Say: *Marco's family is making plans for his birthday party. Could this happen in real life? Yes, this story could happen in real life. What part of the story is this? Yes, it is the middle.*

Go Digital

A Spring Birthday

Genre

Theme

SKILLS TRACE

THEME

Introduce	Unit 6 Week 1
Review	Unit 6 Weeks 3, 4
Assess	Unit 6 Weeks 2, 4

Skill: Theme

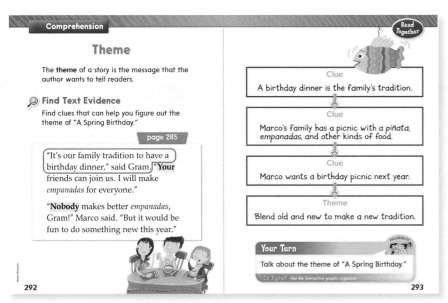

Reading/Writing Workshop, pp. 292–293

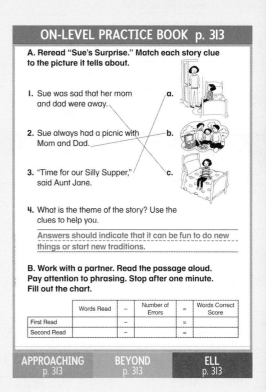
1 Model Tell children that an author usually has a message he or she wants to share. The text and illustrations in the story will have clues about this message. Have children look at pages 292–293 in their Reading/Writing Workshop. Read together the definition of Theme. *The theme of the story is the message that the author wants to tell readers.*

2 Guided Practice/Practice Read together the Find Text Evidence section and model finding clues about the theme in *A Spring Birthday*. Point out the information added to the graphic organizer. *On page 285, we find out that Marco's family has a tradition about a birthday dinner. This information gives us a clue about the author's message. We can add this information to the Theme chart. What other clues can we find to help us identify the theme of the story?*

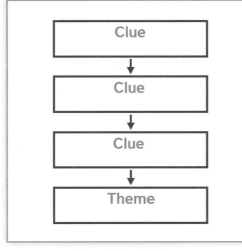

Teaching Poster

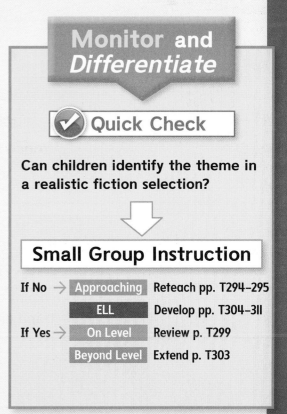

Monitor and *Differentiate*

✓ **Quick Check**

Can children identify the theme in a realistic fiction selection?

⬇

Small Group Instruction

If No → **Approaching** Reteach pp. T294–295
ELL Develop pp. T304–311

If Yes → **On Level** Review p. T299
Beyond Level Extend p. T303

Wonders
Reading/Writing
Workshop

**Reading/Writing
Workshop**

OBJECTIVES

CCSS Write narratives in which they recount two or more appropriately sequenced events, include some details regarding what happened, use temporal words to signal event order, and provide some sense of closure. **W.1.3**

CCSS Use personal, possessive, and indefinite pronouns (e.g., *I, me, my; they, them, their, anyone, everything*). **L.1.1d**

**ACADEMIC
LANGUAGE**

• *describe, detail, pronoun, sentence, tradition*
• Cognates: *describir, detalle, tradición*

MINILESSON 5 Mins

Interactive Writing

Write About the Reading/Writing Workshop

Analyze the Model Prompt Have children turn to page 294 in the **Reading/Writing Workshop**. Kate responded to the prompt: *Write a letter from Marco to his parents thanking them for his great birthday.* Explain to children that the prompt is asking Kate to write a letter from Marco to his parents. To respond to this prompt, Kate found text evidence about Marco's birthday party and made inferences about what Marco would write to his parents.

Find Text Evidence Explain that Kate took notes about what Marco's parents did to prepare for Marco's birthday. Then, Kate used the evidence to write a thank you letter from Marco.

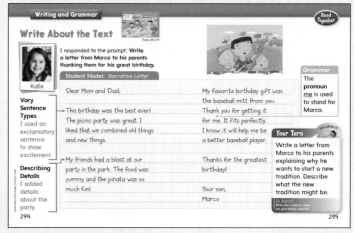

Reading/Writing Workshop

Analyze the Student Model Read the model. Discuss the callouts.

• **Varying Sentence Types** Kate used exclamations and statements to make her letter interesting to read. **Trait: Sentence Fluency**

• **Describing Details** Kate used details from the text to describe the food and the piñata at the party. **Trait: Ideas**

• **Pronouns** Kate correctly used the pronouns *I* and *me*. **Grammar**

Point out that Kate began her letter with a greeting to Marco's parents and ended her letter with the closing "Your son, Marco."

Go Digital

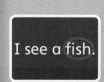

Graphic Organizer

Writing

I see a fish.

Grammar

Your Turn: Write a Letter Say: *Now we will write to a new prompt.* Have children turn to page 295 of the **Reading/Writing Workshop**. Read the Your Turn prompt together. *Write a letter from Marco to his parents explaining why he wants to start a new tradition. Describe what the new tradition might be.*

Find Text Evidence Say: *To answer this prompt, we need to find evidence in the story and the illustrations and take notes. Look at page 291. What does Marco say about his birthday party?* (Marco says it was the best birthday he ever had.) *What does Gram say about traditions?* (Gram says it is fun to mix new and old traditions.) *We can use these details in our letter to Marco's parents.*

Write to a Prompt Say: *Let's begin our letter with a greeting: Dear Mom and Dad.* Write the greeting followed by a comma. *Now let's add a sentence from our notes: It was fun making a new tradition for my birthday!* Write the sentence. Have children brainstorm new traditions Marco could want to start. Pick one and then guide children to think of sentences describing the new tradition to add to the letter. Tell children you will reread the notes to help them complete the letter. Say: *Let's look back and see if we used different types of sentences and details from the story.* Read the final response as you track the print.

For additional practice with the Writing Trait, have children turn to page 318 of the **Your Turn Practice Book**.

Grammar

5 Mins

I and *Me*

1 Review Remind children that the pronoun *I* is used as the subject of a sentence. Remind them that *me* is used after a verb or a word such as *for, at, of, with, to,* or *between*. Display the following sentences:

> I will tie a string around the box. (I)
>
> Gran spent the day with me. (me)

Guide children to circle the pronoun in each sentence.

2 Guided Practice/Practice Display the following sentences. Have children work in pairs to complete each sentence with *I* or *me*.

> My brother and ____ share a bedroom. (I)
>
> Mom helped ____ paint a stripe on my bike. (me)

Talk About It Have partners use *I* and *me* in sentences about traditions in their families.

Daily Wrap Up

- Discuss the Essential Question and encourage children to use the oral vocabulary words. Ask: *What traditions have you read about?*

- Prompt children to discuss what they learned today by asking, *How did the skills you learned today help you become a better reader and writer?*

Materials

Reading/ Writing Workshop
VOLUME 4

Literature Anthology
VOLUME 4

Visual Vocabulary Cards

ancient
drama
effort
movement
tradition
difficult
nobody

before
front
heard
push
tomorrow
your

Teaching Poster

3

Photo Cards

a b c

Word-Building Cards

Response Board

Interactive Read-Aloud Cards

strike

Spelling Word Cards

→ # Build the Concept

MINILESSON
5 Mins

Oral Language

OBJECTIVES

CCSS Read grade-level text orally with accuracy, appropriate rate, and expression. **RF.1.4b**

Review problem and solution

ACADEMIC LANGUAGE
• problem, solution, plot, comma, pause
• Cognates: problema, solución, coma

ESSENTIAL QUESTION
Remind children that this week you have been talking and reading about traditions. Remind them of all the dances they read about and the birthday celebration. Guide children to discuss the question using information from what they have read and discussed throughout the week.

Review Oral Vocabulary
Review the oral vocabulary words *ancient*, *drama*, *effort*, *movement*, and *tradition* using the Define/Example/Ask routine. Prompt children to use the words as they discuss traditions they know.

Visual Vocabulary Cards

Comprehension/ Fluency

ENGLISH LANGUAGE LEARNERS

Retell Guide children to retell by using a question prompt on each page, such as, *What does Gram want to make?* Provide sentence starters for children to complete orally. *Gram wants to make ____.*

Plot: Problem and Solution

1 Explain Tell children they have been learning about identifying theme to help them understand the stories they read. Remind them they have also learned how to look for problems and solutions in the plot. *As we read, we can think about the problems that are presented in the story. We can also look for the solutions the characters come up with. Understanding the problems and how the characters solve them can help us to better understand the story.*

Reading/Writing Workshop

2 Model Display pages 284 and 285 of *A Spring Birthday. I see that Gram wants to make empanadas for Marco's birthday, but Marco wants to try something new for his birthday. This is a problem. How do the characters solve the problem? Let's keep reading to find the solution.*

3 Guided Practice/Practice Reread *A Spring Birthday* with children. Use text evidence to identify problems and solutions.

Phrasing: Commas

1 Explain Tell children that as you read the passage, you will pause slightly when you come to a comma.

2 Model Model reading a section of the Shared Read that has commas. *These sentences have commas. I pause slightly when I come to a comma. Then I continue reading.* Point out how you pause for other punctuation as well.

3 Guided Practice/Practice Have children reread the passage chorally. Remind them to pause slightly when they come to a comma.

Fluency Practice Children can practice using Practice Book passages.

 → # Word Work

Quick Review

Build Fluency: Sound-Spellings

Display the **Word-Building Cards:** *scr, spl, spr, str, thr, shr, wr, kn, gn, au, aw, augh, ew, ue, ui, ow, oy, oi, ar, ore, oar, er, ir, ur, ey, igh, oa, oe, ee, ea.* Have children say the sounds.

Phonemic Awareness

Phoneme Blending

❶ Model Show children how to blend phonemes. *Listen as I say the sounds in a word: /s/ /p/ /l/ /a/ /sh/. Now I'll blend the sounds together and say the word: /sssplllaaash/,* splash. *Let's say the word:* splash.

❷ Guided Practice/Practice Have children practice blending phonemes. Guide practice with the first one. *I'm going to say some words, sound by sound. Blend the sounds together to say the word.*

/s/ /p/ /l/ /i/ /t/   /s/ /p/ /r/ /i/ /ng/   /sh/ /r/ /u/ /g/

/s/ /k/ /r/ /u/ /b/   /s/ /t/ /r/ /ī/ /p/   /th/ /r/ /ō/

Phonics

Blend with Three-Letter Blends

❶ Model Display **Word-Building Cards** *th, r, e, a, d.* Model how to blend the sounds. *These are the letters* th *and* r. *Together they stand for /thr/. These are the letters* ea. *In this word they stand for /e/. This is the letter* d. *It stands for /d/. Let's blend the sounds: /thrrreeed/. The word is* thread. Continue by modeling the words *script, split, spring, straw,* and *shrimp.*

❷ Guided Practice/Practice Review the words and sentences on the Day 3 Phonics Practice Activity with children. Read each word in the first row, blending the sounds, for example: /s/ /t/ /r/ /ē/ /t/; /ssstrrrēēēt/. The word is *street.*

Have children blend each word with you. Prompt children to read the connected text, sounding out the decodable words.

Go Digital

Phonemic Awareness

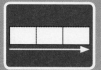

Phonics

Structural Analysis

Handwriting

street	strong	thrill	spring	shrink
strike	thrown	stripe	scrub	splash
stream	screen	threat	thread	straw
scratched	scratching	strolled	strolling	
throwing	throbbed	scrubbed	spraying	

He can stretch the string.

Can you scroll down the screen?

Also online

Day 3 Phonics Practice Activity

Decodable Reader Have children read "Three Shrimp" (pages 73–76) to practice decoding words in connected text.

Structural Analysis

Inflectional Endings -ed, -ing

1 Model Write the words *scrape, scraped, scraping* on the board and read them with children. Underline the letters *-ed* and *-ing*. Remind children that since the word *scrape* ends in final *-e*, the letter *e* was dropped before adding *-ed* or *-ing*.

2 Practice/Apply Help children blend the words *scratch, scratched, scratching, knit, knitted, knitting, spruce, spruced,* and *sprucing.* Point out that adding the letters *-ing* at the end of a word always adds a syllable; adding the letters *-ed* at the end of a word sometimes does.

Corrective Feedback

Corrective Feedback Say: *My turn.* Model blending using the appropriate signaling procedures. Then lead children in blending the sounds. Say: *Do it with me.* You will respond with children to offer support. Then say: *Your turn. Blend.* Have children chorally blend. Return to the beginning of the word. Say: *Let's start over.*

→ # Word Work

Quick Review

High-Frequency Words: Read, Spell, and Write to review this week's high-frequency words: *before, front, heard, push, tomorrow, your.*

MINILESSON 5 Mins
Spelling

OBJECTIVES

 Use conventional spelling for words with common spelling patterns and for frequently occurring irregular words. **L.1.2d**

 Use knowledge of the meaning of individual words to predict the meaning of compound words. **L.2.4d**

Word Sort with Three-Letter Blends

❶ **Model** Display **Word-Building Cards** for *str, spr, spl, scr,* and *thr* to form five columns in a pocket chart. Blend the sounds with children.

Hold up the *splash* **Spelling Word Card.** Say and spell it. Pronounce each sound clearly: /s/ /p/ /l/ /a/ /sh/. Blend the sounds, emphasizing the initial three-letter consonant blend. Repeat this step with *split.* Place the words below the *spl* card.

❷ **Guided Practice/Practice** Have children spell each word. Repeat the process with the other three-letter blends.

Display *know, write, your,* and *heard* in a separate column. Read and spell the words with children. Point out that these spelling words do not begin with three-letter blends.

Conclude by having children orally generate additional words that start with the same three-letter blend. Write the additional words on the board.

Spelling Word Sort

Visual Glossary

Go Digital

MINILESSON 5 Mins
High-Frequency Words

PHONICS/SPELLING PRACTICE BOOK p. 143

before, front, heard, push, tomorrow, your

❶ **Guided Practice** Say each word and have children Read/Spell/Write it. Point out the smaller words *be* in *before* and *you* in *your.*

• Display **Visual Vocabulary Cards** to review this week's words.

| strike | spray | splash | split |
| scrape | three | your | heard |

Write the spelling word that has 4 letters.

1. _____your_____

Write the spelling words that have 5 letters.

2. _____spray_____ 3. _____split_____

4. _____three_____ 5. _____heard_____

Order of 2–5 may vary.

Write the spelling words that have 6 letters.

6. _____strike_____

7. _____scrape_____

8. _____splash_____

Order of 6–8 may vary.

Visual Vocabulary Cards

❷ **Practice** Repeat the activity with last week's word cards.

Build Fluency: Word Automaticity

Have children read the following sentences aloud together at the same pace. Repeat several times.

> Push on the front door.
>
> We heard the band before we saw it.
>
> Can your ship sail around the world?

Word Bank

Review the current and previous words in the word bank. Encourage children to suggest which words should be removed or added back.

MINILESSON
5 Mins

Vocabulary

difficult, nobody

Review Use the **Visual Vocabulary Cards** to review this week's words using the Define/Example/Ask routine. Have partners generate context sentences for each vocabulary word.

Visual Vocabulary Cards

Strategy: Compound Words

1 Model Tell children that compound words are words that are made up of two or more smaller words. You can often use the meaning of the smaller words to figure out what the longer word means. Use *A Spring Birthday* to model how to identify and define a compound word.

Think Aloud In *A Spring Birthday*, I see the compound word *birthday*. The word is made up of the two smaller words *birth* and *day*. *Birth* refers to being born. So, a birthday is the day someone was born. Looking at the two smaller words can often help you sound out the compound word and figure out its meaning.

2 Guided Practice Help children use the strategy with these words: *baseball, snowman, bookbag, grasshopper,* and *notebook*.

3 Practice Have children use the strategy to figure out the meaning of *nobody*. Ask them to find compound words in this week's stories.

Monitor and *Differentiate*

✓ **Quick Check**

Can children read and decode words with three-letter blends?

Can children recognize and read high-frequency and vocabulary words?

Small Group Instruction

If No →	Approaching	Reteach pp. T290–293
	ELL	Develop pp. T304–311
If Yes →	On Level	Review pp. T298–299
	Beyond Level	Extend pp. T302–303

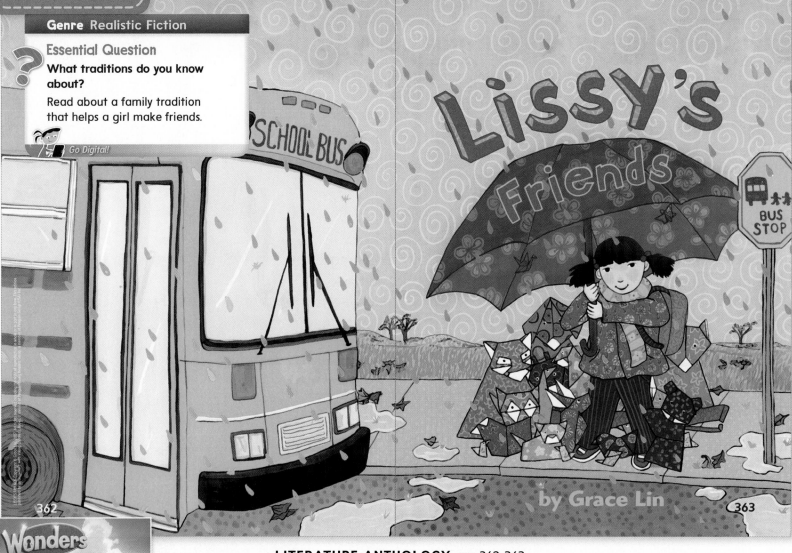

Essential Question

What traditions do you know about?

Read about a family tradition that helps a girl make friends.

Go Digital!

362

363

LITERATURE ANTHOLOGY, pp. 362–363

Literature Anthology

Lissy's Friends

Lexile 460

Close Reading Routine

Read DOK 1–2

• Identify key ideas and details about traditions.
• Take notes and retell.
• Use **A C T** prompts as needed.

Reread DOK 2–3

• Analyze the text, craft, and structure.
• Use *Close Reading Companion*, pp. 187–189.

Integrate DOK 4

• Integrate knowledge and ideas.
• Make text-to-text connections
• Use the Integrate Lesson.

Read

ESSENTIAL QUESTION

Read aloud the Essential Question: *What traditions do you know about?* Tell children that as they read, they should think about Lissy's tradition and how it helps her. Read the title on page 363. Ask: *Who do you predict Lissy's friends are?*

Story Words Read and spell the words *merry-go-round, menu, giraffe, elephant, dragonfly,* and *crane*. Review word meaning as needed. Explain that children will read these words in the story.

Note Taking: Graphic Organizer As children read the selection, guide them to fill in the graphic organizer on **Your Turn Practice Book** page 310.

Lissy was the new girl at school.

364

Nobody talked to her.
Nobody smiled at her.
At the playground, Lissy stood on the
merry-go-round by herself. **1** **2**

365

LITERATURE ANTHOLOGY, pp. 364–365

1 Strategy: Visualize

Teacher Think Aloud I read Lissy is new at school. Nobody talks to her and she is by herself. The picture shows her standing alone on the merry-go-round. I close my eyes and make a picture of Lissy in my mind. I can see her alone. She is watching other children playing together. She can hear them laughing and talking. This helps me imagine what it is like for Lissy.

2 Skill: Theme

Lissy is new at school. What does she do? How might she feel? This information gives you clues about the theme of the story. Let's write these clues on the Theme chart.

A C T Access Complex Text

▶ **What makes this text complex?**

- **Connection of Ideas** Children must connect ideas in the pictures and text. Help them use the pictures to understand who Lissy's friends are.

- **Genre** This story is realistic fiction, but some of it happens in Lissy's imagination. Help children understand the parts that are real and the parts that take place in Lissy's imagination.

Because Lissy ate lunch alone, she was finished **before** lunchtime was over. Since she didn't have anything else to do, Lissy took the lunch menu in **front** of her and began to fold it. Soon, she had made a little paper crane. **3**

366

"Hello," Lissy said to the paper crane. "I will call you Menu, and you will be my friend."

And to her surprise, Menu opened its eyes and blinked at her. Menu looked to the right, then to the left, and fluttered up with its paper wings.

367

LITERATURE ANTHOLOGY, pp. 366–367

Read

3 Skill: Theme

Teacher Think Aloud Lissy eats lunch alone and then makes a paper crane. Since she knows how to make the crane, I think making paper animals is a tradition in her family. I think Lissy makes herself a friend! I will write this clue on our chart.

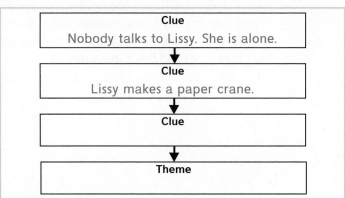

A C T **Access Complex Text**

▶ Genre

Children may think Menu is really alive.

- Remind them this is realistic fiction and is about things that can happen in real life. *What things in the story so far can really happen?*

- Point out Lissy is alone, so she makes a new "friend" and imagines her crane is alive. Explain that Lissy has an active imagination! Ask children if they have active imaginations and what they imagine.

Build Vocabulary page 367
fluttered: waved or flapped

The rest of the day, Lissy smiled a secret smile.

4 **5**

LITERATURE ANTHOLOGY, pp. 368–369

4 Word Choice

Teacher Think Aloud The author uses alliteration in this sentence. The words *smiled, secret,* and *smile* all begin with the /s/ sound. The word *Lissy* has the same sound in it. Using four words together with the /s/ sound gives the sentence a soft, sweet feeling. This helps me understand how Lissy might be feeling.

5 Maintain Skill: Problem and Solution

Remember that realistic fiction stories can have a problem and a solution. Let's think about Lissy. What problem does she have? Turn to a partner and discuss Lissy's problem. Tell how you think she might solve her problem.

Reread

Author's Craft: Author's Purpose

Reread page 369. Why did the author tell us that Lissy smiled a secret smile? (to show that Lissy has a positive point of view; that she is happy with herself for creating the paper friend instead of just being sad)

Build Vocabulary page 369
secret: private

"Did you make any friends in school today?" Mommy asked when Lissy came home.

"Well," Lissy said, patting Menu in her pocket, "I did make one friend." **6**

"Good," Mommy said. "I'm sure you'll make more **tomorrow**." **7**

370

371

LITERATURE ANTHOLOGY, pp. 370–371

Read

6 Author's Craft: Word Choice

Mommy asks Lissy if she made new friends. What does Mommy mean? (Mommy wants to know if Lissy met children at school.) Lissy answers that she made one friend. What does Lissy mean? (She means that she made a crane from paper, and the crane is her friend.) The author uses two different meanings for the phrase *make friends*. Why do you think she does that?

Build Vocabulary page 371
pocket: a pouch on clothing

7 Make and Confirm Predictions

COLLABORATE

Mommy thinks Lissy will make more friends tomorrow. What do you think? Will Lissy make more friends? Will they be paper friends or people friends? Turn to a partner and make predictions about whether Lissy will make more friends.

8 Make and Confirm Predictions

COLLABORATE

Turn to a partner and discuss your predictions. Were you right? Does Lissy make new friends? What friends does she make?

And she did. The next day, Lissy made lots of friends. **8** **9**

372   373

LITERATURE ANTHOLOGY, pp. 372–373

9 Skill: Theme

What is a clue that could help us identify the theme of this story? Let's add the clue to our Theme chart.

Reread

Illustrations

Reread pages 372–373. How does this illustration help you understand the text? (The texts says Lissy made lots of friends. The illustration shows her making new paper animals who look alive. This helps me know that the friends the text tells me about are paper friends.)

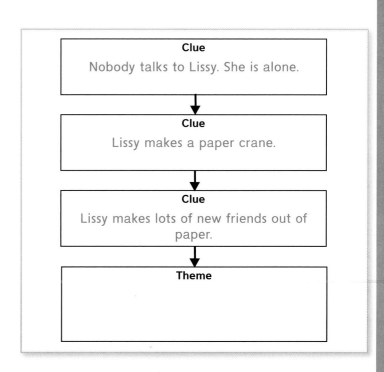

Clue
Nobody talks to Lissy. She is alone.

↓

Clue
Lissy makes a paper crane.

↓

Clue
Lissy makes lots of new friends out of paper.

↓

Theme

Her friends went with her ...

everywhere. **10**

374

375

LITERATURE ANTHOLOGY, pp. 374–375

Read

10 Strategy: Visualize

Teacher Think Aloud Visualizing Lissy helps me understand what she is doing. Close your eyes and make a picture of Lissy in your mind. What do you visualize?

Student Think Aloud I picture Lissy in my mind. She is smiling. She is surrounded by the friends she made by folding paper. Instead of feeling sad, she feels happy. She talks to them sometimes, too.

11 Maintain Skill: Problem and Solution

What was Lissy's problem? Turn to a partner and discuss how Lissy tried to solve it.

A C T Access Complex Text

▶ **Connections of Ideas**

Children must connect details they see in the illustrations with what they read in the text to understand more about Lissy's new friends.

- Have children tell where Lissy is in each picture on pages 374–375. Then have them tell who is with Lissy.

- Reread the text with children. Ask them to name and describe some of Lissy's friends. Then ask them to name some places Lissy's friends go with her.

Build Vocabulary page 375
everywhere: in all places

And Lissy was never alone. **11** **12**

376 377

LITERATURE ANTHOLOGY, pp. 376–377

12 Skill: Theme

Let's review the clues on our Theme chart. Why was Lissy alone before? Why isn't she alone now?

Reread *Close Reading Companion,* 187

Point of View

Reread pages 376–377. How do the text and illustration help you know how Lissy feels? (The text says Lissy was never alone. The illustration shows her smiling while she sleeps. This helps me know that Lissy feels happy and safe with her paper friends.)

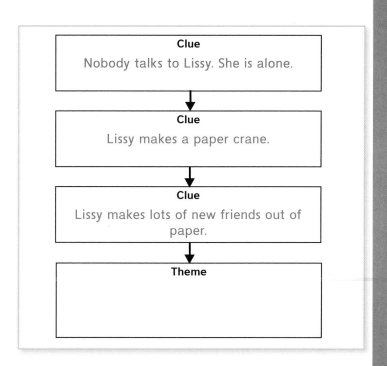

| **Clue** |
| Nobody talks to Lissy. She is alone. |

↓

| **Clue** |
| Lissy makes a paper crane. |

↓

| **Clue** |
| Lissy makes lots of new friends out of paper. |

↓

| **Theme** |
| |

One day, Lissy **heard** a group of kids laughing as they went down the street. They stopped at one house and then another, but they didn't stop at Lissy's.

"Lissy," Mommy called from downstairs, "why don't you go with **your** friends to the playground? I think they are all headed that way."

Lissy looked at her paper friends.

"Yes," she said. "Let's go to the playground."

378   379

LITERATURE ANTHOLOGY, pp. 378–379

Read

13 Compound Words

Compound words are made up of two smaller words. Thinking about the meaning of the two smaller words in a compound word helps us figure out its meaning. Mommy called Lissy from downstairs. Find the word *downstairs* on page 379. What are the two smaller words in *downstairs*? (*down* and *stairs*) What does *downstairs* mean? Now find another compound word on page 379. (*playground*) What are the two smaller words? (*play* and *ground*) What does the compound word mean?

14 Reread

Teacher Think Aloud Mommy asks Lissy why she doesn't go to the playground with her friends. I wonder what Mommy means. Does she mean the children or does she mean Lissy's paper friends? I go back and reread page 371. Now I understand. Mommy thinks Lissy met friends at school. Mommy doesn't know that Lissy made paper friends. Rereading helps me understand that Mommy thinks Lissy will go to the playground with the children. Lissy will really go with her paper friends.

Lissy led her friends down the street and to the playground. **15**

"We'll ride the merry-go-round first," she told them. "Then we can all ride together."

So all the paper animals crowded onto the merry-go-round, and Lissy began to **push** it. Round and round Lissy pushed. She ran so hard she didn't see that her friends were having a **difficult** time staying on … **16**

380

381

LITERATURE ANTHOLOGY, pp. 380–381

---

15 **Structural Analysis: Syllabication**

The word *playground* has two vowel-team syllables: /plā/ and /ground/. Each of these syllables has one vowel sound, even though each syllable has two vowels. Knowing this word is a vowel-team syllable word helps us read it.

16 **Genre: Realistic Fiction**

Remember, this story is realistic fiction. Some things in the story are not realistic and are happening in Lissy's imagination. Turn to a partner and discuss what is really happening and what is happening in Lissy's imagination.

Build Vocabulary page 380
difficult: hard to do

Reread   *Close Reading Companion,* 188

Illustrator's Craft: Point of View

Reread pages 378–279. How does the author/illustrator show what happens as Lissy looks outside? (The text says the friends stopped at one house and then another, but didn't stop at Lissy's. The illustration shows Lissy and her paper friends looking at the children outside. Lissy sees children playing together without her.)

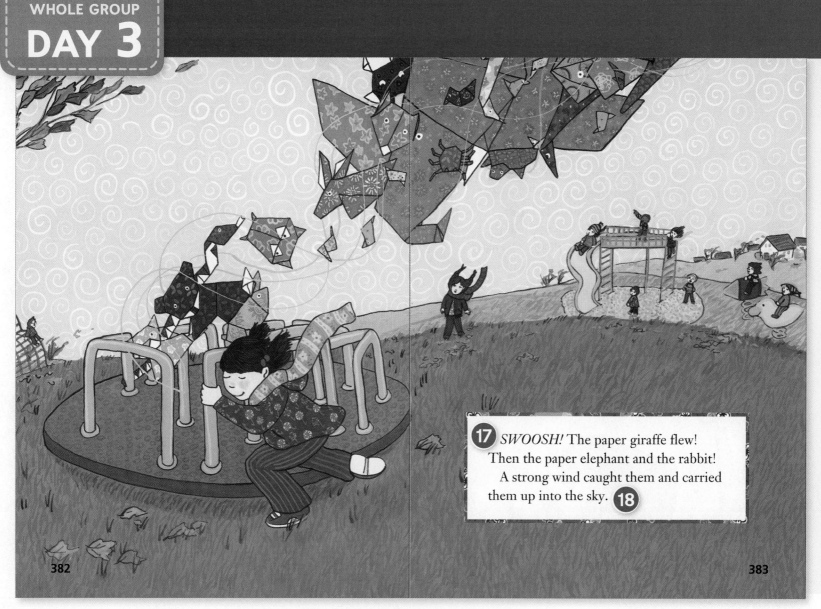

LITERATURE ANTHOLOGY, pp. 382–383

Read

17 Author's Craft: Word Choice

What do you notice about the word *SWOOSH* on page 383? Why do you think the author used all capital letters? Why do you think the author used this word? When you say *swoosh,* it sounds like the sound paper makes when it gets blown away by the wind. Let's say *swoosh* together and make it sound like a swooshing sound.

18 Strategy: Visualize

How does the word *swoosh* help you visualize what happens on these pages? Think of the word as you picture the paper animals being blown off in the air. Can you see them swooshing?

When Lissy jumped on, the merry-go-round was empty! She looked up and saw her paper friends flying away.

"No! Come back!" Lissy cried.
But they couldn't.

"No more friends," Lissy said, and she sat down on the merry-go-round and covered her face with her hands.

384

385

LITERATURE ANTHOLOGY, pp. 384–385

⑲ Skill: Theme

What does Lissy say when her paper friends fly away? ("No! Come back! No more friends.") Show what she does. (covers her face with her hands) How does she feel? After reading page 385, what clue can we add to our Theme chart? Let's add it.

Reread

Key Events

Reread pages 384–385. How do you know something important happens on these pages? (The author uses a lot of exclamation points and says that Lissy says "No more friends" and covers her face with her hands. This must be a very important part of the story.)

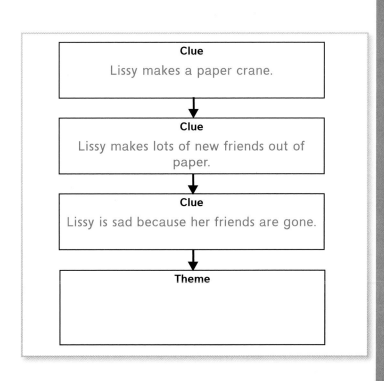

| **Clue** |
| Lissy makes a paper crane. |

↓

| **Clue** |
| Lissy makes lots of new friends out of paper. |

↓

| **Clue** |
| Lissy is sad because her friends are gone. |

↓

| **Theme** |
| |

"Hey, is this yours?" a voice said.

Lissy looked up. There was a girl holding a paper crane. Menu!

"It's neat," the girl said. "Did you make it?"

Lissy looked at the girl. She was smiling at her. Lissy nodded.

"Can you show me how?" the girl asked. "I'm Paige." 20

386

387

LITERATURE ANTHOLOGY, pp. 386–387

Read

20 Skill: Theme

Turn to a partner. Discuss what happens on pages 386–387. Who finds one of Lissy's paper friends? What does she want? What clue can we add to our Theme chart? Let's add the clue.

Build Vocabulary page 386

nodded: shook her head up and down to say "yes"

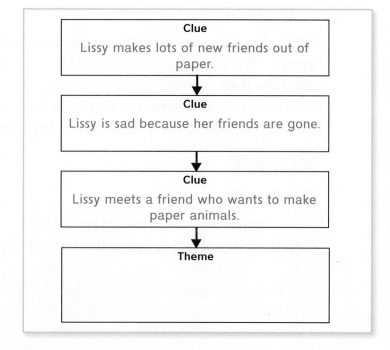

Clue
Lissy makes lots of new friends out of paper.

↓

Clue
Lissy is sad because her friends are gone.

↓

Clue
Lissy meets a friend who wants to make paper animals.

↓

Theme

Paige came over to Lissy's house, and Lissy showed her how to make a paper crane. Then they made a paper fox and dragonfly. They talked and laughed. **21** **22**

388

389

LITERATURE ANTHOLOGY, pp. 388–389

---

21 Strategy: Visualize

COLLABORATE

Turn to a partner. The words say they made a paper dragonfly and fox and that they laughed and talked. Close your eyes and visualize Lissy and her new friend Paige at Lissy's house. Use the words to help imagine what they are doing. What do you see?

22 Maintain Skill: Problem and Solution

What was Lissy's problem at the beginning of the story? (She had no friends.) How did she try to solve her problem? (She made friends out of paper.) How was the problem solved at the end of the story? (She made a real friend.)

Reread   *Close Reading Companion,* 189

Author/Illustrator's Craft

Reread pages 388–389. What clues in the text and illustration help you know that things are different for Lissy now? (The text tells me Paige comes over to Lissy's house. The illustrations show the girls playing and other children watching through the window. I can tell Lissy is making friends.)

Author's Craft: Illustration

Why does the illustration on page 329 show children looking in the window? (to show they are interested in what Paige and Lissy are doing) What does this tell us about how Lissy will get along with the other children from now on? (This tells us Lissy and the children will be friends.)

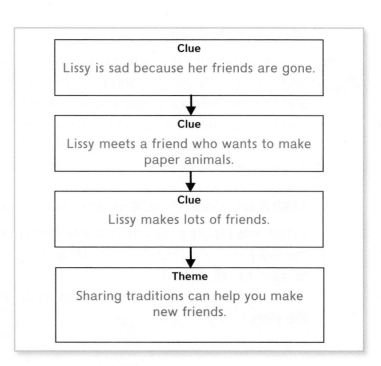

And the next day, Paige pushed Lissy on the merry-go-round with lots and lots of friends.

390

391

LITERATURE ANTHOLOGY, pp. 390–391

Read

Skill: Theme

Complete the Theme chart with children. *What happens at the playground the next day? Let's add this clue to our Theme chart. Now let's reread all our clues. What do you think the theme of the story is? Let's add the theme to our chart.*

Return to Purposes

Review children's predictions. Ask children if their predictions about the story were correct. Guide them to use the evidence in the text to confirm whether their predictions were accurate. Discuss what children learned about traditions.

Clue
Lissy is sad because her friends are gone.

↓

Clue
Lissy meets a friend who wants to make paper animals.

↓

Clue
Lissy makes lots of friends.

↓

Theme
Sharing traditions can help you make new friends.

Meet the Author

Grace Lin

Read aloud page 392 with children. Ask them why they think Grace Lin wrote about the Asian tradition of making origami, or paper animals. *Why do you think Grace Lin wants Asian American kids to be proud of their culture? Why does she also want readers to appreciate Asian traditions? Do you think she succeeds in her goals?*

Author's Purpose

In their Response Journals, have children draw a picture of a family tradition. Have them write a sentence about the picture: *In my family, we _____.*

ILLUSTRATOR'S CRAFT

Focus on Details

Explain that stories use illustrations to give information and to help readers connect ideas.

- Have children look at pictures of Lissy's paper animal friends doing make-believe things, such as opening and closing their eyes and flying. Remind children the story is realistic fiction. *Why does the illustrator show the animals doing make-believe things?*

- Have children discuss the colors and shapes in the art. Ask how the colorful art helps them understand and enjoy the story.

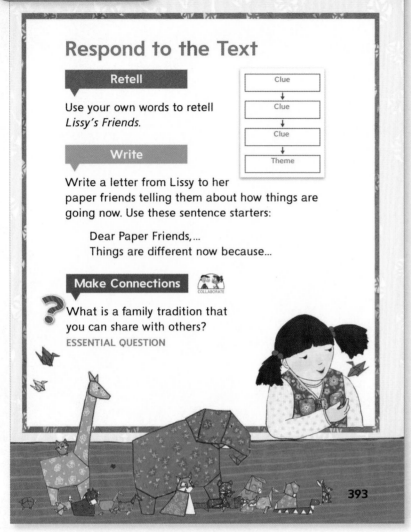

Respond to the Text

Retell

Use your own words to retell *Lissy's Friends*.

Clue
↓
Clue
↓
Clue
↓
Theme

Write

Write a letter from Lissy to her paper friends telling them about how things are going now. Use these sentence starters:

Dear Paper Friends,...
Things are different now because...

Make Connections COLLABORATE

? What is a family tradition that you can share with others?
ESSENTIAL QUESTION

393

LITERATURE ANTHOLOGY, p. 393

Respond to the Text

Retell

Guide children in retelling the story. Remind them that as they read *Lissy's Friends,* they paid attention to clues about the theme, visualized the details, and used the clues to help them identify the theme of the story. Have children use the information they recorded on their Theme chart to help them retell the selection.

Analyze the Text

After children read and retell the selection, have them reread *Lissy's Friends* to develop a deeper understanding of the text by answering the questions on pages 187–189 of the *Close Reading Companion*. For students who need support finding text evidence to support their responses, use the scaffolded instruction from the Reread prompts on pages T269L–T269N.

Write About the Text

Review the writing prompt with students. Remind them to use their responses from the *Close Reading Companion* and cite text evidence to support their answers.

For a full lesson on writing a response supported by text evidence, see pages T270–T271.

Answer: Children's letters will vary, but should include details from the story about what happens after Lissy's paper friends blow away.

Evidence: On 386–387, a girl named Paige brings Menu to Lissy and asks her how to make paper cranes. On 388–389, Paige visits Lissy's house and they make paper animals and laugh together. On page 389, we see that the other children are interested in getting to know Lissy and they will become her friends too. At the end of the story, Lissy is at the park with her new friends.

Integrate

Make Connections
COLLABORATE

Essential Question Answers will vary, but remind children to use text evidence from *Lissy's Friends* to help them think about family traditions they can share with others.

Answer: In my family, we have a special tradition of baking bread. I could invite friends over to learn how to bake bread at my house like Lissy invites Paige over to learn how to make paper cranes.

Evidence: On pages 366–368, Lissy makes a crane out of paper, which is a family tradition. The other children do not know how to make the paper cranes. On pages 386–387, Paige is interested in the paper crane and asks Lissy to teach her how to make one. On pages 388-389, Lissy teaches Paige how to make a paper crane. The girls have fun and become friends.

 CONNECT TO CONTENT

SHARING TRADITIONS

Remind children that this week they have been learning about sharing traditions. Have children discuss the tradition that Lissy shares and how sharing the tradition helps Lissy. Ask partners to tell each other about their own traditions. Encourage them to ask each other how they can share their traditions with friends.

STEM

Literature Anthology

OBJECTIVES

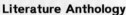 Write narratives in which they recount two or more appropriately sequenced events, include some details regarding what happened, use temporal words to signal event order, and provide some sense of closure. **W.1.3**

Use personal, possessive, and indefinite pronouns (e.g., *I, me, my; they, them, their, anyone, everything*). **L.1.1d**

Use commas in dates and to separate single words in a series. **L.1.2c**

ACADEMIC LANGUAGE

• *letter, sentence types, details, pronouns, comma*

• Cognates: *letra, detalles, coma*

 Independent Writing

5 Mins

Write About the Literature Anthology

Analyze the Prompt Have children turn to page 393 in the **Literature Anthology**. Read the prompt: *Write a letter from Lissy to her paper friends telling them how things are going now.* Say: *The prompt is asking you to write a letter from Lissy to her paper friends to tell them what happened after they blew away. The next step in answering the prompt is to find text evidence and make inferences.*

Find Text Evidence Say: *To answer the prompt, we need to find evidence in the text and the illustrations about what happens after the paper animals blow away. Look at pages 386–387. What happens when Lissy meets Paige?* (Paige brings Menu back to Lissy. Paige asks Lissy to teach her how to make paper cranes, and they become friends. Other children look interested in making paper animals and becoming friends.) Have children take notes as they look for evidence to respond to the prompt.

Write to the Prompt Guide children as they begin their writing.

• **Prewrite** Have children review their notes and plan their writing. Guide them to make a list of things Lissy might want to tell her paper friends and decide which things they want to write about. Then guide children to organize their ideas and choose details to support their writing.

• **Draft** Have children write a response to the prompt. Remind them to begin their letters with a greeting. As children write their drafts, have them focus on the week's skills.

  • **Varying Sentence Types** Use statements, questions, and exclamations to make their writing interesting. **Trait: Sentence Fluency**

  • **Describing Details** Use details to describe events and characters. **Trait: Ideas**

  • **Pronouns** Use the pronouns *I* and *me* correctly. **Grammar**

Tell children they will continue to work on their responses on Day 4.

Go Digital

Present the Lesson

Graphic Organizer

Writing

I see a fish.

Grammar

Grammar

I and *Me*

1 Review Have children look at page 295 in the **Reading/Writing Workshop**. Remind them that *I* is used as the subject and *me* is used after a verb or a word such *as for, at, of, with, to,* or *between.*

Say: *Listen for the pronoun* I *or* me *in this sentence:* Thank you for getting it for me. *Why was* me *used and not* I? (It comes after the word *for* and is not the subject of the sentence.)

2 Guided Practice/Practice Say: *Let's find* I *and* me *in Kate's letter.* Have partners circle the words and write new sentences with *I* and *me.*

Talk About It Have partners work together to explain why Kate chose to use *I* or *me* in each sentence.

Mechanics: Commas in Dates and Letters

1 Explain Remind children that commas have many uses. They are used to separate the date and year when writing a date, and they are used after the greeting and closing in a letter.

2 Guided Practice Prompt children to identify the commas in the following letter.

Saturday, April __, 20__

Dear Champ,

We planted plants today. Every April, we dig in the garden. It is our way to mark the beginning of spring. It was a fun day!

Your friend,

Carl

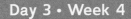
Daily Wrap Up

- Review the Essential Question and encourage children to discuss using the oral vocabulary words. Ask: *What did you learn about making friends?*

- Prompt children to review and discuss the skills they used today. *Give examples of how you used each skill.*

Materials

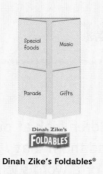

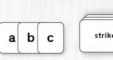

Visual Vocabulary Cards

ancient	before
drama	front
effort	heard
movement	push
tradition	tomorrow
difficult	your
nobody	

Literature Anthology
VOLUME 4

Teaching Poster

a b c

Word-Building Cards

strike

Spelling Word Cards

Dinah Zike's FOLDABLES

Dinah Zike's Foldables®

 → **Extend the Concept** 🔍 CLOSE READING

MINILESSON
5 Mins

Making Paper Shapes

OBJECTIVES

CCSS Distinguish between information provided by pictures or other illustrations and information provided by the words in a text. **RI.1.6**

Review vocabulary

ACADEMIC LANGUAGE
directions, follow, steps, first, last

ESSENTIAL QUESTION

Remind children that this week they have been learning about traditions. Guide children to discuss the Essential Question using information from what they have read and discussed. Use the Visual Vocabulary Cards and the Define/Example/Ask routine to review the oral vocabulary words *ancient, drama, effort, movement,* and *tradition.*

Guide children to use each word as they talk about what they have read and learned about traditions. Prompt children by asking questions.

- Which is more ancient: a radio or a dinosaur bone?
- What would a dance with a lot of drama look like?
- When do you make an effort to do something?
- What is a movement you can make with your hand?
- What is one of your favorite traditions?

Review last week's oral vocabulary words *predict, cycle, creative, frigid,* and *scorching.*

Text Feature: Directions

①Explain Remind children that they can use informational selections to find facts and details about topics such as traditions. Explain that informational text sometimes gives directions—a list of steps that tell you how to do something.

②Model Display Teaching Poster 15. *This set of directions tells you how to plant seeds. The children in the photographs are following these directions.* Read the first two steps in the directions. *I see that the first step is to pack dirt in a pot. The second step is to poke holes in the dirt. The photographs show the child following these steps.*

③Guided Practice/Practice Read together the remaining steps. Guide children to discuss steps 3, 4, and 5. *What should you do after you poke holes in the dirt? What do you do last? What will happen if you follow all of these directions?* Tell children to look for directions in informational text selections.

ENGLISH LANGUAGE LEARNERS SCAFFOLD

Beginning

Use Sentence Frames Use sentence frames to help children identify the steps the people are following. *First, they pack dirt in a _____. Next, they poke holes in the _____. Show me the dirt. Show me the pot.*

Intermediate

Discuss Guide children to focus on the steps in the directions. Have children tell what you must do first, next, and last.

Advanced/High

Describe Prompt children to discuss why it is important to follow all the steps in the process. Ask them what might happen if a person did not do one of the steps.

Genre How-To

Compare Texts
Learn how to make an origami dog.

Making Paper Shapes

See the crane made out of folded paper? Folding paper to make different shapes is called **origami**. People in Asia have made origami for hundreds of years.

Kids learn this art from their mothers, fathers, and grandparents.

394

People in Japan make **decorations** for special days. One **holiday** is the Star Festival. Children sing songs and get treats to eat.

Families hang bright origami in the streets. Kids write wishes on slips of paper and hang them from sticks. They hope their wishes come true. **1**

395

Literature Anthology

LITERATURE ANTHOLOGY, pp. 394–395

Making Paper Cranes

 CLOSE READING

Lexile 510

Compare Texts

As you read and reread "Making Paper Shapes," encourage children to think about the Essential Question. Tell them this selection gives directions for folding paper animals. Point out the words *origami, decoration*, and *holiday*.

Read

❶ Strategy: Visualize

Teacher Think Aloud I close my eyes and visualize, or picture in my mind, the Star Festival. I can see the bright origami hanging in the streets and hear children singing songs.

❷ Text Features: Directions

Look at the numbers in the directions. How many steps are there? (seven) When I follow directions, I follow the steps in order. I also see pictures. The words tell me what to do and the pictures show me.

❸ Text Features: Directions

I will read all of the steps, then go back and start at step 1. The first thing we do is fold the paper in half. Let's do that together. What do we do next? (Fold it in half again.) Let's follow the rest of the steps in order.

Retell

Guide children to use key details to retell the selection.

You can make origami, too. Use these directions to turn a square of paper into a cute dog.

2 **1.** Start with a square of paper. Fold it down in half so it forms a triangle.

2. Fold it in half again, like this. Press down the edge to make a crease.

3

3. Open the paper so you see a crease in the center.

4. Start from the crease and fold down both sides of the paper to make ears. See the dotted line? It shows you where to fold.

396

5. Now your dog will look like this.

6. Fold back the top of your dog so it is flat. Fold back the bottom so it is flat, too.

7. You made a dog! Now you can draw a face on it.

Make Connections
? What might Lissy do with this dog? **Essential Question**

397

LITERATURE ANTHOLOGY, pp. 396–397

Reread

After children retell, have them reread to develop a deeper understanding of the text by annotating and answering the questions on pages 190–192 of the *Close Reading Companion*. For children who need support citing text evidence, use these Reread questions:

- How does the author organize the information in this selection?
- Why did the author write "Making Paper Shapes"?
- How do the photographs help you understand the directions?

Integrate

Make Connections
COLLABORATE

Essential Question Have children use text evidence to tell what Lissy might do with the paper dog from "Making Paper Shapes."

 CONNECT TO CONTENT
SOCIAL STUDIES
TRADITIONS

Remind children that this week they have been reading about traditions. Remind them that making origami is a Japanese tradition. Ask partners to name and discuss some American traditions.

Word Work

Phonemic Awareness

5 Mins — MINILESSON

OBJECTIVES

CCSS Segment spoken single-syllable words into their complete sequence of individual sounds (phonemes). **RF.1.2d**

CCSS Read words with inflectional endings. **RF.1.3f**

CCSS Recognize and read grade-appropriate irregularly spelled words. **RF.1.3g**

Recognize synonyms and antonyms

Phoneme Segmentation

1 Model Show children how to segment words into individual phonemes. *Listen as I say a word:* splash. *Now listen as I say the sounds in the word: /s/ /p/ /l/ /a/ /sh/. There are five sounds. Let's say them together: /s/ /p/ /l/ /a/ /sh/.*

2 Guided Practice/Practice Have children practice segmenting phonemes. *Listen as I say a word. Tell me the sounds you hear in the word. Let's do the first two together: strap, split, throne, scrap, spread, splash, stripe, scream.*

10 Mins — MINILESSON

Phonics/Structural Analysis

Build with Three-Letter Blends

Review *The sounds /str/ can be represented by the letters* str. *We'll use* **Word-Building Cards** *to build words with* str *and other three-letter blends. Place the letters s, t, r, a, n, g, e. Let's blend the sounds together and read the word: /strā¯nj/. Now let's change the* ge *to* d. *Blend the sounds and read the word. Continue with* strap, strip, stripe, strike, strive, thrive, three, threat, thread, thrill, shrill, shred.

> **Decodable Reader** Have children read "A Thrilling Dance" (pages 77–80).

Inflectional Endings *-ed, -ing*

1 Review Write the words *throb, throbbed, throbbing* on the board and read them with children. Remind children that when *-ed* or *-ing* is added to a word that has a short vowel followed by one consonant, the consonant is doubled before adding the ending.

2 Practice Write the following words: *spray, scrape, glue, splash, trace.* Have children work in pairs to construct words that tell about actions in the past and actions happening now by adding *-ed* and *-ing*.

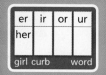

Spelling

Sort Three-Letter Blends

Review Provide pairs of children with copies of the **Spelling Word Cards**. While one partner reads the words one at a time, the other should orally segment the word and then write the word.

Have children correct their own papers. Then have them sort the words by three-letter-blend spelling patterns: *str, spr, spl, scr, thr,* or no three-letter blend.

High-Frequency Words

before, front, heard, push, tomorrow, your

Review Display **Visual Vocabulary Cards** for *before, front, heard, push, tomorrow, your*. Have children Read/Spell/Write each word.

- Point to a word and call on a child to use it in a sentence.
- Review last week's words using the same procedure.

Expand Vocabulary

difficult, nobody

Use the Visual Vocabulary Cards to review *difficult* and *nobody*.

1 Explain S*ynonyms are words that have almost the same meaning. Antonyms are words that have opposite meanings.* Have children generate synonyms and antonyms for *difficult*.

2 Model Write the word *difficult* on the board. Make a two-column chart below the word. Label one column *Synonyms* and the other column *Antonyms*. Say: Difficult *means "hard to do or understand." Another word that means almost the same as* difficult *is* hard. Write the word *hard* in the synonym column. *A word that means the opposite of* difficult *is* easy. Write *easy* in the antonym column.

3 Guided Practice Help children brainstorm other synonyms and antonyms for *difficult* to fill in the chart. Add words children don't list. Have them share sentences using each word.

Monitor and *Differentiate*

✔ **Quick Check**

Can children read and decode words with three-letter blends?

Can children recognize and read high-frequency and vocabulary words?

Small Group Instruction

If No → Approaching Reteach pp. T290–293

ELL Develop pp. T304–311

If Yes → On Level Review pp. T298–299

Beyond Level Extend pp. T302–303

Language Arts

MINILESSON
5 Mins

Independent Writing

Write About the Literature Anthology

Revise

Reread the prompt about the story *Lissy's Friends: Write a letter from Lissy to her paper friends telling them how things are going now.* Have children read their drafts to see if they responded to the prompt. Then have them check for:

- **Varying Sentence Types** Did they use exclamations, statements, and questions to make their writing interesting? **Trait: Sentence Fluency**

- **Describing Details** Did they use details to describe characters and events? **Trait: Ideas**

- **Pronouns** Did they correctly use the pronouns *I* and *me*? **Grammar**

Peer Review Have children work in pairs to do a peer review and read their partner's draft. Ask partners to check that the response includes pronouns, describing details, and varying sentence types. They should take notes about what they liked most about the writing, questions they have for the author, and additional ideas they think the author could include. Have partners discuss these topics by responding to each other's comments. Provide time for them to make revisions.

Proofread/Edit

Have children check for the following:

- Pronouns are used correctly.

- Words are spelled correctly.

- Frequently occurring adjectives are used.

Peer Edit Next, have partners exchange their drafts and take turns reviewing them against the checklist. Encourage partners to discuss and fix errors together.

OBJECTIVES

CCSS With guidance and support from adults, focus on a topic, respond to questions and suggestions from peers, and add details to strengthen writing as needed. **W.1.5**

CCSS Add drawings or other visual displays to descriptions when appropriate to clarify ideas, thoughts, and feelings. **SL.1.5**

CCSS Use commas in dates and to separate single words in a series. **L.1.2c**

ACADEMIC LANGUAGE

- *edit, revise, details, pronoun, sentence types*
- Cognates: *editar, revisar, detalles*

Go Digital

Writing

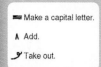

Make a capital letter.

∧ Add.

⌐ Take out.

Proofreader's Marks

I see a fish.

Grammar

Final Draft

After children edit their writing and finish their peer edits, have them write their final draft. Tell children to write neatly so others can read their writing. Or, work with children to explore a variety of digital tools to produce and publish their writing, including collaborating with peers. Have them include details that help make their writing clear. Guide children to add a drawing to their letters.

Teacher Conference As children work, conference with them to provide guidance. Check to make sure they are including describing details and varying sentences types in their letters.

Grammar

I and *Me*

1 **Review** Remind children that *I* is used as the subject of a sentence and *me* is used after a verb or a word such as *for, at, of, with, to,* or *between.*

2 **Practice** Display the following sentences. Have children identify which sentences use *I* and *me* correctly. Have children make corrections where the words are used incorrectly.

> Me like my new blue bedspread. (incorrect; I)
>
> My friend and me played three games. (incorrect; I)

Talk About It Have partners work together to orally generate a question-and-answer dialogue that includes the words *I* and *me.*

Mechanics: Commas in Dates and Letters

1 **Explain** Remind children that commas are used to separate the date and year in a date. Remind them that a comma is used after the greeting and after the closing in a letter.

2 **Guided Practice** Prompt children to insert commas in the following letter.

> April 2, 20__
>
> Dear Grandmother,
>
> We are having a May Day show at school on May 1, 20__. We will sing and dance around a maypole. It is a fun way to bring in spring. I hope to see you soon.
>
> Love,
>
> Tomas

Daily Wrap Up

- Have children discuss the Essential Question using the oral vocabulary words. Ask: *Does our class have any weekly traditions? What are they?*

- Prompt children to discuss the skills they practiced and learned today by asking, *What skills did you use today?*

→ # Integrate Ideas

OBJECTIVES

 CCSS Participate in shared research and writing projects (e.g., explore a number of "how-to" books on a given topic and use them to write a sequence of instructions). **W.1.7**

- Build background knowledge
- Research information using technology

ACADEMIC LANGUAGE
- *tradition, poster, image*
- Cognates: *tradición, imagen*

 # RESEARCH AND INQUIRY

Make a Poster

 Review the steps in the research process. Tell children that today they will do a research project with a partner to learn more about traditions. Explain why teaching each other about traditions is important.

STEP 1 **Choose a Topic**

Guide partners to choose a tradition to research. It may be one they have in their family or one they have heard about that interests them.

STEP 2 **Find Resources**

Discuss how to use the selections, reference materials, and online resources to find information on their chosen tradition. Encourage them to talk to family and community members about traditions. Have them use the Research Process Checklist online.

STEP 3 **Keep Track of Ideas**

Have children record their ideas in a Four-Door Foldable®. Model recording details.

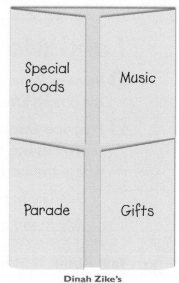

Special foods   Music

Parade   Gifts

Dinah Zike's
FOLDABLES

Go
Digital

Resources Research and Inquiry

Collaborative Conversations

Add New Ideas Review with children that as they engage in partner, small-group, and whole-group discussions, they should:

- stay on topic.
- connect their own ideas to the comments of others.
- look for ways to connect their experiences to the conversation.

STEP 4 Create the Project: Poster

Explain the characteristics of a poster.

- Information A poster can give information. In this project, the poster will give information about a tradition.
- Image A poster can have images that illustrate the information.
- Text A poster can have text. Your poster can have text that tells about your tradition.

Have children create a poster about their chosen tradition.

- Guide them to make a drawing or use photographs.
- Encourage children to write a title and two or three details about the tradition.

INFORMATIVE POSTER

ENGLISH LANGUAGE LEARNERS
ELL SCAFFOLD

Beginning	Intermediate	Advanced/High
Use Sentence Frames Use sentence frames to help children discuss their tradition. For example: *On this day, we eat _____.*	**Discuss** Guide children to focus on the most important details about their tradition. Ask: *Who has this tradition? Are there special foods or music that go with this tradition?*	**Describe** Prompt children to elaborate on their tradition. Ask them whether they have participated in this tradition before. *If so, what did you do? If not, would you like to someday? Why?*

Materials

Reading/ Writing Workshop
VOLUME 4

Literature Anthology
VOLUME 4

Visual Vocabulary Cards
before
front
heard
push
tomorrow
your
difficult
nobody

Teaching Poster

Word-Building Cards

Interactive Read-Aloud Cards

strike
Spelling Word Cards

→ Word Work/Fluency

Go Digital

MINILESSON 5 Mins — Phonemic Awareness

OBJECTIVES

CCSS Orally produce single-syllable words by blending sounds (phonemes), including consonant blends. **RF.1.2b**

CCSS Use conventional spelling for words with common spelling patterns and for frequently occurring irregular words. **L.1.2d**

CCSS Read words with inflectional endings. **L.1.3f**

Phoneme Blending

Review Guide children to blend phonemes to form words. *Listen as I say a group of sounds. Then blend those sounds to form a word.*

/s/ /p/ /l/ /a/ /sh/   /th/ /r/ /ō/ /t/   /s/ /k/ /r/ /u/ /b/   /s/ /p/ /r/ /e/ /d/

Phoneme Substitution

Review Guide children to substitute phonemes. *I am going to say a word. I want you change the initial sound and say the new word.*

map/strap   bit/split   low/throw   tap/scrap

MINILESSON 10 Mins — Phonics/Structural Analysis

Blend and Build with Three-Letter Blends

Review Have children read and say the words *scrape, split, spring, string, throat,* and *shrink.* Then have children use **Word-Building Cards** to build *stream, scream, screen, spree, three, threw, throw.*

Word Automaticity Help children practice word automaticity. Display decodable words and point to each word as children chorally read it. Test how many words children can read in one minute. Model blending words children miss.

Inflectional Endings *-ed, -ing*

Review Have children explain how to add the endings *-ed* and *-ing* to words. Then have children practice writing and reading words with inflectional endings.

Phonemic Awareness

Phonics

Structural Analysis

Visual Glossary

Fluency: Word Automaticity

Spelling

Sort Three-Letter Blends

Review Have children use the **Spelling Word Cards** to sort the weekly words by beginning consonant blend. Remind children that four of the words do not begin with a three-letter blend.

Assess Assess children on their abilities to spell words with three-letter blends *str, spr, spl, scr,* and *thr.* Say each word and provide a sentence. Allow them time to write down the words. To challenge children, provide an additional word with each sound-spelling.

High-Frequency Words

before, front, heard, push, tomorrow, your

Review Display **Visual Vocabulary Cards** for the words. Have children Read/Spell/Write each word and write a sentence with each.

Review Vocabulary

difficult, nobody

Review Write the words and ask children to use each in a sentence. Write the sentences and reinforce word meanings as needed.

Repeat the activity with last week's words or other previously taught words that children need to review.

Monitor and *Differentiate*

 Quick Check

Can children read and decode words with three-letter blends?
Can children recognize and read high-frequency and vocabulary words?

Small Group Instruction

If No →	Approaching	Reteach pp. T290–293
	ELL	Develop pp. T304–311
If Yes →	On Level	Review pp. T298–299
	Beyond Level	Extend pp. T302–303

Fluency

Phrasing: Commas

Review with children that a comma indicates that you should pause slightly while reading. Read aloud from the Shared Read. Have children echo each sentence you read. Point out how you pause at commas. Then have partners reread the selection, working on how they read sentences with commas. Provide feedback as needed.

Language Arts

Literature Anthology

OBJECTIVES

CCSS With guidance and support from adults, use a variety of digital tools to produce and publish writing, including in collaboration with peers. **W.1.6**

CCSS Follow agreed-upon rules for discussions (e.g., *listening to others with care, speaking one at a time about the topics and texts under discussion*). **SL.1.1a**

CCSS Describe people, places, things, and events with relevant details, expressing ideas and feelings clearly. **SL.1.4**

ACADEMIC LANGUAGE

• *present, evaluate, publish*
• Cognates: *presentar, evaluar*

MINILESSON
5 Mins

Independent Writing

Write About the Literature Anthology

Prepare

Tell children they will plan what they will say about their finished writing and drawing to the class. Remind children to:

- Think about the describing details they used to respond to the prompt.
- Think about how they used statements, exclamations, and questions in their letter to make it interesting to read.

Present

Have children take turns giving presentations of their responses to the prompt about the story *Lissy's Friends: Write a letter from Lissy to her paper friends telling them about how things are going now.* If possible, record their presentations so children can self-evaluate. Tell children to:

- Express their ideas clearly, using relevant details from the story.
- Listen carefully and quietly to the presenter.
- Explain the drawing they added to their letter.

Evaluate

Have children discuss their own presentations and evaluate their performance using the presentation rubric.

Use the teacher's rubric to evaluate children's writing. Have children add their writing to their Writer's Portfolio. Encourage children to look back at previous writing. Then have them discuss what they have learned about writing letters. Have children share their observations with a partner.

Publish

After children finish presenting their letters, discuss how the class will compile their letters into a class book. Suggest to children that there are different ways of organizing the letters in the book. Allow children to make decisions on how to best organize the letters. Guide them to use digital tools to create the book. Place the bound book in the reading center so children may read it independently.

Go Digital

Writing

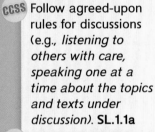

Checklists

I see a fish.

Grammar

MINILESSON 5 Mins

Grammar

I and *Me*

1 Review Have children describe how the pronouns *I* and *me* should be used. Write the following sentence and have children identify the pronouns:

I would like Drew to go to lunch with me. (I, me)

2 Practice Ask: *How do I know the sentence should begin with* I *and not with* me? Write the following sentences and have children choose the correct word to complete each.

Bella and (I, me) sat on the bench. (I)

Jack handed his book to (I, me). (me)

The children asked (I, me) many questions. (me)

(I, Me) hope my friend will play with (I, me). (I, me)

Mechanics: Commas in Dates and Letters

1 Review Remind children that commas are used in dates, and after the greeting and closing in a letter.

2 Practice Display the letter below. Read it aloud. Have children work in pairs to fix the letter.

October 1. 20__ (October 1, 20_)

Dear Dawn (Dear Dawn,)

Have you ever seen a crab hat? My dad came home from a trip to Maine on September 20 20__. He brought me a funny hat. It has a crab on it. I will bring it when I see you next month. It will make you laugh! (September 20, 20_)

Your friend? (Your friend,)

Pat

Daily Wrap Up

- Review the Essential Question and encourage children to discuss using the oral vocabulary words.

- Review with children that the theme of a story is the message the author wants to tell readers.

- Review words with three-consonant blends, including those that begin with *scr, spl, spr, str, thr,* and *shr*.

- Use the Visual Vocabulary Cards to review the Words to Know.

- Remind children that realistic fiction is a made-up story that could happen in real life.

→Integrate Ideas

Close Reading Routine

Read DOK 1–2

- Identify key ideas and details about traditions.
- Take notes and retell.
- Use **A C T** prompts as needed.

Reread DOK 2–3

- Analyze text, craft, and structure.

Integrate DOK 4

- Integrate knowledge and ideas and make text-to-text connections.
- Use the Integrate Lesson.
- Use *Close Reading Companion*, p. 193.

TEXT CONNECTIONS

Connect to the Essential Question

Write the essential question on the board: *What traditions do you know about?* Read the essential question aloud. Tell children that they will think about all of the information that they have learned about traditions. Say: *We have read many selections on this topic. We will compare the information from this week's* **Leveled Readers** *and* A Spring Birthday, **Reading/Writing Workshop** *pages 282–291.*

Evaluate Text Evidence Guide children to review the selections and their completed graphic organizers. Have children work with partners to compare information from all the week's reads. Children can record notes using a Foldable®. Guide them to record information from the selections that helps them to answer the Essential Question.

Dinah Zike's
FOLDABLES
Study Organizer

Sharing Traditions

OBJECTIVES

CCSS Participate in shared research and writing projects. **W.1.7**

Go Digital

Collaborate

RESEARCH AND INQUIRY

Have children create a checklist and review their posters:

- Does their poster tell about a tradition? Does it have all of the information they wanted to show?
- Do they wish to make any last minute changes to the text or the images?
- Have they correctly added images to their poster that illustrate the information?
- Have they taken notes about what they would like to talk about when presenting their posters to the class?

Guide partners to practice sharing their posters with each other. Children should practice speaking and presenting their information clearly.

Guide students to share their work. Prompt children to ask questions to clarify when something is unclear: *What tradition did you learn about? What do you want the poster to show? Why is the tradition you chose important?* Have children use the Presentation Checklist online.

OBJECTIVES

CCSS Identify basic similarities and differences between two texts on the same topic (e.g., in illustrations, descriptions, or procedures). **RI.1.9**

Text to Photography

Read aloud with children the Integrate activity on page 193 of the *Close Reading Companion*. Have partners share reactions to the photograph. Then guide them to discuss how it is similar to the selections they read earlier in the week. Have partners collaborate to complete the Integrate page by following the prompts.

Present Ideas and Synthesize Information

When children finish their discussions, ask for a volunteer from each pair to share the information from their Foldable® and their Integrate pages. After each pair has presented their ideas, ask: *How does learning about these traditions help you answer the Essential Question, What traditions do you know about?* Lead a class discussion asking students to use the information from their charts to answer the Essential Question.

SPEAKING AND LISTENING

OBJECTIVES

CCSS Participate in collaborative conversations with diverse partners about grade 1 topics and texts with peers and adults in small and larger groups. **SL.1.1**

CCSS Build on others' talk in conversations by responding to the comments of others through multiple exchanges. **SL.1.1b**

CCSS Ask and answer questions about key details in a text read aloud or information presented orally or through other media. **SL.1.2**

As children work with partners in their *Close Reading Companion* or on their posters, make sure that students actively participate in the conversation and, when necessary, remind them to use these speaking and listening strategies:

Speaking Strategies

- Have conversations about their work with both peers and adults.
- Work together with diverse partners in small and large groups.
- Speak clearly so that others can easily understand what they are saying.

Listening Strategies

- Listen carefully to others' comments so they can respond with appropriate information. For example, when their discussion partner makes a point they should respond with more relevant information about the topic.
- Listen carefully for specific information in a text read aloud or information presented orally in order to answer questions about the information.
- Listen carefully to text read aloud or information presented orally in order to ask questions about the information.

Approaching Level

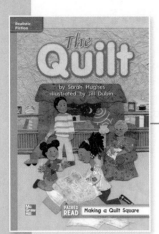

Lexile 380

OBJECTIVES

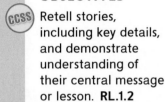

Retell stories, including key details, and demonstrate understanding of their central message or lesson. **RL.1.2**

Identify words and phrases in stories or poems that suggest feelings or appeal to the senses. **RL.1.4**

Distinguish shades of meaning among verbs differing in manner and adjectives differing in intensity by defining or choosing them or by acting out the meanings. **L.1.5d**

Visualize story events

Leveled Reader:
The Quilt

Go Digital

Before Reading

Preview and Predict

Have children turn to the title page. Read the title and the author's name and have children repeat. Preview the selection's illustrations. Prompt children to predict what the selection might be about.

The Quilt

Review Genre: Realistic Fiction

Tell children that realistic fiction is a made-up story that could happen in real life. Remind children of the key features of realistic fiction.

ESSENTIAL QUESTION

Remind children of the Essential Question: *What traditions do you know about?* Set a purpose for reading: *Let's read about special traditions.*

Remind children that as they read a selection, they can ask questions about what they do not understand or want to know more about.

Graphic Organizer

During Reading

Guided Comprehension

As children whisper read *The Quilt,* monitor and provide guidance, correcting blending and modeling the key strategies and skills. Point out the shades of meaning among verbs used in the story's dialogue, such as *said, added, explained,* and *told.*

Strategy: Visualize

Remind children that they can use the words and pictures in the story to help them picture in their minds what is happening. Model the strategy on page 2. Say: *I see the family inside the house. The mom is taking a special quilt out of a box. I can picture the excitement in the room!*

Retell

Skill: Theme

Remind children that the theme is the message the author wants to get across to the reader. As you read, ask: *What clues do we read that tell us about the theme?* Display a Theme chart for children to copy.

Model recording children's answers in the boxes. Have children record the answers in their own charts.

Think Aloud On page 2, we learn that the quilt was started by Leah's great-grandmother. The illustration on page 3 shows quilt squares made with many kinds of cloth scraps. I'll write these events as clues. They will help me figure out the theme or message of the story.

Guide children to use the text and illustrations to complete the chart.

After Reading

Respond to Reading

Have children complete the Respond to Reading on page 12.

Retell

Have children take turns retelling the selection, using the **Retelling Cards** as a guide. Help children make a personal connection by saying: *What is your favorite family tradition? Why do you enjoy it?*

Model Fluency

Read the sentences, one at a time. Have children chorally repeat. Point out to children how you pause when you come to a comma.

Apply Have children practice repeated readings with partners. Provide feedback as needed.

PAIRED READ ...

"Making a Quilt Square"

Make Connections: Write About It · Analytical Writing

Leveled Reader

Before reading, ask children to note that the genre of this text is informational text. Discuss the Compare Texts direction. Ask children to connect information from "Making a Quilt Square" and *The Quilt*. Provide a sentence frame such as: *To make a quilt square, you need to ____.*

Analytical Writing

COMPARE TEXTS

- Have children use text evidence to compare realistic fiction to informational text.

Literature Circles

Lead children in conducting a literature circle using the Thinkmark questions to guide the discussion. You may wish to discuss what children have learned about family traditions from both selections in the Leveled Reader.

Level Up

Level-up lessons available online.

IF children can read *The Quilt* Approaching Level with fluency and correctly answer the Respond to Reading questions,

THEN tell children that they will read another story about family traditions.

- Use pages 2 and 6 of *Latkes for Sam* On Level to model using Teaching Poster 37 to list clues for identifying the theme.

- Have children read the selection, checking their comprehension by using the graphic organizer.

Phonological Awareness

PHONEME BLENDING

TIER 2

OBJECTIVES

 CCSS Orally produce single-syllable words by blending sounds (phonemes), including consonant blends. **RF.1.2b**

I Do Explain to children that they will blend sounds to form words. *Listen as I say three sounds: /th/ /r/ /ē/. I'm going to blend the sounds together: /thrrrēēē/. I blended the sounds and said the word*: three.

 We Do *Listen as I say five sounds: /s/ /t/ /r/ /ē/ /m/. Let's blend the sounds: /ssstrrrēēēmmm/,* stream. *We said the word* stream.

Repeat this routine with the following words:

/s//t//r//e//s/   /s//t//r//ā//n//j/   /s//k//r//u//b/   /s//p//l//i//t/

 You Do *It's your turn. Blend the sounds together to form a word.*

/s//p//r//ā/   /th//r//ō//t/   /s//t//r//u//m/   /s//p//l//a//sh/

PHONEME SEGMENTATION

TIER 2

OBJECTIVES

 CCSS Segment spoken single-syllable words into their complete sequence of individual sounds (phonemes). **RF.1.2d**

I Do Explain to children that they will listen for the sounds in words. *Listen as I say a word*: thread. *I hear four sounds in* thread: */th/ /r/ /e/ /d/.*

 We Do *Let's do it together. Listen as I say a word:* split. *How many sounds do you hear in that word? Yes, there are five sounds: /s/ /p/ /l/ /i/ /t/.*

Repeat this routine with the following words:

screen   splice   strike   threw   thrash

 You Do *Are you ready? Listen carefully. Tell me how many sounds you hear. Then say the sounds.*

splotch   split   sprout   straw   thrown

SYLLABLE ADDITION

OBJECTIVES

Isolate and pronounce initial, medial vowel, and final sounds (phonemes) in spoken single-syllable words. **RF.1.2c**

Add syllables to form new words

I Do
Explain that children will be adding word chunks, or syllables, to the ends of words. *Listen as I say a word:* splat. *I'm going to add the chunk* ter *to the end of* splat *and blend the sounds to make a new word. The new word is* splatter. Splatter *has two chunks,* splat *and* ter. *These chunks are called syllables.*

We Do
Let's try it together. Listen to this word: kit. *Let's add the syllable* ten *to the end of* kit. *Add the syllables together with me:* kit ten, kitten. *We said the new word:* kitten.

Repeat this routine with the following words:

scratch, add *ing*   splint, add *er*   can, add *not*   wrap, add *per*

You Do
Are you ready? I'll say a word and a chunk to add at the end. You blend and say the new word.

stroll, add *er*   scram, add *ble*   scrap, add *y*   strange, add *ly*

PHONEME SUBSTITUTION

OBJECTIVES

Isolate and pronounce initial, medial vowel, and final sounds (phonemes) in spoken single-syllable words. **RF.1.2c**

Substitute vowel sounds to form new words

I Do
Explain to children that they will be substituting initial sounds in words. *Listen carefully as I say a word:* meet. *I'll change the initial sound* /m/ *to* /str/ *to make a new word:* /s/ /t/ /r/ /ē/ /t/. *The new word is* street.

We Do
Let's do one together. The word is trash: /t/ /r/ /a/ /sh/. *Now let's change the initial sound from* /tr/ *to* /spl/. *What is the new word? Yes, the word is* splash.

Repeat this routine with the following word: *sing, change* /s/ *to* /spr/.

You Do
It's your turn. Repeat the word. Then change the initial sound I tell you to make a new word: mow, change /m/ to /thr/fed, change /f/ to /shr/

ELL ENGLISH LANGUAGE LEARNERS

For the **children** who need **phonemic awareness, decoding,** and **fluency** practice, use scaffolding methods as necessary to ensure children understand the meaning of the words. Refer to the Language Transfer Handbook for phonics elements that may not transfer in children's native languages.

CONNECT THREE-LETTER BLENDS AND LETTERS

OBJECTIVES

 Decode regularly spelled one-syllable words. **RF.1.3b**

 I Do Display the **Word-Building Card** *scr. These are the letters* s, c, r. *I am going to trace the letters* s, c, r *while I say* /skr/. *This is the sound I hear at the beginning of the word* scram. *Trace the letters* scr *while saying* /skr/ *five times. Repeat with* spl, spr, str, thr, shr.

 We Do *Now do it with me.* Have children trace the lowercase *scr* in the air while saying /skr/. Trace the letters *scr* five times and say /skr/ with children. Continue with *spl, spr, str, thr, shr.*

 You Do Have children connect the letters *scr* to the sound /skr/ by writing *scr,* while saying /skr/. After children have written *scr* on paper five times, continue with *spl, spr, str, thr, shr.*

Repeat connecting the three-letter blends and their sounds during the week.

BLEND WORDS WITH THREE-LETTER BLENDS

OBJECTIVES

 Decode regularly spelled one-syllable words. **RF.1.3b**

Decode words with three-letter blends *scr, spl, spr, str, thr, shr*

 I Do Display Word-Building Cards *scr, u, b. These are the letters* s, c, r. *They stand for the* /skr/ *sound. Say it with me:* /skr/. *This is the letter* u. *It stands for the* /u/ *sound. This is the letter* b. *It stands for* /b/. *I'll blend the sounds together:* /skrub/, scrub.

 We Do Guide children to blend the sounds and read: *spread, strike, strum, thrift, shrill.*

 You Do Have children blend and decode: *scratch, sprawl, straw, string, splint, throb.*

You may wish to review Phonics with **ELL** using this section.

BUILD WORDS WITH THREE-LETTER BLENDS

OBJECTIVES

Decode regularly spelled one-syllable words. **RF.1.3b**

Build and decode words with three-letter blends *scr, spl, spr, str, thr, shr*

 Display Word-Building Cards *str, a, p. The letters* s, t, r *stand for /str/. The letter* a *stands for /a/. The letter* p *stands for /p/. I will blend these sounds: /strap/. The word is* strap.

 Let's build a different word together. Point to the cards forming *strap. I am going to change the letter* p *to the letter* y. *Remember,* ay *together can stand for /ā/. Let's blend and read the new word: /strā /,* stray.

 Have children continue building and blending words: *strand, strange, strong, string, spring, spread, thread, thrill, shrill.*

Repeat building additional words with three-letter blends.

BLEND WORDS WITH THREE-LETTER BLENDS

OBJECTIVES

Decode regularly spelled one-syllable words. **RF.1.3b**

Decode words with three-letter blends: *scr, spl, spr, str, thr, shr*

 Display Word-Building Cards *thr, ow. The letters* thr *stand for the /thr/ sound. The letters* ow *together stand for /ō/. Listen as I blend the sounds: /thr/ /ō/,* throw. *The word is* throw.

 Let's do some words together. Blend and read the words: *scratch, splat, sprang, sprout, stretch, thrive.*

 Display the words to the right. Have children blend and read the words.

Decodable Reader Have children read "A Thrilling Dance" (pages 77–80).

scrap	scrimp	sprang	spread	spruce
strange	streak	street	stretch	strike
three	throne	shrill	strung	thrash
gnome	flew	nudge	know	suit

Throw the ball three times.

We saw a strange scrap of paper on the street.

You can strum the strings.

BUILD FLUENCY WITH PHONICS

Sound-Spellings Fluency

Display Word-Building Cards: *scr, spl, spr, str, thr, shr, wr, kn, gn, au, aw, augh, ew, ue, ui, ow, oy, oi, ar, ore, oar, er, ir, ur, ey, igh, oa, oe, ee, ea.* Have children chorally say the sounds. Repeat. Vary the pace.

Fluency in Connected Text

Have children review the **Decodable Reader** selections. Identify words with three-letter blends and blend words as needed.

Have partners reread the selections for fluency.

Approaching Level

Structural Analysis

REVIEW INFLECTIONAL ENDINGS *-ed, -ing*

 CCSS

OBJECTIVES

Know and apply grade-level phonics and word analysis skills in decoding words both in isolation and in text. **RF.1.3**

Read words with inflectional endings

 I Do Write the word *scratched* on the board and read it: /skratchd/. *I look at the word* scratched *and I see a word I know,* scratch. *The* -ed *ending tells me that it has already happened. I scratch my arm now. I also scratched my arm yesterday.* Repeat with *scratching.*

 We Do Write *scrubbed. Let's read this word: /skrubd/. If we look at* scrubbed, *is there a word we know? Yes,* scrub. *Write* scrub. *When* -ed *is added to words that end with a vowel and a consonant, we double the consonant. The* -ed *tells us that this is something that already happened. Let's use* scrub *and* scrubbed *in sentences.* Repeat with *scrubbing.*

 You Do Have children work with partners. Give them several words with *-ed* and *-ing* endings. Partners work together to determine the root word and write a sentence that uses each form of the word correctly.

Repeat Have children create sentences using words with *-ed* and *-ing*.

RETEACH INFLECTIONAL ENDINGS *-ed, -ing*

 CCSS

OBJECTIVES

Know and apply grade-level phonics and word analysis skills in decoding words both in isolation and in text. **RF.1.3**

Read and write words with inflectional endings *-ed* and *-ing*

 I Do Write and read the word *splashed*. Underline the letters *ed* in *splashed*. *When* -ed *is added to a verb, it makes the word tell about something that has already happened. If I splashed water, I did it before now.* Repeat with *splashing.*

 We Do Write *serve. Let's add* -ed. *Remember, when a verb ends in* e *we drop the* e *before adding the* ed *ending. Say* served: *served. Now let's use* served *in a sentence. Repeat with* serving.

 You Do Have children add *-ed* and *-ing* to verbs. Guide them to repeat the words as needed. *Now it's your turn. Add* -er *and* -ing *to each word, then say each word and use each word in a sentence.*

stretch   drag   grab   climb   rub   scrub

Words to Know

REVIEW HIGH-FREQUENCY WORDS

OBJECTIVES

 Recognize and read grade-appropriate irregularly spelled words. **RF.1.3g**

Review high-frequency words *before, front, heard, push, tomorrow, your*

 I Do Use the **High-Frequency Word Cards** to **Read/Spell/Write** each high-frequency word. Use each word orally in a sentence.

 We Do Guide children to Read/Spell/Write each word on their **Response Boards**. Work together to generate oral sentences using the words.

 You Do Have children work with a partner to do the Read/Spell/Write routine on their own using the words *before, front, heard, push, tomorrow, your.*

CUMULATIVE REVIEW

OBJECTIVES

 Recognize and read grade-appropriate irregularly spelled words. **RF.1.3g**

Review previously taught high-frequency words

 I Do Display the High-Frequency Word Cards from the previous weeks. Review each word using the Read/Spell/Write routine.

 We Do Have children write the words on their Response Boards. Complete sentences for each word, such as *Close your eyes ____. I am too busy to ____.* Show each card and have children chorally read. Mix and repeat.

 You Do **Fluency** Display the High-Frequency Word Cards. Point to the words in random order. Have children chorally read. Repeat at a faster pace.

REVIEW VOCABULARY WORDS

OBJECTIVES

 Identify real-life connections between words and their uses (e.g., note places at home that are *cozy*). **L.1.5c**

 I Do Display the **Visual Vocabulary Cards** for *difficult* and *nobody*. Review each word using the Define/Example/Ask routine.

 We Do Invite children to act out each word. Then work with them to complete these sentence starters: *It was difficult to ____. Nobody wanted to ____.*

 You Do Have partners write two sentences of their own, using each of the words. Provide assistance as needed.

Comprehension

READ FOR FLUENCY

OBJECTIVES

 Read with sufficient accuracy and fluency to support comprehension. **RF.1.4**

 Read grade-level text orally with accuracy, appropriate rate, and expression. **RF.1.4b**

 I Do Read the first page of the selection. Model using appropriate phrasing. *When I see a comma, I pause.* Reread the second sentence twice, first without pausing at the commas, then pausing.

 We Do Read the rest of the story and have children echo-read each sentence after you. Point out how you pause when you see a comma.

 You Do Have children work with a partner and take turns rereading the passage aloud. Remind them to use phrasing as they read, pausing when they see commas and punctuation marks.

IDENTIFY PLOT

OBJECTIVES

 Describe characters, settings, and major events in a story, using key details. **RL.1.3**

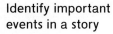 Identify important events in a story

 I Do Remind children that they have been reading a realistic fiction selection. Explain that the plot follows the events that take place in a story. *The plot tells what the characters do and where they go. The plot is what happens during the story.*

 We Do Read the first two pages of the selection aloud. Model identifying and describing the major events. *We read that Sue is at Aunt Jane's. Why is she there? What day is it? What is Sue wondering about?*

 You Do Guide children to read the rest of the Practice Book selection. Prompt them to describe what happens and why it happens.

REVIEW THEME

OBJECTIVES

 Retell stories, including key details, and demonstrate understanding of their central message or lesson. **RL.1.2**

 I Do Explain that the theme of a story is the overall idea. *The theme of a story gives a message about life. When we discover the theme of a story, we understand what is important to the author.*

 We Do Read the selection together. Pause to discuss what the characters do and say. *Where is Sue? Why is she at Aunt Jane's? It's her birthday. What does she wonder about? What is Aunt Jane's birthday tradition? What do you think the author's message is?*

 You Do Have partners reread the selection together. Have children work together as you guide them to complete a Theme chart.

SELF-SELECTED READING

OBJECTIVES

With prompting and support, read prose and poetry of appropriate complexity for grade 1. **RL.1.10**

Apply the strategy and skill to read a text

Read Independently

Have children pick a realistic fiction selection for sustained silent reading. Remind them to:

- think about what the characters do and say.
- identify the major events that happen during the story.
- Identify the message that the author wants to get across to the reader.

Read Purposefully

Have children record the important events on a Theme chart. After reading, guide children to participate in a group discussion about the selection they read. Guide children to:

- share their charts.
- discuss what happens in the story and why.
- explain the clues that helped them identify the theme of the story.

On Level

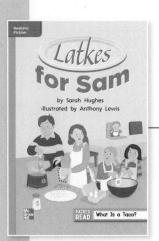

Lexile 410

OBJECTIVES

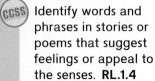 Retell stories, including key details, and demonstrate understanding of their central message or lesson. **RL.1.2**

Identify words and phrases in stories or poems that suggest feelings or appeal to the senses. **RL.1.4**

Distinguish shades of meaning among verbs differing in manner and adjectives differing in intensity by defining or choosing them or by acting out the meanings. **L.1.5d**

Visualize story events

Leveled Reader:
Latkes for Sam

Before Reading

Preview and Predict

Have children turn to the title page. Read the title and the author's name and have children repeat. Preview the selection's illustrations. Prompt children to predict what the selection might be about.

Review Genre: Realistic Fiction

Have children recall that realistic fiction is a made-up story that could happen in real life. Discuss the key features of realistic fiction.

ESSENTIAL QUESTION

Remind children of the Essential Question: *What traditions do you know about?* Set a purpose for reading: *Let's read to find out about two different family traditions.*

Remind children that as they read a selection, they can ask questions about what they do not understand or want to know more about.

During Reading

Guided Comprehension

As children whisper read *Latkes for Sam,* monitor and provide guidance, correcting blending and modeling the key strategies and skills. Point out the shades of meaning among verbs used in the story's dialogue, such as *said, added, explained,* and *told.*

Strategy: Visualize

Remind children that they can use the words and pictures in the story to help them picture what is happening. Model the strategy on page 4. Say: *I visualize everyone in the kitchen getting ready to make latkes. All the food is on the counter. Mom and Emma are wearing aprons.*

Skill: Theme

Remind children that the theme is the message the author wants to share with the reader. As you read, ask: *What clues did we read that tell us about the theme?* Display a Theme chart for children to copy.

Go Digital

Latkes for Sam

Graphic Organizer

Retell

Model recording answers for children. Have children copy the answers into their own charts.

Think Aloud On page 6, Emma's Dad says that making latkes is a tradition in the family. Her mom says she does things the "old way." I can use these clues to figure out the theme.

Prompt children to fill in the chart as they read.

After Reading

Respond to Reading

Have children complete the Respond to Reading on page 12.

Retell

Have children take turns retelling the selection, using the **Retelling Cards** as a guide. Help children make a connection: *What is your favorite food that you eat with your family? When do you have this food?*

Model Fluency

Read the sentences one at a time. Have children chorally repeat. Point out to children how you pause when you come to a comma.

Apply Have children practice reading with partners. Provide feedback as needed.

PAIRED READ ...

"What Is a Taco?"

Make Connections: Write About It ✎ *Analytical Writing*

Before reading, ask children to note that the genre of this selection is informational text. Then discuss the Compare Texts direction. After reading, ask children to make connections between what they learned about making tacos in "What Is a Taco?" and making latkes in *Latkes for Sam*.

Leveled Reader

✎ *Analytical Writing*

COMPARE TEXTS

- Have children use text evidence to compare realistic fiction to informational text.

Literature Circles

Lead children in conducting a literature circle using the Thinkmark questions to guide the discussion. You may wish to discuss what children have learned about traditional foods from both selections in the Leveled Reader.

Level Up

Level-up lessons available online.

IF children can read *Latkes for Sam* On Level with fluency and correctly answer the Respond to Reading questions,

THEN tell children that they will read another story about traditions.

- Use page 5 of *Patty Jumps!* Beyond Level to model using Teaching Poster 37 to list a clue for identifying the theme.

- Have children read the selection, checking their comprehension by using the graphic organizer.

On Level
Phonics

BUILD WORDS WITH THREE-LETTER BLENDS

OBJECTIVES

Decode regularly spelled one-syllable words. **RF.1.3b**

Build and decode words with three-letter blends

 I Do

Display **Word-Building Cards** *str, a, p. These are letters* s, t, r, a, p. *When you see* str *together, they stand for the sound /str/. I will blend the sounds: /strap/,* strap. *The word is* strap.

 We Do

Now let's try it together. Make the word *split* using the Word-Building Cards. *Remember the letters* s, p, l *stand for the /spl/ sound. Let's blend: /split/,* split.

Change the letter i *to* a. *I am going to change the letter* i *to* a. *Let's blend and read the new word: /splat/,* splat. *The new word is* splat.

 You Do

Have children build and blend the words: *stride, strike, stripe, string, spring, spread, thread, thrill, shrill.*

Repeat with additional words with three-letter blends.

Decodable Reader Have children read "Three Shrimp" and "A Thrilling Dance" (pages 73–80).

Words to Know

REVIEW WORDS

OBJECTIVES

Recognize and read grade-appropriate irregularly spelled words. **RF.1.3g**

Review high-frequency words *before, front, heard, push, tomorrow, your,* and vocabulary words *difficult* and *nobody.*

 I Do

Use the **Read/Spell/Write** routine to teach each high-frequency word and vocabulary word. Use each word orally in a sentence.

 We Do

Guide children to Read/Spell/Write each word using their **Response Boards**. Work together to generate oral sentences using the words.

 You Do

Have partners work together using the Read/Spell/Write routine with the words *before, front, heard, push, tomorrow, your,* and the vocabulary words *difficult* and *nobody.* Have partners then write sentences about something they've done with their families. Each sentence must contain at least one high-frequency or vocabulary word.

Comprehension

REVIEW THEME

OBJECTIVES

Retell stories, including key details, and demonstrate understanding of their central message or lesson. **RL.1.2**

 I Do Remind children that the theme of a story is the overall idea. A story's theme is the message the author wants to tell readers.

 We Do Read the first two pages of the selection aloud. Pause to discuss what the characters say and do. *We read about Sue being away from her parents on her birthday. What was her family's tradition? Yes, they always went on a picnic. How might this be a clue to the theme?*

 You Do Guide children to read the rest of the Practice Book selection. Remind them to think about what the characters say and do. Help them identify the theme of the story.

SELF-SELECTED READING

OBJECTIVES

With prompting and support, read prose and poetry of appropriate complexity for grade 1. **RL.1.10**

Apply the strategy and skill to read a text

Read Independently

Have children pick a realistic fiction selection for sustained silent reading. Remind them to:

- think about the actions of the characters.
- identify the key events in the story.
- identify the theme of the story.

Read Purposefully

Have children record the important events of the plot on a Theme chart. After completing the chart, guide partners to:

- share and compare their charts.
- discuss the author's message and the theme of the story.

Beyond Level

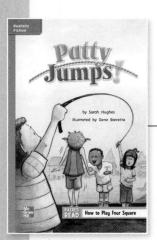

Lexile 440

OBJECTIVES

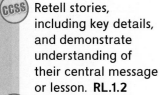 Retell stories, including key details, and demonstrate understanding of their central message or lesson. **RL.1.2**

Identify words and phrases in stories or poems that suggest feelings or appeal to the senses. **RL.1.4**

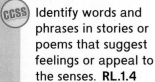 Distinguish shades of meaning among verbs differing in manner and adjectives differing in intensity by defining or choosing them or by acting out the meanings. **L.1.5d**

Visualize story events

Leveled Reader:
Patty Jumps!

Before Reading

Preview and Predict

Read the title and the author's name. Have children preview the title page and the illustrations. Ask: *What do you think this story will be about?*

Review Genre: Realistic Fiction

Have children recall that realistic fiction is a made-up story that could happen in real life. Prompt children to name key characteristics of realistic fiction. Tell them to look for these as they read the Leveled Reader.

ESSENTIAL QUESTION

Remind children of the Essential Question: *What traditions do you know about?* Set a purpose for reading: *Let's find out about jumping rope.*

During Reading

Guided Comprehension

Have children whisper read *Patty Jumps!* Have them place self-stick notes next to difficult words. Remind children that when they come to an unfamiliar word, they can look for familiar spellings. Point out the shades of meaning among verbs used in the story's dialogue, such as *shouts, says, asks, thinks, calls,* and *agrees.*

Monitor children's reading. Stop periodically and ask open-ended questions to facilitate rich discussion, such as *What does the author want you to know about jumping rope in this part of the story?* Build on children's responses to develop deeper understanding of the text.

Strategy: Visualize

Remind children that they can use the words and pictures in the story to help them picture in their minds what is happening. Say: *Think about what you see in the picture and the words you read. Then close your eyes and picture what is happening in the story.*

 Go
Digital

Patty Jumps!

Graphic
Organizer

Retell

Literature Circles

Skill: Theme

Remind children that the theme is the message the author wants to share with the reader. As you read, ask: *What clues helped you figure out the theme?*

Think Aloud As I read, I look for clues that tell what message the author wanted to share by telling this story. To figure out the theme, I look for clues in the details and pictures.

Display a Theme chart for children to copy. Model how to record the information. Have children fill in their charts as they read.

After Reading

Respond to Reading

Have children complete the Respond to Reading on page 12.

Retell

Have children take turns retelling the selection. Help children make a personal connection by writing about a schoolyard game they play. *Tell what the rules are and why you like to play the game.*

Lead children in conducting a literature circle using the Thinkmark questions to guide the discussion. You may wish to discuss what children have learned about traditional games from both selections in the Leveled Reader.

PAIRED READ ...

"How to Play Four Square"

Leveled Reader

Gifted and Talented

SYNTHESIZE Challenge children to make up a new schoolyard game. Encourage them to use ideas from the selections to explain how to play the new game.

EXTEND Have them use facts they learned from the week or do additional research to find out more about other schoolyard games.

Make Connections: Write About It  *Analytical Writing*

Before reading "How to Play Four Square," have children preview the title page and prompt them to identify the genre. Discuss the Compare Texts direction. After reading, have children work with a partner to discuss the information they learned in "How to Play Four Square" and *Patty Jumps!* Ask children to make connections by comparing and contrasting each selection. Prompt children to discuss what they learned about traditional schoolyard games from both selections.

Analytical Writing

COMPARE TEXTS

- Have children use text evidence to compare realistic fiction to informational text.

Vocabulary

OBJECTIVES

 Use sentence-level context as a clue to the meaning of a word or phrase. **L.1.4a**

Understand how to use context clues

 I Do Remind children that context clues can help them figure out the meaning of a word. *When you don't know the meaning of a word, you can look at how the word is used in a sentence.*

 We Do Say this sentence: *Beth's family has a tradition of baking cupcakes on birthdays. Let's use sentence clues to figure out the meaning of the word* tradition. *We know that Beth's family makes cupcakes. Birthdays happen each year. What do you think a tradition is?*

 You Do Have partners take turns orally using the word *tradition* in sentences. Challenge them to include context clues in the sentences.

 Gifted and Talented **Extend** Have partners tell each other stories based on family traditions they know. Encourage them to use the word *tradition* as many times as they can. Challenge them to include context clues in the sentences.

OBJECTIVES

 Use sentence-level context as a clue to the meaning of a word or phrase. **L.1.4a**

Understand how to use context clues

 I Do Remind children that they can use other words in a sentence to figure out the meaning of a word they don't know. Review the meaning of the vocabulary word *difficult*. Then write the sentence: *The thick vines made it difficult for Matt to hike on the trail.* Read the sentence together.

I can use familiar words in the sentence to help me figure out the meaning. I know that Matt was hiking on a trail. But the vines were in the way. I think the word difficult *means "not easy."*

 We Do Have partners take turns using the word *difficult* in sentences. Ask them to draw a simple picture that illustrates their sentences.

 You Do Have partners share their pictures and sentences with the group.

Comprehension

REVIEW THEME

OBJECTIVES

Retell stories, including key details, and demonstrate understanding of their central message or lesson. **RL.1.2**

Remind children that the theme of a story is the overall message. *The theme of the story gives the message the author wants to share. We look at key details and illustrations to determine the theme of a story.*

Guide children in reading the first two pages of the selection aloud. Pause and talk about the setting and Sue's feelings. *How does this information give us clues about the theme of the story?*

Have children read the rest of the selection independently. Remind them to ask themselves: *What is the author's message in this story? What is the story's theme?*

SELF-SELECTED READING

OBJECTIVES

With prompting and support, read prose and poetry of appropriate complexity for grade 1. **RL.1.10**

Apply the strategy and skill to read a text

Read Independently

Have children choose a realistic fiction selection for sustained silent reading. Remind them to think about the characters' actions during the story.

Read Purposefully

Have children record events in a Theme chart. After reading, guide children to:

- share their charts with a partner and discuss how the events connect to the theme of the story.

- record the theme of the story and what they liked most about it in a reading response journal.

Independent Study Ask children to create a poster advertising the book. Discuss with them what the poster should include: title, author, illustration of exciting scene, and a quote or statement to make others interested in reading it.

English Language Learners

Reading/Writing Workshop

OBJECTIVES

Retell stories, including key details, and demonstrate understanding of their central message or lesson. **RL.1.2**

Shared Read:
A Spring Birthday

Before Reading

Build Background

Read the Essential Question: *What traditions do you know about?*

Explain the meaning of the Essential Question: *A tradition can be an idea or event that families pass down through the years. It might be an event that families always do at a certain time, like at a holiday or birthday.*

- **Model an answer:** *When I have a birthday, my family always makes a chocolate cake. We use the same recipe that my grandmother used. This is a special tradition because we make the same cake every year. We all look forward to it.*

- Ask children a question that ties the Essential Question to their own background knowledge. *What are some of your favorite family traditions?* Ask partners to share their answers.

During Reading

Interactive Question-Response

- Ask questions that help children understand the meaning of the text after each paragraph.

- Reinforce the meanings of key vocabulary by providing meanings embedded in the questions.

- Ask children questions that require them to use key vocabulary.

- Reinforce the comprehension strategies and skills of the week by modeling.

Go Digital

A Spring Birthday

Graphic Organizer

A Spring Birthday

Pages 282–283

Point to each word in the title as you read it aloud. Then ask children to repeat the title. *This story is about Marco's birthday. Say the boy's name with me:* Marco. *His birthday is in the spring.*

Point to the illustration. *This picture shows Marco celebrating his birthday with his family.* Point to the piñata. *Do you know what this is called? Yes, a piñata. People hit a piñata with a stick so the surprises inside come out.*

Pages 284–285

Point to the illustration on pages 284 and 285. *Here is Marco's family. Who do you see?* (Marco, Mom, Dad, Gram) Point to the last sentence on page 284. *Let's read what Marco asks: "Can I have a party this year?" He wants something a little different for his birthday.*

However, Gram says that a birthday dinner is a family tradition. She makes empanadas, a pastry with a tasty filling. What does Marco think about Gram's empanadas?

Explain and Model the Strategy *Make a picture in your mind to help you understand the story. Think about story's illustrations and words. What do you see the family doing?*

Tell your partner what you see Marco and his family doing as you visualize the story.

Pages 286–287

Dad has a good idea. Marco can have a birthday picnic. Does Marco like the picnic idea? (yes)

Now let's read page 287. What are Mom, Dad, and Gram doing? (singing a Mexican birthday song) *How do you think Marco feels when he wakes up to his family singing this special song?* (excited, happy)

Explain and Model High-Frequency Words
Write the word *push* and have children say it with you. *Show me how you would push something. What are some things you might need to push?*

Pages 288–289

Look at the picture on page 288. Everyone is having fun at the picnic! On page 289, a piñata hangs above the children. What is Marco doing? (hitting the piñata) *What will happen when the piñata breaks open?* (Treats will fall out.)

Explain and Model Phonics Write these words: *striking, split, shrieked, scrambled.* Say each word and have children repeat it with you. Then circle each three-letter blend and say the sounds: /str/, /spl/, /shr/, /scr/. Have children repeat the words.

Pages 290–291

Marco received a special gift—a baseball mitt. What will he do with his new baseball mitt? (use it in the baseball game tomorrow)

Marco wants to have another birthday picnic next year. Why do you think he wants to mix old and new birthday plans?

Explain and Model the Skill *The theme of a story is what message the author wants to give readers. The theme of this story is mixing old and new to make a tradition. What clues in the story help readers know that?* (piñata; Gram's empanadas; party with family and friends; picnic instead of a dinner party)

After Reading

Make Connections

• Review the Essential Question.

→ English Language Learners

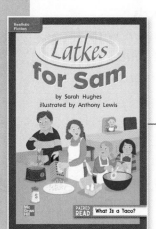

Realistic Fiction

Latkes for Sam
by Sarah Hughes
illustrated by Anthony Lewis

PAIRED READ What Is a Taco?

Lexile 290

OBJECTIVES

(CCSS) Retell stories, including key details, and demonstrate understanding of their central message or lesson. **RL.1.2**

(CCSS) Identify words and phrases in stories or poems that suggest feelings or appeal to the senses. **RL.1.4**

(CCSS) Distinguish shades of meaning among verbs differing in manner and adjectives differing in intensity by defining or choosing them or by acting out the meanings. **L.1.5d**

Visualize story events

Leveled Reader:
Latkes for Sam

Latkes for Sam

Before Reading

Preview

Read the title. Ask: *What is the title? Say it again.* Repeat with the author's name. Preview the illustrations. Have children describe the pictures. Use simple language to tell about each page. Follow with questions, such as *What are the children doing now?*

ESSENTIAL QUESTION

Remind children of the Essential Question: *What traditions do you know about?* Say: *Let's read to find out about latkes and family traditions.* Encourage children to ask for help when they do not understand a word or phrase.

Graphic Organizer

During Reading

Interactive Question-Response

Pages 2–3 *Sam is going to stay overnight at Emma's house. Let's close our eyes and visualize the scene. I see Emma's family greeting Sam. The girls are excited. Talk to a partner about what they say to each other.*

Retell

Pages 4–5 *Where are Emma and Sam?* (kitchen) *Look at the picture. Let's point to each food with a label and say what it is.* (oil; eggs; potatoes; onion) *Emma's family will use these ingredients to make latkes.*

Pages 6–7 *Dad says that latkes are their tradition. What do you think he means?* (Their family cooks and eats latkes as part of their custom.) *Let's find the steps they take to make latkes.* (shred potatoes; add onions; roll potatoes and onions in a towel; mix eggs in at the end)

Pages 8–9 *What is Emma's and Sam's job?* (setting the table) *What is Dad's job?* (cooking latkes) *Let's look at the verbs the author uses with the dialogue: said and added. How would the dialogue change if the author used shouted or interrupted? If a character is shouting, he or she might be yelling at someone. Let's act out what would happen if one character interrupted another character's lines. How can verbs change the story?*

Pages 10–11 *What tradition did we learn about on these pages?* (Sam's tradition of soda bread from Ireland) *What do you think the message is in this story?* (It's good to share cultural traditions with others.)

Go Digital

After Reading

Respond to Reading

Revisit the Essential Question. Ask children to work with partners to fill in the graphic organizer and answer the questions on page 12. Pair children with peers of varying language abilities.

Retell

Model retelling using the **Retelling Card** prompts. Say: *Look at the illustrations. Use details to help you retell the story.* Help children make personal connections by asking, *What is a traditional food you and your family makes?*

Phrasing Fluency

Read the pages in the book, one at a time. Help children echo-read the pages expressively and with appropriate phrasing. Remind them to pause when they see a comma or period.

Apply Have children practice reading with partners. Pair children with peers of varying language abilities. Provide feedback as needed.

PAIRED READ ...

Leveled Reader

"What Is a Taco?"

Make Connections: Write About It *Analytical Writing*

Before reading, tell children to note that this text is nonfiction. Then discuss the Compare Texts direction. After reading, ask children to make connections between what they learned about traditional foods from "What Is a Taco?" and *Latkes for Sam.* Prompt children by providing a sentence frame: *Making tacos and making latkes are alike because ____.*

Analytical Writing

COMPARE TEXTS

• Have children use text evidence to compare realistic fiction to informational text.

Literature Circles

Lead children in conducting a literature circle using the Thinkmark questions to guide the discussion. You may wish to discuss what children have learned about traditional foods from both selections in the Leveled Reader.

Level Up

Level-up lessons available online.

IF children can read *Latkes for Sam* ELL Level with fluency and correctly answer the Respond to Reading questions,

THEN tell children that they will read a more detailed version of the story.

• **USE** pages 7–10 of *Latkes for Sam* On Level to model using Teaching Poster 37 to list clues to the theme.

• **HAVE** children read the selection, checking their comprehension by using the graphic organizer.

Vocabulary

PRETEACH ORAL VOCABULARY

OBJECTIVES

Produce complete sentences when appropriate to task and situation. **SL.1.6**

LANGUAGE OBJECTIVE

Use oral vocabulary words

 I Do Display images from the **Visual Vocabulary Cards** one at a time to preteach the oral vocabulary words *tradition* and *effort*.

 We Do Display each image again and explain how it illustrates or demonstrates the word. Model using sentences to describe the image.

You Do Display the word again. Have partners talk about how the picture shows the word.

Beginning	Intermediate	Advanced/High
Display the Visual Vocabulary Cards and say the words together. Then say a sentence using each word. Have children point to the card and repeat the word.	Write a simple sentence frame for each word. *I made an effort to ____. My favorite tradition is ____.* Help children complete each sentence by writing the word.	Have partners each write a sentence for both of the words. Ask them to draw a picture that illustrates each sentence.

PRETEACH VOCABULARY

OBJECTIVES

Identify real-life connections between words and their use (e.g., note places at home that are *cozy*). **L.1.5c**

LANGUAGE OBJECTIVE

Use vocabulary words

 I Do Display images from the **ELL Visual Vocabulary Cards** one at a time to preteach the vocabulary words *culture* and *share* and follow the routine. Say the word and have children repeat it. Define the word in English.

 We Do Display each image again and explain how it illustrates or demonstrates the word. Model using sentences to describe the image.

 You Do Display the word again and have children say the word, then spell it. Provide opportunities for children to use the words in speaking and writing. Provide sentence starters.

Beginning	Intermediate	Advanced/High
Help children say each vocabulary word and point to the card.	Ask children to repeat and spell each word.	Have children choose a word and draw a picture to illustrate it.

Words to Know

REVIEW WORDS

OBJECTIVES

Recognize and read grade-appropriate irregularly spelled words. **RF.1.3g**

LANGUAGE OBJECTIVE

Use high-frequency words *before, front, heard, push, tomorrow, your,* and vocabulary words *difficult* and *nobody*

 I Do Display the **High-Frequency Word** and **Vocabulary Cards** for *before, front, heard, push, tomorrow, your,* and *difficult* and *nobody*. Read each word. Use the **Read/Spell/Write** routine to teach each word. Have children write the words on their **Response Boards**.

 We Do Write sentence frames on separate lines. Track the print as you guide children to read and complete the sentences: **(1)** *Let's eat lunch before we ____*. **(2)** *The plant is in front of ____*. **(3)** *I heard a ____*. **(4)** *Push the screen ____*. **(5)** *Tomorrow we will ____*. **(6)** *Your bag is ____*. **(7)** *We worked to finish the difficult ____*. **(8)** *Nobody can ____*.

 You Do Display the High-Frequency Word Cards from the previous five weeks. Display one card at a time as children chorally read the word. Mix and repeat. Note words children need to review. Repeat with vocabulary words.

Beginning	Intermediate	Advanced/High
Display the High-Frequency Cards. Say each word together. Then say the words randomly and have children point to the card.	Display the cards. Ask children to choose a card, say the word, and use it in a sentence.	Have children find magazine pictures that illustrate each word. Help them label the pictures with this week's words.

RETEACH HIGH-FREQUENCY WORDS

OBJECTIVES

Recognize and read grade-appropriate irregularly spelled words. **RF.1.3g**

LANGUAGE OBJECTIVE

Use high-frequency words

 I Do Display each Visual Vocabulary Card and say the word aloud. Define the word in English, then in Spanish if appropriate, identifying any cognates.

 We Do Point to the image and explain how it illustrates the word. Have children repeat the word. Engage children in structured partner-talk about the image as prompted on the back of the card. Ask children to chorally say the word three times.

 You Do Display each visual card in random order, hiding the word. Have children identify and define the word in their own words.

Beginning	Intermediate	Advanced/High
Say a word. Have children find its picture. Use the word in a sentence for children to repeat.	Have children complete sentence frames about the pictures.	Have children use the words in sentences about the pictures.

Writing/Spelling

WRITING TRAIT: SENTENCE FLUENCY

OBJECTIVES

With guidance and support from adults, focus on a topic, respond to questions and suggestions from peers, and add details to strengthen writing as needed. **W.1.5**

LANGUAGE OBJECTIVE

Use various types of sentences

 I Do Remind children that there are different types of sentences: statements, questions, and exclamations. Explain that writers use many different types of sentences to make their writing interesting to read.

 We Do Read page 291 of *The Spring Birthday* together. Point out the different sentence types the author used. Then read the first paragraph aloud, substituting with the following statements: *"This is a good birthday,"* Marco said. *"I want to do it next year."* Have partners talk about which sentences make the writing more interesting.

 You Do Have children write about a celebration. Remind them to use different types of sentences to tell about it.

Beginning	Intermediate	Advanced/High
Provide photos for children to describe using various types of sentences.	Provide sentence starters or models for children to refer to as they write.	Challenge children to write one sentence of each type.

THREE-LETTER BLENDS

OBJECTIVES

Use conventional spelling for words with common spelling pattern and for frequently occurring irregular words. **L.1.2d**

LANGUAGE OBJECTIVE

Spell words with three-letter blends *scr, spl, spr, str, thr, shr*

 I Do Read aloud the Spelling Words on page T248. Segment the words into sounds and attach a spelling to each. Point out the three-letter blend. Read aloud, segment, and spell the remaining words. Have children repeat.

 We Do Say a sentence for *strike.* Then say *strike* slowly and ask children to repeat. Have them write the word. Repeat the process for the remaining words.

 You Do Display the words. Have children work with a partner to check their spelling lists. Have children correct misspelled words on their list.

Beginning	Intermediate	Advanced/High
Guide children to trace or copy the words.	Ask children to list the words and circle the three-letter blend in each.	Have partners think of other words with some of the three-letter blends.

Grammar

I AND *ME*

OBJECTIVES
Use personal, possessive, and indefinite pronouns. **L.1.1d**

LANGUAGE OBJECTIVE
Use correct pronouns

Language Transfers Handbook

TRANSFER SKILLS
Korean and Spanish children may omit subject pronouns. Write sentence frames to reinforce the subject pronoun: *I will eat lunch.* Then ask: *Who will eat lunch?* Have children repeat the answer, emphasizing the subject pronoun.

 I Do

Remind children that pronouns take the place of nouns. Write these sentences: *I like to read. Will you read with me?* Underline *I*. *I tells who the sentence is about. This pronoun always uses a capital letter.* Underline *me*. *Me is part of the action of the sentence.*

Remind students that *I* is used as the subject of a sentence and *me* is used after a verb or a word such as *for, at, of, with, to,* or *between.*

 We Do

Write these sentences and help children read them. Underline the pronouns. Reinforce their understanding by saying: *The pronoun* I *tells who the sentence is about. The pronoun* me *is part of the action of the sentence.*

I ride the bus. You can ride the bus with me.

Write the following sentence frames.

_____ *have the box. Bring the box to* _____.

Joy and _____ *went to town. Joy went to town with* _____.

_____ *will bring a snack to the party. Did you get a gift for* _____?

Between Chad and _____, *there were enough books to fill a library!*

 You Do

Pair children and have them complete each sentence frame by using *I* or *me*. Circulate, listen in, and note each child's language use and proficiency.

Beginning	Intermediate	Advanced/High
Use *I* and *me* in sentences about classroom events. Have children repeat the sentences.	Have children use *I* and *me* to tell about something they did with the class earlier in the day or recently.	Have partners use *I and me* in questions and answers about classroom or school events.

PROGRESS MONITORING

Unit 6 Week 4 Formal Assessment	Standards Covered	Component for Assessment
Comprehension Theme	RL.1.2	• *Selection Test* • *Weekly Assessment*
Vocabulary Strategy Compound Words	L.2.4d	• *Selection Test* • *Weekly Assessment*
Phonics Three-Letter Blends *scr, spl, spr, str, thr, shr*	RF.1.3	*Weekly Assessment*
Structural Analysis Inflectional Endings *-ed, -ing*	RF.1.3f	*Weekly Assessment*
High-Frequency Words *before, front, heard, push, tomorrow, your*	RF.1.3g	*Weekly Assessment*
Writing Writing About Text	RL.1.2	*Weekly Assessment*
Unit 6 Week 4 Informal Assessment		
Research/Listening/Collaborating	SL.1.1c, SL.1.2, SL.1.3	• *RWW* • *Teacher's Edition*
Oral Reading Fluency (ORF) **Fluency Goal:** 13-33 words correct per minute (WCPM) **Accuracy Rate Goal:** 95% or higher	RF.1.4a. RF.1.4b, RF.1.4c	*Fluency Assessment*

Using Assessment Results

Weekly Assessment Skills	If . . .	Then . . .
COMPREHENSION	Children answer 0–3 multiple-choice items correctly . . .	. . . assign Lessons 31-33 on Theme from the *Tier 2 Comprehension Intervention online PDFs*.
VOCABULARY	Children answer 0–2 multiple-choice items correctly . . .	. . . assign Lesson 98 on Compound Words from the *Tier 2 Vocabulary Intervention online PDFs*.
PHONICS/ STRUCTURAL ANALYSIS/HFW	Children answer 0–6 multiple-choice items correctly . . .	. . . assign Lesson 72 on Three-Letter Blends, Lesson 66 on Inflectional Ending *-ed*, and Lesson 67 on Inflectional Ending *-ing* from the *Tier 2 Phonics/ Word Study Intervention online PDFs*.
WRITING	Children score less than "2" on the constructed response . . .	. . . reteach necessary skills using Section 13 on Write About Reading from the *Tier 2 Comprehension Intervention online PDFs*.
FLUENCY	Children have a WCPM score of 13 . . .	. . . assign a lesson from Section 1, 9, or 10 of the *Tier 2 Fluency Intervention online PDFs*.
	Children have a WCPM score of 0–12 . . .	. . . assign a lesson from Sections 2–8 of the *Tier 2 Fluency Intervention online PDFs*.

Using Weekly Data

Check your data Dashboard to verify assessment results and guide grouping decisions.

Data-Driven Recommendations

Response to Intervention

Use the children's assessment results to assist you in identifying children who will benefit from focused intervention.

Use the appropriate sections of the *Placement and Diagnostic Assessment* to designate children requiring:

 Intervention Online PDFs    **WonderWorks Intervention Program**

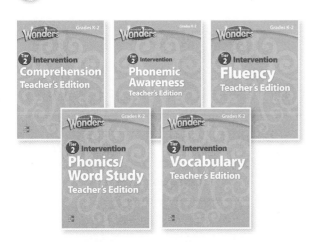

Celebrate America!

Teach and Model
Close Reading and Writing

Big Book and Little Book

Share the Harvest and Give Thanks, 302–311
Genre Nonfiction **Lexile** 680

Reading Writing Workshop

Interactive Read Aloud

"Celebrate the Flag"
Genre: Nonfiction

Practice and Apply
Close Reading and Writing

Literature Anthology

Happy Birthday, U.S.A.!, 398–405
Genre Nonfiction **Lexile** 580

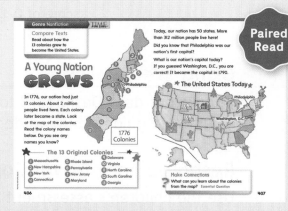

"A Young Nation Grows," 406–407
Genre Nonfiction **Lexile** 390

Differentiated Texts

APPROACHING
Lexile 440

ON LEVEL
Lexile 620

BEYOND
Lexile 660

ELL
Lexile 360

Leveled Readers

Extended Complex Texts

A Picture Book of George Washington
Genre Nonfiction
Lexile 750

How People Learned to Fly
Genre Nonfiction
Lexile 750

Classroom Library

HOW PEOPLE LEARNED TO FLY. Used by permission of HarperCollins Publishers.

Student Outcomes

Close Reading of Complex Text

- Cite relevant evidence from text
- Determine author's purpose
- Retell the text

RI.2.6, RI.1.2

Writing

Write to Sources

- Draw evidence from nonfiction text
- Write opinion text
- Conduct short research on why we celebrate holidays

W.1.1, W.1.7

Speaking and Listening

- Engage in collaborative conversation about celebrating holidays
- Retell and discuss *Share the Harvest and Give Thanks*
- Present information on why we celebrate holidays

SL.1.1c, SL.1.2, SL.1.3

Content Knowledge

- Explore the significance of holidays

Language Development

Conventions

- Use adverbs that tell how

Vocabulary Acquisition

- Develop oral vocabulary

pride	display	design
purpose	represent	

- Acquire and use academic vocabulary

nation	unite

- Use context clues to understand metaphors

L.1.1, L.1.4, L.1.6, L.4.5a

Foundational Skills

Phonics/Word Study/Spelling

- *r*-controlled vowels *air, are, ear*
- *r*-controlled vowel syllables
- fair, pair, bear, wear, spare, share, three, splash, favorite, surprise

High-Frequency Words

favorite	few	gone	surprise
wonder	young		

Fluency

- Appropriate phrasing

Decodable Text

- Apply foundational skills in connected text

RF.1.3, RF.1.3d, RF.1.3e, RF.1.3g, RF.1.4a, RF.1.4b, RF.1.4c

Professional Development

- See lessons in action in real classrooms.
- Get expert advice on instructional practices.
- Collaborate with other teachers.
- Access PLC Resources

Go Digital! www.connected.mcgraw-hill.com.

INSTRUCTIONAL PATH

1 Talk About Celebrating America!

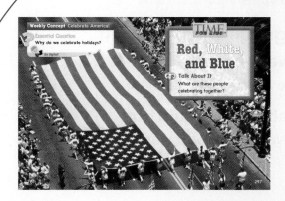

Guide children in collaborative conversations.

Discuss the essential question: *Why do we celebrate holidays?*

Develop academic language.

Listen to "Celebrate the Flag" and reread to understand the importance of the American flag.

2 Read *Share the Harvest and Give Thanks*

Apply foundational skills in connected text. Model close reading.

Read

Share the Harvest and Give Thanks to learn about the harvest season, citing text evidence to answer text-dependent questions.

Reread

Share the Harvest and Give Thanks to analyze text, craft, and structure, citing text evidence.

3 Write About Celebrating the Harvest

Model writing to a source.

Analyze a short response student model.

Use text evidence from close reading to write to a source.

Read and Write About America

Practice and apply close reading of the anchor text.

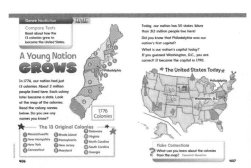

④

Read

Happy Birthday, U.S.A.! to learn about the birth of America.

Reread

Happy Birthday, U.S.A.! and use text evidence to understand how the author presents information.

Integrate

Information about the birth of America.

Write to a Source, citing text evidence to support your opinion of the most important part of the Fourth of July.

⑤

Independent Partner Work

Gradual release of support to independent work

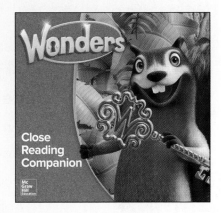

- Text-Dependent Questions
- Scaffolded Partner Work
- Talk with a Partner
- Cite Text Evidence
- Complete a sentence frame.
- Guided Text Annotation

⑥

Integrate Knowledge and Ideas

Connect Texts

Text to Text Discuss how each of the texts answers the question: Why do we celebrate holidays?

Text to Songs Compare information about America in the texts read with "You're a Grand Old Flag."

Conduct a Short Research Project

Create a flag.

DEVELOPING READERS AND WRITERS
Write to Sources: Opinion

Day 1 and Day 2
Shared Writing
- Write about *Share the Harvest and Give Thanks*, p. T330

Interactive Writing
- Analyze a student model, p. T340
- Write about *Share the Harvest and Give Thanks*, p. T341
- Find Text Evidence
- Apply Writing Trait: Ideas: Main Idea and Details, p. T341
- Apply Grammar Skill: Adverbs That Tell *How*, p. T341

Day 3, Day 4 and Day 5
Independent Writing
- Write about *Happy Birthday, U.S.A.!*, p. T348
- Provide scaffolded instruction to meet student needs, p. T348
- Find Text Evidence, p. T348
- Apply Writing Trait: Ideas: Main Idea and Details, T348
- Prewrite and Draft, p. T348
- Revise and Edit, p. T354
- Final Draft, p. T355
- Present, Evaluate, and Publish, p. T360

Grammar

Adverbs that Tell *How*

- Use adverbs that tell *how* to describe what is happening, pp. T331, T341, T349, T355, T361

- Apply grammar to writing, pp. T331, T348, T354, T361

Mechanics: Name Titles (capitals and periods with *Mr., Mrs., Ms., Dr.*)

- Use capitals and periods in name titles (*Mr., Mrs., Ms., Dr.*)

Online PDFs

Grammar Practice, pp. 146–150

Online Grammar Games

Spelling

Words with /âr/air, are, ear

- Spell words with /âr/air, are, ear

Online PDFs

Phonics/Spelling blms
pp. 146–150

Online Spelling Games

SUGGESTED LESSON PLAN

READING		DAY 1	DAY 2
Teach, Model and Apply *Wonders* Reading/Writing Workshop	**Core**	**Build Background** Celebrate America!, T320–T321 **Oral Vocabulary** *pride, display,* T320 **Word Work** T324–T327 • Fluency: Sound-Spellings • Phonemic Awareness: Phoneme Reversal • Phonics/Spelling: Introduce /âr/ *air, are, ear* • High-Frequency Words: *favorite, few, gone, surprise, wonder, young* • Vocabulary: *nation, unite* **Shared Read** *Share the Harvest and Give Thanks,* T328–T329	**Oral Language** Celebrate America!, T332 **Oral Vocabulary** *design, purpose, pride, display, represent,* T332 **Word Work** T334–T337 • Phonemic Awareness: Phoneme Blending • Structural Analysis: *r*-Controlled Vowel Syllables • Vocabulary: *nation, unite* **Shared Read** *Share the Harvest and Give Thanks,* T338-T339 • Genre: Informational Text/Nonfiction, T338 • Skill: Author's Purpose, T339
	Options	**Listening Comprehension** "Celebrate the Flag," T322–T323	**Listening Comprehension:** "Celebrate the Flag," T333 **Word Work** T334–T337 • Phonics/Spelling: Review /âr/, *air, are, ear* • High-Frequency Words

LANGUAGE ARTS			
Writing **Grammar**	**Core**	**Shared Writing** T330 **Grammar** Adverbs That Tell How, T331	**Interactive Writing** T340 **Grammar** Adverbs That Tell How, T341
	Options		

DIFFERENTIATED INSTRUCTION Use your data dashboard to determine each student's needs. Then select instructional supports options throughout the week.

APPROACHING LEVEL

Leveled Reader
It's Labor Day!, T364–T365
"Four Voyages," T365
Literature Circles, T365

Phonemic Awareness
Phoneme
Blending, T366 **TIER 2**
Phoneme Addition, T366 **TIER 2**
Phoneme Deletion, T367
Phoneme Reversal, T367

Phonics
Conect *air, are, ear* to /âr/, T368 **TIER 2**
Blend Words with /âr/, T368 **TIER 2**
Build Fluency with Phonics, T369

Structural Analysis Review *r*-Controlled Syllables, T370

Words to Know Review, T371

Comprehension
Read for
Fluency, T372 **TIER 2**
Identify Main
Idea, T372 **TIER 2**
Review Author's
Purpose, T373
Self-Selected Reading, T373

ON LEVEL

Leveled Reader
It's Labor Day!, T374–T375
"Four Voyages," T375
Literature Circles, T375

Phonics
Build Words with /âr/, T376

DAY 3	**DAY 4**	**DAY 5**
Fluency Phrasing, T343 **Word Work** T344–T347 • Phonemic Awareness: Phoneme Deletion • Phonics/Spelling: Blend Words with /âr/ *air, are, ear* • Vocabulary Strategy: Metaphors **Close Reading** *Happy Birthday, U.S.A.!,* T347A–T347F	**Extend the Concept** T350–T351 • Text Feature: Map, T350 • Close Reading "A Young Nation Grows," T351 **Word Work** T352–T353 • Phonemic Awareness: Phoneme Addition • Structural Analysis: *r*-Controlled Vowel Syllables **Integrate Ideas** • Research and Inquiry, T356–T357	**Word Work** T358–T359 • Phonemic Awareness: Syllable Deletion/Addtion • Phonics/Spelling: Blend and Build Words with /âr/ *air, are, ear* • Structural Analysis: *r*-Controlled Vowel Syllables • High-Frequency Words • Vocabulary: *nation, unite* **Integrate Ideas** • Text Connections, T362–T363
Oral Language Celebrate America!, T342 **Word Work** T344–T347 • Structural Analysis: r-Controlled Vowel Syllables • High-Frequency Words	**Word Work** T352–T353 • Fluency: Sound-Spellings • Phonics/Spelling: Phoneme Addition • High-Frequency Words • Vocabulary: *nation, unite* **Close Reading** *Happy Birthday, U.S.A.!,* T347A–T347F	**Word Work** T358–T359 • Fluency: Phrasing **Integrate Ideas** • Research and Inquiry, T362 • Speaking and Listening, T363
Independent Writing T348 **Grammar** Mechanics: Abbreviations, T349	**Independent Writing** T354 **Grammar** Mechanics: Abbreviations, T355	**Independent Writing** T360 **Grammar** Adverbs That Tell How, T361
Grammar Adverbs That Tell How, T349	**Grammar** Adverbs That Tell How, T355	**Grammar** Mechanics: Abbreviations, T361

BEYOND LEVEL

Words to Know
Review Words, T376

Comprehension
Review Author's Purpose, T377
Self-Selected Reading, T377

Leveled Reader
It's Labor Day!, T378–T379
"Four Voyages," T379
Literature Circles, T379

Vocabulary
Multiple-Meaning Words, T380

Comprehension
Review Author's Purpose, T381
Self-Selected Reading, T381

Gifted and Talented

ENGLISH LANGUAGE LEARNERS

Shared Read
Share the Harvest and Give Thanks, T382–T383

Leveled Reader
It's Labor Day!, T384–T385
"Four Voyages", T385
Literature Circles, T385

Vocabulary
Preteach Oral Vocabulary, T386
Preteach ELL Vocabulary, T386

Words to Know
Review Words, T387
Reteach High-Frequency Words, T387

Writing/Spelling
Writing Trait: Voice, T388
Words with *r*- Controlled Vowels, T388

Grammar
Adverbs That Tell How, T389

DIFFERENTIATE TO ACCELERATE

  Scaffold to **A**ccess **C**omplex **T**ext

IF ▶ the text complexity of a particular selection is too difficult for children

THEN ▶ see the references noted in the chart below for scaffolded instruction to help children Access Complex Text.

Qualitative *Quantitative*
Reader and Task
TEXT COMPLEXITY

	Reading/Writing Workshop	**Literature Anthology**	**Leveled Readers**	**Classroom Library**

Quantitative	Time for Kids: *Share the Harvest and Give Thanks* **Lexile** 680	Time for Kids: *Happy Birthday, U.S.A.!* **Lexile** 580 "A Young Nation Grows" **Lexile** 390	**Approaching Level** **Lexile** 440 **Beyond Level** **Lexile** 660 **On Level** **Lexile** 620 **ELL** **Lexile** 360	*A Picture Book of George Washington* **Lexile** 750 *Ruby Bridges Goes to School: My True Story* **Lexile** 410
Qualitative	**What Makes the Text Complex?** **Foundational Skills** • Decoding with *r*-controlled vowels *air, are, ear,* T324–T325 • Reading words with *r*-controlled vowel syllables, T335 • Identifying high-frequency words, T326–T327 *See Scaffolded Instruction in Teacher's Edition, T324–T325, T326–T327, and T335.*	**What Makes the Text Complex?** • **Purpose,** T347B • **Organization,** T347B, T347D **ACT** *See Scaffolded Instruction in Teacher's Edition, T347B and T347D.*	**What Makes the Text Complex?** **Foundational Skills** • Decoding with *r*-controlled vowels *air, are, ear* • Reading words with *r*-controlled vowel syllables • Identifying high-frequency words *favorite few gone surprise wonder young* *See Level Up lessons online for Leveled Readers.*	**What Makes the Text Complex?** • **Purpose** • **Specific Vocabulary** • **Prior Knowledge** • **Sentence Structure** • **Organization** • **Connection of Ideas** • **Genre** **ACT** *See Scaffolded Instruction in Teacher's Edition, T413–T415.*
Reader and Task	**The** Introduce the Concept lesson on pages T320–T321 will help determine the reader's knowledge and engagement in the weekly concept. See pages T328–T329, T338–T339, T356–T357 and T362–T363 for questions and tasks for this text.	**The** Introduce the Concept lesson on pages T320–T321 will help determine the reader's knowledge and engagement in the weekly concept. See pages T347A–T347F, T351, T356-T357 and T362-T363 for questions and tasks for this text.	**The** Introduce the Concept lesson on pages T320-T321 will help determine the reader's knowledge and engagement in the weekly concept. See pages T364-T365, T374-T375, T378-T379, T384-T385, T356-T357 and T362-T363 for questions and tasks for this text.	**The** Introduce the Concept lesson on pages T320– T321 will help determine the reader's knowledge and engagement in the weekly concept. See pages T413– T415 for questions and tasks for this text.

Monitor and *Differentiate*

 **Quick Check**

To differentiate instruction use the Quick Checks to assess students' needs and select the appropriate small group instruction focus.

Comprehension Strategy Reread, T323

Comprehension Skill Author's Purpose, T339

Phonics *r*-Controlled Vowels *air, are, ear,* T327, T337, T347, T353, T359

High-Frequency Words and Vocabulary T327, T337, T347, T353, T359

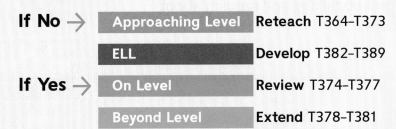

If No → | **Approaching Level** | Reteach T364–T373
| **ELL** | Develop T382–T389
If Yes → | **On Level** | Review T374–T377
| **Beyond Level** | Extend T378–T381

Using Weekly Data

Check your data Dashboard to verify assessment results and guide grouping decisions.

Level Up with Leveled Readers

IF children can read their leveled text fluently and answer comprehension questions

THEN work with the next level up to accelerate children's reading with more complex text.

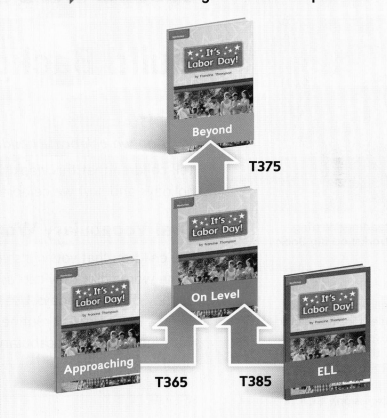

Beyond — T375

On Level

Approaching — T365 | T385 — ELL

ENGLISH LANGUAGE LEARNERS

Small Group Instruction

Use the ELL small group lessons in the *Wonders* Teacher's Edition to provide focused instruction.

Language Development
Vocabulary preteaching, oral vocabulary preteaching, high-frequency word review and reteach, pp. T386–T387

Close Reading
Interactive Question-Response routines for scaffolded text-dependent questioning for reading and rereading the Shared Read and Leveled Reader, pp. T382–T385

Writing
Focus on the writing trait, grammar, and spelling, pp. T388–T389

Additional ELL Support

Use Wonders for English Learners for ELD instruction that connects to the core.

Language Development
My Language Book for ample opportunities for discussions and scaffolded language support

Close Reading
Guided support for the Shared Read, Big Books, and Interactive Read Alouds. Differentiated texts about the weekly concept

Writing
Guided support in Interactive and Independent Writing and writing to sources

Wonders for ELs Teacher Edition and My Language Book

Materials

Reading/Writing Workshop
VOLUME 4

Reading/Writing Workshop Big Book
UNIT 6

Visual Vocabulary Cards
design
display
pride
purpose
represent

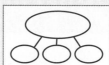

High-Frequency Word Cards
favorite
few
gone
surprise
wonder
young

Teaching Poster

Interactive Read-Aloud Cards

Sound-Spelling Cards

a b c

Word-Building Cards

nation

Vocabulary Cards
nation
unite

Think Aloud Clouds

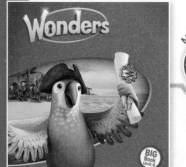

Reading/Writing Workshop Big Book

OBJECTIVES

CCSS Follow agreed-upon rules for discussions (e.g., listening to others with care, speaking one at a time about the topics and texts under discussion). **SL.1.1a**

Discuss the Essential Question

ACADEMIC LANGUAGE
• *celebrate, holiday*
• Cognate: *celebrar*

→ Introduce the Concept

MINILESSON
5 Mins

Build Background

ESSENTIAL QUESTION

Why do we celebrate holidays?

Tell children that this week they will be talking and reading about holidays and how we celebrate them.

Oral Vocabulary Words

Tell children that you will share some words that they can use as they discuss holidays. Use the Define/Example/Ask routine to introduce the oral vocabulary words **display** and **pride**.

Visual Vocabulary Cards

Oral Vocabulary Routine

Define: If you **display** something, you set it out so people can see it.

Example: Grandma displays her pretty seashells in a glass case.

Ask: Do you like to display your art projects? Where do you display them?

Define: **Pride** is a feeling of pleasure or satisfaction with something you have or something you did well.

Example: The soccer team was bursting with pride after they won the championship.

Ask: When have you felt pride? What were you proud of?

Discuss the theme of "Celebrate America!" Have children tell about holidays they have celebrated. *Did you display any special items for the holiday?*

Go Digital

Celebrate America!

Video

Photos

Visual Glossary

Graphic Organizer

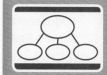

Reading/Writing Workshop, pp. 296–297

Talk About It: Celebrate America!

Guide children to discuss the parade.

- What are the people carrying?

- What do you think this parade celebrates?

- How do you think the people watching feel?

Use Teaching Poster 40 and prompt children to complete the Word Web by sharing words that describe what they see in the photograph.

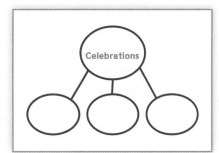

Teaching Poster

Have children look at page 297 of their Reading/Writing Workshop and do the Talk About It activity with a partner.

Collaborative Conversations

Be Open to All Ideas As children engage in partner, small-group, and whole-group discussions, remind them:

- that everyone's ideas are important and should be heard.

- not to be afraid to ask a question if something is unclear.

- to respect the opinions of others.

→ # Listening Comprehension

MINILESSON
10 Mins

Read the Interactive Read Aloud

Connect to Concept: Celebrate America!

"Celebrate the Flag"

Tell children that they will now read a selection about the American flag. Ask: *What does the American flag look like?*

Focus on Oral Vocabulary

Review the oral vocabulary words *display* and *pride*. Use the Define/Example/Ask routine to introduce the oral vocabulary words *design, purpose,* and *represent*. Prompt children to use the words as they discuss holidays

"Celebrate the Flag"

Reread

OBJECTIVES

CCSS Participate in collaborative conversations with diverse partners about grade 1 topics and texts with peers and adults in small and larger groups. **SL.1.1**

- Develop concept understanding
- Develop reading strategy reread

ACADEMIC LANGUAGE

holidays, flag, reread

Oral Vocabulary Routine

<u>Define:</u> The **design** for something is the plan for how it will look.

<u>Example:</u> The design for the park includes a duck pond.

<u>Ask:</u> If you could design a park, what would you include?

Visual Vocabulary Cards

<u>Define:</u> When something has a **purpose**, it has a reason to be there.

<u>Example:</u> The purpose of the text was to teach readers how to make a birdhouse.

<u>Ask:</u> What is the purpose of a car?

<u>Define:</u> When things **represent** other things, they take their place or stand for them.

<u>Example:</u> A smiley face can represent happiness.

<u>Ask:</u> What does a green traffic light represent? What does a red traffic light represent?

Visual Glossary

Retell

Set a Purpose for Reading

- Display the Interactive Read-Aloud Cards.
- Read aloud the title.
- Tell children that you will be reading a selection about the history of the American flag. Tell children to read to find out why the flag looks like it does.

Strategy: Reread

1 **Explain** Tell children that if they do not understand something as they read or listen to a selection, they can go back and read the text again. This is called rereading. This can help them understand the text better and remember the important information.

Think Aloud Rereading tricky parts of a selection can help me to better understand it. Today, as we read "Celebrate the Flag," I will pay attention to which parts I do not understand. Then I will go back and reread those parts.

2 **Model** Read the selection. As you read, use the Think Aloud Cloud to model applying the strategy.

Think Aloud Remember that you can reread parts of the text to make sure you understood correctly. I found the first page confusing. I am not sure that I understood why people display the flag. When I reread the page, I understand that displaying the flag shows our pride at being part of America.

3 **Guided Practice** As you continue to read, pause to ask them which parts of the story they find confusing. *What parts did you have trouble understanding? What can you do to better understand them?* Guide children in rereading parts of the text they did not understand.

Respond to Reading

After reading, prompt children to retell "Celebrate the Flag." Discuss what parts they wanted to reread and how rereading helped them understand the information in the selection.

ENGLISH LANGUAGE LEARNERS SCAFFOLD

Beginning

Engage Display Card 1. *I didn't understand this part. Let's reread it.* Reread the card. *Does the Fourth of July celebrate the beginning of the country? Is the flag a symbol of the country?*

Intermediate

Describe Display Card 2. *I do not understand when the flag is shown. Let's reread the text.* Reread the card. *When and where do people display the flag?* Restate responses.

Advanced/High

Describe Display Card 2. *I do not understand why George Washington wanted a flag. Let's reread this part.* Reread the card. *Can you explain why George Washington designed the flag like he did?*

Monitor and *Differentiate*

 Quick Check

Can children apply the strategy reread?

⬇

Small Group Instruction

If No →	Approaching	Reteach pp. T364–365
	ELL	Develop pp. T382–385
If Yes →	On Level	Review pp. T374–375
	Beyond Level	Extend pp. T378–379

→ # Word Work

Quick Review
Build Fluency: Sound-Spellings
Display the **Word-Building Cards:** *air, are, ear, scr, spl, spr, str, thr, shr, wr, kn, gn, au, aw, augh, ew, ue, ui, ow, oi, oy, ar, ore, oar, er, ir, ur, ey, igh, oa.* Have children say the sounds.

 MINILESSON 5 Mins

Phonemic Awareness

OBJECTIVES

CCSS Decode regularly spelled one-syllable words. **RF.1.3b**

Reverse phonemes to form new words

Phoneme Reversal

1 Model Show children how to reverse phonemes to form new words. *Listen as I blend these sounds: /t/ /a/ /p/, /taaap/, tap. Now I will say the sounds backward and blend them to make a new word. Listen: /p/ /a/ /t/, /paaat/, pat. Repeat with kiss/sick.*

2 Guided Practice/Practice Have children reverse the sounds in the following words. Do the first one together. *Now I am going to say more sounds. Blend the sounds to say a word. Then say the sounds backward and blend them to make another word.*

/m/ /u/ /g/   /p/ /a/ /k/   /s/ /u/ /b/   /n/ /e/ /t/   /s/ /t/ /o/ /p/

MINILESSON 10 Mins

Phonics

Sound-Spelling Card

Introduce /âr/ *air, are, ear*

1 Model Display the *Chair* **Sound-Spelling Card.**
Teach /âr/ spelled *air, are,* and *ear* using *chair, care,* and *wear. This is the Chair Sound-Spelling Card. The sounds are /âr/. These sounds are at the end of the word chair. Listen: /châr/, chair. The /âr/ sounds can be spelled with the letters air as in chair, are as in care, and ear as in wear. Say the sounds with me: /âr/. I'll say /âr/ as I write the letters that stand for the sounds several times.*

2 Guided Practice/Practice Have children practice connecting the letters *air, are,* and *ear* to the sounds /âr/ by writing them. *Now do it with me. Say /âr/ as I write the letters* air. *This time, write the letters* air *five times as you say the /âr/ sounds. Repeat for /âr/ spelled* are *and* ear.

Go Digital

Phonemic Awareness

Chair

Phonics

Handwriting

SKILLS TRACE

*r-*CONTROLLED VOWELS
air, are, ear

Introduce Unit 6 Week 5 Day 1

Review Unit 6 Week 5 Days 2, 3, 4, 5

Assess Unit 6 Week 5

Blend with /âr/ *air, are, ear*

❶ Model Display **Word-Building Cards** *f, air.* Model how to blend the sounds. *This is the letter* f. *It stands for /f/. These are the letters* a, i, r. *Together they stand for /âr/. Listen as I blend these sounds together: /fâr/. Say it with me.* Continue by modeling the words *rare* and *pear.*

❷ Guided Practice/Practice Display the Day 1 Phonics Practice Activity. Read each word in the first row, blending the sounds, for example, /âr/. The word is *air.* Have children blend each word with you. Prompt children to read the connected text, sounding out the decodable words.

air	fair	care	tear	wear	pear
share	chair	hair	bare	blared	dared
wear	wore	bear	bar	star	stare
street	spring	splash	three	write	know

Her red hair blew in the air.

Did that bear stare at Claire?

I will share my pear with Blair.   Also online

Day 1 Phonics Practice Activity

Corrective Feedback

Sound Error Model the sound that children missed, then have them repeat the sound. Say: *My turn.* Tap under the letters and say: *Sounds? /âr/ What are the sounds?* Return to the beginning of the word. Say: *Let's start over.* Blend the word with children again.

 Daily Handwriting

Throughout the week review staying in the lines.

ENGLISH LANGUAGE LEARNERS

Phonemic Awareness: Minimal Contrasts Focus on articulation. Say /âr/ and note your mouth position. Use Sound-Spelling Cards. Repeat for /är/. Have children say both sounds, noticing the differences. Continue with: *fair/far, bear/bar, stare/star.*

Phonics: Variations in Language There is no direct sound transfer for /âr/ in Spanish, Cantonese, Vietnamese, Hmong, Korean, and Khmer. Emphasize /âr/ and show correct mouth position. Practice with Approaching Level phonics lessons.

ON-LEVEL PRACTICE BOOK p. 319

The letters **air** together can make the sound you hear at the end of **chair**.
The letters **are** and **ear** can also make the same sound, as in **share** and **pear**.

Circle the word that completes the sentence. Then write the word.

1. My room is at the top of the ____stairs____.
   (stairs)   stars

2. Ruth has long ____hair____
   heat   (hair)

3. The noise might ____scare____ you.
   scarf   (scare)

4. I think I will ____wear____ a big coat today.
   wrote   (wear)

APPROACHING p. 319	BEYOND p. 319	ELL p. 319

→ # Word Work

 MINILESSON 5 Mins

Spelling

Words with *air, are, ear*

Dictation Use the Spelling Dictation routine to help children transfer their growing knowledge of sound-spellings to writing.

Pretest After dictation, pronounce each spelling word. Say a sentence for each word and pronounce the word again. Ask children to say each word, stretching the sounds, before writing. After the pretest, display the spelling words and write each word as you say the letter names. Have children check their words.

fair	pair	bear	wear	spare
share	three	splash	favorite	surprise

For Approaching Level and Beyond Level children, refer to the Differentiated Spelling Lists for modified word lists.

Go Digital

Spelling Word Routine

they	together
how	eat

High-Frequency Word Routine

school
Visual Glossary

 MINILESSON 5 Mins

High-Frequency Words

favorite, few, gone, surprise, wonder, young

1 Model Display the **High-Frequency Word Cards** *favorite, few, gone, surprise, wonder,* and *young.* Use the Read/Spell/Write routine.

- **Read** Point to and say the word *favorite. This is the word* favorite. *Say it with me:* favorite. *My favorite color is blue.*

- **Spell** *The word* favorite *is spelled* f-a-v-o-r-i-t-e. *Spell it with me.*

- **Write** *Let's write the word in the air as we say each letter:* f-a-v-o-r-i-t-e.

- Follow the same steps for the other words.

- As children spell each word with you, point out irregularities in sound-spellings, such as the /u/ sound spelled *ou* in *young.*

 COLLABORATE • Have partners create sentences using each word.

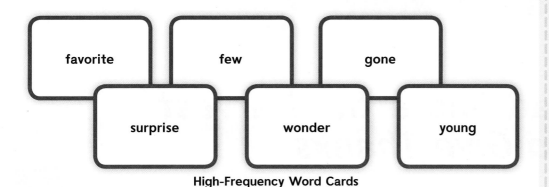

High-Frequency Word Cards

2 **Guided Practice/Practice** Have children read the sentences. Prompt them to identify the high-frequency words in connected text and to blend the decodable words.

1. I **wonder** what your **favorite** food is.

2. I chose a **few** books to **surprise** you.

3. Claire has **gone** to the beach.

4. A kitten is a **young** cat.

Introduce Vocabulary

nation, unite

1 **Model** Introduce the new words using the routine.

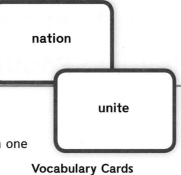

Vocabulary Cards

Vocabulary Routine

<u>Define:</u> A **nation** is a group of people living in one country.

<u>Example:</u> *The United States is a **nation**.*

<u>Ask:</u> What is another **nation** you know? EXAMPLES

<u>Define:</u> To **unite** is to join together.

<u>Example:</u> *The students **unite** to raise money for new playground equipment.*

<u>Ask:</u> Name a word that means the opposite of **unite**. ANTONYM

---

2 **Review** Use the routine to review last week's vocabulary words.

Monitor and *Differentiate*

✓ **Quick Check**

Can children read and decode words with /âr/: *air, are, ear*?

Can children recognize and read high-frequency and vocabulary words?

⬇

Small Group Instruction

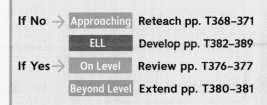

If No →	Approaching	Reteach pp. T368–371
	ELL	Develop pp. T382–389
If Yes →	On Level	Review pp. T376–377
	Beyond Level	Extend pp. T380–381

→ **Shared Read**

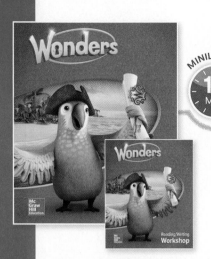

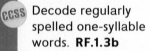

Reading/Writing Workshop Big Book and Reading/Writing Workshop

---

OBJECTIVES

CCSS Decode regularly spelled one-syllable words. **RF.1.3b**

CCSS Recognize and read grade-appropriate irregularly spelled words. **RF.1.3g**

Understand nonfiction genre

ACADEMIC LANGUAGE

• *nonfiction, harvest, feast*

• Cognates: *no ficción, festín*

See pages T382–T383 for Interactive Question-Response routine for the Shared Read.

MINILESSON
10 Mins

Read *Share the Harvest and Give Thanks*

Focus on Foundational Skills

Review the words and letter-sounds in *Share the Harvest and Give Thanks.*

• Have children use pages 298–299 to review high-frequency words *favorite, gone, few, surprise, wonder, young,* and vocabulary words *nation* and *unite.*

• Have children use pages 300–301 to review that *-air, -are,* and *-ear* can stand for the /âr/ sounds. Guide them to blend the sounds to read the words.

• Display the words *celebrate, deer, ears, families, family, festival(s), Kwanzaa, November, parades,* and *Thanksgiving.* Spell each word and model reading each word. Tell children they will be reading the words in the selection.

Read Guide children in reading *Share the Harvest and Give Thanks.* Point out the high-frequency words, vocabulary words, and words in which *-air, -ear,* and *-are* stand for the /âr/ sounds.

Close Reading Routine

| Read | **DOK 1-2**

• Identify key ideas and details about celebrating the harvest.
• Take notes and retell.
• Use A C T prompts as needed.

| Reread | **DOK 2-3**

• Analyze the text, craft, and structure.
• Use the Reread minilessons.

| Integrate | **DOK 4**

• Integrate knowledge and ideas.
• Make text-to-text connections.
• Use the Integrate lesson.

Genre: Informational Text/Nonfiction Tell children that *Share the Harvest and Give Thanks* is an informational text. Informational texts tell about real people, places, things, or events and give important information and interesting details in text, photographs, and illustrations.

Share the Harvest and Give Thanks

READING/WRITING WORKSHOP, pp. 302–311

Lexile 680

Connect to Concept: Celebrate America

ESSENTIAL QUESTION Explain to children that as they read *Share the Harvest and Give Thanks,* they will look for key ideas that will help them answer the Essential Question: *Why do we celebrate holidays?*

- Pages 304–305: What are some ways people celebrate the harvest?
- Pages 306–307: What did people eat at the first Thanksgiving?
- Pages 308–309: What are some ways people celebrate Thanksgiving?
- Pages 310–311: What is Kwanzaa?

Focus on Fluency

With partners, have children read *Share the Harvest and Give Thanks.* Remind them that they can ask themselves questions to make sure they understand what they are reading. Have them use the text, photographs, and illustrations to answer their questions.

Retell Have partners use key ideas and details to retell the selection. Invite them to tell different ways people celebrate the harvest.

Make Connections

Read together Make Connections on page 311. Have partners talk about how they celebrate the harvest using a sentence starter:

> *I celebrate the harvest by...*

Guide children to connect what they have read to the Essential Question.

Shared Writing

Write About the Reading/Writing Workshop

Go Digital

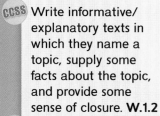

Reading/Writing Workshop

OBJECTIVES

CCSS Write informative/ explanatory texts in which they name a topic, supply some facts about the topic, and provide some sense of closure. **W.1.2**

CCSS Demonstrate command of the conventions of standard English grammar and usage when writing or speaking. **L.1.1**

Identify adverbs that tell how

ACADEMIC LANGUAGE

• *topic, text, details, adverb*

• Cognates: *texto, detalles, adverbio*

Analyze the Prompt Tell children you will work together to write a response to a prompt. Read aloud the prompt: *What are the different ways the harvest is celebrated?* Say: *To respond to this prompt, we need to look at the text, photographs, and illustrations in* Share the Harvest and Give Thanks.

Find Text Evidence Explain that you will reread the text and take notes to help answer the question. Read aloud pages 304–305. *We are looking for ways people celebrate the harvest. On page 304, the text says families celebrate the harvest in lots of ways. On page 305, I see people shopping for food. The text says Thanksgiving is a time that families eat together and give thanks. In my notes, I'll write that Thanksgiving is one way people celebrate the harvest.*

Write to a Prompt Reread the prompt to children. *What are the different ways the harvest is celebrated?* Say: *Our first sentence can tell the topic we are writing about. Let's write our first sentence together: People celebrate the harvest in many ways.* Write the sentence. *As I read our notes, think about which notes tell us the ways people celebrate the harvest.* Track the print as you reread the notes.

Guide children to dictate complete sentences for you to record. Read the final response as you track the print.

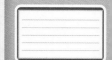

Graphic Organizer

Writing

Grammar

Grammar

Adverbs That Tell How

1 **Explain/Model** Remind children that an adverb is a word that tells more about the action in a sentence. An adverb can tell how an action happened. Many adverbs end in *-ly*. Display the following sentences:

> The cars in the Fourth of July parade drive slowly. The band plays loudly. Clowns run quickly around the floats.

Ask: *How do the cars move?* (slowly) *The adverb* slowly *tells how. How does the band play?* (loudly) *How do the clowns run?* (quickly)

2 **Guided Practice/Practice** Display the sentences below and read them aloud. Prompt children to chorally reread them with you.

Have children work with a partner to identify the adverbs that tell how.

> The teacher spoke softly. (softly)

> She asked the children to neatly hang up their coats. (neatly)

> The children quietly put their things away. (quietly)

OLLABORATE

Talk About It Have partners work together to orally generate sentences with adverbs that tell how.

Link to Writing Say: *Let's look at our writing and see if we used adverbs that tell how an action happened.* Review the Shared Writing for adverbs that tell how. Remind children that adverbs often end in *-ly.* If no adverbs that tell how are in the Shared Writing, work with children to add them and reread the response together.

ENGLISH LANGUAGE LEARNERS SCAFFOLD

Beginning

Demonstrate Comprehension Read the first sentence in the Model activity. Ask: *Did the cars drive slowly?* Continue asking yes-or-no questions with the remaining sentences. Allow children ample time to respond.

Intermediate

Explain Display the Model sentences. For each sentence ask: *Which word tells how?* Clarify responses by providing vocabulary.

Advanced/High

Expand Display the Guided Practice sentences. Ask: *How did you decide which word is an adverb? What question could you ask yourself when you are looking for adverbs that tell how?* Elicit details to support children's answers.

Daily Wrap Up

- Review the Essential Question and encourage children to discuss it using the new oral vocabulary words. Ask: *What holidays have we celebrated at school? How did we celebrate?*

- Prompt children to share the skills they learned. Ask: *How have you used those skills today?*

Materials

Reading/Writing Workshop VOLUME 4

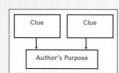
Reading/Writing Workshop Big Book UNIT 6

Visual Vocabulary Cards
design
display
pride
purpose
represent

favorite

High-Frequency Word Cards
favorite
few
gone
surprise
wonder
young

Clue   Clue
Author's Purpose
Teaching Poster

nation

Vocabulary Cards
nation
unite

air are
ear ere
chair
Sound-Spelling Cards

fair
Spelling Word Cards

a b c
Word-Building Cards

Interactive Read-Aloud Cards

→ # Build the Concept

MINILESSON 5 Mins

Oral Language

OBJECTIVES

CCSS Ask and answer questions about key details in a text read aloud or information presented orally or through other media. **SL.1.2**

- Discuss the Essential Question
- Build concept understanding

ACADEMIC LANGUAGE

- *reread, information, details*
- Cognates: *información, detalles*

ESSENTIAL QUESTION

Remind children that this week you've been talking and reading about holidays. Remind them of what they learned about the American flag and how we celebrate the harvest. Guide children to discuss the Essential Question using information from what they read and discussed on Day 1.

Oral Vocabulary Words

Review the oral vocabulary words. Use the Define/Example/Ask routine to review the oral vocabulary words *design, display, pride, purpose,* and *represent.*

- Describe the design of the American flag.
- What would you like to display at home in your room?
- Would you feel pride if you learned to juggle? Why?
- What is the purpose of a toothbrush?
- What does a heart represent on Valentine's Day?

Listening Comprehension

Reread the Interactive Read Aloud

Strategy: Reread

Remind children that as they listen, they can reread parts of the text that they did not understand the first time.

Tell children that you will reread "Celebrate the Flag." Display the Interactive Read-Aloud Cards.

Think Aloud When I read, I can go back and reread parts of the text that confused me. I'm not sure I understand why George Washington chose the colors red, white, and blue. I'll reread that part of the selection. Now I understand that each color represented something George Washington thought was important: white stood for goodness, blue stood for justice, and red stood for bravery.

"Celebrate the Flag"

Make Connections

Discuss partners' responses to "Celebrate the Flag."

- *Why do we see the American flag in so many places?*
- *What might have happened if America did not become independent? Would we still have an American flag?*
- *Do you think George Washington's ideas for the design were good ones? Why or why not?*

Write About It Have children draw a picture of the American flag and write a few sentences about it in their Writer's Notebooks. Guide children by asking questions, such as, *How do you feel when you see the American flag? What does it make you think of?* Have children write continuously for six minutes.

Word Work

Quick Review

Build Fluency: Sound-Spellings
Display the **Word-Building Cards:**
air, are, ear, scr, spl, spr, str, thr, shr, wr, kn, gn, au, aw, augh, ew, ue, ui, ow, oi, oy, ar, ore, oar, er, ir, ur, ey, igh, oa. Have children say the sounds. Repeat, and vary the pace.

 MINILESSON 5 Mins

Phonemic Awareness

OBJECTIVES

CCSS Orally produce single-syllable words by blending sounds (phonemes) including consonant blends. **RF.1.2b**

CCSS Decode two-syllable words following basic patterns by breaking the words into syllables. **RF.1.3e**

Phoneme Blending

❶ **Model** Show children how to orally blend phonemes. *Listen: /f/ /âr/. Now I will blend the sounds together and say the word: /fâr/,* fair. *Let's say the word:* fair.

❷ **Guided Practice/Practice** Have children practice blending phonemes. Do the first two together. *I am going to say some words sound by sound. Blend the sounds together to say the word.*

/p/ /âr/   /ch/ /âr/   /h/ /âr/   /b/ /âr/

/r / /âr/   /k/ /âr/   /s/ /k/ /âr/   /sh/ /âr/

MINILESSON 5 Mins

Phonics

Review /âr/ *air, are, ear*

❶ **Model** Display the *Chair* **Sound-Spelling Card.** Review the sounds /âr/ spelled *air, are,* and *ear* using the words *chair, share,* and *bear.*

❷ **Guided Practice/Practice** Have children practice connecting the letters and sounds. Point to the Sound-Spelling Card. *What are these letters? What sounds do they stand for?*

 ## Go Digital

 **Phonemic Awareness**

 **Phonics**

 **Structural Analysis**

 **Handwriting**

Blend Words with /âr/ *air, are, ear*

1 Model Display **Word-Building Cards** *c* and *are* to form the word *care*. Model how to generate and blend the sounds to say the word. *This is the letter* c. *It stands for /k/. These are the letters* a, r, e. *Together they stand for /âr/. Let's blend: /kâr/. Say it with me:* care. Continue with *pair* and *wear*.

2 Guided Practice/Practice Repeat the routine with children with *dare, pear, hair, bare, scare, tear, bear, chair, rare, barely, airfare.* Note that some of the words sound the same, but have different spellings and meanings.

Build Words with /âr/ *air, are, ear*

1 Model Display the Word-Building Cards *r* and *are.* Blend: /r/ /âr/, /râââr/, *rare.*

- Replace the first *r* with *c* and repeat with *care.*
- Replace *c* with *d* and repeat with *dare.*

2 Guided Practice/Practice Continue with *bare, stare, star, stair, chair, hair, pair, pear, wear, tear, bear.*

ENGLISH LANGUAGE LEARNERS

Build Vocabulary Review the meanings of example words that can be explained or demonstrated in a concrete way. For example, ask children to point to their *hair* and to a *chair.* Model the action for *tear* by tearing a piece of paper and saying, *"I can tear the paper,"* and have children repeat. Provide sentence starters, such as, *I got a scare when ____* for children to complete. Correct grammar and pronunciation as needed.

MINILESSON 5 Mins

Structural Analysis

r-Controlled Vowel Syllables

1 Model Write and read aloud *hairy* and *burning.* Point out that there is an *r*-controlled vowel in each word. Then say the words, clapping for each syllable. Have children repeat. Draw a line between the syllables: *hair/y; burn/ing.* Explain that when a vowel spelling is followed by the letter *r,* the vowel and the *r* will be in the same syllable.

2 Guided Practice/Practice Write the following words: *fairly, target, barely, repair.* Help children divide each word into syllables, read the words, and then use each word in a sentence.

→ Word Work

Spelling
5 Mins MINILESSON

OBJECTIVES
 CCSS Recognize and read grade-appropriate irregularly spelled words. **RF.1.3g**

CCSS Use conventional spelling for words with common spelling patterns and for frequently occurring irregular words. **L.1.2d**

Word Sort with *air, are, ear*

1 Model Display the **Spelling Word Cards** from the Teacher's Resource Book, one at a time. Have children read each word, listening for /âr/.

Make cards for *hair, care,* and *pear* to create a three-column chart. Say each word and pronounce the sounds. Ask children to spell each word.

2 Guided Practice/Practice Have children place each Spelling Word Card in the correct column. Have children read the words in each column. Then call out a word. Have a child find the word card and point to it as the class spells the word.

ANALYZE ERRORS/ARTICULATION SUPPORT

Use children's pretest errors to analyze spelling problems and provide corrective feedback. For example, some children may have difficulty determining which /âr/ spelling to use.

Write words with each spelling on the board and have children circle the /âr/ spelling. Create additional /âr/ word sorts. Point out that some words sound the same but have different spellings. It is necessary to know the meaning of the word to determine which spelling to use.

Go Digital

Spelling Word Sort

High-Frequency Word Routine

school

Visual Glossary

ENGLISH LANGUAGE LEARNERS

Provide Clues Practice spelling by helping children generate more words with /âr/ patterns. Provide clues: *Think of a word that begins with* ch *and rhymes with* fair. Write the word and have children practice reading it. Correct their pronunciation, if needed.

High-Frequency Words
5 Mins MINILESSON

favorite, few, gone, surprise, wonder, young

1 Guided Practice Say each word and have children Read/Spell/Write it. Ask children to close their eyes, picture the word in their minds, and write it the way they see it. Display the high-frequency words for children to self-correct.

- Point out irregularities in sound-spellings, such as the /u/ sound spelled *o* in *wonder*.

2 Practice Add the high-frequency words *favorite, few, gone, surprise, wonder,* and *young* to the cumulative word bank.

COLLABORATE

- Have children work with a partner to create sentences using the words.

- Have children look at the words and compare their sounds and spellings to words from previous weeks.

- Suggest that they write about holidays.

Cumulative Review Review last week's words using the Read/Spell/Write routine.

- Repeat the routine, mixing the words and having children chorally say each one.

MINILESSON

5 Mins

Reinforce Vocabulary

nation, unite

1 Guided Practice Use the **Vocabulary Cards** to review this week's and last week's vocabulary words. Work together with children to generate a new context sentence for each word.

2 Practice Have children work with a partner to orally complete each sentence stem on the Day 2 Vocabulary Practice Activity using this week's and last week's vocabulary words.

---

difficult	nobody	nation	unite

1. Will the two teams ____ to become one team?
2. It is ____ to pick up such a big box!
3. Our ____ is made up of people from many places.
4. ____ likes to be last in line. **Also online**

Day 2 Vocabulary Practice Activity

ON-LEVEL PRACTICE BOOK p. 320

Complete each sentence. Use one of the words in the box.

favorite	few	gone	surprise	wonder	young

1. I like grapes, but pears are my _____ favorite _____ food.

2. Spot is a very _____ young _____ puppy.

3. It will be fun to _____ surprise _____ Mom when she comes home.

4. There are only a _____ few _____ books on my shelf.

5. I _____ wonder _____ what time Dad's plane will land.

6. Mom made cupcakes, but now they are all _____ gone _____

APPROACHING p. 320	BEYOND p. 320	ELL p. 320

Monitor and *Differentiate*

✓ Quick Check

Can children read and decode words with /âr/air, are, ear?

Can children recognize and read high-frequency and vocabulary words?

Small Group Instruction

If No → **Approaching** Reteach pp. T368–371
        ELL Develop pp. T382–389
If Yes → **On Level** Review pp. T376–377
        Beyond Level Extend pp. T380–381

Comprehension

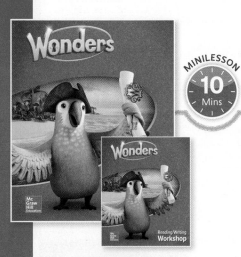

Reading/Writing Workshop Big Book and Reading/Writing Workshop

OBJECTIVES

CCSS Identify the main purpose of a text, including what the author wants to answer, explain, or describe. **RI.2.6**

Understand nonfiction genre

ACADEMIC LANGUAGE
• *nonfiction, author's purpose*
• Cognate: *no ficción*

MINILESSON 10 Mins

Reread *Share the Harvest and Give Thanks*

Genre: Informational Text/Nonfiction

1 Model Tell children they will now reread the nonfiction selection *Share the Harvest and Give Thanks.* Explain that as they read, they will look for information in the text to help them understand the selection.

Review the characteristics of informational nonfiction. It:

• tells about real people, things, places, or events.

• presents facts and information.

• gives important information and interesting details in text, photographs, and illustrations.

Point out that informational text can present information in different ways. *One interesting way writers can share information is with a map. A map can show readers where events take place. This is a way to help readers understand the information.*

Display page 311: *Look at the map. It is a special illustration that shows us where different harvest events take place. The three events shown on the map were all explained in the text. The map helps us understand where they took place.* Explain to children how to use the key.

2 Guided Practice/Practice Display page 311 again. *The map shows three harvest celebrations that happen or happened in the past in different places in the country. Let's find the places in the text that explain each event.* Point out that the informational is all true and the photographs are of real events. *This lets us know this selection is nonfiction.*

Go Digital

Share the Harvest and Give Thanks

Genre

Author's Purpose

SKILLS TRACE

AUTHOR'S PURPOSE

Introduce Unit 6 Week 2

Review Unit 6 Week 5

Assess Unit 6 Weeks 2, 5

Skill: Author's Purpose

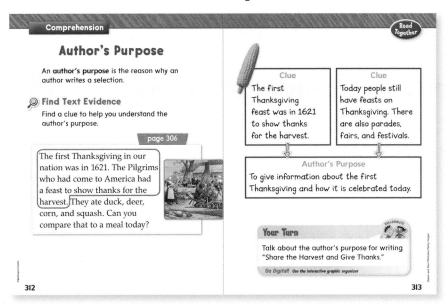

Reading/Writing Workshop, pp. 312–313

ON-LEVEL PRACTICE BOOK p. 325

A. Read the sentences from "Favorite Days." Fill in the circle next to the correct answer.

1. New Year's Day is the first day of the year. The author's purpose is to

  ○ tell how children love to play games.

  ● tell about New Year's Day.

2. Father's Day is in June. The author's purpose is to

  ● tell about Father's Day.

  ○ tell how to make a Father's Day card.

B. Why did the author write "Favorite Days"? Write a sentence.

3. Possible Response: The author's purpose is to tell about special days.

C. Work with a partner. Read the passage aloud. Pay attention to phrasing. Stop after one minute. Fill out the chart.

	Words Read	–	Number of Errors	=	Words Correct Score
First Read		–		=	
Second Read		–		=	

APPROACHING p. 325	BEYOND p. 325	ELL p. 325

1 Model Tell children that authors usually write a nonfiction selection because they want to give information about something. Have children look at pages 312–313 in their Reading/Writing Workshop. Read together the definition of author's purpose. *An author's purpose is the reason why an author writes a selection.*

2 Guided Practice/Practice Read together the Find Text Evidence section and model using clues to find the author's purpose in *Share the Harvest and Give Thanks.* Point out the information added to the graphic organizer. *On page 306, we read about why the first Thanksgiving was celebrated. This information gives an important clue about the author's purpose. This clue is added to the Author's Purpose chart. What other clues can we find in the text to help us understand the author's purpose?*

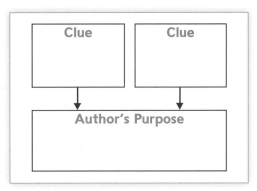

Teaching Poster

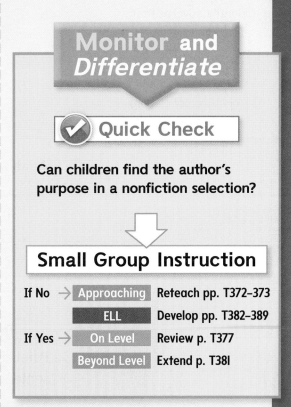

Monitor and *Differentiate*

✓ Quick Check

Can children find the author's purpose in a nonfiction selection?

Small Group Instruction

If No → **Approaching** Reteach pp. T372–373

ELL Develop pp. T382–389

If Yes → **On Level** Review p. T377

Beyond Level Extend p. T381

Write About the Reading/Writing Workshop

Reading/Writing Workshop

OBJECTIVES

CCSS Write opinion pieces in which they introduce the topic or name the book they are writing about, state an opinion, supply a reason for the opinion, and provide some sense of closure. **W.1.1**

CCSS Demonstrate command of the conventions of standard English grammar and usage when writing or speaking. **L.1.1**

Identify adverbs that tell how

ACADEMIC LANGUAGE

• *opinion, concluding statement, adverb*
• Cognates: *opinión, adverbio*

Analyze the Model Prompt Have children turn to page 314 in the **Reading/Writing Workshop**. Grace responded to the prompt: *In your opinion, what is the most interesting way people celebrate the harvest?* Explain to children that the prompt is asking for an opinion about ways people celebrate the harvest. Say: *This prompt is asking for an opinion about which way of celebrating is most interesting.* Point out that Grace responded to the prompt by stating her opinion and using text evidence to give reasons for her opinion.

Find Text Evidence Explain that Grace took notes about the different celebrations in the text. Then, she used her notes to form the opinion that a festival is the most interesting celebration. She found details about festivals in the text to support her opinion.

Graphic Organizer

Writing

Grammar

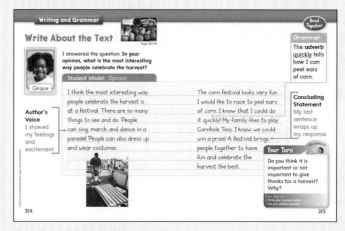

Reading/Writing Workshop

Analyze the Student Model Read the model. Discuss the callouts.

• **Adverbs That Tell How** Grace used the adverb *quickly* to tell how she could peel ears of corn. **Grammar**

• **Author's Voice** Grace showed her feelings and excitement about the festival. **Trait: Voice**

• **Concluding Statement** Grace's last sentence retells her opinion that a festival is the best way to celebrate the harvest. **Trait: Organization**

Point out that Grace's first sentence tells her opinion. Her other sentences give details that support her opinion.

Your Turn: Write an Opinion Say: *Now we will write to a new prompt.* Have children turn to page 315 of the **Reading/Writing Workshop**. Read the Your Turn prompt together. *Do you think it is important or not important to give thanks for a harvest? Why?*

Find Text Evidence Say: *We need to find evidence in the text, photographs, and illustrations and take notes. We'll use our notes to form an opinion about whether it's important or not important to give thanks for a harvest.* Remind children that the illustrations and photographs may contain clues that will help them make inferences.

Write to a Prompt: Guide children to use the notes to help form their opinion. Track the print as you reread the notes. Have children share their opinions and write a first sentence, such as: *It is important to give thanks for a harvest.* Remind children that the prompt asks for reasons to support their opinion. Guide children to form complete sentences that support the opinion in your first sentence as you share the pen with them. Say: *Let's reread our response. Does our response show how we think and feel? Does the last sentence retell our opinion and wrap up our response?* Read the final response as you track the print.

For additional practice with the writing traits, have children turn to page 330 of the **Your Turn Practice Book**.

Grammar

5 Mins MINILESSON

Adverbs That Tell How

① **Review** Remind children that adverbs can tell how an action takes place. Review example adverbs *slowly, quickly, loudly, softly, neatly,* and *gladly.* Write the following sentences:

> We slowly carried the heavy tree.
>
> Then we gladly placed the tree in the hole.
>
> "Happy Arbor Day!" Dad said loudly.

Guide them to circle the adverb that tells how in each sentence.

② **Guided Practice/Practice** Display the sentences below and read them aloud. Have children work in pairs to identify each adverb that tells how.

> Ethan neatly made his bed. (neatly)
>
> Ethan loudly ran down the stairs. (loudly)
>
> He gladly wished his mom a Happy Mother's Day. (gladly)

Talk About It Have partners work together to orally generate sentences about getting ready for school. Have them use adverbs that tell how.

COLLABORATE

ENGLISH LANGUAGE LEARNERS

Explain For each circled adverb in the Review sentences, ask: *How do you know ____ is an adverb?* Have children replace the adverb in each sentence with another adverb that tells how. Repeat correct answers slowly and clearly to the class.

Retell Have children retell what Ethan did in the Practice sentences. For each sentence a child retells, ask how the action happened. Clarify children's responses as needed by providing vocabulary.

Daily Wrap Up

- Discuss the Essential Question and encourage children to use the oral vocabulary words. Ask: *Why do we celebrate Mother's Day? Why do we celebrate Father's Day?*

- Prompt children to discuss what they learned today by asking: *How did the skills you learned today help you write?*

Materials

Reading/Writing Workshop
VOLUME 4

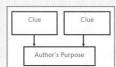

Literature Anthology
VOLUME 4

Visual Vocabulary Cards

design	favorite
display	few
pride	gone
purpose	surprise
represent	wonder
nation	young
unite	

Teaching Poster

Word-Building Cards

Response Board

Spelling Word Cards

Interactive Read-Aloud Cards

Sound-Spelling Cards

(→) Build the Concept

MINILESSON
5 Mins

Oral Language

ESSENTIAL QUESTION

Remind children that this week you are talking and reading about American holidays. Remind them of the harvest celebrations and what they learned about the flag. Guide children to discuss the question using information from what they have read and discussed throughout the week.

Visual Glossary

Review Oral Vocabulary

Review the oral vocabulary words *design, display, pride, purpose,* and *represent* using the Define/Example/Ask routine. Prompt children to use the words as they discuss holidays.

Share the Harvest and Give Thanks

OBJECTIVES

 Describe the connection between two individuals, events, ideas, or pieces of information in a text. **RI.1.3**

Read grade-level text orally with accuracy, appropriate rate, and expression. **RF.1.4b**

Review cause and effect

ACADEMIC LANGUAGE

- *cause, effect, phrasing*
- Cognates: *causa, efecto*

Visual Vocabulary Cards

Comprehension/ Fluency

Connections Within Text: Cause and Effect

1 Explain Tell children they have been learning about identifying the author's purpose in texts they read. Remind them they have also learned how to look for causes and effects. *As we read, we can think about what happened in the selection and why.*

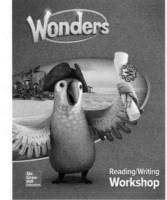

Reading/Writing Workshop

2 Model Display page 306 of *Share the Harvest and Give Thanks. I see the people who came to America had a feast; that is the effect. To find the cause, we can ask ourselves: Why did they have a feast? Because they wanted to show thanks for the harvest. That is the cause. What other causes and effects can we find in the selection?*

3 Guided Practice/Practice Reread *the selection* with children. Use text evidence to identify causes and effects.

Appropriate Phrasing

1 Explain Tell children that as you read, you will pause slightly or stop briefly when you come to certain punctuation marks. Explain that commas indicate you should pause slightly while reading. A period indicates you should stop briefly.

2 Model Read aloud sentences with punctuation in the Shared Read. *This sentence has a comma. I will pause slightly when I come to it. This sentence ends with a period. I will stop briefly when I reach the period. Pausing or stopping for commas and periods helps you know when one idea ends and a new one starts.* Point out how you pause for other punctuation.

3 Guided Practice/Practice Reread the passage. Remind children to pause for commas and stop briefly for periods.

Fluency Practice Children can practice using Practice Book passages.

Word Work

Display the **Word-Building Cards:** *air, are, ear, scr, spl, spr, str, thr, shr, wr, kn, gn, au, aw, augh, ew, ue, ui, ow, oi, oy, ar, ore, oar, er, ir, ur, ey, igh, oa.* Have children say the sounds.

Phonemic Awareness

OBJECTIVES

CCSS Decode regularly spelled one-syllable words. **RF.1.3b**

CCSS Decode two-syllable words following basic patterns by breaking the words into syllables. **RF.1.3e**

Phoneme Deletion

1 Model Show children how to change words by deleting phonemes. *Listen carefully as I say a word:* chair. *The word* chair *has these sounds:* /ch/ /âr/. *I'll take away the first sound* /ch/ *to make a new word:* /âr/, air. *The new word is* air.

2 Guided Practice/Practice Have children practice deleting phonemes to create new words. Do the first two together. *Listen carefully as I say a word. Then say the word without the first sound.*

plate	stall	broom	hair
cloud	strap	scare	bright

Phonics

Blend Words with /âr/ *air, are, ear*

1 Model Display **Word-Building Cards** *b* and *ear.* Model how to blend the sounds. *This is the letter* b. *It stands for the* /b/ *sound. These are the letters* e, a, r. *Together they stand for* /âr/. *Let's blend the sounds:* /bâr/. *The word is* bear. Continue with *hair, scare,* and *repair.*

2 Guided Practice/Practice Review the words and sentences in the Day 3 Phonics Practice Activity with children. Read each word in the first row, blending the sounds, for example: /k/ /âr/; /kâr/. The word is *care.*

Have children blend each word with you. Prompt children to read the connected text, sounding out the decodable words.

Phonemic Awareness

Phonics

Structural Analysis

Handwriting

T344 UNIT 6 WEEK 5

care	fair	dare	stare	tear	air
wear	pear	scare	share	chair	stairs
bare	barely	fair	unfair	hair	hairy

beware   repair   compare   footwear

rarely   prepare   scary   careful

Beware of the mean bears!

Put a spare pair of mittens on the chair. Also online

Day 3 Phonics Practice Activity

Decodable Reader Have children read "A Pair at the Fair" (pages 81–84) and "The Bears Prepare a Feast" (89–92) to practice decoding words in connected text.

Structural Analysis

r-Controlled Vowel Syllables

1 Model Write and read aloud *rarely* and *unfair*. Say the words, clapping for each syllable. Have children repeat. Draw a line between the syllables: *rare/ly; un/fair*. Explain that when a vowel spelling is followed by the letter *r,* the vowel and the *r* will be in the same syllable.

2 Practice/Apply Write: *barely, compare, footwear, airfare,* and *rarely,* and read them with children. Help children divide each word into syllables, and then use each word in a sentence.

Corrective Feedback

Corrective Feedback Say: *My turn.* Model blending using the appropriate signaling procedures. Then lead children in blending the sounds. Say: *Do it with me.* You will respond with children to offer support. Then say: *Your turn. Blend.* Have children chorally blend. Return to the beginning of the word. Say: *Let's start over.*

→ # Word Work

Quick Review

High-Frequency Words: Read, Spell, and Write to review this week's high-frequency words: *favorite, few, gone, surprise, wonder, young.*

MINILESSON
5 Mins

Spelling

OBJECTIVES

CCSS Recognize and read grade-appropriate irregularly spelled words. **RF.1.3g**

CCSS Use conventional spelling for words with common spelling patterns and for frequently occurring regular words. **L.1.2d**

CCSS Explain the meaning of simple similes and metaphors (e.g., *as pretty as a picture*) in context. **L.4.5.a**

air, are, ear Word Families

1 Model Make index cards for *air, are,* and *ear,* and form a three-column chart. Say the sounds with children.

Hold up the *fair* **Spelling Word Card**. Say and spell it. Pronounce each sound clearly. Blend the sounds. Repeat with *pair.* Place the words below the *air* card.

2 Guided Practice/Practice Have children spell each word. Repeat with the *are* and *ear* words. Display the words *three, splash, favorite,* and *surprise* in a separate column. Read and spell the words together with children. Point out that these words do not contain the /âr/ sounds.

Conclude by asking children to orally generate additional words that rhyme with each word. Write the additional words.

Go Digital

Spelling Word Families

school

Visual Glossary

MINILESSON
5 Mins

High-Frequency Words

PHONICS/SPELLING
PRACTICE BOOK p. 148

fair	pair	bear	wear
spare	share	favorite	surprise

A. Read the spelling words in the box. Write the spelling words that match each spelling pattern.

air		are	
1. fair		3. spare	
2. pair		4. share	

In 1–2 and 3–4, order of words may vary.

B. Read aloud the spelling words in the box. Write the spelling words that rhyme with pear.

5. bear	6. wear
7. fair	8. pair
9. spare	10. share

In 5–10, order of words may vary.

favorite, few, gone, surprise, wonder, young

1 Guided Practice Say each word and have children Read/Spell/Write it.

- Display **Visual Vocabulary Cards** to review this week's high-frequency words.

Visual Vocabulary Cards

2 Practice Repeat the activity with last week's word cards.

Build Fluency: Word Automaticity

Have children read the following sentences aloud together at the same pace. Repeat several times.

The young boy has a favorite toy bear.

Few of my friends have gone home.

I wonder what the surprise is!

Word Bank

Review the current and previous words in the word bank. Discuss with children which words should be removed, or added back, from previous high-frequency word lists.

Vocabulary

nation, unite

Review Use the **Visual Vocabulary Cards** to review this week's words using the Define/Example/Ask routine. Have partners generate context sentences for each vocabulary word.

Visual Vocabulary Cards

Strategy: Metaphors

1 Model Tell children that a metaphor is a figure of speech that compares one thing to another. It helps readers picture what something looks, sounds, or feels like. Unlike a simile, it does not use the words *like* or *as*. Use *Share the Harvest and Give Thanks* to model how to identify a metaphor.

Think Aloud In *Share the Harvest and Give Thanks*, a metaphor is used in this sentence: "At the Kentucky Harvest Festival, the corn crop is the star." I know that a *star* can be a popular performer, like a pop star. It can also mean something excellent. That must mean that the corn crop was excellent and it was the most popular crop at the festival.

2 Guided Practice Help children use the strategy to identify the metaphor and meaning of these sentences: *Ron is a giant. Her voice was a lullaby.*

3 Practice Have partners create a metaphor with the word *nation* or look for metaphors in other stories they have read.

Monitor and *Differentiate*

 Quick Check

Can children read and decode words with /âr/air, are, ear?

Can children recognize and read high-frequency and vocabulary words?

Small Group Instruction

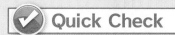

If No →	Approaching	Reteach pp. T368–371
	ELL	Develop pp. T382–389
If Yes →	On Level	Review pp. T376–377
	Beyond Level	Extend pp. T380–381

Genre Nonfiction

 TIME FOR KIDS

Essential Question

Why do we celebrate holidays?

Read about how our country began.

Go Digital!

Happy Birthday, U.S.A.!

Why do we celebrate the Fourth of July?

Whiz! Boom! Bang!

That's the sound of fireworks that tear through the air. Colors light up the sky. Bands play and crowds roar. It's the Fourth of July!

398

Each year, people celebrate the birthday of the United States. It is a day for us all to share. We enjoy **favorite** things such as fireworks, parades, and picnics. This kind of party has **gone** on for over two hundred years. But how did this holiday begin?

1

2

Parades are a favorite way to celebrate July 4th.

399

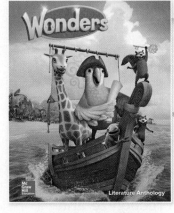

Wonders

Literature Anthology

LITERATURE ANTHOLOGY, pp. 398–399

Happy Birthday, U.S.A.!

CLOSE READING

Lexile 580

Close Reading Routine

Read DOK 1–2

- Identify key ideas and details about celebrating America.
- Take notes and retell.
- Use **A C T** prompts as needed.

Reread DOK 2–3

- Analyze the text, craft, and structure.
- Use *Close Reading Companion*, pp. 194–195.

Integrate DOK 4

- Integrate knowledge and ideas.
- Make text-to-text connections.
- Use the Integrate lesson.

Read

ESSENTIAL QUESTION

Read aloud the Essential Question: *Why do we celebrate holidays?* Read aloud the title. Tell children to predict what they think this selection will be about.

Story Words Read and spell the words *colony, England, Congress, declare, government,* and *independence.*

Note Taking: Graphic Organizer As children read the selection, guide them to fill in **Your Turn Practice Book** page 322.

Build Vocabulary page 398
roar: yell loudly

TIME *FOR KIDS*

In 1775, our **nation** was small. It had just 13 colonies. A colony is like a state, but ruled by a leader far away. This ruler was the king of England. The people in the colonies did not like this. They felt the king's rules were not fair. They felt he did not care if they were happy.

Our country began over 200 years ago.

This is Independence Hall in Philadelphia. Many rules for our nation were written here.

On June 11, 1776, leaders of the **young** colonies met as a group called Congress. The people of the colonies wanted to split away from England. And the leaders wanted to **unite** to make new rules and write their own laws.

400

401

LITERATURE ANTHOLOGY, pp. 400–401

---

① Strategy: Reread

Teacher Think Aloud On page 399, I read people celebrate the birthday of the United States. Does a country have a birthday? I'll reread to see. Pages 398-399 tell about the Fourth of July and what we do on that day. We celebrate the birthday of the United States, so it must mean the Fourth of July.

② Skill: Author's Purpose

The author's purpose is why an author writes a selection, for example, to give information. What information did we read on pages 398–399? Let's put this clue on our Author's Purpose chart.

Build Vocabulary page 401
split: separate; break

Reread   *Close Reading Companion, 194*

Text Structure

Reread pages 399–401. How is the information organized on these pages? (First, we learn what the holiday is about. Then, we learn how it began.)

A C T   Access Complex Text

▶ What makes this text complex?

Purpose The purpose of this text is to provide information. Identifying key details is important to understanding this purpose.

Organization Children should recognize that the historical information in this selection is given in the order it happened.

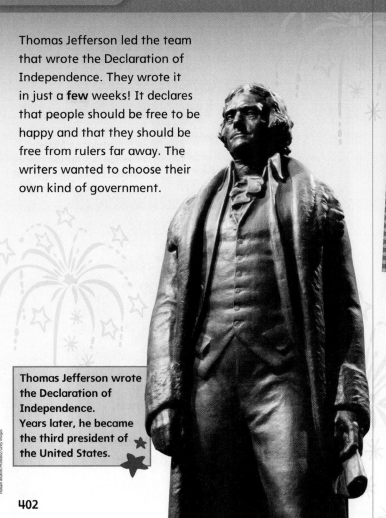

Thomas Jefferson led the team that wrote the Declaration of Independence. They wrote it in just a **few** weeks! It declares that people should be free to be happy and that they should be free from rulers far away. The writers wanted to choose their own kind of government.

Thomas Jefferson wrote the Declaration of Independence. Years later, he became the third president of the United States.

402

TIME FOR KIDS®

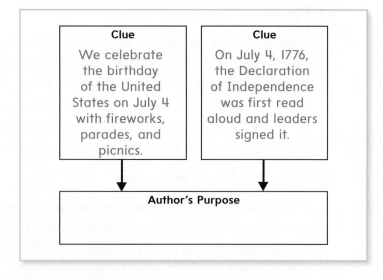

Thomas Jefferson and other leaders in Congress talked about how to split away from England.

Leaders started to sign the Declaration of Independence on July 4, 1776. They sent it to the king of England. He was **surprised** the colonies dared to do this. He did not want the colonies to be free.

The Declaration of Independence was first read out loud on July 4. Music blared and bells rang. One year later, fireworks lit up the sky on July 4.

403

LITERATURE ANTHOLOGY, pp. 402–403

Read

❸ Maintain Skill: Cause and Effect

Talk about what happened when the Declaration of Independence was first read. ("Music blared and bells rang.") How is it similar to how we celebrate the Fourth of July? (We make noise on the Fourth of July, too. We play music, and shoot fireworks.)

❹ Skill: Author's Purpose

Teacher Think Aloud Facts tell me what the writer wants me to know. On pages 402–403, the author tells facts about the Declaration of Independence. What does it have to do with July 4? Let's add to our chart.

Clue	Clue
We celebrate the birthday of the United States on July 4 with fireworks, parades, and picnics.	On July 4, 1776, the Declaration of Independence was first read aloud and leaders signed it.

Author's Purpose

Build Vocabulary page 403
dared: had the courage

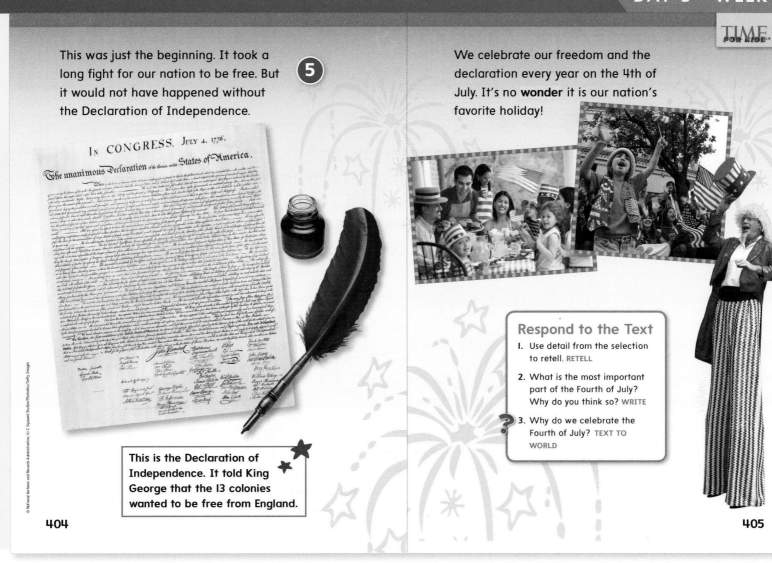

This was just the beginning. It took a long fight for our nation to be free. But it would not have happened without the Declaration of Independence.

5

This is the Declaration of Independence. It told King George that the 13 colonies wanted to be free from England.

404

We celebrate our freedom and the declaration every year on the 4th of July. It's no **wonder** it is our nation's favorite holiday!

Respond to the Text

1. Use detail from the selection to retell. RETELL

2. What is the most important part of the Fourth of July? Why do you think so? WRITE

3. Why do we celebrate the Fourth of July? TEXT TO WORLD

405

LITERATURE ANTHOLOGY, pp. 404–405

A C T Access Complex Text

▶ **Organization**

Remind children that authors often use special signal words and phrases to help readers follow the sequence of events in a text. Explain that in a text that gives historical information these words and phrases often include specific dates.

- Reread pages 400 through 403 with children and guide them in identifying the dates the author uses to show the sequence of events. (p. 400: In 1775; p. 401: On June 11, 1776; p. 403: on July 4, 1776, One year later . . . on July 4)

5 Antonyms

An antonym is a word that means the opposite of another word. Let's look at the word *beginning*. What is the opposite of that word? (ending) Yes, *ending* is an antonym of *beginning*.

Reread   *Close Reading Companion,* 195

Author's Craft: Details

Reread pages 402–403. Why does the author include dates in the text? (to help us understand that the Declaration of Independence was signed long ago and to help us see the order in which events took place)

Read

Skill: Author's Purpose

Review the Author's Purpose chart with children. *We have written down two key clues to help us figure out why the author wrote this selection. If we put them together, we can draw a conclusion about the author's purpose. What is the author's purpose? Let's add it to our Author's Purpose chart.*

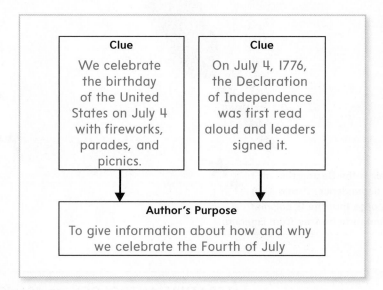

Clue	Clue
We celebrate the birthday of the United States on July 4 with fireworks, parades, and picnics.	On July 4, 1776, the Declaration of Independence was first read aloud and leaders signed it.

Author's Purpose

To give information about how and why we celebrate the Fourth of July

Return to Purposes

Review children's predictions. Ask children if their predictions about the selection were correct. Guide them to use the evidence in the text to confirm whether their predictions turned out to be accurate. Discuss what children learned from the selection. Did they learn anything new about how and why we celebrate the Fourth of July?

Respond to the Text

Read

Retell

Guide children in retelling the selection. Remind them that as they read *Happy Birthday, U.S.A.!*, they figured out the author's purpose for writing the selection and reread when there was something they didn't understand. Have children use the information they recorded on their Author's Purpose charts to help them retell the selection.

Reread

Analyze the Text

After children read and retell the selection, have them reread *Happy Birthday, U.S.A.!* to develop a deeper understanding of the text by answering the questions on pages 194–195 of the *Close Reading Companion*. For children who need support finding text evidence to support their responses, use the scaffolded instruction from the Reread prompts on pages T347B–T347D.

Write About the Text

Review the writing prompt with children. Remind them to use their responses from the *Close Reading Companion* and to cite text evidence to support their answers.

For a full lesson on writing a response supported by text evidence, see pages T348–T349.

<u>Answer:</u> Children should state an opinion about which part of the Fourth of July is most important and give reasons to support their opinion. <u>Evidence:</u> Pages 398–399 and 405 discuss and show fireworks, parades, and picnics. Pages 400–401 describe reasons the colonies wanted to split away from England, while pages 402–404 explain how leaders created and signed the Declaration of Independence.

Integrate

Make Connections
COLLABORATE

Text to World <u>Answer:</u> We celebrate the Fourth of July because it is our nation's birthday. <u>Evidence:</u> On page 403, the text says July Fourth was the day when the Declaration of Independence was first read aloud. Page 405 states that we celebrate the declaration and the fight for freedom that started on July 4, 1776.

ELL

ENGLISH LANGUAGE LEARNERS

Retell Help children by looking at each page of the selection and asking a question, such as, *What is this page about? What did the people want? What did they do?* Provide sentence starters to help children retell the selection, such as, *In 1775, the colonists ____. On June 11, 1776, leaders from the colonies ____. On July 4, 1776, ____. Today we celebrate ____.*

CONNECT TO CONTENT
CELEBRATIONS AND NATIONAL HOLIDAYS

Remind children that this week they have been learning about why we celebrate national holidays. Discuss the historical people and events that holidays such as the Fourth of July commemorate. Prompt children to name symbols and people that we associate with these holidays, such as the American flag and George Washington.

Write About the Literature Anthology

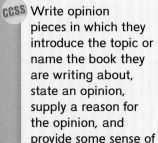

Literature Anthology

OBJECTIVES

CCSS Write opinion pieces in which they introduce the topic or name the book they are writing about, state an opinion, supply a reason for the opinion, and provide some sense of closure. **W.1.1**

CCSS Demonstrate command of the conventions of standard English grammar and usage when writing or speaking. **L.1.1**

- Identify adverbs that tell how
- Use capitalization and periods in title abbreviations

ACADEMIC LANGUAGE

- *opinion, support, voice, adverb, title*
- Cognates: *opinión, voz, adverbio*

Analylyze the Prompt Have children turn to page 405 in the **Literature Anthology**. Read the prompt: *What is the most important part of the Fourth of July? Why do you think so?* Say: *The prompt asks for your opinion about the most important part of the Fourth of July. It also asks you to give reasons that support your opinion. The next step in responding to the prompt is to find text evidence.*

Find Text Evidence Say: *To help us respond to the prompt, we can look for text evidence and take notes about the Fourth of July. We can form an opinion and use that text evidence to support our opinion.* Say: *Look at page 399. The text tells us that the Fourth of July is America's birthday and that it is a day for us all to share. What activities do people do on this holiday?* (People go to fireworks shows, parades, and picnics.) *Look at the photograph of the parade. The children are smiling. This is a clue that helps me know they are having fun celebrating this holiday together.* Have children take notes as they look for evidence to respond to the prompt.

Write to the Prompt Guide children as they begin their writing.

- **Prewrite** Have children review their notes and plan their writing. Guide them to form an opinion about the most important part of the Fourth of July and to think about what reasons from the text they will use to support their opinion.

- **Draft** Have children write a response to the prompt. Remind them that their first sentence should state their opinion. As children write their drafts, have them focus on the week's skills.

  - **Author's Voice** Choose words and punctuation that show how they feel. **Trait: Voice**

  - **Adverbs That Tell How** Include adverbs that tell how. **Grammar**

  - **Concluding Statement** Add a concluding statement that wraps up the ideas in their response and retells their opinion. **Trait: Organization**

Tell children they will continue to work on their responses on Day 4.

Go Digital

Present the Lesson

Graphic Organizer

Writing

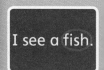
I see a fish.

Grammar

Grammar

Adverbs That Tell How

1 Review Have children look at page 315 in the **Reading/Writing Workshop**. Remind them that adverbs can tell how an action takes place. Have children identify the adverb in the model sentence.

Say: *Name the adverb in this sentence that tells how:* I know that I could do it quickly! Quickly *is an adverb that tells how.*

2 Guided Practice/Practice Guide children to name other adverbs that could replace *quickly* in the sentence *I know I could do it quickly!* Have children write the sentence with new adverbs.

Talk About It Have partners work together to orally generate sentences about their favorite event. Have them use adverbs that tell how.

Mechanics: Abbreviations

1 Model Display *Mr., Mrs., Ms.,* and *Dr.* Remind children that each abbreviation is a name title people use. Explain what each abbreviation stands for. Point out that each title begins with a capital letter and ends with a period.

2 Guided Practice Prompt children to circle the name titles in each sentence.

> Mr. Knight ran up the stairs to see Mrs. Knight. (Mr., Mrs.)
>
> My mom made a pie for Mrs. Post. (Mrs.)

ENGLISH LANGUAGE LEARNERS SCAFFOLD

Beginning

Demonstrate Comprehension Provide sentence frames for partners as they write their responses: *I think _____ is the most important part of the Fourth of July. _____ is important because _____.*

Intermediate

Explain Encourage children to talk about their opinions. Repeat children's responses, correcting grammar or pronunciation as needed. Provide sentence frames, then have children complete them.

Advanced/High

Elaborate Prompt children to add reasons to support their opinions. Ask: *Why do you have that opinion? Let's include those reasons in your response.* Help children transfer these reasons to their writing.

Daily Wrap Up

- Encourage children to discuss the Essential Question using the oral vocabulary words. Ask: *What holidays have you learned about? How do people celebrate them?*

- Prompt children to review and discuss the skills they used today.

Materials

Wonders

Literature Anthology
VOLUME 4

Visual Vocabulary Cards

design
display
favorite
few
gone
nation
pride

purpose
represent
surprise
unite
wonder
young

Teaching Poster

a b c

Word-Building Cards

fair

Spelling Word Cards

Dinah Zike's
FOLDABLES

Dinah Zike's Foldables®

→ # Extend the Concept

CLOSE READING

MINILESSON
5 Mins

A Young Nation Grows

OBJECTIVES

CCSS Know and use various text features (e.g., headings, tables of contents, glossaries, electronic menus, icons) to locate key facts or information in a text. **RI.1.5**

Review vocabulary

ACADEMIC LANGUAGE

- *map, illustrations, parking lot, buses, playground*
- Cognates: *mapa, ilustraciones, buses*

ESSENTIAL QUESTION

Remind children that this week they have been learning about American holidays. Guide children to discuss the question using information from what they have read and discussed. Use the Define/Example/Ask routine to review the oral vocabulary words *design, display, pride, purpose,* and *represent.* Then review last week's oral vocabulary words *ancient, drama, effort, movement,* and *tradition.*

Text Feature: Map

1 Explain Tell children they can use informational selections to find facts and details. Explain that informational text sometimes includes a map—a picture that shows where places are found. A map sometimes has a title that tells about the map and a key that shows what the symbols on the map stand for.

2 Model Display Teaching Poster 19. *This map shows the area around a school. You could use this map to figure out how to get to the different parts of the school.* Point out the building. *The key tells us the building is the school.*

3 Guided Practice/Practice Guide children to identify the features on the map. *Show me which path you would take from the school building to the buses. Show me the playground. How do you know this is the playground?* Tell children to look for maps as they read.

Close Reading

Compare Texts

Tell children that as they read they should think about how the map helps them understand the information in *Happy Birthday, U.S.A.!*

Go Digital

school

Visual Glossary

Teaching Poster

"A Young Nation Grows"

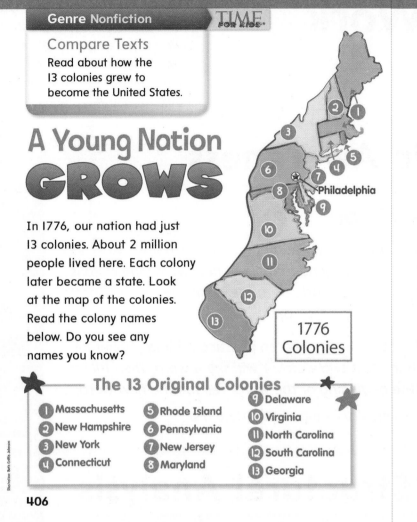

Genre Nonfiction

TIME FOR KIDS

Compare Texts

Read about how the 13 colonies grew to become the United States.

A Young Nation GROWS

In 1776, our nation had just 13 colonies. About 2 million people lived here. Each colony later became a state. Look at the map of the colonies. Read the colony names below. Do you see any names you know?

1776 Colonies

★ The 13 Original Colonies ★

1. Massachusetts
2. New Hampshire
3. New York
4. Connecticut
5. Rhode Island
6. Pennsylvania
7. New Jersey
8. Maryland
9. Delaware
10. Virginia
11. North Carolina
12. South Carolina
13. Georgia

406

Today, our nation has 50 states. More than 312 million people live here!

Did you know that Philadelphia was our nation's first capital?

What is our nation's capital today? If you guessed Washington, D.C., you are correct! It became the capital in 1790.

★ The United States Today ★

Philadelphia

Washington, D.C.

Make Connections

What can you learn about the colonies from the map? **Essential Question**

407

LITERATURE ANTHOLOGY, pp. 406–407

Lexile 390

Read

❶ Skill: Key Details

What was our nation like in 1776? (There were 13 colonies and about 2 million people.) **What is our nation like today?** (Today, there are 50 states and more than 312 million people.)

❷ Text Feature: Map

What does the map on page 406 show? (the original 13 colonies) **How is the map on page 407 different?** (It shows all of the United States today, and it shows where the original 13 colonies fit into the whole nation.)

Retell

Guide children to use key details to retell the selection.

Reread

After children retell, have them reread to develop a deeper understanding of the selection by answering questions on *Close Reading Companion* pages 196–197. For children who need support citing text evidence, use the Reread questions:

- How does the map key help you understand the map?

- How do the maps help you understand how the nation grew?

Integrate

Make Connections

COLLABORATE

Essential Question Have children tell what they learned about the colonies using the map.

→ # Word Work

MINILESSON 5 Mins
Phonemic Awareness

OBJECTIVES

CCSS Decode regularly spelled one-syllable words. **RF.1.3b**

CCSS Use conventional spelling for words with common spelling patterns and for frequently occurring irregular words. **L.1.2d**

CCSS Identify frequently occurring root words (e.g., *look*) and their inflectional forms (e.g., *looks, looked, looking*). **L.1.4c**

Add sounds to form new words

Phoneme Addition

1 Model Show children how to orally add phonemes to words. *Listen as I say a word. Then I will add a sound to make a new word. The word is air. What word will I make if I add /p/ to the beginning of air? That's right, I will make the word /p/ /âr/, pair.*

2 Guided Practice/Practice Have children practice adding phonemes. Guide practice with the first two words. *I will say a word, then I'll say a sound to add to the beginning of the word. Tell me the new word.*

at, /k/   air, /ch/   room, /b/   ring, /sp/   core, /s/

MINILESSON 10 Mins
Phonics/Structural Analysis

Build Words with /âr/ *air, are, ear*

1 Review *The letters* air, are, *and* ear *can stand for the /âr/ sounds. We'll use* **Word-Building Cards** *to build words with the /âr/ sounds.*

Place the letters *t, ear. Let's blend the sounds together and read the word: /târ/. Now let's change the* t *to* w. *Blend the sounds and read the word.* Continue with *pear, bear, bar, bare, care, fare, flare, glare, scare, share, spare, stare, star, stair, pair, hair.*

> **Decodable Reader** Have children read "Lights in the Air" (pages 85–88) and "Leaders Care" (93–96) to practice decoding words in connected text.

r-Controlled Vowel Syllables

1 Review Write the word *dairy* on the board and divide it into syllables. Review how to divide a word into syllables when a vowel in the word is followed by the letter *r*.

2 Practice Write the following words: *barely, prepare, market, dirty, turkey.* Have children work in pairs to divide the words into syllables. Then have them write a sentence with each word.

Go Digital

Phonemic Awareness

Phonics

Structural Analysis

Spelling Word Sort

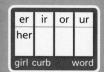

Visual Glossary

Spelling

Word Sort with *air, are, ear*

1 **Review** Provide pairs of children with copies of the **Spelling Word Cards**. While one partner reads the words one at a time, the other partner should orally segment the word and then write the word. After reading all the words, partners should switch roles.

2 **Practice** Have children correct their own papers. Then have them sort the words by ending spelling pattern.

High-Frequency Words

favorite, few, gone, surprise, wonder, young

Review Display **Visual Vocabulary Cards** for high-frequency words: *favorite, few, gone, surprise, wonder, young.* Have children Read/ Spell/Write each word.

- Point to a word and call on a child to use it in a sentence.
- Review last week's words using the same procedure.

Expand Vocabulary

nation, unite

Use the Visual Vocabulary Cards to review *nation* and *unite*.

1 **Explain** Explain to children that words have different forms. Help children generate different forms of this week's words by adding inflectional endings *-ed, -ing,* and *-s or -es.* Review the meaning of each ending.

2 **Model** Model how to add endings to the word *unite.* Write the vocabulary word *unite.* Then write *unites, united,* and *uniting.* Read the words with children. Point out how the different endings change the meaning of *unite.*

3 **Guided Practice** Have children work in pairs to write different forms of *nation.* Then have children share sentences using the words.

Monitor and *Differentiate*

✓ Quick Check

Can children read and decode words with /âr/air, are, ear?

Can children recognize and read high-frequency and vocabulary words?

Small Group Instruction

If No →	Approaching	Reteach pp. T368–371
	ELL	Develop pp. T382–389
If Yes →	On Level	Review pp. T376–377
	Beyond Level	Extend pp. T380–381

→ # Language Arts

Literature Anthology

OBJECTIVES

CCSS With guidance and support from adults, focus on a topic, respond to questions and suggestions from peers, and add details to strengthen writing as needed. **W.1.5**

CCSS Demonstrate command of the conventions of standard English grammar and usage when writing or speaking. **L.1.1**

CCSS Ask questions to clear up any confusion about the topics and texts under discussion. **SL.1.1c**

• Identify adverbs that tell how
• Use capitalization and periods in title abbreviations

ACADEMIC LANGUAGE
• *revise, opinion, voice, title*
• Cognates: *revisar, opinión, voz*

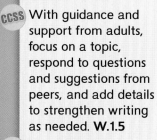
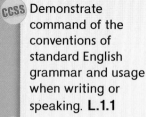
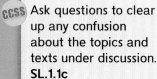

MINILESSON 5 Mins — Independent Writing

Write About the Literature Anthology

Go Digital

Revise

Reread the prompt about the selection *Happy Birthday, U.S.A!*: *What is the most important part of the Fourth of July? Why do you think so?* Have children read their drafts to see if they responded to the prompt. Then have them check for:

- **Author's Voice** Does their response show how they think and feel? **Trait: Voice**

- **Adverbs That Tell How** Did they include adverbs that tell how? **Grammar**

- **Concluding Statement** Does their last sentence wrap up the ideas in their response and retell their opinion? **Trait: Organization**

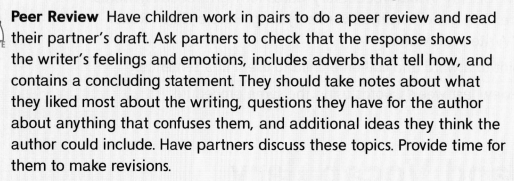

Peer Review Have children work in pairs to do a peer review and read their partner's draft. Ask partners to check that the response shows the writer's feelings and emotions, includes adverbs that tell how, and contains a concluding statement. They should take notes about what they liked most about the writing, questions they have for the author about anything that confuses them, and additional ideas they think the author could include. Have partners discuss these topics. Provide time for them to make revisions.

Proofread/Edit

Have children check for the following:

- Adverbs that tell how are used correctly.
- All sentences express a complete idea.
- Dates and names of people are capitalized.

 Peer Edit Next, have partners exchange their drafts and take turns reviewing them against the checklist. Encourage partners to discuss and fix errors together.

Writing

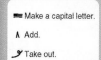

≡ Make a capital letter.
∧ Add.
⤴ Take out.

Proofreader's Marks

I see a fish.

Grammar

Final Draft

After children edit their writing and finish their peer edits, have them write their final draft. Tell children to write neatly so others can read their writing. Or, work with children to explore a variety of digital tools to produce and publish their writing, including collaborating with peers. Have them include details that help make their writing clear and interesting, and add a drawing if needed to make their ideas clear.

Teacher Conference As children work, conference with them to provide guidance. Check to make sure children's responses show what they think and feel, and that they have a concluding sentence.

Grammar

Adverbs That Tell How

❶ **Review** Remind children that some adverbs tell how an action takes place. Ask: *What are some words that tell how?* (Possible responses: slowly, quickly, loudly, softly, neatly, gladly) *How are the words alike?* (They end in -ly.)

❷ **Guided Practice** Display the following sentences. Have children identify the adverbs that tell how.

Mom said I should quickly change my shirt. (quickly)

I slowly looked in the dresser. (slowly)

I found a neatly folded green shirt. (neatly)

I gladly wear green on St. Patrick's Day! (gladly)

❸ **Practice** Have children use the adverbs from the Guided Practice in sentences of their own.

Talk About It Have partners work together to orally generate sentences with adverbs from the Review discussion.

Mechanics: Abbreviations

❶ **Review/Explain** Remind children that name title abbreviations like *Mr., Mrs., Ms.,* and *Dr.* begin with a capital letter and end with a period.

❷ **Practice** Display sentences with errors. Read each aloud. Have children work together to fix the sentences.

Jayden said, "This is my mother, Mrs Smith." (Jayden said, "This is my mother, Mrs. Smith.")

Mr Wong drives the bus to school. (Mr. Wong drives the bus to school.)

Daily Wrap Up

- Have children discuss the Essential Question using the oral vocabulary words. Ask: *What is the purpose of Independence Day, or Fourth of July?*

- Prompt children to discuss the skills they practiced and learned today by asking: *What skills did you use today?*

→ **Integrate Ideas**

Celebrate America!

 CCSS

OBJECTIVES

Participate in shared research and writing projects (e.g., explore a number of "how-to" books on a given topic and use them to write a sequence of instructions). **W.1.7**

- Build background knowledge
- Research information using technology

ACADEMIC LANGUAGE

- *celebrated, origins, meaning*
- Cognates: *celebrar, origenes*

 SCIENCE

RESEARCH AND INQUIRY

 COLLABORATE

Make a Japanese Children's Day Flag

Review the steps in the research process. Tell children they will work with a partner to research Japanese Children's Day. Explain that on this holiday, people fly fish-shaped flags to celebrate the health and happiness of children.

STEP 1 **Choose a Topic**

Guide partners to choose an aspect of Children's Day to research. They might research the origins of the holiday, the meaning of it, or how it is celebrated.

STEP 2 **Find Resources**

Discuss how to use the selections, reference materials, and online sources to find information. Have children use the Research Process Checklist online.

STEP 3 **Keep Track of Ideas**

Have children make a Matchbook Foldable® to record ideas.

fly flags
children's Olympics
sticky rice cakes

Dinah Zike's
FOLDABLES®

Go
Digital

Resources:
Research and
Inquiry

Collaborative Conversations

Be Open to All Ideas Review with children that as they engage in partner, small-group, and whole-group discussions, they should:

- remember that everyone's ideas are important and should be heard.
- not be afraid to ask a question if something is unclear.
- respect the opinions of others.

STEP 4 **Create the Project: Japanese Children's Day Flag**

Explain the characteristics of the flag.

- **Material** The shape of the flag will be cut out of fabric or paper. It will hang from a string.

- **Drawing** The design of the fish's body will drawn on with pencils or markers.

- **Decorations** The flag can include ribbon or cut paper attached as streamers.

Have children create a Japanese fish flag.

- Guide them to draw a colorful fish on a large sheet of paper or fabric.

- Help them cut out the fish and attach a string from which to hang it.

- Have children write a sentence or two, telling what they learned about Children's Day in their research.

ILLUSTRATED FLAG

ENGLISH LANGUAGE LEARNERS
SCAFFOLD

Beginning	Intermediate	Advanced/High
Use Sentence Frames Use sentence frames to help children discuss Japanese Children's Day. For example: *This holiday celebrates ___. People fly ___.*	**Discuss** Guide children to focus on the most important details about the holiday. Ask: *Is this a new holiday or an old tradition? What do people do on this day? What does the fish flag mean?*	**Describe** Prompt children to elaborate on the displayed flags. Ask them to tell how the flags are alike and how they are different.

Materials

Reading/Writing Workshop
VOLUME 4

Literature Anthology
VOLUME 4

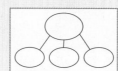

Visual Vocabulary Cards

favorite
few
gone
nation
surprise
unite
wonder
young

Teaching Poster

Interactive Read-Aloud Cards

Spelling Word Cards

a   b   c

Word-Building Cards

Word Work/Fluency

Go
Digital

Phonological Awareness

MINILESSON
5 Mins

Phonological Awareness

OBJECTIVES

CCSS Decode two-syllable words following basic patterns by breaking the words into syllables. **RF.1.3e**

CCSS Use conventional spelling for words with common spelling patterns and for frequently occurring irregular words. **L.1.2d**

Syllable Deletion

Review Guide children to delete syllables in words to form new words. *Listen carefully as I say a word. Then delete a syllable and say the new word.*

barely/bare   unfair/fair   armchair/arm   airfare/air

Syllable Addition

Review Help children add syllables to words to form new words. *Listen as I say a word and a syllable to add to the word. What is the new word?*

hair/hairy   stare/staring   box/boxes   slow/slowly

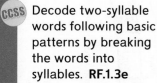
MINILESSON
10 Mins

Phonics/Structural Analysis

Phonics

Blend and Build with /âr/ *air, are, ear*

Review Have children blend and read: *share, wear, air, beware,* and *unfair.* Then have children use **Word-Building Cards** to build *care, scare, spare, stare, share, fare, hare, hair, fair, pair, pear, wear, bear.*

Word Automaticity Help children practice Word Automaticity. Display decodable words and point to each word as children chorally read it. Test how many words children can read in one minute. Model blending words children miss.

Structural Analysis

r-Controlled Vowel Syllables

Review Have children explain how to divide a word into syllables when a vowel in the word is followed by the letter *r.* Then have them practice writing and reading words with *r*-controlled vowel syllables.

Visual Glossary

Fluency: Word Automaticity

Spelling

Word Sort with *air, are, ear*

Review Have children use the **Spelling Word Cards** to sort the weekly words by *r*-controlled vowel spellings.

Assess Assess children on their abilities to spell words in the *air, are, ear* word families. To challenge children, you may wish to provide additional words with the sound-spellings.

High-Frequency Words

favorite, few, gone, surprise, wonder, young

Review Display **Visual Vocabulary Cards** *favorite, few, gone, surprise, wonder, young.* Have children Read/Spell/Write each word. Have children write a sentence with each word.

Review Vocabulary

nation, unite

Review Write *nation* and *unite* on the board. Point to each word and have children use it in a sentence. Write the sentences and reinforce word meanings as necessary. Repeat with last week's words or other previously taught words that children need to review.

Fluency

Appropriate Phrasing

Review Phrasing is how you group words together as you read. Remind them that you also pause briefly when you come to a comma.

Read aloud a few pages of the Shared Read. Have children echo or choral read each sentence. Point out how you pause briefly each time you come to a comma. Then have partners reread the selection, working on how they pause for commas and phrase words appropriately.

Quick Review

Build Fluency: Sound-Spellings
Display the **Word-Building Cards:** *air, are, ear, scr, spl, spr, str, thr, shr, wr, kn, gn, au, aw, augh, ew, ue, ui, ow, oi, oy, ar, ore, oar, er, ir, ur, ey, igh, oa.* Have children say the sounds.

Monitor and *Differentiate*

 Quick Check

Can children read and decode words with /âr/*air, are, ear*?

Can children recognize and read high-frequency words?

Small Group Instruction

If No → | Approaching | Reteach pp. T368–369
| ELL | Develop pp. T382–389
If Yes → | On Level | Review pp. T376–377
| Beyond Level | Extend pp. T380–381

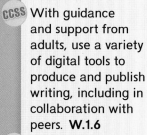

Literature Anthology

OBJECTIVES

CCSS With guidance and support from adults, use a variety of digital tools to produce and publish writing, including in collaboration with peers. **W.1.6**

CCSS Ask and answer questions about key details in a text read aloud or information presented orally or through other media. **SL.1.2**

CCSS Describe people, places, things, and events with relevant details, expressing ideas and feelings clearly. **SL.1.4**

ACADEMIC LANGUAGE

• *present, evaluate, abbreviation, period*
• Cognates: *presentar, evaluar*

Write About the Literature Anthology

Go Digital

Prepare

Tell children they will plan what they will say about their finished writing and drawing to the class. Remind children to:

- Think about how they expressed their feelings in their writing.
- Think about how their concluding sentence wraps up their response.

Present

Have children take turns giving presentations of their responses to the prompt about *Happy Birthday, U.S.A!*: *What is the most important part of the Fourth of July? Why do you think so?* If possible, record their presentations so children can self-evaluate. Tell children to:

- Listen carefully and ask questions about what a speaker says.
- Respond to questions others ask about details in their presentations.
- Speak in complete sentences.

Evaluate

Have children discuss their own presentations and evaluate their performance using the presentation rubric.

Use the teacher's rubric to evaluate children's writing. Have children add their writing to their Writer's Portfolio. Encourage children to look back at previous writing. Guide children to discuss what they learned about the Fourth of July and what they learned about writing an opinion. Have children share their observations with a partner.

Publish

After children finish presenting their work, discuss how the class will publish a class book of their responses. Have children come up with a title and design a cover. Create a table of contents for the book. Guide children to use digital tools to publish writing.

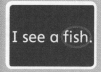
Writing

Checklists

I see a fish.

Grammar

Grammar

Adverbs That Tell How

1 Review Have children describe adverbs that tell how. Write the following sentences and have children identify the adverbs:

> I lay quietly in bed. Then, I quickly jumped up. I'll gladly get up today! Today is the first day of the new year! I get to loudly play drums at the big party. (quietly, quickly, gladly, loudly)

2 Practice Ask: *What question can each adverb answer?* (How?) Have children work in pairs to write sentences using *slowly, softly,* and *neatly.*

Mechanics: Abbreviations

1 Review Remind children that name title abbreviations begin with a capital letter and end with a period.

2 Practice Write the following sentences. Read each aloud. Have children fix the sentences.

> I got my hair cut by ms Neal. (I got my hair cut by Ms. Neal.)
>
> Did dr Drake listen to you breathe? (Did Dr. Drake listen to you breathe?)

Daily Wrap Up

- Review the Essential Question and encourage children to discuss using the oral vocabulary words.

- Review with children that an author's purpose is the reason why an author writes a selection.

- Review words with *r*-controlled vowels *air, are, ear.*

- Use the Visual Vocabulary Cards to review the Words to Know.

- Remind children that nonfiction text tells facts about a topic.

→ Integrate Ideas

Close Reading Routine

Read DOK 1–2

- Identify key ideas and details about holidays and celebrations.
- Take notes and retell.
- Use **A C T** prompts as needed.

Reread DOK 2–3

- Analyze text, craft, and structure.

Integrate DOK 4

- Integrate knowledge and ideas and make text-to-text connections.
- Use the Integrate Lesson.
- Use *Close Reading Companion*, p. 198.

TEXT CONNECTIONS

Connect to the Essential Question

Write the essential question on the board: *Why do we celebrate holidays?* Read the essential question aloud. Tell children that they will think about all of the information they have learned about why we celebrate holidays. Say: *We have read many selections on this topic. We will compare the information from this week's* **Leveled Readers** *and* Share the Harvest and Give Thanks, **Reading/Writing Workshop** *pages 302–311.*

Evaluate Text Evidence Guide children to review the selections and their completed graphic organizers. Have children work with partners to compare information from all the week's reads. Children can record notes using a Foldable®. Guide them to record information from the selections that helps them to answer the Essential Question.

Dinah Zike's
FOLDABLES
Study Organizer

Celebrate America!

OBJECTIVES

CCSS Participate in shared research and writing projects. **W.1.7**

RESEARCH AND INQUIRY

Have children create a checklist and review their projects:

- Does their flag look like a Japanese Children's Day flag?
- Do they wish to make any last minute changes to the flag?
- Have they correctly written sentences about what they learned in their research?
- Have they taken notes about what they would like to talk about when presenting their projects to the class?

Guide partners to practice sharing their projects with each other. Children should practice speaking and presenting their information clearly.

Guide children to share their work. Prompt children to ask questions to clarify when something is unclear: *What did you learn about Japanese Children's Day? What do you want your flag to look like? Why is Japanese Children's Day important?* Have children use the Presentation Checklist online.

Go Digital

Collaborate

Text to Music

Read aloud with children the Integrate activity on page 198 of the *Close Reading Companion*. Have partners share reactions to the song. Then guide them to discuss how it is similar to the selections they read earlier in the week. Have partners collaborate to complete the Integrate page by following the prompts.

Present Ideas and Synthesize Information

When children finish their discussions, ask for a volunteer from each pair to share the information from their Foldable® and their Integrate pages. After each pair has presented their ideas, ask: *How does learning about these traditions help you answer the Essential Question, Why do we celebrate holidays?* Lead a class discussion asking students to use the information from their charts to answer the Essential Question.

SPEAKING AND LISTENING

As children work with partners in their *Close Reading Companion*, or on their projects, make sure that they actively participate in the conversation, and when necessary, remind them to use these speaking and listening strategies:

Speaking Strategies

• Speak at an appropriate volume so that others can easily understand what they are saying.

• Describe the places and things that they are discussing with relevant details.

• Use words that express their ideas and feelings clearly.

Listening Strategies

• Listen quietly as the presenter speaks, and wait until the speaker has finished before asking questions.

• Ask questions in order to get additional information or to clarify something that they might not have understood the first time.

• Ask questions if they are confused about what they hear.

Approaching Level

Lexile 440

OBJECTIVES

 Identify the main purpose of a text, including what the author wants to answer, explain, or describe. **RI.2.6**

Leveled Reader:
It's Labor Day!

Before Reading

Preview and Predict

Have children turn to the title page. Read the title and the author's name and have children repeat. Preview the selection's photographs. Prompt children to predict what the selection might be about.

Review Genre: Informational Text/Nonfiction

Have children recall that informational text gives details about real people, places, events, or things. It gives information in a logical order.

ESSENTIAL QUESTION

Remind children of the Essential Question: *Why do we celebrate holidays?* Set a purpose for reading: *Let's find out why we celebrate Labor Day.*

Remind children that as they read a selection, they can ask questions about what they do not understand or want to know more about.

During Reading

Guided Comprehension

As children whisper read *It's Labor Day!,* monitor and provide guidance, correcting blending and modeling the key strategies and skills.

Strategy: Reread

Remind children that they should reread part of a selection if they do not quite understand something they've read. Model using the strategy on page 2. Say: *I'm not sure I understand when Labor Day is. I'll reread the page slowly.* Reread the page. *Labor Day is the first Monday of September.*

Skill: Author's Purpose

Remind children that the author's purpose is the reason why an author writes a text. An author may write to entertain readers, or to tell information about something. As you read, ask: *What clues tell us why the author wrote this?* Display an Author's Purpose chart for children to copy.

Go Digital

It's Labor Day!

Graphic Organizer

Retell

Literature Circles

Lead children in conducting a literature circle using the Thinkmark questions to guide the discussion. You may wish to discuss what children have learned about holidays from reading the two selections in the Leveled Reader.

Model recording children's answers in the boxes. Have children record the answers in their own charts.

Think Aloud On page 2, I read details about the first Labor Day and when Labor Day is. I can write this information on my chart. These clues help me see that the author is giving information.

Guide children to use the text and photographs to complete the chart.

After Reading

Respond to Reading

Have children complete the Respond to Reading on page 12.

Retell

Have children take turns retelling the selection, using the **Retelling Cards** as a guide. Help children make a personal connection: *Have you celebrated with family and friends in any of these ways? Which one?*

Model Fluency

Read the sentences, one at a time. Have children chorally repeat. Point out to children how to group phrases together, such as "That means" and "it's Labor Day!" on page 2.

Apply Have partners practice reading. Provide feedback as needed.

Level Up

Level-up lessons available online.

IF children can read *It's Labor Day!* Approaching Level with fluency and correctly answer the Respond to Reading questions,

THEN tell children that they will read a more detailed version of the selection.

- Use page 3 of *It's Labor Day!* On Level to model using Teaching Poster 38 to list clues to the author's purpose.

- Have children read the selection, checking their comprehension by using the graphic organizer.

PAIRED READ ...

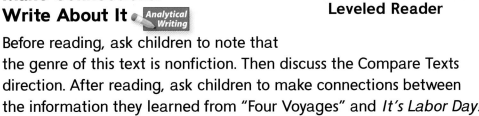

Leveled Reader

"Four Voyages"

Make Connections: Write About It ✏ *Analytical Writing*

Before reading, ask children to note that the genre of this text is nonfiction. Then discuss the Compare Texts direction. After reading, ask children to make connections between the information they learned from "Four Voyages" and *It's Labor Day!* Provide a sentence frame such as: *We can celebrate holidays by ____.*

🔍 FOCUS ON SOCIAL STUDIES

Children can extend their knowledge of workers they know by completing the social studies activity on page 16.

Phonemic Awareness

PHONEME BLENDING

TIER 2

OBJECTIVES

CCSS Orally produce single-syllable words by blending sounds (phonemes), including consonant blends. **RF.1.2b**

I Do Explain to children that they will be blending sounds to form words. *Listen as I say a word sound by sound: /h/ /âr/. Say the sounds with me: /h/ /âr/. I'm going to blend the sounds together: /h/ /âr/, /hâr/, hair. I blended the word* hair.

We Do *Listen as I say the sounds in a word: /s/ /t/ /âr/. Repeat the sounds: /s/ /t/ /âr/. Let's blend the sounds: /sss /t/ /âr/, /ssstâr/,* stare. *We made one word:* stare.

Repeat this routine with the following sounds:

/w/ /âr/   /p/ /âr/   /sh/ /âr/   /f/ /âr/

You Do *It's your turn. Blend the sounds I say together to form a word.*

/d/ /âr/   /k/ /âr/   /r/ /âr/   /b/ /âr/   /s/ /k/ /âr/

Repeat the blending routine with additional *r*-controlled *air, are, ear* words.

PHONEME ADDITION

TIER 2

OBJECTIVES

CCSS Isolate and pronounce initial, medial vowel, and final sounds (phonemes) in spoken single-syllable words. **RF.1.2c**

Add beginning sounds to form new words

I Do Explain to children that they will be adding sounds to make new words. *Listen as I say this word: air. I will add /sh/ to the beginning of* air *to make a new word. Listen: /sh/ /âr/, /shâr/,* share. *I made the word* share.

We Do *Listen as I say the word* race. *Say it with me:* race. *Let's add /b/ to the beginning of* race. *Say it with me: /b/ /rās/. What word do we make when we add /b/ to the beginning of* race? *We get* brace.

Repeat this routine with the following words:

/s/ tear (stare)   /f/ air (fair)   /h/ owl (howl)   /k/ lock (clock)

You Do *I will say a word and a sound. Add the sound and the word to make a new word.*

/s/ pear (spare)   /s/ care (scare)   /ch/ air (chair)   /g/ lair (glare)

Repeat the addition routine with other words.

PHONEME DELETION

OBJECTIVES

Segment spoken single-syllable words into their complete sequence of individual sounds (phonemes). **RF.1.2d**

Delete beginning sounds in words

 I Do Explain to children that they will be deleting beginning sounds in words. *Remember, when you delete a sound, you take a sound away.*

Listen as I say a word: scare, */skâr/. I will take away /s/ from the beginning of* scare. *That leaves /k/ /âr/. Scare without /s/ is* care.

 We Do *Listen as I say a word:* throw. *Say the word with me, /thrō/. Let's take away /th/ from the beginning of* throw. *That leaves /r/ /ō/. Let's blend: /r ō/,* row. *Throw without /th/ is* row. *Repeat this routine with the following words:*

(b)rush   (s)hare   (t)rain   (s)pare

 You Do *It's your turn. Take away the first sound to form a new word.*

(h)air   (p)late   (ch)in   (s)care

PHONEME REVERSAL

OBJECTIVES

Isolate and pronounce initial, medial vowel, and final sounds (phonemes) in spoken single-syllable words. **RF.1.2c**

Reverse sounds in words to form new words

 I Do Explain to children that they will blend sounds to form words, then reverse the sound order to form new words. *I will blend the sounds to form a word: /n/ /a/ /p/, /naaap/,* nap. *Now I will reverse the order of the sounds and blend them: /p/ /a/ /n/, /paaan/,* pan. *When I reverse the sounds in* nap, *I get the word* pan.

 We Do *Listen: /t/ /o/ /p/. Let's blend: /t/ /o/ /p/, /tooop/,* top. *Let's reverse the order of the sounds and blend: /p/ /o/ /t/, /pooot/,* pot. *We get the word* pot *when we reverse* top. *Repeat with the following sounds:*

/b/ /a/ /t/   /n/ /e/ /t/   /k/ /a/ /b/

 You Do *It's your turn. I'll say some sounds. Blend the sounds to say a word. Then reverse the order of the sounds and blend them to say a new word.*

/l/ /ā/ /t/   /p/ /i/ /n/   /p/ /o/ /p/   /k/ /ā/ /m/   /b/ /u/ /s/

 ENGLISH LANGUAGE LEARNERS

For the **children** who need **phonemic awareness**, **decoding**, and **fluency** practice, use scaffolding methods as necessary to ensure children understand the meaning of the words. Refer to the Language Transfers Handbook for phonics elements that may not transfer in children's native languages.

Phonics

CONNECT *air, are, ear* TO /âr/

OBJECTIVES

 Know and apply grade level phonics and word analysis skills in decoding words. **RF.1.3**

 I Do

Display the **Word-Building Card** *air. These are lowercase* a, i, *and* r. *Together they stand for /âr/. I am going to trace the letters* air *while I say /âr/.* Trace the letters *air* while saying /âr/ five times. Repeat for *are* and *ear*.

 We Do

Now do it with me. Have children take turns saying /âr/ while using their fingers to trace lowercase *air*. Then have them say /âr/ as they use their fingers to trace the letters *air* five more times. Repeat for *are* and *ear*.

 You Do

Have children connect the letters *air* to /âr/ by saying /âr/ as they trace lowercase *air* on paper five to ten times. Then ask them to write the letters *air* while saying /âr/ five to ten times. Repeat for *are* and *ear*.

Repeat, connecting the letters *air, are,* and *ear* to /âr/ through tracing and writing the letters throughout the week.

BLEND WORDS WITH /âr/ *air, are, ear*

OBJECTIVES

 Decode regularly spelled one-syllable words. **RF.1.3b**

Blend and decode words with r-controlled *air, are, ear*

 I Do

Display Word-Building Cards *p, ear. This is the letter* p. *It stands for /p/. Say it with me: /p/. These are the letters* a, e, *and* r. *Together they stand for /âr/. Let's say it together: /âr/. I'll blend the sounds together: /pâr/,* pear.

 We Do

Guide children to blend the sounds and read: *pair, hare, wear, share, stair.*

Have children blend and read: *air, bear, bare, fair, fare, spare, wear.*

 You Do

Repeat, blending additional r-controlled *air, are, ear* words.

You may wish to review Phonics with **ELL** using this section.

BUILD WORDS WITH /âr/ *air, are, ear*

OBJECTIVES

(CCSS) Decode regularly spelled one-syllable words. **RF.1.3b**

Build and decode words with *r*-controlled *air, are, ear*

 I Do Display Word-Building Cards *h, air. These are the letters* h, a, i, *and* r. H *stands for* /h/. A, i, *and* r *stand for* /âr/. *I will blend the sounds:* /h/ /âr/, /hâr/, hair. *The word is* hair.

 We Do *Let's do one together.* Place the letter *c* before *hair. Let's blend the new word:* /ch/ /âr/, /châr/, chair.

Change the letters *ch* to *p. Let's blend and read the new word:* /p/ /âr/, /pâr/, pair.

 You Do Have children build and read the words *pear, bear, bare, care, scare, share, hare, ware, wear, swear.*

Repeat, building additional words with *air, are,* and *ear.*

BLEND WORDS WITH /âr/ *air, are, ear*

OBJECTIVES

(CCSS) Decode regularly spelled one-syllable words. **RF.1.3b**

Build and decode words with *r*-controlled *air, are, ear*

 I Do Display Word-Building Cards *f, air. These are the letters* f, a, i, r. F *stands for* /f/. A, i, r *stand for* /âr/. *Listen:* /f/ /âr/, /fâr/, fair. *The word is* fair.

 We Do Blend and read *pair, wear, stair,* and *compare* with children.

 You Do Display the words to the right. Have children blend and read the words.

Decodable Reader Have children read "A Pair at the Fair" (pages 81–84) and "The Bears Prepare a Feast" (89–92).

share	pear	hare	air	bear	affair
glare	chair	pair	rare	aware	square
hair	hay	star	stare	store	scary

shared careful thread wrap marble armchair

Blair had a nightmare about a scary bear.

Who took care of the mare at the fair?

I sat in an airplane chair and ate a pear.

BUILD FLUENCY WITH PHONICS

Sound-Spellings Fluency

Display the following Word-Building Cards: *air, are, ear, scr, spl, spr, str, thr, shr, wr, kn, gn, au, aw, augh, ew, ue, ui, ow, oy, oi, ar, ore, oar, er, ir, ur, ey, igh, oa.* Have children say the sounds. Repeat and vary the pace.

Fluency in Connected Text

Have children review the **Decodable Reader** selections. Identify /âr/ words. Blend words as needed. Have partners reread the selections for fluency.

→ **Approaching Level**

Structural Analysis

REVIEW *r*-CONTROLLED SYLLABLES

OBJECTIVES
 Use knowledge that every syllable must have a vowel sound to determine the number of syllables in a printed word. **RF.1.3d**

Read words with *r*-controlled syllables

 I Do Remind children that a syllable is a word part that has one vowel sound. Write and read the word *airplane*. Repeat the word as you clap the syllables. *I hear two vowel sounds in* airplane, /âr/ *and* /ā/, *so I know* airplane *has two syllables,* air *and* plane. Draw a line between the syllables. *When the letter* r *follows one or two vowels, the vowels and the letter* r *stay in the same syllable.*

 We Do Write and read the word *hairy* and have children repeat. *How many syllables do you hear in* hairy? (2) Underline *air. Remember that when* r *follows one or two vowels, the vowel/s and* r *stay in the same syllable. Let's break* hairy *into syllables:* hair/y. Repeat with *turkey, armchair, surprise,* and *staircase.*

 You Do Have partners divide these words into syllables and then blend the syllables to read the words: *harvest, order, market, party, forest.*

Repeat Ask partners to continue with *hornet, garden,* and *careless.*

RETEACH *r*-CONTROLLED SYLLABLES

OBJECTIVES
 Use knowledge that every syllable must have a vowel sound to determine the number of syllables in a printed word. **RF.1.3d**

Read words with *r*-controlled syllables

 I Do Write and read the syllables *stair* and *case. When a vowel or vowel team is followed by the letter* r, *the* r *affects the vowel sound. When this happens, the vowel and* r *are in the same syllable. I hear* /âr/ *in* stair. Stair *is one syllable.* Case *is a syllable. I hear* /ā/ *in* case. *I will blend the syllables:* /stârkās/, staircase.

 We Do Write and read *surprise.* Surprise *has two syllables,* /sûr/ *and* /prīz/. Draw a line between *sur* and *prise. Let's say the syllables together:* /sûr/ /prīz/. *Now let's blend the syllables to read the word:* /sûr/ /prīz/, /sûrprīz/, surprise.

 You Do *Now it's your turn. Divide the words I say into syllables.*

air/plane   care/ful   tur/tle   pur/ple   ti/ger

Repeat Have partners divide *wearing, hairless, perfect,* and *harvest* into syllables.

Words to Know

REVIEW HIGH-FREQUENCY WORDS

OBJECTIVES

Recognize and read grade-appropriate irregularly spelled words. **RF.1.3g**

Review *favorite, few, gone, surprise, wonder, young*

 I Do Use the **High-Frequency Word Cards** to **Read/Spell/Write** each high-frequency word. Use each word orally in a sentence.

 We Do Guide children to Read/Spell/Write each word on their **Response Boards**. Help them generate oral sentences for the words.

 You Do Have partners work together to Read/Spell/Write the words *favorite, few, gone, surprise, wonder,* and *young*. Ask them to say sentences for the words.

CUMULATIVE REVIEW

OBJECTIVES

Recognize and read grade-appropriate irregularly spelled words. **RF.1.3g**

Review previously taught high-frequency words

 I Do Display the High-Frequency Word Cards from the previous weeks. Use the Read/Spell/Write routine to review each word.

 We Do Guide children to Read/Spell/Write the words on their Response Boards. Have them complete sentence frames. *Before I go tomorrow, I will ____. The children heard their dog ____. My mother, father, and brother love to ____.*

 You Do Have partners display and read the words, then use the words in sentences.

Fluency Display the High-Frequency Word Cards. Point to words in random order. Have children chorally read each word. Repeat at a faster pace.

REVIEW VOCABULARY WORDS

OBJECTIVES

Determine or clarify the meaning of unknown and multiple-meaning words and phrases based on grade 1 reading and content, choosing flexibly from an array of strategies. **L.1.4**

 I Do Display **Visual Vocabulary Cards** for *nation* and *unite*. Review each word using the Define/Example/Ask routine.

 We Do Invite children to name some nations. Then have children stand separately. Ask them to unite into one group. Ask how that helps them understand how states unite to form a nation. Then work with them to complete these sentence starters: **(1)** *A nation is ____.* **(2)** *Sometimes people unite to ____.*

You Do Have partners write two sentences on their own, using each of the words. Provide assistance as needed.

Comprehension

READ FOR FLUENCY

OBJECTIVES

 Read grade-level text orally with accuracy, appropriate rate, and expression. **RF.1.4b**

 I Do Read the first page of the Practice Book selection aloud. Model using appropriate phrasing.

 We Do Read the second page aloud and have children repeat each sentence after you. Point out how you pause slightly when you read a sentence with a comma. Children should also note how you stop briefly for a period.

 You Do Have children read the rest of the selection aloud. Remind them to use appropriate phrasing when they come to certain punctuation.

IDENTIFY MAIN IDEA

TIER
2

OBJECTIVES

 Ask and answer questions about key details in a text. **RL.1.3**

 I Do Remind children that details in an informational text tell about the main idea. *When I read an informational text, I look for details in the pictures and in the words. Then I use those details to help me figure out the main idea, or what the details have in common.*

 We Do Read the first two pages of the Practice Book selection aloud. Pause to discuss details. *What are some details we read? What day is the first day of the year? Those are details that will help me figure out the main idea.*

 You Do Guide children as they read the rest of the Practice Book selection. Prompt them to note details in the words and pictures. Then help them use the details to determine the main idea: People have favorite days of the year.

REVIEW AUTHOR'S PURPOSE

OBJECTIVES

Identify the main purpose of a text, including what the author wants to answer, explain, or describe. **RI.2.6**

Identify author's purpose

 I Do
Remind children that an author has a reason, or purpose, for writing a selection. *When I read an informational text, I ask myself these questions:* Why is the author writing this selection? Does the author want to explain something, describe something, or give me information? *I look for clues that answer my questions. That helps me figure out the author's purpose.*

 We Do
Read the first page of the Practice Book selection together. Pause to discuss clues about the author's purpose. *What did we read about? Yes, we read that some people have favorite days. That's a clue to the author's purpose. The author will give me information.* Record the clue on an Author's Purpose chart.

 You Do
Guide children as they continue to read the selection. Pause to have them identify clues about the author's purpose. Record their responses on the chart.

SELF-SELECTED READING

OBJECTIVES

With prompting and support, read informational texts appropriately complex for grade 1. **RI.1.10**

Identify the main purpose of a text, including what the author wants to answer, explain, or describe. **RI.2.6**

Apply the strategy and skill to read a text

Read Independently

Have children pick an informational text for sustained silent reading. Remind them to:

- look for clues about the author's purpose.
- use the clues to figure out the author's purpose.
- reread to help them understand and remember clues and details.

Read Purposefully

Have children record clues on an Author's Purpose chart. After reading, guide children to participate in a group discussion about the selection they read. Guide children to:

- share the information they recorded on their Author's Purpose charts.
- tell how clues helped them identify the author's purpose.
- explain how rereading helped them understand the selection.

On Level

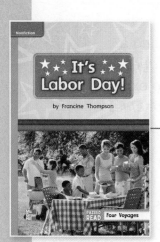

Lexile 620

OBJECTIVES

Identify the main purpose of a text, including what the author wants to answer, explain, or describe. **RI.2.6**

Leveled Reader:
It's Labor Day!

Before Reading

Preview and Predict

Have children turn to the title page. Read the title and author name and have children repeat. Preview the selection's photographs. Prompt children to predict what the selection might be about.

Go Digital

It's Labor Day!

Review Genre: Informational Text/Nonfiction

Have children recall informational text gives facts and details about real people, places, events, or things. Information is presented in a logical order.

ESSENTIAL QUESTION

Remind children of the Essential Question: *Why do we celebrate holidays?* Set a purpose for reading: *Let's read to find out why we celebrate Labor Day.* Remind children that as they read a selection, they can ask questions about what they do not understand.

Graphic Organizer

During Reading

Guided Comprehension

As children whisper read *It's Labor Day!* monitor and provide guidance, correcting blending and modeling the key strategies and skills. Point out the glossary and index on page 15. Tells students they can use the glossary to look up unfamiliar words.

Retell

Strategy: Reread

Remind children that if they miss an important point, they can reread the page. Model using the strategy on page 3. Say: *I want to be sure I understand why we celebrate Labor Day. I'll reread the page.* Reread the page. *I see. We celebrate Labor Day to honor working men and women.*

Skill: Author's Purpose

Remind children that the author's purpose is the reason why an author writes a text, such as to entertain readers, or to tell information about something. As you read, ask: *What clues tell us why the author may have written this?* Display an Author's Purpose chart for children to copy.

Model recording answers for children. Have children copy the answers into their own charts.

Think Aloud As I read, I will look for clues to help me understand the author's purpose. I see on page 3 the author gives information about why we celebrate Labor Day. I'll write this clue in my chart. I'll look to see if other details also give information.

Prompt children to fill in their charts as they read.

After Reading

Respond to Reading

Complete the Respond to Reading on page 11.

Retell

Have children take turns retelling the selection, using the **Retelling Cards** as a guide. Help children make a connection: *Think about the ways to celebrate Labor Day. Which one would you like to do next year?*

Model Fluency

Read the sentences one at a time. Have children chorally repeat. Point out to children how you use particular groups of words.

Apply Have partners practice reading. Provide feedback as needed.

PAIRED READ ...

"Four Voyages"

Make Connections:
Write About It Analytical Writing

Before reading, ask children to note that the genre of this text is nonfiction. Then discuss the Compare Texts direction. After reading, ask children to make connections between the information they learned from "Four Voyages" and *It's Labor Day! What two holidays did we learn about? How are they the same? How are they different?*

Leveled Reader

FOCUS ON SOCIAL STUDIES

Children can extend their knowledge of workers by completing the social studies activity on page 16.

Literature Circles

Lead children in conducting a literature circle using the Thinkmark questions to guide the discussion. You may wish to discuss what children have learned about holidays from reading the two selections in the Leveled Reader.

Level Up

Level-up lessons available online.

IF children can read *It's Labor Day!* On Level with fluency and correctly answer the Respond to Reading questions,

THEN tell children that they will read a more detailed version of the selection.

• Use pages 2 and 3 of *It's Labor Day!* Beyond Level to model using Teaching Poster 38 to list clues to the author's purpose.

• Have children read the selection, checking their comprehension by using the graphic organizer.

On Level

Phonics

BUILD WORDS WITH /âr/

OBJECTIVES

Know and apply grade-level phonics and word analysis skills in decoding words. **RF.1.3**

Decode regularly spelled one-syllable words. **RF.1.3b**

Build and decode words with r-controlled *air, are, ear*

 Display **Word-Building Cards** *h, air. These are the letters* h, a, i, *and* r. *The* a, i, *and* r *together stand for the /âr/ sounds, so the letters stand for /h/ and /âr/. I will blend /h/ and /âr/ together: /hâr/,* hair. *The word is* hair.

 Now let's do one together. Change the letter *h* in *hair* to *p. Let's blend and read the new word: /p/ /âr/, /pâr/,* pair. *The new word is* pair.

 Have children build and blend these words: *fair, fare, care, scare, spare, share, hare, bare, bear, pear.*

Repeat with additional *r*-controlled *air, are, ear* words.

Decodable Reader Have children read "A Pair at the Fair," "Lights in the Air," "The Bears Prepare a Feast," and "Leaders Care" (pages 81–96).

Words to Know

REVIEW WORDS

OBJECTIVES

Recognize and read grade-appropriate irregularly spelled words. **RF.1.3g**

Review high-frequency words *favorite, few, gone, surprise, wonder, young* and vocabulary words *nation* and *unite*

 Use the **Read/Spell/Write** routine to review each high-frequency and vocabulary word. Use each word orally in a sentence.

 Guide children to Read/Spell/Write each word using their **Response Boards**. Then work with the group to generate oral sentences for the words.

 Have partners use the Read/Spell/Write routine on their own using the high-frequency words *favorite, few, gone, surprise, wonder,* and *young* and the vocabulary words *nation* and *unite*. Have partners write sentences about a special day or holiday. Tell them that each sentence should contain at least one high-frequency or vocabulary word.

Comprehension

REVIEW AUTHOR'S PURPOSE

OBJECTIVES

 Identify the main purpose of a text, including what the author wants to answer, explain, or describe. **RI.2.6**

Identify author's purpose

 I Do Remind children that an author's purpose is the reason the author writes a selection. *When I read a selection, I look for clues about the author's purpose. Then I use the clues to help me figure out the purpose.*

 We Do Read the first page of the Practice Book selection aloud. Pause to discuss the author's purpose. *We read a question about favorite days. Why might that clue help you understand the author's purpose?*

 You Do Guide children to read the rest of the Practice Book selection. Remind them to look for clues about the author's purpose. Then invite children to identify the purpose for each page and for the whole selection.

SELF-SELECTED READING

OBJECTIVES

 With prompting and support, read informational texts appropriately complex for grade 1. **RI.1.10**

Apply the strategy and skill to read a text

Read Independently

Have children pick an informational text for sustained silent reading. Remind them to:

- think about the author's purpose for writing the selection.
- reread to help them find clues about the author's purpose.
- use context to confirm or self-correct word recognition and understanding.

Read Purposefully

Have children record details on an Author's Purpose chart. After reading, guide partners to:

- share the information they recorded on their Author's Purpose chart.
- tell how clues helped them identify the author's purpose.
- explain how rereading helped them understand the selection.
- discuss the differences between selections that give information and those that tell stories.

→ Beyond Level

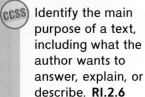

Lexile 660

 OBJECTIVES

Identify the main purpose of a text, including what the author wants to answer, explain, or describe. **RI.2.6**

Leveled Reader:
It's Labor Day!

It's Labor Day!

Graphic Organizer

Before Reading

Preview and Predict

Read the title and author name. Have children preview the title page and the photographs. Ask: *What do you think you will learn about in this text?*

Review Genre: Informational Text/Nonfiction

Have children recall that informational text gives facts and details about real people, places, events, or things. Prompt children to name key characteristics of informational text. Tell them to look for these as they read the Leveled Reader.

ESSENTIAL QUESTION

Remind children of the Essential Question: *Why do we celebrate holidays?* Set a purpose for reading: *Let's find out how and why we celebrate Labor Day.*

During Reading

Guided Comprehension

Have children whisper read *It's Labor Day!* Have them place self-stick notes next to difficult words. Remind children that when they come to an unfamiliar word, they can look for familiar spellings. Point out the glossary and index on page 15. Remind students that they can use the glossary to look up unfamiliar words in the selection.

Monitor children's reading. Stop periodically and ask open-ended questions to facilitate rich discussion, such as, *What does the author want you to know about Labor Day in this part of the text?* Build on children's responses to develop deeper understanding of the text.

Strategy: Reread

Remind children that they can reread the text if they misread something. *Rereading helps you understand part of a text that you may not have understood the first time you read it.*

Skill: Author's Purpose

Remind children the author's purpose is the reason an author writes a text, such as to entertain or tell information about something. As you read, ask: *What clues help you figure out the author's purpose?* Display an Author's Purpose chart for children to copy. Model how to record the information.

Think Aloud Page 2 has the date of the first Labor Day. On page 3 there is information about what Labor Day is. I'll write these clues in my chart to help me identify the reason or purpose the author wrote this text.

Have children fill in their charts as they read.

After Reading

Respond to Reading

Have children complete the Respond to Reading on page 11.

Retell

Have children take turns retelling the selection. Help children make a personal connection by writing about a holiday they enjoy. *Tell what you celebrate on this holiday and how you celebrate it.*

PAIRED READ ...

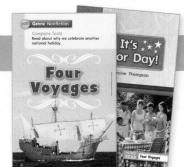

"Four Voyages"

Make Connections: Write About It

Before reading "Four Voyages," have children preview the title page and prompt them to identify the genre. Discuss the Compare Texts direction. After reading, have children work with a partner to discuss the information they learned in "Four Voyages" and *It's Labor Day!* Ask children to make connections by comparing and contrasting each selection. Prompt children to discuss how the celebrations for the holidays are the same and how they are different.

Leveled Reader

FOCUS ON SOCIAL STUDIES

Children can extend their knowledge of workers they know by completing the social studies activity on page 16.

Literature Circles

Lead children in conducting a literature circle using the Thinkmark questions to guide the discussion. You may wish to discuss what children have learned about holidays in both selections in the Leveled Reader.

Gifted and Talented

SYNTHESIZE Challenge children to choose a kind of worker that they would honor on Labor Day. Encourage them to use ideas from the selection.

HAVE them use facts they learned from the week or do additional research to find out more about the specific worker they choose.

Vocabulary

OBJECTIVES

Use sentence-level context as a clue to the meaning of a word or phrase. **L.1.4a**

Determine the meaning of domain-specific words

 Review the meaning of the oral vocabulary word *pride*.

A multiple-meaning word is a word with more than one meaning. *If you feel pride in something, you are proud of it. For example, people take pride in their country.* Pride *also means "a group of lions." Lions live in a pride.*

 Have children say sentences for the different meanings of *pride*.

 Challenge partners to think of or use a dictionary to find at least two meanings for *design*. ("the way something is arranged" and "work out the details of") Then have them say sentences for each meaning.

 Extend Have children draw a picture of a design that they would take pride in. Then have them design a zoo enclosure for a pride of lions. Invite them to discuss their work.

Gifted and Talented

OBJECTIVES

Use sentence-level context as a clue to the meaning of a word or phrase. **L.1.4.a**

 Review the meaning of *nation* with children. Write: *The United States is a nation.* Read the sentence and have children repeat. Discuss what a nation is. *The United States is a nation, or country, that is made up of 50 states. Nation has more than one meaning. Nation can mean "a group of people who live in an area and have the same government." Nation can also refer to a Native American tribe.*

 Use *nation* in sentences to show its different meanings. Have children tell which meaning is used in each sentence. *Sometimes the president speaks to the nation. Many nations are members of the United Nations. The people are part of the Iroquois nation.*

 Have partners use the different meanings of the word *nation* in sentences. Ask them to tell what nation they would like to live in and why. Then have them identify as many Native American nations as they can.

Comprehension

REVIEW AUTHOR'S PURPOSE

OBJECTIVES

Identify the main purpose of a text, including what the author wants to answer, explain, or describe. **RI.2.6**

Identify author's purpose

I Do

Discuss with children what an author's purpose is and how they can figure out the author's purpose. *What are some purposes authors have for writing informational text? How can clues help you figure out the author's purpose?*

We Do

Ask children to read the first page of the Practice Book selection aloud. Pause to discuss the author's purpose. *What is one clue on this page that will help you figure out the author's purpose?*

You Do

Have children read the rest of the Practice Book selection independently. Remind them to look for clues about the author's purpose. Then ask them to identify the purpose for each page and for the whole selection.

SELF-SELECTED READING

OBJECTIVES

With prompting and support, read informational text appropriately complex for grade 1. **RI.1.10**

Apply the strategy and skill to read a text

Read Independently

Have children choose an informational text for sustained silent reading. Tell them that they should use an Author's Purpose chart to record clues about the author's purpose.

Read Purposefully

Have children record the clues in an Author's Purpose chart as they read. After reading, guide children to:

- share the information they recorded on the chart with a partner and discuss the author's purpose.

- record information about the selection in a reading response journal.

Gifted and Talented

Independent Study Have children create posters for their selections. Tell them to include the title, a summary, and the author's purpose on their posters. Ask them to draw pictures to represent what they found the most interesting. Have them write sentences to tell why the information was interesting to them.

→ English Language Learners

Reading/Writing Workshop

OBJECTIVES

CCSS Identify the main purpose of a text, including what the author wants to answer, explain, or describe. **RI.2.6**

Shared Read

Share the Harvest and Give Thanks

Go Digital

Share the Harvest and Give Thanks

Before Reading

Build Background

Read the Essential Question: *Why do we celebrate holidays?*

- Explain the meaning of the Essential Question. *A holiday is a special day. A holiday usually honors a person or an important event. People celebrate holidays in different ways.*

- **Model an answer:** *My family really enjoys the Fourth of July. We like to celebrate the birthday of the United States. We go to a local parade. We have a picnic. We watch fireworks at night. We have lots of fun!*

- Ask children a question that ties the Essential Question to their own background knowledge. *What holiday do you like to celebrate?* Ask partners to share their answers.

Graphic Organizer

During Reading

Interactive Question-Response

- Ask questions that help children understand the meaning of the text after each paragraph.

- Reinforce the meanings of key vocabulary by providing meanings embedded in the questions.

- Ask children questions that require them to use key vocabulary.

- Reinforce the comprehension strategies and skills of the week by modeling.

Share the Harvest and Give Thanks

Pages 302–303

Point to the title. *Listen as I read the title of this selection.* Point to each word as you read it. *Let's read it together:* Share the Harvest and Give Thanks.

Let's read the first sentence on page 303 together: Each year, farmers pick crops from their fields. Crops are plants that we eat. The farmers share or sell the crops. The photo shows a farm stand with lots of harvest foods! What foods do you see? (corn, tomatoes, apples, pumpkins)

Pages 304–305

People in the United States give thanks for the fall harvest. They celebrate a special holiday—Thanksgiving. Say that word with me: Thanksgiving. *It is on the fourth Thursday in November. November is in the fall season. What is the weather like in the fall?* (cooler)

 What harvest foods do you like to eat?

Pages 306–307

The first Thanksgiving was a long time ago. People who came to America were thankful to have food. Point to the third sentence on page 306. *Let's read what they ate:* They ate duck, deer, corn, and squash. *Have you eaten any of those foods? Which ones?*

Point to the photo on page 307. *This family is celebrating Thanksgiving. They are sitting down to a meal. What are they eating?* (turkey, corn, potatoes)

Explain and Model the Skill *The author's purpose is the reason an author wrote a selection. This selection has lots of facts and details about harvest celebrations. The author wrote to help readers learn about harvest celebrations.*

Explain and Model High-Frequency Words
Point to the word *favorite* and have children say it with you. Favorite *means something that you like more than other things. My favorite food is carrots.*

 What is your favorite harvest food?

Pages 308–309

Let's look at the photo on page 308. What do you see? (many people dressed like pilgrims) *These people are acting out the first Thanksgiving. They are wearing costumes.*

Look at the photo on page 309. The photo shows a game that families play. What are the players doing? (trying to throw a bag into a hole)

Explain and Model Phonics Reread page 308. *Listen to these sentences. Raise your hand when you hear a word with the /âr/ sounds.* (fairs, affair, wear)

Pages 310–311

Explain and Model the Strategy *On page 310, I don't understand what Kwanzaa is. I am going to reread to figure out why people celebrate Kwanzaa. Reread the page. Now I understand. Kwanzaa celebrates the harvest season. People celebrate Kwanzaa to give thanks for harvest crops.*

What are people doing in the giant pumpkins? (using them as boats; racing them)

Point to the map on page 311. *What does the key show?* (what the symbols on the map mean)

 How do people celebrate the harvest? (Some celebrate Thanksgiving, others celebrate Kwanzaa. Harvest foods are eaten and thanks is given. There are also parades and games.)

After Reading

Make Connections

• Review the Essential Question.

→ English Language Learners

Lexile 360

 OBJECTIVES

Identify the main purpose of a text, including what the author wants to answer, explain, or describe. **RI.2.6**

Leveled Reader:
It's Labor Day!

Go Digital

It's Labor Day!

Before Reading

Preview

Read the title. Ask: *What is the title? Say it again.* Repeat with the author's name. Preview the photographs. Have children describe the photos. Use simple language to tell about each page. Follow with questions, such as *How does this photo help us learn about Labor Day?*

ESSENTIAL QUESTION

Remind children of the Essential Question: *Why do we celebrate holidays?* Say: *Let's read to find out why we celebrate Labor Day.* Encourage children to ask for help when they do not understand a word or phrase.

Graphic Organizer

During Reading

Interactive Question-Response

Pages 2–3 *In what month is Labor Day?* (September) *We honor workers on Labor Day. How is work different now than in the past?* (The workday was long; no rest; children worked; work was unsafe.)

Pages 4–5 *Work is safer now. What are some laws that protect workers?* (Workers can take breaks; children can't work; children must go to school.) *Why do we celebrate Labor Day?* (to say "thank you" to workers)

Retell

Pages 6–7 *How do some cities celebrate Labor Day?* (with parades, music, a dance) *Talk with your partner about things you might see in a parade.*

Pages 8–9 *Look at the pictures. What are these two families doing?* (having a picnic; eating outside; relaxing) *Labor Day is a day to play. What games do you like to play outside?*

Pages 10–11 *Labor Day is in September, at the end of the summer. How are these people celebrating Labor Day?* (vacationing at the beach) *What other fun ways to celebrate Labor Day did we read about?* (parade, music, dance, picnic, outside games) *Talk with your partner about what happens after Labor Day.* (school starts)

After Reading

Respond to Reading

Revisit the Essential Question. Ask children to work with partners to fill in the graphic organizer and answer the questions on page 12. Pair children with peers of varying language abilities.

Retell

Model retelling using the **Retelling Card** prompts. Say: *Look at the photographs. Use details to help you retell the selection.* Help children make personal connections by asking: *Which way do you think is the most fun way to celebrate Labor Day?*

Phrasing Fluency

Read the pages in the book, one at a time. Help children echo-read the pages expressively and with appropriate phrasing. Point out how they should pause slightly for commas in sentences and stop briefly for periods.

Apply Have children practice reading with partners. Pair children with peers of varying language abilities. Provide feedback as needed.

Literature Circles

Lead children in conducting a literature circle using the Thinkmark questions to guide the discussion. You may wish to discuss what children have learned about holidays from reading the two selections in the Leveled Reader.

Level Up

Level-up lessons available online.

PAIRED READ ...

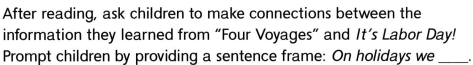

Leveled Reader

"Four Voyages"

Make Connections: Write About It *Analytical Writing*

Before reading, tell chil pecnilWritingdren to note that this text is nonfiction. Then discuss the Compare Texts direction.

After reading, ask children to make connections between the information they learned from "Four Voyages" and *It's Labor Day!* Prompt children by providing a sentence frame: *On holidays we ____.*

IF children can read *It's Labor Day!* ELL Level with fluency and correctly answer the Respond to Reading questions,

THEN tell children that they will read a more detailed version of the selection.

• Use pages 2–3 of *It's Labor Day!* On Level to model using Teaching Poster 38 to list clues to the author's purpose.

• Have children read the selection, checking their comprehension by using the graphic organizer.

FOCUS ON SOCIAL STUDIES

Children can extend their knowledge of workers they know by completing the social studies activity on page 16.

ENGLISH LANGUAGE LEARNERS **T385**

Vocabulary

PRETEACH ORAL VOCABULARY

OBJECTIVES

CCSS Produce complete sentences when appropriate to task and situation. **SL.1.6**

LANGUAGE OBJECTIVE

Use oral vocabulary words

 I Do Display images from the **Visual Vocabulary Cards** one at a time and follow the routine to preteach the oral vocabulary words *pride* and *display*.

 We Do Display the image again and explain how it illustrates or demonstrates the word. Model using sentences to describe the image.

 You Do Display the word again and have partners discuss how this picture demonstrates the word.

Beginning	Intermediate	Advanced/High
Have children draw things they take pride in. Say a sentence about each picture that includes the word *pride*.	Have children draw things they take pride in. Have them tell about their pictures: *I take pride in ___ because ____.*	Challenge partners to draw things they take pride in. Have them create a display of the pictures, then share and discuss.

PRETEACH VOCABULARY

OBJECTIVES

CCSS Participate in collaborate conversations with diverse partners about grade 1 topics and texts with peers and adults in small and larger groups. **SL.1.1**

LANGUAGE OBJECTIVE

Use vocabulary words

I Do Display images from the **ELL Visual Vocabulary Cards** one at a time and follow the routine to preteach the vocabulary words *honor* and *relax*. Say the word and have children repeat it. Define the word in English.

We Do Display the image again and ask children to tell how it illustrates or demonstrates the word. Model using sentences to describe the image.

 You Do Display each word again. Have children say the word and spell it. Have them use the words in speaking and writing. Give sentence starters.

Beginning	Intermediate	Advanced/High
Say a sentence about an image. Have children repeat the sentence and match it to its picture.	Say sentences about the images, leaving out vocabulary words. Have children repeat sentences with the words.	Ask children to use the words to ask and answer questions about the images.

Words to Know

REVIEW WORDS

CCSS OBJECTIVES
Recognize and read grade-appropriate irregularly spelled words. **RF.1.3g**

LANGUAGE OBJECTIVE
Use high-frequency words *favorite, few, gone, surprise, wonder, young,* and vocabulary words *nation, unite*

 I Do

Display the **High-Frequency Word Cards** and **Vocabulary Cards** for *favorite, few, gone, surprise, wonder, young* and *nation* and *unite*. Read each word. Use the **Read/Spell/Write** routine to teach each word. Have children write the words on their **Response Boards**.

 We Do

Write sentence frames on separate lines. Track the print as children read and complete the sentences: **(1)** *My favorite game is ____.* **(2)** *A few of my pals and I like to ____.* **(3)** *When all the food is gone, we ____.* **(4)** *I got a big surprise when ____.* **(5)** *I wonder ____.* **(6)** *The young kitten is ____.* **(7)** *This nation is ____.* **(8)** *If we unite, we ____.*

 You Do

Display the High-Frequency Word Cards from the previous weeks. Display one card at a time as children chorally read the word. Mix and repeat. Note words children need to review. Repeat with vocabulary words.

Beginning	Intermediate	Advanced/High
Display cards and read the words together. Use words in sentences and have children point to the card.	List the words. Have children work together to form and read the words.	List the words and read them together. Give clues and have children name the word.

RETEACH HIGH-FREQUENCY WORDS

 CCSS OBJECTIVES
Recognize and read grade-appropriate irregularly spelled words. **RF.1.3g**

LANGUAGE OBJECTIVE
Use high-frequency words

 I Do

Display each Visual Vocabulary Card and say the word aloud. Define the word in English and, if appropriate, in Spanish. Identify any cognates.

 We Do

Point to the image again and explain how it illustrates or demonstrates the word. Ask children to repeat the word. Engage children in structured partner-talk about the image as prompted on the back of the card. Ask children to chorally say the word three times.

  You Do

Display each visual in random order, hiding the word. Have children identify the word and define it in their own words.

Beginning	Intermediate	Advanced/High
Say a sentence with the word and have children repeat.	Have children complete sentences frames for the words.	Have partners take turns using the words in oral sentences.

English Language Learners
Writing/Spelling

WRITING TRAIT: VOICE

OBJECTIVES

With guidance and support from adults, focus on a topic, respond to questions and suggestions from peers, and add details to strengthen writing as needed. **W.1.5**

LANGUAGE OBJECTIVE

Use personal voice in writing

 Explain that writers often let their personalities show in their work. Writers choose words and punctuation that reflect how they feel about a topic.

We Do Read page 308 of *Share the Harvest and Give Thanks*. The author writes, "In many states, Thanksgiving is a fun affair!" The reader knows that the author thinks how states celebrate Thanksgiving is fun and exciting. Read page 309 and point out the last sentence with the exclamation point.

You Do Have partners write a sentence about how they like to celebrate Thanksgiving or another holiday. Remind them to use words that show how they feel.

Beginning	Intermediate	Advanced/High
Name moods. Have children show that mood on their face and repeat the mood name.	Write a sentence on the board. Name a mood and have children say the sentence in that mood.	Have children convey the same idea (*It is snowing.*) in two different moods.

WORDS WITH *r*-CONTROLLED VOWELS *air, are, ear*

OBJECTIVES

Use conventional spelling for words with common spelling patterns and for frequently occurring irregular words. **L.1.2d**

LANGUAGE OBJECTIVE

Spell words with *r*-controlled vowels *air, are, ear*

 Read the first Spelling Word on page T326. Segment the word into sounds and attach a spelling to each sound. Point out the /âr/ sound and spelling. Read aloud, segment, and spell the remaining words. Have children repeat.

 Say a sentence for the first spelling word on page T326. Then say *fair* slowly. Have children repeat and write the word. Repeat the process for the remaining words.

 Display the words. Have partners check their spelling lists and correct misspelled words on their lists.

Beginning	Intermediate	Advanced/High
Help children say the words and copy them with the correct spelling.	After children have corrected their words, have pairs quiz each other.	Challenge children to think of other words that have the /âr/ sound.

Grammar

ADVERBS THAT TELL HOW

OBJECTIVES

 Demonstrate command of the conventions of standard English grammar and usage when writing or speaking. **L.1.1**

LANGUAGE OBJECTIVE

Understand and use adverbs that tell how

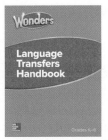

Language Transfers Handbook

TRANSFER SKILLS

Speakers of Haitian Creole, Hmong, and Khmer might use an adjective instead of an adverb. Provide extra support with adverbs that tell how by having children circle the *-ly* at the end and repeat the word stressing the *-ly*. Then have them repeat sentences: *I write neatly. I clap loudly. Please talk quietly.* Have them identify the adverb in each sentence.

 I Do Remind children that adverbs tell about verbs. Review adverbs that tell when. Have children clap. *We clap now. When do we clap? Yes. We clap now.* Now *is an adverb that tells when.* Explain that adverbs can also tell how. Have children clap slowly. Write and read *We clap slowly.* Circle *slowly.* Slowly *tells how we clap.* Slowly *is an adverb that tells how.* Repeat with *quickly* and *loudly.* Point out that many adverbs that tell how end in *-ly*.

 We Do Write the sentences on the board. Have children read each sentence and identify the adverb that tells how.

I walk slowly.

We write neatly in our notebooks.

I will gladly help you.

You may talk softly while you work.

 You Do Write the following sentence frames on the board:

I talk softly when ____. I talk loudly when ____. I walk slowly when ____. I walk quickly when ____.

Have partners complete each sentence frame. Circulate, listen in, and take note of each child's language use and proficiency.

Beginning	Intermediate	Advanced/High
Have children do things slowly, quickly, loudly, and softly. Say sentences without the prepositions. Have children use the correct preposition to complete each sentence.	Show magazine or selection photographs and have children use adverbs that tell how to describe what people, animals, or things do. *The stars shine brightly. The horse runs quickly.* Provide frames as needed.	Ask partners to say as many sentences with adverbs that tell how as they can to describe magazine or selection illustrations. Challenge them to write two sentences.

PROGRESS MONITORING

Unit 6 Week 5 Formal Assessment	Standards Covered	Component for Assessment
Comprehension Author's Purpose	RI.2.6	• *Selection Test* • *Weekly Assessment*
Vocabulary Strategy Metaphors	L.4.5a	• *Selection Test* • *Weekly Assessment*
Phonics *r*-Controlled Vowels *air, are, ear*	RF.1.3	*Weekly Assessment*
Structural Analysis *r*-Controlled Vowel Syllables	RF.1.3d, RF.1.3e	*Weekly Assessment*
High-Frequency Words *favorite, few, gone, surprise, wonder, young*	RF.1.3g	*Weekly Assessment*
Writing Writing About Text	RI.2.6	*Weekly Assessment*
Unit 6 Week 5 **Informal Assessment**		
Research/Listening/Collaborating	SL.1.1c, SL.1.2, SL.1.3	• *RWW* • *Teacher's Edition*
Oral Reading Fluency (ORF) **Fluency Goal:** 13-33 words correct per minute (WCPM) **Accuracy Rate Goal:** 95% or higher	RF.1.4a. RF.1.4b, RF.1.4c	*Fluency Assessment*

Using Assessment Results

Weekly Assessment Skills	If . . .	Then . . .
COMPREHENSION	Children answer 0–3 multiple-choice items correctly . . .	. . . assign Lessons 82–84 on Author's Purpose from the *Tier 2 Comprehension Intervention online PDFs*.
VOCABULARY	Children answer 0–2 multiple-choice items correctly . . .	. . . assign Lesson 113 on Metaphors from the *Tier 2 Vocabulary Intervention online PDFs*.
PHONICS/ STRUCTURAL ANALYSIS/HFW	Children answer 0–6 multiple-choice items correctly . . .	. . . assign Lesson 91 on *r*-Controlled Vowels /âr/ (*air, are, ear, ere*) and Lesson 111 on *r*-Controlled Vowel Syllables from the" *Tier 2 Phonics/Word Study Intervention online PDFs*.
WRITING	Children score less than "2" on the constructed response . . .	. . . reteach necessary skills using Section 13 on Write About Reading from the *Tier 2 Comprehension Intervention online PDFs*.
FLUENCY	Children have a WCPM score of 13 . . .	. . . assign a lesson from Section 1, 9, or 10 of the *Tier 2 Fluency Intervention online PDFs*.
	Children have a WCPM score of 0–12 . . .	. . . assign a lesson from Sections 2–8 of the *Tier 2 Fluency Intervention online PDFs*.

Using Weekly Data

Check your data Dashboard to verify assessment results and guide grouping decisions.

Data-Driven Recommendations

Response to Intervention

Use the children's assessment results to assist you in identifying children who will benefit from focused intervention.

Use the appropriate sections of the *Placement and Diagnostic Assessment* to designate children requiring:

 Intervention Online PDFs

WonderWorks Intervention Program

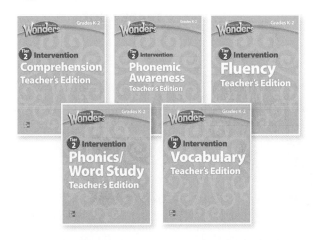

The Big Idea: *How does teamwork help us?*

Student Outcomes

Close Reading of Complex Text
- Cite relevant evidence from text
- Interpret information presented visually
- Navigate links
- Gather relevant information from digital sources

RI.1.5, RI.1.6, RI.1.7

Writing
Write to Sources
- Conduct research
- Select reliable sources
- Write informative text

W.1.2, W.1.7, W.1.8

Speaking and Listening
- Report on a topic
- Listen to presentations
- Ask relevant questions

SL.1.1, SL.1.3

Review and Extend

Reader's Theater

That Goat Has GOT to Go!

Genre Play

Reading Digitally

TIME FOR KIDS "This Land Is Our Land"

Go Digital!

Level Up Accelerating Progress

FROM **APPROACHING** TO **ON LEVEL**

FROM **ON LEVEL** TO **BEYOND LEVEL**

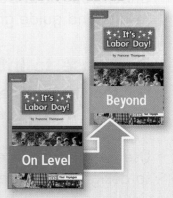

FROM **ENGLISH LANGUAGE LEARNERS** TO **ON LEVEL**

FROM **BEYOND LEVEL** TO **SELF-SELECTED TRADE BOOK**

Advanced Level Trade Book

ASSESS

Presentations

Research and Inquiry
Project Presentations

Project Rubric

Writing
Informative Text Presentations

Writing Rubric

Unit Assessments

UNIT 6 TEST

FLUENCY

Evaluate Student Progress

Use the Wonders online assessment reports to evaluate student progress and help you make decisions about small group instruction and assignments.

SUGGESTED LESSON PLAN

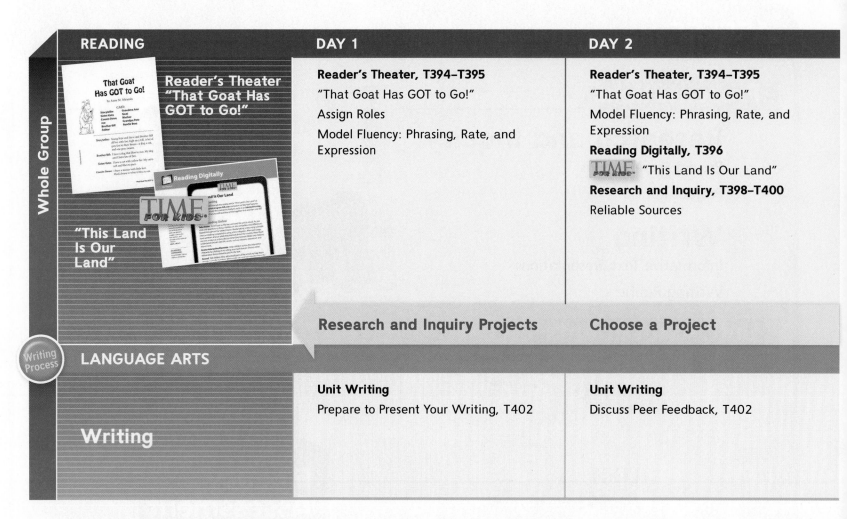

READING	DAY 1	DAY 2

Whole Group

Reader's Theater "That Goat Has GOT to Go!"

"This Land Is Our Land"

DAY 1

Reader's Theater, T394–T395
"That Goat Has GOT to Go!"
Assign Roles
Model Fluency: Phrasing, Rate, and Expression

DAY 2

Reader's Theater, T394–T395
"That Goat Has GOT to Go!"
Model Fluency: Phrasing, Rate, and Expression
Reading Digitally, T396
TIME FOR KIDS "This Land Is Our Land"
Research and Inquiry, T398–T400
Reliable Sources

Research and Inquiry Projects | **Choose a Project**

LANGUAGE ARTS

Writing

Writing Process

Unit Writing
Prepare to Present Your Writing, T402

Unit Writing
Discuss Peer Feedback, T402

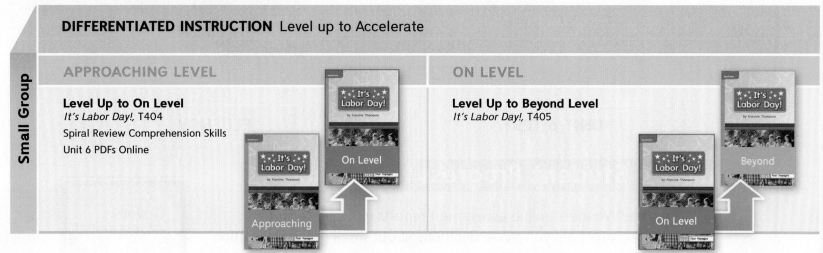

DIFFERENTIATED INSTRUCTION Level up to Accelerate

Small Group

APPROACHING LEVEL

Level Up to On Level
It's Labor Day!, T404
Spiral Review Comprehension Skills
Unit 6 PDFs Online

ON LEVEL

Level Up to Beyond Level
It's Labor Day!, T405

DAY 3	DAY 4	DAY 5
Reading Digitally, T396–T397 TIME FOR KIDS "This Land Is Our Land" Close Reading	**Reader's Theater, T394–T395** Performance	**Research and Inquiry, T398–T399** Presentation ✓ **Unit Assessment, T408–T409** **Wrap Up the Unit, T401**

Research and Inquiry Projects   **Choose a Project** ➤

Unit Writing	Unit Writing	Unit Writing
Unit Writing Rehearse Your Presentation, T402	**Unit Writing** Present Your Writing, T402–T403 Evaluate Your Presentation, T402–T403	**Unit Writing** Portfolio Choice, T403

BEYOND LEVEL

**Level Up to Self-Selected
Trade Book,** T407

ENGLISH LANGUAGE LEARNERS

Level Up to On Level
It's Labor Day!, T406

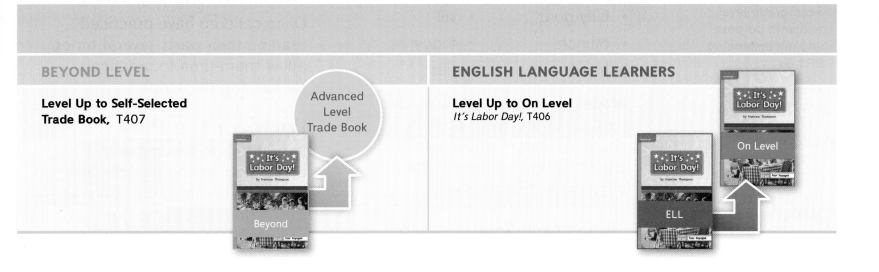

Advanced
Level
Trade Book

That Goat Has GOT to Go!

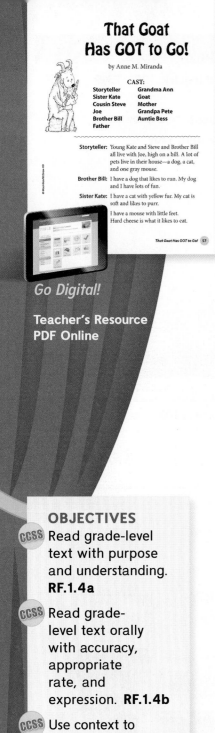

That Goat Has GOT to Go!

by Anne M. Miranda

CAST:

Storyteller	Grandma Ann
Sister Kate	Goat
Cousin Steve	Mother
Joe	Grandpa Pete
Brother Bill	Auntie Bess
Father	

Storyteller: Young Kate and Steve and Brother Bill all live with Joe, high on a hill. A lot of pets live in their house—a dog, a cat, and one gray mouse.

Brother Bill: I have a dog that likes to run. My dog and I have lots of fun.

Sister Kate: I have a cat with yellow fur. My cat is soft and likes to purr.

I have a mouse with little feet. Hard cheese is what it likes to eat.

That Goat Has GOT to Go! 57

Go Digital!

Teacher's Resource PDF Online

OBJECTIVES

CCSS Read grade-level text with purpose and understanding. **RF.1.4a**

CCSS Read grade-level text orally with accuracy, appropriate rate, and expression. **RF.1.4b**

CCSS Use context to confirm or self-correct word recognition and understanding, rereading as necessary. **RF.1.4c**

Introduce the Play

Explain that *That Goat Has GOT to Go!* is a play about pets and what happens when one boy, who has no pet, decides to get a billy goat as a pet. Distribute scripts and the Elements of Drama handout from the **Teacher's Resource PDF Online**.

- Review the features of a play.
- Review the list of characters. Point out that the setting of the play is a house high on a hill, a trail, and a school.

Shared Reading

Model reading the play as children follow along in their scripts.

Focus on Vocabulary Stop and discuss any vocabulary words that children may not know. You may wish to teach:

- billy goat
- munch
- bleat
- sill
- foggy
- hero

Model Fluency As you read each part, state the name of each character and read the part, emphasizing the appropriate phrasing and expression.

Discuss Each Role

- After reading the part of the Storyteller, help children identify what information the Storyteller is giving about the play.
- Ask children to note the repetition of "Bleat, bleat! ____ to eat" each time the Goat speaks.

Assign Roles

Divide the class into two or three casts. The casts can work on their scripts simultaneously. Depending on the number of children, in order for everyone to have a part, you may need to divide the role of Storyteller or Goat between two or more children.

Practice the Play

Have children use highlighters to mark their parts in the script. Each day, allow children time to practice their parts. Pair fluent readers with less fluent readers. Pairs can echo-read or chorally read their parts. As needed, work with less fluent readers to mark pauses in their script, using one slash for a short pause and two slashes for longer pauses.

Throughout the week have children work on the Reader's Theater **Workstation Activity Card 25**.

Once children have practiced reading their parts several times, allow them time to practice performing the script.

Perform the Play

In addition to reading with expression, encourage children to bring the text alive by using facial expressions and some gestures.

- Since there are many characters, you may wish to have each child wear a tag identifying his or her character. Tags can be hung on a string around the neck.
- Talk with the class about ways children could make performances more enjoyable for the audience.

ACTIVITIES

SUM IT UP!

Unlike most of the other Reader's Theater selections, *That Goat Has GOT to Go!* is a play with a clear plot. Have children work with partners and take turns summarizing what happens in the beginning, middle, and end of the play. Provide questions and prompting as needed.

- What happens in the beginning of the play?
- What happens after Joe gets a billy goat as a pet?
- What happens when Joe is at school?
- How does Joe get home?
- What happens when Joe sees his family again?

HOW DOES IT SOUND?

Use an audio recorder to record children's reading of the play. Then have children listen and discuss how the play sounds, what they could do better, and what was good. Discuss possible sound effects children may create. They could:

- create sound effects for when Goat eats things.
- bang on a can and yell for Joe, like Grandma and Grandpa do.
- play a triumphant march or song as Joe is welcomed back home.

ENGLISH LANGUAGE LEARNERS

ELL

- Review the definitions of difficult words and phrases including *got to go, goodness knows, made the going slow, bend, yoo-hoo,* and *hip hooray*.
- Pair an ELL child with a fluent reader who is reading the same part. Have each reader take turns reading the lines.
- Work with ELLs on pronunciation of difficult words and on intonation. As children read, give them corrective feedback and model proper fluency.

Reading Digitally

This Land Is Our Land

Before Reading

Preview Scroll through the online article "This Land Is Our Land" at **http://connected.mcgraw-hill.com** and point out the text features. Explain how to use the interactive features such as an **interactive map**. Tell children that you will read the article together first and then use the features.

Close Reading Online

Take Notes Scroll back to the top and read the article aloud. As you read, ask questions to focus children on the similarities and differences found throughout the United States. Model taking notes using a Details chart or making comparisons using a Venn diagram. After each page, have partners discuss what they learned about the country. Have them use text evidence as they discuss what they learned. Make sure children understand domain-specific words, such as *canyons, steamboat,* and *monuments.*

Access Interactive Elements Help children access the interactive elements by clicking on or rolling over each feature. Discuss what information these elements add to the text.

Reread Tell children they will reread parts of the article to help them answer a specific question: *What might you see if you traveled across the United States?*

Navigate Links to Information Remind children that online texts may include hyperlinks. Hyperlinks help you go from the Web page you are on to another Web page that tells more about the topic.

Model how to use a hyperlink to jump to another Web page. Discuss information on the new Web page.

Before navigating back, demonstrate bookmarking the page so children can return to it at another time.

 OBJECTIVES

CCSS Know and use various text features (e.g., headings, tables of contents, glossaries, electronic menus, icons) to locate key facts or information in a text. **RI.1.5**

 CCSS Write opinion pieces in which they introduce the topic or name the book they are writing about, state an opinion, supply a reason for the opinion, and provide some sense of closure. **W.1.1**

ACADEMIC LANGUAGE
Cut and Paste, Source, Rollover, Interactive

WRITE ABOUT READING *Analytical Writing*

Retell Review children's charts. Model using the information to retell "This Land Is Our Land."

Ask small groups of children to draw the places they read about. Have children write a sentence below each picture that describes the place. Invite them to use their pictures to help them retell the article.

Make Connections Have children compare what they learned about the United States with what they learned about teamwork in other texts they read in this unit.

TAKE A STAND

Honor Our Country

Have children discuss some of the many features of the United States, like mountains, rivers, and monuments.

Ask children if they think it is important for people to protect the land and national monuments. Have partners share opinions. Ask them to use information from the article or linked web pages to support their opinions.

- What happens if the land and water is polluted?
- What can citizens do to protect and honor the natural beauty of the United States?

RESEARCH ONLINE

Use Your Own Words

Explain to children that when they get information from the Internet, they should take notes and use their notes to write information in their own words. Point out that it is not a good idea to just cut and paste information from the Internet. Also remind children that they should check facts by using more than one source.

INDEPENDENT STUDY

Investigate

Choose a Topic Brainstorm questions related to special places in the United States. For example, they might ask: *What are some National Parks and what are they famous for?*

Conduct Internet Research Have children conduct an Internet search. Type in the URL for a child-friendly search engine. Enter key words. Click on a link to go to a site. Have children retell what they learn in their own words.

Present Help children use their research to make a map of famous places in the country or use presentation software to share it with others.

→ Integrate Ideas

Go Digital

Collaborate

Resources: Research and Inquiry

RESEARCH AND INQUIRY

Research and Inquiry

Assign the Projects Divide students into five groups. Assign each group one of the projects or let groups self-select. Before children begin researching, present the minilesson below.

Using Key Words

- Explain that as children research and take notes, they can use key words to locate and record information.

- Explain that key words can list a topic or provide important details about a topic. Guide children to see that they may only need to remember or use particular pieces of information for their project. Model using key words for a topic, such as *tornado*. Then list key words that describe a tornado, such as *twister* and *windstorm*.

CHOOSE A PROJECT!

Go Digital

Resources: Research and Inquiry

A Plan
Research teams will plan a project to make life better in their community, such as picking up litter in a park. Children will write, illustrate, and present their plan. WEEK 1

Interviews
Research team members will interview one another about how people have helped them. Children will practice and present interviews. WEEK 2

A Poster
Research teams will make a poster to show how people can stay safe during an extreme weather event, such as a tornado or drought. WEEK 3

A Report
Research teams will learn about traditions schools have in other countries. These may include first day of school traditions, sports, and lunches. Group members will write a report about one tradition. WEEK 4

A Song
Research teams will research and learn about a holiday so they can write a song about it. They may choose a familiar melody and write verses about how people celebrate. WEEK 5

Locating Information

Explain that key words, or words that provide important details about a topic, can be useful when searching for information.

- Show a page from an encyclopedia. Point out the boldface entry words. Explain that these are key words that indicate what each encyclopedia entry will be about. Explain that their topic might have many key words that they can use to search for information. For example, if their topic is *sports*, children may wish to search for information under the key word *baseball* to find additional information.

- You may wish to demonstrate how key words can be helpful to locate information in online sources. Talk about how key words can help children to find information using search engines.

OBJECTIVES

CCSS With guidance and support from adults, use a variety of digital tools to produce and publish writing, including in collaboration with peers. **W.1.6**

CCSS Participate in shared research and writing projects (e.g., explore a number of "how-to" books on a given topic and use them to write a sequence of instructions). **W.1.7**

CONDUCT THE RESEARCH

Distribute the online Research Roadmap to children. Have them use the roadmap to complete the project.

STEP 1 **Set Research Goals** Discuss the Big Idea and the research project. Each group should develop a research plan that helps focus their research and agree on what the final project should look like.

STEP 2 **Identify Sources** Have groups brainstorm where they can find the information they need. Guide children to focus on sources that will be most helpful for their particular project.

STEP 3 **Find and Record Information** Have children review the strategy for using key words presented on page T398. Then have them do research. Remind children to focus on the information that will help them complete the project.

STEP 4 **Organize and Summarize** After team members have completed their research, they can review the information they collected. Help children decide what information is necessary to complete the project. Help team members summarize their findings and decide on their message. Help them to connect the key ideas of their projects to the unit theme, "Together We Can!"

STEP 5 **Complete and Present** Guide children to complete the project. Ensure children work together to create each part of the project. Encourage them to use various media in their presentations. Have teams take turns presenting their work.

Collaborate Manage and Assign projects online. Students can work with their team online.

→ Integrate Ideas

Review and Evaluate

Distribute the online PDF of the checklists and rubrics. Use the following Teacher Checklist and rubric to evaluate students' research and presentations.

Student Checklist

Research Process

- ☑ Did you choose a research topic?
- ☑ Did you use several sources to find information about your topic?
- ☑ Did you use keywords to search for and record information?

Presenting

- ☑ Did you practice your presentation?
- ☑ Did you speak clearly and loudly enough for others to hear?
- ☑ Did you give important facts and details about your topic?
- ☑ Did you answer the Essential Question?
- ☑ Did you use pictures, audio recordings, or other materials to make your presentation exciting for your audience?

Teacher Checklist

Assess the Research Process

- ☑ Selected a focus.
- ☑ Used sources to gather information.
- ☑ Used time effectively and collaborated well.

Assess the Presentation

- ☑ Presented information clearly and concisely.
- ☑ Maintained a consistent focus by staying on-topic.
- ☑ Used appropriate gestures.
- ☑ Maintained eye contact.
- ☑ Used appropriate visuals and technology.
- ☑ Spoke clearly and at an appropriate rate.

Assess the Listener

- ☑ Listened quietly and politely.
- ☑ Listened actively and asked questions to clarify understanding.

Presentation Rubric

4 Excellent	3 Good	2 Fair	1 Unsatisfactory
• presents the information clearly. • includes many details. • may include many relevant observations.	• presents the information adequately. • provides adequate details. • includes relevant observations.	• attempts to present information. • may offer few or vague details. • may include few or irrelevant personal observations.	• may show little grasp of the task. • may present irrelevant information. • may reflect extreme difficulty with research or presentation.

Wrap Up the Unit

The Big Idea:
How does teamwork help us?

TEXT CONNECTIONS

Connect to the Big Idea

Text to Text Write the Unit Big Idea on the board: *How does teamwork help us?* Remind children that they have been reading selections about how we can work together and collaborate to solve problems and to get things done. Divide the class into small groups. Tell children that each group will compare what they learned about teamwork to answer the Big Idea question. Model how to compare this information by using examples from the **Leveled Readers** and what they have read in this unit's selections.

Collaborative Conversations Have children review their class notes, writing assignments, and completed graphic organizers before they begin their discussions. Ask children to compare information from the unit's selections and presentations. Have children work together to take notes. Explain that each group will use an Accordion Foldable® to record their ideas. Model how to use an Accordion Foldable® to record comparisons of texts. Guide children to focus their conversations on what they learned about teamwork and collaboration.

Dinah Zike's
FOLDABLES
Study Organizer

Present Ideas and Synthesize Information When children finish their discussions ask for volunteers from each group to share their ideas aloud. After each group has presented, ask: *What have we learned about how teamwork and working together can help us?* Lead a class discussion and list children's ideas on the board.

Building Knowledge Have children continue to build knowledge about the Unit Big Idea. Display classroom or library sources and have children search for articles, books, and other resources related to the Big Idea. After each group has presented their ideas, ask: *What does teamwork help us?* Lead a class discussion asking children to use information from their charts to answer the question.

OBJECTIVES

CCSS Integrate information from two texts on the same topic in order to write or speak about the subject knowledgeably. **RI.4.9**

CCSS Follow agreed-upon rules for discussions (e.g., listening to others with care, speaking one at a time about the topics and texts under discussion). **SL.1.1a**

CCSS Build on others' talk in conversations by responding to the comments of others through multiple exchanges. **SL.1.1b**

Go Digital

Resources: Research and Inquiry

Presentations

Giving Presentations

Now is the time for children to share one of their pieces of writing that they have worked on throughout the unit.

You may wish to invite parents or children from other classes to attend the presentations.

Preparing for Presentations

Tell children that they will make preparations to present their writing. Guide children to use digital tools to prepare their work for presentation.

Allow ample time for children to rehearse their presentation. Rereading will help children gain confidence for the presentation.

Children should consider any visuals or props that they may want to use to accompany their writing. Discuss some options.

- Do they have illustrations that accompany their stories, such as those about children working together?

- Do they photos or graphics to accompany their reports, such as those about a favorite holiday?

- Do they have props, such as as ones to accompany their letters or thank-you notes?

Encourage children to practice their presentations with a partner. Share the following Speaking Checklist to help them focus on important parts of the presentation. Discuss each point on the checklist.

Speaking Checklist

Review the Speaking Checklist with children as they practice.

- ☑ Make sure you are confident using your props.
- ☑ Stand up straight.
- ☑ Speak slowly and loudly.
- ☑ Make sure everyone can see your visuals.
- ☑ Read with expression and excitement.

Listening to Presentations

Remind children that they not only will take on the role of a presenter, but they will also be part of the audience for their classmates' presentations. As a listener, children have an important role. Review with them the following Listening Checklist.

Listening Checklist

During the presentation

- ☑ Look at the speaker and listen carefully.
- ☑ Notice how the visuals add interest to the presentation.
- ☑ Think of one positive comment to share about the speaker's presentation.
- ☑ Remain quiet and still during the presentation.

After the presentation

- ☑ Wait until it is your turn to comment.
- ☑ Explain one reason why you liked the presentation.
- ☑ Ask a question if you need to clarify something about the presentation.

Portfolio Choice

Ask children to select one finished piece of writing, as well as a revision to include in their writing portfolio. As children consider their choices, have them use the checklist below.

Published Writing

Does your writing:

- use pronouns and adverbs correctly?
- use varying sentence lengths?
- focus on a main idea?
- use your own voice?
- have few or no spelling errors?

Sample Revisions

Did you choose a revised entry that shows:

- sentences with varying lengths?
- details that support a main idea?
- examples of your own voice?

PORTFOLIO
Children can submit their writing to be considered for inclusion in their digital portfolio. Children's portfolios can be shared with parents.

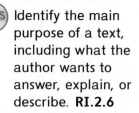

Leveled Reader

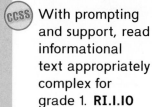

OBJECTIVES

CCSS Identify the main purpose of a text, including what the author wants to answer, explain, or describe. **RI.2.6**

CCSS With prompting and support, read informational text appropriately complex for grade 1. **RI.1.10**

Approaching Level to On Level

It's Labor Day!

Level Up Lessons also available online

Before Reading

Preview Discuss what children remember about the information they learned about Labor Day. Tell them they will be reading a more detailed version of *It's Labor Day!*

High-Frequency Words Use the **High-Frequency Word Cards** to review the high-frequency words. Use the routine on the cards.

A C T During Reading

▶ **Specific Vocabulary** Review the following social studies words that are new to this title. Model how to use the photographs and sentences to determine their meaning. *earned breaks*

▶ **Connection of Ideas** Children may need help recognizing connections between chapters in the higher level. Read the chapter titles. Point out that information in both chapters is about Labor Day, but that Chapter 1 tells what Labor Day is, and Chapter 2 tells ways to celebrate Labor Day. Model how to paraphrase information, then have children retell what they read in each section.

▶ **Organization** The On Level text is divided into chapters, and the information within each chapter is more detailed than the information in the Approaching Level text. Help children identify the main idea of each chapter. Guide them to explain how the facts and details relate to the main idea of the chapter.

After Reading

Ask children to complete the Respond to Reading on page 11 using the new information from the On Level text. After children finish the Paired Read, have them hold Literature Circles.

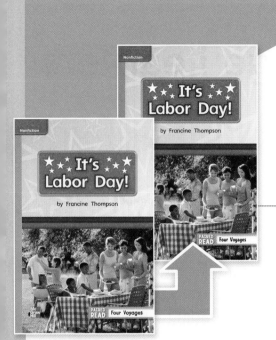

Leveled Reader

On Level
to Beyond Level

It's Labor Day!

Level Up Lessons also available online

Before Reading

Preview Discuss what children remember about Labor Day. Tell them they will be reading a more detailed version of *It's Labor Day!*

High-Frequency Words Use the **High-Frequency Word Cards** to review the high-frequency words. Use the routine on the cards.

A C T During Reading

OBJECTIVES

(CCSS) Identify the main purpose of a text, including what the author wants to answer, explain, or describe. **RI.2.6**

(CCSS) With prompting and support, read informational text appropriately complex for grade 1. **RI.I.I0**

▶ **Specific Vocabulary** Review the following words that are new to this title. Model using sentences and paragraphs to determine word meaning. *forced unsafe written blanket toss over*

▶ **Connection of Ideas** Some pages in the Beyond Level text have multiple paragraphs, and paragraphs provide more details than those in the On Level text. Children may need help recognizing connections between ideas within and between paragraphs. Help children paraphrase each paragraph, then discuss how the paragraphs relate to each other.

▶ **Sentence Structure** The sentence structure at this level is more complex than in the On Level text. To help children understand the information, follow this routine when reading complex or compound sentences, such as the second sentence on page 4:

Read the sentence aloud. *Some laws make sure that workers have safe places to work and that they can take breaks.*

Break down the information into simpler sentences. *Some laws make sure workers have safe places to work. Some laws make sure they can take breaks.*

Have children then read the sentence aloud.

After Reading

Ask children to complete the Respond to Reading on page 11 using the new information from the Beyond Level text. After children finish the Paired Read, have them hold Literature Circles.

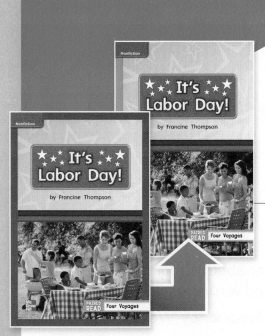

Leveled Reader

OBJECTIVES

 Identify the main purpose of a text, including what the author wants to answer, explain, or describe. **RI.2.6**

CCSS With prompting and support, read informational text appropriately complex for grade 1. **RI.I.IO**

English Language Learners to On Level

It's Labor Day!

Level Up Lessons also available online

Before Reading

Preview Remind children that informational text tells facts about real people, things, and events. Talk about facts they remember about Labor Day, then tell them they will be reading a more detailed version of *It's Labor Day!*

High-Frequency Words Use the **High-Frequency Word Cards** to review the high-frequency words. Use the routine on the cards.

A C T During Reading

▶ **Specific Vocabulary** Help children name elements in each photograph, now that there are no labels. Review the following social studies words that are new to this title. Model how to use the photographs and sentences to determine their meaning. Review any cognates. *holiday earned breaks*

▶ **Connection of Ideas** Children may need help recognizing connections between chapters in the higher level. Read the chapter titles. Point out that information in both chapters is about Labor Day, but that Chapter 1 tells what Labor Day is, and Chapter 2 tells ways to celebrate Labor Day. Model how to paraphrase information, then have children retell what they read in each section.

▶ **Organization** The On Level text is divided into chapters, and the information within each chapter is more detailed than the information in the ELL Level text. Help children identify the main idea of each chapter. Guide them to explain how the facts and details relate to the main idea of the chapter.

After Reading

Ask children to complete the Respond to Reading on page 11 using the new information from the On Level text. After children finish the Paired Read, have them hold Literature Circles.

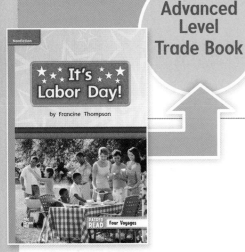

Leveled Reader

OBJECTIVES

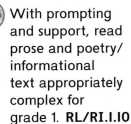 With prompting and support, read prose and poetry/informational text appropriately complex for grade 1. **RL/RI.1.10**

Beyond Level
to Self-Selected Trade Book

Advanced Level Trade Book

Independent Reading

Level Up Lessons also available online

Before Reading

Together with children identify the particular focus of their reading based on the text they choose. Children who have chosen the same title can work together to closely read the selection.

Close Reading

Taking Notes Assign a graphic organizer for children to use to take notes as they read. Reinforce a specific comprehension focus from the unit by choosing one of the graphic organizers that best fits the book.

Examples:	
Fiction	**Informational Text**
Theme	Author's Purpose
Theme chart	Author's Purpose chart

Reread Remind children that as they read, if they do not understand what happened or a piece of information, they can go back and reread. Point out that rereading can also help them remember important information from a selection. Encourage them to write down the events or information from the sections they reread.

After Reading

Write About Text

Have children use their notes, graphic organizers, and the information they shared in their discussions to write a response to the reading.

Examples:	
Fiction	**Informational Text**
Do you like to read books with themes like this one? Why or why not?	What information did you learn that you did not know before you read this book?

SUMMATIVE ASSESSMENT

TESTED SKILLS

✓ COMPREHENSION:
- Theme **RL.1.2**
- Author's Purpose **RI.2.6**
- Plot: Cause and Effect **RL.1.3**
- Text Feature: Headings **RI.1.5**
- Text Feature: Captions **RI.2.5**

✓ VOCABULARY:
- Synonyms **L.4.5c**
- Antonyms **L.4.5c**
- Similes **L.4.5a**
- Metaphors **L.4.5a**

✓ PHONICS/STRUCTURAL ANALYSIS/HIGH-FREQUENCY WORDS:
- Variant Vowel Digraphs /ü/, /ô/ **RF.1.3**
- Silent Letters **RF.1.3**
- Three-letter **RF.1.3**
- r-Controlled Vowels air, are, ear **RF.1.3**
- Suffixes -ful and -less **RF.1.3**
- Inflectional endings -ed, ing **RF.1.3f**
- High-Frequency Words **RF.1.3g**
- Compound Words **RF.1.3**

✓ ENGLISH LANGUAGE CONVENTIONS:
- Pronouns **L.1.1d**
- Possessive Pronouns **L.1.1d**
- Indefinite Pronouns **L.1.1d**
- Adverbs That Tell How **L.2.1e**
- Writing Prompt: Thank-You Note **W.1.2, L.1.1, L.1.2**

Additional Assessment Options

Conduct assessments individually using the differentiated passages in *Fluency Assessment*. Children's expected fluency goal for this Unit is **43–63 WCPM** with an accuracy rate of 95% or higher.

Use the instructional reading level determined by the Running Record calculations for regrouping decisions. Children at Level 14 or below should be provided reteaching on specific Comprehension skills.

Using Assessment Results

TESTED SKILLS	If ...	Then ...
COMPREHENSION	Children answer 0–7 items correctly ...	... reteach tested skills using the *Tier 2 Comprehension Intervention online PDFs.*
VOCABULARY	Children answer 0–3 items correctly ...	... reteach tested skills using the *Tier 2 Vocabulary online PDFs.*
PHONICS/ STRUCTURAL ANALYSIS/HFW	Children answer 0–8 items correctly ...	... reteach tested skills using the *Tier 2 Phonics/Word Study online PDFs.*
ENGLISH LANGUAGE CONVENTIONS	Children answer 0–4 items correctly ...	... reteach necessary skills using the *online Grammar Reproducibles.*
WRITING	Children score less than the benchmark score on the constructed responses ...	... reteach necessary skills using the Write About Reading lessons in the *Tier 2 Comprehension Intervention online PDFs.*
	Children who score less than the benchmark score on the writing prompt ...	... reteach necessary skills using the *online Grammar Reproducibles.*
FLUENCY	Children have a WCPM score of 0–42 ...	... reteach tested skills using the *Tier 2 Fluency Intervention online PDFs.*

Using Summative Data

Check online reports for this Unit Assessment as well as your data Dashboard. Use the data to assign small group instruction for students who are below the overall proficiency level for the tested skills.

Data-Driven Recommendations

Response to Intervention

Use children's assessment results to assist you in identifying children who will benefit from focused intervention. Use the appropriate sections of the *Placement and Diagnostic Assessment* to designate children requiring:

 Intervention Online PDFs

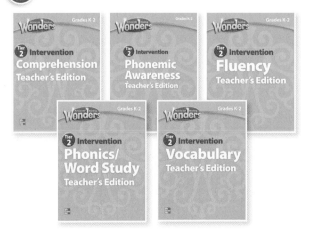

TIER 3 WonderWorks Intervention Program

Reading Complex Text

Your Own Texts

Program Information

Scope and Sequence

Index

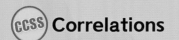Correlations

For Additional Resources

Theme Bibliography

Literature and Informational Text Charts

Word Lists

Web Sites

www.connected.mcgraw-hill.com

READING Complex Text

Close Reading Routine

Read | *What does the text say?*

Select the Text

Depending on the needs of individual children, choose a book to:

- read aloud with children.
- have children read alone.

Model Note-Taking

Invite children to generate questions about aspects of the text that might be confusing for them. Model simple note-taking on the board or on chart paper. Encourage children to note:

- key ideas and details.
- difficult vocabulary words or phrases.
- details that are not clear.
- information that they do not understand.

Together, complete a graphic organizer with important information from the text.

Reread | *How does the author say it?*

Ask Text-Dependent Questions

Reread the text with children and discuss shorter passages from the text. Have children cite text evidence to answer deeper questions about craft and structure. Children should

- talk about and identify text evidence.
- generate questions about the text.

Integrate | *What does the text mean?*

Have children draw a picture or write a short response to the text. Based on their ability, children may respond to the text by writing a short caption for a picture or two or three complete sentences that use evidence from the text to support their ideas.

Children reread to integrate knowledge and ideas and make text-to-text connections. Children should

- work with partners to identify and discuss connections.
- draw a picture and write a short response using text evidence.

Use Your Own Text

Classroom Library lessons available online.

Read-Aloud Books

Read-Alone Books

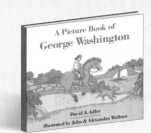

or **Choose from your own Trade Books**

How People Learned to Fly
Genre *Fiction*

Lexile 630

A Picture Book of George Washington
Genre *Nonfiction*

Lexile 750

Ling &Ting: Not Exactly the Same!
Genre *Fiction*

Lexile 390

Frog and Toad Together
Genre *Fiction*

Lexile 330

Teacher's Choice

- Use this model with a text of your choice. Go online for title-specific Classroom Library book lessons.

- Select a Read-Aloud selection or a Read-Alone selection.

- Select a text that provides an opportunity to model application of the comprehension skills and strategies taught during the unit.

- Present an Essential Question. You may want to use the Unit Big Idea: *How does teamwork help us?*

sync tv
Video Preview
studysync

Using the Classroom Library

Selecting a Book For each unit, the classroom library includes two Read-Aloud titles for you to read with the class and two Read-Alone titles for independent reading. There is a mix of fiction and informational nonfiction.

Reading Together Use the Read-Aloud titles to model close reading. Model taking notes, and prompt children to ask and answer text-dependent questions and to participate in writing about the text. You may choose to read the selection in multiple readings.

Independent Reading If children are ready to engage in close reading independently, select a Read-Alone title. Assign the Read-Alone titles and guide children to take notes, ask and answer text-dependent questions, and write about the text.

Use Your Own Text

Read | *What does the text say?*

Read Together

Read the text aloud. You may also invite more advanced readers to select a book to read alone and respond to independently.

Model close reading for children as well as how to take notes. Encourage children to jot down words they do not understand and any questions they have.

Ask Text-Dependent Questions

Ask children to reread a section of the text, or reread it to children, and focus on the following questions. Children should use text evidence in their answers:

Literature

- Is this a book that tells a story or that gives information? Explain your answer.
- What are the plot and setting of the story? Be sure to use the text and illustrations.
- How would you describe the main character(s)?
- What is the main message or lesson of the story?

Informational Text

- What is the main topic? What are the key details?
- What kinds of text features does the author use?
- What reasons does the author give to support points in the text?

Model how to use a graphic organizer, chosen from within the unit, to take notes on important details from the text. Together with children, use the information from the graphic organizer to retell the selection.

 Help children access the complex text features of the text. Scaffold instruction on the following features as necessary:

- Prior Knowledge
- Genre
- Organization
- Connection of Ideas
- Purpose
- Specific Vocabulary
- Sentence Structure

Reread   *How does the author say it?*

Ask Text-Dependent Questions/Generate Questions

- Reread shorter passages of the text with children, focusing on how the author provides information or develops the characters, setting, and plot. Based on the selection you are reading, focus on key elements with the following questions. Remind students to use text evidence in their answers:

Literature

- Who is telling the story on this page? Is it the same person who tells the story on another page?
- What words did the author use to help you understand the character?
- What other story have you read with a similar character or plot? How are the two stories similar? Different?

Informational Text

- How does the author organize the information in this text?
- What reasons does the author give to support points in the text?
- Was the author's use of visuals (photos, graphs, diagrams, maps) effective? Why or why not?

Integrate   *What does the text mean?*

Essential Question

Have children respond to the Essential Question as it relates to the text by drawing a picture and labeling it, writing a caption, or writing two or three complete sentences. Children can work with a partner and use their notes and graphic organizer to locate evidence from the text that can be used to answer the question.

SCOPE & SEQUENCE

	K	1	2	3	4	5	6
FOUNDATIONAL SKILLS							
Concepts About Print/Print Awareness							
Recognize own name							
Understand directionality (top to bottom; tracking print from left to right; return sweep, page by page)	✓						
Locate printed word on page	✓						
Develop print awareness (concept of letter, word, sentence)	✓						
Identify separate sounds in a spoken sentence	✓						
Understand that written words are represented in written language by a specific sequence of letters	✓						
Distinguish between letters, words, and sentences	✓						
Distinguish features of a sentence (first word, capitalization, ending punctuation)							
Identify and distinguish paragraphs							
Match print to speech (one-to-one correspondence)	✓						
Name uppercase and lowercase letters	✓						
Understand book handling (holding a book right-side-up, turning its pages)	✓						
Identify parts of a book (front cover, back cover, title page, table of contents); recognize that parts of a book contain information	✓						
Phonological Awareness							
Recognize and understand alliteration							
Segment sentences into correct number of words							
Identify, blend, segment syllables in words		✓					
Recognize and generate rhyming words	✓	✓					
Identify, blend, segment onset and rime	✓	✓					
Phonemic Awareness							
Count phonemes	✓	✓					
Isolate initial, medial, and final sounds	✓	✓					
Blend spoken phonemes to form words	✓	✓					
Segment spoken words into phonemes	✓	✓					
Distinguish between long- and short-vowel sounds	✓	✓					
Manipulate phonemes (addition, deletion, substitution)	✓	✓					
Phonics and Decoding/Word Recognition							
Understand the alphabetic principle	✓	✓					
Sound/letter correspondence	✓	✓	✓	✓			
Blend sounds into words, including VC, CVC, CVCe, CVVC words	✓	✓	✓	✓			
Blend common word families	✓	✓	✓	✓			

KEY	✓ = Assessed Skill
	Tinted panels show skills, strategies, and other teaching opportunities.

	K	1	2	3	4	5	6
Initial consonant blends		✔	✔	✔			
Final consonant blends		✔	✔	✔			
Initial and medial short vowels	✔	✔	✔	✔	✔	✔	✔
Decode one-syllable words in isolation and in context	✔	✔	✔	✔			
Decode multisyllabic words in isolation and in context using common syllabication patterns		✔	✔	✔	✔	✔	✔
Distinguish between similarly spelled words	✔	✔	✔	✔	✔	✔	✔
Monitor accuracy of decoding							
Identify and read common high-frequency words, irregularly spelled words	✔	✔	✔	✔			
Identify and read compound words, contractions		✔	✔	✔	✔	✔	✔
Use knowledge of spelling patterns to identify syllables		✔	✔	✔	✔	✔	✔
Regular and irregular plurals	✔	✔	✔	✔	✔	✔	✔
Distinguish long and short vowels		✔	✔				
Long vowels (silent *e*, vowel teams)	✔	✔	✔	✔	✔	✔	✔
Vowel digraphs (variant vowels)		✔	✔	✔	✔	✔	✔
r-Controlled vowels		✔	✔	✔	✔	✔	✔
Hard/soft consonants		✔	✔	✔	✔	✔	✔
Initial consonant digraphs		✔	✔	✔	✔	✔	
Medial and final consonant digraphs		✔	✔	✔	✔	✔	
Vowel diphthongs		✔	✔	✔	✔	✔	✔
Identify and distinguish letter-sounds (initial, medial, final)	✔	✔	✔				
Silent letters		✔	✔	✔	✔	✔	✔
Schwa words			✔	✔	✔	✔	
Inflectional endings		✔	✔	✔	✔	✔	✔
Triple-consonant clusters		✔	✔	✔	✔	✔	
Unfamiliar and complex word families				✔	✔	✔	✔
Structural Analysis/Word Analysis							
Common spelling patterns (word families)		✔	✔	✔	✔	✔	✔
Common syllable patterns		✔	✔	✔	✔	✔	✔
Inflectional endings		✔	✔	✔	✔	✔	✔
Contractions		✔	✔	✔	✔	✔	✔
Compound words		✔	✔	✔	✔	✔	✔
Prefixes and suffixes		✔	✔	✔	✔	✔	✔
Root or base words			✔	✔	✔	✔	✔
Comparatives and superlatives			✔	✔	✔	✔	✔
Greek and Latin roots			✔	✔	✔	✔	✔
Fluency							
Apply letter/sound knowledge to decode phonetically regular words accurately	✔	✔	✔	✔	✔	✔	✔
Recognize high-frequency and familiar words	✔	✔	✔	✔	✔	✔	✔
Read regularly on independent and instructional levels							
Read orally with fluency from familiar texts (choral, echo, partner, Reader's Theater)							
Use appropriate rate, expression, intonation, and phrasing		✔	✔	✔	✔	✔	✔
Read with automaticity (accurately and effortlessly)		✔	✔	✔	✔	✔	✔

	K	1	2	3	4	5	6
Use punctuation cues in reading		✓	✓	✓	✓	✓	✓
Adjust reading rate to purpose, text difficulty, form, and style							
Repeated readings							
Timed readings		✓	✓	✓	✓	✓	✓
Read with purpose and understanding		✓	✓	✓	✓	✓	✓
Read orally with accuracy		✓	✓	✓	✓	✓	✓
Use context to confirm or self-correct word recognition		✓	✓	✓	✓	✓	✓

READING LITERATURE

Comprehension Strategies and Skills

	K	1	2	3	4	5	6
Read literature from a broad range of genres, cultures, and periods		✓	✓	✓	✓	✓	✓
Access complex text		✓	✓	✓	✓	✓	✓
Build background/Activate prior knowledge							
Preview and predict							
Establish and adjust purpose for reading							
Evaluate citing evidence from the text							
Ask and answer questions	✓	✓	✓	✓	✓	✓	✓
Inferences and conclusions, citing evidence from the text	✓	✓	✓	✓	✓	✓	✓
Monitor/adjust comprehension including reread, reading rate, paraphrase							
Recount/Retell	✓	✓					
Summarize			✓	✓	✓	✓	✓
Story structure (beginning, middle, end)	✓	✓	✓	✓	✓	✓	✓
Visualize							
Make connections between and across texts		✓	✓	✓	✓	✓	✓
Point of view		✓	✓	✓	✓	✓	✓
Author's purpose							
Cause and effect	✓	✓	✓	✓	✓	✓	✓
Compare and contrast (including character, setting, plot, topics)	✓	✓	✓	✓	✓	✓	✓
Classify and categorize		✓	✓				
Literature vs informational text	✓	✓	✓				
Illustrations, using	✓	✓	✓	✓			
Theme, central message, moral, lesson		✓	✓	✓	✓	✓	✓
Predictions, making/confirming	✓	✓	✓				
Problem and solution (problem/resolution)		✓	✓	✓	✓	✓	✓
Sequence of events	✓	✓	✓	✓	✓	✓	✓

Literary Elements

	K	1	2	3	4	5	6
Character	✓	✓	✓	✓	✓	✓	✓
Plot development/Events	✓	✓	✓	✓	✓	✓	✓
Setting	✓	✓	✓	✓	✓	✓	✓
Stanza				✓	✓	✓	✓
Alliteration						✓	✓
Assonance						✓	✓
Dialogue							

KEY ✓ = Assessed Skill
Tinted panels show skills, strategies, and other teaching opportunities.

	K	1	2	3	4	5	6
Foreshadowing						✔	✔
Flashback						✔	✔
Descriptive and figurative language		✔	✔	✔	✔	✔	✔
Imagery					✔	✔	✔
Meter					✔	✔	✔
Onomatopoeia							
Repetition		✔	✔	✔	✔	✔	✔
Rhyme/rhyme schemes		✔	✔	✔	✔	✔	✔
Rhythm		✔	✔				
Sensory language							
Symbolism							
Write About Text/Literary Response Discussions							
Reflect and respond to text citing text evidence		✔	✔	✔	✔	✔	✔
Connect and compare text characters, events, ideas to self, to other texts, to world							
Connect literary texts to other curriculum areas							
Identify cultural and historical elements of text							
Evaluate author's techniques, craft							
Analytical writing							
Interpret text ideas through writing, discussion, media, research							
Book report or review							
Locate, use, explain information from text features		✔	✔	✔	✔	✔	✔
Organize information to show understanding of main idea through charts, mapping							
Cite text evidence	✔	✔	✔	✔	✔	✔	✔
Author's purpose/Illustrator's purpose							

READING INFORMATIONAL TEXT

Comprehension Strategies and Skills

	K	1	2	3	4	5	6
Read informational text from a broad range of topics and cultures	✔	✔	✔	✔	✔	✔	✔
Access complex text		✔	✔	✔	✔	✔	✔
Build background/Activate prior knowledge							
Preview and predict	✔	✔	✔				
Establish and adjust purpose for reading							
Evaluate citing evidence from the text							
Ask and answer questions	✔	✔	✔	✔	✔	✔	✔
Inferences and conclusions, citing evidence from the text	✔	✔	✔	✔	✔	✔	✔
Monitor and adjust comprehension including reread, adjust reading rate, paraphrase							
Recount/Retell	✔	✔					
Summarize			✔	✔	✔	✔	✔
Text structure	✔	✔	✔	✔	✔	✔	✔
Identify text features		✔	✔	✔	✔	✔	✔
Make connections between and across texts	✔	✔	✔	✔	✔	✔	✔
Author's point of view				✔	✔	✔	✔
Author's purpose		✔	✔				

	K	1	2	3	4	5	6
Cause and effect	✓	✓	✓	✓	✓	✓	✓
Compare and contrast	✓	✓	✓	✓	✓	✓	✓
Classify and categorize		✓	✓				
Illustrations and photographs, using	✓	✓	✓	✓			
Instructions/directions (written and oral)		✓	✓	✓	✓	✓	✓
Main idea and key details	✓	✓	✓	✓	✓	✓	✓
Persuasion, reasons and evidence to support points/persuasive techniques						✓	✓
Predictions, making/confirming	✓	✓					
Problem and solution		✓	✓	✓	✓	✓	✓
Sequence, chronological order of events, time order, steps in a process	✓	✓	✓	✓	✓	✓	✓

Write About Text/Write to Sources

	K	1	2	3	4	5	6
Reflect and respond to text citing text evidence		✓	✓	✓	✓	✓	✓
Connect and compare text characters, events, ideas to self, to other texts, to world							
Connect texts to other curriculum areas							
Identify cultural and historical elements of text							
Evaluate author's techniques, craft							
Analytical writing							
Read to understand and perform tasks and activities							
Interpret text ideas through writing, discussion, media, research							
Locate, use, explain information from text features		✓	✓	✓	✓	✓	✓
Organize information to show understanding of main idea through charts, mapping							
Cite text evidence		✓	✓	✓	✓	✓	✓
Author's purpose/Illustrator's purpose							

Text Features

	K	1	2	3	4	5	6
Recognize and identify text and organizational features of nonfiction texts		✓	✓	✓	✓	✓	✓
Captions and labels, headings, subheadings, endnotes, key words, bold print	✓	✓	✓	✓	✓	✓	✓
Graphics, including photographs, illustrations, maps, charts, diagrams, graphs, time lines	✓	✓	✓	✓	✓	✓	✓

Self-Selected Reading/Independent Reading

	K	1	2	3	4	5	6
Use personal criteria to choose own reading including favorite authors, genres, recommendations from others; set up a reading log							
Read a range of literature and informational text for tasks as well as for enjoyment; participate in literature circles							
Produce evidence of reading by retelling, summarizing, or paraphrasing							

Media Literacy

	K	1	2	3	4	5	6
Summarize the message or content from media message, citing text evidence							
Use graphics, illustrations to analyze and interpret information	✓	✓	✓	✓	✓	✓	✓
Identify structural features of popular media and use the features to obtain information, including digital sources				✓	✓	✓	✓
Identify reasons and evidence in visuals and media message							
Analyze media source: recognize effects of media in one's mood and emotion							
Make informed judgments about print and digital media							
Critique persuasive techniques							

KEY ✓ = Assessed Skill
Tinted panels show skills, strategies, and other teaching opportunities.

WRITING

	K	1	2	3	4	5	6
Writing Process							
Plan/prewrite/identify purpose and audience							
Draft							
Revise							
Edit/proofread							
Publish and present including using technology							
Teacher and peer feedback							
Writing Traits							
Conventions		✓	✓	✓	✓	✓	✓
Ideas		✓	✓	✓	✓	✓	✓
Organization		✓	✓	✓	✓	✓	✓
Sentence fluency		✓	✓	✓	✓	✓	✓
Voice		✓	✓	✓	✓	✓	✓
Word choice		✓	✓	✓	✓	✓	✓
Writer's Craft							
Good topic, focus on and develop topic, topic sentence			✓	✓	✓	✓	✓
Paragraph(s); sentence structure			✓	✓	✓	✓	✓
Main idea and supporting key details			✓	✓	✓	✓	✓
Unimportant details							
Relevant supporting evidence			✓	✓	✓	✓	✓
Strong opening, strong conclusion			✓	✓	✓	✓	✓
Beginning, middle, end; sequence		✓	✓	✓	✓	✓	✓
Precise words, strong words, vary words			✓	✓	✓	✓	✓
Figurative and sensory language, descriptive details							
Informal/formal language							
Mood/style/tone							
Dialogue				✓	✓	✓	✓
Transition words, transitions to multiple paragraphs				✓	✓	✓	✓
Select focus and organization			✓	✓	✓	✓	✓
Points and counterpoints/Opposing claims and counterarguments							
Use reference materials (online and print dictionary, thesaurus, encyclopedia)							
Writing Applications							
Write to sources	✓	✓	✓	✓	✓	✓	✓
Personal and fictional narrative (also biographical and autobiographical)	✓	✓	✓	✓	✓	✓	✓
Variety of expressive forms including poetry	✓	✓	✓	✓	✓	✓	✓
Informative/explanatory texts	✓	✓	✓	✓	✓	✓	✓
Description	✓	✓	✓	✓			
Procedural texts		✓	✓	✓	✓	✓	✓
Opinion pieces or arguments	✓	✓	✓	✓	✓	✓	✓
Communications including technical documents		✓	✓	✓	✓	✓	✓
Research report	✓	✓	✓	✓	✓	✓	✓

	K	1	2	3	4	5	6
Responses to literature/reflection				✓	✓	✓	✓
Analytical writing							
Letters		✓	✓	✓	✓	✓	✓
Write daily and over short and extended time frames; set up writer's notebooks							
Penmanship/Handwriting							
Write legibly in manuscript using correct formation, directionality, and spacing							
Write legibly in cursive using correct formation, directionality, and spacing							

SPEAKING AND LISTENING

Speaking

	K	1	2	3	4	5	6
Use repetition, rhyme, and rhythm in oral texts							
Participate in classroom activities and discussions							
Collaborative conversation with peers and adults in small and large groups using formal English when appropriate							
Differentiate between formal and informal English							
Follow agreed upon rules for discussion							
Build on others' talk in conversation, adding new ideas							
Come to discussions prepared							
Describe familiar people, places, and things and add drawings as desired							
Paraphrase portions of text read alone or information presented							
Apply comprehension strategies and skills in speaking activities							
Use literal and nonliteral meanings							
Ask and answer questions about text read aloud and about media							
Stay on topic when speaking							
Use language appropriate to situation, purpose, and audience							
Use nonverbal communications such as eye contact, gestures, and props							
Use verbal communication in effective ways and improve expression in conventional language							
Retell a story, presentation, or spoken message by summarizing							
Oral presentations: focus, organizational structure, audience, purpose							
Give and follow oral directions							
Consider audience when speaking or preparing a presentation							
Recite poems, rhymes, songs							
Use complete, coherent sentences							
Organize presentations							
Deliver presentations (narrative, summaries, informative, research, opinion); add visuals							
Speak audibly (accuracy, expression, volume, pitch, rate, phrasing, modulation, enunciation)							
Create audio recordings of poems, stories, presentations							

Listening

	K	1	2	3	4	5	6
Identify musical elements in language							
Determine the purpose for listening							
Understand, follow, restate, and give oral directions							
Develop oral language and concepts							

KEY | ✓ = Assessed Skill
Tinted panels show skills, strategies, and other teaching opportunities.

Listen to identify the points a speaker or media source makes							
Listen responsively to oral presentations (determine main idea and key details)							
Ask and answer relevant questions (for clarification to follow-up on ideas)							
Identify reasons and evidence presented by speaker							
Recall and interpret speakers' verbal/nonverbal messages, purposes, perspectives							

LANGUAGE

Vocabulary Acquisition and Use

Develop oral vocabulary and choose words for effect							
Use academic language		✓	✓	✓	✓	✓	✓
Identify persons, places, things, actions		✓	✓	✓			
Classify, sort, and categorize words	✓	✓	✓	✓	✓	✓	✓
Determine or clarify the meaning of unknown words; use word walls		✓	✓	✓	✓	✓	✓
Synonyms, antonyms, and opposites		✓	✓	✓	✓	✓	✓
Use context clues such as word, sentence, paragraph, definition, example, restatement, description, comparison, cause and effect		✓	✓	✓	✓	✓	✓
Use word identification strategies		✓	✓	✓	✓	✓	✓
Unfamiliar words		✓	✓	✓	✓	✓	✓
Multiple-meaning words		✓	✓	✓	✓	✓	✓
Use print and online dictionary to locate meanings, pronunciation, derivatives, parts of speech		✓	✓	✓	✓	✓	✓
Compound words		✓	✓	✓	✓	✓	✓
Words ending in -er and -est		✓	✓	✓	✓	✓	
Root words (base words)		✓	✓	✓	✓	✓	✓
Prefixes and suffixes		✓	✓	✓	✓	✓	✓
Greek and Latin affixes and roots			✓	✓	✓	✓	✓
Denotation and connotation					✓	✓	✓
Word families		✓	✓	✓	✓	✓	✓
Inflectional endings		✓	✓	✓	✓	✓	✓
Use a print and online thesaurus			✓	✓	✓	✓	✓
Use print and online reference sources for word meaning (dictionary, glossaries)		✓	✓	✓	✓	✓	✓
Homographs				✓	✓	✓	✓
Homophones			✓	✓	✓	✓	✓
Contractions		✓	✓	✓			
Figurative language such as metaphors, similes, personification			✓	✓	✓	✓	✓
Idioms, adages, proverbs, literal and nonliteral language			✓	✓	✓	✓	✓
Analogies							
Listen to, read, discuss familiar and unfamiliar challenging text							
Identify real-life connections between words and their use							
Use acquired words and phrases to convey precise ideas							
Use vocabulary to express spatial and temporal relationships							
Identify shades of meaning in related words	✓	✓	✓	✓	✓	✓	✓
Word origins				✓	✓	✓	✓
Morphology				✓	✓	✓	✓

BM7

Skill	1	2	3	4	5	6	7
Choose words, phrases, and sentences for effect							
Choose punctuation effectively							
Formal and informal language for style and tone including dialects							

Conventions of Standard English/Grammar, Mechanics, and Usage

Skill	1	2	3	4	5	6	7
Sentence concepts: statements, questions, exclamations, commands		✓	✓	✓	✓	✓	✓
Complete and incomplete sentences; sentence fragments; word order		✓	✓	✓	✓	✓	✓
Compound sentences, complex sentences				✓	✓	✓	✓
Combining sentences		✓	✓	✓	✓	✓	✓
Nouns including common, proper, singular, plural, irregular plurals, possessives, abstract, concrete, collective		✓	✓	✓	✓	✓	✓
Verbs including action, helping, linking, irregular		✓	✓	✓	✓	✓	✓
Verb tenses including past, present, future, perfect, and progressive		✓	✓	✓	✓	✓	✓
Pronouns including possessive, subject and object, pronoun-verb agreement, indefinite, intensive, reciprocal, interrogative, relative; correct unclear pronouns		✓	✓	✓	✓	✓	✓
Adjectives including articles, demonstrative, proper, adjectives that compare		✓	✓	✓	✓	✓	✓
Adverbs including telling how, when, where, comparative, superlative, irregular		✓	✓	✓	✓	✓	✓
Subject, predicate; subject-verb agreement		✓	✓	✓	✓	✓	✓
Contractions		✓	✓	✓	✓	✓	✓
Conjunctions				✓	✓	✓	✓
Commas			✓	✓	✓	✓	✓
Colons, semicolons, dashes, hyphens						✓	✓
Question words							
Quotation marks			✓	✓	✓	✓	✓
Prepositions and prepositional phrases, appositives		✓	✓	✓	✓	✓	✓
Independent and dependent clauses						✓	✓
Italics/underlining for emphasis and titles							
Negatives, correcting double negatives					✓	✓	✓
Abbreviations			✓	✓	✓	✓	✓
Use correct capitalization in sentences, proper nouns, titles, abbreviations		✓	✓	✓	✓	✓	✓
Use correct punctuation		✓	✓	✓	✓	✓	✓
Antecedents				✓	✓	✓	✓
Homophones and words often confused			✓	✓	✓	✓	✓
Apostrophes				✓	✓	✓	✓

Spelling

Skill	1	2	3	4	5	6	7
Write irregular, high-frequency words	✓	✓	✓				
ABC order	✓	✓					
Write letters	✓	✓					
Words with short vowels	✓	✓	✓	✓	✓	✓	✓
Words with long vowels	✓	✓	✓	✓	✓	✓	✓
Words with digraphs, blends, consonant clusters, double consonants		✓	✓	✓	✓	✓	✓
Words with vowel digraphs and ambiguous vowels		✓	✓	✓	✓	✓	✓
Words with diphthongs		✓	✓	✓	✓	✓	✓

	K	1	2	3	4	5	6
Words with *r*-controlled vowels		✔	✔	✔	✔	✔	✔
Use conventional spelling		✔	✔	✔	✔	✔	✔
Schwa words				✔	✔	✔	✔
Words with silent letters			✔	✔	✔	✔	✔
Words with hard and soft letters			✔	✔	✔	✔	✔
Inflectional endings including plural, past tense, drop final *e* and double consonant when adding -*ed* and -*ing*, changing *y* to *i*		✔	✔	✔	✔	✔	✔
Compound words		✔	✔	✔	✔	✔	✔
Homonyms/homophones			✔	✔	✔	✔	✔
Prefixes and suffixes		✔	✔	✔	✔	✔	✔
Root and base words (also spell derivatives)				✔	✔	✔	✔
Syllables: patterns, rules, accented, stressed, closed, open				✔	✔	✔	✔
Words with Greek and Latin roots						✔	✔
Words from mythology						✔	✔
Words with spelling patterns, word families		✔	✔	✔	✔	✔	✔

RESEARCH AND INQUIRY

Study Skills

	K	1	2	3	4	5	6
Directions: read, write, give, follow (includes technical directions)			✔	✔	✔	✔	✔
Evaluate directions for sequence and completeness				✔	✔	✔	✔
Use library/media center							
Use parts of a book to locate information							
Interpret information from graphic aids		✔	✔	✔	✔	✔	✔
Use graphic organizers to organize information and comprehend text		✔	✔	✔	✔	✔	✔
Use functional, everyday documents				✔	✔	✔	✔
Apply study strategies: skimming and scanning, note-taking, outlining							

Research Process

	K	1	2	3	4	5	6
Generate and revise topics and questions for research				✔	✔	✔	✔
Narrow focus of research, set research goals				✔	✔	✔	✔
Find and locate information using print and digital resources		✔	✔	✔	✔	✔	✔
Record information systematically (note-taking, outlining, using technology)				✔	✔	✔	✔
Develop a systematic research plan				✔	✔	✔	✔
Evaluate reliability, credibility, usefulness of sources and information						✔	✔
Use primary sources to obtain information					✔	✔	✔
Organize, synthesize, evaluate, and draw conclusions from information							
Cite and list sources of information (record basic bibliographic data)					✔	✔	✔
Demonstrate basic keyboarding skills							
Participate in and present shared research							

Technology

	K	1	2	3	4	5	6
Use computer, Internet, and other technology resources to access information							
Use text and organizational features of electronic resources such as search engines, keywords, e-mail, hyperlinks, URLs, Web pages, databases, graphics							
Use digital tools to present and publish in a variety of media formats							

INDEX

A

Abbreviations, 5: T179, T189, T196, T202, T214

Academic Language, Units 1–6: T8, T10, T16, T18, T20, T26, T28, T30, T36, T38, T42, T44, T48, T50, T86, T88, T94, T96, T98, T104, T106, T08, T114, T116, T120, T126, T164, T166, T172, T174, T176, T182, T184, T186, T192, T194, T198, T204, T206, T242, T244, T250, T252, T254, T260, T262, T264, T270, T272, T276, T278, T282, T284, T320, T322, T328, T330, T332, T338, T340, T342, T348, T350, T354, T356, T360, T362. *See also* Vocabulary Acquisition: domain-specific; Vocabulary Acquisition: general vocabulary.

Access Complex Text

connection of ideas, 1: T31, T187, T265, **3:** T187, **4:** T113B, T113F, **5:** T35B, T35D, T113B, T113C, T113H, T113J, T113N, **6:** 35B, T35J, T269B, T269G

genre, 2: T265, **3:** T343, **4:** T347B, **5:** T191B, T191F, T347B, **6:** T269B, T269C

organization, 1: T31, T109, T265, **2:** T31, T187, T343, **3:** T31, T187, **4:** T191B, T191K, T269B, T269G, T269J, T269O, T347B, T347D, **5:** T35B, T35E, T191B, T191C, T269B, T269F, T269I, **6:** T35B, T35C, T113B, T113F, T347B, T347D

prior knowledge, 1: T109, **2:** T265, **3:** T109, T265, **4:** T35B, T35D, **5:** T347D, **6:** T191B, T191F, T191L

purpose, 1: T343, **2:** T187, T343, **3:** T31, T343, **4:** T113B, T113C, **6:** T113B, T113E, T347B

sentence structure, 1: T187, **2:** T31, **4:** T191B, T191C, **5:** T113B, T113E, T113G, T113I, T113O, T269B, T269C

specific vocabulary, 1: T343, **2:** T109, **3:** T109, T265, **5:** T347B, **6:** T35H

Accuracy. *See* Fluency.

Adjectives. *See* Grammar.

Alliteration. *See* Literary Devices and Elements: alliteration.

Alphabet, 1: S6, S12

Alphabetic Order, 1: T257, T267, T275, T281, T292, **4:** T23, T33, T40, T46, T58

Analytical Writing, 2: T53, T63, T67, T73, T131, T141, T145, T151, T287, T297, T301, T307, **3:** T53, T63, T67, T73, T209, T219, T223, T229, **4:** T53, T63, T73, **5:** T53, T63, T73, **6:** T53, T63, T73, T287, T297, T301, T307. *See also* **Write About Reading.**

Answering Questions. *See* Comprehension Strategies: ask and answer questions.

Antonyms. *See* Vocabulary Skills and Strategies.

Approaching Level Options

comprehension, 1: T60–T61, T138–T139, T216–T217, T294–T295, T372–T373, **2:** T60–T61, T138–T139, T216–T217, T294–T295, T372–T373, **3:** T60–T61, T138–T139, T216–T217, T294–T295, T372–T373, **4:** T60–T61, T138–T139, T216–T217, T294–T295, T372–T373, **5:** T60–T61, T138–T139, T216–T217, T294–T295, T372–T373, **6:** T60–T61, T138–T139, T216–T217, T294–T295, T372–T373

fluency, 1: T60, T138, T216, T294, T372, **2:** T60, T138, T216, T294, T372, **3:** T60, T138, T216, T294, T372, **4:** T60, T138, T216, T294, T372, **5:** T60, T138, T216, T294, T372, **6:** T60, T138, T216, T294, T372

high-frequency words, 1: T59, T137, T215, T293, T371, **2:** T59, T137, T215, T293, T371, **3:** T59, T137, T215, T293, T371

Leveled Reader lessons, Units 1–6: T52–T53, T130–T131, T208–T209, T286–T287, T364–T365

Level Up, Units 1–6: T53, T131, T209, T287, T365, T404

phonemic/phonological awareness, Units 1–6: T54–T55, T132–T133, T210–T211, T288–T289, T366–T367

phonics, Units 1–6: T56–T57, T134–T135, T212–T213, T290–T291, T368–T369

self-selected reading, Units 1–6: T61, T139, T217, T295, T373

structural analysis, Units 1–6: T58, T136, T214, T292, T370

words to know, 4: T59, T137, T215, T293, T371, **5:** T59, T137, T215, T293, T371, **6:** T59, T137, T215, T293, T371

Ask and Answer Questions. *See* Comprehension Strategies.

Assessment

checklists

listening, 1: T401, T403, **2:** T401, T403, **3:** T401, **4:** T401, T403, **5:** T401, T403, **6:** T401, T403

portfolio choice, 1: T403, **2:** T403, **3:** T403, **4:** T403, **5:** T403, **6:** T403

presentation, 1: T401, **2:** T401, **3:** T401, **4:** T401, **5:** T401, **6:** T401

project rubric, 1: T401, **2:** T401, **3:** T401, **4:** T401, **5:** T401, **6:** T401

research process, 1: T401, **2:** T401, **3:** T401, **4:** T401, **5:** T401, **6:** T401

speaking, 1: T402, **2:** T402, **3:** T402, **4:** T402, **5:** T402, **6:** T402

end-of-week, Units 1–6: T77A–T77B, T155A–T155B, T233A–T233B, T311A–T311B, T389A–T389B

fluency, 1: T408, **2:** T408, **3:** T408, **4:** T408, **5:** T408, **6:** T408

portfolio, 1: T48, T126, T204, T282, T360, T403, **2:** T48, T126, T204, T282, T360, T403, **3:** T48, T126, T204, T282, T360, T403, **4:** T48, T126, T204, T282, T360, T403, **5:** T48, T126, T204, T282, T360, T403, **6:** T48, T126, T204, T282, T360, T403

Start Smart, 1: S94–S95

Summative Assessment, 1: T408–T409, **2:** T408–T409, **3:** T408–T409, **4:** T408–T409, **5:** T408–T409, **6:** T408–T409

B

C

F

Key 1 = Unit 1

H

I

M

R

W

Common Core State
Standards Correlations

English Language Arts

College and Career Readiness Anchor Standards for READING

The K–5 standards on the following pages define what students should understand and be able to do by the end of each grade. They correspond to the College and Career Readiness anchor standards below by number. The CCR and grade-specific standards are necessary complements—the former providing broad standards, the latter providing additional specificity—that together define the skills and understandings that all students must demonstrate.

Key Ideas and Details

1. Read closely to determine what the text says explicitly and to make logical inferences from it; cite specific textual evidence when writing or speaking to support conclusions drawn from the text.

2. Determine central ideas or themes of a text and analyze their development; summarize the key supporting details and ideas.

3. Analyze how and why individuals, events, and ideas develop and interact over the course of a text.

Craft and Structure

4. Interpret words and phrases as they are used in a text, including determining technical, connotative, and figurative meanings, and analyze how specific word choices shape meaning or tone.

5. Analyze the structure of texts, including how specific sentences, paragraphs, and larger portions of the text (e.g., a section, chapter, scene, or stanza) relate to each other and the whole.

6. Assess how point of view or purpose shapes the content and style of a text.

Integration of Knowledge and Ideas

7. Integrate and evaluate content presented in diverse media and formats, including visually and quantitatively as well as in words.

8. Delineate and evaluate the argument and specific claims in a text, including the validity of the reasoning as well as the relevance and sufficiency of the evidence.

9. Analyze how two or more texts address similar themes or topics in order to build knowledge or to compare the approaches the authors take.

Range of Reading and Level of Text Complexity

10. Read and comprehend complex literary and informational texts independently and proficiently.

English Language Arts

Grade 1

Each standard is coded in the following manner:

Strand	Grade Level	Standard
RL	1	1

Reading Standards for Literature

Key Ideas and Details		McGraw-Hill *Wonders*
RL.1.1	Ask and answer questions about key details in a text.	**READING/WRITING WORKSHOP:** Unit I: 24, 25, 44, 45, 64, 65 **Unit 2:** 44, 45, 84, 85 **Unit 3:** 24, 25, 64, 65 **Unit 4:** 88, 89 **Unit 5:** 130, 131, 190, 191 **Unit 6:** 232, 233, 272, 273 **LITERATURE ANTHOLOGY:** Unit I: 19, 41, 63 **Unit 2:** 21, 43, 81 **Unit 3:** 23, 45, 67, 73 **Unit 4:** 29, 89, 125 **Unit 5:** 155, 195, 225, 255 **Unit 6:** 295, 325, 357, 393 **LEVELED READERS: Unit I, Week I:** *We Like to Share* (O), *Class Party* (B) **Unit I, Week 2:** *A Trip to the City* (O), *Harvest Time* (B) **Unit I, Week 3:** *Mouse's Moon Party* (A), *Pet Show* (O) **Unit 2, Week I:** *Pick Up Day* (A), *Ben Brings the Mail* (O), *At Work with Mom* (B) **Unit 2, Week 2:** *What a Nest!* (A), *Staying Afloat* (O) **Unit 2, Week 4:** *The Sick Tree* (A), *Squirrels Help* (O), *Wow, Kitty!* (B) **Unit 3, Week I:** *Busy's Watch* (A), *Kate Saves the Date!* (O) **Unit 3, Week 2:** *Corn Fun* (A), *Yum, Strawberries!* (O) **Unit 3, Week 3:** *The Magic Paintbrush* (O) **Unit 4, Week I:** *Fly to the Rescue!* (O) **Unit 4, Week 4:** *The Hat* (O) **Unit 5, Week I:** *Nuts for Winter* (A), *Dog Bones* (O), *Spark's Toys* (B) **Unit 5, Week 2:** *Hide and Seek* (O) **Unit 5, Week 4:** *Thump, Jangle, Crash* (A), *Down on the Farm* (O) **Unit 6, Week I:** *Two Hungry Elephants* (A), *What a Feast!* (O) **Unit 6, Week 3:** *Snow Day* (A), *Heat Wave* (O), *Rainy Day Fun* (B) **Unit 6, Week 4:** *The Quilt* (A), *Latkes for Sam* (O) **CLOSE READING COMPANION:** I-3, 8-10, 15-17, 34-36, 41-43, 55-57, 67-69, 74-76, 81-83, 100-103, 121-123, 133-135, 140-142, 154-156, 166-168, 180-182, 187-189 **YOUR TURN PRACTICE BOOK:** 7, 17, 42, 44, 117, 127, 147, 162, 193, 205, 217, 229, 241, 246, 253, 258, 277, 282, 301, 306, 313, 318 **READING WORKSTATION ACTIVITY CARDS:** I, 3, 8, 14, 16, 23, 26, 28 **WRITING WORKSTATION ACTIVITY CARDS:** 9 **INTERACTIVE READ-ALOUD CARDS: Unit I, Week 5:** 2, 4 **Unit 2, Week 2:** 3, 4 **Unit 3, Week 2:** 4 **Unit 3, Week 3:** 4 **Unit 3, Week 5:** 4 **Unit 4, Week I:** 3, 4 **Unit 4, Week 5:** 4 **Unit 5, Week I:** 4 **Unit 5, Week 2:** 4 **Unit 5, Week 4:** 2, 4 **Unit 5, Week 5:** 3, 4 **Unit 6, Week I:** 4 **Unit 6, Week 2:** 2, 4 **Unit 6, Week 3:** 3, 4 **TEACHER'S EDITION: Unit I:** T105, T113B, T113C, T113D, T113E, T113F, T113G, T183, T191B, T191C, T191D, T191E, T191G, T217, T221, T225 **Unit 2:** T269A-T269J, T412-T413, T415 **Unit 3:** T191A-T191J, T412-T413, T415 **Unit 4:** T11, T21, T35C, T35H, T167, T177, T191A-T191P, T269A-T269R, T407, T412-T413, T415 **Unit 5:** T269A-T269P, T245, T255, T261, T269D, T269E, T300, T322, T333, T407, T412-T413, T415 **Unit 6:** T35C, T191A-T191F, T191G-T191L, T191M-T191R, T269A-T269H, T269I-T269R, T407, T412-T413, T415 **www.connected.mcgraw-hill.com: RESOURCES: Units I–6: Student Practice:** Genre Study, Approaching Reproducibles, Beyond Reproducibles, ELL Reproducibles, **Graphic Organizers:** Graphic Organizers, **Cards:** Retelling Cards

Reading Standards for Literature

Key Ideas and Details		McGraw-Hill *Wonders*
RL.1.2	Retell stories, including key details, and demonstrate understanding of their central message or lesson.	**READING/WRITING WORKSHOP:** Unit I: 24, 25, 44, 45, 64, 65 **Unit 4:** 28, 29 **Unit 5:** I50, I51 **Unit 6:** 232, 233, 272, 273, 292, 293 **LITERATURE ANTHOLOGY: Unit I:** I9, 40, 63 **Unit 2:** 21, 42, 81 **Unit 3:** 23, 45, 67 **Unit 4:** 29, I25 **Unit 5:** I55, I95, 255 **Unit 6:** 295, 357, 393 **LEVELED READERS: Unit I, Week 3:** *Pet Show* (O) **Unit 2, Week I:** *Pick Up Day* (A), *Ben Brings the Mail* (O), *At\u0113Work with Mom* (B) **Unit 3, Week 3:** *The Magic Paintbrush* (O) **Unit 4, Week I:** *Fly to the Rescue!* (O), *The Hat* (O) **Unit 5, Week 2:** *Little Blue's Dream* (A), *Hide and Seek* (O) **Unit 5, Week 4:** *Down on the Farm* (O), *Going on a Bird Walk* (B) **Unit 6, Week 4:** *The Quilt* (A), *Latkes for Sam* (O), *Patty Jumps!* (B) **CLOSE READING COMPANION:** I64, I69, I89 **YOUR TURN PRACTICE BOOK:** I38, 274, 277, 282, 3I3 **READING WORKSTATION ACTIVITY CARDS:** 2, 6, I4, I6, 23 **WRITING WORKSTATION ACTIVITY CARDS:** 9 **INTERACTIVE READ-ALOUD CARDS: Unit I, Week 2:** 4 **Unit I, Week 5:** 4 **Unit 2, Week 2:** 3, 4 **Unit 3, Week 2:** 4 **Unit 3, Week 3:** 4 **Unit 3, Week 5:** 4 **Unit 4, Week I:** 3, 4 **Unit 4, Week 5:** 4 **Unit 5, Week I:** 4 **Unit 5, Week 2:** 4 **Unit 5, Week 4:** 4 **Unit 5, Week 5:** 3, 4 **Unit 6, Week I:** 4 **Unit 6, Week 2:** 4 **Unit 6, Week 3:** 4 **TEACHER'S EDITION: Unit I:** S32, TII, T3I, TI09, TTII3I-TII3J, TI87, TI9IF, T269A-T269J, T4I4-T4I5 **Unit 2:** T35I-T35J, T345 **Unit 3:** TII, T3I, TII3J, TI87, TI9II-TI9IJ, T269I **Unit 4:** TII, T35K-T35L, T269R **Unit 5:** TII, T35I, T89, TII3R, T245, T269P, T297, T4I4-T4I5 **Unit 6:** TII, T27, T35B, T35D, T35E, T35N, T89, TI9IQ, TI9IR, T269B, T269C, T269M, T300-T30I **www.connected.mcgraw-hill.com: RESOURCES: Units I–6: Cards:** Retelling Cards **Media:** Fluency Passages **Graphic Organizers:** Graphic Organizers, Think Aloud Clouds **Student Practice:** Approaching Reproducibles, Beyond Reproducibles, ELL Reproducibles
RL.1.3	Describe characters, settings, and major events in a story, using key details.	**READING/WRITING WORKSHOP: Unit 2:** 24, 25, 44, 45, 84, 85 **Unit 3:** 24, 25, 44, 45, 64, 65 **Unit 4:** 28, 29 **Unit 5:** I50, I51, I90, I91 **Unit 6:** 272, 273 **LITERATURE ANTHOLOGY: Unit I:** I9, 41, 63 **Unit 2:** 21, 43, 81 **Unit 3:** 23, 45, 67 **Unit 4:** 29, I25 **Unit 5:** I55, I95, 255 **LEVELED READERS: Unit I, Week I:** *We Like to Share* (O) **Unit I, Week 3:** *Pet Show* (O) **Unit 2, Week I:** *Ben Brings the Mail* (O) **Unit 2, Week 2:** *Staying Afloat* (O) **Unit 2, Week 4:** *The Sick Tree* (A), *Squirrels Help* (O) **Unit 3, Week I:** *Busy's Watch* (A), *Kate Saves the Date!* (O) **Unit 5, Week I:** *Dog Bones* (O) **Unit 6, Week I:** *What a Feast!* (O) **YOUR TURN PRACTICE BOOK:** 42, 44, 50, I04, I07, II4, II7, I24, I27, I44, I47, I54, I57, I90, I93, I98, 202, 205, 2I4, 2I7, 222, 226, 229, 234, 238, 24I, 246, 258, 277, 298, 30I, 306, 3I3, 3I8 **READING WORKSTATION ACTIVITY CARDS:** I, 2, 3, 4, 6, 7, 8, I2, I3, I6, 23, 28 **WRITING WORKSTATION ACTIVITY CARDS:** 9, 23 **INTERACTIVE READ-ALOUD CARDS: Unit 2, Week 2:** 4 **Unit 3, Week 3:** 2 **Unit 3, Week 5:** 2, 4 **Unit 4, Week I:** 4 **Unit 4, Week 5:** 4 **Unit 5, Week I:** 4 **Unit 5, Week 2:** 3, 4 **Unit 5, Week 4:** 2, 4 **Unit 5, Week 5:** 3, 4 **Unit 6, Week I:** 4 **Unit 6, Week 2:** 4 **Unit 6, Week 3:** 3, 4 **TEACHER'S EDITION: Unit I:** T27, T35D-T35F, T35H, TI05, TII3D, TI83 **Unit 2:** T27, T35B, T35E-T35G, T35I, T35J, T5I, T69, T70-T7I, T72-T73, TI05, TII3E-TII3F, TI38, TI39, TI40, TI4I, T27IB-27ID, T296, T297 **Unit 3:** T27, T35B-T35H, T35J, T52-T53, T69, T70-T7I, T72-T73, TII3B-TII3C, TII3G-TII3H, TII3J, TI47, TI48-TI49, TI50 **Unit 4:** T27, T3I, T35E, T35G, T35I, T35L, T52-T53, T60-T6I, T62-T63, T65, T66-T67 **Unit 5:** T27, T3I, T35C-T35D, T35F, T60, T65, TI04-TI05, TI38-TI39, T269C, T269F-T269H, T305, T204, T307, T407, T4I5 **Unit 6:** T35D-T35F, T35I, T35K, TI82-TI83, T2I6 **www.connected.mcgraw-hill.com: RESOURCES: Units I–6: Graphic Organizers:** Graphic Organizers **Cards:** Retelling Cards **Student Practice:** Approaching Reproducibles, Beyond Reproducibles, ELL Reproducibles
Craft and Structure		McGraw-Hill *Wonders*
RL.1.4	Identify words and phrases in stories or poems that suggest feelings or appeal to the senses.	**READING/WRITING WORKSHOP: Unit I:** 7 **Unit 2:** 7 **Unit 3:** 7 **Unit 4:** II **Unit 5:** II3 **Unit 6:** 2I5 **LITERATURE ANTHOLOGY: Unit I:** 84, 85 **Unit 2:** 62, 63 **Unit 3:** 68, 69, 70, 7I, 72, 73 **Unit 4:** 90, 91 **Unit 5:** 222, 223, 224, 225 **Unit 6:** 324, 325 **CLOSE READING COMPANION:** 86, I50, I52, I78 **READING WORKSTATION ACTIVITY CARDS:** 2I **WRITING WORKSTATION ACTIVITY CARDS:** I3, I5 **INTERACTIVE READ-ALOUD CARDS: Unit 3, Week 3:** I **TEACHER'S EDITION: Unit I:** T272-T273 **Unit 2:** TI94-TI95 **Unit 3:** TI8, T35E-T35F, T35I, T76, TI94, TI95A-TI95B **Unit 4:** TI94-TI95 **Unit 5:** T35H, TI95, TI95A-TI95B **Unit 6:** TII6-TII7, T269D **www.connected.mcgraw-hill.com: RESOURCES: Media:** Images

RL.1.5	Explain major differences between books that tell stories and books that give information, drawing on a wide reading of a range of text types.	**LITERATURE ANTHOLOGY: Unit I:** 47, 67, 83, 93 **Unit 2:** 21, 25, 43, 47, 61, 81, 93 **Unit 3:** 23, 27, 45, 66, 89, 101 **Unit 4:** 29, 55, 89, 125, 137 **Unit 5:** 155, 195, 221, 255, 267 **Unit 6:** 295, 323, 357, 393, 405 **LEVELED READERS: Unit I, Week I:** *We Like to Share* (O), *Class Party* (B) **Unit I, Week 2:** *What Can We See?* (A), *AēTrip to the City* (O), *Where I Live,* pp. 13–16 (O), *Harvest Time* (B) **Unit I, Week 3:** *Mouse's Moon Party* (A), *Pet Show* (O), *Polly the Circus Star* (B) **Unit I, Week 4:** *Friends Are Fun* (A, O, B) **Unit I, Week 5:** *We Can Move!* (A, O, B) **Unit 2 Week I:** *Pick Up Day* (A), *Ben Brings the Mail* (O), *At Work with Mom* (B) **Unit 2, Week 2:** *What a Nest!* (A), *Stone Castles,* pp. 13–16 (A), *Staying Afloat* (O), *City Armadillo, Country Armadillo* (B) **Unit 2, Week 3:** *Meerkat Family* (A, O, B) **Unit 2, Week 4:** *The Sick Tree* (A), *Squirrels Help* (O), *Sharing Skills,* pp. 13–16 (B) **Unit 2, Week 5:** *How Maps Help* (A, O, B) **Unit 3, Week I:** *Busy's Watch* (A), *Kate Saves the Date!* (O), *Uncle George Is Coming!* (B) **Unit 3, Week 3:** *How Coquí Got Her Voice* (A), *The Magic Paintbrush* (O), *The Storytelling Stone* (B) **Unit 4, Week I:** *The King of the Animals* (A), *Lions and Elephants,* pp. 13–16 (A), *Fly to the Rescue!* (O), *Animal Traits,* pp. 13–16 (O), *Hummingbird's Wings* (B) **Unit 4, Week 2:** *Penguins All Around* (A, O, B) **Unit 4, Week 4:** *Come One, Come All* (B) **Unit 5, Week I:** *Nuts for Winter* (A), *Dog Bones* (O), *Spark's Toys* (B) **Unit 5, Week 5:** *What Is a Yurt?* (A, O, B) **Unit 6, Week I:** *Two Hungry Elephants* (A), *What a Feast!* (O), *Beware of the Lion!* (B) **Unit 6, Week 4:** *The Quilt* (A), *Latkes for Sam* (O) **TEACHER'S EDITION: Unit I:** SI4, S32, S56, S62, S92, TII3F, T269F **Unit 2:** T26, TII3G, TI9IH, T260, T269E, T338 **Unit 3:** T35E, T269D **Unit 4:** T26, T35H, TII3H, TI9II, T269D, T347D **Unit 5:** T35C, T35J, TII3K, TI82, TI9IL, T269J, T338, T347F **Unit 6:** T26, T35J, TII3L, TI9IR, T269J, T347F www.connected.mcgraw-hill.com: **RESOURCES: Units I–6: Teacher Resources:** Theme Bibliography, Literature/Informational Text Chart, Book Talk, Reader Response **Graphic Organizers:** Graphic Organizers
RL.1.6	Identify who is telling the story at various points in a text.	**READING/WRITING WORKSHOP: Unit 2:** 24, 25, 44, 45, 84, 85 **Unit 3:** 24, 25 **Unit 4:** 88, 89 **Unit 5:** 130, 131 190, 191 **Unit 6:** 272, 273 **LITERATURE ANTHOLOGY: Unit 4:** 125 **Unit 5:** 155 **TEACHER'S EDITION: Unit 3:** T26, TII3B, TII3I **Unit 4:** T26I, T269E-T269F, T269H, T269K, T269O, T269R, T295, T299, T4I5 **Unit5:** T26-T27, T35B-T35E, T35G, T35I-T35J, T395 www.connected.mcgraw-hill.com: **RESOURCES: Graphic Organizers:** Graphic Organizers

Reading Standards for Literature

Integration of Knowledge and Ideas		McGraw-Hill *Wonders*
RL.1.7	Use illustrations and details in a story to describe its characters, setting, or events.	**READING/WRITING WORKSHOP:** Unit 4: 88, 89 **Unit 5:** 130, 131 **LITERATURE ANTHOLOGY:** Unit 1: 63 **Unit 2:** 21, 42, 81 **Unit 3:** 23 **LEVELED READERS:** Unit 1, Week 1: *A Fun Day* (A) **Unit 2, Week 1:** *Pick Up Day* (A), *Ben Brings the Mail* (O), **Unit 6, Week 3:** *Heat Wave* (O) **CLOSE READING COMPANION:** 41, 55, 102, 167, 181 **YOUR TURN PRACTICE BOOK:** 44, 144, 147, 154, 193, 198, 202, 205, 210, 214, 246, 258, 277, 298 **READING WORKSTATION ACTIVITY CARDS:** 2, 4, 28 **INTERACTIVE READ-ALOUD CARDS:** Unit 6, Week 1: 4 **Unit 6, Week 2:** 2, 4 **TEACHER'S EDITION:** Unit 1: T35B-T35D, T38-T39, T104-T105, T113H-T113I, T216 T261 **Unit 2:** T27, T35B-T35E, T113B-T113I T261, T269D, T269G, T269J, T308 **Unit 3:** T35B, T35D, T113D, T141, T167, T191D, T208, T298 **Unit 4:** T11, T35B, T35J, T71, T269G **Unit 5:** T35C, T269D, T269N, T269P, T305, T306-T307, T323 **Unit 6:** T183, T191C, T191E, T191H, T191P, T227, T269G, T269P, T306-T307 www.connected.mcgraw-hill.com: **RESOURCES: Graphic Organizers:** Graphic Organizers; **Media:** Images; Cards: Retelling Cards; Student Practice Approaching Reproducibles 44, 144, 147, 150, 154, 190, 193, 198, 202, 205, 210, 214, 246, 250, 258, 277, 298; Beyond Reproducibles 44, 144, 147, 150, 154, 190, 193, 198, 202, 205, 210, 214, 246, 250, 258, 277, 29, ELL Reproducibles 44, 144, 147, 150, 154, 190, 193, 198, 202, 205, 210, 214, 246, 250, 258, 277, 298
RL.1.8	(Not applicable to Literature)	
RL.1.9	Compare and contrast the adventures and experiences of characters in stories.	**READING/WRITING WORKSHOP:** Unit 2: 24, 25, 44, 45, 84, 85 **Unit 3:** 64, 65 **Unit 4:** 88, 89 **Unit 5:** 130, 131, 150, 151 **Unit 6:** 272, 273 **LEVELED READERS:** Unit 3, Week 3: *How Coquí Got Her Voice* (A), *The Magic Paintbrush* (O) **CLOSE READING COMPANION:** 11-13, 15, 43, 76, 168 **READING WORKSTATION ACTIVITY CARDS:** 23 **INTERACTIVE READ-ALOUD CARDS:** Unit 6, Week 1: 3 **TEACHER'S EDITION:** Unit 1: T128, T206 **Unit 2:** T128 **Unit 3:** T128, T191I, T206 **Unit 4:** T50 **Unit 5:** T50, T128, T284 **Unit 6:** T50, T206 www.connected.mcgraw-hill.com: **RESOURCES: Units 1-6: Graphic Organizers:** Graphic Organizers

Range of Reading and Level of Text Complexity		McGraw-Hill *Wonders*
RL.1.10	With prompting and support, read prose and poetry of appropriate complexity for grade 1.	**WRITING WORKSHOP:** Unit 1: 7, 14-23, 34-43, 54-63 **Unit 2:** 7, 14-23, 34-43, 74-83 **Unit 3:** 7, 14-23, 34-43, 54-63 **Unit 4:** 11, 18-27, 78-87 **Unit 5:** 113, 120-129, 140-149, 180-189 **Unit 6:** 215, 222-231, 262-271, 282-291 **LITERATURE ANTHOLOGY:** Unit 3, Week 2: *The Big Yuca Plant*, 28 **Unit 3, Week 3:** *The Gingerbread Man*, 50 **Unit 3, Week 4:** *Mother Goose Rhymes*, 68 **Unit 4, Week 1:** *How Bat Got Its Wings*, 10 **Unit 4, Week 4:** *When It's Snowing*, 90 **Unit 5, Week 1:** *A Lost Button*, 140 **Unit 5, Week 2:** *Kitten's First Full Moon*, 162 **Unit 5, Week 3:** *Windshield Wipers*, 222 **Unit 6, Week 2:** *Abuelita's Lap*, 324 **Unit 6, Week 3:** *Rain School*, 236 **LEVELED READERS:** Unit 1, Week 4: *I Like to Play*, pp. 13-16 (A, O, B) **Unit 2, Week 3:** *I Live in a House!* (A, O, B) **Unit 4, Week 3:** *Ducklings*, pp. 13-16 (A, O), pp. 12-16 (B) **Unit 5, Week 3:** *Fly Away, Butterfly*, pp. 13-16 (A, O) **Unit 6, Week 2:** *Fire!* pp. 13-16 (A, O); pp. 12-16 (B) **YOUR TURN PRACTICE BOOK:** 5, 6, 15, 16, 25, 26, 35, 36, 42, 45, 46, 55, 56, 65, 66, 75, 76, 85, 86, 105, 106, 115, 116, 125, 126, 145, 146, 155, 156, 191, 192, 203, 204, 215, 216, 227, 228, 239, 251, 252, 275, 276, 299, 311, 312 **READING WORKSTATION ACTIVITY CARDS:** 1, 2, 3, 4, 6, 7, 8, 12, 14, 16, 20, 23, 25, 26, 28 **TEACHER'S EDITION:** Unit 1: T16-T17, T52-T53, T140-T141, T142-T143, T414 **Unit 2:** T16-T17, T35A, T61, T62-T63, T297, T298-T299, T305, T306-T307 **Unit 3:** T65, T66-T67, T94-T95, T113A, T130-T131, T172-T173, T191B, T191C, T195, T195A-T195B, T225 **Unit 4:** T16-T17, T191B, T219, T299, T303, T304-T305, T306-T307 **Unit 5:** T16-T17, T35D, T69, T70-T71, T72-T73, T143, T144-T145, T260-T261, T295, T296, T306-T307 **Unit 6:** T35B, T35H, T61, T62-T63, T151, T217, T303, T407 **LITERATURE BIG BOOKS:** Unit 1, Week 1: *This School Year Will be the Best* **Unit 1, Week 2:** *Alicia's Happy Day* **Unit 1, Week 3:** *Cool Dog, School Dog* **Unit 2, Week 1:** *Millie Waits for the Mail* **Unit 2, Week 2:** *The 3 Little Dassies* **Unit 2, Week 3:** *Babies in the Bayou* **Unit 3, Week 1:** *A Second is a Hiccup* **Unit 3, Week 2:** *Mystery Vine* **Unit 3, Week 3:** *Interrupting Chicken* **Unit 3, Week 4:** *The Last Train* www.connected.mcgraw-hill.com: **RESOURCES: Units 1-6: Teacher Resources:** Theme Bibliography, Literature/Informational Texts Chart **Student Practice:** Approaching Reproducibles, Beyond Reproducibles, ELL Reproducibles

Reading Standards for Informational Text

Key Ideas and Details		McGraw-Hill *Wonders*
RI.1.1	Ask and answer questions about key details in a text.	**READING/WRITING WORKSHOP: Unit I:** 84–85, 104–105 **Unit 2:** 64–65, 104–105 **Unit 3:** 84–85, 104–105 **Unit 4:** 48–49, 68–69 **LITERATURE ANTHOLOGY: Unit I:** 83, 93, 94, 95 **Unit 2:** 61, 88, 89, 91, 93 **Unit 3:** 26, 49, 75, 89, 101, 103 **Unit 4:** 35, 55, 89, 137 **Unit 5:** 221, 267 **Unit 6:** 301, 323, 405 **LEVELED READERS: Unit I, Week 4:** *Friends Are Fun* (A, O, B) **Unit 2, Week 3:** *Meerkat Family* (A, O, B) **Unit 2, Week 5:** *How Maps Help* (A, O, B) **Unit 3, Week 4:** *Schools Then and Now* (A, O, B) **Unit 3, Week 5:** *Apples from Farm to Table* (A, O, B) **Unit 4, Week 2:** *Penguins All Around* (A, O, B) **Unit 4, Week 3:** *Go, Gator!* (A, O, B) **Unit 5, Week 3:** *The Wright Brothers* (A, O, B) **Unit 5, Week 5:** *What Is a Yurt?* (A, O, B) **Unit 6, Week 2:** *Helping Me, Helping You!* (A, O, B) **Unit 6, Week 5:** *It's Labor Day!* (A, O, B) **CLOSE READING COMPANION:** 22-24, 29, 43-45, 62-63, 88-90, 95-96, 107-109, 114-116, 147-149, 154-156, 173-175, 194-196 **YOUR TURN PRACTICE BOOK:** 94, 97, 100, 137, 161, 169, 181, 221, 257, 265, 270, 286, 289, 294, 305, 317, 322, 325, 330 **READING WORKSTATION ACTIVITY CARDS:** 5, 9, 11, 13, 15, 27 **WRITING WORKSTATION ACTIVITY CARDS:** 27, 29, 30 **INTERACTIVE READ-ALOUD CARDS: Unit I, Week 3:** 4 **Unit 2, Week I:** 3, 4 **Unit 2, Week 3:** 1, 4 **Unit 2, Week 4:** 3, 4 **Unit 2, Week 5:** 1, 3, 4 **Unit 3, Week I:** 4 **Unit 3, Week 4:** 4 **Unit 4, Week 2:** 2, 4 **Unit 4, Week 3:** 1, 4 **Unit 4, Week 4:** 3, 4 **Unit 5, Week 3:** 4 **Unit 5, Week 4:** 4 **Unit 6, Week 5:** 3, 4 **TEACHER'S EDITION: Unit I:** T244-T245, T255, T261, T269A-T269J, T322-T323, T332-T333, T338-T339, T343, T347A-T347F, T362, T374-T375, T404, T412-T413 **Unit 2:** T191A-T191H, T218, T347A-T347F, T374, T394-T395, T407, T412-T413, T415 **Unit 3:** T255, T261, T265, T260-T261, T269A-269J, T269I-T269J, T294, T362, T372, T389, T394-T395, T407, T412-T413, T415 **Unit 4:** T89, T99, T105, T113B-T113I, T117B, T130, T140, T144, T148-T149, T167, T183, T191C, T191F, T191H, T208, T216, T218, T222, T227, T228, T347A-T347D **Unit 5:** T167, T191A-T191L, T208, T218, T222, T284, T338-T339, T364, T374, T379, T382-T383 **Unit 6:** T113F-T113J, T113L, T128, T372, T394-T395, T407, T412 www.connected.mcgraw-hill.com: **RESOURCES: Units I–6: Graphic Organizers:** Graphic Organizers, Think Aloud Clouds **Tier 2 Intervention:** Comprehension **Student Practice:** Approaching Reproducibles, Beyond Reproducibles, ELL Reproducibles

Reading Standards for Informational Text

RI.1.2	Identify the main topic and retell key details of a text.	**READING/WRITING WORKSHOP: Unit 2:** 64, 65, 104, 105 **Unit 4:** 48, 49, 68, 69 **LITERATURE ANTHOLOGY: Unit 1:** 83, 93 **Unit 2:** 61, 93 **Unit 3:** 89 **Unit 4:** 55, 89 **Unit 5:** 221 **Unit 6:** 323 **LEVELED READERS: Unit 2, Week 3:** *Meerkat Family* (A, O, B) **Unit 2, Week 5:** *How Maps Help* (A, O, B) **Unit 4, Week 2:** *Penguins All Around* (A, O, B) **Unit 4, Week 3:** *Go, Gator!* (A, O, B) **CLOSE READING COMPANION:** 50, 62, 109 **YOUR TURN PRACTICE BOOK:** 10, 20, 30, 40, 50, 60, 70, 80 90, 100, 110, 120, 138, 150, 186, 198, 210, 274, 277, 282, 310, 313 **READING WORKSTATION ACTIVITY CARDS:** 5, 10, 11, 27 **WRITING WORKSTATION ACTIVITY CARDS:** 24, 27 **INTERACTIVE READ-ALOUD CARDS: Unit 1, Week 3:** 4 **Unit 2, Week 1:** 4 **Unit 2, Week 3:** 2, 4 **Unit 2, Week 4:** 3, 4 **Unit 2, Week 5:** 1, 3, 4 **Unit 3, Week 1:** 4 **Unit 3, Week 4:** 4 **Unit 4, Week 2:** 4 **Unit 4, Week 3:** 1, 4 **Unit 4, Week 4:** 4 **Unit 5, Week 3:** 4 **Unit 6, Week 4:** 4 **Unit 6, Week 5:** 4 **TEACHER'S EDITION: Unit 1:** T261, T265, T269D–269J, T342 **Unit 2:** T167, T182–T183, T191B–T191H, T218–T219, T220–T221, T227, T228–T229, T230–T231, T323, T339, T347E–T347F, T383, T384–T385, T396–T387, T397, T405 **Unit 3:** T269I–T269J, T307, T338–T339, T347C–T347F, T375 **Unit 4:** T89, T105, T113G, T113K, T128–T129, T151, T245, T347B–T347C, T347E–T347F, T379 **Unit 5:** T167, T191H, T191K, T191L, T223, T385, T414–T415 **Unit 6:** T109, T131, T245, T347F, T363 **www.connected.mcgraw-hill.com: RESOURCES: Units 1–6: Graphic Organizers:** Graphic Organizers, Think Aloud Clouds **Tier 2 Intervention:** Comprehension **Student Practice:** Approaching Reproducibles, Beyond Reproducibles, ELL Reproducibles **Cards:** Retelling Cards
Key Ideas and Details		**McGraw-Hill *Wonders***
RI.1.3	Describe the connection between two individuals, events, ideas, or pieces of information in a text.	**READING/WRITING WORKSHOP: Unit 3:** 84, 85, 104, 105 **Unit 4:** 38–47, 108, 109 **Unit 5:** 170, 171, 210, 211 **LITERATURE ANTHOLOGY: Unit 1:** 94, 95 **Unit 2:** 61, 93 **Unit 3:** 49, 89, 101 **Unit 4:** 35, 37–53, 55, 89, 137 **Unit 5:** 221, 267 **Unit 6:** 323 **LEVELED READERS: Unit 2, Week 5:** *How Maps Help* (A, O, B) **Unit 3, Week 5:** *Apples from Farm to Table* (A, O, B) **Unit 4, Week 4:** *Wings*, pp. 13–16 (A) **Unit 4, Week 5:** *Teach a Dog!* (A, O, B) **Unit 5, Week 5:** *What Is a Yurt?* (A, O, B) **Unit 6, Week 5:** *It's Labor Day!* (A, O, B) **CLOSE READING COMPANION:** 90, 93, 140 **YOUR TURN PRACTICE BOOK:** 134, 137, 257, 262, 265, 317 **READING WORKSTATION ACTIVITY CARDS:** 9, 13, 15, 17 **INTERACTIVE READ-ALOUD CARDS: Unit 6, Week 4:** 4 **Unit 6, Week 5:** 3 **TEACHER'S EDITION: Unit 1:** T285, T347B, T347E–T347F, T404–T405, T406 **Unit 2:** T183, T206, T404–T405, T406 **Unit 3:** T261, T269B–T269G, T285, T286–T287, T295, T296–T297, T299, T300–T301, T303, T304–T305, T306–T307, T339, T347B–T347E, T365, T373, T375, T377, T379, T381, T385, T404–T405 **Unit 4:** T105, T109, T113D, T113F, T113H, T339, T347B, T404–T405, T406 **Unit 5:** T183, T187, T191E, T191E, T191H, T191I, T208–T209, T216–T217, T218–T219, T223–T225, T226–T227, T228–T229, T339, T347C, T347E–T347F, T339, T364–T365, T373, T375, T377, T379, T384–T385 **Unit 6:** T95, T113D–T113E, T129, T404–T405, T406 **www.connected.mcgraw-hill.com: RESOURCES: Units 1–6: Student Practice:** Approaching Reproducibles, Beyond Reproducibles, ELL Reproducibles **Graphic Organizers:** Graphic Organizers **Interactive Games & Activities:** Comprehension
Craft and Structure		**McGraw-Hill *Wonders***
RI.1.4	Ask and answer questions to help determine or clarify the meaning of words and phrases in a text.	**CLOSE READING COMPANION:** 31, 44, 124–125, 158 **TEACHER'S EDITION: Unit 2:** T176, T273A, T396 **Unit 3:** T269F **Unit 4:** T113, T113F, T146, T191G, T269, T269G, T347 **Unit 5:** T35, T113C, T269, T269K, T347 **Unit 6:** T40, T113G, T191J **www.connected.mcgraw-hill.com: RESOURCES: Units 1–6: Media:** Visual Glossary **Tier 2 Intervention:** Vocabulary **Interactive Games & Activities:** Vocabulary

Reading Standards for Informational Text

RI.1.5	Know and use various text structures features (e.g., headings, tables of contents, glossaries, electronic menus, icons) to locate key facts or information in a text.	**READING/WRITING WORKSHOP:** Unit 2: 61, 94–103 **Unit 3:** 74–83, 96, 98, 103 **Unit 4:** 43, 45, 47, 98–107 **Unit 5:** 162, 164, 166, 200–209 **Unit 6:** 302–311 **LITERATURE ANTHOLOGY:** Unit 1: 94, 95 **Unit 2:** 59 **LEVELED READERS: Unit 2, Week 5:** *How Maps Help* (B) **Unit 3, Week 4:** *Schools Then and Now* (B) **Unit 4, Week 2:** *Penguins All Around* (B) **Unit 6, Week 5:** *It's Labor Day!* (O,B) **CLOSE READING COMPANION:** 65, 128, 129, 131 **YOUR TURN PRACTCE BOOK:** 19, 29, 49, 59, 69, 99, 109, 119, 139, 149, 161, 173, 197, 209, 221, 233, 269, 281, 305, 329 **READING WORKSTATION ACTIVITY CARDS:** 18, 19, 20 **TEACHER'S EDITION: Unit 1:** T38, T39A–T39B, T338, T347C, T347F, T350–T351, T396, T415 **Unit 2:** T117, T117B, T274–T275, T275B, T338, T347A, T350–T351, T385, T396, T415 **Unit 3:** T260, T273, T273A, T322, T338, T339, T347B–T347C, T347E, T350–T351, T396, T415 **Unit 4:** T38, T39A–T39B, T104, T273, T273B, T284, T338, T339, 347B, 347C, 347E, T396, T415 **Unit 5:** T38–T39, T116, T117A, T396, T415 **Unit 6:** T195, T195A–T195B, T273A, T338, T350, T396, T415 www.connected.mcgraw-hill.com: **RESOURCES: Media:** Images; Time for Kids Online Articles; **Collaborate:** Projects; **Student Practice:** Approaching Reproducibles 19, 29, 49, 59, 69, 99, 109, 119, 139, 149, 161, 173, 197, 209, 221, 233, 269, 281, 305, 329, Beyond Reproducibles 19, 29, 49, 59, 69, 99, 109, 119, 139, 149, 161, 173, 197, 209, 221, 233, 269, 281, 305, 329; ELL Reproducibles 19, 29, 49, 59, 69, 99, 109, 119, 139, 149, 161, 173, 197, 209, 221, 233, 269, 281, 305, 329
RI.1.6	Distinguish between information provided by pictures or other illustrations and information provided by the words in a text.	**READING/WRITING WORKSHOP:** Unit 1: 84, 85, 104, 105 **Unit 2:** 104, 105 **Unit 5:** 210, 211 **CLOSE READING COMPANION:** 23, 48–50, 161, 164 **YOUR TURN PRACTICE BOOK:** 173, 181, 209, 233, 269, 281 **READING WORKSTATION ACTIVITY CARDS:** 20 **INTERACTIVE READ-ALOUD CARDS: Unit 1, Week 1:** 4 **Unit 1, Week 3:** 4 **Unit 1, Week 4:** 4 **Unit 2, Week 1:** 4 **Unit 2, Week 3:** 4 **Unit 2, Week 4:** 4 **Unit 2, Week 5:** 3, 4 **Unit 3, Week 1:** 4 **Unit 3, Week 4:** 4 **Unit 4, Week 2:** 4 **Unit 4, Week 3:** 3, 4 **Unit 4, Week 4:** 2, 4 **Unit 5, Week 3:** 4 **Unit 6, Week 4:** 3, 4 **Unit 6, Week 5:** 4 **TEACHER'S EDITION: Unit 1:** T38–T39, T39B, T269B, T269C, T269E–T269F, T347B–T347C **Unit 2:** T35C, T39A, T191B, T191C, T347D, T350, T351 **Unit 3:** T269D **Unit 4:** T182 **Unit 5:** T182, T273, T338, T347B, T347D, T350–T351 **Unit 6:** T113E–T113F, T113H, T338 www.connected.mcgraw-hill.com: **RESOURCES: Media:** Images; Graphic Organizers; **Student Practice:** Approaching Reproducibles 173, 181, 209, 233, 269, 281, Beyond Reproducibles 173, 181, 209, 233, 269, 281, ELL Reproducibles 173, 181, 209, 233, 269, 281 **Interactive Games & Activities:** Comprehension

Integration of Knowledge and Ideas	McGraw-Hill *Wonders*	
RI.1.7	Use the illustrations and details in a text to describe its key ideas.	**READING/WRITING WORKSHOP:** Unit 1: 104, 105 **Unit 2:** 104, 105 **LITERATURE ANTHOLOGY:** Unit 1: 83, 93, 95 **Unit 2:** 59, 61 **Unit 3:** 49, 89, 103 **LEVELED READERS: Unit 1, Week 1:** *A Fun Day* (A), *Our Classroom Rules*, pp. 13–16 (B) **Unit 3, Week 1:** *Make a Clock*, pp. 13–16 (A) **Unit 3, Week 4:** *Schools Then and Now* (A, O, B) **Unit 4, Week 3:** *Go, Gator!* (A, O, B) **Unit 4, Week 4:** *Wings*, pp. 13–16 (A) **Unit 5, Week 1:** *Sort by Color*, pp. 13–16 (A) **CLOSE READING COMPANION:** 22, 23, 24, 29, 30, 31, 48 **YOUR TURN PRACTICE BOOK:** 99, 137, 166, 169, 174, 181, 186, 221, 233, 269, 281, 294, 305, 317 **READING WORKSTATION ACTIVITY CARDS:** 20 **INTERACTIVE READ-ALOUD CARDS: Unit 1, Week 1:** 1, 2, 4 **Unit 1, Week 3:** 4 **Unit 1, Week 4:** 4 **Unit 2, Week 1:** 4 **Unit 2, Week 3:** 4 **Unit 2, Week 4:** 2, 4 **Unit 2, Week 5:** 3, 4 **Unit 3, Week 1:** 4 **Unit 3, Week 4:** 4 **Unit 4, Week 2:** 4 **Unit 4, Week 3:** 3, 4 **Unit 4, Week 4:** 2, 4 **Unit 5, Week 3:** 4 **Unit 6, Week 4:** 3, 4 **Unit 6, Week 5:** 4 **TEACHER'S EDITION: Unit 1:** T38, T261, T269B–T269G, T304–T305, T306–T307, T347C, T347F, T372–T373, T374–T375 **Unit 2:** T39, T117, T191B–T191D, T191G–T191H, T274–T275, T349B–T349F, T385, T386, T387 **Unit 3:** T39, T117, T117A–T117B, T269D, T269I–T269J, T273, T273A, T273B, T287, T307, T350, T351, T365, T372, T383, T384–T385 **Unit 4:** T38, T149, T150, T167, T191G, T191I, T191O, T229, T245, T339, T365, T374–T375, T384–T385 **Unit 5:** T38–T39, T39A–T39B, T191B, T191D, T228, T347F, T372 **Unit 6:** T31, T38, T39A, T113D–T113I, T113K–T113L, T148–T149, T150–T151, T273, T273A, T338–T339, T347B–T347D, T350–T351, T365, T383 www.connected.mcgraw-hill.com: **RESOURCES: Media:** Images; **Student Practice:** Approaching Reproducibles 99, 100, 137, 166, 169, 174, 181, 186, 221, 233, 269, 270, 281, 294, 305, 317, 330, Beyond Reproducibles 99, 100, 137, 166, 169, 174, 181, 186, 221, 233, 269, 270, 281, 294, 305, 317, 330, ELL Reproducibles 99, 100, 137, 166, 169, 174, 181, 186, 221, 233, 269, 270, 281, 294, 305, 317, 330

Reading Standards for Informational Text

RI.1.8	Identify the reasons an author gives to support points in a text.	**READING/WRITING WORKSHOP:** Unit 6: 252, 253, 312, 313 **LITERATURE ANTHOLOGY:** Unit 6: 323, 405 **LEVELED READERS:** Unit 6, Week 2: *Helping Me, Helping You!* (A, O, B) Unit 6, Week 5: *It's Labor Day!* (A, O, B) **CLOSE READING COMPANION:** 108, 174 **WRITING WORKSTATION ACTIVITY CARDS:** 26 **TEACHER'S EDITION:** Unit 1: T260-T261, T269D-T269F, T285, T363 **Unit 2:** T183, T191G, T207, T363 **Unit 3:** T261, T280, T347D, T330, T363 **Unit 4:** T105, T113F, T113H, T113J, T129, T363 **Unit 5:** T183, T207, T339, T363 **Unit 6:** T104, T105, T113B-T113K, T129, T339, T347B-T347E, T363 www.connected.mcgraw-hill.com: **RESOURCES:** Units 1–6: Cards: Retelling Cards, **Graphic Organizers:** Graphic Organizers
RI.1.9	Identify basic similarities in and differences between two texts on the same topic (e.g., in illustrations, descriptions, or procedures).	**LITERATURE ANTHOLOGY:** Unit 1: 84, 94 **Unit 2:** 22, 44, 61, 62, 82, 94 **Unit 3:** 24, 46, 90, 102 **Unit 4:** 30, 56, 59, 90, 126, 138, 139 **Unit 5:** 156, 201, 222, 256, 268 **Unit 6:** 296, 301, 324, 394, 406 **LEVELED READERS:** Unit 1, Week 5: *What's Under Your Skin?* pp. 13–16 (A, O, B) Unit 2, Week 5: *On the Map,* pp. 13–16 (A, O); pp. 12–16 (B) Unit 3, Week 4: *School Days,* pp. 13–16 (A, O, B) Unit 4, Week 1: *Lions and Elephants,* pp. 13–16 (A, O); pp. 12–16 (B) Unit 4, Week 2: *Penguins All Around* (A, O, B), *Animals Work Together,* pp. 13–16 (A, O), pp. 12–16 (B) Unit 4, Week 5: *Teach a Dog!* (A, O, B), *Working with Dolphins,* pp. 13–16 (A, O), pp. 12–16 (B) **CLOSE READING COMPANION:** 54, 73, 99, 153 **READING WORKSTATION ACTIVITY CARDS:** 22 **TEACHER'S EDITION:** Unit 1: S32, S62, S92, T39B, T50, T128, T206-T207, T284-T285, T351, T362-T363, T379, T385 **Unit 2:** T50-T51, T39B, T117B, T191H, T194, T206-T207, T275B, T284-T285, T350, T353, T358, T359, T362-T363, T367, T381, T387 **Unit 3:** T117B, T273B, T284-T285, T286, T287, T297, T307, T362, T363, T379 **Unit 4:** T39B, T117A, T128, T131, T141, T145, T151, T206, T209, T219, T273B, T284-T285, T287, T297, T301, T307, T350, T351, T362-T363, T365, T375, T379, T385 **Unit 5:** T39B, T117B, T195A, T206-T207, T209, T219, T223, T273B, T284-T285, T297, T301, T350, T362, T365, T375, T385 **Unit 6:** T195B, T206-T207, T273B, T284-T285, T287, T297, T301, T307, T351, T362, T365, T375, T379, T385 www.connected.mcgraw-hill.com: **RESOURCES:** Units 1–6: **Graphic Organizers:** Graphic Organizers **Cards:** Retelling Cards

Range of Reading and Level of Text Complexity		**McGraw-Hill *Wonders***
RI.1.10	With prompting and support, read informational texts appropriately complex for grade 1.	**READING/WRITING WORKSHOP:** Unit 1: 94-103 **Unit 2:** 54-63, 94-103 **Unit 3:** 74-83, 94-103 **Unit 4:** 38-47, 58-67, 98-107 **Unit 5:** 160-169, 200-209 **Unit 6:** 242-251, 302-311 **LITERATURE ANTHOLOGY:** These Units reflect the range of text complexity found throughout the book. **Unit 1, Week 4:** *Friends,* 68 **Unit 2, Week 5:** *Fun with Maps,* 86 **Unit 3, Week 4:** *Long Ago and Now,* 74 **Unit 4, Week 2:** *Animal Teams,* 36 **Unit 4, Week 5:** *Koko and Penny,* 130 **Unit 5, Week 3:** *Thomas Edison, Inventor,* 202 **Unit 6, Week 5:** *Happy Birthday, U.S.A.!,* 398 **LEVELED READERS:** Unit 1, Week 1: *We Share,* pp. 13–16 (O) Unit 2, Week 2: *What a Nest!,* pp. 13–16 (A), *Staying Afloat,* pp. 13–16 (O), *City, Armadillo, Country Armadillo,* pp. 13–16 (B) Unit 3, Week 4: *Schools Then and Now* (A, O, B) Unit 4, Week 3: *Go, Gator!* (A, O, B) Unit 5, Week 1: *Dog Bones,* pp. 13–16 (O) Unit 6, Week 4: *Latkes for Sam,* pp. 13–16 (O) **TEACHER'S EDITION:** Unit 1: T39A, T117, T195A, T250-T251, T269A, T328-T329, T347A, T373, T374-T375, T404-T405, T406-T407 **Unit 2:** T39A, T117A, T172A, T173, T191A, T328-T329, T340-T341, T383, T384-T385, T386-T387, T412-T413, T414 **Unit 3:** T39A, T117A, T250-T251, T269A, T286-T287, T304-T305, T306-T307, T328-T329, T347A, T377, T378-T379 **Unit 4:** T39, T94-T95, T113A, T140-T141, T226-T227, T328-T329, T382-T383 **Unit 5:** T117, T172-T173, T191A, T208-T209, T221, T222-T223, T338-T339, T381, T382-T383, T384-T385 **Unit 6:** T94-T95, T113A, T195A, T273A, T328-T329, T347A **LITERATURE BIG BOOKS:** Unit 1, Week 4: *Friends All Around* Unit 1, Week 5: *Move!* Unit 2, Week 4: *The Story of Martin Luther King, Jr.* Unit 2, Week 5: *Me on the Map* Unit 3, Week 5: *Where Does Food Come From?* www.connected.mcgraw-hill.com: **RESOURCES:** Unit 1: Teacher Resources: Theme Bibliography, Literature/Informational Text Chart **Student Practice:** Approaching Reproducibles, Beyond Reproducibles, ELL Reproducibles

Reading Standards: Foundational Skills

Print Concepts		McGraw-Hill *Wonders*
RF.1.1	Demonstrate understanding of the organization and basic features of print.	
RF.1.1a	Recognize the distinguishing features of a sentence (e.g., first word, capitalization, ending punctuation).	**TEACHER'S EDITION: Unit 1:** S34, S64, T28-T29, T185, T205, T349 **Unit 2:** T88, T166, T331, T341, T349, T361 **Unit 3:** T19, T29, T49 **Unit 4:** T107, T115, T121 **Unit 5:** T97, T107, T115, T127 **www.connected.mcgraw-hill.com: RESOURCES: Units 1–5: Student Practice:** Grammar Practice **Interactive Games & Activities:** Writing & Grammar

Phonological Awareness		McGraw-Hill *Wonders*
RF.1.2	Demonstrate understanding of spoken words, syllables, and sounds (phonemes).	
RF.1.2a	Distinguish long from short vowel sounds in spoken single-syllable words.	**TEACHER'S EDITION: Unit 1:** T168, T196 **Unit 4:** T22, T168, T196, T246 **www.connected.mcgraw-hill.com: RESOURCES: Unit 3: Interactive Games & Activities:** Phonemic Awareness **Cards:** Word-Building Cards **Tier 2 Intervention:** Phonemic Awareness **Unit 4: Interactive Games & Activities:** Phonemic Awareness **Cards:** Word-Building Cards **Tier 2 Intervention:** Phonemic Awareness
RF.1.2b	Orally produce single-syllable words by blending sounds (phonemes) including consonant blends.	**YOUR TURN PRACTICE BOOK:** SS1, SS2, SS6, SS7, SS11, SS13, SS14, SS18, SS19, SS23, SS25, SS26, SS31, SS35, 1, 41, 121, 171 **PHONICS WORKSTATION ACTIVITY CARDS:** 5, 15, 16, 20, 23, 28, 29 **TEACHER'S EDITION: Unit 1:** S53, S65, S71, T32, T55, T91, T110, T132, T168, T178, T210, T280, T289 **Unit 2:** T12, T46, T110, T124, T178 **Unit 3:** T124, T188, T280, T334, T358 **Unit 4:** T32, T46, T178, T202, T280, T344 **Unit 5:** T32, T110, T124, T188, T266, T280, T288, T324-T325, T352, T366-T367 **Unit 6:** T110, T266, T280, T334 **www.connected.mcgraw-hill.com: RESOURCES: Units 1–6: Interactive Games & Activities:** Phonemic Awareness **Student Practice:** Phonics/Spelling Practice, Approaching Reproducibles, Beyond Reproducibles, ELL Reproducibles **Cards:** Word-Building Cards
RF.1.2c	Isolate and pronounce initial, medial vowel, and final sounds (phonemes) in spoken single-syllable words.	**YOUR TURN PRACTICE BOOK:** SS1, SS2, SS6, SS7, SS11, SS13, SS14, SS18, SS19, SS23, SS25, SS26, SS31, SS35, 31, 39, 129, 245 **TEACHER'S EDITION: Unit 1:** S5, S11, S41, T22, T40, T100, T188, T324 **Unit 2:** T22, T40, T54-T55, T100, T118, T132, T168, T188, T198, T212-T213, T246, T258, T276, T290-T291, T369 **Unit 3:** T12, T40, T256, T274 **Unit 4:** T22-T23, T54, T90, T110, T118, T132-T133, T168, T188, T196, T210-T211, T246, T288-T289, T324, T352, T366-T367 **Unit 5:** T12, T22, T40, T168, T256, T274, T288-T289, T334, T366 **Unit 6:** T12, T90, T118, T132-T133, T168, T196, T210-T211, T289, T366-T367 **www.connected.mcgraw-hill.com: RESOURCES: Units 1–6: Interactive Games & Activities:** Phonemic Awareness **Student Practice:** Phonics/Spelling Practice, Approaching Reproducibles, Beyond Reproducibles, ELL Reproducibles **Cards:** Word-Building Cards
RF.1.2d	Segment spoken single-syllable words into their complete sequence of individual sounds (phonemes).	**TEACHER'S EDITION: Unit 1:** S77, S83, T46, T202, T256, T266, T280, T334, T358 **Unit 2:** T46, T124, T202, T280, T324, T358 **Unit 3:** T46, T110, T124, T178, T196, T246, T288, T358, T367 **Unit 4:** T46, T100, T124, T266, T280 **Unit 5:** T46, T202, T334, T358 **Unit 6:** T22, T46, T124, T178, T202, T210, T256, T274, T288, T367 **www.connected.mcgraw-hill.com: RESOURCES: Units 1–6: Interactive Games & Activities:** Phonemic Awareness **Student Practice:** Phonics/Spelling Practice **Tier 2 Intervention:** Phonemic Awareness **Cards:** Word-Building Cards

Phonics and Word Recognition		McGraw-Hill *Wonders*
RF.1.3	Know and apply grade-level phonics and word analysis skills in decoding words.	
RF.1.3a	Know the spelling-sound correspondences for common consonant digraphs (two letters that represent one sound).	**READING/WRITING WORKSHOP: Unit 2:** 72, 73, 92, 93 **PHONICS WORKSTATION ACTIVITY CARDS:** 9, 10 **TEACHER'S EDITION: Unit 2:** T246-T247, T250-T251, T256-T257, T266-T267, T324-T325, T328-T329 **Unit 6:** T168-T169, T172-T173, T179, T188-T189 **YOUR TURN PRACTICE BOOK:** SS25, 13, 18, 23, 25, 26, 28, 29, 31, 33, 49, 91, 93, 103 **www.connected.mcgraw-hill.com: RESOURCES: Unit 2: Tier 2 Intervention:** Phonics **Cards:** Sound-Spelling Cards **Teacher Resources:** Sound-Spelling Songs **Interactive Games & Activities:** Phonics **Student Practice:** Phonics/Spelling Practice, Approaching Reproducibles, Beyond Reproducibles, ELL Reproducibles **Unit 6: Tier 2 Intervention:** Phonics **Cards:** Sound-Spelling Cards **Teacher Resources:** Sound-Spelling Songs **Interactive Games & Activities:** Phonics **Student Practice:** Phonics/Spelling Practice, Approaching Reproducibles, Beyond Reproducibles, ELL Reproducibles

Reading Standards: Foundational Skills

Phonics and Word Recognition		McGraw-Hill *Wonders*
RF.1.3b	Decode regularly spelled one-syllable words.	**READING/WRITING WORKSHOP: Unit 1:** 12, 13, 32, 33, 52, 53, 72, 73, 92, 93 **Unit 2:** 12, 13, 32, 33, 52, 53, 72, 73, 92, 93 **Unit 3:** 12, 13, 32, 33, 52, 72, 73, 92, 93 **Unit 4:** 16, 17, 56, 57, 76, 77, 96, 97 **Unit 5:** 118, 119, 138, 139, 158, 159, 178, 179, 198, 199 **Unit 6:** 220, 221, 240, 241, 260, 261, 280, 281, 300, 301 **YOUR TURN PRACTICE BOOK:** SS3, SS4, SS9, SS15, SS16, SS21, SS22, SS27, SS28, SS33, SS34, 1, 3, 5, 6, 8, 11, 13, 15, 16, 18, 19, 21, 23, 25, 26, 28, 29, 31, 33, 35, 36, 39, 41, 43, 45, 46, 49, 51, 53, 55, 56, 59, 61, 62, 63, 65, 66, 69, 71, 73, 75, 76, 79, 81, 82, 83, 85, 86, 91, 92, 93, 95, 96, 101, 102, 103, 105, 106, 111, 112, 113, 115, 116, 119, 121, 122, 123, 125, 126, 129, 133, 135, 136, 138, 141, 142, 143, 145, 146, 151, 152, 155, 156, 159, 163, 164, 167, 168, 171, 175, 176, 179, 183, 187, 188, 191, 192, 195, 199, 203, 204, 207, 211, 212, 215, 216, 219, 223, 224, 227, 228, 231, 235, 236, 239, 243, 245, 247, 248, 251, 252, 253, 255, 257, 259, 260, 263, 264, 267, 271, 272, 275, 276, 279, 283, 284, 287, 288, 291, 295, 296, 299, 303, 307, 308, 311, 312, 315, 319, 323, 324, 327 **PHONICS WORKSTATION ACTIVITY CARDS:** 3, 6, 7, 8, 9, 10, 11, 12, 13, 14, 15, 16, 17, 18, 19, 20, 21, 22, 23, 24, 25, 26, 27, 28, 29, 30 **TEACHER'S EDITION: Unit 1:** S30, S31, S48–S49, T32–T33, T110–T111, T196, T266–T267, T368–T369 **Unit 2:** T32–T33, T118–T119, T188–T189, T215, T252–T253, T336–T337 **Unit 3:** T16–T17, T168–T169, T266–T267, T324–T325 **Unit 4:** T17, T22–T23, T32–T33, T40–T41, T64, T95, T101, T134–T135, T173, T188–T189, T212–T213, T250–T251, T290–T291, T324–T325, T328–T329, T346 **Unit 5:** T12–T13, T124–T125, T212–T213, T324–T325, T344–T345, T368–T369 **Unit 6:** T16–T17, T22–T23, T32–T33, T40, T46, T56–T57, T64, T90–T91, T94–T95, T100–T101, T134–T135, T142, T168–T169, T172–T173, T188–T189, T196–T197, T202–T203, T212–T213, T246–T247, T250–T251, T256–T257, T266–T267, T274–T275, T290–T291, T298, T324–T325, T328–T329, T334–T335, T344–T345, T352–T353, T368–T369, T376 **www.connected.mcgraw-hill.com: RESOURCES: Units 1–6: Tier 2 Intervention:** Phonics **Cards:** Word-Building Cards, Spelling Word Cards **Interactive Games & Activities:** Phonics **Student Practice:** Approaching Reproducibles, Beyond Reproducibles, ELL Reproducibles
RF.1.3c	Know final -e and common vowel team conventions for representing long vowel sounds.	**READING/WRITING WORKSHOP: Unit 3:** 12–13, 32–33, 72–73 **Unit 4:** 16, 17, 36, 37, 56, 57, 76, 77, 96, 97 **Unit 6:** 220, 221 **YOUR TURN PRACTICE BOOK:** 101, 103, 111, 113, 131, 133, 138, 151, 159, 163, 171, 175, 183, 187, 195, 199, 207, 271, 279, 292 **PHONICS WORKSTATION ACTIVITY CARDS:** 3, 11, 12, 13, 14, 16, 17, 18, 19, 20 **TEACHER'S EDITION: Unit 3:** T12–T13, T16, T17, T22–T23, T32, T33, T40, T46, T56–T57, T64, T90–T91, T100–T101, T110–T111, T118, T124, T134–T135, T142, T210, T246–T247, T256–T257, T266, T267, T274, T290–T291 **Unit 4:** T12–T13, T22–T23, T24, T32–T33, T40, T46, T56–T57, T64, T76, T90–T91, T101, T110–T111, T118–T119, T124–T125, T134, T142, T168–T169, T213, T220, T246–T247, T256–T257, T266–T267, T280, T290–T291, T334, T335, T352–T353, T358–T359, T368–T369, T376, T388 **www.connected.mcgraw-hill.com: RESOURCES: Unit 3: Tier 2 Intervention:** Phonics **Cards:** Word-Building Cards, Spelling Word Cards **Interactive Games & Activities:** Phonics **Student Practice:** Approaching Reproducibles, Beyond Reproducibles, ELL Reproducibles **Unit 4: Tier 2 Intervention:** Phonics **Cards:** Word-Building Cards, Spelling Word Cards **Interactive Games & Activities:** Phonics **Student Practice:** Approaching Reproducibles, Beyond Reproducibles, ELL Reproducibles
RF.1.3d	Use knowledge that every syllable must have a vowel sound to determine the number of syllables in a printed word.	**YOUR TURN PRACTICE BOOK:** 138, 328 **TEACHER'S EDITION: Unit 2:** T179, T257 T267, T275 **Unit 3:** T257 **Unit 4:** T179, T189, T196, T214 **Unit 5:** T335, T370 **Unit 6:** T101, T335, T345, T352, T370 **www.connected.mcgraw-hill.com: RESOURCES: Cards:** Word-Building Cards **Interactive Games & Activities:** Phonics
RF.1.3e	Decode two-syllable words following basic patterns by breaking the words into syllables.	**READING/WRITING WORKSHOP: Unit 2:** 73, 93 **Unit 4:** 56, 57, 76, 77, 94, 95, 96, 97 **Unit 5:** 116, 117, 118, 119, 139, 156, 157, 158, 159, 176, 177, 178, 179, 196, 197, 198, 199 **Unit 6:** 220, 221, 240, 241, 260, 261, 280, 281, 298–301 **YOUR TURN PRACTICE BOOK:** 138, 184, 208, 268, 304, 314, 328 **PHONICS WORKSTATION ACTIVITY CARDS:** 8, 28 **TEACHER'S EDITION: Unit 2:** T257, T267, T275, T281 **Unit 3:** T257, T267, T275, T281 **Unit 4:** T179, T189, T196, T202 **Unit 5:** T335, T345, T352, T358 **Unit 6:** T101, T111, T118, T124, T179, T335, T345, T358 **www.connected.mcgraw-hill.com: RESOURCES: Cards:** Word-Building Cards, Student Practice Approaching Reproducibles 138, 184, 208, 268, 304, 314, 328, Beyond Reproducibles 138, 184, 208, 268, 304, 314, 328, ELL Reproducibles 138, 184, 208, 268, 304, 314, 328

Reading Standards: Foundational Skills

RF.1.3f	Read words with inflectional endings.	**READING/WRITING WORKSHOP:** Unit I: 52, 53, 72, 73, 92, 93 **Unit 2:** 32, 33, 73 **Unit 3:** 32, 33, 72, 92, 93 **Unit 4:** 16, 17, 36, 37, 56, 57, 76, 77 **Unit 5:** II8, I39, I78, I79, I98 **Unit 6:** 240, 260, 261, 280, 281 **YOUR TURN PRACTICE BOOK:** 8, 28, 58, 78, 98, II8, I28, I48, I96, 225, 232, 249, 256, 266, 316 **PHONICS WORKSTATION ACTIVITY CARDS:** 8, I3, I5 **TEACHER'S EDITION: Unit I:** T23, T33, TI79, TI89, TI97, T203 **Unit 2:** T23, T33, T4I, T47, TI79, TI89, TI99, T204, T2I6, T337, T347, T354, T360 **Unit 3:** TI0I, TIII, TII9, TI25, TI79, TI89, T203, T2I4, T335, T345, T352, T358, T370 **Unit 4:** T257, T267, T274, T280, T353 **Unit 5:** TI0I, TIII, TII8, TI24, TI36, T257, T267, T274, T280, T392 **Unit 6:** T40, T257, T267, T274, T280 www.connected.mcgraw-hill.com: **RESOURCES: Units I–6: Cards:** Word-Building Cards **Student Practice:** Phonics/Spelling Practice, Approaching Reproducibles, Beyond Reproducibles, ELL Reproducibles
RF.1.3g	Recognize and read grade-appropriate irregularly spelled words.	**READING/WRITING WORKSHOP: Unit I:** I0, II, 30, 3I, 50, 5I, 70, 7I, 90, 9I **Unit 2:** I0, II, 30, 3I, 50, 5I, 70, 7I, 90, 9I **Unit 3:** I0, II, 30, 3I, 50, 5I, 70, 7I, 90, 9I **Unit 4:** I4, 74, 94 **Unit 5:** II6, I56, I76, I77, I96 **Unit 6:** 2I8, 238, 258, 298, 299 **YOUR TURN PRACTICE BOOK:** I88, 296 **PHONICS WORKSTATION ACTIVITY CARDS:** 28 **TEACHER'S EDITION: Unit I:** TI5, TI6-TI7, T92-T93, T94-T95, TI7I, TI72-TI73, T327, T328-T329 **Unit 2:** TI5, TI6-TI7, T92-T93, T94-T95, TI03, TI7I, TI72-TI73, T249, T250-T25I, T327, T328-T329, T337 **Unit 3:** TI5, TI6-TI7, T25, T93, T94-T95, T249, T250-T25I **Unit 4:** TI4-TI5, TI6-TI7, T47, TII2-TII3, TI80-TI8I, T258-T259, T326-T327 **Unit 5:** TI4, T25, T26, TI7, T92-T93, T94-T95, TI70-TI7I, TI72-TI73, T248-T249, T250-T25I, T346-T347 **Unit 6:** T24-T25, TI02-TI03, T248-T249, T250, T252, T326-T327, T328-T329 www.connected.mcgraw-hill.com: **RESOURCES: Units I–6: Cards:** High-Frequency Word Cards, Spelling Word Cards, Word-Building Cards **Student Practice:** Approaching Reproducibles, Beyond Reproducibles, ELL Reproducibles

Fluency		McGraw-Hill *Wonders*
RF.1.4	Read with sufficient accuracy and fluency to support comprehension.	
RF.1.4a	Read grade-level text with purpose and understanding.	**YOUR TURN PRACTICE BOOK:** SS3, SS4, SS9, SSI5, SSI6, SS2I, SS22, SS27, SS28, SS33, SS34, 5, 6, II, I2, I3, I5, I6, I8, 2I, 22, 23, 25, 26, 28, 3I, 32, 33, 35, 36, 42, 43, 45, 46, 47, 55, 56, 65, 66, 75, 76, 82, 85, 86, 95, 96, 99, I0I, I03, I05, I06, I09, III, II3, II5, II6, I2I, I23, I25, I26, I3I, I32, I33, I35, I36, I38, I39, I4I, I43, I45, I46, I49, I5I, I55, I56, I57, I59, I6I, I63, I67, I68, I69, I7I, I73, I75, I79, I8I, I83, I85, I87, I9I, I92, I93, I95, I97, I99, 203, 204, 205, 207, 209, 2II, 2I5, 2I6, 2I9, 22I, 223, 227, 228, 23I, 233, 235, 239, 24I, 243, 247, 25I, 252, 255, 257, 259, 263, 264, 265, 267, 269, 27I, 275, 276, 277, 279, 28I, 283, 287, 288, 289, 29I, 293, 295, 299, 30I, 303, 305, 307, 3II, 3I2, 3I3, 3I5, 3I7, 3I9, 323, 324, 325, 327, 329 **READING WORKSTATION ACTIVITY CARDS:** I, 2, 3, 4, 5, 6, 7, 8, 9, I0, II, I2, I3, I4, I5, I6, I7, I9, 2I, 22, 23, 24, 25, 26, 27, 28 **TEACHER'S EDITION: Unit I:** TI6-TI7, TI04-TI05, T250-T25I, T328-T329 **Unit 2:** T94-T95, TI82-TI83 **Unit 3:** T94-T95, T284-T285, T394-T395 **Unit 4:** TI04-TI05, TI72-TI73, T394-T395 **Unit 5:** TI6-TI7, T260-T26I, T328-T329, T343, T394-T395 **Unit 6:** T94-T95, TI82-TI83, T328-T329, T343, T344, T395 www.connected.mcgraw-hill.com: **RESOURCES: Units I–6: Student Practice:** Reader's Theater, Approaching Reproducibles, Beyond Reproducibles, ELL Reproducibles
RF.1.4b	Read grade-level text orally with accuracy, appropriate rate, and expression.	**YOUR TURN PRACTICE BOOK:** I57, I69, I8I, I93, 205, 24I, 265, 277, 289, 30I, 3I3, 325 **READING WORKSTATION ACTIVITY CARDS:** 24, 25 **TEACHER'S EDITION: Unit I:** T3I, TII3, TI25, TI9I, T265, T394-T395 **Unit 2:** T3I, T63, TI09, TI4I, TI5I, TI87, T22I, T267, T299, T394-T395 **Unit 3:** T3I, T63, TI4I, TI87, T2I9, T265, T294, T343, T375, T394-T395 **Unit 4:** T3I, T47, TI09, TI87, T203, T2I9, T265, T297, T343, T359, T375, T394-T395 **Unit 5:** T3I, T47, T63, TI09, TI25, TI4I, TI87, T203, T265, T28I, T297, T343, T359, T375, T394-T395 **Unit 6:** T3I, T47, T63, TI09, TI25, TI4I, TI87, T203, T2I9, T28I, T297, T343, T359, T375, T394-T395 www.connected.mcgraw-hill.com: **RESOURCES: Units I–6: Media:** Fluency Passages **Student Practice:** Reader's Theater, Approaching Reproducibles, Beyond Reproducibles, ELL Reproducibles **Tier 2 Intervention:** Comprehension **Interactive Games & Activities:** Fluency
RF.1.4c	Use context to confirm or self-correct word recognition and understanding, rereading as necessary.	**YOUR TURN PRACTICE BOOK:** 53, 73, 83, I03, II2, I23, I32, I33, I42, I52, I64, I75, I76, I83, I87, I88, 20I, 207, 2I2, 2I9, 223, 23I, 236, 237, 243, 259, 272, 284, 295, 296, 303, 308, 3I9 **TEACHER'S EDITION: Unit I:** T39, T394-T395 **Unit 2:** T394-T395 **Unit 3:** T269F, T394-T395 **Unit 4:** TII3, TII3F, T269, T269G, T394-T395 **Unit 5:** T35 **Unit 6:** TII3G www.connected.mcgraw-hill.com: **RESOURCES: Units I–6: Student Practice:** Reader's Theater, Approaching Reproducibles, Beyond Reproducibles, ELL Reproducibles **Media:** Fluency Passages **Interactive Games & Activities:** Fluency

College and Career Readiness Anchor Standards for
WRITING

The K–5 standards on the following pages define what students should understand and be able to do by the end of each grade. They correspond to the College and Career Readiness anchor standards below by number. The CCR and grade-specific standards are necessary complements—the former providing broad standards, the latter providing additional specificity—that together define the skills and understandings that all students must demonstrate.

Text Types and Purposes

1. Write arguments to support claims in an analysis of substantive topics or texts, using valid reasoning and relevant and sufficient evidence.

2. Write informative/explanatory texts to examine and convey complex ideas and information clearly and accurately through the effective selection, organization, and analysis of content.

3. Write narratives to develop real or imagined experiences or events using effective technique, well-chosen details, and well-structured event sequences.

Production and Distribution of Writing

4. Produce clear and coherent writing in which the development, organization, and style are appropriate to task, purpose, and audience.

5. Develop and strengthen writing as needed by planning, revising, editing, rewritings, or trying a new approach.

6. Use technology, including the Internet, to produce and publish writing and to interact and collaborate with others.

Research to Build and Present Knowledge

7. Conduct short as well as more sustained research projects based on focused questions, demonstrating understanding of the subject under investigation.

8. Gather relevant information from multiple print and digital sources, assess the credibility and accuracy of each source, and integrate the information while avoiding plagiarism.

9. Draw evidence from literary or informational texts to support analysis, reflection, and research.

Range of Writing

10. Write routinely over extended time frames (time for research, reflection, and revision) and shorter time frames (a single sitting or a day or two) for a range of tasks, purposes, and audiences.

Common Core State Standards
English Language Arts
Grade 1

Writing Standards

Text Types and Purposes		McGraw-Hill *Wonders*
W.1.1	Write opinion pieces in which they introduce the topic or name the book they are writing about, state an opinion, supply a reason for the opinion, and provide some sense of closure.	**CLOSE READING COMPANION:** 36, 90, 109, 135, 162, 195 **YOUR TURN PRACTICE BOOK:** 60, 140, 150, 222 **READING/WRITING WORKSHOP: Unit 2:** 26-27, **Unit 3:** 86-87, 106-107 **Unit 4:** 50-51 **Unit 5:** 132-133, 212-213 **Unit 6:** 315-316 **READING WORKSTATION ACTIVITY CARDS:** 14 **WRITING WORKSTATION ACTIVITY CARDS:** 4, 11, 26, 30 **TEACHER'S EDITION: Unit 2:** T18, T28-T29, T36, T42 **Unit 3:** T252, T262-T263, T270, T276, T340-T341, T348, T354 **Unit 4:** T96, T106-T107, T114, T120 **Unit 5:** T18, T28-T29, T36, T42, T330, T340-T341, T348, T354 **Unit 6:** T330, T340-T341, T348, T354 www.connected.mcgraw-hill.com: **RESOURCES: Units 1-6: Teacher Resources:** Writer's Checklists/Proofreading Marks
W.1.2	Write informative/explanatory texts in which they name a topic, supply some facts about the topic, and provide some sense of closure.	**CLOSE READING COMPANION:** 24, 50, 57, 83, 90, 96 **YOUR TURN PRACTICE BOOK:** 10, 20, 40, 50, 70, 80, 100, 162, 174, 186, 198, 210, 234, 246, 294, 306 **READING/WRITING WORKSHOP: Unit 1:** 26-27, 46-47, 86-87, 106-107 **Unit 2:** 26-27, 46-47, 66-67, 106-107 **Unit 4:** 70-71, 91-92, 110-111 **Unit 5:** 151-152, 173-174 **Unit 6:** 192-193 **LITERATURE ANTHOLOGY: Unit 2:** 60, 80 **Unit 3:** 44, 88 **Unit 4:** 54 **LEVELED READERS: Unit 4, Week 3:** *Go, Gator!* p. 16 (B) **Unit 5, Week 3:** *The Wright Brothers,* p. 16 (B) **Unit 6, Week 5:** *It's Labor Day!* p. 16 (O, B) **READING WORKSTATION ACTIVITY CARDS:** 10 **SCIENCE & SOCIAL STUDIES WORKSTATION ACTIVITY CARDS:** 9, 19, 27 **READING WORKSTATION ACTIVITY CARDS:** 5, 6, 9, 10, 27, 28, 29 **TEACHER'S EDITION: Unit 1:** T18, T28-T29, T36, T42, T96, T106-T107, T114, T120, T252, T262-T263, T270, T330, T340-T341, T348 **Unit 2:** T18, T96, T106-T107, T114, T120-T121, T126, T174, T184-T185, T192, T252, T262, T270, T330, T340-T341, T348 **Unit 3:** T330 **Unit 4:** T96, T174, T184-T185, T198, T252, T262-T263, T270, T330, T340-T341, T348 **Unit 5:** T18, T96, T106-T107, T114, T174, T184-T185, T192, T330 **Unit 6:** T18, T96, T106-T107, T114, T174, T184-T185, T192, T330 www.connected.mcgraw-hill.com: **RESOURCES: Units 1-6: Teacher Resources:** Writer's Checklists/Proofreading Marks
W.1.3	Write narratives in which they recount two or more appropriately sequenced events, include some details regarding what happened, use temporal words to signal event order, and provide some sense of closure.	**READING/WRITING WORKSHOP: Unit 1:** 66-67 **Unit 2:** 86-87 **Unit 3:** 26-27, 46-47, 66-67 **Unit 4:** 30-31 **Unit 5:** 132-133 **Unit 6:** 234-235, 294-295 **LITERATURE ANTHOLOGY: Unit 3:** 22, 66 **Unit 4:** 124 **Unit 5:** 154, 254 **Unit 6:** 322 **LEVELED READERS: Unit 2, Week 1:** *Ben Brings the Mail,* p. 16 (O,B) **Unit 3, Week 3:** *The Storytelling Stone,* p. 16 (B) **Unit 4, Week 1:** *Fly to the Rescue!* p. 16 (O), *Hummingbird's Wings,* p. 16 (B) **Unit 5, Week 1:** *Spark's Toys* (B) **Unit 6, Week 1:** *Beware of the Lion!* p. 16 (B) **Unit 6, Week 4:** *Patty Jumps!* (B) **CLOSE READING COMPANION:** 17, 57, 69, 76, 83, 102, 156, 168, 189 **YOUR TURN PRACTICE BOOK:** 30, 90, 110, 120, 130, 258, 272, 318, 330 **READING WORKSTATION ACTIVITY CARDS:** 10, 16 **WRITING WORKSTATION ACTIVITY CARDS:** 21, 23 **TEACHER'S EDITION: Unit 1:** T174, T184-T185, T192 **Unit 2:** T252, T262-T263, T270 **Unit 3:** T18, T28-T29, T36, T96, T106-T107, T114, T174, T184-T185, T192 **Unit 4:** T18, T28-T29, T36 **Unit 5:** T252, T262-T263, T270 **Unit 6:** T18, T28-T29, T36, T252, T262-T263, T270 www.connected.mcgraw-hill.com: **RESOURCES: Units 1-6: Teacher Resources:** Writer's Checklists/Proofreading Marks

Writing Standards

Production and Distribution of Writing		McGraw-Hill *Wonders*
W.1.4	(Begins in grade 3)	
W.1.5	With guidance and support from adults, focus on a topic, respond to questions and suggestions from peers, and add details to strengthen writing as needed.	**YOUR TURN PRACTICE BOOK:** 20, 30, 40, 100, 110, 120, 150, 234, 282, 294 **WRITING WORKSTATION ACTIVITY CARDS:** 1, 2, 3, 4, 5, 6, 7, 8, 9, 10, 11, 12, 13, 14, 15, 16, 17, 18, 19, 20, 21, 22, 23, 24, 25, 26, 27, 28, 29, 30 **TEACHER'S EDITION: Unit 1:** T42-T43, T120-T121, T174, T198-T199, T252, T276-T277, T330, T354-T355 **Unit 2:** T42-T43, T120-T121, T174, T198-T199, T252, T276-T277, T330, T354-T355 **Unit 3:** T42-T43, T120-T121, T174, T198-T199, T252, T276-T277, T330, T354-T355 **Unit 4:** T42-T43, T120-T121, T174, T198-T199, T252, T276-T277, T330, T354-T355 **Unit 5:** T42-T43, T120-T121, T174, T198-T199, T252, T276-T277, T330, T354-T355 **Unit 6:** T42-T43, T120-T121, T174, T198-T199, T252, T276-T277, T330, T354-T355 www.connected.mcgraw-hill.com: **RESOURCES: Units 1-6: Graphic Organizers:** Graphic Organizers **Teacher Resources:** Writer's Checklists/Proofreading Marks
W.1.6	With guidance and support from adults, use a variety of digital tools to produce and publish writing, including in collaboration with peers.	**TEACHER'S EDITION: Unit 1:** T36, T48, T114, T122, T126, T192, T204, T270, T282, T348, T360, T397, T398-T399, T400-T401, T402 **Unit 2:** T36, T48, T114, T126, T192, T204, T270, T282, T348, T360, T397, T398-T399, T400-T401, T402 **Unit 3:** T36, T48, T114, T126, T192, T204, T270, T282, T348, T360, T397, T398-T399, T400-T401, T402 **Unit 4:** T36, T48, T114, T126, T192, T204, T270, T282, T348, T360, T397, T398-T399, T400-T401, T402 **Unit 5:** T36, T48, T114, T126, T192, T204, T270, T282, T348, T360, T397, T398-T399, T400-T401, T402 **Unit 6:** T36, T48, T114, T126, T192, T204, T270, T282, T348, T360, T397, T398-T399, T400-T401, T402 www.connected.mcgraw-hill.com: **RESOURCES: Units 1-6: Time for Kids Online Articles, Research & Inquiry:** Weekly Lessons **Teacher Resources:** Writer's Checklists/Proofreading Marks; **Digital Resources and Tools:** Writer's Workspace; Graphic Organizers; My Binder (My Work, My Portfolio); Collaborate (Projects)

Research to Build and Present Knowledge		McGraw-Hill *Wonders*
W.1.7	Participate in shared research and writing projects (e.g., explore a number of "how-to" books on a given topic and use them to write a sequence of instructions).	**TEACHER'S EDITION: Unit 1:** T44-T45, T51, T122-T123, T207, T278-T279, T285, T356-T357, T363, T379, T397, T398-T399, T400-T401 **Unit 2:** T44-T45, T51, T122-T123, T129, T207, T202-T203, T285, T362-T363, T359, T397, T398-T399, T400-T401 **Unit 3:** T44-T45, T51, T122-T123, T129, T200-T201, T207, T278-T279, T285, T356-T357, T363, T397, T398-T399, T400-T401 **Unit 4:** T44-T45, T51, T122-T123, T129, T200-T201, T207, T278-T279, T285, T356-T357, T363, T397, T398-T399, T400-T401 **Unit 5:** T44-T45, T51, T122-T123, T129, T200-T201, T278-T279, T285, T356-T357, T363, T397, T398-T399, T400-T401 **Unit 6:** T44-T45, T51, T122-T123, T129, T200-T201, T207, T278-T279, T285, T356-T357, T363, T397, T398-T399, T400-T401 www.connected.mcgraw-hill.com: **RESOURCES: Units 1-6: Research & Inquiry:** Weekly Lessons **Teacher Resources:** Writer's Checklists/Proofreading Marks **Graphic Organizers:** Foldables
W.1.8	With guidance and support from adults, recall information from experiences or gather information from provided sources to answer a question.	**LEVELED READERS: Unit 1, Week 3:** *A Mouse in the House*, pp. 13-16 (A), *Love That Llama!* pp. 13-16 (O), *Birds That Talk*, pp. 13-16 (B) **Unit 1, Week 4:** *I Like to Play*, pp. 13-16 (A, O, B) **Unit 2, Week 3:** *I Live in a House!* (A, O, B) **Unit 4, Week 2:** *Animals Work Together!* pp. 13-16 (A, O); pp. 12-16 (B) **Unit 4, Week 3:** *Ducklings* (A) **Unit 4, Week 4:** *Let's Look at Insects!* pp. 13-16 (O), *Compare Insects*, pp. 13-16 (B) **Unit 5, Week 2:** *Hello, Little Dipper!* pp. 13-16 (A), *Our Sun Is a Star!* pp. 13-16 (O), *Sunrise and Sunset*, pp. 13-16 (B) **Unit 5, Week 3:** *Fly Away, Butterfly*, pp. 13-16 (A, O); pp. 12-16 (B) **Unit 6, Week 5:** *Four Voyages*, pp. 13-16 (A, O); pp. 12-16 (B) **SCIENCE & SOCIAL STUDIES WORKSTATION ACTIVITY CARDS:** 4, 5, 6, 7, 8, 9, 10, 11, 12, 13, 14, 15, 16, 17, 18, 19, 20, 22, 23, 24, 25, 26, 27, 28, 29, 30 **WRITING WORKSTATION ACTIVITY CARDS:** 1, 2, 3, 4, 5, 6, 7, 8, 9, 10, 11, 12, 13, 14, 15, 16, 17, 18, 19, 20, 21, 22, 23, 24, 25, 26, 27, 29, 30 **INTERACTIVE READ-ALOUD CARDS: Unit 1, Week 3:** 1 **Unit 3, Week 1:** 1, 3 **Unit 5, Week 1:** 3 **Unit 5, Week 2:** 1 **Unit 5, Week 4:** 1 **Unit 6, Week 2:** 1 **Unit 6, Week 5:** 2 **TEACHER'S EDITION: Unit 1:** T200, T398-T399, T400 **Unit 2:** T398-T399, T400 **Unit 3:** T200-T201, T398-T399, T400-T401 **Unit 4:** T122, T398-T399, T400 **Unit 5:** T44, T122, T200-T201, T278, T398-T399, T400 **Unit 6:** T44, T129, T278, T398-T399, T400 www.connected.mcgraw-hill.com: **RESOURCES: Units 1-6: Research & Inquiry:** Weekly Lessons, Note-taking Tools **Graphic Organizers:** Graphic Organizers
W.1.9	(Begins in grade 4)	

Range of Writing		McGraw-Hill *Wonders*
W.1.10	(Begins in grade 3)	

College and Career Readiness Anchor Standards for
SPEAKING AND LISTENING

The K–5 standards on the following pages define what students should understand and be able to do by the end of each grade. They correspond to the College and Career Readiness anchor standards below by number. The CCR and grade-specific standards are necessary complements—the former providing broad standards, the latter providing additional specificity—that together define the skills and understandings that all students must demonstrate.

Comprehension and Collaboration

1. Prepare for and participate effectively in a range of conversations and collaborations with diverse partners, building on others' ideas and expressing their own clearly and persuasively.

2. Integrate and evaluate information presented in diverse media and formats, including visually, quantitatively, and orally.

3. Evaluate a speaker's point of view, reasoning, and use of evidence and rhetoric.

Presentation of Knowledge and Ideas

4. Present information, findings, and supporting evidence such that listeners can follow the line of reasoning and the organization, development, and style are appropriate to task, purpose, and audience.

5. Make strategic use of digital media and visual displays of data to express information and enhance understanding of presentations.

6. Adapt speech to a variety of contexts and communicative tasks, demonstrating command of formal English when indicated or appropriate.

CCSS Common Core State Standards
English Language Arts
Grade 1

Speaking and Listening Standards

Comprehension and Collaboration		McGraw-Hill *Wonders*
SL.1.1	Participate in collaborative conversations with diverse partners about *grade 1 topics and texts* with peers and adults in small and larger groups.	
SL.1.1a	Follow agreed-upon rules for discussions (e.g., listening to others with care, speaking one at a time about the topics and texts under discussion).	**CLOSE READING COMPANION:** 5, 44, 65, 124 **PHONICS WORKSTATION ACTIVITY CARDS:** 3, 10, 11, 12, 17, 18, 19, 20, 22, 23, 24, 30 **READING WORKSTATION ACTIVITY CARDS:** 1, 2, 3, 4, 5, 6, 7, 8, 9, 10, 11, 12, 13, 14, 15, 16, 17, 19, 20, 21, 22, 23, 24, 25, 26, 27, 28 **TEACHER'S EDITION: Unit 1:** T9, T48, T50-51, T87, T128-T129, T165, T282, T284-T285, T360 **Unit 2:** T48, T87, T122, T126, T128-T129, T165, T200, T204, T276-T277, T284-T285, T321, T356, T360, T362-T363, T403 **Unit 3:** T9, T165, T200, T204, T206-T207, T243, T278, T321, T356, T360, T362-T363, T403 **Unit 4:** T48, T87, T122, T126, T165, T200, T243, T278, T284-T285, T356, T403 **Unit 5:** T44, T48, T50-51, T87, T122, T165, T200, T282, T284-T285, T321, T403 **Unit 6:** T48, T87, T122, T126, T165, T200, T206-T207, T282, T321, T356, T403 www.connected.mcgraw-hill.com: **RESOURCES: Units 1–6: Media:** Images, Videos **Collaborative Conversations Videos Teacher Resources:** Speaking and Listening Checklists
SL.1.1b	Build on others' talk in conversations by responding to the comments of others through multiple exchanges.	**READING WORKSTATION ACTIVITY CARDS:** 2, 5, 10, 13, 16 **TEACHER'S EDITION: Unit 1:** T42-T43, T128-T129, T276-T277, T320, T321, T354-T355, T356, T403 **Unit 2:** T9, T42-T43, T44, T49, T50-51, T206-T207, T354-T355, T362-T363, T403 **Unit 3:** T42-T43, T87, T122, T198-T199, T206-T207, T276-T277, T354-T355, T403 **Unit 4:** T50-51, T120-T121, T128, T276-T277, T354-T355, T362-T363, T401, T403 **Unit 5:** T120-T121, T128-T129, T354-T355, T362-T363, T403 **Unit 6:** T42-T43, T198, T278, T284-T285, T403 www.connected.mcgraw-hill.com: **RESOURCES: Units 1–6: Media:** Images, Videos **Teacher Resources:** Speaking and Listening Checklists
SL.1.1c	Ask questions to clear up any confusion about the topics and texts under discussion.	**TEACHER'S EDITION: Unit 1:** T20, T98, T164 **Unit 2:** T128-T129, T204, T242, T282, T284-T285, T403 **Unit 3:** T120-T121, T282, T284-T285, T321, T356, T403 **Unit 4:** T9, T44, T50-51, T96, T106-T107, T122, T206-T207, T276-T277, T282, T403 **Unit 5:** T9, T198-T199, T206-T207, T243, T278, T403 **Unit 6:** T9, T44, T120-T121, T128-T129, T321, T354-T355, T362-T363, T403 www.connected.mcgraw-hill.com: **RESOURCES: Units 1–6: Graphic Organizers:** Graphic Organizers, Think Aloud Clouds **Teacher Resources:** Speaking and Listening Checklists
SL.1.2	Ask and answer questions about key details in a text read aloud or information presented orally or through other media.	**CLOSE READING COMPANION:** 1-3, 11-13, 33, 44-46, 66, 74-76, 97-98, 114-116, 163-164, 187-189 **READING WORKSTATION ACTIVITY CARDS:** 2, 6, 11, 13, 14 **INTERACTIVE READ-ALOUD CARDS: Unit 1, Week 1:** 1, 2, 4 **Unit 1, Week 2:** 1, 3, 4 **Unit 1, Week 3:** 4 **Unit 1, Week 4:** 4 **Unit 2, Week 3:** 4 **Unit 2, Week 4:** 2 **Unit 3, Week 1:** 4 **Unit 3, Week 2:** 4 **Unit 3, Week 3:** 2, 4 **Unit 3, Week 4:** 1, 3, 4 **Unit 3, Week 5:** 4 **Unit 4, Week 1:** 3 **Unit 4, Week 2:** 2, 4 **Unit 4, Week 3:** 1, 3, 4 **Unit 4, Week 4:** 2 **Unit 5, Week 1:** 4 **Unit 5, Week 2:** 4 **Unit 5, Week 3:** 4 **Unit 5, Week 4:** 4 **Unit 5, Week 5:** 4 **Unit 6, Week 1:** 4 **Unit 6, Week 2:** 4 **Unit 6, Week 3:** 4 **Unit 6, Week 4:** 4 **TEACHER'S EDITION: Unit 1:** S8, S14, S26, S38, S44, S50, S56, S68, S74, S80, S86, T48, T50-T51, T198-T199, T206-T207, T245, T255, T284, T403 **Unit 2:** T20, T99, T120-T121, T126, T177, T198-T199, T255, T403 **Unit 3:** T11, T21, T31, T89, T99, T109, T126, T128-T129, T167, T177, T245, T255, T282, T333, T360, T403 **Unit 4:** T11, T21, T89, T99, T126, T167, T177, T255, T282, T284-T285, T333, T403 **Unit 5:** T21, T50-T51, T99, T245, T255, T282, T333, T403 **Unit 6:** T21, T28-T29, T48, T99, T206-T207, T284-T285, T333, T360, T403 www.connected.mcgraw-hill.com: **RESOURCES: Units 1–6: Graphic Organizers:** Think Aloud Clouds **Teacher Resources:** Speaking and Listening Checklists

Speaking and Listening Standards

SL.1.3	Ask and answer questions about what a speaker says in order to gather additional information or clarify something that is not understood.	**TEACHER'S EDITION: Unit I:** TI26, TI65, T206-T207, T243, T282, T284-T285, T360, T403 **Unit 2:** T48, T206-T207, T243, T360, T403 **Unit 3:** T9, T50-T51, TI26, TI28-TI29, T321, T360, T403 **Unit 4:** T9, T48, T87, TI28-TI29, T204, T282, T321, T362-T363, T403 **Unit 5:** T9, TI28-TI29, TI65, T243, T282, T284-T285, T360, T403 **Unit 6:** T9, T48, T50-T51, T204, T321, T362-T363, T403 www.connected.mcgraw-hill.com: **RESOURCES: Units I-6: Research & Inquiry:** Note-taking tools **Graphic Organizers:** Graphic Organizers **Teacher Resources:** Speaking and Listening Checklists

Presentation of Knowledge and Ideas		**McGraw-Hill *Wonders***
SL.1.4	Describe people, places, things, and events with relevant details, expressing ideas and feelings clearly.	**LITERATURE ANTHOLOGY: Unit I:** 47, 63, 85, 86, 94, 95 **Unit 2:** 25, 43, 47 **Unit 5:** 195, 259 **Unit 6:** 392 **LEVELED READERS: Unit I, Week 2:** *My Home,* pp. 13-16 (A), *Where I Live,* pp. 13-16 (O), *Where We Live,* pp. 13-16 (B) **Unit 2, Week 3:** *I Live in a House!* pp. 13-16 (A, O, B) **Unit 2, Week 4:** *The Sick Tree* (A), *Squirrels Help* (O) **Unit 3, Week 4:** *School Days,* pp. 13-16 (A, O); pp. 12-16 (B) **Unit 4, Week I:** *Animal Traits,* pp. 13-16 (O) **Unit 4, Week 5:** *Working with Dolphins,* pp. 13-16 (A, O); pp. 12-16 (B) **Unit 5, Week I:** *Nuts for Winter* (A), *Spark's Toys* (B) **Unit 5, Week 2:** *Hello, Little Dipper!* pp. 13-16 (A), *Our Sun Is a Star!* pp. 13-16 (O), *Sunrise and Sunset,* pp. 13-16 (B) **Unit 6, Week 4:** *The Quilt* (A), *Latkes for Sam* (O) **Unit 6, Week 5:** *Four Voyages,* pp. 13-16 (A, O); pp. 12-16 (B) **READING WORKSTATION ACTIVITY CARDS:** I, 2, 3, 4, 7, 8, 9, 10, 13, 15 **SCIENCE & SOCIAL STUDIES WORKSTATION ACTIVITY CARDS:** 2, 3, 4, 5, 6, 7, 8, 9, 10, 12, 13, 14, 15, 16, 17, 18, 19, 20-30 **WRITING WORKSTATION ACTIVITY CARDS:** I-10, II, 12, 13, 14, 15, 16, 17, 19, 20, 21, 22, 23, 24, 25, 26, 27, 28, 29 **INTERACTIVE READ-ALOUD CARDS: Unit I, Week I:** 2 **Unit I, Week 2:** 3 **Unit I, Week 3:** 3 **Unit 3, Week I:** 2, 3 **Unit 3, Week 2:** I **Unit 6, Week 4:** 3 **TEACHER'S EDITION: Unit I:** S26, S50, S74, T9, T50-T51, T87, T98, TI26, TI28, T204, T282, T284, T321, T360, T362-T363 **Unit 2:** T9, T50-T51, T87, T206-T207, T245, T321, T360, T362-T363 **Unit 3:** T9, T48, T87, T89, TII3J, TI26, TI28-TI29, TI65, T206-T207, T243, T284-T285, T321 **Unit 4:** T9, T48, T50-T51, T87, TI65, T206-T207, T243, T269R, T282, T360, T362-T363 **Unit 5:** T9, T48, T50-T51, T87, TII3R, TI26, TI65, T204, T243, T273, T284-T285, T321, T360, T362-T363 **Unit 6:** T48, T87, TI26, TI77, T243, T282, T360, T362-T363 www.connected.mcgraw-hill.com: **RESOURCES: Unit I: Graphic Organizers:** Graphic Organizers
SL.1.5	Add drawings or other visual displays to descriptions when appropriate to clarify ideas, thoughts, and feelings.	**LITERATURE ANTHOLOGY: Unit I:** 18, 40, 62, 82 **Unit 2:** 20, 42, 80 **Unit 3:** 22, 44, 66, 88 **Unit 4:** 28, 88, 124 **Unit 5:** 194 **Unit 6:** 356, 392 **LEVELED READERS: Unit I, Week 2:** *Where I Live,* pp. 13-16 (O) **Unit 2, Week 3:** *I Live in a House!* pp. 13-16 (A, O, B) **Unit 3, Week 4:** *School Days,* pp. 13-16 (A, O); pp. 12-16 (B) **Unit 4, Week 3:** *Ducklings,* pp. 13-16 (A, O); pp. 12-16 (B) **Unit 5, Week 3:** *Fly Away, Butterfly,* pp. 13-16 (A, O); pp. 12-16 (B) **Unit 6, Week I:** *What a Feast* (O) **YOUR TURN PRACTICE BOOK:** 165, 189, 225, 249, 261, 285 **READING WORKSTATION ACTIVITY CARDS:** I, 2, 3, 4, 5, 6, 7, 8, 9, 10, II, 12, 13, 15, 17, 19, 20, 23, 26, 27, 28 **SCIENCE & SOCIAL STUDIES WORKSTATION ACTIVITY CARDS:** 2, 3, 4, 5, 6, 7, 8, 9, 10, 12, 13, 14, 15, 16, 17, 18, 19, 20, 21, 22, 23, 24, 25, 26, 27, 28, 29, 30 **WRITING WORKSTATION ACTIVITY CARDS:** I, 2, 3, 4, 5, 6, 7, 9, 10, 13, 14, 17, 19, 20, 21, 22, 23, 24, 25, 26, 27, 28, 29 **TEACHER'S EDITION: Unit I:** T43, T45, T48, T51, T48, TI21, TI23, TI26, TI28-TI29, TI91J, T204, T279, T284-T285, T355, T360, T398-T399 **Unit 2:** T43, T48, T50-T51, TI21, T282, T284-T285 **Unit 3:** T48, TI21, TI26, TI98, TI99, T204, T277, T279, T282, T284-T285, T360, T362-T363 **Unit 4:** T42-T43, T48, TI21, TI23, TI26, TI28-TI29, TI99, T204, T282, T354-T355, T357, T360 **Unit 5:** T43, TI21, TI23, TI26, TI28-TI29, TI99, T204, T206-T207, T276-T277, T282, T360 **Unit 6:** T43, T48, TI21, TI23, TI26, TI28-TI29, T204, T276-T277, T282, T360
SL.1.6	Produce complete sentences when appropriate to task and situation.	**LEVELED READERS: Unit 3, Week I:** *Busy's Watch* (A), *Kate Saves the Date!* (O), *Uncle George Is Coming!* (B) **Unit 5, Week 2:** *Sunrise and Sunset,* pp. 13-16 (B) **Unit 6, Week I:** *Two Hungry Elephants* (A) **Unit 6, Week 2:** *Fire!* pp. 13-16 (A, O); pp. 12-16 (B) **YOUR TURN PRACTICE BOOK:** 2, 12, 17, 22, 32, 51, 52, 58, 61, 62, 71, 72, 81, 91, 92, 93, 101, III, 151, 165, 189, 211, 221, 225, 249 **SCIENCE & SOCIAL STUDIES WORKSTATION ACTIVITY CARDS:** 2, 4, 5, 6, 7, 8, 9, 12, 14, 15, 17, 18, 19, 20, 23, 24, 25, 26, 27 **WRITING WORKSTATION ACTIVITY CARDS:** I, 2, 3, 4, 5, 6, 7, 8, 9, 10, II, 12, 13, 14, 15, 16, 17, 18, 19, 20-30 **INTERACTIVE READ-ALOUD CARDS: Unit I, Week 4:** 3 **Unit I, Week 5:** I **Unit 2, Week 3:** 3 **Unit 3, Week 4:** 2 **Unit 4, Week 2:** I **Unit 4, Week I:** I **Unit 5, Week 5:** 2 **Unit 6, Week 3:** I **TEACHER'S EDITION: Unit I:** S5, SI4, TI9, T37, T43, T48, TI75, TI85, TI93, T206-T207, T341, T355, T362-T363 **Unit 2:** T9, TI9, T29, TI28-TI29, TI75, TI93, T354 **Unit 3:** T37, T43, T48, T87, TI65, T204, T253, T271, T362-T363 **Unit 4:** T9, TI07, TI91, T253, T263, T282, T284-T285, T321, T360 **Unit 5:** TI9, T29, T42-T43, T48, TI26, TI85, TI99, T204, T206-T207, T277, T362-T363 **Unit 6:** T9, TI9, T29, T42-T43, TI28-TI29, TI65, TI98-TI99, T206-T207, T243, T253, T360, T263

College and Career Readiness Anchor Standards for LANGUAGE

The K–5 standards on the following pages define what students should understand and be able to do by the end of each grade. They correspond to the College and Career Readiness anchor standards below by number. The CCR and grade-specific standards are necessary complements—the former providing broad standards, the latter providing additional specificity—that together define the skills and understandings that all students must demonstrate.

Conventions of Standard English

1. Demonstrate command of the conventions of standard English grammar and usage when writing or speaking.

2. Demonstrate command of the conventions of standard English capitalization, punctuation, and spelling when writing.

Knowledge of Language

3. Apply knowledge of language to understand how language functions in different contexts, to make effective choices for meaning or style, and to comprehend more fully when reading or listening.

Vocabulary Acquisition and Use

4. Determine or clarify the meaning of unknown and multiple-meaning words and phrases by using context clues, analyzing meaningful word parts, and consulting general and specialized reference materials, as appropriate.

5. Demonstrate understanding of word relationships and nuances in word meanings.

6. Acquire and use accurately a range of general academic and domain-specific words and phrases sufficient for reading, writing, speaking, and listening at the college and career readiness level; demonstrate independence in gathering vocabulary knowledge when encountering an unknown term important to comprehension or expression.

Common Core State Standards
English Language Arts
Grade 1

Language Standards

Conventions of Standard English		McGraw-Hill *Wonders*
L.1.1	Demonstrate command of the conventions of standard English grammar and usage when writing or speaking.	
L.1.1a	Print all upper- and lowercase letters.	**YOUR TURN PRACTICE BOOK:** SS5, SS8, SS12, SS17, SS20, SS24, SS29, SS32, SS36 **TEACHER'S EDITION: Unit 1:** T13, T91, T169, T247 **Unit 2:** T13, T91, T120, T169, T247, T325 **Unit 3:** T13, T91, T169, T247, T276 **Unit 4:** T13, T42, T91, T169, T247, T325 **Unit 5:** T13, T91, T169, T247 **Unit 6:** T13, T91, T169, T247 www.connected.mcgraw-hill.com: **RESOURCES: Unit 1: Student Practice:** Grammar Practice, Approaching Reproducibles, Beyond Reproducibles, ELL Reproducibles **Interactive Games & Activities:** Writing & Grammar
L.1.1b	Use common, proper, and possessive nouns.	**READING/WRITING WORKSHOP: Unit 2:** 27, 47, 67, 87, 107 **YOUR TURN PRACTICE BOOK:** 2, 32, 49, 59, 92, 102, 112, 132, 152, 165, 176, 213, 237, 248, 261, 272, 273, 284, 296, 297, 321 **PHONICS WORKSTATION ACTIVITY CARDS:** 5 **TEACHER'S EDITION: Unit 2:** T19, T28-T29, T37, T43, T97, T107, T115, T175, T184-T185, T193, T199, T205, T253, T262-T263, T271-T272, T276-T277, T281 **Unit 3:** T42 **Unit 4:** T199, T276 **Unit 5:** T36, T42, T121, T114, T198 **Unit 6:** T120 www.connected.mcgraw-hill.com: **RESOURCES: Unit 2: Student Practice:** Grammar Practice, Approaching Reproducibles, Beyond Reproducibles, ELL Reproducibles **Interactive Games & Activities:** Writing & Grammar **Unit 4: Student Practice:** Grammar Practice, Approaching Reproducibles, Beyond Reproducibles, ELL Reproducibles **Interactive Games & Activities:** Writing & Grammar **Unit 5: Student Practice:** Grammar Practice, Approaching Reproducibles, Beyond Reproducibles, ELL Reproducibles **Interactive Games & Activities:** Writing & Grammar
L.1.1c	Use singular and plural nouns with matching verbs in basic sentences (e.g., *He hops; We hop*).	**READING/WRITING WORKSHOP: Unit 3:** 47, 87 **Unit 4:** 31, 51 **YOUR TURN PRACTICE BOOK:** 2, 8 **PHONICS WORKSTATION ACTIVITY CARDS:** 5 **TEACHER'S EDITION: Unit 2:** T106, T017 **Unit 3:** T97, T106, T107, T252-T253, T262-T263, T270-T271, T276-T277, T283-T284 **Unit 4:** T18-T19, T28-T29, T36-T37, T42-T43, T48-T49, T114 **Unit 5:** T42 www.connected.mcgraw-hill.com: **RESOURCES: Units 3: Student Practice:** Grammar Practice, Approaching Reproducibles, Beyond Reproducibles, ELL Reproducibles **Interactive Games & Activities:** Writing & Grammar **Unit 4:** Approaching Reproducibles, Beyond Reproducibles, ELL Reproducibles, Grammar Practice, Interactive Games & Activities (Writing & Grammar)
L.1.1d	Use personal, possessive, and indefinite pronouns (e.g., *I, me, my; they, them, their; anyone, everything*).	**READING/WRITING WORKSHOP: Unit 6:** 235, 254, 255, 275, 295 **YOUR TURN PRACTICE BOOK:** SS3, SS4, SS9, SS15, SS16, SS21, SS22, SS27, SS28, SS33, SS34, 32, 152, 296, 308, 309 **WRITING WORKSTATION ACTIVITY CARDS:** 21 **TEACHER'S EDITION: Unit 6:** T18, T19, T28-T29, T36-T37, T42-T43, T48-T49, T96-T97, T106-T107, T114-T115, T121, T127, T175, T185, T193, T198, T199, T205, T252-T253, T262-T263, T270-T271, T276, T277, T283 www.connected.mcgraw-hill.com: **RESOURCES: Unit 6: Student Practice:** Grammar Practice, Approaching Reproducibles, Beyond Reproducibles, ELL Reproducibles **Interactive Games & Activities:** Writing & Grammar

Language Standards

Conventions of Standard English		McGraw-Hill *Wonders*
L.1.1e	Use verbs to convey a sense of past, present, and future (e.g., *Yesterday I walked home; Today I walk home; Tomorrow I will walk home*).	**READING/WRITING WORKSHOP:** Unit 3: 27, 47, 67 **Unit 4:** 71, 91 **YOUR TURN PRACTICE BOOK:** 58, 78, 225 **PHONICS WORKSTATION ACTIVITY CARDS:** 5 **TEACHER'S EDITION: Unit 3:** T96–T97, T106–T107, T114–T115, T120–T121, T127–T128, T175, T185, T193, T198, T199, T205, T252–T253, T263, T271, T276, T277, T283 **Unit 4:** T19, T29, T42, T43, T49, T175, T185, T193, T198, T199, T205, T252–T253, T262–T263, T271, T276–T277, T282–T283 **Unit 5:** T198 www.connected.mcgraw-hill.com: **RESOURCES: Unit 3: Student Practice:** Grammar Practice, Approaching Reproducibles, Beyond Reproducibles, ELL Reproducibles **Interactive Games & Activities:** Writing & Grammar **Unit 4: Student Practice:** Grammar Practice, Approaching Reproducibles, Beyond Reproducibles, ELL Reproducibles **Interactive Games & Activities:** Writing & Grammar
L.1.1f	Use frequently occurring adjectives.	**READING/WRITING WORKSHOP: Unit 5:** 152–153, 173 **YOUR TURN PRACTICE BOOK:** SS15, SS16, SS33, SS34, 22, 42, 52, 62, 92, 102, 112, 122, 132, 142, 152, 153, 164, 165, 176, 185, 189, 201, 212, 213, 236, 237, 248, 256, 272, 293, 309 **WRITING WORKSTATION ACTIVITY CARDS:** 17, 22, 25 **TEACHER'S EDITION: Unit 5:** T96–T97, T106–T107, T114–T115, T120–T121, T126–T127, T174–T175, T184–T185, T192–T193, T198–T199, T204–T205 **Unit 6:** T276 www.connected.mcgraw-hill.com: **RESOURCES: Unit 5: Student Practice:** Grammar Practice, Approaching Reproducibles, Beyond Reproducibles, ELL Reproducibles **Interactive Games & Activities:** Writing & Grammar
L.1.1g	Use frequently occurring conjunctions (e.g., *and, but, or, so, because*).	**READING/WRITING WORKSHOP: Unit 5:** 133 **YOUR TURN PRACTICE BOOK:** SS15, SS16, SS21, SS22, 164 **TEACHER'S EDITION: Unit 5:** T18–T19, T28–T29, T36–T37, T42–T43, T48–T49 **Unit 6:** T120 www.connected.mcgraw-hill.com: **RESOURCES: Unit 5: Student Practice:** Grammar Practice, Approaching Reproducibles, Beyond Reproducibles, ELL Reproducibles **Interactive Games & Activities:** Writing & Grammar
L.1.1h	Use determiners (e.g., articles, demonstratives).	**READING/WRITING WORKSHOP: Unit 5:** 193 **YOUR TURN PRACTICE BOOK:** SS3, SS4, SS9, SS15, SS16, SS21, SS22, SS27, SS28, SS33, SS34 **TEACHER'S EDITION: Unit 5:** T252–T253, T262–T263, T270–T271, T276–T277, T282–T283 **Unit 6:** T42 www.connected.mcgraw-hill.com: **RESOURCES: Unit 5: Student Practice:** Grammar Practice, Approaching Reproducibles, Beyond Reproducibles, ELL Reproducibles **Interactive Games & Activities:** Writing & Grammar
L.1.1i	Use frequently occurring prepositions (e.g., *during, beyond, toward*).	**READING/WRITING WORKSHOP: Unit 5:** 213 **YOUR TURN PRACTICE BOOK:** SS9, SS33, SS34, 72, 92, 122, 142, 152, 164, 176, 308 **TEACHER'S EDITION: Unit 5:** T330–T331, T340–T341, T348–T349, T354–T355, T360–T361 **Unit 6:** T198 www.connected.mcgraw-hill.com: **RESOURCES: Unit 5: Student Practice:** Grammar Practice, Approaching Reproducibles, Beyond Reproducibles, ELL Reproducibles **Interactive Games & Activities:** Writing & Grammar
L.1.1j	Produce and expand complete simple and compound declarative, interrogative, imperative, and exclamatory sentences in response to prompts.	**READING/WRITING WORKSHOP: Unit 1:** 107 **Unit 5:** 132–133 **Unit 6:** 294–295 **YOUR TURN PRACTICE BOOK:** 2, 12, 17, 22, 51, 52, 58, 61, 62, 70-71, 72, 80-81, 90-91, 92, 93, 100-101, 110-111, 120, 130, 140, 148, 150-151, 162, 165, 174, 186, 189, 198, 210-211, 221, 222, 225, 234, 246, 249, 258, 261, 270, 282, 285, 294, 306, 314, 318, 330 **PHONICS WORKSTATION ACTIVITY CARDS:** 1, 2, 4, 9, 10, 11, 12, 15, 17, 18, 19, 22, 23, 29, 30 **SCIENCE & SOCIAL STUDIES WORKSTATION ACTIVITY CARDS:** 2, 4, 5, 6, 7, 8, 9, 12, 14, 15, 17, 18, 19, 20, 23, 24, 25, 26, 27, 28, 30 **WRITING WORKSTATION ACTIVITY CARDS:** 1, 2, 3, 4, 5, 6, 7, 8, 9, 10, 11, 12, 13, 14, 15, 16, 17, 18, 19, 20, 21, 22, 23, 24, 25, 26, 27, 28, 29, 30 **TEACHER'S EDITION: Unit 1:** T19, T28–T29, T37, T43, T49, T51, T120, T175, T185, T193, T198–T199, T205, T253, T263, T271, T276–T277, T283, T354, T361 **Unit 2:** T42, T198 **Unit 3:** T42 **Unit 4:** T276, T354 **Unit 5:** T19, T29, T37, T43, T49, T120, T276, T354 **Unit 6:** T42, T198, T354 www.connected.mcgraw-hill.com: **RESOURCES: Unit 1: Student Practice:** Grammar Practice, Approaching Reproducibles, Beyond Reproducibles, ELL Reproducibles **Interactive Games & Activities:** Writing & Grammar **Graphic Organizers:** Graphic Organizers **Teacher's Resources:** Writer's Checklists/Proofreading Marks
L.1.2	Demonstrate command of the conventions of standard English capitalization, punctuation, and spelling when writing.	**YOUR TURN PRACTICE BOOK:** 10, 20, 30, 40, 50, 60, 70, 80, 90, 100, 110, 120, 130, 140, 150, 162, 174, 186, 198, 210, 222, 234, 246, 258, 270, 282, 294, 306, 318, 330 **TEACHER'S EDITION: Unit 1:** T37 **Unit 3:** T330, T340, T348, T354–T355, T360

Language Standards

L.1.2a	Capitalize dates and names of people.	READING/WRITING WORKSHOP: Unit 2: 86-87 TEACHER'S EDITION: Unit 1: T42 Unit 2: T253, T263, T271, T277, T283 Unit 3: T120 Unit 4: T97, T175, T185, T192, T205 Unit 5: T42, T175, T185, T193, T199, T205, T276 Unit 6: T97, T107, T120, T114-T115, T120-T121, T126-T127, T354 www.connected.mcgraw-hill.com: RESOURCES: Units 1-6: Student Practice: Grammar Practice, Interactive Games & Activities: Writing & Grammar Teacher Resources: Writer's Checklists/Proofreading Marks
L.1.2b	Use end punctuation for sentences.	READING/WRITING WORKSHOP: Unit 1: 47, 87, 107 TEACHER'S EDITION: Unit 1: T97, T107, T115, T121, T127, T175, T185, T193, T205, T253, T263, T271, T277, T283, T285, T331, T341, T349, T355, T361, T366 Unit 2: T198, T331, T341, T349, T355, T361 Unit 3: T198, T276, T354 Unit 4: T97, T107, T114, T115, T120-T121, T127-T128 Unit 5: T97, T107, T115, T120-T121, T127, T276 Unit 6: T120, T198, T270 www.connected.mcgraw-hill.com: RESOURCES: Units 1-5: Student Practice: Grammar Practice, Interactive Games & Activities: Writing & Grammar Teacher Resources: Writer's Checklists/Proofreading Marks
L.1.2c	Use commas in dates and to separate single words in a series.	READING/WRITING WORKSHOP: Unit 3: 27 TEACHER'S EDITION: Unit 2: T19, T28, T29, T37, T43, T49 Unit 3: T19, T28, T29, T36-T37, T42-T43, T49, T175, T185, T192, T198-T199, T204-T205, T253, T262-T263, T271, T276, T277, T283 Unit 4: T331, T341, T348-T349, T354-T355, T360-T361 Unit 6: T175, T185, T193, T198, T199, T205, T253, T263, T263, T270-T271, T276-T277, T282-T283 www.connected.mcgraw-hill.com: RESOURCES: Units 1-6: Student Practice: Grammar Practice, Interactive Games & Activities: Writing & Grammar Teacher Resources: Writer's Checklists/Proofreading Marks
L.1.2d	Use conventional spelling for words with common spelling patterns and for frequently occurring irregular words.	YOUR TURN PRACTICE BOOK: 196, 232, 256 PHONICS WORKSTATION ACTIVITY CARDS: 1, 2, 3, 4, 5, 6, 7, 8, 9, 10, 11, 12, 13, 14, 15, 16, 17, 18, 19, 20, 21, 22, 23, 24, 25, 26, 27, 28, 29, 30 TEACHER'S EDITION: Unit 1: T14, T24, T34, T41, T47, T92, T170, T196, T274 Unit 2: T25, T92, T93, T112, T113, T120, T190, T191 Unit 3: T34, T35, T103, T120, T180, T181, T258, T259, T326, T327 Unit 4: T92, T93, T170, T171, T268, T269, T336, T337, T346, T347, T354 Unit 5: T14, T47, T119, T180, T353 Unit 6: T41, T125, T248, T276, T281, T326, T327, T359 www.connected.mcgraw-hill.com: RESOURCES: Units 1-6: Student Practice: Phonics/Spelling Practice, Approaching Reproducibles, Beyond Reproducibles, ELL Reproducibles Interactive Games & Activities: Phonics Cards: Spelling Word Cards, Sound-Spelling Cards Teacher Resources: Sound-Spelling Songs
L.1.2e	Spell untaught words phonetically, drawing on phonemic awareness and spelling conventions.	PHONICS WORKSTATION ACTIVITY CARDS: 1, 2, 3, 4, 5, 6, 7, 8, 9, 10, 11, 12, 13, 14, 15, 16, 17, 18, 19, 20, 21, 22, 23, 24, 25, 26, 27, 28, 29, 30 TEACHER'S EDITION: Unit 1: T14, T92, T170, T248, T326 Unit 2: T14, T92, T170, T248, T276, T326 Unit 3: T15, T92, T170, T248, T326 Unit 4: T15, T42, T170, T248, T326 Unit 5: T14, T92, T170, T248, T326, T354 Unit 6: T14, T92, T170, T248, T326 www.connected.mcgraw-hill.com: RESOURCES: Units 1-6: Student Practice: Phonics/Spelling Practice, Approaching Reproducibles, Beyond Reproducibles, ELL Reproducibles Interactive Games & Activities: Phonemic Awareness Cards: Spelling Word Cards, Sound-Spelling Cards Teacher Resources: Sound-Spelling Songs

Knowledge of Language		McGraw-Hill *Wonders*
L.1.3	(Begins in grade 2)	

Vocabulary Acquisition and Use		McGraw-Hill *Wonders*
L.1.4	Determine or clarify the meaning of unknown and multiple-meaning words and phrases based on *grade 1 reading and content,* choosing flexibly from an array of strategies.	
L.1.4a	Use sentence-level context as a clue to the meaning of a word or phrase.	READING/WRITING WORKSHOP: Unit 4: 15, 35, 55, 75, 95 Unit 5: 117, 137, 157, 177, 197 Unit 6: 218, 239, 259, 279, 299 YOUR TURN PRACTICE BOOK: 194 INTERACTIVE READ-ALOUD CARDS: Unit 1, Week 1: 3 Unit 4, Week 2: 3 Unit 5, Week 3: 3 Unit 6, Week 3: 2 TEACHER'S EDITION: Unit 1: T195A Unit 2: T39A, T113C, T224, T269G, T273A Unit 3: T39A, T113F, T269F, T273A Unit 4: T113, T113F, T117A, T191J, T269, T269H Unit 5: T35, T39, T117, T224, T273A Unit 6: T39, T113G, T146, T195A, T273A, T302 www.connected.mcgraw-hill.com: RESOURCES: Units 1-6: Student Practice: Approaching Reproducibles, Beyond Reproducibles, ELL Reproducibles Interactive Games & Activities: Vocabulary Cards: Visual Vocabulary Cards

Language Standards

Vocabulary Acquisition and Use		McGraw-Hill *Wonders*
L.1.4b	Use frequently occurring affixes as a clue to the meaning of a word.	**YOUR TURN PRACTICE BOOK:** 172, 206, 218, 242, 254 **PHONICS WORKSTATION ACTIVITY CARDS:** 17 **TEACHER'S EDITION: Unit 4:** T101, T111, T118, T124, T136 **Unit 5:** T146, T191, T269, T269K **Unit 6:** T23, T33, T58, T191J www.connected.mcgraw-hill.com: **RESOURCES: Units 3–6: Student Practice:** Approaching Reproducibles, Beyond Reproducibles, ELL Reproducibles **Interactive Games & Activities:** Vocabulary **Cards:** Visual Vocabulary Cards
L.1.4c	Identify frequently occurring root words (e.g., *look*) and their inflectional forms (e.g., *looks, looked, looking*).	**YOUR TURN PRACTICE BOOK:** 118, 128, 148, 196, 266, 316 **TEACHER'S EDITION: Unit 4:** T146, T347, T347D **Unit 5:** T113C, T269K, T347 **Unit 6:** T41, T119, T191J, T197 www.connected.mcgraw-hill.com: **RESOURCES: Units 3–6: Student Practice:** Approaching Reproducibles, Beyond Reproducibles, ELL Reproducibles **Interactive Games & Activities:** Vocabulary **Cards:** Visual Vocabulary Cards
L.1.5	With guidance and support from adults, demonstrate understanding of figurative language, word relationships and nuances in word meaning.	
L.1.5a	Sort words into categories (e.g., colors, clothing) to gain a sense of the concepts the categories represent.	**TEACHER'S EDITION: Unit 4:** T191G, T191H **Unit 6:** T35K, T191M www.connected.mcgraw-hill.com: **RESOURCES: Units 1–6: Cards:** High-Frequency Word Cards, Visual Vocabulary Cards **Teacher Resources:** Word Games and Activities, Word Lists **Interactive Games & Activities:** Vocabulary
L.1.5b	Define words by category and by one or more key attributes (e.g., a duck is a bird that swims; a *tiger* is a large cat with stripes).	**TEACHER'S EDITION: Unit 4:** T191G, T191H **Unit 6:** T35K, T191M www.connected.mcgraw-hill.com: **RESOURCES: Units 1–6: Cards:** High-Frequency Word Cards, Visual Vocabulary Cards **Teacher Resources:** Word Games and Activities, Word Lists **Interactive Games & Activities:** Vocabulary
L.1.5c	Identify real-life connections between words and their use (e.g., note places at home that are *cozy*).	**TEACHER'S EDITION: Unit 1:** T20, T30, T194 **Unit 2:** T38, T39A, T116 **Unit 3:** T30, T38, T116 **Unit 4:** T186, T332 **Unit 5:** T186, T194, T264, T272 **Unit 6:** T30, T264 www.connected.mcgraw-hill.com: **RESOURCES: Units 1–6: Cards:** High-Frequency Word Cards, Visual Vocabulary Cards **Teacher Resources:** Word Games and Activities, Word Lists **Interactive Games & Activities:** Vocabulary
L.1.5d	Distinguish shades of meaning among verbs differing in manner (e.g., *look, peek, glance, stare, glare, scowl*) and adjectives differing in intensity (e.g., large, gigantic) by defining or choosing them or by acting out the meanings.	**YOUR TURN PRACTICE BOOK:** 177, 189, 230 **TEACHER'S EDITION: Unit 4:** T191D, T191G, T302 **Unit 5:** T113 **Unit 6:** T191K www.connected.mcgraw-hill.com: **RESOURCES: Units 1–6: Cards:** High-Frequency Word Cards, Visual Vocabulary Cards **Teacher Resources:** Word Games and Activities, Word Lists **Interactive Games & Activities:** Vocabulary
L.1.6	Use words and phrases acquired through conversations, reading and being read to, and responding to texts, including using frequently occurring conjunctions to signal simple relationships (e.g., *because*).	**WRITING WORKSTATION ACTIVITY CARDS:** 26 **INTERACTIVE READ ALOUD CARDS: Unit 1:** Weeks 1–4 **Unit 2:** Weeks 1–4 **Unit 3:** Weeks 1–4 **Unit 4:** Weeks 1–4 **Unit 5:** Weeks 1–4 **Unit 6:** Weeks 1–4 **TEACHER'S EDITION: Unit 1:** T30, T38, T66, T108, T116, T194, T254, T255, T264, T332, T342 **Unit 2:** T20, T30, T38, T98, T108, T116, T176, T186, T194, T264, T272, T332 **Unit 3:** T20, T30, T38, T108, T116, T176, T186, T194, T254, T264, T272, T332, T342, T397 **Unit 4:** T20, T30, T98, T108, T116, T176, T186, T194, T254, T264, T272, T332 **Unit 5:** T20, T30, T38, T98, T108, T116, T176, T186, T194, T254, T264, T272, T332, T342 **Unit 6:** T20, T30, T38, T98, T108, T116, T176, T186, T194, T254, T264, T272, T332, T342 www.connected.mcgraw-hill.com: **RESOURCES: Units 1–6: Student Practice:** Grammar Practice **Interactive Games & Activities:** (Writing & Grammar) **Cards:** Retelling Cards, Visual Vocabulary Cards